Between Secularization and Reform

Brill's Studies
in Intellectual History

The titles published in this series are listed at *brill.com/bsih*

Between Secularization and Reform

Religion in the Enlightenment

Edited by

Anna Tomaszewska

BRILL

LEIDEN | BOSTON

Cover illustration: *Release from Deception* (*Il Disinganno*, 1753–1754), by Francesco Queirolo. Location: Cappella Sansevero in Naples, also known as the Chapel of Santa Maria della Pietà.

The Library of Congress Cataloging-in-Publication Data is available online at https://catalog.loc.gov
LC record available at https://lccn.loc.gov/2022027926

Typeface for the Latin, Greek, and Cyrillic scripts: "Brill". See and download: brill.com/brill-typeface.

ISSN 0920-8607
ISBN 978-90-04-45871-0 (hardback)
ISBN 978-90-04-52337-1 (e-book)

Printed by Printforce, United Kingdom

Contents

Acknowledgments   VII
Notes on Contributors   VIII

1   Between Secularization and Reform: An Introduction   1
    Anna Tomaszewska and Hasse Hämäläinen

PART 1
Enlightenment and Secularization

2   Theological Revolution and the Entangled Emergence
    of Enlightenment Secularization   15
    Jeffrey D. Burson

3   If Men Were Angels: Reason and Passion in the Enlightenment   46
    Dominic Erdozain

4   The Triumph of Theocracy: French Political Thought, God,
    and the Question of Secularization in the Age of Enlightenment   68
    Damien Tricoire

5   Secularization in the Dutch Enlightenment: The Irrelevance
    of Philosophy   101
    Wiep van Bunge

PART 2
The Religion(s) of the Enlightenment

6   The Ways of Clandestinity: Radical Cartesianism and Deism
    in Robert Challe (1659–1721)   131
    Gianni Paganini

7   More Voltaire Than Rousseau? Deism in the Revolutionary Cults
    of Reason and the Supreme Being   160
    Mathias Sonnleithner

8   D'Holbach and Deism   197
         Hasse Hämäläinen

9   'A Matter of Dangerous Consequence': Molyneux and
         Locke on Toland   219
         Ian Leask

         PART 3
         Religious Enlighteners and Radical Reformers

10   Locke's Reasonable Christianity: A Religious Enlightener's
         Theology in Context   237
         Diego Lucci

11   Does Quakerism Qualify as Kantian Enlightened Religion?   266
         Stephen R. Palmquist

12   Radical Critics and Religious Enlighteners: The Cases
         of Edelmann and Kant   294
         Anna Tomaszewska

13   The Gospel of the New Principle: The Marcionian Leitmotif in Kant's
         Religious Thought in the Context of Thomas Morgan and the German
         Enlightenment   319
         Wojciech Kozyra

         Index   349

Acknowledgments

This volume is a result of research seminar meetings, held from 2020 until 2022 at the Institute of Philosophy of the Jagiellonian University in Kraków, predominantly in an online format due to the COVID-19 pandemic, within the research project *Between Secularization and Reform. Religious Rationalism in the Late 17th Century and in the Enlightenment*, funded by the National Science Centre in Poland (grant no. UMO-2018/31/B/HS1/02050) and in which I worked as the PI. The organization of the seminar would not have been possible for me without the collaboration of Hasse Hämäläinen, Marta Kwaśnicka, and Damian Barnat. I would also like to thank Hasse Hämäläinen, Izabela Zwiech, Malwina Mus-Frosik, and Aeddan Shaw, as well as the readers and editors for Brill, in particular Ivo Romein and Dinah Rapliza, for their helpful assistance in preparing this volume.

Anna Tomaszewska

Notes on Contributors

Jeffrey D. Burson
is Professor of History, Georgia Southern University.

Dominic Erdozain
is Visiting Scholar at Candler School of Theology, Emory University.

Hasse Hämäläinen
is Research Associate at the Institute of Philosophy, Jagiellonian University in Kraków.

Wojciech Kozyra
is a PhD student at the Faculty of Philosophy, University of Warsaw.

Ian Leask
is Lecturer in Philosophy at the School of Theology, Philosophy, and Music, Dublin City University.

Diego Lucci
is Professor of Philosophy and History at the American University in Bulgaria.

Gianni Paganini
is Professor of the History of Philosophy at the University of Piedmont (Vercelli) and Fellow at the Research Centre of the Accademia dei Lincei (Rome).

Stephen R. Palmquist
is Professor of Philosophy, associated with Hong Kong Baptist University.

Mathias Sonnleithner
is a PhD student in History at Martin Luther University of Halle-Wittenberg and Research Assistant at the Department of History at the University of Trier.

Anna Tomaszewska
is Assistant Professor at the Institute of Philosophy, Jagiellonian University in Kraków.

Damien Tricoire
is Professor of Early Modern History at the University of Trier.

Wiep van Bunge
is Professor of the History of Philosophy at Erasmus University Rotterdam.

CHAPTER 1

Between Secularization and Reform: An Introduction

Anna Tomaszewska and Hasse Hämäläinen

In her once much-discussed book *Nomad. From Islam to America: A Personal Journey through the Clash of Civilizations* (2010), Ayaan Hirsi Ali, a Somali activist for human rights and a public atheist, builds her narrative, addressing multiculturalism, on the opposition between religion, especially in its fundamentalist guise, and Western values epitomized by the Enlightenment, which she defines as "a worldview that came into being mainly in reaction to a particular religion, Christianity, and a particular institution of Christianity, the Roman Catholic Church."[1] In a similar vein, the Catholic Pope John Paul II featured the Enlightenment as "a movement of dissent from the Christian faith ... based on rationalistic premises."[2] This perceived opposition between Enlightenment and religion, brought up by authors representing otherwise different worldviews, would usually be thematized by means of the notion of secularization, designating the loss of significance of religious faith in both the public sphere and private lives.[3]

Though this *cliché* narrative on Enlightenment and religion, as we shall shortly see, has not been completely disavowed, much has been done to provide a more nuanced description of the relation between the two. This volume shares in the critical approach towards the narrative at issue, though without

---

1 Ayaan Hirsi Ali, *Nomad. From Islam to America: A Personal Journey through the Clash of Civilizations* (New York: 2010), 206.

2 John Paul II, "Address of His Holiness John Paul II at the Conclusion of the International Colloquium on 'Enlightenment Today'," https://www.vatican.va/content/john-paul-ii /en/speeches/1996/august/documents/hf_jp-ii_spe_19960810_illuminismo-oggi.html [Accessed 9.10.2021].

3 According to Charles Taylor, theories of secularization describe "our relation to a transcendent God" as "displaced at the centre of social life," the displacement being tracked to a "decline" of "faith in this God." *A Secular Age* (Cambridge, Mass.: 2007), 20. Taylor endows the notion of "secularity" with a triple meaning: (1) "the retreat of religion in public life," (2) "the decline in belief and practice," and (3) "the change in the conditions of belief." Ibid., 423. For a concise explanation of what "secularization" means, see Hasse Hämäläinen and Anna Tomaszewska, "Editors' Introduction," in: *The Sources of Secularism: Enlightenment and Beyond*, eds. Anna Tomaszewska and Hasse Hämäläinen (Cham: 2017), 3–5.

offering a wholesale rejection of the secularization thesis. Contributions collected in this book picture the multiple transformations of the notion of religion and the idea of religiosity in the "Age of Lights," a period in the history of ideas spanning from the second half of the 17th and throughout the 18th century.[4] Like the *Enlightened Religion* (2019),[5] the volume centers on a reconceptualization undergone by religion in that period, yet it goes beyond that book's thematic scope and regional borders and attempts to capture the Enlightenment religion (or religions) within an area delineated, so to say, between secularization and reform.

Recent research on the Enlightenment has parsed it into categories designed to capture particular aspects, if not the essence, of its intellectual agenda. Accordingly, David Sorkin has advocated the category of the "religious Enlightenment." This is the idea that "the Enlightenment was not only compatible with religious belief but conducive to it. The Enlightenment made possible new iterations of faith." In the wake of these developments, "religion lost neither its place nor its authority in European society and culture."[6] The religious Enlightenment attempted to follow the middle course between commitment to enlightened values and confessional creeds. Represented by figures such as William Warburton, Jacob Vernet, Moses Mendelssohn or Adrien Lamourette, it created a "transnational and multiconfessional" movement,[7] seeking to ground "reasonable belief" on both reason and Scripture, read as a source of truths that could transcend but not contradict reason.[8] Besides promoting toleration based on natural law,[9] the religious Enlightenment fostered a culture of engagement in the public sphere and advocated the idea of a state religion, and thereby sustained "the last attempt by European states to use *reasonable religion* … as the cement of society."[10] Sorkin's considerations cast new light on the origins

---

4   This is not a place to venture a comprehensive definition of the Enlightenment or attempt to provide a periodization of the epoch. Yet we should remember the distinction between "Enlightenment" understood as an epoch in the history of human thought, and "enlightenment" as the process of a deep transformation of minds, values, and mores both at the individual and the societal level. For a thorough treatment of the latter as a process that determined the ideological setup of the epoch, as well as debates on the meaning of the concept, see *What Is Enlightenment? Eighteenth-Century Answers and Twentieth-Century Questions*, ed. James Schmidt (Berkeley: 1996).

5   *Enlightened Religion: From Confessional Churches to Polite Piety in the Dutch Republic*, eds. Joke Spaans and Jetze Touber (Leiden: 2019).

6   David Sorkin, *The Religious Enlightenment. Protestants, Jews and Catholics from London to Vienna* (Princeton: 2008), 3.

7   Ibid., 19.

8   Ibid., 11–13.

9   Ibid., 11. Cf. also ibid., 270, 285.

10   Ibid., 21.

of political liberalism, which, as he contends, should be traced back to both organized religion and opposition to it.[11]

The attempts to reconcile reason and faith were not the only way religion would manifest its presence in the Enlightenment. Thus, Anton Matytsin and Dan Edelstein have argued that even the atheistic critique of Christianity was firmly attached to the conceptual scaffolding of the Christian theology and religion. In this picture, "atheism emerged as a philosophical alternative not from a tradition of 'free thought' and clandestine literature but from 'deeply learned Christian culture.'"[12] Yet the atheistic critique would exploit different aspects of the Christian intellectual culture. According to Alan Charles Kors, the Jesuits' investigation of atheistic arguments of ancient Epicureans for the sake of refuting them, encouraged by Pierre Gassendi's philosophical work, made "encounters with deep Epicurean perspectives far more common" among the learned. A consequence of tolerating the discussion of atheistic arguments was that the critics of the Church would be granted public space for presenting new and more convincing versions of those arguments.[13] Charly Coleman, in turn, has contended that many atheistic thinkers adopted their principal philosophical goal from the Christian mystics – and the goal was the pursuit of "self-dispossession."[14] This focus would connect François de Sales, Jeanne-Marie Guyon, and later François Fénelon with Spinoza and d'Holbach.[15] Both atheists and mystics were opposed by the Jesuits and the religious establishment, whose interest, in the view of their critics, was to support "a cult of spiritual individualism in which men and women exercise ownership of the world by right of their privileged relationship to divinity."[16]

Scholars of the Catholic Enlightenment, like Ulrich Lehner, have made the point that it was by the ecclesiastics themselves that the enlightened values would be shaped and promoted.[17] Jeffrey Burson has argued that the emergence of the Enlightenment witnessed the entanglement of the *philosophes'*

---

11   See ibid.

12   Anton M. Matytsin and Dan Edelstein, "Introduction," in *Let There Be Enlightenment. The Religious and Mystical Sources of Rationality*, eds. Anton M. Matytsin and Dan Edelstein (Baltimore: 2018), 2.

13   Alan Charles Kors, *Epicureans and Atheists in France, 1650–1729* (Cambridge, Eng.: 2016), 49.

14   Charly Coleman, *The Virtues of Abandon: An Anti-Individualist History of the French Enlightenment* (Stanford: 2014), 127.

15   Ibid., 48–9.

16   Ibid., 137.

17   See Ulrich L. Lehner, *The Catholic Enlightenment. The Forgotten History of a Global Movement* (New York: 2016). For a collection of essays on various national types of the Catholic Enlightenment, see Ulrich L. Lehner and Michael Printy (eds.), *A Companion to the Catholic Enlightenment in Europe* (Leiden: 2010).

religious criticism, theological polemics within the Church itself, and media-
tory attempts by "enlightened" priests such as Abbé Claude Yvon.[18] In the Protestant context, the spread of heterodoxy effected by the activity of "Spinozists
from the pulpit," such as Johann Heinrich Schulz, and radical Pietists, such as
Johann Christian Edelmann, would accompany mere scriptural exegesis.[19] The
Bible, as Jonathan Sheehan has tried to demonstrate, would thereby turn into a
cultural "medium," with its purely theological content becoming gradually dis-
solved, yet without this process being conducive to the loss of the Scriptures'
impact on Western secularized societies.[20]

An account of the Enlightenment, competitive to the "religious" one, reads
the epoch through the lens of the category of the "secular." For Margaret Jacob,
the Enlightenment "made the secular world its point of departure," as a result
of which "the purpose of human life" would start to be determined "without
necessary reference to a transcendent order."[21] Jacob, who is to be credited
for reintroducing to contemporary intellectual history the idea of the "radical Enlightenment,"[22] charts the changing ways of thinking about religion in
the late 17th and throughout the 18th centuries, zooming in on private figures of deists, pantheists, attendees of masonic lodges, and investigators of
world religions whose work contributed to a new understanding of religion
as a cultural phenomenon. Among other developments, Jacob tracks down
the sources of this new understanding to Bernard Picart and Jean-Frederic
Bernard's *Ceremonies et coutumes religieuses de tous les peuples du monde*.[23]
Yet she does not construe the Enlightenment as an attempt to relegate religion
from both public and private affairs, but rather links the secularizing processes
with attempts to "defang religion of its bellicosity,"[24] crucial to prevent devas-
tating conflicts like the Thirty Years War.

Charles Taylor's idea of religion being located within an "immanent frame"
also suggests a far-reaching transformation of the social and cultural role of
religion in early modernity, rather than its demise. The concept of "immanent

---

18   Jeffrey D. Burson, *The Culture of Enlightening. Abbé Claude Yvon and the Entangled
      Emergence of the Enlightenment* (Notre Dame: 2019).
19   See Wiep van Bunge and Wim Klever (eds.), *Disguised and Overt Spinozism around 1700*
      (Leiden: 1996).
20   See Jonathan Sheehan, *The Enlightenment Bible: Translation, Scholarship, Culture*
      (Princeton: 2005).
21   Margaret C. Jacob, *The Secular Enlightenment* (Princeton: 2019), 1–2.
22   Margaret C. Jacob, *The Radical Enlightenment: Pantheists, Freemasons and Republicans*
      (London: 1981).
23   See Jacob, *The Secular Enlightenment*, 13–14, 95–6.
24   See Margaret C. Jacob, "How Radical Was the Enlightenment? What Do We Mean by
      Radical?" *Diametros* 40 (2014): 99–114.

frame," coined by Taylor in his *A Secular Age* (2007), forms part of the description of a process whereby a religious life would become only one of many existential options.[25] For Taylor, the Enlightenment is not the sole trigger of the secularizing tendency which would be driven by a variety of factors, in particular, the "disenchantment" of the world brought together with the development of modern science, the emergence of deism, mainly in the Catholic part of Europe, and Christian reform movements. The secular world would not be founded on atheism and irreligion, although, according to Taylor, some of the constituents of the secularizing tendency, such as deism, may provide a "halfway house" to atheism.[26]

Relatedly, there emerges the problem of religious heterodoxy: sharing the zeal of the "Protestant Counter-Reformation" or "Radical Reformation,"[27] disappointed especially with the course taken by the Lutheran Church, a number of heterodox writers – like already mentioned Edelmann and Schulz, or earlier Jarig Jelles, the supposed author of the preface to Spinoza's *Opera posthuma* (1677) – would draw on ideas characteristic of religious criticism, to be found also in Spinoza's *Theological-Political Treatise* (1670) and Gottfried Arnold's *Kirchen- und Ketzerhistorie* (1700). Were heterodox thinkers merely reformers or also secularizers? Did they express their thoughts openly or would they rather use the religious idiom to convey anti-religious ideas? Winfried Schröder warns against conflating heterodoxy with atheism; occasionally, he argues, it is even unclear whether a figure commonly deemed an unbeliever, such as Kazimierz Łyszczyński, a Polish author of *De non-existentia Dei*, actually advanced an atheistic stance or only collected arguments undermining the existence of God.[28] Gianni Paganini's research on clandestine manuscripts, that is, works such as *Theophrastus redivivus*, *De tribus impostoribus magnis*, and *Symbolum sapientiae sive Cymbalum mundi*, can also help to build a case against interpreting heterodox authors as smuggling anti-religious ideas under the cover of religious idiom. For if such ideas had already been freely circulating among reading audience in the form of clandestine writings, did the

---

25   For Taylor's exposition of the "immanent frame" as a condition in which "we come to understand our lives as taking place within a self-sufficient immanent order; or better, a constellation of orders, cosmic, social and moral," see *A Secular Age*, 543.

26   Ibid., 270.

27   See Frederick C. Beiser, *The Fate of Reason. German Philosophy from Kant to Fichte* (Cambridge, Mass.: 1987), 50–2, and Henri Krop, "The Secularism of Spinoza and His Circle," in *The Sources of Secularism: Enlightenment and Beyond*, eds. Anna Tomaszewska and Hasse Hämäläinen (Cham: 2017), 75.

28   Winfried Schröder, *Ursprünge des Atheismus. Untersuchungen zur Metaphysik- und Religionskritik des 17. und 18. Jahrhunderts*, 2nd ed. (Stuttgart: 2012), 21–44, in particular 32–7 on Łyszczyński.

heterodox thinkers really need to resort to as much as doublespeak to market subversive ideas which they could as well have published anonymously?[29]

However, some scholars hold that the Enlightenment was essentially atheistic, and the key category capturing this feature is that of "radicalism." Leo Strauss, who was one of the first to herald this approach, defined the "radical Enlightenment," in his early book *Die Religionskritik Spinozas* (1930), in terms of the critique of revealed religion.[30] This was meant to imply that the Enlightenment was essentially anti-religious, since any "in-between positions," such as religious heterodoxy or deism, would be for Strauss, as Jonathan Israel reports, "merely forms of self-deception and illusion or else deliberate evasion and misleading of others, a morally questionable and dubious approach to philosophizing to which he accused Voltaire and Hume of being excessively inclined."[31]

Likewise, according to Peter Gay, "the Enlightenment was a single army with a single banner," which pursued a rejection of Christianity and metaphysical speculation that he thought had stifled scientific, political, and social progress in Europe for many centuries.[32] Gay claims that the thinking of Voltaire and Hume, as well as of Kant and Rousseau, was not essentially different from the atheism of Diderot and d'Holbach. All these thinkers would display "coherence" and "continuity" with one another and share "devotion to modern science and the hostility to Christianity."[33] The roots of this hostility were to be found in the Italian Renaissance and its admiration of pagan philosophy.[34] The fragmentation of the Christian world as a result of the Protestant Reformation, together with the progress of natural science in the 17th and 18th centuries, had only injected much-needed vigor and self-confidence into this hostile attitude.[35] Although they disagreed with one another regarding the finer details of their arguments, the *philosophes* across Europe wanted to recover "the organized habit

---

29   Gianni Paganini, "Enlightenment before the Enlightenment: Clandestine Philosophy," *Ethica e politica / Ethics and Politics* 20/3 (2018): 183–200. See also: Gianni Paganini, Margaret C. Jacob, John Christian Laursen (eds.), *Clandestine Philosophy. New Studies on Subversive Manuscripts in Early Modern Europe, 1620–1823* (Toronto: 2020).

30   Leo Strauss, *Spinoza's Critique of Religion*, trans. Elsa M. Sinclair (New York: 1982), 35.

31   Jonathan I. Israel, "Leo Strauss and the Radical Enlightenment," in *Reading between the Lines – Leo Strauss and the History of Early Modern Philosophy*, ed. Winfried Schröder (Berlin: 2015), 17.

32   Peter Gay, *Enlightenment: An Interpretation*, vol. 1: *The Rise of Modern Paganism* (New York: 1966), 7–8.

33   Ibid., 17–18.

34   Ibid., 257–268.

35   Ibid., 280.

of criticism," characteristic of the ancient Hellenistic philosophy, and apply it to tearing down the justifications of the existing metaphysical systems.[36]

Jonathan Israel has divided the Enlightenment into two blocks: "radical" and "moderate."[37] This division is based on how the 18th-century philosophers received or appropriated Spinoza. According to Israel, Spinozist radical ideas, which originated either directly from Spinoza or from the *cercle Spinoziste* that developed and expanded his thoughts, were more crucial to the emergence of the Enlightenment than the factors mentioned by Gay.[38] Israel argues that only the radical block promoted true Enlightenment by adopting the complete package of Spinozist ideas (in one formulation, "toleration, personal freedom, democracy, racial equality, sexual emancipation and the universal right to knowledge"[39]). All that the moderate block did was to cherry-pick some elements of this Spinozist package and water them down to make them appear compatible with the traditional forms of Christianity. Therefore, the moderates do not deserve the credit for promoting Enlightenment that Gay has given them. According to Israel, only a few explicitly atheistic French *philosophes* – d'Holbach, Helvétius, and Diderot – would be enlighteners proper. In the end, Hume, Rousseau, Voltaire, and other moderates only empowered the reactionary Counter-Enlightenment by creating a false appearance that religion can be compatible with the Enlightenment.[40]

Whichever aspect of the Enlightenment one regards as prevailing – the religious, the secular or the radical – we claim that some general observations may hold true for any of these perspectives. First and foremost, in the "age of reason," one can witness a growing interest in religion, and that from different sides: critics, apologists, and reformers emerge alongside investigators of religious customs, recruiting themselves from among both the laity and the clergy. Rather than a background that enables a shared worldview and understanding of the purpose of an individual's life, religion becomes problematized as a subject of debates.

---

36 Ibid., 121, see also ibid., 130–4.

37 See, e.g., Jonathan I. Israel, *The Enlightenment that Failed: Ideas, Revolution and Democratic Defeat, 1748–1830* (Oxford: 2019), 7–20.

38 Ibid., 93–107. Israel maintains that only the combination of Epicureanism and Reformation with Spinozism enabled these two to contribute to the radical Enlightenment.

39 Jonathan I. Israel, *Enlightenment Contested: Philosophy, Modernity and the Emancipation of Man, 1670–1752* (Oxford: 2006), 11.

40 See the argument unfolding in: Jonathan I. Israel, *A Revolution of the Mind: Radical Enlightenment and the Intellectual Origins of Modern Democracy* (Princeton: 2009), c. 5.

Secondly, as a result of these debates, not only does the concept of religion undergo transformation, but also the relation between reason and faith must be renegotiated. In particular, those who would often be assessed as proposing a "reconciliation" between reason and religion, and who can be labelled "moderate" or "religious" enlighteners, following the idiom of Israel and Sorkin – such as John Locke, Immanuel Kant or even Voltaire and Hermann Samuel Reimarus – consider religion from the viewpoint of a critical reason, thus not as believers who try to understand the basic tenets of their faith, like Augustine and Thomas Aquinas, but as thinkers who seek rational justification for any theistic belief. The latter approach brings with it a reassessment of *revealed* religion and, in the case of Christianity, the surfacing of heterodox forms of faith, challenging the suprarational component of religion, present in such doctrines as Trinity, Incarnation and the bodily Resurrection of Jesus. The challenging of the suprarational or "mysterious" components of religion encourages reconceiving it in terms acceptable for the critical reason. The core of religion will now be reduced to a set of fundamental, rationally justifiable ethical precepts, a move that can also entail a kind of deification of the rational. The trust deposited in the divine being will hence find its practical manifestation in following one's duties to oneself and others. Thus "purified," Christianity can be seen as encouraging "justice and charity,"[41] aspiring to become a universal religion and the basis of peaceful coexistence of individuals in a political community. But rationalizing religion can also mark the incipient process of secularization – of diluting religion, divested of its sacramental, mysterious, and institutional dimensions, in rational activity. This ambiguity of the Enlightenment undertaking of religious reform constitutes a main theme that this volume purports to explore.

The book is divided into three parts. Part One, "Enlightenment and Secularization," addresses the well-entrenched bias, prevalent among intellectual historians and influential among scholars of the 18th century, towards connecting the Enlightenment with the process of secularization the aftermath of which we are supposed to witness in contemporary culture. Countering this established view, Jeffrey D. Burson argues that the emergence of the Enlightenment was deeply entangled in religious and theological controversies, which makes secularization no more than a contingent outcome of early modern cultural and scientific revolution and religious practice. Dominic Erdozain attempts to rectify the errors dominating perception of the

---

41   Benedict de Spinoza, "Theological-Political Treatise," in *Complete Works*, trans. Samuel
        Shirley (Indianapolis: 2002), 392.

Enlightenment in that he argues that the main protagonists of the period would not only embark on a programme of religious reform, but also devise a whole host of measures allowing to temper the excessive pretense of reason. These measures, originating in the Christian culture, albeit heterodox, would find their institutional expression in the American political system. Taking France as an example, Damien Tricoire also demonstrates that the claim about the Enlightenment standing at the headwaters of secularization is far from adequate: the strong impetus towards reforms that would transform into a revolution sprang from an intensive search for a political and social order that placed a transcendent God at its centre. Moving on to the 18th-century Dutch Republic, we can see that it was not philosophy that contributed to the gradual abandoning of Christian views and practices, but rather the elites' engagement with the values and lifestyle of Antiquity, as Wiep van Bunge argues, pointing out that the radical Enlightenment spearheaded by Spinoza petered out too soon to exert much of the significant influence on society.

Part Two, titled "The Religion(s) of the Enlightenment," includes chapters highlighting critical alternatives to revealed religion. Gianni Paganini draws on clandestine philosophical manuscripts as the source of radical religious criticism vital for the emergence of a new conception of religion, that is, a rational religion. He illustrates this development with the example of an early-Enlightenment radical Cartesian – Robert Challe, whose rational religion, construed independently from Spinozism and Lockean empiricism, would aspire to a universal reach. Mathias Sonnleithner argues that the French revolutionaries did not call religion as such into question; rather, appealing to the Cult of Reason and the Cult of the Supreme Being, devised by the *philosophes*, they championed a natural religion and occasionally even supported the idea of a reciprocal relation between God and human beings as a useful political tool. Hasse Hämäläinen challenges a received interpretation of baron d'Holbach, an Enlightenment radical, as a critic of both theism and deism, and contends that since the arguments presented in the *System of Nature* fail to refute Voltaire's deism conclusively, theoretically the baron could accept deism as a "reasonable" religion. Ian Leask's case study of the correspondence between John Locke and William Molyneux on the "irreligious" tenets of John Toland, regarded as a pantheist or deist, adumbrates the emergence of a modern argument for exempting religious opinions from the authority of civil magistrates, unmasking the crisis of theocracy at the turn of the 17th and 18th centuries and drawing on the secularizing potential of the Enlightenment conceptions of religion.

Part Three, dedicated to "Religious Enlighteners and Radical Reformers," captures various aspects of the Enlightenment attempt to reform religion along rational lines. Accordingly, Diego Lucci discusses John Locke's religious views as an example of moralist soteriology based on Scripture which purports to show that natural reason and biblical revelation are mutually sustaining and complementary. He argues that Locke provides an original and internally consistent version of Protestant Christianity influenced by heterodox traditions, such as Socinianism and Arminianism. Stephen Palmquist considers possible conceptual affinities between Immanuel Kant's "enlightened religion" and Quakerism, an example of radical religious reformation initiated by George Fox. One of the affinities consists in both Kant and the Quakers perceiving the world peace as a main goal of religion; the quasi-mystical tendencies of Kant's religion are paralleled by Quakerism's focus on silent worship. Anna Tomaszewska's comparative essay on Kant and Johann Christian Edelmann highlights some radical consequences of the rationalist religious reform. Drawing on philological analyses of Scripture, Edelmann identifies God with reason that reveals itself in all human beings equally, rendering historical revelation in the person of Jesus superfluous. Likewise, as she points out, Kant associates the "Son of God" with the moral ideal in our reason which cannot be equated with any particular person on pain of the ideal becoming motivationally inefficient. Finally, Wojciech Kozyra analyzes the relations between Christianity and Judaism in the German Enlightenment, including Moses Mendelssohn's religious Enlightenment view on the eligibility of Judaism for modernization. Setting Kant's ideas against those of an English deist, Thomas Morgan, he highlights Kant's Marcionian commitment to morally revolutionize Christianity at the cost of discarding its Jewish heritage.

References

Beiser, Frederick C., *The Fate of Reason. German Philosophy from Kant to Fichte* (Cambridge, Mass.: 1987).

Burson, Jeffrey D., *The Culture of Enlightening. Abbé Claude Yvon and the Entangled Emergence of the Enlightenment* (Notre Dame: 2019).

Coleman, Charly, *The Virtues of Abandon: An Anti-Individualist History of the French Enlightenment* (Stanford: 2014).

Gay, Peter, *Enlightenment: An Interpretation*, vol. 1: *The Rise of Modern Paganism* (New York: 1966).

Hämäläinen, Hasse, and Anna Tomaszewska, "Editors' Introduction," in *The Sources of Secularism: Enlightenment and Beyond*, eds. Anna Tomaszewska and Hasse Hämäläinen (Cham: 2017), 1–17.

Hirsi Ali, Ayaan, *Nomad. From Islam to America: A Personal Journey through the Clash of Civilizations* (New York: 2010).

Israel, Jonathan I., *The Enlightenment that Failed: Ideas, Revolution and Democratic Defeat, 1748–1830* (Oxford: 2019).

Israel, Jonathan I., "Leo Strauss and the Radical Enlightenment," in *Reading between the Lines – Leo Strauss and the History of Early Modern Philosophy*, ed. Winfried Schröder (Berlin: 2015), 9–28.

Israel, Jonathan I., *A Revolution of the Mind: Radical Enlightenment and the Intellectual Origins of Modern Democracy* (Princeton: 2009).

Israel, Jonathan I., *Enlightenment Contested: Philosophy, Modernity and the Emancipation of Man, 1670–1752* (Oxford: 2006).

Jacob, Margaret C., *The Secular Enlightenment* (Princeton: 2019).

Jacob, Margaret C., "How Radical Was the Enlightenment? What Do We Mean by Radical?" *Diametros* 40 (2014): 99–114.

Jacob, Margaret C., *The Radical Enlightenment: Pantheists, Freemasons and Republicans* (London: 1981).

John Paul II, "Address of His Holiness John Paul II at the Conclusion of the International Colloquium on 'Enlightenment Today,'" https://www.vatican.va/content/john-paul-ii/en/speeches/1996/august/documents/hf_jp-ii_spe_19960810_illuminismo-oggi.html [Accessed 9.10.2021].

Kors, Alan Charles, *Epicureans and Atheists in France, 1650–1729* (Cambridge, Eng.: 2016).

Krop, Henri, "The Secularism of Spinoza and His Circle," in *The Sources of Secularism: Enlightenment and Beyond*, eds. Anna Tomaszewska and Hasse Hämäläinen (Cham: 2017), 73–99.

Lehner, Ulrich L., *The Catholic Enlightenment. The Forgotten History of a Global Movement* (New York: 2016).

Lehner, Ulrich L., and Michael Printy (eds.), *A Companion to the Catholic Enlightenment in Europe* (Leiden: 2010).

Matytsin, Anton M., and Dan Edelstein, "Introduction," in *Let There Be Enlightenment. The Religious and Mystical Sources of Rationality*, eds. Anton M. Matytsin and Dan Edelstein (Baltimore: 2018), 1–20.

Paganini, Gianni, "Enlightenment before the Enlightenment: Clandestine Philosophy," *Ethica e politica / Ethics and Politics* 20/3 (2018): 183–200.

Paganini, Gianni, Margaret C. Jacob, and John Christian Laursen (eds.), *Clandestine Philosophy. New Studies on Subversive Manuscripts in Early Modern Europe, 1620–1823* (Toronto: 2020).

Schmidt, James (ed.), *What Is Enlightenment? Eighteenth-Century Answers and Twentieth-Century Questions* (Berkeley: 1996).

Schröder, Winfried, *Ursprünge des Atheismus. Untersuchungen zur Metaphysik- und Religionskritik des 17. und 18. Jahrhunderts*, 2nd ed. (Stuttgart: 2012).

Sheehan, Jonathan, *The Enlightenment Bible: Translation, Scholarship, Culture* (Princeton: 2005).

Sorkin, David, *The Religious Enlightenment. Protestants, Jews and Catholics from London to Vienna* (Princeton: 2008).

Spaans, Joke, and Jetze Touber (eds.), *Enlightened Religion: From Confessional Churches to Polite Piety in the Dutch Republic* (Leiden: 2019).

Spinoza, Benedict de, "Theological-Political Treatise," in *Complete Works*, trans. Samuel Shirley (Indianapolis: 2002), 383–583.

Strauss, Leo, *Spinoza's Critique of Religion*, trans. Elsa M. Sinclair (New York: 1982).

Taylor, Charles, *A Secular Age* (Cambridge, Mass.: 2007).

Van Bunge, Wiep, and Wim Klever (eds.), *Disguised and Overt Spinozism around 1700* (Leiden: 1996).

PART 1

Enlightenment and Secularization

∵

Theological Revolution and the Entangled Emergence of Enlightenment Secularization

Jeffrey D. Burson

In his now famous retrospective on the nature of the cultural revolution that had unfolded before him by 1784, Immanuel Kant asked the question "What is Enlightenment?" and proposed his now well-known response that "enlightenment" (*Aufklärung*) was the process by which one struggles to free oneself from one's "self-incurred minority" (WA, 8:35). Kant further opined, however, that vital to this steep ascent from minority or immaturity was the obligation to elevate one's "own understanding ... in religious matters, without another's guidance" (WA, 8:40), transcending thereby the stultifying constraints of confessional religiosity. When Kant invoked the words of the Roman poet Horace by challenging his readers to "dare to know" (*sapere aude*), he was articulating a sentiment then common to contemporaries of his age across Europe and the Atlantic world: that living in an age of enlightenment and pursing cultural maturity entailed moral, social, individual, and even theological improvement.[1] Daring to know, as Kant implied, was a quest for enlightenment at once rational and religious. Yet, the Enlightenment is still often interpreted – and not at all inaccurately – as an important locus of modern secularization. But, even after decades of attempts to rethink the Enlightenment's origins, diversity, or distinctively religious varieties, the question of exactly how secularization took root in the soil of the Enlightenment era remains somewhat elusive. Was secularization an essential characteristic of Enlightenment as defined by contemporaries, or did categories of the secular find themselves redefined as contingent, even accidental outcomes of 18th-century cultural history? Kant's essay provides us with important clues in our own quest to effectively address this dilemma precisely because it points us toward a more expansive definition of *Aufklärung* than the ones most commonly employed by most popular or scholarly approaches presently available.

In an effort to address this question, and from the perspective of the social history of ideas, this chapter traces elements of the entangled intellectual

---

[1] Immanuel Kant, "An Answer to the Question: What Is Enlightenment?" in *Practical Philosophy*, ed. Mary J. Gregor (New York: 1996), 11–22.

genealogy that informed members of the "sect of philosophy" (as their contemporary critics often referred to them) in the middle third of the 18th century. In so doing, I am in no way denying the existence or importance of Enlightenment secularization, nor do I suggest that the secular Enlightenment lacks historical agency.[2] Instead, I argue that the origins and emergence of the Enlightenment are inextricably entangled with religiously inspired debates and theological controversies. In tracing this entangled genealogy of Enlightenment, this chapter reveals, first, that the expansive commerce in texts and debates – even that associated with what some refer to as the radical Enlightenment – effectively possessed religious origins.[3] Second, I argue that the secularization aptly associated with certain "varieties of Enlightenment experience" (to quote Dale Van Kley) might just as profitably be considered as one unlikely outcome of broader shifts associated with an early modern cultural revolution affecting both theology and religious practice – one far longer than conventionally defined.[4]

Undoubtedly, many significant disagreements divided the diverse partisans of national, regional, or dynastic varieties of Enlightenment thought.[5] Yet, the willingness of Voltaire, d'Alembert, Diderot, and a host of other figures (despite their differences) to anchor human happiness and useful knowledge in pursuit of natural reason was rooted in the late 17th- and early 18th-century preoccupation with discerning and reviving *prisca theologia*, or the pure theology

---

2 For a recent and important narrative history of the "secular Enlightenment," see Margaret C. Jacob, *The Secular Enlightenment* (Princeton: 2019).

3 This chapter was originally delivered as the keynote for the virtual symposium, "Between Secularization and Reform: Religion in the Enlightenment" convened at Jagiellonian University, Kraków, Poland (October 8–9, 2020); it further expands upon points I originally developed at greater length in my recent book, Jeffrey D. Burson, *The Culture of Enlightening: Abbé Claude Yvon and the Entangled Emergence of the Enlightenment* (Notre Dame: 2019), notably 1–36, 274–281. The author gratefully acknowledges Anna Tomaszewska and Hasse Hämäläinen, co-organizers of the symposium, for inviting me to expand on my keynote address. I also gratefully acknowledge University of Notre Dame Press, for allowing me to revise and expand upon aspects of my earlier research in the form of this contribution.

4 For compatible views of the Enlightenment as a cultural revolution, see Vincenzo Ferrone, *The Enlightenment: History of an Idea* (Princeton: 2015); on the notion of "varieties of Enlightenment," see Dale K. Van Kley, "The Varieties of Enlightened Experience," in *God in the Enlightenment*, eds. William J. Bulman and Robert G. Ingram (Oxford: 2016), 278–316.

5 Jean Haechler, *L'Encyclopédie: Les combats et les hommes* (Paris: 1998); Robert Darnon, "Policing Writers in Paris circa 1750," *Representation* 5 (1984): 1–34; Frank A. Kafker, *The Encyclopedists as a Group: A Collective Biography of the Authors of the Encyclopédie* (Oxford: 1996); also Jeffrey D. Burson, "The Crystallization of Counter-Enlightenment and Philosophe Identities: Theological Controversy and Catholic Enlightenment in Pre-Revolutionary France," *Church History* 77/4 (2008): 955–1002.

of humankind's original and, it was thought, most natural religion. Often relegated to the peripheral world of the early Enlightenment, this quest for natural theology proved to be of preeminent concern to many members of the early modern Republic of Letters until well into the 18th century, even if the content or identity of pure theology differed greatly from one writer to the next. When considered in this light, the secularization most often associated with the Enlightenment evolved organically from many early modern theological controversies. Thus, the contributions of even the most "radical" partisans of Enlightenment emerged from a laicization and deconfessionalization of theology characteristic of the Enlightenment.[6] If this notion of Enlightenment as a revolution in theology seems paradoxical, it is largely because of the equally paradoxical persistence of largely Christian assumptions about theology tacitly perpetuated in many mainstream historical treatments of Enlightenment secularization. In early-modern confessional Catholicism or Protestantism, theology was the science (in the original sense of *scientia*) of God achieved by modes of thought, piety, and practice appropriated via the mediation of confessional religious authorities. Confessional authority meant the totality of Catholic magisterium perpetuated and elaborated through apostolic succession and the priesthood; in the case of Protestantism, it meant the salvific grace and illumination presumed to be conveyed through the Bible. The Enlightenment did indeed undermine theology in these traditional, confessional senses of the term. But, in another sense, the emergence of Enlightenment secularization traces its origins to a revolution in theology, if one historicizes the concept of theology itself, as Jonathan Sheehan has recently done, as the discursive field of truth "claims that appear in time ... under specific mediated circumstances."[7] In what follows, I have adapted and broadened Sheehan's historicization of theology, defining it as the epistemological investigation, polemical defense, practical application, or lived experience of humanity's presumed relationship to an ultimate reality, in order to show more specifically how Enlightenment secularization is less usefully defined as the opposite of religion and theology, and more aptly viewed (in a manner reminiscent of Charles Taylor, Jonathan Sheehan, Charly Coleman,

---

6   Burson, *Culture of Enlightening*, especially at 372–381; see also William J. Bulman, "Introduction: Enlightenment for the Culture Wars," in *God in the Enlightenment*, eds. William J. Bulman and Robert G. Ingram (New York: 2016), 1–41; also Brad S. Gregory, "The Reformation Origins of the Enlightenment's God," in *God in the Enlightenment*, 201–214.

7   Jonathan Sheehan, "Thomas Hobbes, D.D.: Theology, Orthodoxy, and History," *Journal of Modern History* 88/2 (2016): 274.

and the late Carl Becker) as a transformation or transposition of theological categories, and as the deconfessionalization and pluralization of truth claims.[8]

1   **Historiographical Hurdles I: *E pluribus unam Lucem, vel ex unam
         Lucem Pluribus*?**

Any topic that addresses the Enlightenment immediately encounters the lack
of firm consensus over how best to characterize the *siècle des lumières*, and at
a time when the importance of the Enlightenment has enjoyed a kind of popular resurgence among journalists, politicians, and public intellectuals.[9] The
Enlightenment is often still defined, in a manner reminiscent of either Peter
Gay or Ernst Cassirer, as a predominantly 18th-century cultural and intellectual phenomenon that optimistically promoted a spirit of critical inquiry, and
assumed the improvability or perfectibility of human nature by the popular-
izing of empirical reason and new methods of natural philosophy. Publicists,
philosophers, and statesmen associated with the Enlightenment often insisted
on the pervasive application of empirical methods to practical problems of
political economy, human society, and history, all for the purpose of maximizing happiness and moral improvement. Further, some noteworthy reformers
associated with the Enlightenment, as the late Peter Gay once argued, found
themselves motivated by "modern paganism," whether in the form of attacks
on religious orthodoxy and orthopraxis, or in their promotion of secularism, atheism, or materialism. This lengthy, comprehensive characterization
of the Enlightenment has by turns been praised or blamed as the founding
myth for modern society: praised, insofar as the period is taken to stand at the
headwaters of individualism, democratization, and human rights; or blamed,

---

8   Carl Becker, *The Heavenly City of the Eighteenth-Century Philosophers*, 2nd ed. (New
     Haven: 2003); Charles Taylor, *A Secular Age* (Cambridge, Mass.: 2007); Jonathan Sheehan,
     "Enlightenment, Religion, and the Enigma of Secularization," *American Historical Review* 108
     (2003): 1061–1080; Charly Coleman, "Resacralizing the World: The Fate of Secularization in
     Enlightenment Historiography," *Journal of Modern History* 82/2 (2010): 368–395, and Charly
     Coleman, *The Virtues of Abandon: An Anti-Individualist History of the French Enlightenment*
     (Stanford: 2014); see also Michael Warner, Jonathan Van Antwerpen and Craig Calhoun (eds.),
     Varieties of Secularism in a Secular Age (Cambridge, Mass.: 2013); and Amos Funkelstein,
     *'Secular Theology' in a Modern Age: Theology and the Scientific Imagination from the Middle
     Ages to the Seventeenth Century* (Princeton: 1986).
9   The juxtaposition of fragmented scholarly consensus about the Enlightenment, with the
     recent, increasingly popular tendency to double down on the Enlightenment as an ori-
     gin story for modern, secular, scientific values and political liberalism is also addressed by
     Antoine Lilti, *L'héritage des Lumières: Ambivalences de la modernité* (Paris: 2019), 7–32.

inasmuch as critics have also attributed to it the most profound crises and crimes of the 20th and now 21st centuries.[10]

Criticisms of this univocal or unitary picture of the Enlightenment now abound. For one thing, 18th-century scholars have long noted that Gay's particular conception of the Enlightenment was perhaps an overly self-congratulatory product of Anglo-American Cold War historiography – an observation recently underscored by Caroline Winterer's book on the American Enlightenment.[11] Moreover, many now consider the French Enlightenment, from which Gay derived most members of his "family of *philosophes*," to have been an exceptional case because of its precocious anti-clericalism after the middle third of the 18th century.[12] Indeed, throughout Europe and its geographical or colonial peripheries – peripheries that, as Richard Butterwick, Simon Davies, and Gabriel Espinoza remind us, were often as important as the supposedly central French case – most of the philosophers, promoters, and popularizers of enlightened ideas were neither uniformly anti-clerical nor atheistic materialists, as J.G.A. Pocock's work instructively noted long ago. In response to such criticisms, then, a number of historians whose contributions dominated the 1980s to early 2000s instead preferred to speak of an ever-multiplying array of separate enlightenments divided most commonly by national, imperial, or confessional variants.[13]

---

10   Peter Gay, *The Enlightenment: An Interpretation*, vol. 1: *The Rise of Modern Paganism* (New York: 1966); Ira O. Wade, *The Structure and the Form of the French Enlightenment* (Princeton: 1987). For more critical adherents of the unitary Enlightenment thesis, see Jean-François Lyotard, *The Postmodern Condition: A Report on Knowledge*, trans. Geoff Bennington and Brian Massumi (Minneapolis: 1984), xxiii–xxiv, 29–31; Michel Foucault, "What Is Enlightenment?" in *The Foucault Reader*, ed. Paul Rabinow (New York: 1984), 32–51; Max Horkheimer and Theodore Adorno, *The Dialectic of Enlightenment: Philosophical Fragments*, trans. Edmund Jephcott (Los Angeles: 2012); see also Edward Said, *Orientalism* (New York: 1979); on "Enlightenment" and the centrality of broader human happiness, see Ritchie Robertson, *The Enlightenment: The Pursuit of Happiness, 1680–1790* (New York: 2021), 1–41.

11   Caroline Winterer, *American Enlightenments: Pursuing Happiness in the Age of Reason* (New Haven: 2016), 10–11.

12   Annie Jourdain, *La Révolution, une exception française?* (Paris: 2004); Dale K. Van Kley, *The Religious Origins of the French Revolution from Calvin to the Civil Constitution, 1560–1791* (New Haven: 1996); Jeffrey D. Burson, *The Rise and Fall of Theological Enlightenment: Jean-Martin de Prades and Ideological Polarization in Eighteenth-Century France* (Notre Dame: 2010); Jonathan I. Israel, *Enlightenment Contested: Philosophy, Modernity, and the Emancipation of Man, 1670–1752* (Oxford: 2011).

13   Richard Butterwick, Simon Davies and Gabriel Sánchez Espinoza (eds.), *Peripheries of the Enlightenment* (Oxford: 2008); J.G.A. Pocock, *Barbarism and Religion*, vol. 1: *The Enlightenments of Edward Gibbon, 1737–1764* (Cambridge, Eng.: 1999); Roy Porter, *The Creation of the Modern World: The Untold Story of the British Enlightenment* (New York:

But the plural enlightenments thesis has generated its own series of justifiable criticisms. The notion of national enlightenments, for example, is far from satisfying for at least two reasons. First, the transnational or even global connections among writers, publishers, and travelers spanning the 18th-century effectively challenge any pretense that an assortment of relatively homogenous national schools of enlightenment can be consistently identified. Second, the debate over when to situate the origins of modern nationalism further complicates the temptation to apply such an arguably anachronistic concept (such as the concept of nation) to an era before the late 18th century.[14] And then there is a practical, pedagogical concern associated with the proliferation of plural enlightenments: if one slices a loaf of bread finely enough, the bread vanishes and one is left with nothing but an assortment of messy and indiscriminate crumbs – indigestible and of little nutritive value to students, or to the general populace alike. Thus, to bifurcate the Enlightenment too much is to lead one to the precipice of a more nihilistic, and potentially quite inaccurate conclusion – that there was no Enlightenment at all.

Parallel to this process of questioning both the plural and the unitary Enlightenment paradigms, however, has been a largely fruitful effort to account for the origins of how the Enlightenment, as presently conceived, relates to the stories told by its diverse participants. Dan Edelstein's short but crucial work, *The Enlightenment: A Genealogy* (2010) first attempted to focus

---

2000); Franco Venturi, *Settecento Riformatore*, vol. 3: *La prima crisi dell'Antico Regime, 1768–1776* (Turin: 1979); Michael Printy, *Enlightenment and the Creation of German Catholicism* (Cambridge, Eng.: 2007), 1–22; Marc R. Forster, *Catholic Germany from the Reformation to the Enlightenment* (Basingstoke: 2007); Richard Butterwick, *The Polish Revolution and the Catholic Church, 1788–1792* (Oxford: 2012).

14   Roy Porter and Mikuláš Teich (eds.), *The Enlightenment in National Context* (Cambridge, Eng.: 1981). This introduction can neither fully nor adequately address the full panoply of diverse "enlightenments" more recently identified by scholars. See also Dan Edelstein (ed.), *The Super Enlightenment: Daring to Know Too Much?* (Oxford: 2010). Similar examinations of the mystical and occult side of the 18th century are offered by David Allen Harvey, *Beyond Enlightenment: Occultism and Politics in Modern France* (DeKalb: 2005), and more recently, Anton M. Matytsin and Dan Edelstein (eds.), *Let There Be Enlightenment: The Religious and Mystical Sources of Rationality* (Baltimore: 2018), 1–23. Others situate the Enlightenment within the cultural circulation characterizing the Atlantic world; see Susan Manning and Francis Cogliano (eds.), *The Atlantic Enlightenment* (London: 2007), 1–35. On the growing body of scholarship on Eastern European and Orthodox styles of Enlightenment, see Larry Wolff, *The Enlightenment in the Orthodox World* (Athens: 2001); Paschalis M. Kitromilides (ed.), *Enlightenment and Religion in the Orthodox World* (Oxford: 2016); on Rousseau and the "Platonic Enlightenment," see David Lay Williams, *Rousseau's Platonic Enlightenment* (University Park: 2007).

on the elements that French *philosophes* and *Encyclopédistes* drew upon in their process of retrospectively explaining and justifying their activities to themselves and to readers. This historiographical focus on narratological or intellectual genealogies – in short, how participants explained and contextualized what they were doing – parallels earlier investigations by James Schmidt and Darrin M. McMahon into the somewhat ironic and often retrospective constructions of the Enlightenment by Counter-Revolutionary apologists, or by later 19th- and 20th-century partisans and critics.[15] Vincenzo Ferrone's book, *The Enlightenment: An Interpretation* ultimately underscores the conclusions of Edelstein, Schmidt, and McMahon, but elegantly points up a persisting dilemma: that scholarly treatments of the 18th century still suffer from the interweaving of the philosophical *mythos* of the Enlightenment shaped by later events and philosophical perspectives, with the empirical history of the "Enlightenment" itself.[16]

These many complex caveats notwithstanding, many impressive scholars have nevertheless persisted in approaching the Enlightenment (as a whole, or in its more "radical Enlightenment" incarnations) as a uniquely important wellspring of modernity.[17] In all fairness, these efforts often reflect the abiding concern that many of the Enlightenment's most cherished contributions to humanity are increasingly under siege. In an age that seems disturbingly unable or unwilling to remember the best of the century of lights, I can only profess my sympathy with those who seek to protect some of the best fruits of the Enlightenment from further erosion. But I share William J. Bulman's recent caution that merely doubling down on the excessively tidy narrative of the Enlightenment as harbinger of modern secularization may not be the most productive response in these perilous times.[18]

---

15   Dan Edelstein, *The Enlightenment: A Genealogy* (Chicago: 2010), 1–44. For works arguing that the concept of the Enlightenment was at least in part the creation of later Revolutionary, Counter-Revolutionary, or 19th- and 20th-century history, see James G. Schmidt (ed.), *What Is Enlightenment? Eighteenth-Century Answers to Twentieth-Century Questions* (Berkeley: 2006); Darrin M. McMahon, *Enemies of Enlightenment: The French Counter-Enlightenment and the Making of Modernity* (Oxford: 2001).

16   Ferrone, *The Enlightenment*, vii–xvi, 3–6, 155–172.

17   Jonathan I. Israel, *Democratic Enlightenment: Philosophy, Revolution, and Human Rights, 1750–1790* (Oxford: 2011), 558–572; Anthony Pagden, *The Enlightenment and Why It Still Matters* (New York: 2013).

18   William J. Bulman, introduction to William J. Bulman and Robert G. Ingram (eds.), *God in the Enlightenment*, 8.

2   **Historiographical Hurdles II: Varieties of Religious Enlightenment and Their Critics**

Beginning with Pocock's suggestion that an "Enlightenment without *philosophes*" existed in England, likely existed elsewhere, and was perhaps more friendly to confessional Catholic or Protestant impulses than had been the case in France, scholars set forth on a quest to investigate clergy and devout laypersons, not as enemies of the Enlightenment, but as engaged participants in its most important 18th-century developments.[19] Thus, it has now become commonplace to speak of various styles of "religious Enlightenment" (to invoke David Sorkin's important book of the same title).[20] But, historical taxonomies of discrete confessional or religious enlightenments have also generated their own share of justifiable critique. One representative example of this observation concerns the scholarship on the Catholic Enlightenment – an interpretive paradigm that has been relevant to many facets of my own work over the years. No scholar has done more in recent years to revive and develop the scholarship on the Catholic Enlightenment than Ulrich L. Lehner. Lehner's important synthesis has recently defined "Catholic Enlightenment" rather capaciously as a movement forged primarily by Catholic clergy who aimed "to use the newest achievements of philosophy and science to defend the essential dogmas of Catholic Christianity by explaining them in a new language." Thereby, as Lehner continues, participants in Catholic Enlightenment sought to "reconcile Catholicism with modern culture."[21]

As Professor Lehner has more recently clarified, his notion of a Catholic Enlightenment "movement" must be understood to have encompassed a range of preoccupations and priorities associated with early modern global Catholicism. Speaking too coherently or hypostatically about a Catholic Enlightenment, as Lehner himself insists, is to fundamentally mistake the

---

19   Pocock, *Barbarism and Religion*, 9.

20   David Sorkin, *The Religious Enlightenment: Protestants, Jews, and Catholics from London to Vienna* (Princeton: 2008); Adam Sutcliffe, *Judaism and the Enlightenment* (Cambridge, Eng.: 2005); Shmuel Feiner, *The Jewish Enlightenment*, trans. Chaya Naor (Philadelphia: 2004). The centrality of religious debates to the origins of the Enlightenment is also freshly and insightfully covered in Anton M. Matytsin, *The Specter of Skepticism in the Age of Enlightenment* (Baltimore: 2016).

21   Ulrich L. Lehner, *The Catholic Enlightenment: The Forgotten History of a Global Movement* (New York: 2016), 7; see esp. 1–13; Ulrich L. Lehner, "The Many Faces of the Catholic Enlightenment," in *Companion to the Catholic Enlightenment in Europe*, eds. Ulrich L. Lehner and Michael Printy (Leiden: 2010), 1–61.

diversity of Enlightenment Catholicism.[22] It is, in my view, problematic chiefly because insisting too emphatically on the coherence of the Catholic Enlightenment movement risks eliding very substantive and contentious divisions dividing enlightened Catholics amongst themselves. Dale K. Van Kley's recent work, *Reform Catholicism and the International Suppression of the Jesuits in Enlightenment Europe*, for example, vocally addresses this contentious diversity at the heart of even Enlightenment Catholicism. Van Kley's research has framed the 18th century as an era of "plural lights" cutting across, not merely the once tidy Enlightenment project, but also across the religious Enlightenment within Catholic Europe.[23] Van Kley's understanding of Reform Catholicism clearly intersects with certain strands of what has often been understood as the Catholic Enlightenment, but, he contends, it was most often quite distinct from and opposed to the types of engagement common to other 18th-century Enlightenment Catholics. For example, Jesuits and those most favorable to them proved remarkably adept at revering the ancients while subtly moving beyond them through their eclectic appropriation methods and findings from the new natural philosophy. Descartes and Malebranche (to a modest extent), as well as Bacon, Locke, and Newton (to a somewhat greater extent) all by turns found themselves integrated into the scholarship of many 18th-century Jesuits in France who nevertheless remained faithful to their self-avowed Scholastic-Aristotelian roots, but in ways that updated and adapted them to new intellectual terrain. Jesuits and their fellow travelers within the 18th-century Catholic Church generally accepted the feasibility of social and individual progress through reason as well as through revelation. For the many writers influenced by the Jesuits, attending to the improvement of humanity through innovations in political economy, natural philosophy, and even through a kind of comparative anthropology, would promote human happiness in this life, just as sound theology informed and refined by those same pursuits would assure it in the next.[24] In Van Kley's view, then, the

---

22   Ulrich L. Lehner and Shaun Blanchard, "Introduction: The World of Catholic Enlightenment," in *The Catholic Enlightenment: A Global Anthology*, eds. Ulrich L. Lehner and Shaun Blanchard (Washington, D.C.: 2021), 1–18.

23   Dale K. Van Kley, *Reform Catholicism and the International Suppression of the Jesuits in Enlightenment Europe* (New Haven: 2018), notably 1–57; also, Dale K. Van Kley, "From the Catholic Enlightenment to the *Risorgimento:* The Debate between Nicola Spedalieri and Pietro Tamburini, 1791–1797," *Past and Present* 224/1 (2014): 112.

24   On the burgeoning science of comparative religion as a "new science," see Guy Stroumsa, *A New Science: The Discovery of Religion in the Age of Reason* (Cambridge, Mass.: 2010); also Aleksandra Porada, "Sources of Knowledge, Sources of Doubts: The Emergence of Modern Religious Studies and the French Enlightenment," in *The Sources of Secularism: Enlightenment and Beyond*, eds. Anna Tomaszewska and Hasse Hämäläinen (Cham: 2017),

controversies between supporters of Jansenists and Jesuits render the notion of a coherent movement of Catholic Enlightenment impossible, or at least highly problematic, once the 1750s–1760s brought with it a wave of suppressions and expulsions of the Jesuits from Catholic Europe and the Atlantic World, and set the stage for an acceleration of philo-Jansenist, Gallican-inspired Reform Catholicism. At best, he implies that the earlier, more coherent Catholic Enlightenment, such as it was, fractured at midcentury into at least two potentially competing tendencies, and perhaps, two largely incompatible Catholic Enlightenments – one Jansenist-friendly and the other, more favorable to or influenced by Jesuits and later ex-Jesuit ultramontanists.[25]

But even this duality within 18th-century Catholicism risks fraying at its edges depending on the periodization and national milieu in question. For many Jesuits shared with their rivals among the Jansenists a sincere fascination with historical apologetics – a fascination that unites them with the Benedictines of St Maur.[26] Affinities to philo-Jesuit proclivities notwithstanding,

---

141–167; on Jesuits in the Enlightenment, see Jeffrey D. Burson, "Introduction: The Culture of Jesuit Erudition in an Age of Enlightenment," *Journal of Jesuit Studies* 6/3 (2019): 387–415; Joan-Pau Rubiés, "The Jesuits and the Enlightenment," *The Oxford Handbook of the Jesuits*, ed. Ines G. Županov (Oxford: 2019), 855–890; Jeffrey D. Burson, "Between Power and Enlightenment: The Cultural and Intellectual Context of the Jesuit Suppression in France," in *The Jesuit Suppression in Global Context: Causes, Events, and Consequences*, eds. Jeffrey D. Burson and Jonathan Wright (Cambridge, Eng.: 2015), 40–64; on Jesuits in the origins of comparative religious studies, see Stroumsa, *A New Science*, 16–28, 41–64, 145–158; Dale K. Van Kley, "Robert R. Palmer's *Catholics and Unbelievers in Eighteenth-Century France*: An Overdue Tribute," in *Sacred and Secular Agency in Modern France: Fragments of Religion*, ed. Sanja Perovic (London: 2011), 16; an expanded version of this piece was first published as Dale K. Van Kley, "Robert R. Palmer's *Catholics and Unbelievers in Eighteenth-Century France*," *Historical Reflections/ Réflexions historiques* 37/3 (2011): 18–37; Jean Ehrard, *L'Idée de nature en France dans la première moitié du XVIIIᵉ siècle* (Geneva: 1981), 438–440. For additional foundational works on the Jesuits, see John W. O'Malley, "Jesuit Schools and the Humanities: Yesterday and Today," *Studies in the Spirituality of the Jesuits* 47/1 (2015): 1–34; John W. O'Malley, *The First Jesuits* (Cambridge, Mass.: 1993).

25   Dale K. Van Kley, *The Jansenists and the Expulsion of the Jesuits from France, 1757–1765* (New Haven: 1975), 4–5, 230–7; Dale K. Van Kley, *The Damiens Affair and the Unraveling of the Ancien Régime, 1750–1770* (Princeton: 1984), 99–165; Van Kley, *The Religious Origins of the French Revolution*, 5–13, 34–45, 89–109, 122–139, 180–3, 253–290, 297–267. For further development of the relationship between these religious controversies and the development of the *philosophes*, and of the attendant radicalization of the Enlightenment, see Burson, *The Rise and Fall of Theological Enlightenment* and Burson, "The Crystallization of Counter-Enlightenment and Philosophe Identities," 955–1002.

26   Rene-Joseph Tournemine, "Discours sur les Études de la Compagnie in doctrinis glorificate Dominum Par l'Etude des sciences rendés vous capable de glorifier le Seigneur" (Paris: s.a.), BnF: Nouvelles acquisitions Françaises, 10946, fols. 303–383. On transnational connections between French and German Benedictines with an emphasis on the

the Benedictines adapted a range of theological innovations, some of which were often much closer to those of philo-Augustinian Reform Catholicism. Furthermore, the evidence of popular 18th-century Catholic apologists, especially those in France, drew upon elements of both Jansenist-adjacent and Jesuit-adjacent styles of Enlightenment Catholicism. A famous example of this abiding complexity is evident in the work of the apologist Abbé Noël Antoine Pluche. Pluche's best-selling apologetic, *La Spectacle de la Nature*, drew on Huguenot, Jesuit, Oratorian, and other more radical philosophers. Pluche himself originally opposed the papal bull *Unigenitus* just as Jansenists did, yet his insistence that God enlisted "the understanding and use of created things" to conduct humankind to salvation and "teach reason through the help of the senses" was actually far more reminiscent of Jesuit theologians and philosophers such as Claude G. Buffier.[27]

While by no means exhaustive, the above examples serve to illustrate that the pluralization of the Enlightenment into religious enlightenments – and the further inter-confessional and intra-confessional dissection of Sorkin's originally more nuanced idea of a separate "spectrum" of religious Enlightenment – brings us back to the same problem with which we began.[28] How, then, can one grapple with what Hasse Hämäläinen and Anna Tomaszewska refer to as the "sources of secularism" in the Enlightenment, when the scholarly consensus regarding Kant's original query, "What is Enlightenment?" has seemingly so completely evaporated?[29]

---

distinctiveness of the German Benedictines, however, see Ulrich L. Lehner, *Enlightened Monks: The German Benedictines 1740–1803* (Oxford: 2011); on the importance of Oratorians in disseminating new methods and findings of natural philosophy in smaller towns and cities, see René Taton et al. (eds.), *Enseignement et diffusion des sciences en France au XVIIIᵉ siècle* (Paris: 1964), 67–75.

27 Abbé Noël-Antoine Pluche, "Discours préliminaire sur la necessité d'une Révélation," in *La Spectacle de la Nature, ou, entrétiens sur les particularités de l'histoire naturelle, qu'ont parus les plus propres à rendre les jeunes-gens curieux et à leur former l'esprit* (Paris: 1736–1742), vol. 5, 95–6; vol. 8, 1–20, 312–436; cf. Claude G. Buffier, *Traité des Premières vérités et de la source de nos jugements*, in *Oeuvres philosophiques de P. Buffier* (Paris: 1843), pars. III, cap. i., sectio. 406; and pars. I, cap. xxi, sectio. 337; Didier Masseau, *Les ennemis des philosophes: L'antiphilosophie au temps des Lumières* (Paris: 2000), 224–7.

28 Sorkin, *Religious Enlightenment*, 19–21.

29 Hasse Hämäläinen and Anna Tomaszewska, "Editors' Introduction," in: *The Sources of Secularism: Enlightenment and Beyond*, 1–17.

3   Transcending the Impasse: Theological Transformations
       and the Entangled Emergence of the Enlightenment

One way around this impasse is to consider the socio-cultural history of Enlightenment as an entangled process. Writing a more methodologically self-conscious *histoire croisée* of Enlightenment, as I have attempted to do recently, is to remain attentive to the fact that, as two principal theorists of *l'histoire croisée*, Michael Werner and Bénédicte Zimmermann have put it, "entities, persons, practices, or objects that are intertwined" in history "do not necessarily remain intact and identical in form" by their entanglement. Instead, their interactions mutually transform one another.[30] In other words, separate enlightenments (be they secular, religious, radical, national or otherwise) created and transformed one another through time and space – they were neither fully separate nor temporally static spectra or movements amenable to a stable taxonomy or characterization. When viewed in this way, theological debates over the nature of faith often emerge from the sources as ironic origins of the Enlightenment, just as texts and debates produced by what some have called the radical Enlightenment have just as often served as important catalysts for the reconstruction of religious belief and practice.[31]

The almost accidental and contingent secularizing implications of early modern discourse are evident even when we briefly consider the sources and reception of Baruch Spinoza's early work. While the primacy of Spinoza's role in the crafting of a supposedly modern and radical materialism has been exaggerated, one certainly cannot soundly deny the role that appropriations (or even unfounded accusations) of *"Spinozisme"* played in the intellectual genealogy of materialist naturalism and secularization. Radical understandings of Spinoza, for example, were one important harbinger and source for the young Diderot at mid-century.[32]

---

30   Michael Werner and Bénédicte Zimmermann, "Beyond Comparison: *Histoire croisée* and the Challenge of Reflexivity," *History and Theory* 45 (2006): 38, 45. For compatible perspectives on the plasticity of the category of "Enlightenment," and the risk that historical taxonomies often abstract, transcend, or transgress the past as experienced, see Wolfgang Schmale, *Das 18 Jarhundert* (Vienna: 2012); see for details, Burson, *Culture of Enlightening*, 1–25; and Jeffrey D. Burson, "Entangled History and the Concept of Enlightenment," *Contributions to the History of Concepts* 8/2 (2013): 1–24.

31   See also Damien Tricoire, "The Fabrication of the *Philosophe*: Catholicism, Court Culture, and the Origins of Enlightenment Moralism in France," *Eighteenth-Century Studies* 51/4 (2018): 453–477.

32   Andrew S. Curran, *Diderot and the Art of Thinking Freely* (New York: 2019), 49–125, 133–5, 142–176; for a more pluralistic interpretation of the radical Enlightenment from a variety of influences, including (but not at all limited to) Spinoza, see Jeffrey D. Burson,

But even with regard to the earliest reception of Spinoza in the Netherlands, as studies by Jetze Touber and Rienk Vermij persuasively argue, religiously inspired controversies informed both the content and reception of Spinoza's work.[33] Spinoza's *Tractatus theologico-politicus* and the polyvalence of its reception among both radical *philosophes* and orthodox writers illustrates, first, the risk of anachronism involved with prematurely and too casually reading later, starker juxtapositions of secularism and religion into 17th- and 18th-century developments. Second, the reception of Spinoza illustrates the very gradual and contingent process by which theological controversies drove philosophical debates and almost accidentally gave rise to forces of philosophical radicalization within the Enlightenment.

Among the earliest theaters for the reception of Spinoza's work was from within the contentious dispute among Dutch Reformed theologians over the application of historical-critical insights into biblical hermeneutics. Gijsbert Voetius (1589–1676) and his heirs among the "Voetians" began to focus on the practical application of biblical teaching to the lives of everyday believers. Often opposed to the Voetians were the Cocceians, as intellectual descendants of Johannes Cocceius (1603–1669) were called. Though just as sincere and constant in their outward adherence to Dutch Calvinist orthodoxy, the Cocceian method of approaching and teaching it was to insist that the most recent critical scholarship was a significant consideration as part of continuous and critical examination of the biblical text. The Cocceians' reinterpretation of the Bible in light of recent scholarship drew criticism from the Voetians as early as the 1670s. Indeed, the polemical controversy between Cocceians and Voetians within the Dutch Republic informed the context in which Spinoza's *Tractatus theologico-politicus* was originally received into Christian theology. In effect, Voetians began attacking the Cocceians for pioneering exactly the kind of historico-critical exegesis that they believed had led to Spinoza. While many Cocceians responded to these accusations by writing some of the very first public refutations of Spinoza, others such as Frederik van Leenhof (1647–1712) actually defended Spinoza's *Tractatus* for being fundamentally in accord with biblical teaching. The conclusion, for some of these pro-Spinozan

---

"*Unlikely Tales of Fo and Ignatius*: Rethinking the Radical Enlightenment through French Appropriation of Chinese Buddhism," *French Historical Studies* 38/3 (2018): 391–420.

33   Jetze Touber, "God's Word in the Dutch Republic," in *God in the Enlightenment*, 157–181; for accusations of Spinozism among antinominians in the Dutch Republic, see Rienk Vermij, "The Political Theory of the Libertines: Manuscripts and Heterodox Movements in the Early-Eighteenth-Century Dutch Republic," *Clandestine Philosophy: New Studies on Subversive Manuscripts in Early Modern Europe, 1620–1823*, eds. Gianni Paganini, Margaret C. Jacob and John Christian Laursen (Los Angeles: 2020), 143–159.

Calvinists – very much in the spirit of Spinoza's own interpretation – was that the gospel of Jesus Christ revealed within the New Testament was much closer to the universal dictates of natural reason than the dogmatic accretions of both Catholic and Protestant theologies had claimed. Here we can see how Spinoza's radicalism was further telegraphed in between the lines of Dutch Calvinist refutations, even as other Dutch Cocceians seized on the theological and historical-critical dimensions of Spinozan thought as natural allies in defense of Reformed orthodoxy.[34]

But, even from its inception, Spinoza's one-substance materialism and his conception of the natural order as a singular self-evolving substance, had far more to do with the reformulation of theocentric notions of the cosmos than with its subversion. In this sense, as historian of philosophy Przemysław Gut has argued, materialism was not even the primary emphasis of Spinozan substantial monism. Many of Spinoza's arguments in the *Tractatus theologicopoliticus*, and in Part I of the *Ethics*, instead reveal that divine causality and the characteristics of the human mind could each be embodied within the natural order itself. Thus, Spinoza's *Ethics* revealed that the absolute philosophical necessity of God's nature was the immanent cause of nature's end and vitality.[35] "Spinoza's numerous objections to theism did not aim at negating the deity," Gut contends, but instead "constituted an attempt to purify religion from the ... anthropomorphic vision of God."[36] Insofar as Spinoza's work became a source for the radical secularization of Enlightenment, then, it did so ironically, in a way that belied its origins as an attempt "to rehabilitate" religion "by the deification of the natural world."[37] Even Jonathan Israel has recently given a nod to the theological dimensions of Spinozan thought when he writes in the *Oxford Handbook of Early Modern Theology* that "Dutch and German Spinozism certainly *was* [emphasis original] a distinct, coherent, and rival theology.... Consequently, both the religious and irreligious wings of the Radical Enlightenment can be said to have shared a quasi-theological dimension."[38] Spinoza's philosophical perspective – much like the whole of

---

34   For this summary of the Voetian and Cocceian controversies and their influence on Spinozan appropriation in the Netherlands, I am indebted to the discussion in Touber, "God's Word in the Dutch Republic," 157–181.

35   Przemysław Gut, "The Legacy of Spinoza: The Enlightenment according to Jonathan Israel," *Diametros: An Online Journal of Philosophy* 40 (2014): 57–64.

36   Ibid., 63.

37   Ibid.

38   Jonathan I. Israel, "Spinoza and Early Modern Theology," in *The Oxford Handbook of Early Modern Theology, 1600–1800*, eds. Ulrich L. Lehner, Richard A. Muller and A.G. Roeber (Oxford: 2016), 583–8.

the Enlightenment in all of its various avatars – was thus pregnant with potential both for nascent secularization and for entirely new forms of religious experience and praxis realized much later in the 18th and 19th centuries.

However radical in its appropriation by many and however immanentist and heterodox in its approach, Spinoza's theology/philosophy also emerged from engagement with a complex and global genealogy, including artifacts of much earlier theological and philosophical debates of the medieval Mediterranean. The *Guide for the Perplexed* by Maimonides (Moses ben Maimon, ca. 1135–1204), the Arabic-speaking Jewish Aristotelian philosopher and medieval rabbi, was well known to Spinoza, Leibniz, Malebranche, Newton, and Bayle, thanks to a Latin edition newly translated from Arabic in 1629 at Basel. While the influence of Maimonides on Spinoza was hardly exceptional in the late 17th century, Spinoza's contention that the vitality of substance was synonymous with the divine creative life force appears to have been inspired by Maimonides's notion of the "World Soul" – an originally Middle Platonic and Neoplatonic idea translated into both Jewish and medieval Christian theological discourse thanks to the mediation of the Muslim philosopher Abu Nasr Muhammad ibn Muhammad al-Farabi (al-Farabi; 872 – ca. 950).[39]

Spinoza's notion of a natural religion accessible to all peoples based in the natural light of reason also closely resembled what Maimonides understood to be the basis for the so-called Laws of Noah – thought by many late 17th century polymaths to have contained the foundational principles of both civil law and natural religion granted to all peoples and passed down as the religion of the biblical patriarchs reflected in the epic of Genesis. As Guy Stroumsa has observed, Maimonides was of particular interest to both Catholic and Protestant erudition because of his participation in an influential earlier medieval rabbinical debate (translated into 17th- and 18th-century culture by Oxford and Cambridge Hebraists) over how many of the commandments in the Torah reflected a long-lost purpose based in natural reason. Maimonides had contributed to this debate, and he concluded that all of God's commandments originally reflected rational motivations that must also have served a utilitarian purpose. The shadow of these medieval rabbinical debates (and of the Maimonidean arguments more specifically) remains visible in the rather pervasive notions – common to nearly every 18th-century enlightener (Catholic, Protestant, or radical) – that the original religion of humanity must have been

---

39   Steven Nadler, *Spinoza's Heresy: Immortality and the Jewish Mind* (Oxford: 2001), 68; on al-Farabi's thought within the broader context of early Islamic philosophy, see Sari Nusseibeh, *The Story of Reason in Islam* (Stanford: 2017), 120–141.

fundamentally synonymous with the law of nature, and that true religion was, and ought to be, socially cohesive and useful to society.[40]

Beyond its partial rootedness in the medieval groundswell of theological speculation commonly constructed by Muslims, Jews, and Christians alike, the Spinozan system additionally owed much to traditions of ancient vitalistic materialism revived by Renaissance Hermeticism, Epicureanism, and atomism after the 16th century.[41] Authors of clandestine texts – such as John Toland, in his *Pantheisticon*, or M. Foucroy, who likely penned *Doutes sur la religion* – underscored the ancient genealogy and commensurability of these various traditions of materialism. This classical tradition of materialism, seemingly so ubiquitous in the cosmologies of so many of the world's most ancient peoples, affirmed Toland's conclusions, suggesting that God was merely the force or sentient energy animating the universe, and that this seemingly foundational tenet of the universal religion had been affirmed by ancient cosmologies the world over.[42] In effect, the pages of numerous clandestine manuscripts synthesized these ancient cosmologies with the fruits of the new science, ongoing confessional polemics, and the insights of contemporary philosophers including Spinoza.[43] In some sense, therefore, clandestine texts constitute just one significant laboratory for the cultural and theological revolution which, among other outcomes, gave rise to Enlightenment secularization. Such texts reveal more than just the proliferation of Spinozan thought (even at times in ways that Spinoza himself would not have anticipated): they further allow us to consider the entanglement of radical and orthodox religious works, as 18th-century writers worked out the cultural, historical, and political implications of what were, originally, theological and metaphysical debates.[44]

---

40 Stroumsa, *New Science*, 45–9, 87, 92–7.

41 Sarah Ellenzweig, "Richard Bentley's *Paradise Lost* and the Ghost of Spinoza," in *God in the Enlightenment*, 257–277.

42 Miguel Benítez, *La Face cachée des Lumières: Recherches sur les manuscrits philosophiques clandestins de l'âge classique* (Paris: 1996), 191–5.

43 Burson, *"Unlikely Tales of Fo and Ignatius,"* 396; Aram Vartanian, "Quelques réflexions sur le concept d'âme dans la littérature clandestine," in *Le Matérialisme du XVIIIᵉ siècle et la littérature clandestine*, ed. Olivier Bloch (Paris: 1982), 162.

44 The relationship between clandestine manuscripts and the history of printed texts continues to be complex. Ira Wade completed the first, most complete list of around one hundred manuscripts located throughout French and other European repositories. This list, which has informed foundational works published by Miguel Benítez, Margaret C. Jacob, and Jonathan I. Israel, continues to expand and presently includes over two thousand manuscripts. Scholars continue to locate new manuscripts while also mapping their circulation, emendation, and relationship to print editions. Ira O. Wade, *The Clandestine Organization and Diffusion of Philosophic Ideas in France from 1700 to 1750* (New York: 1967), 11–21; for a list of repositories and an early approximation of when each manuscript

As Ann Thomson and Roland Mortier have noted elsewhere, many of the works comprising the clandestine corpus addressed, or directly blossomed from within important metaphysical or religious debates. But, by the dawn of the 18th century, clandestine texts further interlaced these issues with developments in political thought and medical science.[45] Vitalistic styles of materialism, forged from much earlier religious and philosophical debates and contained within influential clandestine texts (for example, *L'Ame matérielle*, *Sentiments des philosophes sur la nature de l'âme*, and Mirabaud's *De l'âme et de son immortalité*), were actually hybrid discourses constructed from several different sources. Texts produced by Jesuits and travelers suggesting a more universal history of philosophy and religion; Spinozan metaphysics; the Renaissance Hermeticism that informed Toland and Anthony Collins as much as Spinoza; debates about the soul ignited by Cartesians; and Gassendo-Epicurean definitions of mind as emergent from a species of subtle matter: all of these sources played a role as the discursive context for the shaping of Enlightenment vitalistic materialism.[46]

---

was likely composed, see 263–275; for additional texts, see Miguel Benítez, "Liste et localisation des traités clandestins," in *Le Matérialisme du XVIIIe siècle et la littérature clandestine*, 17–25.

45   Claude Buffier, *Traité des premières vérités*, ed. Louis Rouquayrol (Paris: 2020), and notably also, Professor Rouquayrol's useful introduction, 11–63; Ann Thomson, "Qu'est-ce qu'un manuscrit clandestin?" in *Le Matérialisme du XVIIIe siècle et la littérature clandestine*, 15; Roland Mortier, "Conclusions," in *Le Matérialisme du XVIIIe siècle et la littérature clandestine*, 275; Jeffrey D. Burson, "The Polyvalence of Heterodox Sources and Eighteenth-Century Religious Change," in *Clandestine Philosophy*, 328–351; Margaret C. Jacob, "The Enlightenment Critique of Christianity," in *The Cambridge History of Christianity*, vol. 8, eds. Stewart J. Brown and Timothy Tackett (Cambridge, Eng.: 2006), 265–282.

46   Jean Baptiste de Mirabaud, *De l'âme et de son immortalité*, vol. 1 (London: 1751), 6–8; Alain Niderst (ed.), *L'Ame matérielle* (Paris: 1969), 50, 52, 118, 222–234; Dennis Des Chene, *Life's Form: Late Aristotelian Conceptions of the Soul* (Ithaca: 2000), 168–9, 199–202; Ann Thomson, "Toland, Dodwell, Swift and the Circulation of Irreligious Ideas in France: What Does the Study of International Networks Tell Us about the 'Radical Enlightenment,'" in *Intellectual Journeys: The Translation of Ideas in England, France and Ireland*, eds. Lise Andries and Frederic Ogee (Oxford: 2013), 162–4; Ann Thomson, *Bodies of Thought: Science, Religion, and the Soul in the Early Enlightenment* (Oxford 2008; repr. 2010), 29–65; Ann Thomson, *L'âme des Lumières: Le débat sur l'être humain entre religion et science Angleterre-France, 1690–1760* (Paris: 2013), 161–238; for the "animal spirits" and the root of the more radical, materialist reading of Descartes, see René Descartes, *Passions de l'âme*, article IV, in *Oeuvres philosophiques de Descartes*, vol. 3, ed. Ferdinand Alquié (Paris: 1973), 959, 965, 973; Jürgen Osterhammel, *Unfabling the East: The Enlightenment's Encounter with Asia* (Princeton: 2019); David Allen Harvey, *The French Enlightenment and Its Others: The Mandarin, the Savage, and the Invention of the Human Sciences* (Basingstoke: 2012); and Florence C. Hsia, *Sojourners in a Strange Land: Jesuits and their Scientific Missions in Late Imperial China* (Chicago: 2009); on the role of travelers, see Henry Liebersohn,

Refocusing our attention, then, on the impact of these developments in just one area – the development of the French Enlightenment – will allow us to observe how the fruits of more than a half century of clandestine manuscripts suddenly found their way into print and reached a more widespread readership.[47] The latter half of the 1740s and into the 1750s proved to be increasingly alarming decades to authorities within France and its already deeply faction-ridden Gallican Church. La Mettrie's *L'Homme machine* (1745), Diderot's *Pensées philosophiques* (1746) (a book that did much to incite the wrath of the Jesuits over his growing editorial importance to the *Encyclopédie*), Montesquieu's *L'Esprit des lois* (1748), and Buffon's *L'Histoire naturelle* (1749) all swiftly became available before 1751.[48] Yet, the more radical edges to these and other important works associated with the mid-century French Enlightenment were not intrinsic to radical philosophy as such. Rather, French readers saw – and found increasingly convincing – the potentially radical implications of a convergence between religious debates over natural theology, the universal

---

The Traveler's World: Europe to the Pacific (Cambridge, Mass.: 2006); Vartanian, "Quelques réflexions sur le concept d'âme dans la littérature clandestine," in *Le Matérialisme du XVIIIᵉ siècle et la littérature clandestine*, 149–165. For a vital reassessment of the role of Epicureanism during the 18th century, see Alan C. Kors, *Epicureans and Atheists in France* (Cambridge, Eng.: 2015); also Alan C. Kors, *Naturalism and Unbelief in France* (Cambridge, Eng.: 2015); Pierre Gassendi, *Metaphysical Colloquy, or Doubts and Rebuttals Concerning the Metaphysics of René Descartes with His Replies*, trans. Craig B. Brush (New York: 1972), 275–8.

47   See discussion in Wade, *Clandestine Origin and Diffusion of Philosophic Ideas in France*, 1–21, 263–5, 274; Jonathan I. Israel, *Radical Enlightenment: Philosophy and the Making of Modernity, 1650–1750* (Oxford: 2001), 684–701; Robert Shackleton, "When Did the French *Philosophes* Become a Party?" *Bulletin of the John Rylands University Library of Manchester* 60 (1977): 189–193; César Chesneau du Marsais, *Examen de la religion, ou Doutes sur la religion dont on cherche l'éclaircissement de bonne foi* (Oxford: 1998). Growing concern for such publication was becoming increasingly evident by the mid-1730s in the Jesuit *Mémoires de Trévoux*; see, for example, André Rouillé, "La Psychometre ou Réflexions sur les différens caractères de l'Ésprit par Mylord Anglois," *Mémoires de Trévoux* (mai 1735): 712–713; René-Joseph Tournemine, "Lettre du P. Tournemine de la Compagnie de Jésus à M.*** sur l'immatérialité de l'âme et les sources de l'incrédulité," *Mémoires de Trévoux* (mai 1735): 1915–1917; see also specific responses to the rash of publications of formerly clandestine philosophical essays in the book review essay, "On Fontenelle, *Nouvelles libertés de penser*; Mirabaud, *Sentimens des philosophes sur la nature de l'âme*; Fontenelle, *Traité de la liberté*; Chesneau du Marsais, *Réflexions sur l'âme et sur l'existence de Dieu*," *Mémoires de Trévoux* (août 1743): 2267–2271.

48   Julien Offray de La Mettrie, *L'Homme machine* (1745; repr. Amsterdam: 1966); François Toussaint, *Les Moeurs* (Amsterdam: 1748); Georges Louis Leclerc, Comte de Buffon, *Histoire naturelle générale et particulière*, *Oeuvres complètes de Buffon*, vol. 6 (Paris: 1774); Charles Louis de Sécondat, Baron de la Brède et de Montesquieu, *De l'Ésprit des lois* (1748; repr. Paris: 1950).

history of philosophy, and the fruits of the scientific revolution. The receptivity of readers to these more radical implications required entanglement with contingent socio-political factors: chiefly, France's erratic foreign policy, financial difficulties, intraconfessional strife between Jesuits and Jansenists, and a new wave of both religious and intellectual persecution that swept the realm between ca. 1750 and 1765. But the result was a wholesale realignment of the Francophone Enlightenment. This realignment derived from religious, metaphysical, and theological origins, as much as from purely philosophical ones, or from social changes in reading taste and commerce studied in isolation from the history of ideas. In many ways, even the habit of distinguishing sharply between philosophy and theology, while relegating the latter to a private sphere of faith and suprarational (or irrational) speculation, reveals itself to be a major *consequence* of the Enlightenment, not its cause. Similarly, the sweeping impact of the radical edges of the Enlightenment, especially as pedaled and popularized by members of the sect of philosophy in France, can be more effectively understood as an *outcome* of the cultural and theological transformations previously discussed. They were not precisely the cause and *sine qua non* of the Enlightenment, or of a distinct radical Enlightenment.

Diderot's own intellectual journey and influence on the public sphere during the 1750s to 1770s affords still another prime example of the fruits of the Enlightenment's entangled emergence from theological and metaphysical speculation, and his literary output has, among other things, much to do with the redrawing of the boundaries between philosophy and theology. In a way that owed something to Spinoza, to forms of Epicurean materialism, and to medical vitalism in the tradition of the Montpellier physicians, Diderot's article, "Spinosisme" and his *Eléments de physiology* (unpublished within his lifetime) ascribed vitality and sensitivity to all matter, and conceived of the universe as a self-directing, self-evolving organism.[49] Derived in part from the animism of ancient Greco-Roman theology and in part from the medieval Jewish rabbinical theology of Maimonides, Spinozan notions had entered into

---

49   Ellenzweig, "Richard Bentley's *Paradise Lost* and the Ghost of Spinoza," in *God in the Enlightenment*, 272; Paul Vernière, *Spinoza et la pensée française avant la Révolution*, vol. 2 (Paris: 1954), 560; Elizabeth A. Williams, *A Cultural History of Medical Vitalism in Enlightenment Montpellier* (Aldershot: 2003), 3–11, 147–177, 275–281, 305–328; Elizabeth A. Williams, *The Physical and the Moral: Anthropology, Physiology, and Philosophical Medicine in France, 1750–1850* (Cambridge, Eng.: 1994), 1–46; Henri Lefebvre, *Diderot ou les affirmations fondamentales du matérialisme* (Paris: 1999), 112–116, 131–155; Charles T. Wolfe, "Epigenesis as Spinozism in Diderot's Biological Project," in *The Life Sciences in Early Modern Philosophy*, eds. Ohad Nachtomy and Justin E.H. Smith (Oxford: 2014), 192–6; Pierre-François Moreau, "Spinoza's Reception and Influence," in *The Cambridge Companion to Spinoza*, ed. Don Garrett (Cambridge, Eng.: 1996), 418–419.

17th-century Dutch theological controversies over Calvinist hermeneutics, and into the esoteric theologies of clandestine manuscripts. From thence, they became one of the tools available to Diderot when he sought to sculpt more utilitarian understandings of natural religion and philosophy without recourse to traditional institutions of confessional theology. This was most certainly a process of secularization at work, but it was also a prominent example of a transformation and laicization of theological questioning associated with the long theological revolution of the 16th to 19th centuries. Enlightenment secularization, in short, reveals itself to be not "post-theological" *per se*, but rather, a post-confessional, post-Christian, and post-clerical turn in the history of both religion and culture derived from that longer theological revolution.[50]

In the hands of even the most self-consciously radical enlighteners, unveiling the vast uncharted territory of hidden knowledge universally available to all humanity through reason while disseminating these truths before an expanding readership became the principal sacrifice offered up by the new species of philosopher exemplified by Diderot – an offering dedicated to the ultimate happiness of humanity. As the article "Philosophe" in the *Encyclopédie* phrased it, "[The philosopher] burns incense to [civil society], honors it by his probity, by an exact attention to his duties and by a sincere desire not to be an unusual or burdensome member of it."[51] As Lynn Hunt has recently suggested, the progressive and perhaps ultimately perfectible happiness of society, valorized by late 18th-century writers and increasingly legitimized by an empathically-sensed desire to actualize an individual's natural rights in law and *morale*, began to displace God from the center of the emergent Enlightenment of the *philosophes*.[52] But Hunt's insight does not exclusively betoken the abandonment of theology for philosophy; instead, it articulates the result of a new phase in the religious and theological history of the Euro-Atlantic community – one with arguably global dimensions because of the 19th- and 20th-century commingling of the *philosophe* notion of Enlightenment with the fruits of related

---

50   Jonathan Sheehan, *The Enlightenment Bible: Translation, Scholarship, Culture* (Princeton: 2005), xi; Sheehan's later work cited in n. 7 proceeds more openly and consistently from the assumption that Enlightenment secularization is not post-theological as such, but more particularly, post-theological in the sense of confessional Christian theology.

51   "Philosophe," in *Encyclopédie*/ARTFL, 12:509–510, http://encyclopedie.uchicago.edu/ [Accessed 12.05.2020]. For English translation, see Lynn Hunt, *Writing History in a Global Era* (New York: 2014), 83.

52   Hunt, *Writing History*, 83–100; also, Lynn Hunt, *Inventing Human Rights* (New York: 2007).

cultural awakenings throughout Eurasia, perhaps in the manner posited by Sebastian Conrad.[53]

In fact, Diderot's longtime co-editor of the *Encyclopédie*, Jean d'Alembert, in his lengthy harangue against the persecutors of the *Encyclopédie*, well captures this oft-overlooked way in which the radicalized Enlightenment, co-opted and galvanized by the midcentury Francophone Enlightenment, effectively disseminated a new species of theology. In d'Alembert's estimation, reason was not opposed to religion as such; instead, d'Alembert's satirical rhetoric merely redefined the notion of "religion." His was a philosophy that remained handmaiden of theology, but of a theology purified by the expurgation of superstition:

> The *Encyclopédie* is assumed to have been a society formed to destroy morality and religion, and the authors are accused of contradicting one another.... They have been reproached for having said (with Saint Paul) that the worship we render to God must be reasonable; with Father Malebranche that the good of men is in pleasure (as if the word "pleasure" is to be defined only as the pleasures of the senses); with the most respectable authors that intolerance and persecution are contrary to the spirit of Christianity; and finally with the most powerful of our kings, and with the first Parlement of this realm, that legitimate authority is founded on the contract made between subjects and sovereigns.[54]

This passage unmasked the hypocrisy and self-interest of traditional religious elites by compelling the reader to ponder the consonance between philosophical Enlightenment, purified Christianity, and true religion. In other words, d'Alembert, in the good company of many *philosophes*, and in accord with many thoughtful Catholic and Protestant reformers of the time, continued to argue that the purest theology of humanity was, at its core, synonymous with the pure spirit of Christianity, and with the quest for sound philosophy purged of superstition and corruption.[55] In words borrowed from du Marsais earlier

---

53   Sebastian Conrad, "Enlightenment in Global History: An Historiographical Critique," *American Historical Review* 117/4 (2012): 999–1027, esp. at 1005–1022; see also Sebastian Conrad, "The Global History of the Enlightenment," in *An Emerging Modern World, 1750–1850*, eds. Sebastian Conrad and Jürgen Osterhammel (Cambridge, Mass.: 2018), 485–526.

54   Jean d'Alembert, "Avertissement sur cette nouvelle édition," in *Discours préliminaire de l'Encyclopédie* (Amsterdam: 1763; repr. Paris: 1965), 7–8.

55   See also, "Que les souverains méprisent et ignorent les disputes de religion, et elles ne deviendront ni turbulentes ni funestes. Qu'ils favorisent les progrès de la raison, et ces disputes deviendront ridicules ... Aux intérêts de la seule religion veritable ... doit tender,

in the century, Voltaire went so far as to proclaim that the apostles of *prisca theologia* were in fact the *philosophes* of his time – the bringers of the "love of wisdom" into a world long darkened by priests, theologians, and ancient, barbarous, philosophical systems.[56]

4 Conclusion

Scholars still too often succumb to the habit of investigating religious discourse in so far as it borrowed or adapted Enlightenment tropes; or they investigate the Enlightenment in so far as it encouraged people to live "without reference to God."[57] While each of these approaches remains useful in significant ways, they nevertheless can obscure as much as they illuminate because of the shared, tacit assumption that participants in religious and secular Enlightenments were, by and large, alien others who borrowed from discrete intellectual tool boxes. But the secular and religious transformations of the age were inextricably of a piece with the same process of theological and cultural revolution already unfolding throughout the Enlightenment period and beyond. Vincenzo Ferrone has aptly described this larger cultural revolution from which *Aufklärung* emerged:

> [T]he Enlightenment was ... perhaps first and foremost, an extraordinary religious revolution. It radically changed the Western way of seeing the relationship between man and God, for it overturned the hierarchy of primary interests, exploring man's autonomy and liberty and consequently his responsibility instead of taking the traditional providential view of human existence. From the historical point of view, this was due not so much to the Enlightenment's atheistic and materialistic propaganda – which was a fairly circumscribed phenomenon, despite its importance – as to its redefinition of the image, function and meaning of God and religion.[58]

---

autant qu'il est possible, à détruire et à saper les autres, non par la force, mais par le raisonnement et la persuasion." Jean d'Alembert, "Fragment sur la véritable religion," in Charles Henry (ed.), *Oeuvres et correspondences inédites* (Geneva: 1967), 1 and 3.

56 "Philosophe," in *Encyclopédie*, vol. 12, 511–515; also Voltaire, "L'introduction générale aux Questions sur l'*Encyclopédie* par des amateurs," in *Oeuvres Complètes*, vol. 17 (Paris: 1878), 3–5.

57 Jacob, *The Secular Enlightenment*, 1.

58 Ferrone, *The Enlightenment*, 102.

Charly Coleman has further noted that "French mystics and materialists drew on analogous arguments, and at times identical terminologies, in their efforts to undermine the individual's claims to active self-determination." Late 18th-century culture, then, engaged in a process of "resacralization" that "valorize[d] the immanent relations between human beings and the world." Secularization, in Coleman's view as well as my own, needs to be understood as "a contingent, multidimensional process." It was a process that in many respects actually "originated within religion itself."[59] If recent scholarship on the French Revolution – indeed to a degree, the age of Atlantic Revolutions more generally – is duly considered, the Revolutionary period only accelerated and intensified ways in which individuals experienced the sacred through collective action, ritual, zeal for revolutionary virtue, and rights discourse. Taking a cue from Emile Durkheim and Lynn Hunt, Blake Smith has proclaimed the French Revolution "a spiritual phenomenon, a manifestation of the sacred," the "legacy and commemoration" of which "has become a religion with rituals, festivals, and idols" of its own.[60] Taking its cue more from Tocqueville and Charles Taylor than from Durkheim, the essays in the recent volume edited by Bryan Banks and Erica Johnson amount to a very similar claim that the global impact of the French Revolution's secularizing language was "a recalibration of the religious in the modern world, rather than its death knell."[61] Nor, it needs be said, was this recalibration of the sacred an entirely Francophone, Enlightenment, or Revolutionary affair. Recent work by historian of philosophy Alexander J.B. Hampton on Friedrich Schlegel, Friedrich von Hardenberg, and Friedrich Hölderlin has convincingly suggested that the religious revolution of the late Enlightenment continued, informing attempts by German Romantics "to forge a new metaphysics and epistemology of transcendence," focused on aesthetics, poetry, and imaginative creativity, and thereby, to "reinvent modern religion."[62]

These reflections on the current state of the field suggest that the "secular Enlightenment"[63] is just one historically significant result of a cultural

---

59 All quotes from Coleman, *Virtues of Abandon*, 11–12.

60 Blake Smith, "The Sacred French Revolution: Emile Durkheim, Lynn Hunt, and Historians," in *Age of Revolutions*, eds. Bryan Banks, Cindy Ermus et al. (2019), www.ageofrevolutions. com [Accessed 12.4.2021].

61 Bryan Banks and Erica Johnson, introduction to *The Revolution and Religion in Global Perspective*, eds. Bryan Banks and Erica Johnson (Cham: 2017), x.

62 Alexander J.B. Hampton, *Romanticism and the Re-Invention of Modern Religion: The Reconciliation of German Idealism and Platonic Realism* (Cambridge, Eng.: 2019), 9, see also 1–9.

63 Jacob, *The Secular Enlightenment*, 263–5.

revolution possessing both European and global origins and impacts; one that can be considered to have unfolded throughout the breadth of the late 16th to 19th centuries; and one that transformed theological assumptions, religious experience, and emotional regimes, much as it did methods of natural philosophy and the normative assumptions of moral and political thought.[64]

References

Banks, Bryan, and Erica Johnson (eds.), *The Revolution and Religion in Global Perspective* (Cham: 2017).

Becker, Carl, *The Heavenly City of the Eighteenth-Century Philosophers*, 2nd ed. (New Haven: 2003).

Benítez, Miguel, *La Face cachée des Lumières: Recherches sur les manuscrits philosophiques clandestins de l'âge classique* (Paris: 1996).

Benítez, Miguel, "Liste et localisation des traités clandestins," in *Le Matérialisme du XVIIIᵉ siècle et la littérature clandestine*, ed. Olivier Bloch (Paris: 1982), 17–25.

Buffier, Claude G., *Traité des Premières vérités et de la source de nos jugements*, in *Oeuvres philosophiques de P. Buffier*, ed. Francisque Brouiller (Paris: 1843).

Buffier, Claude, *Traité des premières vérités* (Paris: 2020).

Buffon, Georges Louis Leclerc, Comte de, "Histoire naturelle générale et particulière," *Oeuvres complètes de Buffon*, vol. 6 (Paris: 1774).

Bulman, William J., "Introduction: Enlightenment for the Culture Wars," in *God in the Enlightenment*, eds. William J. Bulman and Robert G. Ingram (New York: 2016), 1–41.

Burson, Jeffrey D., "Between Power and Enlightenment: The Cultural and Intellectual Context of the Jesuit Suppression in France," in *The Jesuit Suppression in Global Context: Causes, Events, and Consequences*, eds. Jeffrey D. Burson and Jonathan Wright (Cambridge, Eng.: 2015), 40–64.

Burson, Jeffrey D., "The Polyvalence of Heterodox Sources and Eighteenth-Century Religious Change," in *Clandestine Philosophy: New Studies on Subversive Manuscripts in Early Modern Europe, 1620–1823*, eds. Gianni Paganini, Margaret C. Jacob and John Christian Laursen (Los Angeles: 2020), 328–351.

Burson, Jeffrey D., "The Crystallization of Counter-Enlightenment and Philosophe Identities: Theological Controversy and Catholic Enlightenment in Pre-Revolutionary France," *Church History* 77/4 (2008): 955–1002.

---

64   Burson, *The Culture of Enlightening*, 372–382; see also Jeffrey D. Burson, "Process, Contingency, and Cultural Entanglement: Toward a Post-Revisionism in Enlightenment Historiography," *Journal of the Western Society for French History* 47 (2021): http://hdl.handle.net/2027/spo.0642292.0047.001 [Accessed 20.9.2021].

Burson, Jeffrey D., *The Culture of Enlightening: Abbé Claude Yvon and the Entangled Emergence of the Enlightenment* (Notre Dame: 2019).

Burson, Jeffrey D., "Entangled History and the Concept of Enlightenment," *Contributions to the History of Concepts* 8/2 (2013): 1–24.

Burson, Jeffrey D., "Introduction: The Culture of Jesuit Erudition in an Age of Enlightenment," *Journal of Jesuit Studies* 6/3 (2019): 387–415.

Burson, Jeffrey D., "Process, Contingency, and Cultural Entanglement: Toward a Post-Revisionism in Enlightenment Historiography," *Journal of the Western Society for French History* 47 (2021): http://hdl.handle.net/2027/spo.0642292.0047.001 [Accessed 21.9.2021].

Burson, Jeffrey D., *The Rise and Fall of Theological Enlightenment: Jean-Martin de Prades and Ideological Polarization in Eighteenth-Century France* (Notre Dame: 2010).

Burson, Jeffrey D., "*Unlikely Tales of Fo and Ignatius*: Rethinking the Radical Enlightenment through French Appropriation of Chinese Buddhism," *French Historical Studies* 38/3 (2018): 391–420.

Butterwick, Richard, *The Polish Revolution and the Catholic Church, 1788–1792* (Oxford: 2012).

Butterwick, Richard, Simon Davies, and Gabriel Sánchez Espinoza (eds.), *Peripheries of the Enlightenment* (Oxford: 2008).

Coleman, Charly, "Resacralizing the World: The Fate of Secularization in Enlightenment Historiography," *Journal of Modern History* 82/2 (2010): 368–395.

Coleman, Charly, *The Virtues of Abandon: An Anti-Individualist History of the French Enlightenment* (Stanford: 2014).

Conrad, Sebastian, "Enlightenment in Global History: An Historiographical Critique," *American Historical Review* 117/4 (2012): 999–1027.

Conrad, Sebastian, "The Global History of the Enlightenment," in *An Emerging Modern World, 1750–1850*, eds. Sebastian Conrad and Jürgen Osterhammel (Cambridge, Mass.: 2018), 485–526.

Curran, Andrew, *Diderot and the Art of Thinking Freely* (New York: 2019).

D'Alembert, Jean, "Avertissement sur cette nouvelle édition," in *Discours préliminaire de l'*Encyclopédie (Amsterdam: 1763; repr. Paris: 1965), 5–8.

D'Alembert, Jean, "Fragment sur la véritable religion," in *Oeuvres et correspondences inédites* (Geneva: 1967), 1–8.

Darnon, Robert, "Policing Writers in Paris circa 1750," *Representation* 5 (1984): 1–34.

Descartes, René, *Passions de l'âme*, in *Oeuvres philosophiques de Descartes*, vol. 3 (Paris: 1973).

Des Chene, Dennis, *Life's Form: Late Aristotelian Conceptions of the Soul* (Ithaca: 2000).

Du Marsais, César Chesneau, *Examen de la religion, ou Doutes sur la religion dont on cherche l'éclaircissement de bonne foi* (Oxford: 1998).

Edelstein, Dan, *The Enlightenment: A Genealogy* (Chicago: 2010).

Edelstein, Dan (ed.), *The Super Enlightenment: Daring to Know Too Much?* (Oxford: 2010).

Ehrard, Jean, *L'Idée de nature en France dans la première moitié du XVIIIᵉ siècle* (Geneva: 1981).

Ellenzweig, Sarah, "Richard Bentley's *Paradise Lost* and the Ghost of Spinoza," in *God in the Enlightenment*, eds. William J. Bowman and Robert Ingram (Oxford: 2016), 257–277.

Feiner, Shmuel, *The Jewish Enlightenment*, trans. Chaya Naor (Philadelphia: 2004).

Ferrone, Vincenzo, *The Enlightenment: History of an Idea* (Princeton: 2015).

Forster, Michael R., *Catholic Germany from the Reformation to the Enlightenment* (Basingstoke: 2007).

Foucault, Michel, "What Is Enlightenment?" in *The Foucault Reader*, ed. Paul Rabinow (New York: 1984), 32–51.

Funkelstein, Amos, *'Secular Theology' in a Modern Age: Theology and the Scientific Imagination from the Middle Ages to the Seventeenth Century* (Princeton: 1986).

Gassendi, Pierre, *Metaphysical Colloquy, or Doubts and Rebuttals Concerning the Metaphysics of René Descartes with His Replies*, trans. Craig B. Brush (New York: 1972).

Gregory, Brad S., "The Reformation Origins of the Enlightenment's God," in *God in the Enlightenment*, eds. William J. Bulman and Robert G. Ingram (New York: 2016), 201–214.

Gut, Przemysław, "The Legacy of Spinoza: The Enlightenment according to Jonathan Israel," *Diametros: An Online Journal of Philosophy* 40 (2014): 99–114.

Haechler, Jean, *L'Encyclopédie: Les combats et les hommes* (Paris: 1998).

Hämäläinen, Hasse, and Anna Tomaszewska, "Editors' Introduction," in *The Sources of Secularism: Enlightenment and Beyond* (Cham: 2017), 1–17.

Hampton, Alexander J.B., *Romanticism and the Re-Invention of Modern Religion: The Reconciliation of German Idealism and Platonic Realism* (Cambridge, Eng.: 2019).

Harvey, David Allen, *Beyond Enlightenment: Occultism and Politics in Modern France* (DeKalb: 2005).

Harvey, David Allen, *The French Enlightenment and Its Others: The Mandarin, the Savage, and the Invention of the Human Sciences* (Basingstoke: 2012).

Horkheimer, Max, and Theodore Adorno, *The Dialectic of Enlightenment: Philosophical Fragments*, trans. Edmund Jephcott (Los Angeles: 2012).

Hsia, Florence C., *Sojourners in a Strange Land: Jesuits and their Scientific Missions in Late Imperial China* (Chicago: 2009).

Hunt, Lynn, *Inventing Human Rights* (New York: 2007).

Hunt, Lynn, *Writing History in a Global Era* (New York: 2014).

Israel, Jonathan I., *Democratic Enlightenment: Philosophy, Revolution, and Human Rights, 1750–1790* (Oxford: 2011).

Israel, Jonathan I., *Enlightenment Contested: Philosophy, Modernity, and the Emancipation of Man, 1670–1752* (Oxford: 2011).

Israel, Jonathan I., *Radical Enlightenment: Philosophy and the Making of Modernity, 1650–1750* (Oxford: 2001).

Israel, Jonathan I., "Spinoza and Early Modern Theology," in *The Oxford Handbook of Early Modern Theology, 1600–1800*, eds. Ulrich L. Lehner, Richard A. Muller, and A.G. Roeber (Oxford: 2016), 577–593.

Jacob, Margaret C., "The Enlightenment Critique of Christianity," in *The Cambridge History of Christianity*, eds. Stewart J. Brown and Timothy Tackett, vol. 8 (Cambridge, Eng.: 2006), 265–282.

Jacob, Margaret C., *The Secular Enlightenment* (Princeton: 2019).

Jourdain, Annie, *La Révolution, une exception française?* (Paris: 2004).

Kafker, Frank A., *The Encyclopedists as a Group: A Collective Biography of the Authors of the Encyclopédie* (Oxford: 1996).

Kant, Immanuel, "An Answer to the Question: What Is Enlightenment?" in *Practical Philosophy*, ed. Mary J. Gregor (New York: 1996), 11–22.

Kitromilides, Paschalis M. (ed.), *Enlightenment and Religion in the Orthodox World* (Oxford: 2016).

Kors, Alan Charles, *Epicureans and Atheists in France* (Cambridge, Eng.: 2015).

Kors, Alan Charles, *Naturalism and Unbelief in France* (Cambridge, Eng.: 2015).

La Mettrie, Julien Offray de, *L'Homme machine* (1745; repr. Amsterdam: 1966).

Lehner, Ulrich L., *The Catholic Enlightenment: The Forgotten History of a Global Movement* (New York: 2016).

Lehner, Ulrich L., *Enlightened Monks: The German Benedictines 1740–1803* (Oxford: 2011).

Lehner, Ulrich L., "The Many Faces of the Catholic Enlightenment," in *Companion to the Catholic Enlightenment in Europe*, eds. Ulrich L. Lehner and Michael Printy (Leiden: 2010), 1–61.

Lehner, Ulrich L., and Shaun Blanchard, "Introduction: The World of Catholic Enlightenment," in *The Catholic Enlightenment: A Global Anthology*, eds. Ulrich L. Lehner and Shaun Blanchard (Washington, DC: 2021), 1–18.

Liebersohn, Henry, *The Traveler's World: Europe to the Pacific* (Cambridge, Mass.: 2006).

Lilti, Antoine, *L'héritage des Lumières: Ambivalences de la modernité* (Paris: 2019).

Lyotard, Jean-François, *The Postmodern Condition: A Report on Knowledge*, trans. Geoff Bennington and Brian Massumi (Minneapolis: 1984).

Manning, Susan, and Francis Cogliano (eds.), *The Atlantic Enlightenment* (London: 2007).

Masseau, Didier, *Les ennemis des philosophes: L'antiphilosophie au temps des Lumières* (Paris: 2000).

Matytsin, Anton M., *The Specter of Skepticism in the Age of Enlightenment* (Baltimore: 2016).

Matytsin, Anton M., and Dan Edelstein (eds.), *Let There Be Enlightenment: The Religious and Mystical Sources of Rationality* (Baltimore: 2018).

McMahon, Darrin M., *Enemies of Enlightenment: The French Counter-Enlightenment and the Making of Modernity* (Oxford: 2001).

Mirabaud, Jean Baptiste de, *De l'âme et de son immortalité*, vol. 1 (London: 1751).

Montesquieu, Charles Louis de Sécondat, Baron de la Brède et de, *De l'Ésprit des lois* (1748; repr. Paris: 1950).

Moreau, Pierre-François, "Spinoza's Reception and Influence," in *The Cambridge Companion to Spinoza*, ed. Don Garrett (Cambridge, Eng.: 1996), 408–434.

Mortier, Roland, "Conclusions," in *Le Matérialisme du XVIIIe siècle et la littérature clandestine*, ed. Olivier Bloch (Paris: 1982), 275–7.

Nadler, Steven, *Spinoza's Heresy: Immortality and the Jewish Mind* (Oxford: 2001).

Niderst, Alain (ed.), *L'Ame matérielle* (Paris: 1969).

Nusseibeh, Sari, *The Story of Reason in Islam* (Stanford: 2017).

"On Fontenelle, *Nouvelles libertés de penser*; Mirabaud, *Sentimens des philosophes sur la nature de l'âme*; Fontenelle, *Traité de la liberté*; Chesneau du Marsais, *Réflexions sur l'âme et sur l'existence de Dieu*," *Mémoires de Trévoux* (1743): 2267–2271.

Osterhammel, Jürgen, *Unfabling the East: The Enlightenment's Encounter with Asia* (Princeton: 2019).

O'Malley, John W., "Jesuit Schools and the Humanities: Yesterday and Today," *Studies in the Spirituality of the Jesuits* 47/1 (2015): 1–34.

O'Malley, John W., *The First Jesuits* (Cambridge, Mass.: 1993).

Pagden, Anthony, *The Enlightenment and Why It Still Matters* (New York: 2013).

"Philosophe," in *Encyclopédie*/ARTFL, vol. 12, 509–510; http://encyclopedie.uchicago .edu/ [Accessed 12.05.2020].

Pocock, J.G.A., *The Enlightenments of Edward Gibbon, 1737–1764*, vol. 1 (Cambridge, Eng.: 1999).

Porada, Aleksandra, "Sources of Knowledge, Sources of Doubts: The Emergence of Modern Religious Studies and the French Enlightenment," in *The Sources of Secularism: Enlightenment and Beyond*, eds. Anna Tomaszewska and Hasse Hämäläinen (Cham: 2017), 141–167.

Porter, Roy, *The Creation of the Modern World: The Untold Story of the British Enlightenment* (New York: 2000).

Porter, Roy, and Mikuláš Teich (eds.), *The Enlightenment in National Context* (Cambridge, Eng.: 1981).

Pluche, Abbé Noël-Antoine, "Discours préliminaire sur la necessité d'une Révélation," in *La Spectacle de la Nature, ou, entrétiens sur les particularités de l'histoire naturelle, qu'ont parus les plus propres à rendre les jeunes-gens curieux et à leur former l'esprit*, 9 vols. (Paris: 1736–1742).

Printy, Michael, *Enlightenment and the Creation of German Catholicism* (Cambridge, Eng.: 2007).

Robertson, Ritchie, *The Enlightenment: The Pursuit of Happiness, 1680–1790* (New York: 2021).

Rouillé, André, "La Psychometre, ou Réflexions sur les différens caractères de l'Ésprit par Mylord Anglois," *Mémoires de Trévoux* (1735): 712–713.

Rubiés, Joan-Pau, "The Jesuits and the Enlightenment," *The Oxford Handbook of the Jesuits*, ed. Ines G. Županov (Oxford: 2019), 855–890.

Said, Edward, *Orientalism* (New York: 1979).

Schmale, Wolfgang, *Das 18 Jarhundert* (Vienna: 2012).

Schmidt, James G. (ed.), *What Is Enlightenment? Eighteenth-Century Answers to Twentieth-Century Questions* (Berkeley: 2006).

Shackleton, Robert, "When Did the French *Philosophes* Become a Party?" *Bulletin of the John Rylands University Library of Manchester* 60 (1977): 181–199.

Sheehan, Jonathan, *The Enlightenment Bible: Translation, Scholarship, Culture* (Princeton: 2005).

Sheehan, Jonathan, "Enlightenment, Religion, and the Enigma of Secularization," *American Historical Review* 108 (2003): 1061–1080.

Sheehan, Jonathan, "Thomas Hobbes, D.D.: Theology, Orthodoxy, and History," *Journal of Modern History* 88/2 (2016): 249–274.

Smith, Blake, "The Sacred French Revolution: Emile Durkheim, Lynn Hunt, and Historians," in *Age of Revolutions*, eds. Bryan Banks et al. (2019), www.ageofrevolutions.com [Accessed 12.4.2021].

Sorkin, David, *The Religious Enlightenment: Protestants, Jews, and Catholics from London to Vienna* (Princeton: 2008).

Stroumsa, Guy, *A New Science: The Discovery of Religion in the Age of Reason* (Cambridge, Mass.: 2010).

Sutcliffe, Adam, *Judaism and the Enlightenment* (Cambridge, Eng.: 2005).

Taton, René, et al. (eds.), *Enseignement et diffusion des sciences en France au XVIIIe siècle* (Paris: 1964).

Taylor, Charles, *A Secular Age* (Cambridge, Mass.: 2007).

Thomson, Ann, *L'âme des Lumières: Le débat sur l'être humain entre religion et science Angleterre-France, 1690–1760* (Paris: 2013).

Thomson, Ann, *Bodies of Thought: Science, Religion, and the Soul in the Early Enlightenment* (Oxford: 2008; repr. 2010).

Thomson, Ann, "Qu'est-ce qu'un manuscrit clandestin?" in *Le Matérialisme du XVIIIe siècle et la littérature clandestine*, ed. Olivier Bloch (Paris: 1982), 13–16.

Thomson, Ann, "Toland, Dodwell, Swift and the Circulation of Irreligious Ideas in France: What Does the Study of International Networks Tell Us about the 'Radical Enlightenment,'" in *Intellectual Journeys: The Translation of Ideas in England, France and Ireland*, eds. Lise Andries and Frederic Ogee (Oxford: 2013), 159–175.

Tournemine, René-Joseph, "Discours sur les Études de la Compagnie in doctrinis glorificate Dominum par l'Etude des sciences rendés vous capable de glorifier le Seigneur" (Paris: s.a.), BnF: Nouvelles acquisitions Françaises, 10946, fols. 303–383.

Tournemine, René-Joseph, "Lettre du P. Tournemine de la Compagnie de Jésus à M.*** sur l'immatérialité de l'âme et les sources de l'incrédulité," *Mémoires de Trévoux* (1735): 1915–1917.

Touber, Jetze, "God's Word in the Dutch Republic," in *God in the Enlightenment*, eds. William J. Bulman and Robert G. Ingram (Oxford: 2016), 157–181.

Toussaint, François, *Les Moeurs* (Amsterdam: 1748).

Tricoire, Damien, "The Fabrication of the *Philosophe:* Catholicism, Court Culture, and the Origins of Enlightenment Moralism in France," *Eighteenth-Century Studies* 51/4 (2018): 453–477.

Van Kley, Dale K., *The Damiens Affair and the Unraveling of the Ancien Régime, 1750–1770* (Princeton: 1984).

Van Kley, Dale K., "From the Catholic Enlightenment to the *Risorgimento*: The Debate between Nicola Spedalieri and Pietro Tamburini, 1791–1797," *Past and Present* 224/1 (2014): 109–162.

Van Kley, Dale K., *The Jansenists and the Expulsion of the Jesuits from France, 1757–1765* (New Haven: 1975).

Van Kley, Dale K., *Reform Catholicism and the International Suppression of the Jesuits in Enlightenment Europe* (New Haven: 2018).

Van Kley, Dale K., *The Religious Origins of the French Revolution from Calvin to the Civil Constitution, 1560–1791* (New Haven: 1996).

Van Kley, Dale K., "Robert R. Palmer's *Catholics and Unbelievers in Eighteenth-Century France*: An Overdue Tribute," in *Sacred and Secular Agency in Modern France: Fragments of Religion*, ed. Sanja Perovic (London: 2011), 13–36.

Van Kley, Dale K., "The Varieties of Enlightened Experience," in *God in the Enlightenment*, eds. William J. Bulman and Robert G. Ingram (Oxford: 2016), 278–316.

Vartanian, Aram, "Quelques réflexions sur le concept d'âme dans la littérature clandestine," in *Le Matérialisme du XVIIIᵉ siècle et la littérature clandestine*, ed. Olivier Bloch (Paris: 1982), 149–165.

Venturi, Franco, *La prima crisi dell'Antico Regime, 1768–1776*, vol. 3 (Turin: 1979).

Vermij, Rienk, "The Political Theory of the Libertines: Manuscripts and Heterodox Movements in the Early-Eighteenth-Century Dutch Republic," in *Clandestine Philosophy: New Studies on Subversive Manuscripts in Early Modern Europe, 1620–1823*, eds. Gianni Paganini, Margaret C. Jacob, and John Christian Laursen (Los Angeles: 2020), 143–159.

Vernière, Paul, *Spinoza et la pensée française avant la Révolution*, 2 vols. (Paris: 1954).

Voltaire, "L'introduction générale aux Questions sur l'*Encyclopédie* par des amateurs," in *Oeuvres Complètes*, vol. 17 (Paris: 1878), 3–5.

Wade, Ira O., *The Clandestine Organization and Diffusion of Philosophic Ideas in France from 1700 to 1750* (New York: 1967).

Wade, Ira O., *The Structure and the Form of the French Enlightenment*, 2 vols. (Princeton: 1987).

Warner, Michael, Jonathan Van Antwerpen, and Craig Calhoun (eds.), *Varieties of Secularism in a Secular Age* (Cambridge, Mass.: 2013).

Werner, Michael, and Bénédicte Zimmermann, "Beyond Comparison: *Histoire croisée* and the Challenge of Reflexivity," *History and Theory* 45 (2006): 30–50.

Williams, David Lay, *Rousseau's Platonic Enlightenment* (University Park: 2007).

Williams, Elizabeth A., *A Cultural History of Medical Vitalism in Enlightenment Montpellier* (Aldershot: 2003).

Williams, Elizabeth A., *The Physical and the Moral: Anthropology, Physiology, and Philosophical Medicine in France, 1750–1850* (Cambridge, Eng.: 1994).

Winterer, Caroline, *American Enlightenments: Pursuing Happiness in the Age of Reason* (New Haven: 2016).

Wolfe, Charles T., "Epigenesis as Spinozism in Diderot's Biological Project," in *The Life Sciences in Early Modern Philosophy*, eds. Ohad Nachtomy and Justin E.H. Smith (Oxford: 2014), 181–201.

Wolff, Larry, *The Enlightenment in the Orthodox World* (Athens: 2001).

CHAPTER 3

If Men Were Angels: Reason and Passion in the Enlightenment

Dominic Erdozain

The notion of a secular Enlightenment obscures some of its most interesting features, among them the concept of sin. Champions and critics alike have been prone to an oversimplification of the Enlightenment as an "age of reason," a decisive release from theological bondage, with an insufficient recognition of its moral complexity and subtlety. At its worst, this leads either to a triumphalist account of Promethean emancipation or to the doom-laden perspective of conservative and theological commentators of the Enlightenment as a rude assault on religious faith. Together, these opposing but kindred perspectives contribute to tribalism in academia and culture war in politics and journalism, as one side embraces and another side recoils from the "birth of the modern." The outcome is thus not only an intellectual impoverishment but often a coarsening of political discourse. In the United States, for example, the intellectual substrate of political conservatism has been an attack on the soulless pragmatism of the Lockean social contract, and a sense of nervous embarrassment at the secular proclivities of Thomas Jefferson, the author of the Declaration of Independence.[1] Where popular writers have attempted to "Christianize" the nation's founding documents, with clumsy and often dishonest methodologies,[2] intellectual conservatives have been content to write off the Enlightenment as a wrong turn of history: a cult of reason that led to the "me generation" and to the tyrannies of the modern state.[3] The subtlety with which a thinker such as Edmund Burke appraised the philosophy of the Enlightenment has, it seems, given way to crisp and binary judgments, which would hold Voltaire and Rousseau as progenitors of the atrocities of the 20th century. It is no exaggeration to say that some traditions of conservatism, moral theory and political theology have been defined by contempt for "the

---

1 Gillis J. Harp, *Protestants and American Conservatism: A Short History* (New York: 2019).

2 Francis A. Schaeffer, *How Should We Then Live? The Rise and Decline of Western Thought and Culture* (Old Tappan: 1976).

3 Richard M. Weaver, *Ideas Have Consequences* (Chicago: 2013); John Ralston Saul, *Voltaire's Bastards: The Dictatorship of Reason in the West* (New York: 1993).

© KONINKLIJKE BRILL NV, LEIDEN, 2022 | DOI:10.1163/9789004523371_004

Enlightenment project,"[4] educating readers to abhor and resist the movement's alluring simplicity.

In this chapter, I want to challenge the perspective that would reduce the Enlightenment to a naked assertion of reason, highlighting instead the rich and supple anthropology at the heart of the movement. In short, I want to argue that, far from decisively rejecting the Christian doctrine of sin, Enlightenment philosophy reconceived it as the tyranny of the passions – a force that challenged, hedged, and qualified the expectations of reason. Indeed, I want to argue, reason itself was a principle that recognized its own vulnerability and the continuing need for external resources, in the form of education, political regulation, and religious faith. The focus of this chapter is on the second of those three resources: politics and political theory. My hope is that an appreciation of Enlightenment thought as a creative response to the problem of passion can lead to more fruitful analysis of the social contract and the obligations of political engagement. The framers of the US polity – the context and focus of my study – were neither pessimists nor optimists. They were, to an extent rarely appreciated by their admirers or detractors, realists – and their realism was grounded in this textured and implicitly theological account of human nature.

1   "Obvious Truths": Reason as Faith

While ideological predilections clearly play their part, there is a more mundane methodological dimension to the failure of scholarship to acknowledge the theology at work within reason. Many of the foundational principles of the Enlightenment had their gestation and tutelage in sectarian Christianity: the radical fringe of Christendom. Unacquainted with the rudiments of church history, let alone these outer reaches of spirituality, students of philosophy are inclined to think of the discoveries of Locke or Spinoza as creations *ex nihilo*. But this is where much of the work was done. As the English historian Christopher Hill argued in his groundbreaking study, *The World Turned Upside Down: Radical Thought in the English Revolution*, it is easy to feel yourself in the company of Voltaire in the anti-clerical literature of the 1640s, or to feel that you are reading a first draft of Rousseau on the "General Will" as you encounter the democratic and immanentist metaphysics of Gerard Winstanley and the

---

4 Alasdair C. MacIntyre, *After Virtue: A Study in Moral Theory* (London: 1985); William T. Cavanaugh, *The Myth of Religious Violence: Secular Ideology and the Roots of Modern Conflict* (New York: 2009).

"Diggers."[5] These were rude and often untutored radicals, with a deep familiarity with the Bible. From that source, they developed a concept of faith as a law "written on the heart" – an "inner light" that transcended clerical authorities and written sources, including the Bible itself.

It was for this reason, Hill demonstrates, that radical Christians were the most trenchant critics of the written text itself, and its deployment as a pillar of political authority. Building upon the Bible's own distinction between the "spirit" and "letter" of the law, as developed by Jesus Christ in the Sermon on the Mount and in the epistles of St Paul, such radicals reduced Christianity to a certainty of salvation by faith and an irrefragable doctrine of love. This became their platform of criticism – the solid ground from which they would assault what they regarded as the perversions of ecclesiastical authority and abuses of the Bible. Radicals sometimes burned copies of the Bible in protest against the idea that the book, the written, translated and much-copied text, somehow represented "the word of God." No, they insisted, the word of God was the breath of the Holy Spirit known in the heart. This "inner light" transcended all earthly or "carnal" mediators – a critical term in radical theology. "Carnal" was a word used by Paul the Apostle to denote sin, the world and, literally, "the flesh." So radical theology effectively inverted the categories of ecclesiastical order by identifying religion – especially violent religion – as the fallen realm of the flesh, and identifying true divinity with an internal, personal, unmediated experience of God.

One of the most famous instances of this "inversion" was the occasion when George Fox, founder of the "Society of Friends," derisively dubbed "Quakers," paced around an English Church all but mocking the authority of Scripture. People will say that "Christ" says this and the apostles say that, Fox challenged, *"But what canst thou say?"*[6] Could ink and parchment rival the majesty of the voice within? Was God a piece of paper? His audience – including his future bride, Margaret Fell – was initially appalled by the irreverence, until they understood his point.

"Art thou a child of the Light, and hast thou walked in the Light, and what thou speakest, is it inwardly from God?"[7] For the man or woman of faith, Fox contended, it was an insult to live by scraps of quotations and mottled verses. When the heart burns with the love of God, Fox suggested, it does not need

---

5   Christopher Hill, *The World Turned Upside Down: Radical Ideas During the English Revolution* (Harmondsworth: 1978).

6   George Fox, *Journal of George Fox Being an Historical Account of the Life, Travels, Sufferings, Christian Experiences, and Labour of Love* (London: 1852), 358.

7   Ibid.

or desire the pedantry of words. The Word of God was not the same as these copied and cobbled pretenders, he argued in a position that became standard in the radical milieu. And this Word, translated from "*logos*" in the Greek, was often called "Reason." Gerard Winstanley even substituted the word "Reason" for "God" – explaining: "I am made to change the name from God to Reason, because I have been held under darknesse by that word as I see many people are."[8] What he meant was that, since "God" had been claimed and owned by an oppressive religious establishment, and used to justify persecution, he had to reject the term. The word had to go for the principle to live. This led to the paradox of ardent and zealous Christians, acknowledging Christ as their savior, dismantling the vocabulary of orthodoxy. After all, they pointed out, Jesus had spent a large part of his earthly ministry in running disputes with the Temple authorities and teachers of the law – a central theme of the Fourth Gospel, the Gospel of John, which was the radicals' Bible. Christ himself was at war with clerical presumption, including such metaphysical oddities as the doctrine of the Trinity, they argued. Could anything more alien to this brusque and earthy moral teacher who called himself "The Son of Man" be imagined? – wondered the Christian dissidents, who implicitly identified the doctrine with practices of persecution. The same phenomenon was visible in the Dutch Republic, another seedbed of the Enlightenment.[9]

As Andrew Fix argued in a study of the Dutch Collegiants, which parallels Hill's work on the English radicals, reason, faith and "light" were often interchangeable terms in the radical milieu. Reason as a mental faculty was freighted with Christian assumptions about charity, love of neighbors, and the duty of truthfulness. One of the most intriguing aspects of this phenomenon was the tendency to attribute to the faculty of reason properties traditionally identified with the Holy Spirit – the third "person" of the Trinity – and the "accusing" conscience of the mystical tradition of Christian spirituality. This ministry of self-critique and self-awareness, in other words, was gradually transferred from the external agency of the Holy Spirit to the internal discipline of reason. Yet the boundaries blurred. In the world of the Collegiants, a body of churchless Christians that included Baruch Spinoza among its circle, "reason was spiritualized almost as much as spirit was rationalized."[10]

---

8   David Loewenstein, "Gerrard Winstanley and the Diggers," in *The Oxford Handbook of Literature and the English Revolution*, ed. Laura Lunger Knoppers (Oxford: 2012), 335.

9   See Leszek Kolakowski, *The Two Eyes of Spinoza and Other Essays on Philosophers* (South Bend: 2004), 82.

10   Andrew C. Fix, *Prophecy and Reason: The Dutch Collegiants in the Early Enlightenment* (Princeton: 1991), 192.

A key source for this mystical-rationalist tradition was the first chapter of the fourth Gospel, which described Jesus Christ as the "Word," or eternal "*Logos*," taking on flesh and coming into the world. The passage implies that this word or light, however, was already existent in the minds of humans, the difference now being that the light was assuming physical form: "The light that lighteth every man," states John 1:9, was coming into the world. This was nothing less than a proof text for Christian rationalists, appearing again and again in dissident literature. The meaning, or claim, was that the light was active and preexistent in every attentive soul. And although Christ (the Word) came into the world to teach in a more visible and tangible manner, part of that teaching, evidenced in the Sermon on the Mount, was that the inner testimony of truth was more potent and revealing than the plodding precepts of "the law." Christian rationalists, in other words, had a scriptural foundation for their independent and fissiparous piety: the Kingdom of God is *within* you. Who, then, needs churches, priests and rituals? Christian spirituality – of an intense, not attenuated form – was thus the motor of philosophical dissent. It was the hottest spirituality that produced the most dynamic dissent. Rejection of ecclesiastical authority often came from people with the strongest sense that sacred ideas, Christian ideas, had been violated by institutional religion, and that purity and wisdom must now retreat to the unsullied chambers of conscience and reason. It was the people who were serious about their faith that often had the most to say about the corruptions of Christendom. Natural law was never very natural. It was loaded with religious assumptions.

Since reason was often identified as the voice of God or the Holy Spirit, the language of secularization is premature. As I have argued in relation to Spinoza and the Huguenot philosopher, Pierre Bayle – two giants of the early Enlightenment mistakenly secularized by scholars such as Jonathan Israel – "atheism" was more often an accusation than an affirmation.[11] The concept of a secular Enlightenment, in other words, is one that has drawn more sustenance from the critics of the movement's pioneers than the thinkers themselves. This means that scholars such as Jonathan Israel and the hugely influential Quentin Skinner have been drawing their conclusions from polemicism, clerical denunciation and, sometimes, outright abuse to build their picture of a secular, unbelieving Enlightenment. If the overwhelming judgment of their contemporaries was that Hobbes, Spinoza or Bayle was an atheist, this must have been true, argue such scholars. The "context" has to define the "text," urges Skinner, and people are always claiming to believe in God, just to stay out of trouble. The problem, of course, is that philosophers such as Spinoza and Bayle did not just

---

11   Dominic Erdozain, "A Heavenly Poise: Radical Religion and the Making of the Enlightenment," *Intellectual History Review* 27/1 (2017): 71–96.

include God as an adventitious gloss or a rhetorical decency: their ideas were molded by faith. And where sincerity is disputed by scholars, it is surely better to give the benefit of the doubt to the writers themselves rather than their militant critics. It is, at the very least, awkward that this notion of a secular and godless Enlightenment promoted by scholars such as Jonathan Israel is so dependent on the unfriendly verdicts of critics: on polemical denunciation rather than the philosophy itself. It is one thing to allow the context to interpret the text, but quite another to allow a writer's enemies to define his or her meaning. The same thing was true of Mary Wollstonecraft, as Barbara Taylor has argued with some force: a profoundly religious thinker unduly secularized by her critics and modern admirers alike.[12]

Apart from the inherent injustice of erasing religious motivation from those for whom it mattered dearly, the Promethean approach leaves us with a dry, unrealistic and overly intellectualized vision of reason. The philosophers are intellectuals first and moralists second, if at all, on this reading. Intellectual history is the triumph of intellect over the fog of superstition, a steady ascent from the misty lowlands of religion. But as John Locke warned in a luminous passage written in 1695, this intellectual hauteur, this determination to write religion out of the history of reason, is at once ahistorical and conducive to bickering. We would, he suggests, all get along a lot better if we could acknowledge common roots. "[B]ecause what we see we see with our own Eyes," he writes, "we are apt to over-look or forget the help we had from others, who shewed it us, and first made us see it."[13] The passage is worth quoting in full:

> He that Travels the Roads now, applauds his own strength and legs, that have carried him so far in such a scantling of time; And ascribes all to his own Vigor, little considering how much he owes to their pains, who cleared the Woods, drained the Bogs, built the Bridges, and made the Ways passable; without which he might have toiled much with little progress. A great many things which we have been bred up in the belief of from our Cradles, (and are Notions grown Familiar and, as it were Natural to us, under the Gospel,) we take for unquestionable obvious Truths, and easily demonstrable; without considering how long we might have been in doubt or ignorance of them, had Revelation been silent. And many are beholden to Revelation, who do not acknowledge it.[14]

---

12 Barbara Taylor, *Mary Wollstonecraft and the Feminist Imagination* (Cambridge: 2003).
13 John Locke, *The Reasonableness of Christianity: As Delivered in the Scriptures* (Oxford: 1999), 155.
14 Ibid., 156.

That was his message to the philosophers. Next, he turns to the theologians, advising them that: "'Tis no diminishing to Revelation, that Reason gives its Suffrage too to the Truths Revelation has discovered." Yet the burden of his argument fell upon philosophy and the belief that those "obvious truths" of reason would not be quite so obvious without some sort of grounding faith. It is, he concludes, "our mistake to think, that because Reason confirms them to us, we had the first certain knowledge of them from thence, and in that clear Evidence we now possess them."[15]

Reason, then, has a history. It is neither the clean deliverance from superstition imagined by secular philosophy nor the monster of faithless presumption feared by anti-modernist theology. And as Locke argued with equal emphasis in both his religious and political writing: reason is a work in progress. While attempting to fill the boots of religious dogma, catechism and confessional – to be the perfect husband and the man of all seasons – reason often falls short. Although it would like to be fully autonomous, never to bend its knee or confess its sins before God or man, it had not even approached that moment of perfection and maturity. The lesson of history – ancient and modern – was that "humane reason unassisted, failed Men in its great and Proper business of *Morality*." The "natural light" of conscience, though present in every soul, was too often dormant, making, as Locke put it, "slow progress, and little advance in the World."[16] This was why humans would still need the bannisters and signposts of religion, and perhaps a spirituality.

More importantly for the political philosopher: this was why societies need laws. The paradox was that a political philosophy premised upon liberty and human choice was, in many ways, skeptical of the human capacity to fulfill its potential. One of the reasons philosophers such as Locke were eager to keep reason in touch with religion – or at least to acknowledge its roots – was to foster the kind of humility that could make rational agents receptive to the assistance and guidance of the law. Certain truths or principles may now be "obvious" but living up to them is not easy. This recognition was not only made by the skeptics and pessimists of the Enlightenment such as Bayle and his successor, David Hume. It was made by the alleged apostles of reason, such as Voltaire and Jean-Jacques Rousseau. Emancipated as they were from much of the terminology of Christian theology, such writers were keenly aware of the perils of "egoism" and "self-love." They developed a rationalism and a political philosophy fully conversant with the problem of passion. And it was this balance, this tension, that inspired the founders of the American political system with its dialectic of hope and realism, liberty and law. I will first sketch the continuity

---

15   Ibid., 156–7.
16   Ibid., 149–150.

of this consciousness of sin in some key thinkers of the European Enlightenment before analyzing its role in the American founding. Locke was right – reason was a child of theology: a heavenly certitude in fallen flesh.

2   The Limits of Reason and the Problem of Passion

The 18th century balanced confidence with doubt. It followed Bayle in wondering whether the new castles of certitude were as solid as Descartes, Spinoza or Malebranche claimed. In their darker moments, they wondered whether the new god of reason was as fickle and irresponsible as the old God of theology. Was reason, perhaps, a polite word for passion: a cover for something darker? How can we be so sure that this voice within is anything more than the eloquence of the flesh? This rugged and cautious skepticism, writes Peter Gay, was the working principle of the 18th-century Enlightenment. The Enlightenment, he contends, "was not an Age of Reason but a Revolt against Rationalism."[17] One cannot grasp the mood of the period, Gay suggests, without eavesdropping on James Boswell and Samuel Johnson, as they wandered out of church one morning musing on Bishop Berkeley's metaphysical idealism. To say that all experience is perception was manifestly absurd, they agreed, but how could such ideas be refuted? At this point in the conversation, Samuel Johnson decided to kick a rock, and he did so with such violence that he almost fell backwards, reported Boswell. "I refute it thus," was the triumphant verdict.[18]

One had to live in the real world. In the 18th century, Lockean empiricism eclipsed Cartesian rationalism as the groundwork of philosophy: experience above theory, observation over idea. And part of this attitude of retreat and retrenchment was a perception of the degree to which rational judgments are prone to emotional interference: the confusion of affection and passion. Such forces were not necessarily to be distrusted, and a great deal of 18th-century epistemology harnessed its sails to the reliability of "sentiment." But in moral and political philosophy, the movement was in the opposite direction, towards a recognition of the fallibility of reason even in the loftiest of souls. "Reason," Pierre Bayle had famously written, "is like a runner, who doesn't know the race is over" – a phrase that captured the combined energy and naivety of the new god of the philosophers.[19] It was a sentiment that Voltaire and David Hume made their own.

---

17   Peter Gay, *The Enlightenment: The Rise of Modern Paganism* (New York: 1995), 141.
18   Ibid., 180.
19   Elisabeth Labrousse, *Bayle* (Oxford: 1983), 61.

Voltaire is a fascinating example. As an advocate of natural law against the pretensions of theology, he was a true believer. This "bright ethereal spark of heavenly fire," this "generous flame," as he described the conscience in his poem on natural law, was a true judge and a true guide to mortal humanity. Natural law was steady and strong where superstition and dogmatic theology was vain and capricious. Yet a parallel strand of his thinking was a cold dread that conscience was not up to its task. In Voltaire's philosophical novel, *Candide*, the redoubtable "Martin" (modeled on Bayle) expresses his distaste for the honeyed idealism of the 17th century in three words: "I have lived."[20] As Voltaire mused in his *Philosophical Dictionary*: "There is a natural law; but it is still more natural to many people to forget or neglect it."[21] In *Candide*, Voltaire steered an intriguing line between the facile optimism of the philosophers – personified by the pompous, prattling "Pangloss" – and the inhumanity of Augustinian theologies of original sin. "[Men] were not born wolves," insisted one of his characters; "they have *become* wolves; God has given them neither cannon of four-and-twenty pounders nor bayonets; and yet they have made cannon and bayonets to destroy one another."[22] This, I think, was a critical expression of Voltaire's own position as it developed against the backdrop of ecclesiastical oppression and what he regarded as philosophical folly. Augustine and his cruel, unworthy doctrine of "original sin" had to go. The idea that human beings were only fit for destruction, he argued, was offensive and dangerous. Yet a philosophy of affirmation, with no room for sin, was almost as hazardous. Voltaire satirized the pretensions of reason with as much force as the cruelties of theology.

Prompted in no small part by the disagreeable example of Jean-Jacques Rousseau, a man who wrote soaring works on natural law yet abandoned his own children on the steps of a Paris orphanage, Voltaire developed a profound skepticism of the reliability of unassisted reason. His polemical pamphlet, aimed at Rousseau, *How Citizens Feel* (1762), captured the complaint. It is one thing to talk about conscience; it is another thing to act upon it. Natural law, he argued in several other works, is a potent diagnostic tool but it cannot always deliver the cure. As a man of fierce loathings, who struggled with the Christian duty of forgiveness, Voltaire was acutely sensitive to the shortcomings of a morality of reciprocity: doing to others as they do to you. In his epic poem on Henry IV, the clement King who ended France's Wars of Religion, and in his

---

20   Voltaire, *Candide*, trans. Shane Weller (New York: 1991), 69.

21   Voltaire, "Natural Law," in *Philosophical Dictionary*, Part 1, *The Works of Voltaire. A Contemporary Version*, vol. 6, trans. William F. Fleming (New York: 1901), 64.

22   Voltaire, *Candide*, 9.

South American play, *Alzire*, Voltaire dramatized the contrast between a sterile philosophy of just deserts and the liberating power of "mercy." The message of *Alzire* was that if vengeance may be justified under a strict reading of natural law, it cannot enable people to live at peace. Voltaire said that he wrote *Alzire* "with a view of showing how far superior the spirit of true religion is to the light of nature."[23] The reciprocities of natural law will eventually come back to hurt the person who stands on his rights, Voltaire argues. Mercy is greater than justice. These are Christian ideas.

Voltaire developed this argument in one of his later works, *The Sage and the Atheist*, which included a dialogue between a descendant of William Penn and a Native American Chief, who advocated the killing and scalping of enemies. Voltaire used the English Quaker – called "Freind" in his story – to advocate for the higher wisdom of forgiveness. In the story, Freind restores and forgives his own, errant son – a dissolute rake called "Johnny" modeled on the vices of the English aristocracy. Voltaire's parable was nothing less than an elaboration of the story of the "Prodigal Son," as recorded in the Gospel of Luke, in the New Testament.[24]

The Sage and the Atheist was one of Voltaire's later works and it reflects his anxiety about the perils of materialism and atheism, as well as containing his critique of natural law. Although Voltaire was more explicit than many of his contemporaries on the need for some sort of "revealed" religion – even if it was revealed by him – this concern to supplement or repair reason was widely felt. And Rousseau himself, effulgent on natural law in the "Profession of Faith of a Savoyard Vicar" – a long interlude in *Emile* – was more restrained in his political writing. It was as if the conscience burned with radiance next to the fallen deity of dogma, but it flickered with worrying uncertainty in the friction of society. Indeed, the distinction between nature and society was fundamental to the emergence of the social contract theory. People may be born good, with just and laudable self-respect, argued Rousseau, but society ruins them. The difference between self-love ("*amour-soi*") and pride or self-regard ("*amour-propre*") was fundamental, for Rousseau, and the latter had to be tamed. *Amour-propre* – variously rendered as pride, egoism, or honor – was the disease that sets in when humans grow up, rub shoulders with their peers and develop instincts of envy and rivalry. Under the pressure of *amour-propre*, Rousseau argues, we all become vain and self-conscious: unreliable in duty and decency. Pride, "less out of real need than in order to put himself above others,

---

23   Voltaire, "Alzire," in *The Works of Voltaire*, vol. 9, 4.
24   Voltaire, "L'Histoire de Jenni ou le Sage et l'Athée," in *Œuvres complètes de Voltaire*, vol. 26, ed. Louis Moland (Paris: 1877), 523–376.

inspires in all men a wicked tendency to harm one another,"[25] writes Rousseau. It was the real cause of those "national wars, battles, murders, and reprisals that make nature tremble and offend reason, and all those horrible prejudices that rank the honor of shedding human blood among the virtues."[26] So whatever could be achieved by education and moral training in the long term, faster remedies were required.

Liberal theory, from Locke to Thomas Jefferson, was at once hopeful and positive about human reason, and anxious to fill the void between potential and actuality. Although Enlightenment philosophers rarely used the word, their evolving faith in representative government and the rule of law emerged from a keen sense of what theologians called "sin." Just as reason and the "inner light" of conscience bore the marks of Christian spirituality in the seventeenth century, Enlightenment anthropology was suffused with that corresponding Christian idea of fallenness. This balance between dignity and weakness, human worth and human propensity to fall, was the premise of representative government.

3   Sin and the Social Contract

As early as the 1640s, advocates of representative government warned of the danger of erecting a new kind of kingship on the ruins of the old. Groups such as the English "Levellers" understood tyranny to be a propensity of human nature rather than an accident of blood or birth. Indeed, to suggest that only crowned monarchs were prone to a lust for unlimited power was to produce an inverted form of the monarchist fallacy: the belief that some humans are created fundamentally different to others. It was not just kings who had to be brought down to earth, argued the Levellers, it was the "thing king."[27] The thing king was the instinct of domination: a hunger to rule. What princes did by "prerogative," ordinary men would do by impulse. In fact, monarchs were nothing more than winners in a state of nature, strong men in ermine. Kings, argued pioneers of republican thought, such as John Lilburne and Richard Overton, were really nothing more than yesterday's warriors. They were knights and chieftains who put a gloss on their power by inventing rituals of permanence and preeminence, coopting religion to sanctify the fraud.

---

25   Jean Jacques Rousseau, "Discourse on the Origin and Foundations of Inequality among Men," in *Basic Political Writings*, trans. Donald A. Cress (Indianapolis: 2011), 77.

26   Ibid., 80.

27   Rachel Foxley, *The Levellers: Radical Political Thought in the English Revolution* (Manchester: 2013), 199.

The aristocracy, so-called, were the knights and soldiers who assisted their conquests and were rewarded with titles, land and a no less conjured status. But no sooner had one seen through the fraud, exposed the myth, than the ground below began to crumble: "where they dare ... all Men would be Tyrants," warned the Whig philosopher Thomas Gordon in *Cato's Letters*.[28] A stable republic had to prepare for the worst.

Given his importance to the liberal tradition, and to the American polity in particular, it is fascinating how profoundly John Locke engaged with this problem of passion and aggression. Locke is so frequently associated with a post-theological worldview, and a rationality of property and gain, that it is startling how alert he was to the tyranny of the ordinary mortal. I would suggest that he is restating a theological problem rather than superseding it. Locke's fulsome statements on equality, and his bold assertions of natural right, come in the context of despotism and arbitrary power, as he defends the common man against the pretended authority of hereditary monarchs. But having asserted nature against artifice and pretense, he addresses the "inconveniences" of this dangerous and brutal estate. Locke's *Second Treatise of Government* is a cumbrous and repetitive work, but it charts a decisive transition from a state of nature to a state of society, and from there to the settled conditions of civil government. A state of nature, he argues, is only a clenched fist away from a state of war, and it is to avoid this condition that humans put "themselves under government." Here, the shortcomings of natural law are instantly apparent. For although the law of nature is "plain and intelligible to all rational creatures,"[29] writes Locke, "yet men, being biassed by their interest, as well as ignorant for want of study of it, are not apt to allow of it as a law binding to them in the application of it to their particular cases."[30] They make exceptions for themselves, seeing what they want to see. As he explains: "For the law of nature being unwritten, and so nowhere to be found but in the minds of men, they who, through passion or interest, shall miscite, or misapply it, cannot so easily be convinced of their mistake where there is no established judge."[31] Indeed: "men being partial to themselves, passion and revenge is very apt to carry them too far, and with too much heat in their own cases, as well as negligence and unconcernedness, make them too remiss in other men's."[32]

---

28 *Cato's Letters: Or, Essays on Liberty, Civil and Religious, and Other Important Subjects*, vol. 2 (London: 1755).

29 John Locke, *Two Treatises of Government* (Norwalk, CT: 1991), 192–3.

30 Ibid., 193.

31 Ibid., 198–9.

32 Ibid., 193.

Even the rosiest advocates of natural law would have to admit that "the greater part" of humankind are "no strict observers of equity and justice."[33] Whatever the credentials of natural law in a pre-political environment, Locke doubted that anyone would want to plant the security of the community upon such uncertain ground. Few could object to the claim that it is "unreasonable for men to be judges in their own cases, that self-love will make men partial to themselves and their friends; and, on the other side, ill-nature, passion, and revenge will carry them too far in punishing others."[34] It was to avoid this predicament that governments came to be: "For the end of civil society being to avoid and remedy those inconveniencies of the state of Nature, which necessarily follow from every man's being judge in his own case by setting up a known authority to which every one of that society may appeal upon any injury received."[35] As Locke concludes, with a sigh of relief: "God hath certainly appointed government to restrain the partiality and violence of men."[36]

Locke renders the instability of the ordinary citizen in the same language with which he critiqued the divine right of kings. Laws were to provide sanctuary from the "inconstant, uncertain, unknown, arbitrary will" of other men.[37] That was where freedom began. "For who could be free," he wonders, "when every other man's humour might domineer over him?"[38] "Freedom, then, is not," Locke insists, "'a liberty for every one to do what he lists, to live as he pleases, and not to be tied by any laws'; but freedom of men under government is to have a standing rule to live by, common to every one of that society, and made by the legislative power erected in it."[39] Liberty was almost synonymous with the rule of law: "For liberty is to be free from restraint and violence from others, which cannot be where there is no law."[40]

Somehow, this sensitivity to the fallibility of human nature has eluded a great deal of the scholarship on the emergence of American republicanism. Scholars such as Gordon Wood have emphasized virtue to the point of neglecting this emphasis almost entirely. This is partly due to an overstatement of the classical roots of American republicanism, and partly due to a misunderstanding of the Enlightenment itself. "For the revolutionary generation," writes Wood,

---

33   Ibid., 192.
34   Ibid., 132.
35   Ibid., 172.
36   Ibid., 132.
37   Ibid., 137.
38   Ibid., 154.
39   Ibid., 137.
40   Ibid., 154.

"America became the Enlightenment fulfilled,"[41] which he reads as virtue-in-action. "No generation in American history," he suggests, "has ever been so self-conscious about the moral and social values necessary for public leadership."[42]

This may be true, but few generations were as conscious of the difficulty of realizing such values and the danger of relying upon them. The American Founders preached virtue and planned for vice. Few political systems have been so carefully molded around the expectation that citizens will fall short of their ideals. A key text was *Cato's Letters*, which popularized Lockean social contract theory and was widely read in the colonies in the decade before the Revolution. "[T]he writings of Trenchard and Gordon ranked with the treatises of Locke as the most authoritative statement of the nature of political liberty," writes Bernard Bailyn.[43]

One of the central themes of these letters was the need to work with the grain of human nature and to recognize the pervasiveness of selfish ambition. "[H]e who knows little of human Nature," warned Thomas Gordon, "will never know much of the affairs of the World, which every where derive their Motion and Situation from the Humours and Passions of Men."[44] The "Constitution which trusts more than it needs to any Man, or Body of Men," he warned, "has a terrible Flaw in it, and is big with the Seeds of its own Destruction."[45] "The Experience of every Age convinces us, that we must not judge of Men by what they ought to do, but by what they will do."[46]

Humans were the creatures that thought one thing, said another, and did a third. "They are naturally Innocent, and yet fall naturally into the Practice of Vice; and the greatest Instances of Virtue and Villainy are to be found in one and the same Person; and perhaps one and the same Motive produces both."[47] "Man," continued Gordon in a passage redolent of Voltaire, "is a Mixture of Contrarieties, imperious and supple, sincere and false, fearful and bold, merciful and cruel: He can sacrifice every Pleasure to the getting of Riches, and all his Riches to a Pleasure: He is fond of his Preservation, and yet sometimes eager after his own Destruction: He can flatter those he hates, and destroy those he loves."[48] "It fills me with Concern," he continued, "when I consider how Men

---

41   Gordon S. Wood, *The Radicalism of the American Revolution* (New York: 1993), 191.

42   Ibid., 197.

43   Bernard Bailyn, *The Ideological Origins of the American Revolution* (Cambridge, Mass.: 1992), 36.

44   *Cato's Letters*, vol. 1 (London: 1724), 243.

45   *Cato's Letters*, vol. 2, 55.

46   Ibid., 230.

47   *Cato's Letters*, vol. 1, 245–6.

48   Ibid., 245.

use one another; and how wretchedly their Passions are employ'd."[49] The lesson was that "we must not judge of one another by our fair Pretensions and best Actions ... since many a Man, long thought honest, has at length proved a Knave."[50] The problem was egoism or self-love. "Of all the Passions which belong to humane Nature," averred Gordon, "*Self-love* is the strongest, and the Root of all the rest; or, rather, all the different Passions are only several Names for the several Operations of Self-love." This intoxicating principle "*makes a Man the Idolater of himself, and the Tyrant of others.*"[51]

This was theological language, aimed at the follies of wishful thinking. In a parallel argument, made in an influential treatise on standing armies, Trenchard counseled against the worship of leaders. "I am afraid we don't live in an Age of Miracles," he wrote, with mournful realism. People may speak of "the Publick Good" but there was "too much Dross mix'd with their Constitutions for such refin'd Principles" to be relied upon. Even "our Heroes are made of a coarser Alloy."[52]

Yet *Cato's Letters* struck a more positive note in attempting to harness this realism to the public good. The solution, in the liberal tradition, would not be authority, or a reinvented monarchy, along the lines of Hobbes's *Leviathan*. It would be sound and responsive government. "All these Discoveries and Complaints of the Crookedness and Corruption of human Nature," maintained Gordon, "are made with no malignant Intention to break the Bonds of Society."[53] The aim was to "preserve Justice and Equality in the World"[54] by devising a system that could bear the load: placing "Checks," not chains, upon the "Wolfish Nature" of man.[55] For "Men, thus formed and qualified, are the Materials for Government," whether we like it or not, "and the Art of political Mechanism is, to erect a firm Building with such crazy and corrupt Materials." Just as the "strongest Cables are made out of loose Hemp and Flax," continued Trenchard with an inspired analogy, a republic could grow strong on ambition, drawing tensile strength from the primordial strife.[56]

---

49   Ibid., 246.
50   Ibid., 252.
51   Ibid., 245.
52   John Trenchard, *An Argument, Shewing That a Standing Army Is Inconsistent with a Free Government and Absolutely Destructive to the Constitution of the English Monarchy* (London: 1697), 17.
53   *Cato's Letters*, vol. 2, 53.
54   Ibid., 55–6.
55   *Cato's Letters*, vol. 1, 262.
56   *Cato's Letters*, vol. 2, 237.

It was a brilliant metaphor – strong cable made from "crazy and corrupt Materials" – and this sentiment of strength from weakness was widely echoed in the American literature. Abigail Adams claimed no originality when she told her husband, in a classic exchange of 1776: "Remember, all men would be tyrants if they could."[57] Even Jefferson, the closest to a "Pangloss" among the founders, knew the difference between admiring virtue and banking on it. Explaining his support for legal reform in Virginia, Jefferson denied that a desire to humanize the penal code betrayed a naïve faith in human nature: "The fantastical idea of virtue & the public good being a sufficient security to the state against the commission of crimes," he wrote in 1776, "I assure you was never mine. It is only the sanguinary hue of our penal laws which I meant to object to. Punishments I know are necessary, & I would provide them, strict & inflexible, but proportioned to the crime.... Let mercy be the character of the lawgiver," Jefferson continued, "but let the judge be a mere machine. The mercies of the law will be dispensed equally & impartially to every description of men."[58]

The same held true in Jefferson's philosophical writings, where he defined "Self-interest, or rather Self-love, or Egoism," as the nemesis of virtue. It is, he writes, "against this enemy that are erected the batteries of moralists and religionists." It was true that nature "hath implanted in our breasts a love of others, a sense of duty to them, a moral instinct in short, which prompts us irresistibly to feel and to succour their distresses." "The creator," he added, "would indeed have been a bungling artist, had he intended man for a social animal, without planting in him social dispositions." It was also true that humans possessed free will, and the passions that war against morality. Where conscience falters, "the rewards and penalties established by the laws" fill the void. Government, guided by the will of the people, acts *in loco parentis*. It is reason where reason fails.[59]

In a contribution to the American Philosophical Society, Jefferson suggested that "the will of the majority," embodied in the law, functioned as "the Natural law of every society." The law was a national conscience, "the only sure guardian of the rights of man." As he concluded with a phrase redolent of Rousseau's notion of the general will: "Let us then, my dear friends, for ever bow down to the general reason of the society."[60]

---

57   Charles Francis Adams (ed.), *Familiar Letters of John Adams and His Wife Abigail Adams during the Revolution. With a Memoir of Mrs. Adams* (New York: 1876).

58   Thomas Jefferson, *Writings*, vol. 2: *Letters* (Norwalk, CT: 1993), 756–7.

59   Thomas Jefferson, *Jefferson's Extracts from the Gospels:* The Philosophy of Jesus *and* The Life and Morals of Jesus (Princeton: 1983), 356–7.

60   Thomas Jefferson, *Writings*, vol. 1: *Autobiography, A Summary View of the Rights of British America, Notes on the State of Virginia, Public Papers, Addresses, Messages, and Replies, Miscellany* (Norwalk, CT: 1993), 491.

This tension between affirming human life and distrusting private judgment was the central insight of Cesare Beccaria's *Essay on Crimes and Punishments*, widely lauded among the Founders, including Jefferson.[61] Beccaria, counting himself among "humble and peaceable lovers of reason,"[62] constructed his appeal for rational laws around what might be termed a democratic theory of tyranny: a sprightly sensitivity to "the physical despotism of every individual."[63] "The judges," he wrote, "receive [the laws] as the result of a tacit or express oath which the united wills of the subjects have made to the sovereign as bonds necessary to curb and control the domestic turbulence of particular interests."[64] Law, once again, was reason to the unreason of the human heart – that wayfaring vessel, blown and buffeted by "the winds of human passions."[65] Among these "miserable" passions was the genteel toxin of honor. "There is," wrote Beccaria, "a noteworthy contradiction between, on the one hand, the civil laws, which are the jealous guardians of, above all, the citizen's person and goods, and on the other, the laws of, what is called, honour, in which pride of place is given to opinion."[66] Honor, "since it arose only after the formation of society," was the friendly face of barbarism, for it "represents an instantaneous return to the state of nature and a temporary withdrawal of oneself from the laws."[67] It was one thing for a society to outgrow "private duels,"[68] but all trace of vengeance had to be purged from the law. This meant the abolition of "the punishment of death."[69]

Nobody articulated the vision of government-as-rescue with more crusading intensity than Thomas Paine, whose pamphlet *Common Sense* electrified the colonies in the spring of 1776. "Government, like dress, is the badge of lost innocence," wrote Paine, with an elegant precis of the Lockean theory. "For were the impulses of conscience clear, uniform, and irresistibly obeyed, man would need no other lawgiver; but that not being the case, he finds it necessary to

---

61   See John D. Bessler, "Revisiting Beccaria's Vision: The Enlightenment, America's Death Penalty, and the Abolition Movement," *Northwestern Journal of Law & Social Policy* 4/2 (2009): 195–328.

62   Cesare Beccaria, "On Crimes and Punishments," in *On Crimes and Punishments and Other Writings*, ed. Richard Bellamy, trans. Richard Davies (Cambridge 1995), 8.

63   Ibid., 27.

64   Ibid., 14.

65   Ibid., 26.

66   Ibid.

67   Ibid., 27.

68   Ibid., 28.

69   Ibid., 66.

surrender up a part of his property to furnish means for the protection of the rest."[70] This was the social contract: the holy transfer from "natural liberty" to the "prudence" and "common interest" of civil order. The hard truth was that if "society is produced by our wants," "government" is produced "by our wickedness," advised Paine: "the former promotes our happiness positively by uniting our affections, the latter negatively by restraining our vices."[71]

The classic statement of this stony yet hopeful realism came from James Madison, the primary architect of the Constitution. Defending a system of government that placed greater restraints upon individual liberty than the Articles of Confederation, by which the new nation had hitherto been governed, Madison turned to the problem of sin: "But what is government itself," he wondered, "but the greatest of all reflections on human nature? If men were angels, no government would be necessary. If angels were to govern men, neither external nor internal controls on government would be necessary."[72] Few people seemed to perceive how profoundly their minds were guided by "self-love" – how their "passions" controlled their "opinions." It was no good bragging that the factions of European courts were unknown in America, he warned in *Federalist* #10. "The latent causes of faction are," he said, "sown in the nature of man."[73]

Madison's co-warrior in the constitutional debate, Alexander Hamilton, adopted the same stance of wizened realism. In 1775 he quoted a passage from David Hume, a philosopher who made a career bringing dreamers down to earth. "In contriving any system of government," Hume had written, "and fixing the several checks and controuls of the constitution, every man ought to be supposed a knave; and to have no other end in all his actions, but private interest. By this interest, we must govern him, and by means of it, make him co-operate to public good, notwithstanding his insatiable avarice and ambition."[74]

Humans were the creatures that mapped the heavens but died over gambling debts. A government had to be alive to both proclivities. "[M]en are ambitious, vindictive, and rapacious," Hamilton wrote in *Federalist* #6. To expect otherwise was "to disregard the uniform course of human events, and to set at defiance the accumulated experience of ages." For "the love of power or the desire of pre-eminence and dominion" were human, not European, propensities, alive

70   Thomas Paine, "Common Sense: Addressed to the Inhabitants of America," in *The Writings of Thomas Paine* (New York: 1894), 69.

71   Ibid.

72   James Madison, Alexander Hamilton, John Jay, *The Federalist Papers* (London: 1987), 319–320.

73   Ibid. 124.

74   Alexander Hamilton, *The Papers of Alexander Hamilton* (Columbia: 1961), 95.

in republics as well as monarchies.[75] "Have republics in practice been less addicted to war than monarchies?" he wondered.[76] The ancients had been falsely eulogized. Nations and individuals were too often intoxicated by "pride." "When the sword is once drawn, the passions of men observe no bounds of moderation." When pride is "wounded" and "resentment" felt in the soul, men will go "to any extremes necessary to avenge the affront or to avoid the disgrace of submission."[77] As Hamilton affirmed in a critical passage:

> To judge from the history of mankind, we shall be compelled to conclude that the fiery and destructive passions of war reign in the human breast with much more powerful sway than the mild and beneficent sentiments of peace; and that to model our political systems upon speculations of lasting tranquility, is to calculate on the weaker springs of the human character.[78]

Finally, the doyen of battle-scarred realism was John Adams, a man who knew ambition from the inside. Always the least utopian of the founders, Adams once responded to Jefferson's vexed idealism with a vivid metaphor: "A burned Child dreads the Fire." Thinking of Europe, Jefferson had asked "How the Apostacy from National Rectitude can be Accounted for."[79] Why did nations act "on the Principle 'that Power was Right'"?[80] Adams responded with a treatise on human nature. Although he believed "there are such things" as "human Reason and human Conscience," history showed that they were "not a Match, for human Passions, human Imaginations and human Enthusiasm."[81] As he continued, in a passage worthy of Hume:

> Our Passions, Ambition, Avarice, Love, Resentment etc. possess so much metaphysi[c]al Subtilty and so much overpowering Eloquence, that they insinuate themselves into the Understanding and the Conscience and convert both to their Party. And I may be deceived as much as any of them, when I say, that Power must never be trusted without a Check.[82]

---

75   Madison et al., *The Federalist Papers*, 104.
76   Ibid., 106.
77   Ibid., 152–3.
78   Ibid., 228–9.
79   Lester J. Cappon (ed.), *The Adams-Jefferson Letters. The Complete Correspondence between Thomas Jefferson and Abigail and John Adams* (Chapel Hill: 1987), 461.
80   Ibid., 462.
81   Ibid., 461.
82   Ibid., 463.

That was in 1816, but the note of disenchantment was not new. Although his *Thoughts on Government* (1776) were bullish on the possibility of national virtue, the case for balanced government rested on a stronger sensitivity to the potential for tyranny in ordinary people. The importance of a bicameral legislature reflected this concern that a single body made up of like-minded men would function as a king: "A single assembly," warned Adams, "is liable to all the vices, follies and frailties of an individual – subject to fits of humor, starts of passion, flights of enthusiasm, partialities, or prejudice – and consequently productive of hasty results and absurd judgments. And all these errors ought to be corrected and defects supplied by some controlling power."[83] "We may boast that *we* are the chosen people," Adams sighed, "we may even thank God that we are not like other men; but, after all, it will be but flattery, and the delusion, the self-deceit of the Pharisee."[84]

These are striking statements because they are so alien to both our inherited notion of the Enlightenment as an age of unbounded optimism and the doctrines of American exceptionalism to which the words of the Founders have been so frequently misapplied. The framers of the US polity eulogized the law because they understood the limitations of reason and the paucity of saints. In this, they were faithful interpreters of Locke, Voltaire and Rousseau. This legacy was not, as scholars such as Gordon Wood suggest, one that stood against their Christian or theological background. Nor was it a paradox that thinkers such as Jefferson and Benjamin Rush remained preoccupied to the point of obsession with questions of scriptural interpretation. Their Enlightenment proclivities grew out of their theological, indeed Christian, sensibilities. And whatever they chose to call it, they still had a doctrine of sin. Their Enlightenment was thus part of a tradition of reform, not secularization. The child retained the features of the parent.

References

Adams, Charles Francis (ed.), *The Works of John Adams, Second President of the United States: With a Life of the Author, Notes and Illustrations*, vol. 6 (Boston: 1851).

Adams, Charles Francis (ed.), *Familiar Letters of John Adams and His Wife Abigail Adams during the Revolution. With a Memoir of Mrs. Adams* (New York: 1876).

---

83   John Adams, "Thoughts on Government," in: *The Political Writings of John Adams. Representative Selections* (Indianapolis: 2003), 87.

84   Charles Francis Adams (ed.), *The Works of John Adams, Second President of the United States: With a Life of the Author, Notes and Illustrations*, vol. 6 (Boston: 1851), 467.

Adams, John, "Thoughts on Government," in: *The Political Writings of John Adams. Representative Selections* (Indianapolis: 2003), 83–92.

Bailyn, Bernard, *The Ideological Origins of the American Revolution* (Cambridge, Mass.: 1992).

Beccaria, Cesare, "On Crimes and Punishments," in *On Crimes and Punishments and Other Writings*, trans. Richard Davies (Cambridge 1995), 1–114.

Bessler, John D., "Revisiting Beccaria's Vision: The Enlightenment, America's Death Penalty, and the Abolition Movement," *Northwestern Journal of Law and Social Policy* 4/2 (2009): 195–328.

Cappon, Lester J. (ed.), *The Adams-Jefferson Letters. The Complete Correspondence between Thomas Jefferson and Abigail and John Adams* (Chapel Hill: 1987).

Cato's Letters, vol. 1 (London: 1724).

Cato's Letters: Or, Essays on Liberty, Civil and Religious, and Other Important Subjects, vol. 2 (London: 1755).

Cavanaugh, William T., *The Myth of Religious Violence: Secular Ideology and the Roots of Modern Conflict* (New York: 2009).

Erdozain, Dominic, "A Heavenly Poise: Radical Religion and the Making of the Enlightenment," *Intellectual History Review* 27/1 (2017): 71–96.

Fix, Andrew C., *Prophecy and Reason: The Dutch Collegiants in the Early Enlightenment* (Princeton: 1991).

Fox, George, *Journal of George Fox Being an Historical Account of the Life, Travels, Sufferings, Christian Experiences, and Labour of Love* (London: 1852).

Foxley, Rachel, *The Levellers: Radical Political Thought in the English Revolution* (Manchester: 2013).

Gay, Peter, *The Enlightenment: The Rise of Modern Paganism* (New York: 1995).

Hamilton, Alexander, *The Papers of Alexander Hamilton* (Columbia: 1961).

Harp, Gillis J., *Protestants and American Conservatism: A Short History* (New York: 2019).

Hill, Christopher, *The World Turned Upside Down: Radical Ideas During the English Revolution* (Harmondsworth: 1978).

Jefferson, Thomas *Writings*, vol. 1: *Autobiography, A Summary View of the Rights of British America, Notes on the State of Virginia, Public Papers, Addresses, Messages, and Replies, Miscellany* (Norwalk, CT: 1993).

Jefferson, Thomas, *Writings*, vol. 2: *Letters* (Norwalk, CT: 1993).

Jefferson, Thomas, *Jefferson's Extracts from the Gospels:* The Philosophy of Jesus *and* The Life and Morals of Jesus (Princeton: 1983).

Kolakowski, Leszek, *The Two Eyes of Spinoza and Other Essays on Philosophers*, trans. Zbigniew Janowski (South Bend: 2004).

Labrousse, Elisabeth, *Bayle* (Oxford: 1983).

Locke, John, *Two Treatises of Government* (Norwalk, CT: 1991).

Locke, John, *The Reasonableness of Christianity: As Delivered in the Scriptures* (Oxford: 1999).

Loewenstein, David, "Gerrard Winstanley and the Diggers," in *The Oxford Handbook of Literature and the English Revolution*, ed. Laura Lunger Knoppers (Oxford: 2012), 327–345.

MacIntyre, Alasdair C., *After Virtue: A Study in Moral Theory* (London: 1985).

Madison, James, Alexander Hamilton, John Jay, *The Federalist Papers* (London: 1987).

Paine, Thomas, "Common Sense: Addressed to the Inhabitants of America," in *The Writings of Thomas Paine* (New York: 1894).

Rousseau, Jean Jacques, "Discourse on the Origin and Foundations of Inequality among Men," in *Basic Political Writings*, trans. Donald A. Cress (Indianapolis: 2011), 27–92.

Saul, John Ralston, *Voltaire's Bastards: The Dictatorship of Reason in the West* (New York: 1993).

Schaeffer, Francis A., *How Should We Then Live? The Rise and Decline of Western Thought and Culture* (Old Tappan: 1976).

Taylor, Barbara, *Mary Wollstonecraft and the Feminist Imagination* (Cambridge, Eng.: 2003).

Trenchard, John, *An Argument, Shewing That a Standing Army Is Inconsistent with a Free Government and Absolutely Destructive to the Constitution of the English Monarchy* (London: 1697).

Voltaire, *Candide*, trans. Shane Weller (New York: 1991).

Voltaire, "L'Histoire de Jenni ou le Sage et l'Athée," in *Œuvres complètes de Voltaire*, vol. 26 (Paris: 1877), 523–376.

Voltaire, *The Works of Voltaire. A Contemporary Version*, 21 vols. (New York: 1901).

Weaver, Richard M., *Ideas Have Consequences* (Chicago: 2013).

Wood, Gordon S., *The Radicalism of the American Revolution* (New York: 1993).

CHAPTER 4

The Triumph of Theocracy: French Political Thought, God, and the Question of Secularization in the Age of Enlightenment

Damien Tricoire

In significant parts of scholarship, Enlightenment culture is deemed to be "secular." This interpretation is for example central for Margaret Jacob's recent magnum opus that crowns decades of prolific and stimulating scholarship. While she does not endorse the idea that there was a process of secularization running in the West from the 18th century to the present, she claims that the Enlightenment "shifted attention away from religious questions toward secular ones" and sought "answers in secular terms." Thanks to the Enlightenment, it became normal to live "without constant reference to God," to concentrate on the "here and now," and to think about society and politics "without necessary reference to a transcendent order."[1]

There is some truth in this narrative. A growing minority of men and women surely began to think about the social and political order without any reference to God. In this chapter, however, I intend to draw a different picture of Enlightenment culture. I claim that on the whole, 18th-century French thought about politics may have shown opposite tendencies to those identified by Jacob. Instead of a declining reference to a transcendent order, French Enlightenment political thought experienced an intensive search for a political and social order that would put God at its very centre. Furthermore, it was precisely this transcendent conception of politics and society that gave the French Enlightenment a strong impetus towards reforms, and lastly – a revolutionary potential.

It is not to say that it is illegitimate to speak of "secularization" in the 18th century. If, like Charles Taylor, we understand this term to mean the decline of confessional dogmas and practices and the increasing possibility of a choice of religious beliefs, then the Enlightenment and the French Revolution were indeed intertwined with a process of secularization.[2] However, the term

---

1 Margaret C. Jacob, *The Secular Enlightenment* (Princeton: 2019), 1–2.
2 Charles Taylor, *A Secular Age* (Cambridge, Mass.: 2007).

"secularization" is somewhat misleading because it can mean very different, indeed even contrary things: a decline of religious worldviews, a growing separation between religion and other social subsystems (for example art or politics), or an appropriation of religious ideas by non-clerical actors. In the last instance (appropriation), secularization means not a decline of religious ideas, but the contrary – an increase of their social and political relevance. This is, in my view, what we can observe widely in 18th-century France: Enlightenment culture saw a massive appropriation by laypersons of religious ideas formulated originally by clerics.

Making this claim means departing from long-established and impressive scholarly traditions, of which Jacob is one of the most illustrious heirs. The classical grand narratives of Enlightenment history assert that there was a secularization in the sense of a decline of religious beliefs, an orientation towards the world, and a declining importance of the divine for society and politics. To pick up only some of the most famous theses, Pierre Brunet and Alexandre Koyré saw the Enlightenment as a product of the "Scientific Revolution," and Peter Gay equated the Enlightenment with "neo-paganism."[3] The French Revolution is commonly interpreted as the result of a "dechristianisation" and a "desacralisation" of the political order.[4] When the role of religion in revolutionary politics is mentioned, the scholars usually have in mind a political religion without transcendence.[5]

Recently, however, something has been changing in historiography. A growing number of studies are exploring the life and thought of Christian Enlightenment authors and revolutionaries.[6] Following the lead of Carl Becker, some

3 Pierre Brunet, *L'Introduction des théories de Newton en France au XVIIIᵉ siècle, avant 1738* (Geneva: 1970); Alexandre Koyré, "The Significance of the Newton Synthesis," *Archives internationales d'histoire des sciences* 11 (1950): 291–311; Peter Gay, *The Enlightenment: An Interpretation*, 2 vols. (New York: 1966).

4 Michel Vovelle, *Religion et Révolution: La déchristianisation de l'an II* (Paris: 1976); Michel Vovelle, *La Révolution contre l'Église: de la raison à l'etre suprême* (Brussels: 1988).

5 Alexis de Tocqueville, *L'Ancien Régime et la Révolution* (Paris: 1988), 105–9; Albert Mathiez, *Les Origines des cultes révolutionnaires* (Geneva: 1977); Mona Ozouf, *La Fête révolutionnaire 1789-1799* (Paris: 1976), 414–474.

6 Jeffrey D. Burson, "The Catholic Enlightenment in France from the Fin de Siècle Crisis of Consciousness to the Revolution, 1650–1789," in *A Companion to the Catholic Enlightenment in Europe*, eds. Ulrich L. Lehner and Michael Printy (Leiden: 2010), 62–125; Ulrich Lehner, *The Catholic Enlightenment: The Forgotten History of a Global Movement* (New York: 2016); Jeremy D. Popkin and Richard H. Popkin (eds.), *The Abbé Grégoire and his World* (Dordrecht: 2000); Alyssa Goldstein Sepinwall, *The Abbé Grégoire and the French Revolution: The Making of Modern Universalism* (Berkeley: 2005); Caroline Chopelin-Blanc, *De l'apologétique à l'Église constitutionnelle: Adrien Lamourette (1742-1794)* (Paris: 2009); Katrina Jennie-Lou

historians are exploring the Christian imprint on 18th-century secular thought. But even in this scholarship, the Enlightenment still appears largely secular, and its Christian imprints are mostly considered as unconscious influences or as accidental products of religious controversies.[7]

Much remains to be done. What is still largely missing is an in-depth study of the place of God in the political thought of authors who did not write and fight as theologians, clerics, and Christians, and who were indeed often deists, that is who wanted to restore the natural religion. It is the goal of this chapter to give insights into the ideas expressed by authors who might appear at first glance as "secular," and who have not played – usually for good reasons – a significant role in the scholarship about the religious or Catholic Enlightenment, or about revolutionary Catholicism. I will focus on their conception of political law as an emanation from God and will hold that they affirmed the theocratic principle of the superiority of divine law, a fundamental idea in Christian reform movements since the Hussites. Theocracy was strongly rejected by many French Enlightenment philosophers and later revolutionaries, but in the sense of direct government by God or of a government by priests. "Enlightened" theocracy was understood as an order based on divine legislation. To be sure, the law referred to by these authors was not the divine *positive* law present in Scripture; it was rather the *natural* law, which had authority precisely because it was divine. The awareness of the theocratic thinking of the Enlightenment provides thus insights into the "natural republicanism" and "social naturalism" highlighted by Dan Edelstein. It helps to understand better that in the 18th century, thinking about individual rights was embedded in a long tradition of theological thinking about natural law as a divine order. It is this tradition of thought that also explains, among other reasons, why the French Revolution did not have

Wheeler, "Rabaut Saint-Étienne and the Huguenot Fight for Religious Freedom," in *Revolution as Reformation: Protestant Faith in the Age of Revolutions, 1688–1832*, eds. Peter C. Messer and William Harrison Taylor (Tuscaloosa: 2021), 96–112; Joseph Byrnes, *Priests of the French Revolution: Saints and Renegades in a New Political Era* (University Park: 2014); Nigel Aston, *Religion and Revolution in France* (Basingstoke: 2000); Rodney Dean, *L'Assemblée Constituante et la Réforme Ecclésiastique, 1790: La constitution civile du Clergé du 12 juillet et le serment ecclésiastique du 27 novembre* (Paris/London: 2014).

7   Carl L. Becker, *The Heavenly City of the Eighteenth-Century Philosophers* (New Haven: 1932); Robert Roswell Palmer, *Catholics and Unbelievers in 18th Century France* (Princeton: 2016); Alan Charles Kors, *Atheism in France, 1650–1729: The Orthodox Sources of Disbelief* (Princeton: 1990). According to Jeffrey D. Burson ("Introduction: The Culture of Jesuit Erudition in an Age of Enlightenment," *Journal of Jesuit Studies* 6/3 (2019): 387–415), the Enlightenment is an "accidental progeny of religious debates." In his recent work on Abbé Yvon, Burson takes this idea further and emphasizes the theological character of anti-Christian polemics in the 18th century: Jeffrey D. Burson, *The Culture of Enlightening: Abbé Claude Yvon and the Entangled Emergence of the Enlightenment* (Notre Dame: 2019), 379–381.

a fundamentally liberal character. Social and political order could not be the result of negotiation and compromise. The divine laws had to be imposed, and possibly with violent means.[8]

1   Secular and Religious Values in Pre-Modern Europe

The interpretation of the Enlightenment era as an age of secularization partly derives from common misconceptions about pre-modern societies. When Jacob claims that – thanks to the Enlightenment – it was no longer necessary to make "constant reference to God," she follows a caricature of earlier societies. In fact, medieval and early modern men and women did *not* refer constantly to God when they thought about the political and social order. Religious norms were only one of several ways to judge politics, social order, and morality; indeed, the existing normative systems commonly entered into conflict. For example, whereas the Gospel encouraged forgiveness, violence was usually considered perfectly legitimate for defending one's honour. "Secular" values like honour, military glory, dynasty, or the common good were major political norms and powerful instruments to legitimate policies. It was often unclear whether they were compatible with divine order, but this does not seem to have bothered most political actors. Transcendence was regularly referred to, but only as one point of reference among others.[9]

In the 17th and early 18th centuries, the dominant stream of Catholic moral theology did not call for a strict application of religious norms. Numerous Jesuits, and many other clerics, had a probabilistic approach in moral and political matters – that is, they adopted an ethic admitting that actions could be justified by "probable" reason, even if "more probable" reasons could be invoked.[10] Probabilism was extremely tolerant towards established social practices that conflicted with religious norms: some authors even justified, to a certain extent, the killing of a slanderer if the victim of calumny was not able to restore his honour in another way. Norms concerning personal and family honour were deemed reasonable, even if they were not the "most probable" norms.[11] Probabilistic thought thus accepted a plurality of norms, and secular values. It even held that norms might change with societal changes, and that

---

8   Dan Edelstein, *The Terror of Natural Rights: Republicanism, the Cult of Nature, and the French Revolution* (Chicago: 2009); Dan Edelstein, *On the Spirit of Rights* (Chicago: 2019).

9   Hillard von Thiessen and Arne Karsten (eds.), *Normenkonkurrenz in historischer Perspektive* (Berlin: 2015).

10   Damien Tricoire, "What was the Catholic Reformation? Marian Piety and the Universalization of Divine Love," *The Catholic Historical Review* 103 (2017): 20–49.

11   Jean-Louis Quantin, *Le Rigorisme chrétien* (Paris: 2001), 45–75.

this was legitimate to a certain extent. In a similar fashion, a certain variation across space was widely accepted. Jesuits adapted Christianity to non-European cultures: beginning in the late 16th century, they merged Confucianism and Catholicism in China, and "accommodated" religious practice to caste society in India.[12] In political theory, this tendency to make religious norms compatible with secular ones, and to accept a plurality of norms, found expression in treatises on the reason of state, which also became a Jesuit speciality. In this stream of Catholic political thought, the state had its own morality stemming from natural law.[13]

Across centuries, Christian Europe had experienced many strong reactions against common divergences between secular and religious norms. Long before the 18th century, most people clearly did recognize secular norms as valid, and it was the diverse reform movements since the High Middle Ages, which were often considered heresies by the Roman Church, that struggled for a strict application of religious norms and an eradication of the many secular ones. Such movements often interpreted the gap between established secular norms and religious ones as a sign that the world was corrupted, and that the end of times was near.[14] This struggle continued with undiminished vigour in the 18th century, the era of the Great Awakening in the Protestant world, and of Jansenism in the Catholic one.

We shall not assume, therefore, that people thought less of God when reflecting upon their life and society in the 18th century than in previous periods. Indeed, at the dawn of the Enlightenment, the thinking on society and politics was diverse. While it was common to conceive of political order as something established by God, there were conflicting views about the degree of human autonomy and about which kind of divine norms which society should be based on.

One major current of thought claimed that men were largely free to set positive laws. This was especially the case of authors influenced by the Roman law. Since antiquity, legal theory has distinguished between natural and positive

---

12   Ronnie Po-chia Hsia, *A Jesuit in the Forbidden City: Matteo Ricci, 1552–1610* (Oxford: 2011); David Mungello, *Curious Land: Jesuit Accommodation and the Origins of Sinology* (Stuttgart: 1985); Antje Flüchter, "Pater Pierre Martin – ein 'Brahmane aus dem Norden.' Jesuitische Grenzgänger in Südindien um die Wende zum 18. Jahrhundert," *Zeitenblicke* 11 (2012), http://www.zeitenblicke.de/2012/1/ [Accessed 6.03.2018].

13   Harro Höpfl, *Jesuit Political Thought: The Society of Jesus and the State, c. 1540–1630* (Cambridge: 2004).

14   Overview: Andreas Pečar and Damien Tricoire, "Introduction: Reformations, Prophecy and Eschatology," in *Early Modern Prophecies in Transnational, National and Regional Contexts*, ed. Lionel Laborie (Leiden: 2020), 1–22.

(human) law. It has held that natural law defines the rights and duties arising from human nature, but that these rights and duties can be modified by social imperatives. Thus, for the classical authors, positive law could contradict and nullify natural law. Under natural law, men were considered free and equal, but according to positive law, they could be masters and slaves. The state of nature and the civil state were largely dissociated. This way of thinking was lively in the 17th century. For Hugo Grotius, positive law took priority over natural law because natural law had primarily regulated a state of nature that had been lost forever. For this reason, slavery was in his eyes a perfectly legitimate institution.[15]

On the other side, a second group of authors asserted the primacy of positive *divine* law. For those influenced by St Augustine, including numerous Protestants in early modern times, original sin had largely destroyed knowledge of natural law, and it had also damaged the human ability to identify this law. God had then resorted to positive law (Revelation) to remind humans of the principles of good and evil. In the view of these authors, society was to be judged by the standards of Scripture.[16]

A third group of authors stood in the tradition of Thomist natural law theory. Thomism was a current of theological-philosophical thought that originated in 13th-century universities and was still flourishing in Catholic universities in the early modern era. It was associated most closely with the works of Thomas Aquinas, who was canonized in 1323 and elevated to the rank of the Father of the Church in 1567. Aquinas clearly affirmed the primacy of natural over human positive law, and later Thomist law theory followed this prioritization. Transcendence also played a major role in Thomist political thought, but in a different way than for the authors of the second group described above: for the early modern Thomists, the divine norms were to be found in nature, which had been created by God.

Aquinas himself had asserted the right of resistance of subjects to a tyrant who flouts the natural rights established by God.[17] This idea was successful during the Renaissance, and it was developed by neo-Thomist theologians at the University of Paris, and by both Protestant and Catholic authors, who

---

15   Charles Edwards, "The Law of Nature in the Thought of Grotius," *The Journal of Politics* 32 (1970): 784–807; Stephen Darwall, "Grotius at the Creation of Modern Moral Philosophy," *Archiv für Geschichte der Philosophie* 94 (2012): 296–325.

16   Robert Dyson, *St. Augustine of Hippo: The Christian Transformation of Political Philosophy* (London: 2005), 36; Knud Haakonssen, *Natural Law and Moral Philosophy: From Grotius to the Scottish Enlightenment* (Cambridge, Eng.: 1996).

17   Jean-Paul Coujou, "Political Thought and Legal Theory in Suárez," in *A Companion to Francisco Suárez*, ed. Victor Salas (Boston: 2015), 40.

called for resistance against royal power in the 16th century.[18] Around 1600, the Jesuit Francisco Suárez asserted the primacy of natural laws over civil (human positive) laws and loudly vindicated the right of subjects to resist tyranny.[19] Suárez, like many Jesuits, was optimistic about man's ability to understand natural law. According to him, natural law was written in the heart of every man and, through conscience, could be felt as well as conceived by the intellect. He insisted that even in the social state, which was the consequence of man's fall from grace, human positive laws had to be judged by the yardstick of the natural law. Thus, a tyrant who did not respect the principles of natural law could be deposed if necessary.

In contrast, in the 17th century, a fourth group of authors used natural law theory to legitimize strong princely power. This option was attractive for heterodox Lutherans seeking to assert the autonomy of the state from the (Lutheran) church because they were attacked by their orthodox coreligionists. According to late 17th-century Pietist theorists, such as Samuel Pufendorf and Christian Thomasius, natural law had practical relevance and normative value in society but was primarily an invitation to respect the positive laws established by legitimate authorities – because the establishment of positive law was itself an imperative of natural law. In their view, political power emanated from (divine) natural order and was autonomous from the Church, whose teaching was derived from divine positive law (that is, Scripture).[20]

2   The Primacy of Divine Order in Late 17th-Century French Thought

Which of these views, then, prevailed in the dominant French Enlightenment culture? While the authors of the French Enlightenment usually did not hold that social and political institutions were to be judged by the yardstick of Scripture – indeed most of them were strongly hostile to that idea – the stream of thought that gained particular importance was *not* the most secular one. A "secular" stream of thought, following the definition by Margaret Jacob, would have largely dissociated the human and divine orders, with a strong distinction between natural and positive law – like the first current of

---

18   Edelstein, *On the Spirit of Rights.*

19   Francisco Suárez, *Defensio Fidei III. Principatus politicus o la soberania popular* (Madrid: 1965), 34–6.

20   Thomas Ahnert, *Religion and the Origins of the German Enlightenment: Faith and Reform of Learning in the Thought of Christian Thomasius* (Rochester: 2006); Diethelm Klippel, *Politische Freiheit und Freiheitsrechte im deutschen Naturrecht des 18. Jahrhunderts* (Paderborn: 1976); Taylor, *A Secular Age*, 125–130.

thought described above, influenced by the Roman law. Likewise, the stream of thought developed by Pietist natural law theorists, that gave to the state and its law great autonomy, did not prevail in France. It was, rather, the stream that stemmed from Thomism and claimed the superiority of divine natural law over the human positive ones that gained prominence. Indeed, many French Enlightenment authors radicalized the claim that human law should follow the divine order. Among earlier Thomist thinkers, like Suárez, natural law only set out the general aims of society – the common good – but then gave men some latitude to develop positive law, and various institutions, on a contractual basis. In this way, the domain of natural law was superior, but on the whole limited, compared to the broader domain of positive law.[21] This changed in 18th-century France, as we shall see.

The first step in this direction was made by a group of authors who gathered in the late 17th century around the Versailles court preacher Bossuet, and who called themselves *"philosophes."* Until that time, the idea of a superiority of divine natural over human positive law was primarily a "scholastic" one, that is an idea anchored in university tradition. It was above all relevant in the circles of certain religious orders like the Dominicans and the Jesuits. In order to gain political relevance, it was necessary for this current of thought to leave these narrow circles. This happened in France at the end of the 17th century, when the idea of divine natural laws became increasingly an instrument of social and political criticism. This conception of natural law was in tune with the reformist impulses of a group of the Bossuet circle. These Catholic "philosophers," including Claude Fleury, François Fénelon, Jean Mabillon, Jean de La Bruyère, Antoine Galland, Charles Perrault, Jean Racine, and Nicolas Boileau, defended the idea that society should be reformed by applying the precepts of a natural order of divine origin. This notion led these authors to criticize harshly the established social practices and institutions. The philosophers of Bossuet's circle rejected (among other things) luxury, the arrogance of the great, and the pursuit of glory on the battlefield, and they deplored the misery of the people. Thus, in *Caractères de Théophraste* [...] *avec Les Caractères ou les Mœurs de ce siècle* (1688), La Bruyère set up classical Athens as a model society. He saw in ancient Athens an admirable free republic whose inhabitants led a simple and virtuous life, far superior to the depraved life of his

---

21   Haakonssen, *Natural Law*, 16–24; Oliver Bach, Norbert Brieskorn and Gideon Stiening, "'Nam lex naturalis in homine est, quia non est in deo': Das Naturrechtsdenken des Francisco Suárez," in *Die Naturrechtslehre des Francisco Suárez*, eds. Oliver Bach, Norbert Brieskorn and Gideon Stiening (Berlin: 2017), 3–21; Kurt Seelmann, "Zur historischen Wandelbarkeit des Naturrechts," in *Die Naturrechtslehre*, 213–232; Coujou, "Political Thought," 29–71.

contemporaries at the Versailles court. This Athenian social order, based on personal merit, civic virtue, industry, and paternalistic rule, was, according to La Bruyère, closer to nature and more reasonable than that of contemporary France. In particular, La Bruyère attacked the venality of offices, the wealth of the tax collectors (*fermiers généraux*), the separation between the common people and the higher estates, and the lack of public squares, promenades, baths, fountains, and theatres. Boileau, to whom he was close, denounced in his satirical writings the pedantry of scholars, the exaggerated severity of Jansenists, the corrupting sophisms of Jesuits, the ignorance and libertinism of courtiers, the chaotic life of townspeople, and the corruption of merchants and magistrates.[22]

Fénelon, who left the "philosophers'" circle in 1694 because of a violent dispute with Bossuet, portrayed in his famous educational novel *Télémaque* (1692/1699) different societies violating or respecting the natural and divine order. The frugal life of the shepherds of Betica, the flourishing Crete, and the industry of the trading city of Tyre are presented as different models. But it is especially the chapters on the Kingdom of Salente that attracted the attention of contemporaries. In the description of a corrupt Salente, they saw a thinly veiled criticism of Ludovician France, followed by Fénelon's proposed path to reform: The philosopher Mentor, an incarnation of Athena who accompanies the young prince Telemachus, transforms Salente. Telemachus rules as a paternalistic and virtuous prince who heeds Mentor's advice, restoring peace, eliminating luxury, and renewing "industry."[23]

Although the authors within Bossuet's circle are – apart from Fénelon perhaps – rarely considered protagonists of Enlightenment history, they made important contributions. Firstly, as seen in *Télémaque*, they invented the model of the Enlightenment philosopher – a committed intellectual who brings progress by fighting for the application of natural law. Secondly, they defended many of the key ideas of the 18th-century Enlightenment culture. They developed an anthropology that synthesized Augustinian (Jansenist) and semi-Pelagian (Jesuit) ideas.[24] They rejected the Jesuit probabilistic and

---

22   Damien Tricoire, "The Fabrication of the *philosophe*: Catholicisms, Court Culture and the Origins of the Enlightenment Moralism," *Journal for Eighteenth-Century Studies* 51–54 (2018): 453–477.

23   François Fénelon, *Les Aventures de Télémaque* (Paris: 1987), 155–174, 193–222, 247–271, 321–351.

24   On the different Catholic streams, see Jeffrey Burson, "Introduction: Catholicism and Enlightenment, Past, Present, and Future," in *Enlightenment and Catholicism in Europe: A Transnational History*, ed. Jeffrey Burson (Notre Dame: 2014), 1–37.

accommodationist approach, which was too lax in their eyes. But they did not share the severity of the Jansenists, who considered that human nature was wholly corrupted by original sin, and that man should submit to divine positive laws even when they contradicted the most established customs. The Versailles philosophers tended to defend a moderate rigorism. According to them, man was driven by passions more than by reason, but, if they remained natural and were not perverted, these passions could lead him to the common good. God had made man both a being of passion and of reason; man was capable of understanding natural laws and could follow the inclination of his conscience which pointed him in the right direction.[25]

The conception of natural law by the philosophers of Bossuet's circle represented a turning point in French intellectual history. Their call for a more rigorous application of divine norms did not come from a fringe or oppositional group like the Jansenists, but from intellectuals and dignitaries among the elite of the kingdom, surrounding the royal family. Nor was it a scholarly discourse conducted in Latin and preoccupied with theological, philosophical, or legal subtleties like those constrained to the scholastic tradition. The thinking of the new philosophers was entirely practical, and in some ways more pastoral than theological. The works of Racine, Boileau, La Bruyère, or Fénelon constituted an "*honnête*" literature, that is, a literature meeting the criteria of a good society that rejected the "pedantry" of academics. They quickly became classics and provided 18th-century authors not only with aesthetic models, but also with the model of the committed intellectual, working for the reform of society and for the moralization of its members. Such otherwise different *philosophes* as Voltaire, Rousseau, and Diderot were deeply influenced alike by this quest for morality. It was through their writings that the idea of the necessary application of natural laws became a keystone of French philosophical thought, expanding (not shrinking) references to God in political and social life.[26]

---

25 François-Xavier Cuche, *Une pensée sociale catholique: Fleury, La Bruyère et Fénelon* (Paris: 1991); Tricoire, "The Fabrication."

26 Ibid. On Fénelon's huge influence, see Jacques Le Brun, Christoph Schmitt-Maass, Stefanie Stockhorst and Doohwan Ahn (eds.), *Fénelon in the Enlightenment: Traditions, Adaptations and Variations* (Amsterdam: 2014); Charly Coleman, *Virtues of Abandon: An Anti-Individualist History of the French Enlightenment* (Stanford: 2014).

3   Enlightenment Theocratic Thought

In his *Questions sur l'Encyclopédie* (1774), Voltaire writes: "Theocracy should be everywhere; for every man or prince, or boatman, must obey the natural & eternal laws which GOD has given him."[27] For Rousseau, too, theocracy is a good system – as long as it is not based on superstition.[28] Raynal adds: "The best government, if it were possible for it to be maintained in its purity, would be theocracy."[29] What had happened to make these famous philosophers speak so highly of theocracy, and even to support an openly theocratic project?

By the middle of the 18th century, the desire to establish an order that was both natural and divine had intensified, particularly under the influence of philosophers whom contemporaries named "*économistes*" and whom posterity calls "physiocrats." Although apparently without direct links to the Bossuet circle, physiocrats took over the idea of the superiority of divine natural law over human positive law and affirmed it more strongly than ever. The kind of theocracy propagated as a political and social model by François Quesnay, the father of physiocracy, was not direct government by God or government by priests, but a social and political order that closely followed divine laws. In his article "Despotism of China" (1767), Quesnay makes a direct case for his vision of "theocracy":

> The laws which constitute society are not of human institution. The legislative power, often disputed between the sovereign and the nation, belongs primitively to neither of them; its origin is in the supreme will of the Creator ... ; from this confusion have come all the irregular and extravagant constitutions of governments, devised by men too uneducated for theocracy, which has invariably fixed by weights and measures the reciprocal rights and duties of men united in society.[30]

Under Quesnay's pen, "theocracy" takes on a very positive meaning, and this reduces human agency to a minimum. Quesnay continues to elaborate that the "Almighty [has] regulated and provided for everything in the general order

---

27   Voltaire, "Théocratie. Gouvernement de Dieu ou des Dieux," in *Questions sur l'Encyclopédie par des amateurs*, vol. 4 (Geneva: 1774), 444.

28   Jean-Jacques Rousseau, *Du contrat social* (Paris: 1992 [first edition 1762]), 163.

29   Guillaume-Thomas Raynal, *Histoire philosophique et politique du commerce et des établissements des européens dans les deux Indes*, vol. 4 (Geneva: 1782), 196.

30   François Quesnay, "Despotisme de la Chine," in *Œuvres économiques et philosophiques, accompagnées des éloges et d'autres travaux biographiques par différents auteurs* (Frankfurt: 1888), 642 (first published in *Ephémérides du Citoyen*, March–June 1767).

of the universe: men can only add disorder."[31] In any well-ordered political system, he explains, sovereign authority may issue laws, but these positive laws must not go beyond what the natural law prescribes: "Positive laws, if they are just, are therefore only exact deductions, or simple commentaries on those primitive laws which everywhere ensure their execution as far as possible."[32] Legislation cannot be a creative act, or the result of a negotiation between men: it "requires only the physical study of the fundamental laws of society, instituted invariably and in perpetuity by the Author of nature, on the part of those who govern, and of those who are governed."[33] Just laws follow "the sovereign and decisive rule of absolute right and wrong, of moral good and evil," and "imprint themselves on the hearts of men, they are the light that enlightens them and controls their conscience." All dissension and all conflict disappear when society follows the divine prescriptions inscribed in nature: "Divine legislation must therefore extinguish all dissension over the legislation itself, and subject the executing authority and the nation to this supreme legislation."[34]

To demonstrate what a society that follows these natural and divine laws (i.e., a "theocratic" society) would look like, Quesnay launches into a description of China. According to him, "Chinese despotism," an absolute government regulated by laws, is the best of all political systems because it strictly follows natural divine law. This "government, which is the oldest, most humane, most extensive and most flourishing that has ever existed in the universe,"[35] is based on the cult of the Supreme Being. The Chinese, he continues, recognize that

> He is the creator of all that exists, the father of peoples; he is an independent being who can do everything, who knows the deepest secrets of our hearts; he governs the universe, and foresees, moves backwards, forwards and determines at his will all the events of this world; His holiness equals his omnipotence, and his justice equals his sovereign goodness; the poor man in his thatched cottage, the king on a throne which he [God] overturns at will, experience his equity equally and receive the punishment due to their crimes.[36]

---

31   Ibid.
32   Ibid., 643.
33   Ibid., 644.
34   Ibid. On Quesnay's conception of natural law, see François Quesnay, "Le droit naturel" (septembre 1765), in: Œuvres, 359–377.
35   Quesnay, "Despotisme de la Chine," 627.
36   Ibid., 586.

This belief is, for Quesnay, a fundamental law of the Chinese empire. It plays an essential role in the establishment of order and virtue because it ensures that all, the humble as well as the emperors, submit to the laws of the Creator, towards whom they show great piety. These laws are contained in a few books that every Chinese man, great or humble, studies. The people are thus given moral instruction in thrift, frugality, industry, civility, decorum, and respect for the law. Everything is done to promote the virtue both of the governed and of the rulers and administrators. The result, writes Quesnay, is that agriculture is flourishing, while taxation (which applies only to land) is accepted. The ruler has all the power to do good, and none to do evil. He is beloved as a father, and he himself loves his subjects as his own children. The subjects make use of the right of remonstrance with great freedom without the emperor taking offence. The penal laws are mild but strictly enforced by courts that are free and know no corruption.[37]

Quesnay's theory gave a new turn to the history of natural law in France. Although the members of Bossuet's circle had already demanded a greater application of natural laws, and a thorough reform of society on that basis, their vision had not been theocratic. Like Suárez, they had left room for man to define social and political institutions as long as they remained in harmony with natural law. Fénelon had thus presented several divergent examples of societies in harmony with the divine order. Quesnay, on the other hand, reduced human freedom to a minimum. He believed that there could be only one political and social system in accordance with natural law. His theocracy was a new type. The Hussites in the 15th century, or the English regicides of 1649, among others, had proposed a theocracy based on the idea of a superiority of divine positive law (Scripture). Quesnay, however, based political and social order on natural law alone.

Quesnay's ideas were taken up by a whole series of philosophers, including Le Mercier de La Rivière, the author of *L'Ordre naturel et essentiel des sociétés politiques* (1767). For this "*économiste*," "the natural and essential order of society is simple, obvious and unchangeable."[38] It has been defined once and for all by the Creator: "God is the first Author of positive laws."[39] According to Le Mercier de La Rivière, "the Author of nature has not left them [the legislators] the laws to be made; but he presents them with ready-made laws."[40] For this

---

37   Ibid., 585–622.
38   Pierre-Paul Le Mercier de La Rivière, *L'Ordre naturel et essentiel des sociétés politiques* (London: 1767), 37.
39   Ibid., 105.
40   Ibid., 120.

reason, "the [human] Legislator only applies the natural and essential laws to the different cases that it is possible to foresee."[41] This is why political authority could only be despotic: in this divine order, there was no room for negotiation, compromise between social groups, or the popular will.[42] Similarly, national traditions, the ancient constitution of the kingdom, and particular habits and customs could not be legitimate. The divine law was uniform and unalterable.

This absolute superiority of divine laws over human ones gave strong impulses towards reform in physiocratic thought. In particular, it called on these authors to reject trade barriers, feudal rights, *corvée*, serfdom, and – for some of them – colonial slavery. In the long run, the *économistes'* aim was to abolish any institution that did not fit with natural order: an order based on the ownership of land, constituted by independent and virtuous agricultural producers, under the tutelary authority of an absolute sovereign subject only to immutable laws.[43]

Physiocracy was far from being a marginal stream of thought in 18th-century France, and its centrality is being rediscovered in recent scholarship.[44] Physiocracy soon became indeed highly influential among the administrative and political elites of the Old Regime, and among the *philosophes*. With Turgot, physiocracy came to power in France in 1774, albeit for a short period of time. Physiocracy had an enormous impact on colonial policy. It is not exaggerated to claim that the very Enlightenment idea of a civilizing policy was a product of physiocracy, which took inspiration in this matter from Jesuit missionary ideas.[45]

Physiocracy also had a major impact on many authors who are not categorized usually as "physiocrats." Voltaire's surprisingly positive view of theocracy is a clear testimony of such an influence. The same can be said of Raynal and Diderot's critique of some forms of colonialism and pleas for an enlightened colonial expansion in their famous *Histoire des deux Indes*.[46] Although Diderot

---

41 Ibid., 105.

42 Ibid., 142–200.

43 Turgot's reform projects: *Œuvres de Turgot et documents le concernant*, especially vols. 2–4 (Paris: 1919–1924). On the critique of slavery, see Dupont de Nemours, "Observations sur l'esclavage des nègres," *Éphémérides du citoyen* 6 (1771): 162–246.

44 See, for example, Edelstein, *Terror*; Edelstein, *On the Spirit of Rights*; Pernille Røge, *Économistes and the Reinvention of Empire: France in the Americas and Africa, c. 1750–1802* (Cambridge: 2019).

45 Damien Tricoire, "Les Lumières, l'idéologie coloniale et Madagascar: Aux origines de la mission civilisatrice," in *Les Lumières, l'esclavage et l'idéologie coloniale: XVIIIᵉ–XXᵉ siècles*, ed. Pascale Pellerin (Paris: 2020), 85–98; Røge, *Économistes*, 24–63.

46 Røge, *Économistes*, 102–3. On the *Histoire des deux Indes'* critique of some forms of colonialism and endorsement of others see also Damien Tricoire, "Raynal's and Diderot's

is not commonly perceived as influenced by physiocracy, he was a broker between Le Mercier de La Rivière and the Russian court, and in his unofficial position as a royal censor in France, Diderot had approved *L'Ordre naturel et essentiel des sociétés politiques*. Contrary to the idea, dominant in scholarship, that Diderot was always an enemy of strong monarchical power, he praised in high terms Le Mercier de La Rivière's political system: in a letter to his friend Falconet in 1768, he claimed that Le Mercier de La Rivière had elucidated "the secret of the happiness of states."[47]

4   The Influence of Theocratic Thought on Materialist and Agnostic Authors

Diderot's case suggests that the physiocratic idea of a supremacy of (divine) natural rights over positive (human) ones influenced even at least some materialist authors. While the physiocratic system was based upon the idea of theocracy, it could also function without references to transcendence. This transformation of physiocratic thought is visible in the writings of a small minority of authors and can be termed "secularization" – but it still contributed to a growing social and political relevance of ideas with religious fundaments, not to their marginalization. In this respect, the case of Condorcet, who played an important role in the French Revolution, is highly significant.

If Condorcet was not a declared atheist, he seems to have been an agnostic. He was above all a rationalist, who did not accept any truth that could not be demonstrated by "natural light." Condorcet believed that it was impossible to demonstrate the existence of God. He was thus openly hostile to the religious ideas of Rousseau, who argued that man should believe in God because such belief consoles him, and that one could deduce from God's goodness that everything on earth was for the best.[48] Condorcet was preoccupied by the problem of theodicy, and he found it difficult to conceive that general laws were always wise. An example of his skepticism appears in a letter to his physiocratic friend and patron Turgot, for whom natural laws could only be good because they

---

Patriotic History of the Two Indies, or The Problem of Anti-Colonialism in the Eighteenth Century," *The Eighteenth Century* 59 (2018): 429–448.

47   Diderot to Falconet, July 1767, in Denis Diderot, *Oeuvres: Édition établie par Laurent Versini*, vol. 5: *Correspondance* (Paris: 1997), 747.

48   Jean Antoine Nicolas de Caritat de Condorcet, "Sur la loi naturelle," in *Œuvres de Condorcet: Nouvelle impression en facsimilé de l'édition de Paris 1847–1849*, vol. 4 (Stuttgart: 1968), 221; see also Jean Antoine Nicolas de Caritat de Condorcet, "Éloge de Pascal," in *Œuvres*, vol. 3, 576 and "Remarques sur les *Pensées* de Pascal," in *Œuvres*, vol. 3, 640.

were of divine origin.[49] Unlike Turgot, Condorcet did not believe that natural laws regulated everything. While he did not subscribe to "skeptical" and relativistic moral thinking, he accepted that there could be different sexual morals as long as the woman consented.[50] Faced with this assertion, Turgot replied as a good *économiste*: "I do not believe that morality in itself can ever be local. Its principles are everywhere founded on the nature of man and his relations with his fellow men, which do not vary ... "[51] It is thus clear that not only did Condorcet not share the ideas of the physiocrats on the divine origin of natural laws, but that he was not convinced that natural laws always guarantee happiness and form a code that governs all human relations.

Despite these disagreements with physiocrats, Condorcet also believed that French society and the French state needed to be reshaped in order to enforce natural laws. In *Réflexions sur les affaires publiques* (1789), for example, he takes a position in the debates on the form of deliberation of the Estates-General. Here, he argues that neither "ancient usages" nor "ancient capitulations" should be respected, but rather that "a form of convocation, regulated solely according to natural law, which admits neither prescription nor local differences" should be introduced.[52] He measures any idea against the "rigorous principles of natural law" and the "true principles of statehood," among which he counts "natural equality."[53] His conception of law thus has many similarities with that of physiocratic authors, even though he did not consider nature as the emanation of a just and good deity. How could this be?

In fact, Condorcet's writings display a direct influence of physiocracy. He was an intimate friend of Turgot, and one of his closest collaborators. It was under the influence of Turgot, who was 16 years his senior, that Condorcet became involved in social and economic issues. Between the end of the 1760s and the revolution, he wrote a number of papers in support of the physiocratic reform projects. In particular, he argued for the liberalization of the grain trade and for the legalization of the civil status of Protestants. His fight for greater gender equality and against slavery was in line with the thinking of Turgot and

---

49   Condorcet à Turgot, 7 juin 1772, "Correspondance avec Turgot," in *Œuvres*, vol. 1, 200.

50   Condorcet à Turgot, 13 décembre 1773, "Correspondance avec Turgot," in *Œuvres*, vol. 1, 221–2.

51   Turgot à Condorcet, 28 décembre 1773, "Correspondance avec Turgot," in *Œuvres*, vol. 1, 227.

52   Jean Antoine Nicolas de Caritat de Condorcet, *Réflexions sur les affaires publiques, par une société de citoyens* (s.l.: 1789), 19–20.

53   Condorcet, *Réflexions sur les affaires publiques*, 14–15, 19.

some physiocrats.[54] In his correspondence with Turgot, Condorcet – despite the kinds of disagreement voiced in the letter above – expressed strong support for the projects of his friend, minister, and patron.[55]

In his *Vie de Turgot* (1786), Condorcet repeatedly emphasized a trait that he particularly admired in his deceased protector: according to Condorcet, all of Turgot's thought and political action were aimed at ensuring the triumph of natural law. Still *Maître des requêtes*, Turgot "[f]orced to judge those cases where the letter of the law seemed contrary to natural law, whose superiority over all laws he recognised ... he believed he had to take it as a guide in his opinion," but "the majority preferred a positive law which seemed clear, to a more sacred law."[56] In his article "Fondation" for the *Encyclopédie*, or in a work on mines and quarries, Condorcet found that Turgot drew "such clear consequences from the most general and certain principles of natural law,"[57] and had "managed to see" that "the entire system of civil laws" could be "deduced from these same principles."[58] As a minister, Turgot had restored "to the grain and flour trade its natural liberty" and attacked "all kinds of oppression," thereby giving "back to men a part of those natural rights, which no constitution can legitimately take away from them."[59]

In *Vie de Turgot*, Condorcet shows great admiration for Turgot's philosophical system. He strongly approves of Turgot's idea that the state "must be subordinated to the more essential, more sacred duty of preserving the exercise of citizens' rights."[60] Condorcet follows Turgot when he declares that laws "can only be legitimate if they fulfil two conditions: firstly, that they emanate from a legitimately instituted power; secondly, that they do not violate in any way the natural rights that they must preserve,"[61] and places a clear emphasis on the latter criteria. Condorcet approves the physiocratic criticism of the republicans, who believe "that all laws must be made by a legitimate and just power."[62] He adds:

> If we suppose that men are subject to laws, none of which violates any of their rights, and that all, on the contrary, contribute to ensuring their

---

54   Condorcet acknowledges that his pleas for more gender equality were influenced by Turgot and physiocracy: Jean Antoine Nicolas de Caritat de Condorcet, "Vie de Turgot," in *Œuvres*, vol. 5, 188. The first French abolitionist writings were of physiocratic inspiration: Dupont de Nemours, "Observations."

55   Condorcet, *Œuvres*, vol. 1, 248–268.

56   Ibid., 16–17.

57   Ibid., 24, 46 (citation).

58   Ibid., 46.

59   Ibid.,77.

60   Ibid., 83.

61   Ibid., 181.

62   Ibid.

enjoyment, it will matter little to these men whether these laws have received their sanction in a public form, or only by tacit consent. The essential thing is not popular participation, but the application of natural law.[63]

For Condorcet, who is both summarizing and approving Turgot here, this means that "[e]verything must necessarily change": the laws on marriage, on succession, on trade and industry, on taxation. The "humiliating distinctions between the classes of citizens" must disappear, and even the vices.[64] To this end, public education and freedom of the press must be introduced.[65]

5   God, Conscience and Political Order in Rousseau's Thought

Condorcet's case shows that even some agnostic authors took over central tenets of the Enlightenment theocratic thought. Such secularization of religious political ideas is observable in the 18th century, but it did not become a dominant feature of intellectual life. The most influential currents of French Enlightenment were, on the contrary, directly and openly influenced by theocratic thinking. This is at least what appears not only from the history of physiocracy, but also from the history of another stream of thought that became highly popular in the second half of the 18th century: republicanism, especially in its Rousseauian version.

Rousseau differed from physiocrats in his conception of the ways to find the good principles of social and political order. According to Rousseau, nature is not a code of law that can be deciphered by reason. But this does not make him less theocratic in his conception of the just society: like Suárez, Bossuet, and Quesnay, Rousseau postulates that it is through his conscience that man finds eternal laws which are superior to the positive laws established in society. It is therefore necessary to "return to nature" – not to a hypothetical state of nature, but to a divine order that can be found by listening to one's conscience, which allows men to be one with themselves and to bridge the gap between being and appearing. For Rousseau, as for the physiocrats, there is an imperative to apply natural laws, and this imperative is divine: according to both Rousseau and Quesnay, it is the Supreme Being who has placed conscience within us. For this reason, divinity is present to man, and accompanies him in his quest for truth and goodness, so long as he is willing to listen to his conscience. According to

---

63   Ibid., 182.
64   Ibid., 196–7.
65   Ibid., 203, 207–8.

Rousseau, Jesus Christ is the archetype of man returning to nature by following his conscience. Rousseau holds that the Gospel presents laws drawn from
nature, and (taking leave from major Christian dogmas) explains that the Gospel
was revealed by God, albeit indirectly and without supernatural intervention, by
means of human conscience, which he conceives as a divine instrument.[66]

This religious, indeed mystical,[67] dimension in Rousseau's thought is essential for understanding several of his major philosophical works. In proposing
a hypothetical vision of natural man in the *Discours sur l'origine et les fondements de l'inégalité parmi les hommes* (1754), Rousseau's overt aim was to distinguish between divine institutions and the artifices added by humans:

> Now, without the serious study of man, of his natural faculties, and of
> their successive developments, one will never be able to make these dis-
> tinctions, and to separate in the present constitution of things what the
> divine will has done from what human art has claimed to do.[68]

In this way, the political concepts expressed in *Du contrat social* can also be
linked to Rousseau's religious ideas. According to Rousseau, history was a process of moving away from the divine order.[69] But, as he outlines a theoretical
model of a just political society, Rousseau arrives at the conclusion that any
social order, if it is to be free from corruption, can only be built upon the moral
order revealed by God. Indeed, the ideal political community is based on the
general will, which is not the sum of particular wills, which are tainted by passions, and therefore cannot be the result of negotiation or compromise. As an
expression of the intrinsic interests of society in general, the general will is discovered by following one's conscience, the instrument that the Supreme Being
uses to guide the human being.

This theocratic conception of the good law reveals a gap between Rousseau's
ideas and our common conception of democracy in the 21st-century western
world. For Rousseau, law-making is not really a creative process. Since good
laws are an expression of God's imprint on man, they are discovered rather
than invented. For this reason, legislating is an exceptional act. Rousseau imag-
ines a legislator setting laws for several centuries and having them approved by
the people. Politics is then above all the work of magistrates who apply the law,

---

66   Christian Jacquet, *La pensée religieuse de Jean-Jacques Rousseau* (Leuven: 1975), especially
      37–143.
67   Coleman, *Virtues*, 203–247.
68   Jean-Jacques Rousseau, *Discours sur l'origine et les fondements de l'inégalité parmi les hom-
      mes: Discours sur les sciences et les arts* (Paris: 1971), 163.
69   Rousseau, *Discours sur l'origine*, 249–257.

and who are regularly confirmed in their function by the popular assembly. This conception of law as an institution that is indirectly of divine origin (at least if it is good) explains why one of the criteria by which Rousseau judges the quality of laws is their durability. The closer the laws are to the natural order, the more they preserve society from the corruption of time, and the more durable they are. Finally, this conception of law explains why Rousseau thinks that the belief in a Supreme Being who rewards and punishes in the afterlife, as well as a public cult, are necessary for the proper functioning of the state. Anyone who does not subscribe to the civil religion must be banished, or even punished by death.[70]

In Rousseau's system, democracy is ultimately first and foremost a means of establishing divine laws, and the people have a voice as acclaimers of the divine order. With such a theory, Rousseau was following a long and controversial tradition within Europe of legitimizing popular participation that was formulated in the Middle Ages. The adage "*Vox populi, vox Dei*" was used in politics repeatedly from the 11th century onwards to justify the election of dignitaries by acclamation, and somewhat later – from the late Middle Ages onwards – to justify the right of resistance to princely power.[71] It gave rise to political controversies during the Fronde in the mid-17th century.[72] In England, the formula was used to legitimize resistance to James II, and later to vindicate the 1688 revolution against the Jacobites. Its latter use was promoted notably through the treatise *Vox populi, vox Dei*, which continued to circulate in numerous editions throughout the 18th century.[73] The formula is found, as well, in the titles of English political pamphlets, and in some French titles, through 1789.[74]

---

70   Jean-Jacques Rousseau, *Contrat social*, above all 57, 61–8, 134–8, 158–168. The idea of the general will stems from the idea of God's general will: Patrick Riley, *The General Will Before Rousseau. The Transformation of the Divine into the Civic* (Princeton: 1986).

71   George Boas, *Vox Populi: Essays in the History of an Idea* (Baltimore: 1969), 3–26; Alain Boureau, "L'adage Vox populi, vox Dei et l'invention de la nation anglaise (VIIIe–XIIe siècle)," *Annales. Histoire, Sciences Sociales* 47 (1992): 1071–1089.

72   *Question, si la voix du peuple est la voix de Dieu?* (s.l.: 1649); *Que la voix du peuple est la voix de Dieu. Contre le sentiment de celuy qui nous a proposé une Question toute contraire* (Paris: 1649); *Remède aux malheurs de l'Estat de France, au sujet de la question Si la voix du peuple est la voix de Dieu* (Paris: 1649).

73   *Vox Populi, Vox Dei, or, Englands general lamentation for the dissolution of the Parliament* (s.l.: 1681); *Vox populi, vox Dei: being true maxims of government* [...] (London: 1709).

74   Jacob Henriques, *Vox populi, vox Dei, &c. The petition and proposal of Jacob Henriques to the Honourable House of Commons, for paying the national debt* (London: 1749); Alexander Dalrymple, *Vox populi vox Dei. Lord Weymouth's appeal to a general court of India proprietors considered* (London: 1769); *Le Peuple au roi: vox populi vox Dei* (s.l.: 1789).

6   "The Cooperators of Providence": Mably

God was not only the cornerstone of Rousseau's moral-political system. God also played a major role in the thought of Mably – another influential French author influenced by classical republicanism.[75] Keith Michael Baker comments that Abbé de Mably urged the French to finally exercise their will and to create a fundamental law for themselves.[76] But it appears that this fundamental law was, for the ecclesiastic Mably, above all to be dictated by nature, and ultimately, by God himself. This is at least what Mably suggests in *De la législation ou Principe des lois* (1776), which presents a dialogue between a Swede and an Englishman, in which the former largely dominates. The Scandinavian defends the introduction of sumptuary laws and fulminates against the corrupting power of money, which destroys the public spirit. Mably takes up the *topoi* of classical republicanism here.[77] While Mably should not be misunderstood as an opponent of foreign trade, or an early proponent of communism – a common misleading interpretation[78] – the denunciation of the deleterious effects of luxury is omnipresent in his work. He wrote his voluminous historiographical work from the point of view of a moralist and a legislator.[79] Looking at his religious thought can therefore help us to understand better the republican conception of social order and the law in 18th-century France.

In *De la législation*, the idea of a divine order is central. Mably speaks through the mouth of the Swede: "there is neither good policy nor good laws in a society, unless it conforms to the intentions of providence ... Let us therefore try to know these intentions, instead of studying ourselves to satisfy our passions."[80] According to the Swede, before discussing laws, one must listen to one's heart and go back to the principles, which are none other than the intentions of Providence. These principles are eternal and universal, and contrast with the "monstrous variety of governments, laws, usages, customs"[81] throughout the

---

75   Johnson Kent Wright, *A Classical Republican in Eighteenth-Century France: The Political Thought of Mably* (Stanford: 1997).

76   Keith Michael Baker, *Inventing the French Revolution: Essays on French Political Culture in the Eighteenth Century* (Cambridge, Eng.: 1999), 86–106.

77   Gabriel Bonnot de Mably, "De la législation ou Principes des lois," in *Collection complète des œuvres de l'abbé de Mably*, vol. 9 (Paris: 1794).

78   Julie Ferrand and Arnaud Orain, "Abbé de Mably on Commerce, Luxury, and 'Classical Republicanism,'" *Journal of the History of Economic Thought* 39/2 (2017): 199–221.

79   Stéphane Pujol, "Histoire, morale et politique chez Mably," in *Les philosophes et l'histoire au XVIIIᵉ siècles*, ed. Muriel Brot (Paris: 2011), 123–148.

80   Mably, "De la législation," 14–15.

81   Ibid., 24.

world. This diversity comes from the fact that people have followed their passions. But nature has punished them for their errors, and they are unhappy. "Providence" could not make "different kinds of happiness for the ancients and for us, for Asia, Africa, America and Europe."[82]

In following their hearts, legislators must "look upon themselves as co-operators with providence."[83] They must prevent us from turning away from the purpose for which the Supreme Being created us. Mably insists that we cannot deviate from "the order of providence," from "those eternal laws which preceded the birth of cities and societies and which ... are but the supreme reason of God himself ... "[84] God "necessarily does everything for the best," says the Swede.[85] In *De la législation*, as in Rousseau's writings, belief in the divinity and in post-mortem rewards and punishments, as well as a public cult, are deemed necessary for the maintenance of virtue, because they encourage citizens to listen to their conscience (or "heart") and not to their passions: "if there is no God, there is no morality."[86] This idea can also be found in Quesnay's writing on China.

Of course, the natural order that Mably sketches through the words of the Swede is not that of the physiocrats. Unlike those authors, the Swede does not believe that property rights and social inequality are natural. On the contrary, he believes that "providence has not allowed the feeling of equality to be outraged."[87] This idea can be found in many of Mably's works. Much more than the physiocrats, he insists that nature demands simplicity and frugality. His condemnation of luxury is also more radical than that of the Bossuet circle. He attacks the inequality of wealth more clearly, which, as he believes, alters the natural sentiments of the human heart. The happiness of a people, in his view, does not come from opulence, nor from the degree of the cultivation of land. Also, unlike the economists, Mably did not believe that the executive and legislative powers should be in the same hand. In an article against the physiocrats, Mably demolished Quesnay's idyllic picture of China, saying, "I fear that your natural order is unnatural!"[88]

---

82   Ibid., 26.
83   Ibid., 30.
84   Ibid., 32, 34.
85   Ibid., 57.
86   Ibid., 389.
87   Ibid., 54.
88   Gabriel Bonnot de Mably, "Doutes proposés aux philosophes économistes sur l'ordre naturel et essentiel des sociétés politiques," in *Collection complète des œuvres de l'abbé de Mably*, vol. 10 (Paris: 1794).

Nevertheless, Mably's conception of law has similarities with that of the economists. Like the latter, Mably reduces human freedom to a minimum: the plurality of social and political systems is for him fundamentally illegitimate because it is incompatible with the idea of the divine order. What is essential, therefore, is perhaps less the popular will than submission to an eternal order. Moreover, Mably, like the physiocrats, considered natural laws to be the expression of the will of a just deity, and concluded that positive laws can only be good if they are the application of divine laws. While strongly influenced by Thomistic scholastic thought, the republicans – like the physiocrats – gave a theocratic turn to the natural law theories that had prevailed in the 16th and 17th centuries: for these Enlightenment writers, the diversity of political and social systems was a scandal, and tradition no longer carried any weight as a principle for legitimizing institutions. Divine law had become a political principle superior to any other.

7   Republican Theocratic Thought in the French Revolution

What impact did this conception of law and social order have on the French Revolution? It is important to be careful not to see the revolutionaries as simply applying programmes developed in the Enlightenment. Baker has thus somewhat overstated the case by presenting Mably as the inventor of the "script" of the French Revolution: although Mably did anticipate that the Estates-General would be convened in the face of financial problems, and that the deputies would reform the political system, he did not have in mind the creation of the National Assembly or the abolition of the privileges of the Old Regime. He only imagined the establishment of a monarchy tempered by the estates.[89] As for the political system set out in *Du contrat social*, it differs greatly from the constitutions and political systems that were established successively after 1789. Moreover, one must be careful not to see in Rousseau's work a proposal for the reform of all political communities; the model he developed seems to be applicable only to small republics, and *Du contrat social* was most certainly a work in which Rousseau took a position in Genevan political debates.[90]

---

89   Baker, *Inventing*, 86–106; Stéphanie Roza, "L'abbé de Mably, entre modérantisme et radicalité," *Tangence* 106 (2014): 37–8.

90   Richard Whatmore, "Rousseau and the *représentants*: The Politics of the *Lettres de la montagne*," *Modern Intellectual History* 3 (2006): 1–29; Helena Rosenblatt, "Rousseau's Gift to Geneva," *Modern Intellectual History* 3 (2006): 65–73; Simone Zurbuchen, "Die Theorie der Institutionen im Contrat Social und das Modell der Genfer Verfassung," in *Jean-Jacques Rousseau im Bann der Institutionen*, eds. Konstanze Baron and Harald Bluhm (Berlin: 2016), 147–167.

Nevertheless, Mably and Rousseau were major references during the French Revolution, and their conceptions of the social and political order influenced the thinking of many revolutionaries.[91] As the revolutionaries appropriated the ideas of these and other Enlightenment philosophers, they modified many of these ideas extensively. But when they argued for a recasting of the political and social order, it was usually on a largely faithful reproduction of the philosophers' theocratic conceptions of law.

The case of Brissot, who was himself an Enlightenment philosopher before becoming a major revolutionary politician, is illuminating in this respect. Natural laws play an important role in his thinking from his early work. In his curious and provocative *Recherches philosophiques sur le droit de propriété* (1780), Brissot, then 26, attacked the unequal distribution of wealth in the name of natural and divine law. According to him, the right to property is a natural right, but only in the sense that nature gives every living being the right to consume what it needs to survive. This applies to humans, animals, and even plants. All living beings form an indissoluble chain, and the division between species is chimerical. For Brissot, the tiger has a property right over man, and even cannibalism is legitimate in the state of nature. Brissot thus challenges land ownership in the name of divine law:

> Jacques claims to be the possessor of a garden. Does he have more right than Pierre? No, certainly not. Jacques' parents have, in truth, passed on this inheritance to him in their estate. But by virtue of what title did they themselves possess it? The Supreme Being has given the earth to all men: he has not said to this one, you shall have these thirty acres; to that one, enjoy these immense meadows.[92]

Of course, Brissot specifies that he is "speaking here only for the state of nature." In the civil state, considerations push to guarantee property:

> for in the social state, the situation is very different. Without doubt, in this state, to make a piece of land fertile, it is necessary to make advances

---

91   Gordon H. McNeil, "The Cult of Rousseau and the French Revolution," *Journal of the History of Ideas* 6 (1945): 197–212; Nathalie-Barbara Robisco, *Jean-Jacques Rousseau et la Révolution française: une esthétique de la politique, 1792–1799* (Paris: 1998); Roger Barny, *Le droit naturel à l'épreuve de l'histoire: Jean-Jacques Rousseau dans la Révolution (débats politiques et sociaux)* (Paris: 1995); Florence Gauthier, "De Mably à Robespierre, un programme économique égalitaire," *Annales historiques de la Révolution française* 57 (1985): 265–289.

92   Jacques-Pierre Brissot de Warville, *Recherches philosophiques sur le droit de propriété considéré dans la nature* [...] (s.l.: 1780), 42–3.

& work. Without doubt it is right that he who has worked should enjoy the fruit of his labours.

Agriculture is the foundation of the State; but to make it flourish, the farmer must be assured of the right to enjoy the fruits of his labour. Without this favour attached to property, there can be no cultivation of land ...[93]

However, the fact remains that the distribution of wealth in current societies violates, according to Brissot, the natural law that property should be limited by the human beings' physical needs:

Judges of nations, you whom societies have chosen to protect their laws ... until when will you be inconsistent and cruel? When will you stop violating the laws of nature? ... Must it be necessary, then, that in order to respect civil property, which is only a social usurpation, [the poor] should perish from hunger?[94]

Thus, according to Brissot, the natural law – God's gift of the earth to all men – remains valid in the social state, since it sets narrow limits to property rights.

Like that of Rousseau, Brissot's philosophy is marked by faith in the Divinity that created the earth. This concordance between Brissot's thought and that of the Genevan philosopher is not due to chance: Brissot often makes explicit reference to Rousseau to justify his views. As he states in *De la vérité* (1782), while reason cannot prove the existence of God, "moral instinct" and the resulting happiness reveal to the philosopher that there is a Supreme Being, and only this belief can lead to the good:

I therefore set reason aside, & follow only my moral instinct, only the voice of happiness. I am happy when I work for the good of my fellow men ... I am happy when I believe I am under the eye of a Supreme Being, when I believe I see him smile at my feeble efforts and encourage them; I am happy when I invoke him, when I pray to him; & I only pray to him driven by an irresistible need, by pleasure: he is my master, I give him an account, we converse; & in this conversation, in the hope that he gives me, I draw new strength, a greater energy ... Where will you draw yours, O you who believe in nothing? ... You are indifferent [*vous êtes de glace*]

---

93   Ibid., 106–7.
94   Ibid., 109–110.

for everything that is not you; truth is foreign to you; & its search requires a passionate soul [*une ame de feu*].[95]

Brissot believes that Christianity is based on a deception, but, like Rousseau, he thinks that the maxims of the Gospel and of St Paul are sublime and have been drawn from nature.[96]

For Brissot, as for Rousseau and Mably, natural laws are superior to the traditions of the kingdom because they were instituted by God. This also applies to the respect that rulers must show towards public opinion (a "system, which is that of God himself," writes Brissot).[97] It is the divine institution of natural laws, derived from the Christian conception of divinity taken over by deism, that forms the basis of Brissot's political ideals. But Brissot no longer felt the need to spell out these premises in his 1789 writings. Thus, in his *Précis adressé à l'assemblée générale des électeurs de Paris, pour servir à la rédaction du cahier de doléances de cette ville* (1789), Brissot pleads for the electors of Paris to ask for the drafting of "an enunciative act of the essential rights, inherent to men in society," a declaration that "can be contained in this line: All men are born free & equal in rights."[98] In fact, this last statement had been self-evident for centuries to jurists trained in Roman law. But for Brissot and his contemporaries, it had taken on a new meaning: it no longer simply meant that men were born free and equal in rights, but that they remained so in society, whatever might happen, because it was God who had instituted these rights. It is striking that Brissot could afford not to justify the superiority of natural law over positive law, so obvious did this superiority seem to him and his contemporaries in 1789. A century of writings on the laws of the Creator, and especially physiocratic and republican thought, had left their mark.

According to many revolutionaries, divine law was the cornerstone of the new political order they sought to establish. In the debate of August 1789 about the Declaration of the Rights of Man and of the Citizen, Abbé Grégoire called for the Supreme Being to be mentioned in the preamble. There was

---

95   Jacques-Pierre Brissot de Warville, *De la vérité ou Méditations sur les moyens de parvenir à la vérité dans toutes les connaissances humaines* (Neuchâtel: 1782), 212.

96   Jacques-Pierre Brissot de Warville, *Lettres philosophiques sur St Paul, sur sa doctrine politique, morale et religieuse et sur plusieurs points de la religion chrétienne, considérés politiquement* [...] (Neuchâtel: 1783), 25–7.

97   Jacques-Pierre Brissot de Warville, "Lettre adressée à M. le Comte de M***, par M ... sur le plan de M. Turgot," Sur les assemblées provinciales, in *Œuvres posthumes de Turgot, ou Mémoire de M. Turgot sur les administrations provinciales* [...] (Lausanne: 1787), 101.

98   Jacques-Pierre Brissot de Warville, *Précis adressé à l'assemblée générale des électeurs de Paris, pour servir à la rédaction du cahier de doléances de cette ville* (s.l.: 1789), 4–5.

no consensus on this question. Many revolutionaries would have recognized explicitly that man derives his rights from God, and some even placed the Decalogue in the preamble to the Declaration. A minority, on the other hand, thought that a mention of the Supreme Being was superfluous or even harmful.[99] In the end, the deputies recognized that God was responsible for the natural laws they were implementing, and integrated the following words into the preamble of the Declaration of Rights: "The National Assembly recognizes and declares, in the presence and under the auspices of the Supreme Being, the following rights of Man and Citizen." In the famous painting by Jean-Jacques François Le Barbier, as well as in the engravings based on it, the Declaration is placed under the divine eye, which is underlined by an angel on the right with a hand gesture. At the top left, an allegorical figure of France, freed from its chains, also turns towards the deity. The text is engraved on a double table inspired by the iconography of the tables of the law. In the medieval scholastic tradition, and again by Suárez, the Decalogue was considered an expression of natural law. Through iconography, the Declaration of the Rights of Man is presented as a covenant between God and the French nation, an idea that several contemporaries such as François-Henri de Virieu, Mirabeau-Tonneau, and – a little later – Maximilien Robespierre formulated explicitly.[100] One of the latter's most striking projects was the *Fête de l'Être suprême*, which was directly inspired by Rousseau's idea that a political society could not survive without publicly acknowledging that it was based on divine laws.[101]

8   Conclusion

The example of French political thought and political culture in the second half of the 18th century shows major flaws in the classical interpretations of the Enlightenment era as an age of secularization. To be sure, there was a pluralization of religious ideas in France, and Christianity was on the defensive. But ideas about a transcendent order did not lose their political significance. We observe rather a triumph of religious ideas, which operated in two ways. A minority of materialist and agnostic authors developed a secularized version

---

99   See the debates in *Archives Parlementaires* (AP), vol. 8, August 1789 (Paris: 1875).
100   Virieu: AP, vol. 8: 462 (20 août 1789); Mirabeau-Tonneau: ibid.; Robespierre: for example, AP, vol. 20: 407 (18 floréal, an II/7 mai 1794) or *Réimpression de l'ancien Moniteur*, vol. 20: 683 ("Discours de Maximilien Robespierre, président de la Convention nationale, au peuple réuni pour la fête de l'Etre suprême, 20 prairial, an II/8. Juni 1794").
101   Jonathan Smyth, *Robespierre and the Festival of the Supreme Being: The Search for a Republican Morality* (Manchester: 2016).

of the natural law theory, taking over some central tenets of Thomism but stripping them of the mention of God. Many more authors and revolutionary politicians consciously defended a theocratic programme, under the influence of either physiocracy or republicanism. These theocratic foundations of French political thought manifested manifold undemocratic tendencies (like in physiocracy) or illiberal ones (like in republicanism). Theocratic thought makes the French Revolution appear much more similar to the English Revolution of 1648–1649 than we would expect at first glance. Like the 17th-century English revolutionaries, Brissot and Robespierre worked to build the City of God.

References

Ahnert, Thomas, *Religion and the Origins of the German Enlightenment: Faith and Reform of Learning in the Thought of Christian Thomasius* (Rochester: 2006).

Archives Parlementaires de 1787 à 1860 (AP), eds. Jérôme Mavidal and Émile Laurent (Paris: 1875).

Aston, Nigel, *Religion and Revolution in France* (Basingstoke: 2000).

Bach, Oliver, Norbert Brieskorn and Gideon Stiening, "'Nam lex naturalis in homine est, quia non est in deo': Das Naturrechtsdenken des Francisco Suárez," in *Die Naturrechtslehre des Francisco Suárez*, eds. Oliver Bach, Norbert Brieskorn and Gideon Stiening (Berlin: 2017), 3–21.

Baker, Keith Michael, *Inventing the French Revolution: Essays on French Political Culture in the Eighteenth Century* (Cambridge, Eng.: 1999).

Barny, Roger, *Le droit naturel à l'épreuve de l'histoire: Jean-Jacques Rousseau dans la Révolution (débats politiques et sociaux)* (Paris: 1995).

Becker, Carl L., *The Heavenly City of the Eighteenth-Century Philosophers* (New Haven: 1932).

Boas, George, *Vox Populi: Essays in the History of an Idea* (Baltimore: 1969).

Boureau, Alain, "L'adage Vox populi, vox Dei et l'invention de la nation anglaise (VIIIe–XIIe siècle)," *Annales. Histoire, Sciences Sociales* 47 (1992): 1071–1089.

Brissot de Warville, Jacques-Pierre, "Lettre adressée à M. le Comte de M***, par M ... sur le plan de M. Turgot," in *Œuvres posthumes de Turgot, ou Mémoire de M. Turgot sur les administrations provinciales* [...] (Lausanne: 1787), 99–112.

Brissot de Warville, Jacques-Pierre, *De la vérité ou Méditations sur les moyens de parvenir à la vérité dans toutes les connaissances humaines* (Neuchâtel: 1782).

Brissot de Warville, Jacques-Pierre, *Lettres philosophiques sur St Paul, sur sa doctrine politique, morale et religieuse et sur plusieurs points de la religion chrétienne, considérés politiquement* [...] (Neuchâtel: 1783).

Brissot de Warville, Jacques-Pierre, *Précis adressé à l'assemblée générale des électeurs de Paris, pour servir à la rédaction du cahier de doléances de cette ville* (s.l.: 1789).

Brissot de Warville, Jacques-Pierre, *Recherches philosophiques sur le droit de propriété considéré dans la nature* [...] (s.l.: 1780).

Brunet, Pierre, *L'Introduction des théories de Newton en France au XVIIIᵉ siècle, avant 1738* (Geneva: 1970).

Burson, Jeffrey, "Introduction: Catholicism and Enlightenment, Past, Present, and Future," in *Enlightenment and Catholicism in Europe: A Transnational History*, ed. Jeffrey Burson (Notre Dame: 2014), 1–37.

Burson, Jeffrey D., "Introduction: The Culture of Jesuit Erudition in an Age of Enlightenment," *Journal of Jesuit Studies* 6 (2019): 387–415.

Burson, Jeffrey D., "The Catholic Enlightenment in France from the Fin de Siècle crisis of Consciousness to the Revolution, 1650–1789," in *A Companion to the Catholic Enlightenment in Europe*, eds. Ulrich L. Lehner and Michael Printy (Leiden: 2010), 62–125.

Burson, Jeffrey D., *The Culture of Enlightening: Abbé Claude Yvon and the Entangled Emergence of the Enlightenment* (Notre Dame: 2019).

Byrnes, Joseph, *Priests of the French Revolution: Saints and Renegades in a New Political Era* (University Park: 2014).

Chopelin-Blanc, Caroline, *De l'apologétique à l'Église constitutionnelle: Adrien Lamourette (1742–1794)* (Paris: 2009).

Coleman, Charly, *Virtues of Abandon: An Anti-Individualist History of the French Enlightenment* (Stanford: 2014).

Condorcet, Jean Antoine Nicolas de Caritat de, *Œuvres de Condorcet: Nouvelle impression en facsimilé de l'édition de Paris 1847–1849*, 12 vols. (Stuttgart: 1968).

Condorcet, Jean Antoine Nicolas de Caritat de, *Réflexions sur les affaires publiques, par une société de citoyens* (s.l.: 1789).

Coujou, Jean-Paul, "Political Thought and Legal Theory in Suárez," in *A Companion to Francisco Suárez*, ed. Victor Salas (Boston: 2015), 29–71.

Cuche, François-Xavier, *Une pensée sociale catholique: Fleury, La Bruyère et Fénelon* (Paris: 1991).

Dalrymple, Alexander, *Vox populi vox Dei: Lord Weymouth's appeal to a general court of India proprietors considered* (London: 1769).

Darwall, Stephen, "Grotius at the Creation of Modern Moral Philosophy," *Archiv für Geschichte der Philosophie* 94 (2012): 296–325.

Dean, Rodney, *L'Assemblée Constituante et la Réforme Ecclésiastique, 1790: La constitution civile du Clergé du 12 juillet et le serment ecclésiastique du 27 novembre* (Paris: 2014).

Diderot, Denis, *Oeuvres. Édition établie par Laurent Versini*, 5 vols. (Paris: 1997).

Dupont de Nemours, "Observations sur l'esclavage des nègres," *Éphémérides du citoyen* 6 (1771): 162–246.

Dyson, Robert, *St. Augustine of Hippo: The Christian Transformation of Political Philosophy* (London: 2005).

Edelstein, Dan, *On the Spirit of Rights* (Chicago: 2019).

Edelstein, Dan, *The Terror of Natural Rights: Republicanism, the Cult of Nature, and the French Revolution* (Chicago: 2009).

Edwards, Charles, "The Law of Nature in the Thought of Grotius," *The Journal of Politics* 32 (1970): 784–807.

Fénelon, François, *Les Aventures de Télémaque* (Paris: 1987 [first edition 1699]).

Ferrand, Julie, Arnaud Orain, "Abbé de Mably on Commerce, Luxury, and 'Classical Republicanism'," *Journal of the History of Economic Thought* 39 (2017): 199–221.

Flüchter, Antje, "Pater Pierre Martin – ein 'Brahmane aus dem Norden'. Jesuitische Grenzgänger in Südindien um die Wende zum 18. Jahrhundert," *Zeitenblicke* 11 (2012), http://www.zeitenblicke.de/2012/1/ [Accessed 6.03.2018].

Gauthier, Florence, "De Mably à Robespierre, un programme économique égalitaire," *Annales historiques de la Révolution française* 57 (1985): 265–289.

Haakonssen, Knud, *Natural Law and Moral Philosophy: From Grotius to the Scottish Enlightenment* (Cambridge, Eng.: 1996).

Henriques, Jacob, *Vox populi, vox Dei, &c. The petition and proposal of Jacob Henriques to the Honourable House of Commons, for paying the national debt* (London: 1749).

Höpfl, Harro, *Jesuit Political Thought: The Society of Jesus and the State, c. 1540–1630* (Cambridge, Eng.: 2004).

Jacob, Margaret C., *The Secular Enlightenment* (Princeton: 2019).

Jacquet, Christian, *La pensée religieuse de Jean-Jacques Rousseau* (Leuven: 1975).

Klippel, Diethelm, *Politische Freiheit und Freiheitsrechte im deutschen Naturrecht des 18. Jahrhunderts* (Paderborn: 1976).

Kors, Alan Charles, *Atheism in France, 1650–1729: The Orthodox Sources of Disbelief* (Princeton: 1990).

Koyré, Alexandre, "The Significance of the Newton Synthesis," *Archives internationales d'histoire des sciences* 11 (1950): 291–311.

Le Brun, Jacques, Christoph Schmitt-Maass, Stefanie Stockhorst and Doohwan Ahn (eds.), *Fénelon in the Enlightenment: Traditions, Adaptations and Variations* (Amsterdam: 2014).

Le Mercier de La Rivière, Pierre-Paul, *L'Ordre naturel et essentiel des sociétés politiques* (London: 1767).

Le Peuple au roi: vox populi vox Dei (s.l.: 1789).

Lehner, Ulrich, *The Catholic Enlightenment: The Forgotten History of a Global Movement* (New York: 2016).

Mably, Gabriel Bonnot de, *De la législation ou Principes des lois* (= *Collection complète des œuvres de l'abbé de Mably*, vol. 9) (Paris: 1794).

Mably, Gabriel Bonnot de, "Doutes proposés aux philosophes économistes sur l'ordre naturel et essentiel des sociétés politiques," in *Collection complète des œuvres de l'abbé de Mably*, vol. 11 (Paris: 1794), 1–256.

Mathiez, Albert, *Les Origines des cultes révolutionnaires* (Geneva: 1977).

McNeil, Gordon H., "The Cult of Rousseau and the French Revolution," *Journal of the History of Ideas* 6 (1945): 197–212.

Mungello, David, *Curious Land: Jesuit Accommodation and the Origins of Sinology* (Stuttgart: 1985).

Ozouf, Mona, *La Fête révolutionnaire 1789–1799* (Paris: 1976).

Palmer, Robert R., *Catholics and Unbelievers in 18th Century France* (Princeton: 2016).

Pečar, Andreas, Damien Tricoire, "Introduction: Reformations, Prophecy and Eschatology," in *Early Modern Prophecies in Transnational, National and Regional Contexts*, ed. Lionel Laborie (Leiden: 2020), 1–22.

Po-chia Hsia, Ronnie, *A Jesuit in the Forbidden City: Matteo Ricci, 1552–1610* (Oxford: 2011).

Popkin, Jeremy D., and Richard H. Popkin (eds.), *The Abbé Grégoire and His World* (Dordrecht: 2000).

Pujol, Stéphane, "Histoire, morale et politique chez Mably," in *Les philosophes et l'histoire au XVIIIᵉ siècles*, ed. Muriel Brot (Paris: 2011), 123–148.

Quantin, Jean-Louis, *Le Rigorisme chrétien* (Paris: 2001).

Que la voix du peuple est la voix de Dieu. Contre le sentiment de celuy qui nous a proposé une Question toute contraire (Paris: 1649).

Quesnay, François, *Œuvres économiques et philosophiques, accompagnées des éloges et d'autres travaux biographiques par différents auteurs* (Frankfurt: 1888).

Question, si la voix du peuple est la voix de Dieu? (s.l.: 1649).

Raynal, Guillaume-Thomas, *Histoire philosophique et politique du commerce et des établissements des européens dans les deux Indes*, vol. 4 (Geneva: 1782).

Remède aux malheurs de l'Estat de France, au sujet de la question Si la voix du peuple est la voix de Dieu (Paris: 1649).

Riley, Patrick, *The General Will Before Rousseau: The Transformation of the Divine into the Civic* (Princeton: 1986).

Robisco, Nathalie-Barbara, *Jean-Jacques Rousseau et la Révolution française: une esthétique de la politique, 1792–1799* (Paris: 1998).

Røge, Pernille, *Économistes and the Reinvention of Empire: France in the Americas and Africa, c. 1750–1802* (Cambridge, Eng.: 2019).

Rosenblatt, Helena, "Rousseau's Gift to Geneva," *Modern Intellectual History* 3 (2006): 65–73.

Rousseau, Jean-Jacques, *Discours sur l'origine et les fondements de l'inégalité parmi les homme: Discours sur les sciences et les arts* (Paris: 1971 [first edition 1755]).

Rousseau, Jean-Jacques, *Du contrat social* (Paris: 1992 [first edition 1762]).

Roza, Stéphanie, "L'abbé de Mably, entre modérantisme et radicalité," *Tangence* 106 (2014): 29–50.

Seelmann, Kurt, "Zur historischen Wandelbarkeit des Naturrechts," in *Die Naturrechtslehre des Francisco Suárez*, eds. Oliver Bach, Norbert Brieskorn and Gideon Stiening (Berlin: 2017), 213–232.

Sepinwall, Alyssa Goldstein, *The Abbé Grégoire and the French Revolution: The Making of Modern Universalism* (Berkeley: 2005).

Smyth, Jonathan, *Robespierre and the Festival of the Supreme Being: The Search for a Republican Morality* (Manchester: 2016).

Suárez, Francisco, *Defensio Fidei III. Principatus politicus o la soberania popular* (Madrid: 1965).

Taylor, Charles, *A Secular Age* (Cambridge, Mass.: 2007).

Thiessen, Hillard von, Arne Karsten (eds.), *Normenkonkurrenz in historischer Perspektive* (Berlin: 2015).

Tocqueville, Alexis de, *L'Ancien Régime et la Révolution* (Paris: 1988).

Tricoire, Damien, "The Fabrication of the *philosophe*: Catholicisms, Court Culture and the Origins of the Enlightenment Moralism," *Journal for Eighteenth-Century Studies* 51–54 (2018): 453–477.

Tricoire, Damien, "Les Lumières, l'idéologie coloniale et Madagascar: Aux origines de la mission civilisatrice," in *Les Lumières, l'esclavage et l'idéologie coloniale: XVIIIᵉ–XXᵉ siècles*, ed. Pascale Pellerin (Paris: 2020), 85–98.

Tricoire, Damien, "Raynal's and Diderot's Patriotic History of the Two Indies, or The Problem of Anti-Colonialism in the Eighteenth Century," *The Eighteenth Century* 59 (2018): 429–448.

Tricoire, Damien, "What Was the Catholic Reformation? Marian Piety and the Universalization of Divine Love," *The Catholic Historical Review* 103 (2017): 20–49.

Turgot, Anne-Robert-Jacques, *Œuvres de Turgot et documents le concernant*, 5 vols. (Paris: 1919–1924).

Voltaire, "Théocratie. Gouvernement de Dieu ou des Dieux," in *Questions sur l'Encyclopédie par des amateurs*, vol. 4 (Geneva: 1774), 441–4.

Vovelle, Michel, *Religion et Révolution: La déchristianisation de l'an II* (Paris: 1976).

Vovelle, Michel, *La Révolution contre l'Église: de la raison à l'etre suprême* (Brussels: 1988).

Vox populi, vox Dei: being true maxims of government [...] (London: 1709).

Vox Populi, Vox Dei, or, Englands general lamentation for the dissolution of the Parliament (s.l.: 1681).

Whatmore, Richard, "Rousseau and the *représentants*: The Politics of the *Lettres de la montagne*," *Modern Intellectual History* 3 (2006): 1–29.

Wheeler, Katrina Jennie-Lou, "Rabaut Saint-Étienne and the Huguenot Fight for Religious Freedom," in *Revolution as Reformation: Protestant Faith in the Age of Revolutions, 1688–1832*, eds. Peter C. Messer and William Harrison Taylor (Tuscaloosa: 2021), 96–112.

Wright, Johnson Kent, *A Classical Republican in Eighteenth-Century France: The Political Thought of Mably* (Stanford: 1997).

Zurbuchen, Simone, "Die Theorie der Institutionen im Contrat Social und das Modell der Genfer Verfassung," in *Jean-Jacques Rousseau im Bann der Institutionen*, ed. Konstanze Baron and Harald Bluhm (Berlin: 2016), 147–167.

CHAPTER 5

Secularization in the Dutch Enlightenment: The Irrelevance of Philosophy

Wiep van Bunge

According to Max Weber's celebrated secularization hypothesis, modernity, essentially characterized by rationalization, inevitably leads to a gradual abandonment of religion.[1] This process of the so-called "disenchantment," or so Weber felt, is not peculiar to the West, but for a variety of reasons struck first in Europe. Today, Weber's thesis has lost much of its former appeal. In a series of publications on Dutch religious history, Peter van Rooden has demonstrated that it was precisely during the 18th-century Enlightenment that the complete confessionalization of the Dutch population was achieved.[2] During the early 17th century, a sizeable minority of the Dutch populace were not affiliated with any church, but by the end of the 18th century, nearly all Dutchmen at least officially belonged to one church or another. It was only during the Enlightenment that being a proper Dutch *burger* came to demand allegiance to a particular, preferably Reformed, creed. Van Rooden has highlighted several different factors that were involved in this process, including the gradual transfer of the care for the poor from the state to the church and the rapidly declining appeal of individualistic, spiritual varieties of Protestantism by the end of the 17th century. (Spinoza's plea in favor of a *vera religio*, based on a "*credo minimum*" came at a time such a conception was actually losing ground.[3]) From the empirical point of view, secularization was simply not a major issue in the 18th-century Dutch Republic.

Of course, it could be argued that the continuing allegiance to some sort of Christianity by the large majority of the Dutch well into the 18th century and beyond should not worry us unduly, as scholars and philosophers – or

---

1   Max Weber, *Wissenschaft als Beruf* (Munich: 1917).

2   Peter T. van Rooden, *Religieuze regimes. Over godsdienst en maatschappij in Nederland, 1570–1990* (Amsterdam: 1996) and "Godsdienst en nationalisme in de achttiende eeuw: het voorbeeld van de Republiek," in *Vaderland. Een geschiedenis vanaf de vijftiende eeuw tot 1940*, eds. Nicolaas C.F. van Sas (Amsterdam: 1999), 201–236. See also Joris van Eijnatten, *Liberty and Concord. Religious Toleration and the Public in the Eighteenth-Century Netherlands* (Leiden: 2003).

3   Peter T. van Rooden, "Spinoza's Bijbeluitleg," *Studia Rosenthaliana* 18 (1984): 120–133.

theologians – may have well developed publicly or clandestinely strictly secular ideas, arguments or views which were completely at odds with the general picture outlined above. The fact is, however, that they hardly ever did. Early 19th-century Dutch Church historians were grateful for being able to conclude that "Deism" and "naturalism" did not have any serious impact on the Dutch, and to Philip Willem van Heusde, a celebrated Utrecht professor in history, Greek, and philosophy from 1803 to his death in 1839, this was a matter of considerable relief: because the Dutch Enlightenment had remained at heart a Protestant affair, the Dutch had fortunately never fallen victim to the horrors perpetrated during the French Revolution, or so he felt.[4] The debates that had been raging in the Dutch Republic towards the end of the previous century had been of a political nature.[5] This is not to say that secularization is a vacuous concept in the Dutch context. Today the Dutch inhabit a largely secularized society as a result of the momentous developments which took place during the 1960s and '70s. By the early 1960s, the Netherlands was still among the most confessionalized nations of Europe, but the intellectual history of the Dutch Republic has little to offer to anyone interested in the causes of our current predicament.[6]

Of course, there was at least one important sense in which secularization did matter in the early modern Dutch Republic: by the end of the 18th century, unbelievers were no longer criminally charged. In 1668, one of Spinoza's Amsterdam friends, Adriaan Koerbagh, was sentenced to imprisonment and hard labor after merely having wanted to publish a book about revealed religion, and he died in prison within a year.[7] By the end of the 18th century, however, the highly original satirist Pieter van Woensel, a travel writer and medical doctor in the Dutch army, was perfectly happy to profess his atheism without having to suffer any legal consequences.[8] Recently, Hans Trapman has

---

4 Oene Noordenbos, *Het atheïsme in Nederland in de negentiende eeuw. Een kritisch overzicht* (Rotterdam: 1931); Philip W. van Heusde, *De school van Polybius of geschiedkunde voor de negentiende eeuw* (Amsterdam: 1841), 230–4.

5 Edwina Hagen, "Een zaal van staatsmannen, niet van godgeleerden. Godsdienstige sentimenten in de Nationale Vergadering," in Frans Grijzenhout, Nicolaas C.F. van Sas, and Wyger Velema (eds.), *Het Bataafse experiment. Politiek en cultuur rond 1800* (Nijmegen: 2013), 125–153.

6 Peter T. van Rooden, "Secularization in the Netherlands," *Kirchliche Zeitgeschichte* 11 (1998): 34–40.

7 Adriaan Koerbagh, *A Light Shining in Dark Places, to Illuminate the Main Questions of Theology and Religion*, trans. Michiel Wielema (Leiden: 2011); Bart Leeuwenburgh, *Het noodlot van een ketter. Adriaan Koerbagh, 1633–1669* (Nijmegen: 2013).

8 Ivo Nieuwenhuis, "The Eccentric Enlightenment of Pieter van Woensel," *De Achttiende Eeuw* 45 (2012): 177–191, and Ivo Nieuwenhuis, *Onder het mom van satire. Laster, spot en ironie in Nederland, 1780–1800* (Hilversum: 2014). See also René Bakker, *Reizen en de kunst van*

unearthed a 1798 atheist adaptation in Dutch of Erasmus' *Praise of Folly*, by a major in the Dutch army, Johan van der Wyck.[9] He too was left alone. By the end of the century, the majority of politicians involved in drawing up the new constitutions, first of the Batavian Republic and subsequently of the Kingdom of the Netherlands, established in 1813, agreed that State and Church needed to be *separated* in a way the Dutch Republic had never managed to achieve, as the Dutch Reformed Church had kept its status as a "privileged" church. Yet, as Van Rooden has argued, this separation was no assault on the Church in any way.[10] On the contrary, it served to make an end to the discrimination of religious *minorities*, including the Jews.

The concerns over the secular consequences of academic research as such were as old as the Republic itself, for soon after the establishment of the University of Leiden in 1575 it had managed to hire the famous Flemish scholar Justus Lipsius.[11] In 1584 Lipsius published his famous *De Constantia* and immediately eyebrows were raised over its lack of references to the Bible or, for that matter, to the Fathers of the Church. A former Catholic, the ease with which he served his Lutheran and Calvinist employers only added to the suspicions concerning the depth of his allegiance to Christianity. Lipsius was essentially a Stoic, and he was not the only Leiden scholar whose immersion in Antiquity raised suspicions among strict Calvinists. Soon, the wayward manner in which Joseph Scaliger, his successor at Leiden, set out to redraw biblical chronology also raised questions.[12] Significantly, we find most of his more daring observations in the *Scaligeriana*, a collection of remarks made in the company of his students.[13] Apparently, Scaliger had been extremely skeptical about the textual integrity of the New Testament, and in private he was only too happy to admit that as far as he was concerned and with the exception of

---

      het schrijven. Pieter van Woensel in het Ottomaanse Rijk, de Krim en Rusland 1784–1789 (Zeist: 2008).

9   Hans Trapman, *Wijze dwaasheid. Vijfhonderd jaar Lof der zotheid in Nederland* (Amsterdam: 2011), c. 6.

10   Van Rooden, *Religieuze regimes*, c. 1.

11   See, for instance, Christopher Brooke, *Philosophic Pride. Stoicism and Political Thought from Lipsius to Rousseau* (Princeton: 2012), c. 1.

12   Anthony Grafton, *Joseph Scaliger. A Study in the History of Classical Scholarship*, 2 vols. (Oxford: 1983–1993). See Mark Somos, *Secularisation and the Leiden Circle* (Leiden: 2012), but also Dirk van Miert, *The Emancipation of Biblical Philology in the Dutch Republic, 1590–1670* (Oxford: 2018), 11–13.

13   Anthony Grafton, "Close Encounters of the Learned Kind. Joseph Scaliger's Table Talk," *American Scholar* 57 (1988): 581–8; Van Miert, *The Emancipation of Biblical Philology*, 36–52.

a genius such as Calvin, theology did not amount to much.[14] It was only to be expected that as a Protestant classicist he thought little of St. Jerome's Vulgate version of the Bible, but he actually made fun of the Fathers of the Church, and even Augustine, who had known neither Greek nor Hebrew, was ridiculed by Scaliger. He classified the *Confessiones* as a "pauvre livre."[15]

The first issue of the *Scaligeriana* was only published in 1666 and by that time the cynical political realism expressed by Tacitus in particular had become all the rage among Dutch poets, such as P.C. Hooft, and students of Scaliger, such as Grotius and Daniel Heinsius.[16] By the second half of the 17th century, Isaac Vossius, one of the editors of the *Scaligeriana*, would return to the subject of Global Chronology, questioning such biblical stories as the Flood. Notoriously, it was rumored that he much preferred Ovid over the Bible, and it was King Charles II, whom he served as librarian, who was reported as having claimed that Vossius was one of the most curious men he had ever met as he was ready to believe anything as long as it was not in the Bible.[17] One of Vossius' most radical classicist friends, Adriaan Beverland, shared some of Vossius' tastes and in 1678 published a commentary on the Fall, which to his mind was essentially a story about *coïtus interruptus*, for it had been the discovery of sexual intercourse which had led to Adam's fall from grace.[18] Beverland was immediately censured and banned from the Dutch Republic – he left for England – but we know that his book was studied.[19] Among some Italian classicists, reverence

---

14   *Scaligeriana, sive Excerpta ex ore Josephi Scaligeri* (Geneva: 1666), 333–4.

15   *Scaligeriana*, 16.

16   Jan Waszink, "Your Tacitism or Mine? Modern and Early Modern Conceptions of Tacitism and Tacitus," *History of European Ideas* 36 (2010): 375–385, and Jan Waszink, "Lipsius and Grotius: Tacitism," *History of European Ideas* 39 (2013): 151–168.

17   David S. Katz, "Isaac Vossius and the English Biblical Critics," in *Scepticism and Irreligion in the Seventeenth and Eighteenth Centuries*, eds. Richard H. Popkin and Arjo Vanderjagt (Leiden: 1993), 142–184. See also Eric Jorink, "'Horrible and Blasphemous'. Isaac La Peyrère, Isaac Vossius and the Emergence of Radical Biblical Criticism in the Dutch Republic," in *Nature and Scripture in the Abrahamic Religions. Up to 1700*, eds. Jitse M. van der Meer and Scott Mandelbrote, vol. 1 (Leiden: 2008), 429–450; Eric Jorink and Dirk van Miert (eds.), *Isaac Vossius (1618–1689). Between Science and Scholarship* (Leiden: 2012); Tim Wauters, "*Libertinage érudit* and Isaac Vossius. A Case Study," *The Journal for Early Modern Cultural Studies* 11 (2012): 37–53.

18   Adriaan Beverland, *De Peccato Originali kat' exochên sic nuncupato Dissertatio* (Leiden: 1678). See R. De Smet, *Hadrianus Beverlandus (1650–1716). Non unus e multis peccator. Studie over het leven en werk van Hadriaan Beverland* (Brussels: 1988); Karen E. Hollewand, *The Banishment of Beverland. Sex, Sin, and Scholarship in the Seventeenth-Century Dutch Republic* (Leiden: 2019).

19   Piet Steenbakkers, Jetze Touber, Jeroen van de Ven, "A Clandestine Notebook (1678–1679) on Spinoza, Beverland, Politics, the Bible and Sex," *Lias* 38 (2011): 225–365.

for Antiquity and curiosity about pre-Christian sexual *mores* had become all the rage much earlier and we know that during the early Enlightenment in the Dutch Republic an indigenous pornographic tradition thrived for several decades.[20] The anonymous production of the material involved complicated censorship, but even such a distinguished and well-connected Utrecht professor of Classics as Franciscus Burman had to be careful. His 1709 edition of Petronius' *Satyricon* got him into serious trouble, and it appears that his career was only saved because he was able to move to a chair in Leiden.[21] One of the fiercest theological disputes raging during the second half of the century was the so-called "Socratic War" on the virtue of pagans.[22] In 1693 Pierre Bayle's suggestion that a society of virtuous atheists was conceivable cost him his job as professor at the Rotterdam Illustrious School, and many decades later the issue was still hotly disputed.[23] One of the reasons Beverland's little book on the Fall caused such an uproar was of course that it almost coincided with the publication of Spinoza's *Opera Posthuma*, which included his *Ethics*, in 1677. The latter's *Tractatus theologico-politicus* (1670) had been censored as early as 1674 and the authorities were decidedly uncomfortable over the proliferation of radical ideas. During the early Dutch Enlightenment such ideas were hardly uncommon.

By the early 2000s, a new narrative of the early Dutch Enlightenment crystallized, drawing attention well beyond the halls of academia. According to this new narrative, the essentially moderate, deeply Protestant enlightened discourse coming into its own during the 18th century was preceded by an early radical Enlightenment, spearheaded by Spinoza. In Jonathan Israel's *Radical Enlightenment* of 2001 – and in my own much more modest *From Stevin to Spinoza*, published almost simultaneously, as well as in Michiel Wielema's *The March of the Libertines* – several new lines of research converged, including the recovery initiated by French Spinoza experts of Spinoza's "modernity" as well as

20   Karl Enenkel, "Neo-Latin Erotic and Pornographic Literature (c. 1400–c. 1700)," in *Brill's Encyclopaedia of the Neo-Latin World*, eds. Philip Ford, Jan Bloemendal and Charles Fantazzi (Leiden: 2014), 487–501; Inger Leemans, *Het woord is aan de onderkant. Radicale ideeën in Nederlandse pornografische romans, 1670–1700* (Nijmegen: 2002).

21   Floris Verhaart, *Classical Learning in Britain, France, and the Dutch Republic, 1690–1750. Beyond the Ancients and the Moderns* (Oxford: 2020), 70–92.

22   Ernestine van der Wall, *Socrates in de hemel? Een achttiende-eeuwse polemiek over deugd, verdraagzaamheid en de vaderlandse kerk* (Hilversum: 2000).

23   Pierre Bayle, *Pensées diverses sur la comète* (Paris: 2007), 288–292. For the philosophical background, see John Marenbon, *Pagans and Philosophers. The Problem of Paganism from Augustine to Leibniz* (Princeton: 2015); Jean-Michel Gros, "Bayle and the Question of the Salvation of the Infidels," in *Inexcusabiles. Salvation and the Virtues of the Pagans in the Early Modern Period*, ed. Alberto Frigo (Cham: 2020), 127–144.

the growing recognition of his impact on a string of late 17th-century Dutch and French freethinkers in particular.[24] In addition, Israel insisted on the unique relevance of philosophy for this period in particular. By highlighting the crucial relevance of the debates provoked by Spinoza's *Tractatus theologico-politicus* and the *Ethics*, he managed to question both the traditional chronology of the European Enlightenment and its geography. According to Israel, instead of starting moderately during either the 1680s or the 1720s and radicalizing after the middle of the century, the European Enlightenment started "with a Bang," in a very radical way, as Spinoza's monist metaphysics, secular moral philosophy, and democratic politics implied a frontal assault on the ideological underpinnings of the *Ancien Régime*. What is more, it did not get underway somewhere on the London – Paris axis, but in the Dutch Republic, the most tolerant, egalitarian and intellectually innovative European nation of the time – the country, for instance, which not just served as the most adventurous publishing hub, but which also accommodated the first academic reception of Cartesianism as an alternative to Aristotelianism.[25] Instead of concentrating on Locke and Montesquieu, let alone Newton and Voltaire, Israel argued, we should focus on Spinoza and his Dutch friends and followers, and on Bayle.

It remains to be seen, however, how much sense it makes to present Dutch Spinozism as an essentially atheist and materialist movement.[26] According to Israel, Spinozism was indeed a secularizing phenomenon, but while Spinoza was of course *something* of an atheist and while his critique of revealed religion was widely held to be outrageous and very dangerous indeed, it is not as if he removed God from his philosophical vocabulary and many of his Dutch followers were deeply devout Christians – *Chrétiens sans Église*, as Leszek Kołakowski

24   Jonathan I. Israel, *Radical Enlightenment. Philosophy and the Making of Modernity, 1650–1750* (Oxford: 2001) and Jonathan I. Israel, *Enlightenment Contested. Philosophy, Modernity and the Emancipation of Man, 1670–1752* (Oxford: 2006); Wiep van Bunge, *From Stevin to Spinoza. An Essay on Philosophy in the Seventeenth-Century Dutch Republic* (Leiden: 2001); Michiel Wielema, *The March of the Libertines. Spinozists and the Dutch Reformed Church (1660–1750)* (Hilversum: 2004). The most comprehensive survey of the history of Dutch Spinozism is now Henri Krop, *Spinoza. Een paradoxale icoon van Nederland* (Amsterdam: 2014). See more recently Jonathan Israel and Martin Mulsow (eds.), *Radikalaufklärung* (Frankfurt a.M.: 2014) and Steffen Ducheyne (ed.), *Reassessing the Radical Enlightenment* (London: 2017).

25   Andrew Pettegree and Arthur der Weduwen, *The Bookshop of the World. Making and Trading Books in the Dutch Golden Age* (New Haven: 2019); Theo Verbeek, *La querelle d'Utrecht. René Descartes et Martin Schoock* (Paris: 1988), and Theo Verbeek, *Descartes and the Dutch: Early Reactions to Cartesian Philosophy, 1637–1650* (Carbondale: 1992).

26   Wiep van Bunge, *Spinoza Past and Present. Essays on Spinoza, Spinozism, and Spinoza Scholarship* (Leiden: 2012), c. 11.

famously called them.[27] What does seem clear is that in the Dutch Republic this radical Enlightenment petered out in the early 18th century. Yes, there definitely was such a thing as an early, radical Dutch Enlightenment, but it was a short-lived phenomenon and the two major interpretations we have about the later Dutch Enlightenment more or less agree about the near complete irrelevance of philosophy to the 18th-century Dutch culture. Both Joost Kloek and Wijnand Mijnhardt's *1800: Blauwdrukken voor een samenleving* and Niek van Sas' *De Metamorfose van Nederland*, which jointly concentrate on the latter half of the century, basically argue that the main subject of the Dutch enlightened discourse concerned the sad state of the ailing Dutch Republic itself.[28] In none of these highly sophisticated accounts of the later Dutch Enlightenment does philosophy matter greatly.

Any attempt to come to terms with the Dutch Enlightenment must surely take its point of departure from the Golden Age of the Dutch Republic, when the Dutch, as the British ambassador Sir William Temple famously put it in 1672, were "the fear of some, the envy of others, and the wonder of all their neighbours."[29] In 1764, however, while a student in Utrecht, James Boswell averred in a letter to home: "Were Sir William Temple to revisit these Provinces, he would scarcely believe the amazing alterations which they have undergone."[30] Apparently, something had gone seriously wrong, and many more similar quotations could be collected. Still in 1713 Anthony Collins claimed that in the United Provinces, *"Free-thinking* is in its greatest perfection."[31] Yet following a costly military stalemate with France and the resulting economic demise, the same year Anthony Collins still felt the Dutch pointed the way intellectually, at the Utrecht Peace Treaty, the French diplomat Melchior de Polignac assured his Dutch counterparts: "nous avons parlé chez vous, sur vous, sans vous."[32] As early as the 1730s, Voltaire was (famously but probably falsely) reported as having quipped that the Dutch Republic was packed with "canaux, canards, canaille."[33] Forty years later, Diderot felt that "La

27   Leszek Kolakowski, *Chrétiens sans Église. La Conscience religieuse et le lien confessionnel au XVIIᵉ siècle* (Paris: 1969).

28   Joost J. Kloek and Wijnand W. Mijnhardt, *1800: Blauwdrukken voor een samenleving* (The Hague: 2001); Nicolaas C.F. van Sas, *De metamorfose van Nederland. Van oude orde naar moderniteit, 1750–1900* (Amsterdam: 2004).

29   Sir William Temple, *Observations upon the United Provinces of the Netherlands* (Cambridge, Eng.: 1932), xi.

30   Frederick A. Pottle (ed.), *Boswell in Holland, 1763–1764* (Melbourne: 1952), 281.

31   Anthony Collins, *A Discourse of Free-Thinking, Occasion'd by the Rise and Growth of a Sect Call'd Free-Thinkers* (London: 1713), 27.

32   Peet H.J.M. Theeuwen, *Pieter 't Hoen en De Post van den Neder-Rhijn* (Hilversum: 2002), 49.

33   Jeroom Vercruysse, *Voltaire en Hollande* (Geneva: 1966), 25–6.

nation est superstitieuse, ennemie de la philosophie et de la liberté de penser en matière de religion."[34]

By the 1730s, Dutch public opinion started to acknowledge the loss of prestige the Republic was now beginning to suffer abroad. After a relatively successful career as a Francophone editor of such journals as *La Bagatelle* and *Le Misanthrope*, Justus van Effen launched his *Hollandsche Spectator*, a popular weekly in which again and again the Dutch decline was diagnosed as indicative of a loss of *moral* fibre.[35] As Van Effen inspired countless "Spectatorials" echoing his insistence on the need to return to the *burgerlijke* virtues that inspired previous generations of Dutchmen, it should come as no surprise that Mijnhardt has highlighted the 18th-century Dutch obsession with national decline, most poignantly evident perhaps from the remarkable stagnation of the Dutch population figures: while in France, Britain and the Holy Roman Empire the size of the population grew rapidly, in the Dutch Republic it did not.[36] By the end of the century the country was still inhabited by a little over two million people – the same figure reached already by 1700. By the second half of the 18th century in particular foreign immigration virtually came to a halt.[37] During the late 16th and the 17th centuries hundreds of thousands of Germans, Scandinavians, French Protestants and Iberian Jews had added to the indigenous workforce, but by the 18th century, other destinations had become much more popular.

The refusal of Mijnhardt and many other Dutch historians to include the Refuge in the Dutch Enlightenment seems less warranted: although the Refuge was and remained for quite some time Francophone, during the 18th century, French just happened to be the second modern language of all educated Europeans. To exclude Bayle from the Dutch Enlightenment, along with most of the work of Van Effen, Elie Luzac, Isaac de Pinto, Frans Hemsterhuis, and Belle van Zuylen, to name just the most obvious examples, merely because they wrote in French, seems questionable.[38] As far as Bayle is concerned, he

---

34   Denis Diderot, *Oeuvres complètes*, vol. 17 (Nendeln: 1966), 428.

35   Wiep van Bunge, *From Bayle to the Batavian Revolution. Essays on Philosophy in the Eighteenth-Century Dutch Republic* (Leiden: 2019), c. 4.

36   Wijnand W. Mijnhardt, "The Dutch Enlightenment: Humanism, Nationalism, and Decline," in *The Dutch Republic in the Eighteenth Century. Decline, Enlightenment, and Revolution*, ed. Margaret C. Jacob and Wijnand W. Mijnhardt (Ithaca: 1992), 197–223.

37   Leo Lucassen and Jan Lucassen, *Winnaars en verliezers. Een nuchtere balans van vijfhonderd jaar migratie* (Amsterdam: 2012), c. 5.

38   Van Bunge, *From Bayle to the Batavian Revolution*, c. 1. On the Refuge, see most recently David van der Linden, *Experiencing Exile. Huguenot Refugees in the Dutch Republic, 1680–1700* (Farnham: 2015).

spent nearly his entire working career in Rotterdam, published exclusively in Holland and continued to be read by the Dutch until well into the century. According to Mijnhardt and Van Sas, it should be added, the real Dutch Enlightenment only materialized during the second half of the century, as the location of the Dutch enlightened discourse largely coincided with the sudden emergence from 1750 to 1800 of some 500 literary, scientific and philanthropic societies, some of which exist to this day, such as the Haarlem *Maatschappij der Wetenschappen* and the Leiden *Maatschappij der Nederlandse Letterkunde*.[39] The overriding joint concern of the Dutch over the state of the nation rendered their efforts largely irrelevant to foreign observers not primarily interested in diagnosing, let alone remedying, such a primarily local phenomenon as Dutch decline. This essentially inward-looking attitude also helps to explain the failure of the Dutch Enlightenment to raise much interest among the Dutchmen today. While both the Golden and the Iron Age, that is, the 17th and the 19th centuries, still play a prominent part in our collective memory, the Silver Age of the 18th century is largely ignored by the general public. Perhaps its cultivation of explicitly *burgerlijke* virtues was not very much conducive to its popularity, especially among students of Dutch history and literature, many of whom appear to feel that 18th-century Dutch *burgerlijkheid* was slightly boring.[40]

As far as the part played by philosophy is concerned, Cartesianism and Spinozism were rapidly replaced during the 1720s, both at university and among the wider reading public, by Newtonianism. Over the past few years, Dutch Newtonianism has at last received the attention it deserves.[41] Willem Jacob 's Gravesande and Pieter van Musschenbroek led the way producing brilliant introductions and clarifications to this new natural philosophy, which by the

---

39   Wijnand W. Mijnhardt, *Tot Heil van 't Menschdom. Culturele genootschappen in Nederland, 1750–1815* (Amsterdam: 1988).

40   Remieg Aerts and Henk te Velde (eds.), *De stijl van de burger. Over Nederlandse burgerlijke cultuur vanaf de Middeleeuwen* (Kampen: 1998); Joost J. Kloek and Karin Tilmans (eds.), *Burger. Een geschiedenis van het begrip 'burger' van de Middeleeuwen tot de 21ste eeuw* (Amsterdam: 2002).

41   Rienk Vermij, "The Formation of the Newtonian Natural Philosophy. The Case of the Amsterdam Mathematical Amateurs," *The British Journal for the History of Science* 26 (2003): 183–200; Ernestine van der Wall, "Newtonianism and Religion in the Netherlands," *Studies in History and Philosophy of Science* 35 (2004): 493–514; Eric Jorink and Ad Maas (eds.), *Newton and the Netherlands. How Isaac Newton was Fashioned in the Netherlands* (Amsterdam: 2012); Steffen Ducheyne, "'ias Gravesande's Appropriation of Newton's Natural Philosophy," *Centaurus* 56 (2014): 31–55 and 97–120; van Bunge, *From Bayle to the Batavian Revolution*, c. 6.

middle of the century had triumphed all over Europe.[42] Bernard Nieuwentijt in particular went out of his way to demonstrate that Isaac Newton's natural philosophy was particularly suited to replace Spinozism, as it represented a genuinely mathematical way of thinking and because it confirmed the obvious truth of physico-theology – a genre that became hugely popular throughout the century.[43] The swift Dutch reception of Newtonianism added considerably to the status of the universities of Leiden and Utrecht in particular. In 1734 Voltaire famously moved to Leiden for instruction in the finer details of Newton's natural philosophy and as late as 1765, according to the *Encyclopédie* at least, Leiden still topped the European rankings.

From a philosophical point of view, the popularity of Newton's natural philosophy soon started to present something of a problem, too, as its main proponents throughout the century gradually turned into natural *scientists*. Arguably the most stunning aspect of 's Gravesande's long career at Leiden was his lack of involvement in any political or religious polemic. From a comparative perspective, this is all the more remarkable as nearly all major 17th-century professors of philosophy were definitely part of some political party and committed to some theological school of thought. By the end of the century, Dutch professors even wrote polemical pamphlets in Dutch. It could be argued, and it has been argued, however, that this new lack of polemical ambition was precisely the point of Newtonianism: at last a "self-less," "value-free," essentially mathematical view of the world had become available, confirmed by impartial observation and illustrated by objective experiments.[44] But all the while, no Newtonian moral or political philosophy was produced, in the way

---

42   See, for instance, Willem Jacob 's Gravesande, *Physices Elementa Mathematica, experimentis confirmata, sive Introductio ad Philosophiam Newtonianam*, 2 vols. (Leiden: 1720–1721), *Philosophiae Newtonianae Institutiones in usus academicos* (Leiden: 1723) and *Oeuvres philosophiques et mathématiques*, 2 vols. (Amsterdam: 1774); Petrus van Musschenbroek, *Elementa physicae conscripta in usus academicos* (Leiden: 1734), *Institutiones logicae, praecipue comprehendentes artem argumentandi* (Leiden: 1748) and *Primae lineae theologiae naturalis secundum normam emendatione ontologiae et pneumatologiae* (Leiden: 1756).

43   Bernard Nieuwentijt, *Het regt gebruik der werelt beschouwingen, ter overtuiginge van ongodisten en ongelovigen aangetoont* (Amsterdam: 1715) and *Gronden van zekerheid, of de regte betoogwyse der wiskundigen, So in het denkbeeldige als in het zakelyke* (Amsterdam: 1720). See Jan Bots, *Tussen Descartes en Darwin. Geloof en natuurwetenschap in de achttiende eeuw in Nederland* (Assen: 1972); Rienk Vermij, *Secularisering en natuurwetenschap in de zeventiende en achttiende eeuw* (Amsterdam: 1991); Eric Jorink, *Reading the Book of Nature in the Dutch Golden Age, 1575–1715* (Leiden: 2010), c. 7.

44   Ad Maas, "The Man Who Erased Himself. Willem Jacob 's Gravesande and the Enlightenment," in *Newton and the Netherlands*, 113–138.

previous generations had at least attempted to write Cartesian ethics, politics, and even theologies.

Meanwhile, one school of thought which did provoke a series of political rows from the middle of the century was Wolffianism.[45] It was the late Michiel Wielema who was the first scholar to point to a remarkable number of appointments at 18th-century Dutch universities of German Wolffian lawyers and philosophers, such as Samuel Koenig, Nicolaus Engelhard, Frederick Adolf van der Marck and Friedrich Wilhelm Pestel, and a surprising number of Dutch translations becoming available during the 1760s in particular of Christian Wolff's views on natural law.[46] Interestingly, both liberal and conservative Dutch thinkers quoted Wolff at length, including the poet Christina de Neufville and the novelist Betje Wolff (who occasionally made fun of her own "Wolffianism"). Apparently, Newton's popularity did not prevent the continuing appeal of rationalism as a major school of thought in the Dutch Republic. As a matter of fact, the first main revolutionary active in the Dutch Republic, Joan Derk van der Capellen tot den Poll, the author of the inflammatory *Aan het volk van Nederland* (1781), was a close personal friend and a great admirer of Van der Marck.[47] None of these Wolffians were prepared to abandon Christianity. Johannes Petsch, the author of many translations of *Wolffiana* into Dutch, was a former minister of the Moravian Brethren and it would seem that none of the Dutch Wolffians abandoned Christianity, although Betje Wolff was widely held to be a "Socinian."[48] Of course, by the 1760s Socinianism was dead and buried as a movement, after Samuel Crell, in the 1730s, had actually joined the Amsterdam Remonstrants. Betje Wolff was one of the last so-called "Collegiants," coming together at Rijnsburg, just as some of Spinoza's friends had done a century before. But "Socinian" Collegiants were definitely no atheists. Remarkably, in the course of the 18th century, many of the more liberal Protestant sects that had blossomed during the Golden Age more or less evaporated, as the Dutch Reformed Church gradually grew into a large,

---

45   Van Bunge, *From Bayle to the Batavian Revolution*, c. 7.

46   Michiel Wielema, *Ketters en verlichters. De invloed van het spinozisme en het wolffianisme op de Verlichting in Nederland, in het bijzonder in de gereformeerde theologie* (PhD, Vrije Universiteit Amsterdam: 1999).

47   Johannes Lindeboom, *Frederik Adolf van der Marck, een achttiende-eeuwsch leeraar van het natuurrecht* (The Hague: 1947); Clifford H.J. Jansen, *Natuurrecht of Romeins recht. Een studie over leven en werk van F.A. van der Marck (1719–1800) in het licht van de opvattingen van zijn tijd* (Leiden: 1987); Willem J. Zwalve, "Het Recht en de Verlichting. De juridische hoogleraar Frederik Adolf van der Marck (1719–1800)," in *Om niet aan onwetendheid en barbarij te bezwijken. Groningse geleerden, 1614–1989*, ed. Guillaume A. van Gemert, Johanna Schuller tot Peursum-Meijer and Arie J. Vanderjagt (Hilversum: 1989), 83–100.

48   Van Eijnatten, *Liberty and Concord in the United Provinces*, 389–398.

truly national Protestant community, allowing room for considerable theological diversity.

As far as the later stages of the Dutch Enlightenment are concerned, there is shared agreement among the experts that even when during the 1780s it did acquire a radical, revolutionary edge, there is little, if any, evidence of Spinoza's radical Enlightenment having had anything to do with it and it would seem that the violent theological disputes that in the previous century split Arminians and Gomarists, and Voetians, and Cocceians, were now replaced by *political* disputes. But again, even the most radical "Patriots" or "Batavians" still regarded themselves as Christians.[49] Indeed, some of the most revolutionary causes, such as the fight against slavery, were fought on the basis of Christian notions regarding the essential equality of God's creatures.[50] By this time, besides Wolffianism, also the American Revolution and the writings of Richard Price, Joseph Priestley, and to some extent of Rousseau, were inspiring growing opposition to the political *status quo* in the Dutch Republic. By the end of the century, Thomas Paine became available in Dutch.[51] Some of the Dutch revolutionaries involved appear to have held very liberal theological views, but there is no evidence for any late 18th-century Spinozist or atheist offensive. The Dutch interest in, for instance, the writings of the baron d'Holbach was so limited that the authorities did not even take the trouble to censure them, at a time, moreover, at which censorship was definitely tightening.[52] The connection between naturalist metaphysics and a democratic political agenda, which lies at the heart of Israel's conception of the radical Enlightenment, failed to materialize in the dying days of the Dutch Republic.

As will only be too familiar, the so-called Batavian Revolution of 1787 actually preceded the French Revolution, but failed miserably as the King of Prussia, father-in-law to *stadhouder* William V, intervened with a military force entering Dutch territory.[53] In this context, it makes little sense to spell out the

---

49   Ernestine van der Wall, "Geen natie van atheïsten. Pieter Paulus (1753–1796) over godsdienst en mensenrechten," *Jaarboek van de Maatschappij der Nederlandse Letterkunde* (1996): 45–58.

50   See, for instance, Willem Anthony Ockerse, *Verhandeling over de Vrage: In Welken zin kunnen de Menschen gezegd worden Gelijk te Zijn?* (Haarlem: 1793).

51   Paul van Gestel, "*De verbasteringen van het Christendom*. Joseph Priestley (1733–1804) en de Nederlandse Verlichting," *De Achttiende Eeuw* 30 (1998): 3–29, and Paul van Gestel, "Dutch Reactions to Thomas Paine's *Age of Reason*," *Studies on Voltaire and the Eighteenth Century* 378 (1999): 271–301.

52   Van Bunge, *From Bayle to the Batavian Revolution*, c. 12.

53   Joost Rosendaal, *De Nederlandse Revolutie. Vrijheid, volk en vaderland, 1783–1799* (Nijmegen: 2005); Wilfried Uiterhoeve, *Koning, keizer, admiraal. 1810: De ondergang van het keizerrijk*

extremely complicated subsequent train of events, including the French inva-
sion of 1795, the inauguration of the Batavian Republic, to be replaced by the
Napoleonic Kingdom of Holland, and finally, in 1813, by the Kingdom of the
Netherlands, heralding the return of the House of Orange at the heart of Dutch
politics. Looking back, it would seem that philosophy was not completely irrelevant to 18th-century Dutch culture. Besides the obvious European significance of Bayle's work and of Dutch Newtonianism for the history of physics,
we have to acknowledge the real presence of Dutch Wolffianism in the political
debates leading up to the Batavian Revolution which in the end, after decades
of chaos and foreign interventions, resulted in a new nation state, replacing
the essentially late medieval Republic of United Provinces.

Yet, on the whole, the conclusion that Dutch philosophers *failed* in the Dutch
Republic as well as its Enlightenment seems inescapable. Again: just compare
the 1600s to the 1700s. First, Dutch 17th-century Aristotelian philosophy professors, such as Franco Burgersdijk, were extremely successful in introducing
their students to a conceptual vocabulary which gave them access to the sciences of the day.[54] In addition, it bolstered the efforts of the Dutch Calvinists
in their polemical opposition to Roman Catholicism, and to each other, of
course. By the middle of the century, Aristotelianism started to disintegrate,
Descartes' philosophy took over this essentially preparatory part, articulating
a metaphysics, as well as a method enabling scientists to launch their mech-
anicist alternatives to Peripateticism. In addition, it was to inspire a number of
radical Cartesians to turn to subjects Descartes himself had been careful *not* to
explore in any detail, such as *political* philosophy.[55] Add Hobbes to the equa-
tion, and the programme of Spinoza and his friends starts to make sense: they
were out, essentially, to develop a philosophy enabling them, or so they hoped,
to put an end both to the political and the theological disputes that were tearing the Republic apart.[56] This was what the early, radical Enlightenment was
all about – or so it would seem: finding a conceptual vocabulary which, now
that the *Ethica ordine geometrico demonstrata* was available, would achieve
political and theological *Concordia*.

Holland (Nijmegen: 2010); Ido de Haan, Paul den Hoed and Henk te Velde (eds.), *Een nieuwe staat. Het begin van het Koninkrijk der Nederlanden* (Amsterdam: 2013).

54 Van Bunge, *From Stevin to Spinoza.*

55 Arthur Weststeijn, *Commercial Republicanism in the Dutch Golden Age. The Political Thought of Johan and Pieter de la Court* (Leiden: 2012).

56 Wiep van Bunge, "*Concordia Res Parvae Crescunt.* The Context of Seventeenth-Century Dutch Radicalism," in *The Dutch Legacy. Radical Thinkers of the Seventeenth Century and the Enlightenment*, ed. Sonja Lavaert and Winfried Schröder (Leiden: 2017), 16–34.

Against this background, the history of philosophy in the 18th-century Dutch Republic was much less adventurous. Dutch philosophers of the time consistently chose *to ignore* the religious concerns of the day, and it was only by the final quarter of the century that some of them got involved into politics. Consider the career of Frans Hemsterhuis, arguably the only 18th-century Dutch thinker besides Bayle and 's Gravesande who reached a European audience, especially in Germany, inspiring such authors as Jacobi, Goethe, and as some would have it, Kant.[57] He definitely was an interesting figure in the rise of aesthetics and an obvious proponent both of the 18th-century culture of sensibility and of late 18th-century Philhellenism: following Winckelmann, he was one of the first European scholars to confirm the superiority of the Greek over Roman culture. But he was active during the 1760s and 1770s, when the Dutch Republic was rapidly falling apart. As a high-ranking civil servant to the *Raad van State*, moreover, he was at the heart of the imminent collapse of the country, and yet he stubbornly refused to address any of the issues involved. Instead, he preferred to study Greek vases and cultivate his own "moral organ," as he called it. Neither, incidentally, was he prepared to address any theological issues. What is more, Hemsterhuis knew and cared very little about some of the main Enlightenment *philosophes* and their writings – he was actually proud *not* to have read Locke, and in private letters he frankly admitted being largely ignorant about modern metaphysics.[58] Much has been made of the part he is supposed to have played in the German *Pantheismusstreit* of the 1780s, but privately he conceded hardly to be in a position to do so and the only contemporary philosopher whose work he knew well was Rousseau.

Arguably more importantly, the sorry fate of Dutch Kantianism also appears to indicate the conservative nature of Dutch philosophy by the end of the 18th century, and this will bring us back to the theme of secularization, for the early history of the Dutch reception of Kant seems to confirm the extent to which theological concerns at the time still outweighed philosophical arguments. Kant's work was known in the Netherlands at an early stage already and at Königsberg he even had a Dutch student, Dirk van Hogendorp, brother to the more famous Gijsbert Karel, one of the architects of the 1813 Kingdom.[59] But

---

57   Heinz Mönkemeyer, *François Hemsterhuis* (Boston: 1975); Marcel F. Fresco, Loek Geeraedts, and Klaus Hammacher (eds.), *Frans Hemsterhuis (1721–1790). Quellen, Philosophie und Rezeption* (Münster: 1995); Claudia Melica (ed.), *Hemsterhuis. A European Philosopher Rediscovered* (Naples: 2005).

58   Van Bunge, *From Bayle to the Batavian Revolution*, c. 8.

59   Edwin van Meerkerk, *De gebroeders Van Hogendorp. Botsende idealen in de kraamkamer van het koninkrijk* (Amsterdam: 2013).

despite the efforts launched by Paulus van Hemert and Johannes Kinker in particular, Dutch academic philosophers chose to ignore Kant's Copernican Revolution, and the more generally educated public swiftly grew bored with Kant.[60] In part, their reluctance is very understandable, of course, and it is not as if by 1800 British and French academics were ready to unanimously embrace German Idealism. They were not, and it is easy to see why the wider reading public of Dutchmen with an interest in philosophy was not affected by Kant. For Kant's *Critiques* were indeed relentlessly academic, the object of his critique being philosophy itself. His "transcendental turn" was largely a response to the problem created by the triumph of Newtonianism, which had turned the practice of natural philosophy into what we call today physics, that is, essentially autonomous natural science. His critique resulted in the definition of a new professional competence of academic philosophers facing the loss of "natural philosophy" from their curriculum, and it was only to be expected that the wider public did not get too excited over these academic achievements.

Once Kant started addressing issues with a wider moral and political relevance, as he did perhaps most notably in his *Zum ewigen Frieden* of 1795, in particular Van Hemert's failure to raise support for Kant's cosmopolitanism appears to indicate quite clearly the sad state of Dutch academia by the end of the century, as well as the pretty desperate self-assessment of the Dutch intelligentsia.[61] It was not for the lack of trying: Van Hemert was a tireless editor and lecturer, active in all sorts of societies, and a well-connected freemason. From 1798 to 1803 he published his *Magazijn voor de critische wijsgeerte*, a journal exclusively aimed at the promotion of Kant's critical philosophy and from 1804 to 1808 he even published a ten-volume popular journal, entitled *Lektuur bij het ontbijt en de thetafel*, largely dedicated to the cause of Kantian cosmopolitanism.[62] But Van Hemert found it increasingly difficult to find any audience, and by the 1810s he simply gave up and stopped publishing altogether. The main

---

60   Michiel Wielema, "Die erste niederländische Kant Rezeption, 1786–1850," *Kant-Studien* 79
      (1988): 450–466; Ernst-Otto Onnasch, "Immanuel Kants Philosophie in den Niederlanden,
      1785–1804," in *Kant der Europäer. Europäer über Kant*, eds. Steffen Dietsch and Lorenz
      Grimoni (Duisburg: 2010), 70–96. On Kinker, see André Hanou, *Sluiers van Isis. Johannes
      Kinker als voorvechter van de Nederlandse Verlichting, 1790–1845*, 2 vols. (Deventer: 1988).
61   Van Bunge, *From Bayle to the Batavian Revolution*, c. 11.
62   Paulus van Hemert (ed.), *Magazijn voor de critische wijsgeerte en de geschiedenis van
      dezelve*, 6 vols. (Amsterdam: 1799–1803) and *Lektuur bij het ontbijt en de thetafel*, 10 vols.
      (Amsterdam: 1804–1808). See Annemieke Kouwenberg, "Kant in den Niederlanden:
      Lektuur bij het ontbijt en aan de thetafel (1804–1808). Praktischer Kantianismus für
      Anfänger," in *Nur Narr? Nur Dichter? Über die Beziehungen von Literatur und Philosophie*,
      eds. Roland Duhamel and Guillaume van Gemert (Würzburg: 2008), 143–164; Jan Verweij,

reason, meanwhile, why the most prominent Dutch academic philosophers of the day, such as Daniel Wyttenbach, Dionysius van de Wijnpersse and Van Heusde squarely rejected Kant, was their allegiance to the primacy of revealed religion: Kant's proposal to consider religion *innerhalb der Grenzen der bloßen Vernunft* was widely held to degrade Revelation and the same authors who by the end of the Enlightenment were trying to define the essence of "Dutchness" were adamant that whatever else Dutchmen might have been, they were, first and foremost, essentially Protestants.

Let us not forget, however, that around the turn of the century Dutch universities were going through a deep crisis and would soon be subject to fundamental reforms. The modern research university as we know it today would only come into its own during the second half of the 19th century and in the Netherlands the number of students had been dropping dramatically already for decades. Foreign students now started to evade Leiden and Utrecht. Part of the problem was of course their continuing commitment to lecturing in Latin – which around the turn of the century was getting slightly silly and had largely been abandoned already in Germany. In the Netherlands it would only be abolished in 1876.[63] Latin perfectly suited classicists such as Wyttenbach, at the time a famous professor at Leiden who felt that philosophy basically came down to studying Ancient Philosophy, and who appears to have felt that Kantianism was simply too recent a phenomenon to bother his students with, but it hardly contributed to the academic reception of more modern strands of thought.[64]

By the early 1800s both Kant's cosmopolitanism and his realignment of theology also failed to attract any substantial audience in the Netherlands as its intelligentsia had almost universally embraced a new-found nationalism, which very much included the notion that a proper Dutchman was a *Protestant*. This self-perception was to a considerable extent the product of the collapse of the Republic and its subsequent annexation by the French: cosmopolitanism had always been regarded an essentially French invention,

---

     Kant-tekening van een Horrearius. De rol van het Magazyn voor de critische Wijsgeerte en de Geschiedenis van Dezelve *(1798–1803) in de Kantreceptie* (Nijmegen: 2012).

63   Joke Roelevink, "Het Babel van de geleerden. Latijn in het Nederlandse universitaire onderwijs van de achttiende en de negentiende eeuw," *Jaarboek van de Maatschappij der Nederlandse Letterkunde* (1990): 33–41.

64   See, for instance, Eclecticus (Dionysius van de Wijnpersse), *Eenige Bespiegelingen der Kantische Wijsgeerte* (The Hague: 1805). See Carl von Prantl, "Daniel Wyttenbach als Gegner Kants," in *Sitzungsberichte der philosophisch-philologischen und historischen Classe der Königlich Bayerischen Akademie der Wissenschaften zu München* (1877), 264–286.

indicative of France's imperialist tendencies.[65] As early as the 1730s, when Van Effen launched his *Hollandsche Spectator*, educated Dutchmen had been warned against the effeminate, treacherous, and ultimately unwholesome morals of the French.[66] From the 1770s onwards a remarkable series of very detailed analyses were published, probing the essence of the national character of the Dutch. Faced with the imminent collapse of the country as they knew it, the Dutchmen were now being told that not all was lost: again and again they were instructed to return to their original nature as solid, honest, freedom loving, and God fearing Protestants. The authors of these countless *Karakterschetsen* are now completely forgotten, but at the time they were hailed as major authorities, from IJsbrand van Hamelsveld and Engelbertus Engelberts to Willem Anthony Ockerse and Van Heusde. Their message was unequivocal: yes, our country is suffering. In the 1780s we had been defeated spectacularly by the British navy and trampled over by the Prussians, after which we were invaded by the French, and culturally we are no longer a match even for the Germans – whose culture their 17th-century ancestors had still regarded as backward, as the Holy Roman Empire had largely been inhabited by illiterates.[67] But we *are* Dutchmen.

Around 1800, all contemporary commentaries appear to have agreed: as Dutchmen we inhabit a small country, but perhaps we are best advised to face this fact and take a second look at what it means to be Dutch. Let us embrace the fact that we are, indeed, a simple people, but we have remained "natural." We may not excel in such hazardous endeavours as speculative metaphysics, Ockerse argued in 1798, but "still waters run deep," or so he told his readers.[68] What is more, after having been through such tough times as we Dutchmen have lately been experiencing, we should first of all be proud to be Dutch and not be seduced by idle talk coming either from France or from Germany about global citizenship and universal human rights. Van Heusde, a hugely popular professor of philosophy at Utrecht from 1803 to 1839, fully agreed, confirming

---

65   Margaret C. Jacob, *Strangers Nowhere in the World. The Rise of Cosmopolitanism in Early Modern Europe* (Philadelphia: 2006).

66   Kloek and Mijnhardt, *1800. Blauwdrukken voor een samenleving*, c. 11.

67   Engelbertus (Matthias Engelberts), *Verdediging van de eer der Hollandsche natie* (Amsterdam: 1763); Willem Anthony Ockerse, *Ontwerp tot eene algemeene character-kunde*, 3 vols. (Utrecht: 1788–1797); IJsbrand van Hamelsveld, *De Zedelijke Toestand der Nederlandsche Natie op het einde van de achttiende eeuw* (Amsterdam: 1791). See Jacques Bos, "Verval, deugd en Nederlandse eigenheid. Karakter als politiek-antropologische categorie in de achttiende eeuw," *De Achttiende Eeuw* 39 (2007): 7–24.

68   Ockerse, *Ontwerp tot eene algemeene characterkunde*, vol. 3, 122.

that anyone interested in pursuing a really critical philosophy was best advised *not* to study Kant and his pupils, but the Greeks instead, not least because classical philosophy did not endanger the main tenets of the Dutch Reformed Church and what he dubbed "common sense."[69] In short, both Kant's transcendental project and his cosmopolitanism were rejected by the Dutch as modern Dutch nationalism took precedence by the early 19th century, in which religion continued to play a crucial part. To the extent this nationalism was instrumental in establishing a kingdom that was actually much more modern than many experts for a long time were prepared to admit, this was essentially a legal achievement.[70] All the major players from Van der Capellen tot den Poll to Van Hogendorp were lawyers.[71] Similarly, the modern Protestantism which emerged at the end of the century was the result of theological efforts.[72] The Dutch "modernist" theology, elaborating on the German *Aufklärungstheologie*, would only come into its own in the course of the 19th century, but we know for a fact that already during the final quarter of the 18th century, sermons held in Dutch reformed congregations clearly took heed of some of the enlightened critiques of "prejudices" relating to, say, God's intentions with the earthquake of Lisbon.[73]

In Hemsterhuis, we seem to encounter an 18th-century Dutch philosopher who had abandoned this traditional adherence to the Reformed creed. His

---

69   See, e.g., Philip W. van Heusde, *Brieven over het beoefenen der wijsgeerte, inzonderheid in ons Vaderland en in onze tijden* (Utrecht: 1837), 41. See also Piet P. de Quay, *De genoegzaamheid van het natuurlijk gezond verstand. Prijsverhandelingen over godsdienst, zedenkunde en burgerlijke maatschappij in Nederland aan het einde der 18e eeuw* (Den Haag: 2000).

70   Van Sas, *De metamorfose van Nederland*, c. 26, and van Sas, "De Republiek voorbij. Over de transitie van republicanisme naar liberalism," in *Het Bataafse experiment*, 65–100.

71   Some further, recent attempts to assess the Dutch Revolutionary Age and its aftermath: Matthijs Lok, *Windvanen. Napoleontische bestuurders in de Nederlandse en Franse Restauratie (1813–1820)* (Amsterdam: 2009); Joris Oddens, *Pioniers in schaduwbeeld. Het eerste parlement van Nederland, 1796–1798* (Nijmegen: 2012); Mart Rutjes, *Door gelijkheid gegrepen. Democratie, burgerschap en staat in Nederland, 1795–1801* (Nijmegen: 2012); Bart Verheijen, *Nederland onder Napoleon. Partijstrijd en natievorming, 1801–1813* (Nijmegen: 2017).

72   See most recently Ernestine van der Wall and Leo Wessels (eds.), *Een veelzijdige verstandhouding. Religie en Verlichting in Nederland, 1650–1850* (Nijmegen: 2007); Jan Wim Buisman (ed.), *Verlichting in Nederland, 1650–1850. Vrede tussen rede en religie?* (Nijmegen: 2013).

73   Jan Willem Buisman, *Tussen vroomheid en Verlichting. Een cultuurhistorisch en –sociologisch onderzoek naar enkele aspecten van de Verlichting in Nederland (1755–1810)* (Zwolle: 1992); Jelle Bosma, *Woorden van een gezond verstand. De invloed van de Verlichting op de in het Nederlands uitgegeven preken van 1750 tot 1800* (Nieuwkoop: 1997).

contemporaries could not fail to notice the absence of biblical references in his work, which consisted of Platonic dialogues and "Letters," many of which were addressed to the Princess Galitzine, whom he had met at The Hague, and who served as his "Diotima" – the famous character from Plato's *Symposium*.[74] But his worldview was not so much the outcome of any philosophical secularism, as the product of his Philhellenism, the movement commonly associated with Hemsterhuis' German contemporary Johann Joachim Winckelmann.[75] He may not have been the sensual heathen Winckelmann was, yet both Winckelmann's and Hemsterhuis' Garden of Eden was called Athens. Van Heusde, Hemsterhuis' only major Dutch pupil, however, went out of his way to render Hemsterhuis' "Socratic Philosophy" fit for Protestant consumption.[76] Admittedly, this took some effort as Christian theology did not figure prominently in the work of Hemsterhuis. It would seem that, in a sense, Hemsterhuis was part of a Dutch tradition that was, perhaps, more interesting from the perspective of intellectual secularization than the history of Dutch philosophy. While he was no academic, his father Tiberius was a very famous Leiden classicist – the Dutch 18th-century flowering of Greek studies would soon be attributed to the so-called *Schola Hemsterhusiana*.[77] Perhaps Van Heusde was right when he argued that ever since Erasmus "the Petrarch of the North," it had been Classical Antiquity which constituted "the Philosophy of our nation."[78]

In a series of recent publications, Wyger Velema has established the extent to which late 18th-century political authors in the Dutch Republic were still completely enthralled with the classical Republican vocabulary, which would

---

74   Frans Hemsterhuis, *Lettres de Socrate à Diotime. Cent cinquante lettres du philosophe néerlandais Frans Hemsterhuis à la princesse de Gallitzin* (Frankfurt a.M.: 2007) and Frans Hemsterhuis, *Oeuvres philosophiques* (Leiden: 2015).

75   The literature is huge. See most notably Eliza M. Butler, *The Tyranny of Greece over Germany* (Cambridge: 1935) and more recently Katherine Harloe, *Winckelmann and the Invention of Antiquity* (Oxford: 2013), and Anthony Andurand, *Le Mythe grec allemand. Histoire d'une affinité elective* (Rennes: 2013).

76   Philip W. van Heusde, *De Socratische School of Wijsbegeerte voor de negentiende eeuw*, 4 vols. (Utrecht: 1834–1839).

77   Jan G. Gerretzen, *Schola Hemsterhusiana. De herleving der Grieksche studiën aan de Nederlandsche universiteiten in de achttiende eeuw van Perizonius tot en met Valckenaer* (Nijmegen: 1940).

78   Van Heusde, *Brieven over het beoefenen der wijsgeerte*, 30. See Henri Krop, "De Wijsbegeerte der Ouden als norm van Hemsterhuis tot Van Heusde," in *De Oudheid in de Achttiende Eeuw*, ed. Alexander J.P. Raat, Wyger R.E. Velema, and Claudette Baar-de Weerd (Utrecht: 2012), 103–114.

only lose its appeal in the aftermath of the French Revolution.[79] As mentioned, one of the very few late 18th-century authors who quite openly advertised their atheism was Pieter van Woensel. He was no philosopher and made fun of the fashionable *philosophes* among his contemporaries. He had been destined to become a minister but after a year at the Remonstrant Seminary, he was expelled for "gross indecency," upon which he moved to Leiden, where he studied medicine, before enjoying a fine career in the Dutch armed forces. It would seem his journeys through the Islamic world in particular only confirmed the relative status Christianity held in his eyes and it seems no coincidence that one of Pieter van Woensel's favorite titles was Lucretius' *De rerum natura*, a book that was first translated into Dutch in 1701 by an Amsterdam regent who was rumored to be something of a Spinozist.[80] It was, however, only during the second half of the 1800s that the Dutch movement of modern freethinkers emerged, consisting of Marxists, Darwinists, and, of course, Spinozists.[81]

References

Aerts, Remieg, and Henk te Velde (eds.), *De stijl van de burger. Over Nederlandse burgerlijke cultuur vanaf de Middeleeuwen* (Kampen: 1998).

Andurand, Anthony, *Le Mythe grec allemand. Histoire d'une affinité elective* (Rennes: 2013).

Bakker, René, *Reizen en de kunst van het schrijven. Pieter van Woensel in het Ottomaanse Rijk, de Krim en Rusland 1784–1789* (Zeist: 2008).

Bayle, Pierre, *Pensées diverses sur la comète* (Paris: 2007).

Beverland, Adrian, *De Peccato Originali kat' exochên sic nuncupato Dissertatio* (Leiden: 1678).

---

79   Wyger R.E. Velema, *Republicans. Essays on Eighteenth-Century Dutch Political Thought* (Leiden: 2007); Wyger R.E. Velema, *Omstreden Oudheid. De Nederlandse achttiende eeuw en de klassieke politiek* (Amsterdam: 2010); Wyger R.E. Velema, "Antiquity and Modernity in the Eighteenth Century. The Case of the Dutch Republic," in *De Oudheid in de Achttiende Eeuw*, 17–29; Wyger R.E. Velema, "Oude waarden. Over de terugkeer van de klassieke oudheid in de Verlichtingshistoriografie," *Tijdschrift voor Geschiedenis* 127 (2014): 229–246; Wyger R.E. Velema, "The Enlightenment and the Past. Old Controversies and New Perspectives," *De Achttiende Eeuw* 46 (2014): 7–26.

80   Lucretius, *De natuur van de dingen*, trans. Piet Schrijvers (Groningen: 2008), 536–612.

81   Siebe Thissen, *De spinozisten. Wijsgerige beweging in Nederland (1850–1907)* (Den Haag: 2000).

Bos, Jacques, "Verval, deugd en Nederlandse eigenheid. Karakter als politiek-antropologische categorie in de achttiende eeuw," *De Achttiende Eeuw* 39 (2007): 7–24.

Bosma, Jelle, *Woorden van een gezond verstand. De invloed van de Verlichting op de in het Nederlands uitgegeven preken van 1750 tot 1800* (Nieuwkoop: 1997).

Bots, Jan, *Tussen Descartes en Darwin. Geloof en natuurwetenschap in de achttiende eeuw in Nederland* (Assen: 1972).

Brooke, Christopher, *Philosophic Pride. Stoicism and Political Thought from Lipsius to Rousseau* (Princeton: 2012).

Buisman, Jan Wim (ed.), *Verlichting in Nederland, 1650–1850. Vrede tussen rede en religie?* (Nijmegen: 2013).

Buisman, Jan Willem, *Tussen vroomheid en Verlichting. Een cultuurhistorisch en – sociologisch onderzoek naar enkele aspecten van de Verlichting in Nederland (1755–1810)* (Zwolle: 1992).

Butler, Eliza M., *The Tyranny of Greece over Germany* (Cambridge: 1935).

Collins, Anthony, *A Discourse of Free-Thinking, Occasion'd by the Rise and Growth of a Sect Call'd Free-Thinkers* (London: 1713).

De Haan, Ido, Paul den Hoed, and Henk te Velde (eds.), *Een nieuwe staat. Het begin van het Koninkrijk der Nederlanden* (Amsterdam: 2013).

De Quay, Piet P., *De genoegzaamheid van het natuurlijk gezond verstand. Prijsverhandelingen over godsdienst, zedenkunde en burgerlijke maatschappij in Nederland aan het einde der 18e eeuw* (Den Haag: 2000).

De Smet, Rudolf, *Hadrianus Beverlandus (1650–1716). Non unus e multis peccator. Studie over het leven en werk van Hadriaan Beverland* (Brussels: 1988).

Diderot, Denis, *Oeuvres complètes*, 20 vols. (Nendeln: 1966).

Ducheyne, Steffen, "'s Gravesande's Appropriation of Newton's Natural Philosophy," *Centaurus* 56 (2014): 97–120.

Ducheyne, Steffen (ed.), *Reassessing the Radical Enlightenment* (London: 2017).

Eclecticus (Dionysius van de Wijnpersse), *Eenige Bespiegelingen der Kantische Wijsgeerte* (The Hague: 1805).

Enenkel, Karl, "Neo-Latin Erotic and Pornographic Literature (c. 1400–c. 1700)," in *Brill's Encyclopaedia of the Neo-Latin World*, eds. Philip Ford, Jan Bloemendal, and Charles Fantazzi, (Leiden: 2014), 487–501.

Engelbertus (Matthias Engelberts), *Verdediging van de eer der Hollandsche natie* (Amsterdam: 1763).

Fresco, Marcel F., Loek Geeraedts, and Klaus Hammacher (eds.), *Frans Hemsterhuis (1721–1790). Quellen, Philosophie und Rezeption* (Münster: 1995).

Gerretzen, Jan Gerard, *Schola Hemsterhusiana. De herleving der Grieksche studiën aan de Nederlandsche universiteiten in de achttiende eeuw van Perizonius tot en met Valckenaer* (Nijmegen: 1940).

Grafton, Anthony, *Joseph Scaliger. A Study in the History of Classical Scholarship*, 2 vols. (Oxford: 1983–1993).

Grafton, Anthony, "Close Encounters of the Learned Kind. Joseph Scaliger's Table Talk," *American Scholar* 57 (1988): 581–8.

Gros, Jean-Michel, "Bayle and the Question of the Salvation of the Infidels," in *Inexcusabiles. Salvation and the Virtues of the Pagans in the Early Modern Period*, ed. Alberto Frigo (Cham: 2020), 127–144.

Hagen, Edwina, "Een zaal van staatsmannen, niet van godgeleerden. Godsdienstige sentimenten in de Nationale Vergadering," in *Het Bataafse experiment. Politiek en cultuur rond 1800*, eds. Frans Grijzenhout, Nicolaas C.F. van Sas, and Wyger Velema (Nijmegen: 2013), 125–153.

Hanou, André, *Sluiers van Isis. Johannes Kinker als voorvechter van de Nederlandse Verlichting, 1790–1845*, 2 vols. (Deventer: 1988).

Harloe, Katherine, *Winckelmann and the Invention of Antiquity* (Oxford: 2013).

Hemsterhuis, Frans, *Oeuvres philosophiques* (Leiden: 2015).

Hemsterhuis, Frans, *Lettres de Socrate à Diotime. Cent cinquante lettres du philosophe néerlandais Frans Hemsterhuis à la princesse de Gallitzin* (Frankfurt a.M.: 2007).

Hollewand, Karen E., *The Banishment of Beverland. Sex, Sin, and Scholarship in the Seventeenth-Century Dutch Republic* (Leiden: 2019).

Israel, Jonathan I., *Enlightenment Contested. Philosophy, Modernity and the Emancipation of Man, 1670–1752* (Oxford: 2006).

Israel, Jonathan I., *Radical Enlightenment. Philosophy and the Making of Modernity, 1650–1750* (Oxford: 2001).

Israel, Jonathan I., and Martin Mulsow (eds.), *Radikalaufklärung* (Frankfurt a.M.: 2014).

Jacob, Margaret C., *Strangers Nowhere in the World. The Rise of Cosmopolitanism in Early Modern Europe* (Philadelphia: 2006).

Jansen, Clifford H.J., *Natuurrecht of Romeins recht. Een studie over leven en werk van F.A. van der Marck (1719–1800) in het licht van de opvattingen van zijn tijd* (Leiden: 1987).

Jorink, Eric, *Reading the Book of Nature in the Dutch Golden Age, 1575–1715* (Leiden: 2010).

Jorink, Eric, "'Horrible and Blasphemous.' Isaac La Peyrère, Isaac Vossius and the Emergence of Radical Biblical Criticism in the Dutch Republic," in *Nature and Scripture in the Abrahamic Religions. Up to 1700*, eds. Jitse M. van der Meer and Scott Mandelbrote, vol. 1 (Leiden: 2008), 429–450.

Jorink, Eric, and Ad Maas (eds.), *Newton and the Netherlands. How Isaac Newton was Fashioned in the Netherlands* (Amsterdam: 2012).

Jorink, Eric, and Dirk van Miert (eds.), *Isaac Vossius (1618–1689). Between Science and Scholarship* (Leiden: 2012).

Katz, David S., "Isaac Vossius and the English Biblical Critics," in *Scepticism and Irreligion in the Seventeenth and Eighteenth Centuries*, eds. Richard H. Popkin and Arjo Vanderjagt (Leiden: 1993), 142–184.

Kloek, Joost J., and Wijnand W. Mijnhardt, *1800: Blauwdrukken voor een samenleving* (The Hague: 2001).

Kloek, Joost J., and Karin Tilmans (eds.), *Burger. Een geschiedenis van het begrip 'burger' van de Middeleeuwen tot de 21ste eeuw* (Amsterdam: 2002).

Koerbagh, Adriaan, *A Light Shining in Dark Places, to Illuminate the Main Questions of Theology and Religion*, trans. Michiel Wielema (Leiden: 2011).

Kolakowski, Leszek, *Chrétiens sans Église. La Conscience religieuse et le lien confessionnel au XVIIe siècle* (Paris: 1969).

Kouwenberg, Annemieke, "Kant in den Niederlanden: *Lektuur bij het ontbijt en aan de thetafel* (1804–1808). Praktischer Kantianismus für Anfänger," in *Nur Narr? Nur Dichter? Über die Beziehungen von Literatur und Philosophie*, eds. Roland Duhamel and Guillaume van Gemert (Würzburg: 2008), 143–164.

Krop, Henri, *Spinoza. Een paradoxale icoon van Nederland* (Amsterdam: 2014).

Krop, Henri, "De Wijsbegeerte der Ouden als norm van Hemsterhuis tot Van Heusde," in *De Oudheid in de Achttiende Eeuw*, eds. Alexander J.P. Raat, Wyger R.E. Velema, and Claudette Baar-de Weerd (Utrecht: 2012), 103–114.

Leemans, Inger, *Het woord is aan de onderkant. Radicale ideeën in Nederlandse pornografische romans, 1670–1700* (Nijmegen: 2002).

Leeuwenburgh, Bart, *Het noodlot van een ketter. Adriaan Koerbagh, 1633–1669* (Nijmegen: 2013).

Lindeboom, Johannes, *Frederik Adolf van der Marck, een achttiende-eeuwsch leeraar van het natuurrecht* (The Hague: 1947).

Lok, Matthijs, *Windvanen. Napoleontische bestuurders in de Nederlandse en Franse Restauratie (1813–1820)* (Amsterdam: 2009).

Lucassen, Leo, and Jan Lucassen, *Winnaars en verliezers. Een nuchtere balans van vijfhonderd jaar migratie* (Amsterdam: 2012).

Lucretius, *De natuur van de dingen*, trans. Piet Schrijvers (Groningen: 2008).

Maas, Ad, "The Man Who Erased Himself. Willem Jacob 's Gravesande and the Enlightenment," in *Newton and the Netherlands. How Isaac Newton was Fashioned in the Netherlands*, eds. Eric Jorink and Ad Maas (Amsterdam: 2012), 113–138.

Marenbon, John, *Pagans and Philosophers. The Problem of Paganism from Augustine to Leibniz* (Princeton: 2015).

Melica, Claudia (ed.), *Hemsterhuis. A European Philosopher Rediscovered* (Naples: 2005).

Mijnhardt, Wijnand W., "The Dutch Enlightenment: Humanism, Nationalism, and Decline," in *The Dutch Republic in the Eighteenth Century. Decline, Enlightenment, and Revolution*, eds. Margaret C. Jacob and Wijnand W. Mijnhardt (Ithaca: 1992), 197–223.

Mijnhardt, Wijnand W., *Tot Heil van 't Menschdom. Culturele genootschappen in Nederland, 1750–1815* (Amsterdam: 1988).

Mönkemeyer, Heinz, *François Hemsterhuis* (Boston: 1975).

Nieuwenhuis, Ivo, *Onder het mom van satire. Laster, spot en ironie in Nederland, 1780–1800* (Hilversum: 2014).

Nieuwenhuis, Ivo, "The Eccentric Enlightenment of Pieter van Woensel," *De Achttiende Eeuw* 45 (2012): 177–191.

Nieuwentijt, Bernard, *Gronden van zekerheid, of de regte betoogwyse der wiskundigen, So in het denkbeeldige als in het zakelyke* (Amsterdam: 1720).

Nieuwentijt, Bernard, *Het regt gebruik der werelt beschouwingen, ter overtuiginge van ongodisten en ongelovigen aangetoont* (Amsterdam: 1715).

Noordenbos, Oene, *Het atheïsme in Nederland in de negentiende eeuw. Een kritisch overzicht* (Rotterdam: 1931).

Ockerse, Willem Anthony, *Verhandeling over de Vrage: In Welken zin kunnen de Menschen gezegd worden Gelijk te Zijn?* (Haarlem: 1793).

Ockerse, Willem Anthony, *Ontwerp tot eene algemeene characterkunde*, 3 vols. (Utrecht: 1788–1797).

Oddens, Joris, *Pioniers in schaduwbeeld. Het eerste parlement van Nederland, 1796–1798* (Nijmegen: 2012).

Onnasch, Ernst-Otto, "Immanuel Kants Philosophie in den Niederlanden, 1785–1804," in *Kant der Europäer. Europäer über Kant*, eds. Steffen Dietsch and Lorenz Grimoni (Duisburg: 2010), 70–96.

Pettegree, Andrew, and Arthur der Weduwen, *The Bookshop of the World. Making and Trading Books in the Dutch Golden Age* (New Haven: 2019).

Pottle, Frederick A. (ed.), *Boswell in Holland, 1763–1764* (Melbourne: 1952).

Roelevink, Joke, "Het Babel van de geleerden. Latijn in het Nederlandse universitaire onderwijs van de achttiende en de negentiende eeuw," *Jaarboek van de Maatschappij der Nederlandse Letterkunde* (1990): 33–41.

Rosendaal, Joost, *De Nederlandse Revolutie. Vrijheid, volk en vaderland, 1783–1799* (Nijmegen: 2005).

Rutjes, Mart, *Door gelijkheid gegrepen. Democratie, burgerschap en staat in Nederland, 1795–1801* (Nijmegen: 2012).

's Gravesande, Willem Jacob, *Physices Elementa Mathematica, experimentis confirmata, sive Introductio ad Philosophiam Newtonianam*, 2 vols. (Leiden: 1720–1721).

's Gravesande, Willem Jacob, *Philosophiae Newtonianae Institutiones in usus academicos* (Leiden: 1723).

's Gravesande, Willem Jacob, *Oeuvres philosophiques et mathématiques*, 2 vols. (Amsterdam: 1774).

Somos, Mark, *Secularisation and the Leiden Circle* (Leiden: 2012).

Steenbakkers, Piet, Jetze Touber, Jeroen van de Ven, "A Clandestine Notebook (1678–1679) on Spinoza, Beverland, Politics, the Bible and Sex," *Lias* 38 (2011): 225–365.

Temple, Sir William, *Observations upon the United Provinces of the Netherlands* (Cambridge, Eng.: 1932).

Theeuwen, Peet H.J.M., *Pieter 't Hoen en De Post van den Neder-Rhijn* (Hilversum: 2002).

Thissen, Siebe, *De spinozisten. Wijsgerige beweging in Nederland (1850–1907)* (Den Haag: 2000).

Trapman, Hans, *Wijze dwaasheid. Vijfhonderd jaar Lof der zotheid in Nederland* (Amsterdam: 2011).

Uiterhoeve, Wilfried, *Koning, keizer, admiraal. 1810: De ondergang van het keizerrijk Holland* (Nijmegen: 2010).

Van Bunge, Wiep, *From Bayle to the Batavian Revolution. Essays on Philosophy in the Eighteenth-Century Dutch Republic* (Leiden: 2019).

Van Bunge, Wiep, "*Concordia Res Parvae Crescunt.* The Context of Seventeenth-Century Dutch Radicalism," in *The Dutch Legacy. Radical Thinkers of the Seventeenth Century and the Enlightenment*, eds. Sonja Lavaert and Winfried Schröder (Leiden: 2017), 16–34.

Van Bunge, Wiep, *Spinoza Past and Present. Essays on Spinoza, Spinozism, and Spinoza Scholarship* (Leiden: 2012).

Van Bunge, Wiep, *From Stevin to Spinoza. An Essay on Philosophy in the Seventeenth-Century Dutch Republic* (Leiden: 2001).

Van der Linden, David, *Experiencing Exile. Huguenot Refugees in the Dutch Republic, 1680–1700* (Farnham: 2015).

Van der Wall, Ernestine, "Newtonianism and Religion in the Netherlands," *Studies in History and Philosophy of Science* 35 (2004): 493–514.

Van der Wall, Ernestine, *Socrates in de hemel? Een achttiende-eeuwse polemiek over deugd, verdraagzaamheid en de vaderlandse kerk* (Hilversum: 2000).

Van der Wall, Ernestine, "Geen natie van atheïsten. Pieter Paulus (1753–1796) over godsdienst en mensenrechten," *Jaarboek van de Maatschappij der Nederlandse Letterkunde* (1996): 45–58.

Van der Wall, Ernestine, and Leo Wessels (eds.), *Een veelzijdige verstandhouding. Religie en Verlichting in Nederland, 1650–1850* (Nijmegen: 2007).

Van Eijnatten, Joris, *Liberty and Concord. Religious Toleration and the Public in the Eighteenth-Century Netherlands* (Leiden: 2003).

Van Gestel, Paul, "Dutch Reactions to Thomas Paine's *Age of Reason*," *Studies on Voltaire and the Eighteenth Century* 378 (1999): 271–301.

Van Gestel, Paul, "*De verbasteringen van het Christendom.* Joseph Priestley (1733–1804) en de Nederlandse Verlichting," *De Achttiende Eeuw* 30 (1998): 3–29.

Van Hamelsveld, IJsbrand, *De Zedelijke Toestand der Nederlandsche Natie op het einde van de achttiende eeuw* (Amsterdam: 1791).

Van Hemert, Paulus, *Lektuur bij het ontbijt en de thetafel*, 10 vols. (Amsterdam: 1804–1808).

Van Hemert, Paulus (ed.), *Magazijn voor de critische wijsgeerte en de geschiedenis van dezelve*, 6 vols. (Amsterdam: 1799–1803).

Van Heusde, Philip W., *De school van Polybius of geschiedkunde voor de negentiende eeuw* (Amsterdam: 1841).

Van Heusde, Philip W., *Brieven over het beoefenen der wijsgeerte, inzonderheid in ons Vaderland en in onze tijden* (Utrecht: 1837).

Van Heusde, Philip W., *De Socratische School of Wijsbegeerte voor de negentiende eeuw*, 4 vols. (Utrecht: 1834–1839).

Van Meerkerk, Edwin, *De gebroeders Van Hogendorp. Botsende idealen in de kraamkamer van het koninkrijk* (Amsterdam: 2013).

Van Miert, Dirk, *The Emancipation of Biblical Philology in the Dutch Republic, 1590–1670* (Oxford: 2018).

Van Musschenbroek, Petrus, *Elementa physicae conscripta in usus academicos* (Leiden: 1734).

Van Musschenbroek, Petrus, *Institutiones logicae, praecipue comprehendentes artem argumentandi* (Leiden: 1748).

Van Musschenbroek, Petrus, *Primae lineae theologiae naturalis secundum normam emendatione ontologiae et pneumatologiae* (Leiden: 1756).

Van Rooden, Peter T., "Godsdienst en nationalisme in de achttiende eeuw: het voorbeeld van de Republiek," in *Vaderland. Een geschiedenis vanaf de vijftiende eeuw tot 1940*, ed. Nicolaas C.F. van Sas (Amsterdam: 1999), 201–236.

Van Rooden, Peter T., "Secularization in the Netherlands," *Kirchliche Zeitgeschichte* 11 (1998): 34–40.

Van Rooden, Peter T., *Religieuze regimes. Over godsdienst en maatschappij in Nederland, 1570–1990* (Amsterdam: 1996).

Van Rooden, Peter T., "Spinoza's Bijbeluitleg," *Studia Rosenthaliana* 18 (1984): 120–133.

Van Sas, Nicolaas C.F., *De metamorfose van Nederland. Van oude orde naar moderniteit, 1750–1900* (Amsterdam: 2004).

Van Sas, Nicolaas C.F., "De Republiek voorbij. Over de transitie van republicanisme naar liberalisme," in *Het Bataafse experiment. Politiek en cultuur rond 1800*, eds. Frans Grijzenhout, Nicolaas C.F. van Sas, and Wyger Velema (Nijmegen: 2013), 65–100.

Velema, Wyger R.E., "Oude waarden. Over de terugkeer van de klassieke oudheid in de Verlichtingshistoriografie," *Tijdschrift voor Geschiedenis* 127 (2014): 229–246.

Velema, Wyger R.E., "The Enlightenment and the Past. Old Controversies and New Perspectives," *De Achttiende Eeuw* 46 (2014): 7–26.

Velema, Wyger R.E., "Antiquity and Modernity in the Eighteenth Century. The Case of the Dutch Republic," in *De Oudheid in de Achttiende Eeuw*, eds. Alexander J.P. Raat, Wyger R.E. Velema, and Claudette Baar-de Weerd (Utrecht: 2012), 17–29.

Velema, Wyger R.E., *Omstreden Oudheid. De Nederlandse achttiende eeuw en de klassieke politiek* (Amsterdam: 2010).

Velema, Wyger R.E., *Republicans. Essays on Eighteenth-Century Dutch Political Thought* (Leiden: 2007).

Verbeek, Theo, *Early Reactions to Cartesian Philosophy, 1637–1650* (Carbondale: 1992).

Verbeek, Theo, *La querelle d'Utrecht. René Descartes et Martin Schoock* (Paris: 1988).

Vercruysse, Jeroom, *Voltaire en Hollande* (Geneva: 1966).

Verhaart, Floris, *Classical Learning in Britain, France, and the Dutch Republic, 1690–1750. Beyond the Ancients and the Moderns* (Oxford: 2020).

Verheijen, Bart, *Nederland onder Napoleon. Partijstrijd en natievorming, 1801–1813* (Nijmegen: 2017).

Vermij, Rienk, "The Formation of the Newtonian Natural Philosophy. The Case of the Amsterdam Mathematical Amateurs," *The British Journal for the History of Science* 26 (2003): 183–200.

Vermij, Rienk, *Secularisering en natuurwetenschap in de zeventiende en achttiende eeuw* (Amsterdam: 1991).

Verweij, Jan, *Kant-tekening van een Horrearius. De rol van het* Magazyn voor de critische Wijsgeerte en de Geschiedenis van Dezelve *(1798–1803) in de Kantreceptie* (Nijmegen: 2012).

Von Prantl, Carl, "Daniel Wyttenbach als Gegner Kants," *Sitzungsberichte der philosophisch-philologischen und historischen Classe der Königlich Bayerischen Akademie der Wissenschaften zu München* (1877): 264–286.

Waszink, Jan, "Lipsius and Grotius: Tacitism," *History of European Ideas* 39 (2013): 151–168.

Waszink, Jan, "Your Tacitism or Mine? Modern and Early Modern Conceptions of Tacitism and Tacitus," *History of European Ideas* 36 (2010): 375–385.

Wauters, Tim, "*Libertinage érudit* and Isaac Vossius. A Case Study," *The Journal for Early Modern Cultural Studies* 11 (2012): 37–53.

Weber, Max, *Wissenschaft als Beruf* (Munich: 1917).

Weststeijn, Arthur, *Commercial Republicanism in the Dutch Golden Age. The Political Thought of Johan and Pieter de la Court* (Leiden: 2012).

Wielema, Michiel, *The March of the Libertines. Spinozists and the Dutch Reformed Church (1660–1750)* (Hilversum: 2004).

Wielema, Michiel, *Ketters en verlichters. De invloed van het spinozisme en het wolffianisme op de Verlichting in Nederland, in het bijzonder in de gereformeerde theologie* (PhD, Vrije Universiteit Amsterdam: 1999).

Wielema, Michiel, "Die erste niederländische Kant Rezeption, 1786–1850," *Kant-Studien* 79 (1988): 450–466.

Zwalve, Willem J., "Het Recht en de Verlichting. De juridische hoogleraar Frederik Adolf van der Marck (1719–1800)," in *Om niet aan onwetendheid en barbarij te bezwijken. Groningse geleerden, 1614–1989*, eds. Guillaume A. van Gemert, Johanna Schuller tot Peursum-Meijer, and Arie J. Vanderjagt (Hilversum: 1989), 83–100.

PART 2

The Religion(s) of the Enlightenment

∵

The Ways of Clandestinity: Radical Cartesianism and Deism in Robert Challe (1659–1721)

Gianni Paganini

1   Clandestine Philosophy: An Overview

Over the last fifty years, knowledge about the clandestine world of ideas has improved significantly and has brought about a real historiographical revolution, giving rise to new interpretive paradigms. To name just three of them, we owe to the works of Margaret Jacob[1] the term and the idea of "radical Enlightenment" based on the Anglo-Dutch context, while Martin Mulsow has coined the term "heterodox underground" as a melting pot of modernity in the *"Frühaufklärung."*[2] Another paradigm, born from this kind of research, is that of "radical libertinism" that I proposed to distinguish the most audacious and clandestine forms of French 17th-century freethinking from the works of authors such as La Mothe Le Vayer and Gabriel Naudé who practiced the art of simulating and dissimulating in order to stay on the public stage of the *Ancien Régime*, while cautiously advancing new heterodox ideas.[3] In practice, these new proposals have supplanted older categories such as "crisis of the European conscience," "pre-enlightenment," and "erudite libertinism." Jonathan Israel, in particular, has taken up again the idea of "radical Enlightenment" and

---

1   Margaret C. Jacob, *The Radical Enlightenment: Pantheists, Freemasons, and Republicans* (London: 1981; 2nd ed.: 2003).

2   Martin Mulsow, *Moderne aus dem Untergrund. Radikale Frühaufklärung in Deutschland 1680–1720* (Hamburg: 2002). English translation: *Enlightenment Underground: Radical Germany, 1680–1720* (Charlottesville: 2015). See also the reviews by Gianni Paganini: "Modernità dalla clandestinità," *Giornale Critico della Filosofia Italiana* 84 (2005): 172–180; and John Christian Laursen, *Journal of the History of Philosophy* 41 (2003): 419–420. Martin Mulsow has now reissued a revised edition of that volume and added a second volume, under this general title: *Radikale Frühaufklärung in Deutschland 1680–1720*, vol. 1: *Moderne aus dem Untergrund*; vol. 2: *Clandestine Vernunft* (Göttingen: 2018).

3   Gianni Paganini, "Wie aus Gesetzgebern Betrüger werden. Eine philosophische Archäologie des 'radikalen' Libertinismus," in *Radikalaufklärung*, eds. Jonathan Israel and Martin Mulsow (Berlin: 2014), 49–91.

developed it into that of "democratic Enlightenment,"[4] stressing above all the universality of reason – with all its consequences – that distinguishes "radicals" from "moderate" thinkers. In so doing, he included the contribution of clandestine literature in the development of this new radicalism. Thus, we have witnessed a propitious moment for studies during which the quantitative growth of knowledge (also documented by two specific book series dedicated to the *clandestina* in France and in Germany, respectively, led by Antony McKenna[5] and Winfried Schröder[6]) has resulted in a qualitative mutation of paradigms in the history of ideas.

These clandestine philosophical manuscripts[7] form an appreciable *corpus*: more than 290 texts corresponding to some 2,000 manuscript copies owned by public and private European and North American libraries, most of them dating back to the 17th and 18th centuries, but some also to the beginning of the 19th century.[8] It should be noted that the clandestine philosophical manuscript is an early modern literary genre *par excellence*: there is nothing like it

---

4   See Jonathan I. Israel, *Radical Enlightenment: Philosophy and the Making of Modernity, 1650–1750* (Oxford: 2001), esp. 684–703 on clandestine literature; Jonathan I. Israel, *Enlightenment Contested: Philosophy, Modernity, and the Emancipation of Man, 1670–1752* (Oxford: 2006); Jonathan I. Israel, *Democratic Enlightenment: Philosophy, Revolution, and Human Rights 1750–1790* (Oxford: 2011), esp. 1–35 on clandestine manuscripts. For an overview of the research on this topic, see these collections of articles: *Qu'est-ce que les Lumières "radicales"? Libertinage, athéisme et spinozisme dans le tournant philosophique de l'âge classique*, eds. Catherine Secrétan, Tristan Dagron, and Laurent Bove (Paris: 2007); Jonathan I. Israel and Martin Mulsow (eds.), *Radikalaufklärung* (Berlin: 2014) and Steffen Ducheyne (ed.), *Reassessing the Radical Enlightenment* (London: 2018).

5   Series: "Libre pensée et Littérature clandestine" (Paris: H. Champion). McKenna edits with Pierre-François Moreau the specialized periodical *La Lettre clandestine* (Paris: Presses de la Sorbonne and then Classiques Garnier) as well as "Libertinage et Philosophie au XVIIe siècle" (Presses de l'Université de Saint-Etienne; then Paris: Classiques Garnier).

6   Series: "Freidenker der deutschen Aufklärung" (Stuttgart: Frommann-Holzboog).

7   For an overview of recent research on clandestine philosophical manuscripts, see Gianni Paganini, Margaret C. Jacob, and John Christian Laursen (eds.), *Clandestine Philosophy. New Studies on Subversive Manuscripts in Early Modern Europe, 1620–1823* (Toronto: 2020). Of course, there were other kinds of clandestine texts: religious, satirical, political, erotic, which were prohibited due to their contents but were not philosophical, even in a broader meaning of this term. For a historical definition of the category, see Gianni Paganini, "What Is a Clandestine Philosophical Manuscript?," in *Clandestine Philosophy*, 3–19. For their philosophical import, see Winfried Schröder, "Why, and to What End, Should Historians of Philosophy Study Early Modern Clandestine Texts?," in *Clandestine Philosophy*, 23–36.

8   For a synthetic history of this literature, see Gianni Paganini, *Les Philosophies clandestines à l'âge classique* (Paris: 2005); new expanded Italian edition: *Introduzione alle filosofie clandestine* (Rome: 2008).

either in the Middle Ages or in the Renaissance. It is only in the years straddling the 16th and 17th centuries that Jean Bodin (considered to be the author of the most famous deist work criticizing religion, the *Colloquium Heptaplomeres*), or anonymous authors (e.g., the author of the *Quatrains du déiste*, around 1620, and the one of *Theophrastus redivivus*, in 1659) entrusted to this form of communication ideas and works that could never be printed and published in their time.

Clearly, the existence of the "clandestine philosophical manuscript" itself is in part a consequence of and in part a reaction to historical circumstances that are typical of modernity: the invention and expansion of printing, against which the manuscript served as an alternative and surrogate channel for texts that were unquestionably impossible to print; the close alliance of throne and altar that significantly conditioned intellectual life; the creation of increasingly efficient and restrictive forms of preventive censorship of books, which meant that new ways had to be found to circumvent the web of repression; and, finally, the growing autonomy of minor or major "intellectuals," who were often forced to lead a double life or in any case to conceal their ideas, revealing them at the very most to a restricted and carefully selected group by spreading manuscript texts and copies of their subversive works. All these factors led the heterodox authors to privilege manuscript expression and communication over the printed book and sometimes the same texts that circulated in printed form where it was possible had to shift to manuscript form where censorship was stricter.

In terms of their approach to philosophical and religious issues, we can classify the manuscripts roughly into three large families: the deist tradition, the pantheist, and the atheist. The first is grounded in the *Colloquium Heptaplomeres*, attributed to Jean Bodin, and the *Origo et fundamenta religionis christianae* (both at the end of the 16th century), and a little afterwards (around 1620) in the so-called *Quatrains du déiste*. The second tradition culminates in *L'Esprit de Spinosa*, which circulated in different versions under the title *Traité des trois imposteurs*. The third tradition has as its archetype the huge *Theophrastus redivivus* (almost one thousand pages), anonymous and dated to 1659, conserved in four different manuscripts, all in Latin, and not published until 1981–1982.[9]

---

9   *Theophrastus redivivus*, first and critical edition with commentary, eds. Guido Canziani and Gianni Paganini, 2 vols. (Florence: 1981–1982). See also the study by Tullio Gregory, *Theophrastus redivivus. Erudizione e ateismo nel Seicento* (Naples: 1979).

Another "modern" characteristic of philosophical clandestinity was its transversality among the social classes of the *Ancien Régime*. The collectors or authors of philosophical manuscripts included princes (e.g., Prince Eugene of Savoy, general of the imperial Habsburg army and a prominent collector of forbidden works, both printed and in manuscript), nobles, soldiers, diplomats, magistrates fully integrated into the political structures (e.g., Jean Bodin, mentioned above), clergymen both Catholic (the parish priest Jean Meslier) and Calvinist (minister Yves de Vallone), *abbés* (Jean Terrasson), tutors and intellectuals (du Marsais), and renowned academics (Fontenelle and Fréret).[10]

Thanks to the clandestine manuscripts, we can speak of an "Enlightenment before the Enlightenment," and in some cases even before that radical Enlightenment that Jonathan Israel started with Spinoza. This is the case of the *Colloquium Heptaplomeres*, written in the last decade of the 16th century and immediately spread in almost one hundred copies (the first printed version dates back to 1859 only), but also the case of *Theophrastus redivivus*, written in 1659 and to be considered the first large treatise of atheism in early modern philosophy, half a century before Jean Meslier and longer before the works by Diderot and d'Holbach.

Certainly, the *corpus* of philosophical manuscripts is varied and heterogeneous; it includes texts of just a few pages as well as much longer treatises. Also, these manuscripts varied in terms of the quality of their philosophical arguments: in some cases, those arguments are short, almost propagandistic, but in other cases they deservedly accompany and at times boldly anticipate Enlightenment philosophical ideas. As we have already seen about *Theophrastus redivivus*, the case of atheism is exemplary:[11] the first treatise in the history of early modern philosophy that openly, explicitly, and comprehensively supports the thesis of atheism is not a printed book but a clandestine manuscript of mid-17th century. The same thing could be said about the idea of "natural religion," or deism, which appears first in the clandestine manuscripts (the *Colloquium*, the *Quatrains du déiste*, Challe's work) and only later in the texts of Voltaire, Hume, and the early Diderot. Also, the program of a natural history of religion, which traces its genealogy in terms of completely natural and human factors, appeared and was developed brilliantly first in some clandestine manuscripts well before Hume adopted this title for his work dated 1755.

---

10   On this question see the rich dossier in *La Lettre clandestine* 12 (2003): 13–222, on *Lecteurs et collectionneurs de textes clandestins à l'âge classique*.

11   See Gianni Paganini, "The First Philosophical Atheistic Treatise: *Theophrastus redivivus* (1659)," in *Clandestine Philosophy*, 37–83.

These clandestine texts are "philosophical" in a broad sense; they discuss metaphysical, religious, and moral topics from a critical perspective and based fundamentally on what the authors consider to be the criterion of reason as opposed to authority, tradition, revelation. From the end of the Renaissance to the Libertine period and the birth of the Enlightenment, these manuscripts crossed eras of important cultural and philosophical transformations. We cannot speak of "clandestine philosophy" in the singular because the authors drew on different traditions and concepts: they referred to the skepticism of Montaigne and Bayle, to the rationalism of Descartes or Malebranche, to the metaphysics of Spinoza, or to the materialistic approach of Hobbes, or yet again to the empiricism of Locke. Likewise, there were different philosophical orientations: from skepticism to atheism, from deism to materialism, from Spinozism to pantheism. Had Leo Strauss ever taken into consideration these clandestine texts, he would have realized that the "forbidden" manuscripts in early modern times allowed freer, more direct, and more "radical" intellectual processing than the printed but encrypted texts that had to be read "between the lines" in his study *Persecution and the Art of Writing* (1952).

In conclusion of this point, we can claim that the epoch in which the clandestine manuscripts were written and in which they flourished preceded what is viewed as the "official" start of the Enlightenment in the 1720s and 1730s, that is, the period between the publication of the *Lettres persanes* (1721) by Montesquieu and the *Lettres philosophiques* (1734) by Voltaire. The clandestine communication of ideas certainly continued after the 1730s, but the impression is that it was more a quantitative expansion than a qualitative creation of original ideas. And after the 1750s, thanks also to the growing efficacy of the publishing industry abroad and to the spread of book trafficking, printed editions of the clandestine texts that had before circulated as manuscripts more and more multiplied.

2 Challe's Challenge to, and Reworking of, Malebranche's Philosophy

Israel placed Spinoza's philosophy at the origins of radical Enlightenment, but a comparable importance must also be assigned to Descartes' philosophy and Cartesianism, when they were suitably reworked to become the vehicle of non-conformist, anti-religious and subversive ideas, most often against the intentions of Descartes and the "orthodox" Cartesians. The turning point impressed by Cartesianism (at times more his disciple Malebranche than Descartes himself) can also be seen in the transformation of clandestine deism. There is a profound difference in the constitution of deistic ideas before and after Descartes.

Already in Bodin's *Colloquium*, the "religion of nature" or the "religion of reason" (of which Toralba – one of the seven characters of the dialogue – is the interpreter) is distinguished from, and contrasts with, revealed religions (this is the specific trait of "radical" deism, although this term – which was already in use in the French language of the 16th century – is not used in the Latin prose of the *Colloquium*). However, the meaning of terms such as "nature" and "reason," and therefore the meaning of natural and rational religion, are still linked in Bodin to the classical philosophy (in particular, Cicero and Stoicism). Furthermore, Toralba does not hesitate, to support his position, to refer to the "old" and "pure" religion of the biblical patriarchs. This natural religion (in the double meaning of being the most rational and at the same time the most ancient, going back to Adam and Abraham) is opposed by Toralba, due to its universality, to the definition of the Mosaic Judaism as a restricted national religion, charged with holy texts, clerical apparatus, ceremonial, national and political values. Bodin's natural religion has thus a twofold foundation: rational and biblical, even if the latter is limited to the origins of the entire humankind before the election of single privileged people.[12]

The arrival and assertion of Cartesianism, and especially of Malebranche's philosophy, constitutes a decisive break in the development of clandestine deism, since the notions of reason are identified with the criterion of intellectual evidence (clear and distinct ideas). Malebranche conveyed the bulk of Cartesianism and represented the defining feature of a number of some major manuscript treatises, like the works of Robert Challe, Jean Terrasson and the *Examen de la religion* of du Marsais.[13]

The influence of Malebranche's philosophy was felt most powerfully within the radical deist currents even at the cost of a somewhat paradoxical reversal. Conceived as a support for Christian rationalism, this philosophy was transformed in the writings of these clandestine authors into a powerful springboard for anti-Christian rationalism, albeit of a non-atheistic nature. Having been produced by the effort of combining reason and revelation into a coherent theological system, Malebranche's philosophy ultimately provided the clandestine deists of the beginning of the century with the conceptual instruments most suited to elaborating a subversive version of natural religion. Thanks to the reworking of the Cartesian heritage, natural religion was

---

12   On Bodin's *Colloquium*, see Gianni Paganini, "Jean Bodin's Universalism and the Twofold Foundations of Natural Religion: A New Reading of the *Colloquium Heptaplomeres*," *Maimonides* (2022): 145–173.

13   For an overview of this "radical Malebranchism," see Gianni Paganini, "Les voies du malebranchisme clandestin: Challe, Dumarsais, Terrasson," in *Liberté de conscience et arts de penser (XVIe–XVIIIe siècle). Mélanges en l'honneur d'Antony McKenna*, eds. Christelle Bahier-Porte, Pierre-François Moreau and Delphine Reguig (Paris: 2017), 705–719.

no longer conceived as the foundation or common denominator of the historical religions, but it became their formidable adversary, especially with respect to the Christian religion. Challe is the example of this turning upside down of Cartesian rationalism, read through, and at the same time against, Malebranche.

The life of Robert Challe remains something of a mystery and his *Mémoires* do nothing to elucidate these mysteries. We will therefore restrict ourselves to considering the proven facts of his biography and then present his critique of Christianity.

Robert Challe was born in Paris in 1659 in a petty bourgeois milieu, and he was the first in his family to know how to sign his name. He studied at the *Collège de la Marche* and then worked with an uncle notary. He knew very well the social environment of jurists. It seems that he entered the army at the time of the Dutch war and that he participated in the siege of Saint-Omer and the battle of Mont-Cassel (1677). On 2 May 1681, his father died and, the following year, Challe made his first campaign in Acadie, in Canada; he remained there during the following two years, in the service of the *Compagnie des pêches sedentaires de l'Acadie*. On a last trip in 1687, it seems that he was taken prisoner there by the English army and transferred to London.

Coming back, ruined, to France in 1688, he embarked again, in February 1690, as the King's *écrivain extraordinaire*, aboard a ship of the *Compagnie des Indes*. He made a stopover in the Antilles and returned to the port of Lorient on 20 August 1691. During this voyage he kept three diaries (intended for Minister Seignelay, his uncle and protector, and himself) and a compilation of the three accounts, probably compiled around 1715, was published in 1721, a few months after his death.[14] In 1713, his great novel, *Les Illustres Françaises*, was published in The Hague. It was in 1716 that Challe wrote his *Mémoires*, a curious mixture of memories, elements of a chronicle of the reign of Louis XIV, and fables. Challe spent a short time in the prisons of Le Châtelet (from 5 June to 12 August 1717). After his release, he retired to Chartres, where he died, and was buried there on 27 January 1721.[15]

---

14   Robert Challe, *Journal d'un voyage fait aux Indes orientales, par une escadre de six vaisseaux commandés par M. Du Quesne, depuis le 24 février 1690 jusqu'au 20 août 1691, par ordre de la Compagnie des Indes orientales* (Rouen: 1721). See by now the modern edition: *Journal d'un voyage fait aux Indes orientales (du 24 février 1690 au 10 août 1691)*, 2 vols. (Paris: 2002).

15   See Geneviève Artigas-Menant, "Anonymat et autobiographie intellectuelle: Robert Challe," in *Du secret des clandestins à la propagande voltairienne*, ed. Geneviève Artigas-Menant (Paris: 2001), 65–160; Frédéric Deloffre (ed.) *Autour de Robert Challe. Actes du colloque de Chartres (20–22 juin 1991)* (Paris: 1993); Jacques Cormier, Jan Herman and Paul Pelckmans (eds.), *Robert Challe: sources et héritage* (Paris: 2003); Jacques Cormier, *L'Atelier de Robert Challe* (Paris: 2010).

In Challe we see the formation of a "radical" Cartesian who partly followed Malebranche only to go beyond him, with the aim of radicalizing his basic principles (univocity of moral notions, primacy of wisdom and therefore of reason, regularity and simplicity of divine ways). Challe refused to follow Malebranche in his philosophical theology (that included original sin, sacrificial redemption, and the vision of ideas in God). In this rejection, Challe went back to find the original inspiration of Cartesianism, with its eminent role of reason, opposition of understanding to memory and, thus, to history and tradition. In particular, he rejected the merger of philosophy with theology, of which Malebranche had been the protagonist in the second half of the 17th century. By reading Challe, one enters the laboratory where an anti-Christian philosophy was developed out of Cartesian rationalism and oriented towards the idea of rational religion, yet independent of Spinozism, on one hand, and Lockean empiricism, on the other.

The *Difficultés sur la religion proposées au Père Malebranche*[16] were drafted shortly before or after 1710 and diffused only by the way of manuscript copies. It seems that they did not circulate widely as we have found out so far only five copies. The work was printed by the *coterie holbachique* in 1767 with the title of *Le Militaire philosophe*, after a reworking and substantial additions that transformed it in an atheist work. The last chapter, in particular, written by d'Holbach himself, replaced the fourth section of Challe's text, where deistic conceptions were most developed.

In the *Lettre dédicatoire*, addressed to Father Malebranche, the author introduces himself as a moderately learned man, but not as a professional philosopher. He announces that in this work he will assume "a liberated character, indifferent and unconstrained by any political considerations; a purely natural character, a wild character, whose mind has not been sullied by any conception or assumption."[17] His work consists of four books, the first of which contains "the things that opened my eyes"; he reviews all of the major themes within Protestant polemics – and often those elements are borrowed directly from Pierre Bayle, including the critique of the popish power, the abuse of dispensations and indulgences, "the ostentation, the pride, the debauchery, the vanity, the greed, the intrigues and politics of that court [at the Vatican],"[18] the hypocrisy of the missionaries, the acts of persecution undertaken against the Jews

---

16   All references relate to this edition: Robert Challe, *Difficultés sur la religion proposées au Père Malebranche* (Geneva: 2000). All translations from the French original text are mine (G.P.).

17   Ibid., 71.

18   Ibid., 74.

and heretics while blatantly disregarding the rights of conscience – all of the areas in which the Catholic Church could be compared to ancient paganism and idolatry of the Indians and the Americans. As a soldier, Challe had been employed in the *dragonnades* directed against the Huguenots – "what cruel memory!"[19] – and these excesses, supported by the priests, compelled him, he says, to reread the New Testament, the Fathers of the Church and a number of theologians, "which, in truth, had a negative effect"; he then turned to the "Christian philosophers," "who had an even more negative effect."[20]

This denunciation of Christian apologetics is founded on what would be later called deism; in other words, a particular understanding of God, "which no one questions,"[21] having the features of rationality and universality and, what is more, independent of any historical or supposedly revealed religion.[22] In fact, Challe rejects any "artificial religion," based on historical facts and testimonies, and not on rational proofs. The opposition between what is rational and what is just historical is strongly stated thus:

> It was then [in a more mature age] that I examined, not as a historian or as a critic, which is an unending task and tells us nothing, but as a philosopher, as a man who, seriously wanting to find the truth, searches for it hard, in its source and in its principles, and not in those uncertain and muddled facts where superstition is painted with the same features and the same colours as truth; neither in books where we find the pros and cons, the yes and the no, and which even the most skilful men never understand perfectly, but in the right reason which always speaks clearly and uniformly, even to the simplest minds.[23]

Challe draws his guiding principle from the Cartesian philosophy of Malebranche in particular, as it allows him to contrast the truths of reason, and therefore of the natural religion stemming from it, with all the "artificial religions," which are based merely on "books" and historical testimonies. The second book of the *Difficultés* consists of a systematic denunciation of the "artificial" religions in the name of the evidence provided by rational proofs: "No fact is capable of removing an obvious certainty. The artificial religions are based on facts. Therefore, they are doubtful. Thus, by following them, we

---

19   Ibid., 86.
20   Ibid., 87.
21   Ibid., 88.
22   Ibid.
23   Ibid., 93.

are in danger of falling into error."[24] Faith is rejected. Challe states that he does not "believe" in God; he "knows" Him, and based on the characteristics of this infinitely perfect being, he condemns the "absurdities" of the Christian religion and enumerates the articles of his rational religion. In opposition to the biased, conditional and always uncertain persuasion induced by the "facts" and the documents relating them, the author of the *Difficultés* presents his conviction based on simple reason: "I take the human reason common to the whole human race as my sole authority."[25]

After the third book, devoted to refuting the arguments offered by the Christian apologists – among whom Pascal plays a prominent role – the fourth contains his *"système de religion fondé métaphysiquement sur les lumières naturelles et non sur des faits"* ("system of religion metaphysically founded on natural light and not on facts").[26] This system is reliant on proving the existence of God through the wonders of nature. It would be absurd to imagine that everything occurs by chance; the order of nature necessitates a creator God.[27] His primary attributes are wisdom and power, eternity and immensity, and of course we ought to love Him "with a supreme reverence mixed with fear and a kind of joy and pleasure."[28]

> This being which all men have present in their mind and heart, almost without realizing it, is felt and known very vividly at the slightest warning. Then a mediocre attention makes us find that it is the necessary, independent, immense, eternal being, the author of all things, who is himself the essence of all things, and who penetrates the universe without occupying it, who limits it and overcomes it.[29]

There is, therefore, no room for atheism in the *Difficultés*, despite the adulterate printed version published by d'Holbach.

While keeping to reason the guarantee afforded by the divine origins of *les lumières naturelles*, this rationalism is shorn of the most daring metaphysical innovations of Malebranche. Nevertheless, it proves to be strong enough to dispense with any form of historical or revealed, or specifically "artificial," mediation, relying only on the work of pure reason. One of the most clear Malebranchian traits consists in the fact that Challe emphasizes the univocity

24   Ibid., 175.
25   Ibid., 115.
26   Ibid., 555.
27   Ibid., 569.
28   Ibid., 573.
29   Ibid., 569.

in man and God, albeit to varying degrees and different extensions from one to the other. "Evidence must be preferred to uncertainty, clarity to obscurity," and, therefore, "God is just from the justice that we know ourselves."[30] For him it follows that it is "highly doubtful" "that such a book [as the Bible] is the work of God, and that such a man [as Moses] might possess His specific commands."[31] In fact, all of the books alleged to be sacred and all of the religions that pretend to be revealed show up with specific claims that are incompatible with the universality of true reason. Worse still, they present us with contradictions, mysteries or outright absurdities, which are absolutely impossible to reconcile with the authority of reason, whose source, as we have seen, is directly divine. Malebranchism is then metaphysically lightened (first of all, Challe does not commit himself to the doubtful theory of the vision of ideas in God), separated from Christian theology to which it had been married, but still underpins some pillars of Challe's system, such as the primacy of reason, its univocity and the requirement of regularity and simplicity in the divine action.

Another 17th-century philosopher and theologian is directly attacked: Blaise Pascal. What we are witnessing in Challe's work is the elimination of the argument embodied in Pascal's "wager," although the author's name is not explicitly mentioned. Indeed, it is the scrutiny of rational arguments that highlights the disproportion between the two stakes in the wager, so that only reason, and not bet, can provide men with a safe choice:

> Between two dangerous propositions, between two opposing parties, where great risks are involved, nothing less than a proof will suffice to convince a wise man. To make God out of three distinct parts, even if He is not composed of them; to love God, even if it is not true that he is God … is as dangerous as disbelieving all of these things if they are true.[32]

And even if the Pascalian argument were valid (which it is not), it would still be necessary to determine which of the numerous religions we ought to adopt in our wager, since "this reasoning is identical in the mouth of the mufti and the pope, the rabbi and the talapoin, the parish priest and the minister." Wager's argument is therefore "a ghost of an argument that decides nothing."[33]

---

30   Ibid., 148.
31   Ibid., 151.
32   Ibid., 150.
33   Ibid., 105.

3   Reason's Religion against Artificial Religion

Armed with a cast-iron theological guarantee, as in the best Cartesian tradition, Challe proposes a syllogism whose objective is to validate beyond any
shadow of a doubt the power of human reason, causing it to flow from an
enlightened conception of the divine and of its relationship with the humankind. The dogmatic rationalism of the treatise is based on the Malebranchian
principle according to which divine reason is directly accessible to human reason, although the author of the *Difficultés* does not wish to commit himself to
supporting a complex and overly sophisticated doctrine such as that of the
vision of ideas in God, which was the core of Malebranche's theological epistemology. Challe prefers, instead, more flexible and general formulations, such
as the recommendation, when seeking truth, "to enter into oneself," in order to
consult "the perfect being with whom our intelligence is united."[34] As Challe
writes in a syllogistic form:

> Everything done by an infinitely powerful and infinitely wise being is
> perfect in relation to its end.
> The infinitely wise and infinitely powerful being has given us reason
> with which to distinguish truth from error.
> Reason therefore allows us to distinguish truth from error.[35]

When it comes to history, and not to reason, Challe sets out arguments worthy
of a Pyrrhonist, such as the following: "All facts are uncertain. The artificial
religions are based on facts. Therefore, they are uncertain. Thus, by following
them, we are in danger of being in error."[36] All the time Challe contrasts "seeing" and "knowing" with "believing."

The *Difficultés* ultimately invalidate all the "artificial" religions, using another
argument, also typically Malebranchian in nature, according to which "God
always takes the simplest and shortest path," which means that He "has not
taken the path of books and human speech," with the consequence that the
religions based on these "have not come through the ways of God." In other
words, "they have not come from God."[37] In an entirely coherent manner, this
approach leads to a "refutation of the faith"[38] and a demolition of Christian
theology, including the rationalist form that it had assumed in the thought of

---

34   Ibid., 569.
35   Ibid., 145.
36   Ibid., 175.
37   Ibid., 215.
38   Ibid., 239.

Malebranche. Challe describes this under the highly ironic heading: "The admirable discoveries of the Christian philosophers by the light of the Gospel."[39]

> To believe is not to know, it is not to see: to believe implies uncertainty. I mean demonstratively knowing, I mean seeing from the point of view of the mind, for which I know no term, since those of understanding, and of comprehending do not express this view. I know, I see that the three angles of a triangle are equal to two rights, I believe that Alexander defeated Darius, and conquered Persia.
>
> Metaphysical truths, essential truths, eternal and necessary, are seen from this view of the mind, they are present in it, it holds them, it looks at them, it ponders them, it considers them, so to speak, it turns them, and it handles them. They leave no doubt, no shadow of uncertainty, we are entirely convinced with the most perfect assurance. This conviction is not susceptible of more or less, it is located at the last degree, we are sure that we will never change on this article, namely that all intelligent beings and God himself sees the same thing. One must not have either fear or hope of finding the opposite.[40]

The *Difficultés* also contain several major theses of prior clandestine deism, such as the rejection of the concept of the corruption of nature as a consequence of sin, and the resultant superfluity of a redeemer. The very foundations of the Christian theology based on sin, sacrifice and redemption are destroyed by this rejection. To explain evil or bad behaviors, in place of original sin, Challe creates a theoretical apparatus that clearly reminds us of the Cartesian and mechanist philosophy of the 17th century. Although men are not always just or rational, this may be explained in his view by the duality of body and soul that constitutes their nature, without the necessity of relying, as in Malebranche, on the concept of Adam's sin that would have changed the subordination of the senses to the mind and brought about disorder instead of an orderly relation:

> It is fundamental to man to possess and to experience conflict because he is essentially composed of different parts, but this combination, considered as a whole, is correctly balanced ... To rational minds, it is a beautiful, natural and simple machine, whose contradictions constitute its essence, and render it capable of shooting arrows with a violence and speed that

---

39   Ibid., 506.
40   Ibid., 175.

the strength of man is not capable of attaining; this being the objective and intention of the inventor, whose goal is unique and very simple.[41]

Moreover, if we reflect on the univocal concept of justice that man shares with God, we are forced to admit that "the narrative of Adam's sin destroys itself,"[42] since it involves the transfer of punishment to those who were not responsible for the transgression.

Man is composed of a mechanical body and an insubstantial, and consequently immortal, spirit; he possesses in himself the sense of right and wrong independently of any human convention. Similarly, he also experiences in himself the undeniable sense of freedom: "Man is absolutely free in all of his actions," even when "swept away by the most violent passion."[43] The man God has created exists in order to administer His justice. This is his "final cause."[44] Challe then provides a summary of his system:

> Let us therefore restrict ourselves to the indisputable general principles that there is a God who is the author of all things, who will reward virtue and punish vice; that there is no other virtue than to love God within one's self, from the bottom of one's heart and with all the effort of which our minds are capable, and secondly to behave on every occasion towards other men in the way that we might reasonably expect others to behave towards us, all for the purpose of earning the approval of God; and, finally, that the contrary is the vice that God condemns and punishes; in short, there is no religion other than that which is dictated to us by pure reason, dispassionately, without self-interest and without any prompting, and no virtue except justice, and no vice except injustice.[45]

Going back below Malebranche's theological philosophy, Challe gets rid of occasionalism, the particular theory of causality espoused by the Oratorian, and rediscovers a Cartesian view of man, both governed by the mechanical laws but free in his will. For Challe, occasionalism turns out to be "obscure" and "curious," and fundamentally useless for understanding human conduct. While retaining a certain metaphysical dualism in the human "compound," the author sees in it neither a drama nor the consequences of sin, but the result of a nature that needs a certain tension between different elements to reach the

---

41   Ibid., 507.
42   Ibid., 520.
43   Ibid., 600–9.
44   Ibid., 609–613.
45   Ibid., 700.

balance. Here dualism is "naturalized," in the sense that it holds no theological or pejorative meaning due to a supposed original fall.

4   Critique of Christianity

Some recent commentaries have sought to interpret the *Difficultés* either as a stage in Challe's hypothetical "spiritual career" or as the simple, although admittedly brutal and spontaneous, reaction of a Catholic shocked by the corruption of his church. In our view, this is to forget both the philosophical foundations and the virulently anti-Christian character of the manuscript. Challe's religion is, as Geneviève Artigas-Menant has explained, "devoid of Christ, devoid of revelation, devoid of redemption, devoid of dogma, devoid of miracles, devoid of saints, devoid of clergy, devoid of the pope."[46] Indeed, the author of the *Difficultés* – according to the version found in the Munich manuscript, the most complete that we possess – is not Catholic because he is not Christian. He supplies his own highly specific criticisms of all the dogmas and articles of the Christian faith. This is not straightforward anti-clericalism, even though certain colourful passages constitute admirable examples of anti-clerical invective, but an orchestrated attack against the whole of Christianity, and the Bible in particular.

He denounces the New Testament in this way:

> Nothing is more ill-conceived, disordered, disconnected, poorly expressed, poor language, unnecessary repetitions, omissions of essential elements; nothing is more defective, contradictions, gibberish, misquotations, etc.[47]

Challe rejects the very notion of a redeemer who would actually leave men as they are; with all their ceremonies, the Christians fail to modify their behavior.[48] The narrative of the birth of Christ is a "fiction," as is its genealogy.[49] Nor is there anything remarkable about Christ's morality:

> He said nothing new, nothing that the Jews might not ordinarily have preached ... All of these proverbs, these parables, these teachings, baptism, and even that which we call the Eucharist or the Lord's Supper are merely

---

46   Geneviève Artigas-Menant, "La prière dans les *Difficultés sur la religion*," in *Autour de Robert Challe*, 270.

47   Challe, *Difficultés sur la religion*, 343–4.

48   Ibid., 353–4.

49   Ibid., 354–9.

old ceremonies drawn from Jewish custom. Any reasonable sayings there might be, anything good, and clearly expressed, were employed by J.C. in the same way that our peasants often speak, sometimes randomly, and highly pertinently.[50]

Christianity, according to Challe, has contributed nothing to social life. On the contrary, it has generated poverty, through the growth of the clergy and religious orders.

The narrative of the death, resurrection and ascension of Jesus Christ suffers the same fate at the hands of our author; the Trinity is an "extravagant" dogma; the Last Judgment, a "calamity,"[51] predestination an incomprehensible paradox.[52] Satan is reduced to a folkloric animal;[53] the miracles of Christ and his apostles are mere fables;[54] the fulfilment of the prophecies, a skillful and ambiguous application of the texts.[55] More generally, there is a profound incompatibility between reason and the content of Christian belief, with every effort to reconcile them (such as that of Malebranche, whom he addresses directly) being doomed to failure.

There is no doubt: the author is not Christian, and his deistic system is incompatible with the Christian religion. According to Challe, man is sufficient in himself. Hence, his reason and his conscience allow him to earn his salvation, and, in accordance with his justice and the laws that he himself has established, God owes this salvation to man and cannot refuse it to him.

5   "A System of Religion Based Metaphysically on the Light
     of Nature and Not on Facts"

There is also a *pars construens* in Challe's work. Having dismantled the very concept of revealed religion (in Book II), and destroyed Christian theology (principally in Book III), the author of the *Difficultés* does not shy away from a more constructive task. Accordingly, in Book IV he presents "a system of religion based metaphysically on the light of nature and not on facts."[56] The "system" described in the manuscript is rooted in the argument of order in the universe, which is sufficient, he states, to demonstrate the existence of

---

50   Ibid., 361–2.
51   Ibid., 405–420.
52   Ibid., 420–1.
53   Ibid., 422.
54   Ibid., 426–443.
55   Ibid., 444–452.
56   Ibid., 555.

a supreme divine intelligence and to overcome the "obstinate or deranged freethinkers," who are persuaded that the "machine of the world" can be explained by "the moving force," or "blind strength," of matter.[57] In opposition to them, Challe re-establishes the great truths of the most refined philosophical theology,[58] despite the difficulties making the creation an incomprehensible idea. He asserts that the attributes of God are essentially wisdom and power, while goodness is subsumed within His justice; that "the immediate object of the designs of God" is man, while "the material and mechanical universe" is governed solely by the autonomous laws of physics; that the soul is spiritual and immortal. "Man," concludes Challe, "is absolutely free in all of his actions."[59] Thus, he is not subject to material necessity, nor to the species of theological determinism embodied in predestination, flatly rejected by the author of the *Difficultés*. The principal argument that Challe adduces in favor of human freedom is that of an internal "sentiment":

> The sentiment one has of one's own freedom, and that of others, is a spiritual sentiment, independent of the senses, which, far from being opposed by reasoning based on first principles, possesses in itself the purest light of reason whose power is felt generally by all men, and for which there is always opportunity for it to be tested.[60]

Therefore, morality represents one of the fundamental elements within the "system," which is all the more important given that Challe maintains the thesis of a God judging with equity and rewarding human actions. Indeed, he makes it the basis of his natural religion, while rejecting the concept of eternal punishment, which is in his view entirely contrary to the attributes of justice and goodness characteristic of God. Contrary to the Spinozist tendency, which preferred an impersonal divinity, inextricably interwoven with the world, Challe appears to reconnect with the concept of a personal God, who is free but also profoundly rational, in accordance with Malebranche's principle of conformity to the order established by reason. This is why, as Malebranche had already previously done, Challe also breaks with the Cartesian doctrine of the free creation of eternal truths by God ("believing that the essences are arbitrary" is, in his opinion, "an extravagance and an absurdity"[61]), with all that such a doctrine entails from both a speculative perspective ("He [God] can

---

57   Ibid., 564.
58   Ibid., 569.
59   Ibid., 601.
60   Ibid.
61   Ibid., 650–1.

indeed make a circle from a square, but he cannot make a square circle"[62]) and a moral point of view (the notions of good and evil would depend on God's will). The polemic against Descartes concerning this point is particularly clear and indicative of the decisive change effected by Malebranche in relation to the concept of God, since the Oratorian too rejected this voluntarist aspects of Descartes' philosophy.

> If it is true that Mr. Descartes ever said the opposite, as I believe I have heard he said, I would bet everything except my eternal salvation, he unleashed an extravagance and an absurdity that he saw well that no one would adopt, and in which cultivated people would not believe him capable of giving, to get away from the cries of the priests, who would cry that his philosophy was not favorable to religion.[63]
>
> Wanting to deepen the essences by dint of reasoning, and piling up subtleties upon subtleties, is to tire oneself out looking for what one holds. But why is this so? What are essences? A thing may or may not be, but once it is, it is a certain thing. Can it be otherwise? It is the simpler things that are most easily and clearly understood, and yet that we can explain less.[64]

According to Challe, the principle of the fundamental univocity of reason can never be disregarded, and the same must, therefore, also apply to the univocity of the moral attributes between God and man. This principle constitutes the true cornerstone of the entire structure of his work. In other words, if we abandon this univocity, God becomes "a deceiver, the very essence of deception, who has given men the clearest and most distinct opinions against truth."[65] Although there are differences of degree in reason and morality, such as from the less perfect to the more perfect, it is nevertheless legitimate to assert that human justice "is of the same species as divine justice."[66] Conversely, if we create a gulf between man and God, and if we affirm that "the justice of God is entirely different from what we mean by the word 'justice', and even actually the opposite," we will be constrained to say the same thing regarding His existence and all of His attributes.[67] Hence, God would ultimately exist "while not existing," His freedom would be transformed into "necessity," His power would

---

62   Ibid.
63   Ibid.
64   Ibid.
65   Ibid., 516.
66   Ibid., 520.
67   Ibid., 519.

become powerlessness, His wisdom a way of "acting without choice and out of necessity." In other words, we would fall back into the abyss of Spinozism. Even a "doctor of fantasies" who sought to defend such theses would finally have to bow to the evidence of reason and admit "that God is just in accordance with the justice familiar to us" since "that which is in God is more perfect, but it is still the same concept."[68]

In Challe's work, regardless of whether he is referring to Descartes, for his thesis about the creation of eternal truths, or Pascal, charged with being a "great papist genius and religious bigot" for having called "our justice despicable justice on account of original sin,"[69] or the histrionic supporters of the "horror of that predestination,"[70] the accusation of deception is continually turned against the philosophers and theologians that overemphasize the motifs of God's transcendence, to the point of asserting a fully-fledged heterogeneity, or divergence in meaning, of reason between the creatures and the creator. These philosophers ultimately make God "the author of evil," akin to a tyrant. In conclusion, "in the system established by the Christians, and perhaps that of all the false religions," it proves impossible to "justify the divinity" when faced with the existence of evil.[71] By contrast, "in natural law," writes Challe, "my salvation is easy,"[72] and God cannot be blamed if I behave badly.

All the difficulties surrounding the existence of evil that Pierre Bayle had expanded upon in the *Dictionnaire*, are resolved, in Challe's opinion, in an interpretation that situates both the goodness of God and human freedom at the center of philosophy, against the "horrors" and "monstrous ideas" espoused by some Christian theologians. The author of the *Difficultés* summarizes his fundamentally optimistic view of man, imbued with a strong sense of the power of liberty illuminated by reason, as follows:

> Everything that God has done is most just and good. He has made beings capable of good and evil. He has given them knowledge of both. He has given them the capacity to choose between them, and the grounds for this choice by informing them of what the outcome would be. Reason and conscience have dictated all of this.[73]

---

68   Ibid.
69   Ibid., 515.
70   Ibid., 687.
71   Ibid., 673.
72   Ibid., 674.
73   Ibid.

6   A New Moral and Public Religion

Strongly armed with this reason of Malebranchian origin, which invites us to conceive of God as "fundamental justice," Challe identifies "the foundation of all morality" in the certainty that He "will judge us in accordance with a sovereign and precise equity, and that our only concern is, consequently, the practice of virtue."[74] It is not indicated in the manuscript how this retribution will be made, nor is any view on the afterlife advanced. In any case, God is the ultimate warrantor of the idea of justice in the world.

This idea forms the basis not only of the "system," but also of the practical implementation of effective communal life. Challe baulks at a heavy institutionalizing of natural religion and explicitly refuses the notion of a clergy specially designated for that purpose. He nevertheless envisages a genuine reform of beliefs, built on a handful of visible institutions yet reduced to a minimum: a highly simplified catechism, written into "a few lines" and governed by "pure reason," a "worship" that allows the "interior religion" to be displayed to the outside in all of its purity, public assemblies overseen by "a few of the wisest, most virtuous, and most enlightened people," with the very strict proviso that they fulfil "their vocation as ministers."[75]

He even acknowledges the utility of sculpting clearly expressed formulae of natural religion in marble or bronze. These are, however, merely concessions to the external requirements of communal life, the heart of religion remaining rational knowledge and the virtuous practice of the good, which – according to the author – would still be possible even if God did not exist; even in this case, the atheists "would still have an understanding of good and evil. They would not, however, have the same motivations for making their choices,"[76] since they would be deprived of the promise of punishments and rewards in the hereafter.

The "religion" preached by Challe also has a domestic dimension, since he charges the "head of the family" with performing a "short meditation" in front of the family members, inviting them to examine their actions and to repent, and finally to offer a "prayer," "in order to give the children and most uncouth members of the household a form, not of a dangerous ideal, but of an example to be imitated, and not followed to the letter."[77] In truth, genuine worship is dependent solely on the intelligence and will of the individual, but is useful to

---

74   Ibid., 577.
75   Ibid., 710.
76   Ibid., 673.
77   Ibid., 702.

reinforce common belief about God and morality by some simple rituals that are rather forms of meditation or self-examination.

> We do not need any exterior [worship], and a specific interior one is not absolutely necessary. The common feeling about worshiping God and planning to do only what He approves of is enough. But it is good to devote a quarter of an hour a day to remembering His principles in order to strengthen oneself in his own resolution to be faithful to God; especially, to get motivated about the true repentance of the cases in which one has missed. This makes that the evening is preferable to the morning.[78]

Malebranche's influence had already surfaced on occasion among the philosophical manuscripts, as a bit earlier in the treatise by Yves de Vallone (*La Religion du Chrétien conduit par la raison éternelle*, ca. 1704–1705), but it is only with the *Difficultés* of Robert Challe that, for the first time, one is confronted with a form of deism deeply influenced by the reading of Malebranche.[79] Of course, Challe is highly selective in his theoretical choices and his concerns are far removed from the original speculative orientation of Malebranche vis-à-vis positive Christian theology. His interest is in pure philosophy, and he rejects the "philosophical" explanations of the revealed theology that Malebranche had developed at length on the subjects of original sin, the distribution of grace, occasionalism, incarnation, redemption, and theodicy. Besides simplifying Malebranche's metaphysics and recovering its original Cartesian inspiration, Challe disentangles reason from faith, which Malebranche had on the contrary tried to melt in one single complex.

In Challe's view, faith is not a source of rational truth. It is, on the contrary, depicted as "a monster to be opposed, a monster stranger and less imaginable than the mythical chimera."[80] In philosophy, the author of the *Difficultés* remains nevertheless impervious to philosophical contributions of a different origin. Thus, Spinoza is rejected as an "atheist" who introduced "fate and necessity into men's actions";[81] Locke is never mentioned, and neither is his empiricism. The same distance is maintained in relation to the classic libertine themes. The moral relativism and skepticism of these authors, their

---

78   Ibid.
79   In Yves de Vallone's text, Malebranchian ideas are mingled with a prevailing influence from Spinoza's philosophy (see Paganini, *Introduzione alle filosofie clandestine*, 60–8).
80   Challe, *Difficultés*, 239.
81   Ibid., 57.

manipulation of religion for political aims, their frequent recourse to the topics of deception and imposture in the analysis of beliefs, their attempts at historical reconstructions are overshadowed by an ethical intellectualism based
on reason as a universal criterion. For his trust in the norm of universal reason
in almost every field of human activity (religion, morals, and society), Robert
Challe represents the link between Cartesianism and Enlightenment and since
his "*Système de religion fondé métaphysiquement sur les lumières naturelles*"
is radical indeed, he features also as a link between Cartesian deism and radical Enlightenment. Only a true project of political reformation is missing in the
Réflexions, even though the strong criticism of intolerance and the alliance
between throne and altar contains an explicit condemnation of the Catholic
and monarchical *Ancien Régime*, in the form it took on under the reign of Louis
XIV. As we are going to see in the conclusions, this kind of "radical" deism is
not devoid of significant consequences at the level of a new sociability, which
is strongly opposed to the old and hierarchical sociability of the French ecclesiastical regime.

7   Complicating Historical Categories: How to Become Radical while
        Being Cartesian and Deist

The narratives of the Enlightenment seem to be currently polarized between
two different versions: on the one hand, the radical, fundamentally secular,
Spinozist and democratic version advocated by Jonathan Israel; on the other
hand, a renewed attention to the religious Enlightenment, in its various confessional and philosophical variants.[82] Cartesianism and deism have both
paid the price of this polarization. Of the first, the supporters of "radicalism"
have valued at most the materialistic potential of Descartes' physics (in the
wake of the famous study by Aram Vartanian[83]) or the idea of a universally
accessible reason, against the elitism of the "moderates." Of the second, the
anti-Christian charge has been rightly underlined, but at the same time its
providentialism has often been associated with a social and political function

---

82   See William J. Bulman and Robert G. Ingram (eds.), *God in the Enlightenment* (Oxford: 2016);
      David Sorkin, *The Religious Enlightenment: Protestants, Jews, and Catholics from London to
      Vienna* (Princeton: 2008); Jeffrey D. Burson and Ulrich L. Lehner (eds.), *Enlightenment
      and Catholicism. A Transnational History* (Notre Dame: 2014); Jeffrey D. Burson, *The Rise
      and Fall of Theological Enlightenment: Jean-Martin de Prades and Ideological Polarization
      in Eighteenth-Century France* (Notre Dame: 2010).
83   Aram Vartanian, *Diderot and Descartes. A Study of Scientific Naturalism in the Enlighten-
      ment* (Princeton: 1953).

in support of the social order. In comparison with classical Protestant and Catholic theologies, deism seems furthermore to be poor in contents and most often devoid of authentic religious significance. Besides, clandestine deism has been neglected by the classic and more recent histories of 18th-century ideas, whose paradigms continue to be Voltaire on the French side[84] and the so-called "deists" on the English one.

Wayne Hudson has pointed out that deism, like atheism, is not a natural kind, having different meanings in different contexts, and that it must therefore be historicized.[85] In fact, deists ranged from the simple statement of the existence of a first cause, not necessarily transcendent to the world (think of various forms of pantheism) to the doctrine that God intervenes in the world, and this again in different ways: as a creator, as an architect, or as a judge that is supposed to retribute human actions. It is clear thus that one single standard attribution of definitional account is historically mistaken, yet one core meaning is recurrent from the age of Bodin to that of Challe and then Voltaire: insofar as deism is a natural and rational religion, it is not only independent of, but also contrasts with, any particular revelation, claiming that natural reason is enough to reach a right conception of divinity, to rule human morality and so to provide "salvation," however one means that (in mundane or extramundane terms). Moreover, divine retribution, when it is accepted, is conceived rather as a motivational support enforcing the dictates of reason than as the true core of the moral law.

Considering the wide range of positions that deism encompasses (maybe it would be better to speak of deisms, plural), and the necessity of finding more complex patterns to define it in historical terms (of course, there is not some sort of an "essence" of deism), the choice of focusing on the figure of Robert Challe has a particular value: it is not only due to fill a gap in scholarship (this author is rarely studied in comprehensive histories of 18th-century deism), but it also has the ambition of contributing to redesign the divide between "radical" and "moderate" Enlightenment, "religious" and "secular" 18th-century philosophy.

---

84 Still now, the most comprehensive history of French deism is: Christopher J. Betts, *Early Deism in France. From the So-Called 'deistes' of Lyon (1564) to Voltaire's* Lettres philosophiques *(1734)* (The Hague: 1984), 137–156 on Challe; more recently, the special issue of *La Lettre clandestine* 21 (2013) on "Déismes et déistes à l'âge classique," 11–304. For a European perspective, see Winfried Schröder (ed.), *Gestalten des Deismus in Europa. Günter Gawlick zum 80. Geburtstag* (Wiesbaden: 2013).

85 Wayne Hudson, Diego Lucci and Jeffrey R. Wigelsworth (eds.), *Atheism and Deism Revalued. Heterodox Religious Identities in Britain, 1650–1800* (Farnham: 2014), esp. 19–23.

The Challe "case" complicates and upsets these too general partitions and it is a pity, and it is worth bringing to the attention of Enlightenment scholars, outside the circles of the history of French literature where it is more considered. Challe's "anomalies" with respect to the prevailing narratives of the birth of the Enlightenment are evident and very significant. We can summarize them in four points.

a.   From a philosophical point of view, Challe represents both a "challenge" to, and at the same time a "revival" of, Malebranche and Cartesianism. From these authors he takes up some relevant themes (intransigent rationalism, the universality of reason as opposed to the particularity of history and positive religions, soul-body dualism, a spiritual and perfectionist conception of God, divine retribution) (Challe, however, refuses as unjust the idea of eternal punishment). On the other hand, Challe refuses Malebranche's mixture of philosophy and theology that ended up theologizing reason. Thus, the vision of ideas in God, the history of original sin and redemption, occasionalism and distribution of grace are Malebranche's main topics that are expunged from the "system of natural religion." On many points the author of the *Difficultés* returns to the original inspiration of Descartes leaving aside the major theological innovations suggested by Malebranche. In this sense we can speak of "radical Cartesianism"[86] in a double meaning: (i) the author goes back to the "roots" of this philosophy (prominence of understanding, search for intellectual evidence, universality of reason): (ii) he uses this philosophical Cartesianism to discredit the credentials of positive religions and in particular against Christianity. So doing, instead of putting philosophy at the service of Christian theology, as Malebranche on the contrary did, he turns philosophical evidence against historical, traditional and supposedly transcendent values of any faith. In the name of reason and natural light, Challe proposes a refined conception of divinity and morality that only partly sides with Malebranche, when he rejects, like him,

---

86   Tad Schmaltz adopted the label "radical Cartesianism" to describe the reception of Descartes by Desgabets and Régis (see Tad Schmaltz, *Radical Cartesianism: The French Reception of Descartes* (Cambridge, Eng.: 2002), 1–18). My categorization is altogether different from that of Schmaltz. According to him, Desgabets and Régis are "radical" in that they retain Descartes' voluntarism (free creation of essences) and claim that all human thought derives from the soul-body union. There is in them nothing that even from far could hint to the topic of natural and rational religion, and – as we have seen – free creation of essences is rejected by Challe. This latter is not even mentioned either in Schmaltz's book or in the more recent *Oxford Handbook of Descartes and Cartesianism*, eds. Steven Nadler, Tad Schmaltz and Delphine Antoine-Mahut (Oxford: 2019).

Descartes' theological voluntarism (free creation of eternal truths). This kind of voluntarism would represent, according to Challe, a threat to reason and morality, making them depend on an arbitrary decision of God. Therefore, his relation with Malebranche is complex and twofold: on the one hand, Challe takes from him all that can strengthen the role of reason and purify the idea of God and religion from any arbitrariness contrary to rationality and justice; on the other, he turns the requirements of this same rationality against the synthesis of philosophy and Christian theology made by Malebranche.

b.   From the religious point of view, Challe's rational religion or deism (take care, however, that he never uses this term which will come into vogue later with Voltaire and with the translation of the English deists) contains an authentic religious nucleus: a precise conception of God as creator and judge (He has arranged the physical world, but it does not seem that providence plays any role in human history): certainly, the architect of the universe but also a perfect being. Its main function is to guarantee the validity of reason (human reason is homogeneous to divine reason and enlightened by it) and to ensure the foundations of morality. However, since the attainment of moral knowledge is the result of rational research, without any special revelation, Challe can declare, following Bayle, that even the atheist is capable of conceiving the basic moral notions. This rational God is the object of love, reverence, fear and joy, but all these feelings are basically founded on reason: "there is no religion other than that which is dictated by pure reason, dispassionately, without self-interest," as well as virtues are condensed in justice.[87] For all these reasons, Challe's deistic religiosity cannot be equivocated as a camouflage or an instrumental ideology aimed at ensuring social order and political stability. For his sincerity and authentic philosophical belief in a rational God and thanks to his Cartesian formation, Challe definitely parted company with the ambiguities and double-sided positions of the French libertines.

c.   Challe is one of the most radical and clear-cut anti-Christian authors, but he is not an atheist. Due to his philosophical origins, his battle takes place mainly on a philosophical-rational ground, rather than a historical-exegetical one (as happens instead in many English deists). This strong opposition of reason and history, which Challe inherits from Descartes and Malebranche, makes him impervious to the search for historical explanations of the origins of positive religions, an attempt that was

---

87   Challe, *Difficultés*, 700.

already present in libertine texts or in a clandestine atheist one like the *Theophrastus redivivus*. It cannot therefore be said that its Cartesian foundations and its deistic orientation contributed to "moderate" the polemic against established religions, rather they gave it a strongly philosophical feature, inspired by what Bayle called "the culture of evidence."

d.   From the ideological point of view, the foundations of Challe's arguments are democratic, not in a political but social sense, to the extent that he addresses human reason that Descartes had declared to be present in everyone. The author abandons elitism that characterized philosophical speculation and to a large extent also free thought between the Middle Ages, the Renaissance and the early 17th century. Differently from Spinoza (who is rejected by Challe), these democratic roots do not find a corresponding political development in the *Difficultés*. As we have already said, there is no explicit political project in the *Difficultés*. However, one should not underestimate the social and indirectly political import of Challe's deism. In fact, the author does not limit himself to proposing theoretical arguments.[88] His project also contains social forms of public worship, a "catechism of reason" for less cultivated people, prayer as a form of meditation, assembly meetings for the teaching of fundamental truths and a sort of domestic preaching managed by the head of the family. All this without sacred books, institutional clergy, priestly hierarchy and institutional organization. Taking into account the importance that the model of institutional church had in the *Ancien Régime* and particularly in France, as a pillar of the social and political order, Challe's proposal for a publicly practiced rational religion has a double interest: on the one hand, it gives concreteness to the deistic ideal, often accused of abstractness, and makes it accessible not only to intellectuals and educated elite, but also to the people; on the other, it breaks the alliance between throne and altar by re-establishing religious sociability on an egalitarian and democratic basis. The whole ritual and ceremonial apparatus are reduced to minimum, all the more so as Challe claims the superiority of interior worship, understood as moral meditation. More than a civil religion with a political value, in Challe's work we find out a moral religion with social value, while the political consequences remain implicit, being in any case outside the scope of the *Difficultés*. Before the full Enlightenment, rarely, not even the most radical thinkers have

---

88   For an analysis of the social virtue as it is advocated by Challe and counterposed to traditional and religious virtues, see Susana Maria Seguin, "Sociabilité philosophique et philosophie clandestine: le cas Robert Challe," in *Robert Challe et la sociabilité de son temps*, ed. Maria Susana Seguin (Montpellier: 2005), 129–139.

thought of giving public, universal and democratic visibility to the religion of reason against, and in the place of, institutional faiths. It is true that Challe's proposal remains as it is only a suggestion, but it is remarkable for its universality, at least in principle. Contemporary comparable forms of heterodox sociability (think of the Freemasonry or the "*sodalitas*" evoked by Toland in the *Pantheisticon*) were all limited to restricted societies, with a strong esoteric and mystical connotation, far removed from Challe's plain and open rationalism.[89]

In conclusion, can one be deist, Cartesian, religious, democratic in the social sense, universalist and at the same time a "radical" thinker, without being Spinozist and also before Voltaire? The Challe case leads us to answer: yes, one can.

References

Artigas-Menant, Geneviève, "Anonymat et autobiographie intellectuelle: Robert Challe," in *Du secret des clandestins à la propagande voltairienne*, ed. Geneviève Artigas-Menant (Paris: 2001), 65–160.

Artigas-Menant, Geneviève, "La prière dans les *Difficultés sur la religion*," in *Autour de Robert Challe. Actes du colloque de Chartres (20–22 juin 1991)*, ed. Frédéric Deloffre (Paris: 1993), 257–270.

Betts, Christopher J., *Early Deism in France. From the So-Called 'deistes' of Lyon (1564) to Voltaire's* Lettres philosophiques *(1734)* (The Hague: 1984).

Bulman, William J., Robert G. Ingram (eds.), *God in the Enlightenment* (Oxford: 2016).

Burson, Jeffrey D., *The Rise and Fall of Theological Enlightenment: Jean-Martin de Prades and Ideological Polarization in Eighteenth-Century France* (Notre Dame: 2010).

Burson, Jeffrey D., Ulrich L. Lehner (eds.), *Enlightenment and Catholicism. A Transnational History* (Notre Dame: 2014).

Canziani, Guido, Gianni Paganini (eds.), *Theophrastus redivivus*, 2 vols. (Florence: 1981–1982).

Challe, Robert, *Difficultés sur la religion proposées au Père Malebranche* (Geneva: 2000).

Challe, Robert, *Journal d'un voyage fait aux Indes orientales, par une escadre de six vaisseaux commandés par M. Du Quesne, depuis le 24 février 1690 jusqu'au 20 août 1691, par ordre de la Compagnie des Indes orientales* (Rouen: 1721); the modern edition: *Journal d'un voyage fait aux Indes orientales (du 24 février 1690 au 10 août 1691)*, 2 vols. (Paris: 2002).

Cormier, Jacques, *L'Atelier de Robert Challe* (Paris: 2010).

---

89   For an overview of the period, see Gianni Paganini, *De Bayle à Hume. Tolérance, hypothèses, systèmes* (Paris: 2022).

Cormier, Jacques, Jan Herman and Paul Pelckmans (eds.), *Robert Challe: sources et héritage* (Paris: 2003).

Deloffre, Frédéric (ed.), *Autour de Robert Challe* (Paris: 1993).

Ducheyne, Steffen (ed.), *Reassessing the Radical Enlightenment* (London: 2018).

Gregory, Tullio, *Theophrastus redivivus. Erudizione e ateismo nel Seicento* (Napoli: 1979).

Hudson, Wayne, Diego Lucci and Jeffrey R. Wigelsworth (eds.), *Atheism and Deism Revalued. Heterodox Religious Identities in Britain, 1650–1800* (Farnham: 2014).

Israel, Jonathan I., *Democratic Enlightenment: Philosophy, Revolution, and Human Rights, 1750–1790* (Oxford: 2011).

Israel, Jonathan I., *Enlightenment Contested: Philosophy, Modernity, and the Emancipation of Man, 1670–1752* (Oxford: 2006).

Israel, Jonathan I., *Radical Enlightenment: Philosophy and the Making of Modernity, 1650–1750* (Oxford: 2001).

Israel, Jonathan I., Martin Mulsow (eds.), *Radikalaufklärung* (Berlin: 2014).

Jacob, Margaret C., *The Radical Enlightenment: Pantheists, Freemasons, and Republicans* (London: 1981; 2nd ed.: 2003).

La Lettre clandestine 21 (2013): "Déismes et déistes à l'âge classique."

La Lettre clandestine 12 (2003): "Lecteurs et collectionneurs de textes clandestins à l'âge classique."

Laursen, John Christian, "Moderne aus dem Untergrund: Radikale Frühaufklärung in Deutschland, 1680–1720 (review)," *Journal of the History of Philosophy* 3/41 (2003): 419–420.

Mulsow, Martin, *Radikale Frühaufklärung in Deutschland 1680–1720*, 2 vols. (Göttingen: 2018).

Mulsow, Martin, *Moderne aus dem Untergrund. Radikale Frühaufklärung in Deutschland, 1680–1720* (Hamburg: 2002). English translation: *Enlightenment Underground: Radical Germany, 1680–1720* (Charlottesville: 2015).

Nadler, Steven, Tad Schmaltz and Delphine Antoine-Mahut (eds.), *Oxford Handbook of Descartes and Cartesianism* (Oxford: 2019).

Paganini, Gianni, *De Bayle à Hume. Tolérance, hypothèses, systèmes* (Paris: 2022).

Paganini, Gianni, "Jean Bodin's Universalism and the Twofold Foundations of Natural Religion: A New Reading of the *Colloquium Heptaplomeres*," *Maimonides* (2022): 145–173.

Paganini, Gianni, "What Is a Clandestine Philosophical Manuscript?," in *Clandestine Philosophy. New Studies on Subversive Manuscripts in Early Modern Europe, 1620–1823*, eds. Gianni Paganini, Margaret C. Jacob and John Christian Laursen (Toronto: 2020), 3–19.

Paganini, Gianni, "The First Philosophical Atheistic Treatise: *Theophrastus redivivus* (1659)," in *Clandestine Philosophy. New Studies on Subversive Manuscripts in Early Modern Europe, 1620–1823*, eds. Gianni Paganini, Margaret C. Jacob and John Christian Laursen (Toronto: 2020), 37–83.

Paganini, Gianni, "Les voies du malebranchisme clandestin: Challe, Dumarsais, Terrasson," in *Liberté de conscience et arts de penser (XVIe–XVIIIe siècle). Mélanges en l'honneur d'Antony McKenna*, eds. Christelle Bahier-Porte, Pierre-François Moreau and Delphine Reguig (Paris: 2017), 705–719.

Paganini, Gianni, "Wie aus Gesetzgebern Betrüger werden. Eine philosophische Archäologie des 'radikalen' Libertinismus," in *Radikalaufklärung*, eds. Jonathan Israel and Martin Mulsow (Berlin: 2014), 49–91.

Paganini, Gianni, *Les Philosophies clandestines à l'âge classique* (Paris: 2005); new expanded Italian edition: *Introduzione alle filosofie clandestine* (Rome: 2008).

Paganini, Gianni, "Modernità dalla clandestinità," *Giornale Critico della Filosofia Italiana* 84 (2005): 172–180.

Paganini, Gianni, Margaret C. Jacob and John Christian Laursen (eds.), *Clandestine Philosophy. New Studies on Subversive Manuscripts in Early Modern Europe, 1620–1823* (Toronto: 2020).

Schmaltz, Tad, *Radical Cartesianism: The French Reception of Descartes* (Cambridge, Eng.: 2002).

Schröder, Winfried, "Why, and to What End, Should Historians of Philosophy Study Early Modern Clandestine Texts?," in *Clandestine Philosophy. New Studies on Subversive Manuscripts in Early Modern Europe, 1620–1823*, eds. Gianni Paganini, Margaret C. Jacob and John Christian Laursen (Toronto: 2020), 23–36.

Schröder, Winfried (ed.), *Gestalten des Deismus in Europa. Günter Gawlick zum 80. Geburtstag* (Wiesbaden: 2013).

Secrétan, Catherine, Tristan Dagron and Laurent Bove (eds.), *Qu'est-ce que les Lumières "radicales"? Libertinage, athéisme et spinozisme dans le tournant philosophique de l'âge classique* (Paris: 2007).

Seguin, Susana Maria, "Sociabilité philosophique et philosophie clandestine: le cas Robert Challe," in *Robert Challe et la sociabilité de son temps*, ed. Maria Susana Seguin (Montpellier: 2005), 129–139.

Sorkin, David, *The Religious Enlightenment: Protestants, Jews, and Catholics from London to Vienna* (Princeton: 2008).

Vartanian, Aram, *Diderot and Descartes. A Study of Scientific Naturalism in the Enlightenment* (Princeton: 1953).

CHAPTER 7

More Voltaire Than Rousseau? Deism in the Revolutionary Cults of Reason and the Supreme Being

Mathias Sonnleithner

It was raining cats and dogs in Paris on 11 July 1791. Hence, the celebration of Voltaire's apotheosis started several hours later than planned,[1] and by the end of the day, the cardboard copy of Jean-Antoine Houdon's famous Voltaire statue was missing its head.[2] But it was not only the weather that did not play along with the aims of the organizers. In the preceding months, there had been again and again ideological and practical discussions of whether Voltaire's remains could be brought from his grave in the Scellières Abbey to Paris. The date was postponed again and again.[3] But, all in all, Voltaire's transfer to the Pantheon seemed inevitable for many revolutionaries. Many journals and pamphlets called Voltaire a forerunner of the revolution.[4] Not least, his supposed fight against every prejudice was brought into focus. A celebration in honor of the one who signed his letters often with "crush the infamous,"[5] had therefore to be understood as a provocative answer to the pope who anathematized the whole revolution in spring 1791.[6] The revolutionary theater, too, remembered Voltaire as "the protector of the innocent victims of fanaticism."[7] Therefore,

---

1 See *Archives parlementaires de 1787 à 1860. Recueil complet des débats législatifs & politiques des chambres françaises. Première série (1787 à 1799)*, vol. 28 (Paris: 1887), 121. In the following, I will refer to this edition by the abbreviation *AP*.

2 See Raymond Rockwood, "The Legend of Voltaire and the Cult of the Revolution, 1791," in *Ideas in History. Essays Presented to Louis Gottschalk by His Former Students*, eds. Richard Herr and Harold T. Parker (Durham: 1965), 125.

3 See for the chronology of events Rockwood, "Voltaire," 111–121.

4 See, for instance, the statements cited in Renée Waldinger, *Voltaire and Reform in the Light of the French Revolution* (Geneva: 1959), 82–4, and in Rockwood, "Voltaire," 129.

5 Unless otherwise stated, all translations are my own.

6 Two days after the National Assembly decreed the feast, the *Chronique de Paris* declared that it would be "a triumph of reason over error and impostures." Cited in Rockwood, "Voltaire," 117. According to some sources cited in ibid., 128, there were some iconoclastic acts against images of the popes. Rockwood shows that the anti-clerical front was not the only one the festival was directed against. The flight of the king just a few days earlier leads to the construction of Voltaire as an anti-monarchical thinker.

7 Rockwood, "Voltaire," 113.

according to Raymond Rockwood, the feast was planned in correspondence with Greek and Roman pagan models, and was free from "traditional religious motifs."[8] Rockwood calls it "a mirror of secular devotion."[9] He even claims at one point that Voltaire held an "extreme anti-religious position,"[10] suggesting that there was, in a sense, an intrinsic connection between Voltaire's philosophical thinking and his veneration in revolutionary festive culture.

That the festival planners were concerned with a demonstration of (supposed) classical republican strength can hardly be denied. The choice of the name "Pantheon" for the place where Voltaire (and other important personalities) was to be transferred already speaks for this demonstration. Ardent anticlericalism can also be conceded to this festival.[11]

It would be completely wrong, however, to assert that religion played no positive role at all in the festivities. Almost nothing of this role is documented by Rockwood, but in the contemporary descriptions of the festival it is clear that religious elements showed up on the most different levels: anecdotally,[12] meteorologically,[13] and above all in the planned course of the festival itself. Even the hymn of the festival that was sung at several stations, with a text by Marie-Joseph Chénier and a melody by François-Joseph Gossec, culminated in the following stanzas:

> Great whole, Sovereign God, Nature, Providence,
> Only unchanging and only unlimited being,
> Uncreated creator, supreme intelligence,
> Goodness, Justice, Eternity.

---

8   Ibid., 123.

9   Ibid., 126.

10   Ibid., 112.

11   According to Mona Ozouf, "Voltaire," in *Dictionnaire critique de la Révolution française*, eds. François Furet and Mona Ozouf, vol. 4: *Idées* (Paris: 1992), 527, it was the first revolutionary festival entirely without the participation of the clergy.

12   See *Journal de Paris* 194 (13 July 1791): 778–9: "In the midst of a great number of citizens who had rushed over, a priest shouted with fury: GOD WILL BE AVENGED [sic!]. No anger erupted against this priest; it was said: if he believes that God is offended by the tributes paid to the genius, he is very miserable, and we must have pity on him; if he wants to raise errors that he does not share, he is very guilty, but he is no longer to be feared, and he was gently dismissed."

13   See *Journal de Paris* 194 (13 July 1791): 779: "The Heavens like the People undoubtedly favoured this Apotheosis of Voltaire, but the elements, that is to say, the rain seemed to want at least to delay it."

You made Liberty, Man made Slavery;
But often in his century an inspired mortal
Preserves the sacred deposit of your sublime work
For the following centuries.

God of Liberty, always cherish France;
Fertilize our fields, protect our ramparts;
Grant us peace, and happy abundance
And the eternal Empire of the Arts.

Give us Virtues, Talents, Enlightenment,
Love of our duties, respect for our Rights,
A pure Liberty, and Tutelary Laws
And mores worthy of our Laws.[14]

Voltaire was obviously meant to be such an "inspired mortal,"[15] and was commemorated as someone who preserved the liberty originally given by God and thus created the possibility for God to remain connected to France. Voltaire was described as a fighter for the true religion and that meant that he was a fighter on two fronts: against atheism and against fanaticism. The sarcophagus, pulled by 12 horses on a giant chariot through the muddy streets of Paris, bore (and bears to this day) the inscription:

---

14   *Hymne. Sur la translation du corps de Voltaire au Panthéon. Par M. J. Chénier; Représentant du peuple. Musique de Gossec* (Paris, Bibliothèque nationale de France [BnF], VM7-16910) (s.l.: 1791); a slightly altered, but in content completely identical text version is offered by *Chronique de Paris* 195 (14 July 1791): 788. On the hymn and its tradition, see Pierre Constant, *Les hymnes et chansons de la Révolution* (Paris: 1904), 205–8. In addition, another hymn may have been sung, the text of which came directly from Voltaire himself and was also set to music by Gossec. Religious echoes can be found in this text as well. See Constant, *Hymnes*, 208–213, and Marie-Louise Biver, *Fêtes révolutionnaires à Paris* (Paris: 1979), 42. The lyrics can be found in *Courrier de Paris dans les 83 départemens* 26/12–13 (13 July 1791): 193.

15   This is taken to the extreme by a clergyman who, as a deputy for the religious district of Châtillon-sur-Seine in the National Assembly, demands that Voltaire's remains be transferred to Palestine as a prophet. This speech is shouted down because of its too Christian implications. Factually, however, a certain prophethood of Voltaire is already confirmed in the speech held by the deputy Christin, who obviously knew Voltaire personally. He informed the National Assembly that Voltaire had often told him about premonitions of a revolution. See *AP* 25 (Paris: 1886), 661.

He fought against Atheists and Fanatics
He inspired Tolerance
He demanded Human Rights Against the Servitude of Feudalism.[16]

Quotations from Voltaire's own works, as they were used in the festival, also made clear that his own references to God were quite important. Two separate revolutionary societies each carried a banner emblazoned with verses from Voltaire's play *Le fanatisme ou Mahomet le Prophète* (1743).[17] This was one of Voltaire's five most frequently performed plays in the period between 1789 and 1792, and many spectators would have recognized the quotes.[18] Both referred clearly to God. The one society ran under the motto:

Exterminate, great God, from the earth where we are
All those who take pleasure in spilling the blood of men.[19]

The other used a motto much quoted during the revolution:

All mortals are equal: it is not birth,
It is only virtue that makes the difference.[20]

The context of the latter quote in Voltaire's play clearly indicated the equality of men as guaranteed by the gaze of God:

Do you not know yet, weak and superb man,
That the insensible insect buried under the grass,
And the imperious eagle that soars above the sky,
Shall return into nothingness in the eyes of the Eternal Being?[21]

---

16 See, for instance, the engraving from Jean Baptiste Félix Massard, *Inscriptions du char pour la translation de Voltaire le XI juillet MDCCXCI* (BnF, G-162361) (Paris: 1791).

17 See Voltaire, *Œuvres complètes de Voltaire. Nouvelle édition*, vol. 4 (Paris: 1877), 106–162. In the following, I will refer to this edition of Voltaire's works by the abbreviation *œcv*.

18 See Ling-Ling Sheu, *Voltaire et Rousseau dans le théâtre de la Révolution française (1789–1799)* (Brussels: 2005), 16–20.

19 *Feuille villageoise* 43 (21 July 1791): 108. It seems interesting here, that the journal cites the quote slightly incorrectly. In *Mahomet*, act 3, scene 8, Zopire says: "Exterminate, great Gods ..." Cf. *œcv* 4, 139. It is unclear whether the revolutionary society itself quoted it wrong (perhaps for some monotheistic purpose?) or the journal. According to Sheu, *Voltaire*, 28, it was these two verses, among others, that were not allowed to be performed during the Terror, because they could have been misinterpreted as criticism of Robespierre.

20 *Feuille villageoise* 43 (21 July 1791): 108. Cf. *œcv* 4, 114.

21 *œcv* 4, 113–114.

Taking all these indications together, it can be said that the festival planners blatantly intended an anti-clerical festival for Voltaire, but hardly an anti-religious one. Indeed, a purely secular festival in which religion played no public role at all would not have been possible. In the planners' eyes, such a festival would have contradicted Voltaire himself.

It is this perspective of the revolutionaries that I would like to reconstruct in the following chapter: How did (some of) the actors of the French Revolution refer to Voltaire and Rousseau? On which Voltairean and Rousseauean concepts did they focus? What kind of Voltaire and Rousseau did they (re)construct? It is not my purpose, then, to present Voltaire's and Rousseau's own full philosophical positions concerning God and religion, but rather those that were attributed to them by their near contemporaries.

It is sufficient to point out here that in the work of both *philosophes* quite different views on religion can be found.[22] However, both commonly assumed a natural order instituted by God. The way human beings correspond to this original order is called "natural religion." Voltaire's concept of and approach to God can be assessed as rather rationalistic, while Rousseau's may be characterized as affective. Nevertheless, both *philosophes* can be described as deists – albeit of different varieties[23] – who strictly distinguished a natural religion from the revealed and positive religions. They emphatically pleaded for the former against the latter. The historiography on deism largely agrees on this assessment of the two men, but – and in contrast to it – scholars focused on the French Revolution and its origins see almost no role at all for Voltaire's and Rousseau's deistic ideas.

---

22   For Voltaire, the work of René Pomeau, *La religion de Voltaire* (Paris: 1969) has still to be mentioned above all. See also Jean Dagen, "Quel besoin Voltaire a-t-il de Dieu?" *La Lettre clandestine* 21 (2013): 213–227. For Rousseau, see Pierre-Maurice Masson, *La religion de Jean-Jacques Rousseau*, 3 vols. (Paris: 1916); Albert Schinz, *La pensée religieuse de Rousseau et ses récents interprètes* (Northampton, Mass.: 1928); Christian Jacquet, *La pensée religieuse de Jean-Jacques Rousseau* (Louvain: 1975); Ghislain Waterlot (ed.), *La théologie politique de Rousseau* (Rennes: 2010); Marie-Hélène Cotoni, "Mécréant ou chrétien? Les paradoxes dans la pensée religieuse de Jean-Jacques Rousseau," in *Jean-Jacques Rousseau (1712–2012): Matériaux pour un renouveau critique*, ed. Christophe Van Staen (Brussels: 2012), 143–157; Marie-Hélène Cotoni, "La polémique contre les modernes matérialistes dans les professions de foi théistes de Rousseau," *La Lettre clandestine* 21 (2013): 191–211; Geneviève Di Rosa, *Rousseau et la Bible: pensée du religieux d'un philosophe des Lumières* (Leiden: 2016). For both, see in addition: Ourida Mostefai and John T. Scott (eds.), *Rousseau and L'infâme: Religion, Toleration, and Fanaticism in the Age of Enlightenment* (Amsterdam: 2009).

23   See Robert S. Tate, "Rousseau and Voltaire as Deists: A Comparison," *L'Esprit Créateur* 9 (1969): 175–186.

The historiography of the French Revolution focuses on Voltaire's and Rousseau's respective influence in the field of political ideas. There, the hypothesis that the *philosophes* of the Enlightenment had a direct impact on the developments of the revolution is as old as the historiography itself. From the very beginning, Voltaire and Rousseau were the focus of interest.[24] It was the revolutionaries themselves who adopted Voltaire and Rousseau as their own and acknowledged the two as the "first authors of the Revolution."[25] As a result, the effect of the Enlightenment's concepts of liberty, equality, and sovereignty on the revolution has been treated many times and also quite critically.[26]

Besides such a conceptional approach, there are plenty of studies which deal with the revolutionary reception of the personalities of Voltaire and Rousseau.[27] However, here, too, their political theories are often in the center

---

24   See, for instance, Jules Michelet, *History of the French Revolution*, trans. C. Cocks (London: 1847), 55: "WHEN [sic!] those two men have passed, the Revolution is accomplished in the intellectual world. ... The Revolution is on her march, with Rousseau and Voltaire still in front." Cf. Jules Michelet, *Histoire de la Revolution française*, vol. 1 (*Œuvres complètes de J. Michelet*) (Paris: 1897), 108. For other examples, see Ozouf, "Voltaire," 523–4, and Bernard Manin, "Rousseau," in *Dictionnaire critique de la Révolution française*, eds. François Furet and Mona Ozouf, vol. 4: *Idées* (Paris: 1992), 457–8.

25   It was Condorcet who used this characterization for Voltaire, and Sébastien Mércier for Rousseau. See James Swenson, *On Jean-Jacques Rousseau: Considered as One of the First Authors of the Revolution* (Stanford: 2000), 11.

26   The literature on this subject, which in the meantime has become immense, can only be referred to here with a very small selection: Daniel Mornet, *Les origines intellectuelles de la Révolution française: 1715–1787* (Paris: 1933); François Furet, *Penser la Révolution française* (Paris: 1978); Margaret C. Jacob, *The Radical Enlightenment: Pantheists, Freemasons and Republicans* (London: 1981); Keith Michael Baker, *The French Revolution and the Creation of Modern Political Culture*, vol. 1: *The Political Culture of the Old Regime* (Oxford: 1987); Thomas E. Kaiser, "This Strange Offspring of *Philosophie*: Recent Historiographical Problems in Relating the Enlightenment to the French Revolution," *French Historical Studies* 15 (1988): 549–562; Keith Michael Baker, *Inventing the French Revolution: Essays on French Political Culture in the Eighteenth Century* (Cambridge, Eng.: 1999); Jonathan I. Israel, *Democratic Enlightenment: Philosophy, Revolution, and Human Rights 1750–1790* (Oxford: 2012); Jonathan I. Israel, *Revolutionary Ideas: An Intellectual History of the French Revolution from* The Rights of Man *to Robespierre* (Oxford: 2014); Andreas Pečar and Damien Tricoire, *Falsche Freunde: War die Aufklärung wirklich die Geburtsstunde der Moderne?* (Frankfurt a.M.: 2015).

27   See, for instance, Waldinger, *Voltaire*; Carol Blum, *Rousseau and the Republic of Virtue: The Language of Politics in the French Revolution* (Ithaca: 1986); Roger Barny, *Rousseau dans la Révolution: le personnage de Jean-Jacques et les débuts du culte révolutionnaire (1787–1791)* (Oxford: 1986); Nathalie-Barbara Robisco, *Jean-Jacques Rousseau et la Révolution française: une esthétique de la politique 1792–1799* (Paris: 1998); Holger Ross Lauritsen and Mikkel Thorup (eds.), *Rousseau and Revolution* (London: 2011); Daniel Schönpflug, "La faute à

of interest. In the case of Voltaire, religion plays a role with regard to the religious tolerance debates concerning the *Déclaration des droits de l'homme et du citoyen* in 1789 and, on the other hand, concerning the destruction of church structures, dechristianization, and anti-clericalism. In the case of Rousseau, the main issue is the question of the political instrumentalization of religion, and here above all the reception of the corresponding paragraphs of his *Contrat social*.[28] For both, the quasi-religious cults of their persons are also often studied.[29] Yet their personal religious convictions, philosophy of religion in a narrower sense, and the foundational role of both in their philosophical writings are rarely mentioned with respect to these authors.

In addition, historiography has become accustomed to a particular schema that is not entirely wrong, but nevertheless reductive. Voltaire is often associated with a first phase of the revolution, considered more liberal (1789–1791); Rousseau with a second (from 1793 at the latest), characterized by ideology and terror.[30] An instrumentalized religion seems to fit better into this last phase than into the first. Above all, the hypothesis that Rousseau's philosophy was only increasingly received since 1793 has already been contradicted several times and on a broad source basis.[31] It can therefore be taken for granted that

Voltaire? Secularizations and the Origins of the French Revolution," in *Redefining the Sacred: Religion in the French and Russian Revolutions*, eds. Daniel Schönpflug and Martin Schulze Wessel (Frankfurt a.M.: 2012), 25–50; Oliver Hidalgo, "Voltaire und Rousseau: Zwei Antipoden im Kontext der Aufklärung und ihre Bedeutung für die Französische Revolution," in *Das Jahrhundert Voltaires: Vordenker der europäischen Aufklärung*, eds. Norbert Campagna and Rüdiger Voigt (Baden-Baden: 2020), 48–68.

28   See, for instance, Michaël Culoma, *La religion civile de Rousseau à Robespierre* (Paris: 2010).

29   For Voltaire, see Raymond Rockwood, *The Apotheosis of Voltaire during the French Revolution*, unpublished Ph.D. Dissertation (Chicago: 1931); Rockwood, "Voltaire." For Rousseau, see Barny, *Rousseau*; Joan MacDonald, *Rousseau and the French Revolution 1762–1791* (1965; repr. London: 2013); Swenson, *On Jean-Jacques Rousseau*; Gordon H. McNeil, "The Cult of Rousseau and the French Revolution," *Journal of the History of Ideas* 6 (1945): 197–212.

30   On the development of the assumption during the 19th century and its formulation in Louis Blanc, see François Furet, *Jean-Jacques Rousseau and the French Revolution: Jan-Patočka Memorial Lecture of the IWM 1994* (Vienna: 1994), 14–17. By counting citations, Renato Galliani, "Voltaire et les autres philosophes dans la Révolution: les brochures de 1791, 1792, 1793," *Studies on Voltaire and the Eighteenth Century* 174 (1978): 69–112, has supported this thesis quantitatively. Ozouf, "Voltaire," 534, problematizes Galliani's purely quantitative method but ultimately comes to a similar conclusion.

31   See above all Barny, *Rousseau*; Swenson, *On Jean-Jacques Rousseau*, 161–7.

Rousseau was an important inspiration[32] for many different politicians of the revolution (and even "anti-revolutionaries")[33] from the very beginning.

However, the research on the revolutionary Voltaire and Rousseau seems to confirm Roger Chartier's theory that neither the enlightened *philosophes*, nor their ideas, originated the revolution, but that, conversely, the revolutionaries invented the Enlightenment in an anachronistic way for their own legitimation.[34] In *Les Origines culturelles de la Révolution Française*, Chartier wrote:

> When they brought together (not without debate) a pantheon of ancestors including Voltaire, Rousseau, Mably, and Raynal, when they assigned a radically critical function to philosophy (if not to all the Philosophes), the revolutionaries constructed a continuity that was primarily a process of justification and a search for paternity. Finding the "origins" of the event in the ideas of the century ... would be a way of repeating, without knowing it, the actions of the persons involved in the event itself and of holding as established historically a filiation that was proclaimed ideologically.[35]

Similarly, this chapter does not ask whether the revolutionary constructs of "Voltaire" and "Rousseau" reflect an adequate representation of Voltaire's and Rousseau's philosophies. Rather, the point is to explore the Voltaire and the Rousseau of the French Revolution and to ask why these *philosophes* were received in particular ways. In contrast to Chartier, however, I show that the two *philosophes* did not (only) have "a radically critical function," at least in the field of religion, but also a so-to-speak positive and constructive one: Voltaire and Rousseau were called upon as key witnesses of a certain conception of God, and they were used authoritatively as such thinkers of God in the revolutionary cults to enforce this image of God as generally binding on society.

---

32 Using the term "inspiration," Manin, "Rousseau," 479, points out that while the revolutionaries certainly made use of some concepts and set pieces from Rousseau's works, they hardly ever came close to implementing Rousseau's entire political theory.

33 See, above all, Barny, *Rousseau*; Gordon H. McNeil, "The Anti-Revolutionary Rousseau," *The American Historical Review* 58 (1953): 808–823.

34 See Roger Chartier, *The Cultural Origins of the French Revolution*, trans. Lydia G. Cochrane (Durham: 1991). Cf. Roger Chartier, *Les origines culturelles de la Révolution française* (Paris: 1990).

35 Chartier, *Origins*, 5. Cf. Chartier, *Origines*, 17. In the French original, the list of the *philosophes* additionally includes Buffon and Helvétius.

At the same time, I am linking two fields of research that have hardly been thought together so far. Scholars of deism, usually strongly oriented towards the history of ideas, have largely failed to ask about a "practiced" deism: Did deism exist as an applied religion beyond its high literature? On the other hand, research on the French Revolution still suffers from the deficit of an adequate religious-historical description of the so-called revolutionary cults. Admittedly, there was such an attempt at the beginning of the 20th century with the groundbreaking studies of Alphonse Aulard and Albert Mathiez,[36] which can still be read with great profit today. However, a certain "blind spot" can be traced from both writers into today's studies on the topic – although written in great polemic to each other, Aulard and Mathiez shared the unquestioned presupposition that politics and religion in the 18th century were already separate fields in a modern sense.[37] This means that both scholars took a strongly instrumental understanding of religion[38] and assumed that the revolutionary elites were acting politically – and according to political precepts – even if they invoked religion to achieve certain goals.[39] Ultimately, therefore, they were concerned with a political religion. This view can also be found in the works of Mona Ozouf in the 1970s, which strongly influenced and fertilized research on revolutionary cults. There is much to be said for her hypothesis of a transfer of sacrality from traditional religion to state institutions, but she, too, ultimately underestimates the autonomy of religion.[40]

---

36   François-Alphonse Aulard, *Le culte de la raison et le culte de l'être suprême: 1793–1794. Essai historique* (Paris: 1892); Albert Mathiez, *Les origines des cultes révolutionnaires: 1789–1792* (Paris: 1904); Albert Mathiez, "Robespierre et le culte de l'Être suprême," *Annales révolutionnaires* 3 (1910): 209–238.

37   Scholars often tend to equate Christianity with religion, and therefore infer that anti-clerical or anti-Christian positions are criticisms of religion *per se*. Large parts of the 18th century were undoubtedly anti-clerical, but that does not necessarily imply it was also anti-religious.

38   See, for instance, Mathiez, *Origines*, 64.

39   Regarding these supposed aims, the views of Aulard and Mathiez diverge. While Aulard, *Culte*, viii assumed that through religion the French people should be united as a community against external enemies, Mathiez, *Robespierre*, 213, presumed that the aim was to establish a free, equal, and just society.

40   See, especially, Mona Ozouf, *La fête révolutionnaire: 1789–1799* (Paris: 1976). In this book she bundles all her essays from previous years. There are a lot of more recent studies deeply influenced by Ozouf, for instance, David A. Bell, *The Cult of the Nation in France: Inventing Nationalism, 1680–1800* (Cambridge, Mass.: 2001). Chartier, *Origines*, 155–160, too, believes that a transfer of sacrality took place.

By focusing on the revolutionary construction of Voltaire and Rousseau as thinkers of God, I will show that for at least some revolutionaries it was rather the other way round. They often used political means to enforce their religious convictions. Thus, they did not seek political religion, but acted on the basis of theopolitical reasoning. In doing so, I will also argue that Robespierre's sharp distinction between the two main cults of the French Revolution – the Cult of Reason (mainly in the fall and winter of 1793/94) and the Cult of the Supreme Being (in the late spring and summer of 1794) – is hardly tenable.

1   Robespierre's Farewell to Voltaire?

Cult and festivals constituted one of the main institutions the revolutionaries used to establish their conception of religion. Before fall 1793, there were already a couple of newly constructed festivals. Some of them tried to integrate the traditional church festival culture, others were in strong opposition to it.[41] The festival in honor of Voltaire described at the beginning was only one of many to come. From the fall of 1793, large parts of the movement leading revolutionary festival culture across France began to identify under a common motto: "Cult of Reason." This movement was decidedly anti-clerical and was intertwined with a larger social movement, which scholars named dechristianization, that was opposed to the clergy and certain Christian ideas. Robespierre soon opposed the Cult of Reason by accusing its protagonists of atheism. With his speech and the decree of 18 Floréal Year 2 (7 May 1794), which was passed by the National Convention, he opposed them with the "Cult of the Supreme Being." The Cult of the Supreme Being was connected with an elaborated festival calendar; it also established the two dogmas "God exists" and "the soul is immortal" as legally binding and thus took its place as a kind of "state cult."[42] The initiation festival of this cult, the Festival of the Supreme Being, took place across France on 20 Prairial Year 2 (8 June 1794).[43]

---

41   An insight into the most important revolutionary festivals is offered by Biver, *Fêtes*, and by Ozouf, *Fête*.

42   See the Discours and the Decree of 18 Floréal Year 2 (7 May 1794) in *AP* 90 (Paris: 1972), 132–141. Cf. Maximilien Robespierre, *Œuvres de Maximilien Robespierre*, vol. 10 (Paris: 1967), 442–465. In the following, I will refer to this edition of Robespierre's works by the abbreviation *ŒRob*.

43   See Aulard, *Culte*, 297–354; Ozouf, *Fête*, 172–192; Jonathan Smyth, *Robespierre and the Festival of the Supreme Being: The Search for a Republican Morality* (Manchester: 2016).

Scholars largely agree that Robespierre borrowed from Rousseau's philosophy and his idea of a civil religion for the Cult of the Supreme Being.[44] Robespierre did not mention Rousseau by name in his speech of 18 Floréal, but it was deeply inspired by Rousseau's language[45] and also referred very clearly to him in one paragraph when he recalls

> [a]mong those who, at the time of which I am speaking, were celebrated as literary men and philosophers, there was a man who by his nobleness of soul and greatness of character showed himself worthy of being the teacher of mankind. He attacked tyranny openly; he spoke with rapture of the Deity; his manly and dignified eloquence painted, in glowing colors, the charms of virtue.[46]

This unique soul, character, sincerity, this eloquence and this strong connection to the *vertu* – Robespierre used here all those *clichés* which were strongly bonded to Rousseau at least since his death.[47]

Other contemporaries also recognized Rousseau's central position to the Cult of the Supreme Being. In a letter of thanks from the Section *"Droits-de-l'homme"* read at the National Convention on 6 Prairial Year 2 (25 May 1794), the delegation acknowledged a link between Rousseau and the establishment of the cult through "the principles of Socrates, of Rousseau about the existence of a Supreme Being, about the immortality of the soul."[48] Also, on 11 June 1794, only two days after the Festival of the Supreme Being, a report was presented to the Committee of Public Safety in which the responsible commission endorsed a sculptor's project to create an "image of Rousseau discovering nature," for it

---

44   See Aulard, *Culte*; Mathiez, *Origines*; Culoma, *La religion civile*; and many more. Solitary voices that Robespierre had become less a student than a critic of Rousseau, especially at the time of the Terror, have more political issues in mind; see, for instance, Andrew Levine, "Robespierre: Critic of Rousseau," *Canadian Journal of Philosophy* 8 (1978): 543–557; similarly, Smyth, *Festival*, 19.

45   See Israel, *Revolutionary Ideas*, 561–5.

46   Paul H. Beik (ed.), *The French Revolution. Selected Documents* (London: 1970), 307. Cf. AP 90, 137, and *ŒRob* 10, 455.

47   See Barny, *Rousseau*, 56–78.

48   AP 90, 631. On the not uncommon connection between Rousseau and Socrates, see for instance, also the graphic *Arrivée de J.J. Rousseau aux champs elisées* (BnF, IFN-6950589), where Rousseau is received by Socrates at the Elysium; also the manuscript *Socrate et Jean-Jacques, ou parallèle de Jean-Jacques Rousseau avec Socrate* (BnF, MS-6099), cit. after McNeil, "Cult," 198; for parallelism already in Rousseau's lifetime, see Raymond Trousson, *Rousseau et sa fortune littéraire* (Paris: 1977), 47–8, and Mark Hulliung, *The Autocritique of Enlightenment: Rousseau and the Philosophes* (Cambridge, Mass.: 1994), 225–7.

was nature (as Rousseau had exclaimed) that reminded people of "the benefits and the existence of the Divinity."[49] Likewise, the Parisian Jacobins thanked the National Convention for the decree of 18 Floréal, pointing out that only those could be "true Jacobins"

> who highly profess these articles, which should not be considered as dogmas of religion but as sentiments of sociability, "without which," says Jean-Jacques, "it is impossible to be a good citizen; *the existence of the Divinity, the life to come, the sanctity of the social contract and of laws!*" ... No one can be forced to believe them: but whoever dares to say that he does not believe them, rises up against the French people, the human race and nature.[50]

This echoed both the words of Robespierre and of Rousseau's *Contrat social*. Robespierre saw Rousseau as the real *philosophe* precisely because his virtuous attitude

> defended those consoling dogmas which reason supplies to support the human heart; the purity of his doctrine, drawn from nature and from a profound hatred of vice, as well as his invincible scorn for the intriguing sophists who usurped the name of philosophers, drew upon him the hatred and persecution of his rivals and of his false friends.[51]

Thus, in his defense of those consolatory dogmas (here, Robespierre surely meant the two dogmas he proclaimed himself in his speech: the existence of God and the immortality of the soul), Rousseau stood alone against those false *philosophes* who "have prostituted themselves to factions, and especially to the Orleans party; the others have taken refuge in a cowardly neutrality."[52]

As he was the only *philosophe* for Robespierre, Rousseau was the first "true Jacobin" for the Parisian Jacobins, because he unabashedly professed the pure doctrine. In the latter's eyes, all those who did not profess the pure doctrine could not have been "true Jacobins."

---

49 Paris, Archives Nationales de France, AF/II/66, 489, No. 27, fol. IV–2r.

50 *AP* 90, 389. Similarly, the Revolutionary Committee in Sarlat (*AP* 91 [Paris: 1976], 257), and already before 18 Floréal, the *société populaire* in Perriers (*AP* 90, 559). Incidentally: referring to Rousseau by his first name was quite common at the time of the revolution.

51 Beik, *Revolution*, 307. Cf. *AP* 90, 137, and *ŒRob* 10, 455. Already in a speech held on 27 April 1792, Robespierre ascribed this unique position to Rousseau; see *ŒRob* 8 (Paris: [1954]), 309.

52 Beik, *Revolution*, 308. Cf. *AP* 90, 137, and *ŒRob* 10, 455.

In the passage of the *Contrat social* to which the Parisian Jacobins referred, Rousseau promised banishment to those who do not believe in these dogmas (so-to-speak the "false Jacobins"):

> While not having the ability to obligate anyone to believe them, the sovereign can banish from the state anyone who does not believe them. It can banish him not for being impious but for being unsociable, for being incapable of sincerely loving the laws and justice, and of sacrificing his life, if necessary, for his duty.[53]

Robespierre in his speech of 18 Floréal, in turn, did not pursue the actual banishment of the false *philosophes*[54] – among whom he certainly included Voltaire[55] – but he condemned them sharply and silenced their names in his speech and in doing so,[56] he dismissed their relevance to the revolution.[57]

2   Voltaire's Comeback, Part 1: A Grammatical Proof of God

The outstanding position of Rousseau for the Cult of the Supreme Being; knowledge of the difficult relationship between Voltaire and Rousseau; the

53   Jean-Jacques Rousseau, *Basic Political Writings*, trans. Donald A. Cress (Indianapolis: 1987), 226. Cf. Jean-Jacques Rousseau, *Collection complète des œuvres de J.J. Rousseau*, vol. 1 (Geneva: 1782), 354. In the following, I will refer to this edition of Rousseau's works by the abbreviation *ŒRous*.

54   On the contrary, Robespierre objected to banishment explicitly as a general practice. Jullien, a member of the Jacobins and a commissioner of the Committee of Public Safety, had prepared a thank-you letter on behalf of the Jacobin Club to the National Convention for the decree of 18 Floréal. He demanded, among other things, that all who did not believe in God must be banished. Robespierre was in favor of this letter in principle but required the deletion of that very passage: "There are truths that must be presented with care, such as the truth professed by Rousseau, that all those who do not believe in divinity must be banished from the Republic. ... I believe that this truth should be left in Rousseau's writings, and should not be put into practice." *ŒRob* 10, 467.

55   See Ozouf, "Voltaire," 531–2.

56   In the very next passage of this speech, Robespierre mentioned Condorcet, Hébert, Danton, and a few other names, but these are all persons who were his direct contemporary political opponents and are treated as such, not as *philosophes*. See *AP* 90, 137. Cf. *ŒRob* 10, 456.

57   Another example appeared in his speech held on 5 Nivôse Year 2 (25 December 1793). Regarding the "revolutionary government," Robespierre argued that the revolution was so new that nothing could be learned about it from the books of the *philosophes*. See *ŒRob* 10, 274.

two-phase liberal/terror (Voltaire/Rousseau) division of the revolution; and the absence of references to Voltaire in the speech of 18 Floréal – all have prevented scholars from asking about Voltaire's role for the Cult of the Supreme Being, and have led some even to assert that this cult was fundamentally opposed to Voltaire.[58] This negation of Voltaire's role is contradicted, however, by the fact that Robespierre used a formula in his speech of the 18 Floréal that strongly suggested Voltaire in a positive sense. In a staccato of questions, Robespierre included: who would benefit from the spread of atheism? – and ventured an answer, in which he concluded that to deny the existence of God and the immortality of the soul was nothing but a pitiful sophism, because – and here he recalled clearly a familiar Voltairean formula – "if the existence of God and the immortality of the soul were only dreams, they would still be the most sublime conceptions of the human mind."[59]

The same argument that the existence of God, even if only thought up by man, is a self-evident thought was already used by Robespierre in his speech of 1 Frimaire Year 2 (21 November 1793). In this discourse he had already developed certain basic features of his religious conception, and he used this argument to assert the concept of God as a popular one, and thus as a conception appropriate to the revolution because it was opposed to aristocratic atheism. The respective paragraph culminates in a line from Voltaire's *Épitre à l'auteur du livre des trois imposteurs* (1769): "If God did not exist, it would be necessary to invent him."[60] Already in this speech from November 1793, Robespierre did not mention Voltaire's name in a single syllable, nor had he even indicated that this phrase was not his own. He did not seem to need Voltaire's authority by name at this point, or possibly he did not want to use it in order not to be misunderstood as Voltaire's follower.

However, I think that a third possibility is even more likely: Robespierre could assume that everyone was aware of whom he was quoting. In general, Voltaire's phrase was known. For instance, Voltaire was defended against the accusation of atheism by a priest in the play *La France régénérée* by Pierre-Jean-Baptiste Chaussard, which was performed for the first time on 14 September 1791, with exactly this sentence.[61] In a pamphlet from Year 2 (1793/94) with the title *Culte philosophique* a certain De La Bastays, who calls himself a physicist and

---

58   See, for instance, Georges Labica, *Robespierre: Eine Politik der Philosophie* (Hamburg: 1994), 85.

59   Beik, *Revolution*, 305. Cf. *AP* 90, 135, and *ŒRob* 10, 452.

60   *ŒRob* 10, 197. The original in Voltaire can be found in *œcv* 10 (Paris: 1877), 403.

61   Pierre-Jean-Baptiste Chaussard, *La France régénérée; pièce épisodique en vers et à spectacle, précédée d'un prologue* (BnF, YF-8582) (Paris: 1791), 32.

philosopher, presented his ideas about natural religion and the appropriate cult and thereby located himself quite clearly in the debates about the Cult of Reason.[62] In his eyes, the concept of God and the following concept of an after-life cannot be removed from human hearts because they are engraved there. According to De La Bastays, Voltaire had also seen it that way:

> A great Philosopher (Voltaire) [sic!], to whom we partially owe our sub-lime revolution, as well as the advantages which will result from it, since by the charms of his writings he has made instruction general, said: That if there were no God, it would be necessary to create one, and this sub-lime genius certainly cannot be accused of too much credulity.[63]

De La Bastays thus strengthened the argument by pointing out that because Voltaire was not really known for his "credulity," this confession was to be taken all the more seriously. In some other prints, whose authors were clergymen and expressed themselves critically against supposedly atheistic tendencies, the sentence can also be found.[64] It is difficult to judge whether they opposed the Cult of Reason as a whole or only meant very specific persons. But it is also possible that they saw themselves as advocates of a Cult of Reason and contributed their ideas on such a cult to the public. Be that as it may, such texts prove that Voltaire's phrase circulated at the time and was often attributed to him.

In the immediate timeframe of Robespierre's 1 Frimaire speech, there were several references to the phrase in circles around the Cult of Reason. Thus, for example, in an article in Camille Desmoulin's journal *Le Vieux Cordelier* only a few days after the speech (which, however, did not directly address the speech at all), the sentence was associated with Voltaire.[65] On 29 November 1793, a festival of reason was celebrated in the Temple of Reason housed at the former Cathedral of Chartres. In a short theatrical performance, Voltaire and Rousseau were enacted together as critics of the Church, putting down fanaticism, and a little before this vignette, Voltaire had been quoted in a flaming speech in favor

---

62   The BnF dates the printing in its catalog to the year 1792, but this does not match the indication "Year 2" on the last page. The BnF copy bears the handwritten indication 1793 at the title (which can possibly also be read as 1792).
63   Lebeschu De La Bastays, *Culte philosophique* (BnF, LB41-846) (Paris: Year 2 [1793/94]), 1–2.
64   See Galliani, "Voltaire," 106.
65   *Le Vieux Cordelier* 2 (20 Frimaire Year 2 [12 December 1793]): 21.

of the existence of God: "If God ..."[66] The next month, Voltaire's motto was also quoted explicitly in the context of the Cult of Reason in a speech that the National Convention deputy Desrues gave to the *assemblée électorale* of the Paris department on 25 December 1793.[67]

Such references suggest that Robespierre could assume that everybody knew whom he quoted in his speech. They also suggest that he was not at great pains to distance himself from Voltaire, as he could easily have used another phrase (one by Rousseau for example). Certainly, other supporters of the Cult of the Supreme Being found a champion for their cause in Voltaire. The quotation continued to be circulated throughout 1794. For instance, in the Festival of the Supreme Being in Dun-sur-Auron (Departement Cher) a member of the *société populaire* emphasized the consoling function of the idea of God and pitied the atheists. Then he urged others to shout "with that immortal philosopher, who with the biting weapon of mockery mortally wounded fanaticism and prepared the days of enlightenment: 'If God did not exist, it would be necessary to invent him.'"[68] In such configurations, Voltaire was thus cited both as a fighter against fanaticism (i.e., Catholicism) and against atheism.

It should be summarized here that Voltaire is quoted in the context of both the Cult of Reason and the Cult of the Supreme Being with a single sentence from his prolix work. This phrase is well suited to portraying him as an advocate for the existence of God. If we look at the sentence a little more closely, we can see how well suited it is for the revolutionaries' claims to rationality, and for deployment in the intellectual games of the time. The sentence itself embodies logical (rational) and practical proofs of God. Incidentally, following its grammatical composition, the first part of the sentence actually acknowledges that God exists. But the sentence still provides "proof" *via* a null hypothesis: even if he did not (so to speak: even if the grammar goes wrong), then nothing would be closer than to assume that he does exist. But let us take a step back from this sentence.

---

66 *Récit de la fête célébrée pour l'inauguration du temple de la Raison, dans la ci-devant cathédrale de Chartres, le 9 frimaire, l'an 2e. de la République, une & indivisible* (BnF, LB41-3552) (Chartres: 1793), 9. In this speech a second quotation of Voltaire can be found, which is also exceedingly interesting and originates from *Le Pour et le Contre* (1722): "If I am not a Christian, it is to love you better, to serve you more worthily." œcv 9 (Paris: 1877), 361.

67 See Galliani, "Voltaire," 106.

68 De Lamerville, *Discours prononcé le jour de la fête de l'Être suprême dans la commune de Dun-sur-Auron, et dont le peuple a voté l'impression* (BnF, LB41-5417) (Bourges: s.a.), 5.

3   Voltaire's Comeback, Part 2: The Right Way to Adore God

There are further indications that Voltaire still played an important role in
the year 1794 and for the Cult of the Supreme Being. After 18 Floréal, *sociétés
populaires* all over France sent protocols of consecration feasts to the National
Convention, in which busts of "great men" and revolutionary martyrs were
erected in the communities' meeting places (often former churches). These
were mostly busts of Lepeletier, Marat, Chalier, Brutus, Rousseau, and Voltaire.
Such dedication ceremonies are recorded in the minutes of the National
Convention, for example, for the *sociétés populaires* of Bellevue-les-Bains
(now Bourbon-Lancy; Department of Saône-et-Loire),[69] Bury (Department of
Oise)[70] and Noyon (also Department of Oise).[71] The accompanying letter of the
latter society quite explicitly links the veneration of the "great men" with the
Cult of the Supreme Being:

> It was when our hearts were warmed by the love of the virtues of which
> these great men had given the example to the Universe, that we renewed
> the oath to be republican and free, and that we received the decree by
> which you recognize the Supreme Being and the immortality of the soul.
> Everything in nature proves this great truth.[72]

In the visual propaganda of the revolution, too, Voltaire and Rousseau were
found as united combatants for the Cult of the Supreme Being. On the right
side of an anonymous print,[73] Rousseau concentrates completely on the children who surround him. This showed Rousseau's uncontested authority concerning education in the revolution, mainly because of his *Emile*. In addition,
a beehive on his side symbolizes the importance of nature for his philosophy.
Voltaire, on the other side, looks directly at the observer. He looks old but spry
and is surrounded by art and cultural objects. He thus represents the importance of culture, especially for the adult human being (as the observer of the
picture). On the pedestal of the statue of Brutus, which stands before him, is
engraved a quotation from Voltaire's play *Brutus*: "Gods, give us death rather
than slavery."[74] Since Brutus is one of the key figures of republicanism in the

---

69   See *AP* 92 (Paris: 1980), 216.
70   See *AP* 92, 232.
71   See *AP* 92, 234.
72   *AP* 92, 234.
73   *Être suprême Peuple souverain République française* (Paris: 1794), Paris, Musée Carnavalet,
      Inv.-No. G.26963.
74   Voltaire, *Le Brutus*, act 4, scene 7. Cf. *ŒCV* 2 (Paris: 1877), 371.

French Revolution, the plea for death rather than slavery here is likely to be understood as the republican idea of sacrifice for the liberty of the fatherland. But whether it can be reconciled with such an idea of a somehow sacred fatherland or goes beyond it, the phrase in any case refers explicitly to the gods – just as Voltaire and Rousseau themselves do in the picture: Both philosophers point their fingers at the Supreme Being, symbolized by a luminous eye surrounded by a snake biting its tail (a symbol for eternity), and identified below with the words "Supreme Being." One can interpret that Rousseau explains the way to God to the children, but Voltaire explains it to the adult observer. In any case, the picture draws a connection between the concept of God and the political morality of virtue with the help of Voltaire's (not Rousseau's) quotation. This confirms to a certain extent Aulard's assertion, according to which

> one had only to leaf through Voltaire to find a thousand deist arguments. In their preaching, the officers of the new cult had to quote more than once and indeed quoted these verses from the *Poëme sur la loi naturelle*:
> This sovereign law in China, in Japan,
> Inspired Zoroaster, enlightened Solon.
> From one end of the world to the other, it speaks, it cries:
> Adore a God, be just and cherish your fatherland.[75]

In the previous section, I described Voltaire's phrase about the existence of God as logical. In comparison, the verse "Adore a God, be just and cherish your fatherland," selected by Aulard, seems more emotional in its exclamational form. It calls for an affective-worshipful attitude towards God. Of course, this does not necessarily contradict the above sentence, but the emphasis is less on the question of knowing God and more on the question of the behavior towards God (and fatherland).

This verse, as Aulard has indicated but hardly elaborated, appeared often in the Cult of the Supreme Being. Thus, a banner at a festival in honor of the Supreme Being at Le Mans on 19 Floréal Year 2 (8 May 1794) was inscribed on one side with that very phrase and on the other with the motto: "Tribute given to the Supreme Being."[76] In an extensive songbook of 1794 entitled *Hymnes du*

---

75 Aulard, *Culte*, 6. Voltaire's *Poëme sur la loi naturelle* (1752), sometimes also referred to as *La religion naturelle*, can be found in œcv 9, 441–460, here, 445. Very similar to the last verse is a phrase in Voltaire's *Profession de foi des théistes* (1768) in œcv 27 (Paris: 1879), 56. There, however, the demand for love of the fatherland is missing.

76 Cited after Almire René Jacques Lepelletier, *Histoire complète de la province du Maine depuis les temps les plus reculés jusqu'à nos jours*, vol. 2 (Paris: 1861), 350. This festival is extremely early, if Lepelletier's given date of 19 Floréal is correct. Robespierre first

Républicain à l'Éternel, Voltaire's verse was put into the mouth of nature. As the "Interpreter of heaven," nature addresses humans with this phrase.[77] Voltaire's words were also referred to in a curious-seeming book that legitimized the change of street names in the spirit of the revolution in the city of La Rochelle with rambling explanations of the new names.[78] In the explanation devoted to the *Rue de la Morale*, the author linked morality to the confession of the existence of God and the immortality of the soul. (The same claim Robespierre made on 18 Floréal.) Then he asserted that at all times and among all peoples of the earth there has been one fundamental principle: "Adore a God & be just."[79] In the article on the *Rue de Voltaire*, in turn, the author defended Voltaire against possible attacks. The fictional accusation against Voltaire concerned his dealings with the powerful. The author countered this, on the one hand, by pointing out that Voltaire stayed close to the powerful to better influence their thoughts. On the other hand, he noted that Voltaire was always the protector and liberator of the oppressed (Calas and Sirven are mentioned). In addition, Voltaire had turned with verve against the clergy and the Church, but not without also constructively formulating "sane ideas & consoling truths." Thus, he had represented "aloud the existence of God, the sweet pleasures of virtue, the necessity of the pains and rewards of another life" in his writings.[80]

The double dogma of the Cult of the Supreme Being (the existence of God and immortality of the soul) is thus often legitimized with reference to Voltaire. If one evaluates this particular quotation as a kind of concentrated expression of Voltaire's deism, as Aulard did, then it can be assumed that the proponents of the Cult of the Supreme Being ultimately saw themselves as deists, insofar as they tried to establish Voltaire's (and Rousseau's) supposed religion.

Yet the same quotation can also be traced to the movement against which Robespierre installed his Cult of the Supreme Being (because he regarded its

---

instituted the cult on 18 Floréal and scheduled a nationwide feast for the Supreme Being on 20 Prairial Year 2 (8 June 1794). Unfortunately, I have not been able to locate Lepelletier's own source to verify his information. However, the date of the feast does not really play a crucial role for my argumentation here.

77   *Hymnes du Républicain à l'Éternel* (BnF, YE-24340) (Paris: Year 2 [1793/94]), 61.

78   These *Notices sur la nouvelle Nomenclature des Rues de la Rochelle* (BnF, LK7-3464) (La Rochelle: Year 3 [1794/95]) date – according to the indication "Year 3" (1794/95) and the excerpts of the decisions of the city council contained therein (2 Frimaire Year 3 [22 November 1794]) – to the end of 1794. This would have been after Robespierre's fall. However, the content of it fits very well into the context of the Cult of the Supreme Being.

79   *Notices*, 309. The phrase quoted here is the abridged version from Voltaire's *Profession de foi des théiste*.

80   *Notices*, 201–2.

alleged atheism as harmful and wanted to prevent it): the Cult of Reason. At Mello, the verse was written in large letters over the statue of Liberty "near the Temple's vault."[81] At Strasbourg, the *accusateur public* (the former priest Eulogius Schneider), in his address on the Feast of Reason, bundled in Voltaire's words "all your religion," after mocking the religions of revelation.[82] The *société populaire* in Soissons even developed a kind of constitutional text for its local Cult of Reason. Its second article regulated the appearance of its place of worship:

> The temple where they will assemble will be dedicated to truth and will bear this inscription: Temple of truth, consecrated to God and to the fatherland. On the door of this temple this epigraph will be inscribed: Do not do to others what you do not want to be done to yourself. And these four verses:
>   Among enlightened people a man is equal to a man;
>   both good and evil are commonly shared;
>   the happiness of life is understood through three laws:
>   Adore a God, be just and cherish your fatherland.[83]

In the Temple of Reason at Fresnay,[84] Saint-Aignan,[85] and Chaumont,[86] the verse was also emblazoned prominently in the worship space, along with others.[87] At Chaumont, moreover, busts of Brutus, Marat, Lepeletier, Chalier, Rousseau, and Franklin are joined by one of Voltaire. All of them were crowned with laurel wreaths by young girls during the inauguration

---

81   *AP* 86 (Paris: 1965), 145.

82   *Description de la fête de la Raison, célébrée pour la première fois à Strasbourg, le jour de la 3e décade de brumaire de l'an 2e de la République une, indivisible et démocratique* (BnF, LB41-3528) (Strasbourg: s.a.), 9–10.

83   *AP* 80 (Paris: 1912), 401.

84   See Auguste Le Guicheux, *Chroniques de Fresnay, Assé-le-Boisne, Douillet, Montreuil-le-Chétif, Saint-Aubin-de-Locquehay, Saint-Georges-le-Gaultier, Saint-Léonard-des-Bois, Saint-Ouen-de-Mimbré, Saint-Paul-le-Gaultier, Saint-Victeur* (Le Mans: 1877), 249.

85   See Jean Jacques Delorme, *Histoire de la ville de Saint-Aignan (Loir-et-Cher)* (Saint-Aignan: 1846), 304.

86   See *AP* 83 (Paris: 1961), 720.

87   So far inexplicable remains to me the fact that at all three places not only this verse of Voltaire, but also other verses of other writers (Colardeau, Crébillon, Helvétius) were attached. And in fact exactly the same verses. There was possibly some kind of manual for the transformation of churches into temples of reason, in which this selection of words was recommended.

feast of the Temple of Reason.[88] These findings strengthen the results I presented above: As with the phrase "If God …," Voltaire appeared both in the Cult of Reason and in the Cult of the Supreme Being with the quotation "Adore a God …" as a *philosophe* for whom the idea of God played a central role.

4   Voltaire's Reconciliation with Rousseau in the Mystical Adoration of God

How exactly God was understood in each case is hard to know on the basis of the mostly very brief contextual statements. However, at least the implied relationship to the deity becomes manifest in places. Thus, in a theatrical sequence performed during the inauguration feast of the Temple of Reason in Chaumont, three old wise men appeared, the first of whom prayed to the Supreme Being and the third invited the participants to hand over the "attributes of fanaticism and tyranny" to the purifying fire in front of the temple. The middle one recited the following four-verse stanza:

> Far from deciding anything about this Supreme Being,
> Let us keep, while adoring him, a profound silence.
> His nature is immense and confuses the human mind;
> To know what he is, one would have to be him.[89]

God is portrayed here as ultimately incomprehensible in rational terms, and the only adequate way for human beings to deal with him is through adoration in silence. At Chaumont, these verses were in no way associated with Voltaire and the somehow mystical words hardly fit with the biting mockery and cutting rationality so often associated with Voltaire – nor are they to be found in his writings[90] – but contemporaries attributed them to Voltaire

---

88   See *AP* 83, 720.
89   See *AP* 83, 720.
90   Rather, their origin is somewhat obscure. I found the verses in Charles-François-Nicolas Le Maître de Claville, *Traité du vrai mérite de l'homme*, vol. 2 (Amsterdam: 1738), 167, in the 8th chapter, "De la morale." Whether Le Maître is the author of them, however, is uncertain. According to Henri Perrochon, "Noé-Antoine-Abraham Bonjour (1731–1807): politique, stratégie et histoire des religions," *Revue historique vaudoise* 80 (1972): 42, the Swiss politician Noé Antoine Abraham Bonjour attributes the verses to the Lausanne philosophy professor Jean-Pierre de Crousaz (1663–1750). Unfortunately, I could not find the verses in Crousaz's work so far. In a slightly modified version, the *Dictionnaire critique de la langue française* by Abbé Féraud, vol. 3 (Marseille: 1788), 128, attributes the verse to Antoine-Louis de Chalamont de La Visclède (1692–1760). Also in his work I have not found the stanza.

nevertheless. Perhaps this was a misattribution because the verses could be read as an elaboration of the verse from the *Poëme de la loi naturelle*, or maybe they were deliberately claimed to mobilize Voltaire's authority. In any case, in Cassius Quillet's report to the *société populaire* of Rochefort on the Festival of the Supreme Being in 1794, this aphorism was explicitly attributed to Voltaire. Having already offered the audience a rather free interpretation of our well-known adoration-verse from the *Poëme de la loi naturelle*,[91] Quillet implicitly argued with the help of Voltaire's *Essai sur les mœurs* (1756) that the clerics in any positive religion speak "a mysterious jargon" by which they "abused the simplicity of the people to declare themselves as the immediate representatives of the divinity, & as charged with interpreting its oracles."[92]

But in nature as well as in the own conscience, "everywhere the invisible hand of a supreme being is felt."[93] And to this claim Quillet added the above-mentioned motto with explicit reference to Voltaire. However, he shortened it by the first verse and introduced it instead with the hint that this rule applies, "if our reason gives in to the evidence, if we recognize a god." He obviously seemed to believe that he had provided such evidence with his reference to the order of the universe. Quillet thus used this stanza to outline not the form of God-recognition, but rather the form of God-worship that follows it: the true Cult of the Supreme Being would then be one that takes place in "profound silence." Quillet put it this way, asserting an agreement between Voltaire and Rousseau regarding the nature of worship: "The only cult that can be pleasing to him [sc. Supreme Being] is that of justice and probity, a pure heart, says J.-J. Rousseau, is the true temple of the divinity."[94] Here Quillet quoted (almost) correctly how Rousseau culminated the speech of the Vicaire Savoyard to Émile with this advice:

> My son, keep your soul in a condition where it always desires that there be a God, and you shall never doubt it. What is more, whatever decision you may make, bear in mind that the true duties of religion are independent of the institutions of men; that a just heart is the true temple of the

---

91 Cassius Quillet, *Rapport fait à la Societé révolutionnaire, de Rochefort, au nom de sa commission des fêtes décadaires* (London, British Library, 936.f.7.[14.]) (Rochefort: 1794), 2–3: "To sanctify the divinity is to honor one's parents, to love one's brothers, to cherish one's fatherland; it is to contract the obligation to be just, humane, generous and patriotic; to raise one's heart to the supreme being, to recognize one's origin, to admit that all men are children of the same father, that tyrants are the destroyers of the world, & that fraternal friendship is the first affection of reasonable beings."

92 Quillet, *Rapport*, 3.

93 Ibid., 4.

94 Ibid.

divinity; that in every country and in every sect the sum of the law is to love God above everything and one's neighbor as oneself; that no religion is exempt from the duties of morality; that nothing is truly essential other than these duties; that inner worship is the first of these duties; and that without faith no true virtue exists.[95]

Quillet thus connected his supposedly rationalistic proof of God, which he drew from the observation of nature, with Rousseau's inward worship of God. The missing link of this connection is the quotation that Quillet foisted on Voltaire: The rational knowledge of God must be followed by a profound, worshipful silence. He thus strengthened Rousseau's supposed religious position with a particular understanding of Voltaire based on a borrowed quotation. At the same time, he thus asserted the unity of the two *philosophes* on the question of religion. Whether Quillet's interpretation agreed to Voltaire's and Rousseau's positions or glossed over certain differences is not important here.[96] It is decisive that Voltaire and Rousseau *both* were invoked as authorities for the same conception of God. Obviously, their philosophies could thus be understood by the revolutionaries in exactly the same way:[97] God can be known in nature and

---

95   Jean-Jacques Rousseau, *Emile: or On Education*, trans. Allan Bloom (New York: 1979), 311–312. Cf. *Œuvres* 5 (Geneva: 1782), 107.

96   Without being able to give a profound discussion of the literature here, it should be pointed out that older research assumed a clear difference between Voltaire's and Rousseau's positions on the question of religion. See, for instance, Gustave Lanson, *Histoire de la littérature française* (Paris: 1898) or Norman Torrey, *The Spirit of Voltaire* (New York: 1938). At the latest since the 1960s, voices emerged that emphasized the similarities and located the differences more on a linguistic-stylistic level, the respective historical contexts of the texts, or a personal level. See, for instance, Ralph A. Leigh, "From the *Inégalité* to *Candide*: Notes in a Desultory Dialogue between Rousseau and Voltaire (1755–1759)," in *The Age of the Enlightenment: Studies Presented to Theodore Besterman*, ed. William Henry Barber (Edinburgh: 1967), 66–92; John Pappas, "Le Rousseauisme de Voltaire," *Studies on Voltaire and the Eighteenth Century* 57 (1967): 1169–1181; Arnold Ages, "Voltaire Rousseauiste?" *University of Windsor Review* 3 (1967): 62–8; Tate, "Rousseau and Voltaire"; more recently, Urs Marti-Brander, *Rousseaus Schuld: Essays über die Entstehung philosophischer Feindbilder* (Basel: 2015), 13–27. In recent years, however, there has been a comeback of the difference hypothesis. See, for instance, Noel Parker, "Religion and Politics: Voltaire's and Rousseau's Enlightenment Strategies," *Distinction: Scandinavian Journal of Social Theory* 7 (2006): 93–115; Hidalgo, "Voltaire." This back and forth of research might have many causes, but among them perhaps not least that Voltaire and Rousseau saw themselves, due to personal animosities, as more divergent than they were perceived by some of their contemporaries.

97   Hidalgo, "Voltaire," advances the interesting hypothesis that it was precisely due to the dissimilarity of Voltaire's and Rousseau's philosophical standpoints regarding religion that they could both be claimed by the revolution at the same time. The revolutionaries could refer to them in a complementary way, as it were, each moderating the other's

in one's conscience, and his worship is accomplished through *vertu*, understood as an attitude of justice resting deeply in inwardness.

Before we go a step further, it is important to highlight that scholars usually describe deism as a form of religion that reduces God to a sort of watchmaker. In this view, God created the world and gave it an initial impetus – just as a watchmaker builds a watch and sets it in motion. Quillet's conception of God, however, seems to have been different, for he insisted that men must "please" the Supreme Being by behaving in a certain way. But if it is necessary to please him, it follows that the Supreme Being can also be displeased and that his whim depends precisely on men's behavior. The theological principle underlying such relationship between men and God is often called "*do ut des.*" While Quillet formulates this principle in a rather implicit way, we find it expressed very clearly in the feast in the Temple of Reason at Chaumont, mentioned above. The prayer of the first elderly man contains, for instance, the following lines:

> Great God, if from now on the earth is your altar,
> If the wall of your temple is the enclosure of the sky,
> If France serves you and has only you for master,
> It is that between the man and you all has just disappeared,
> It is because he has risen up to his author.
> ...
> Watch over us, preserve our fatherland,
> This rock, victorious over the waves and the furious winds;
> May the lightning bolt, the thunderbolt in splinters,
> Leave the mountain and not shake it.[98]

The meaning of these verses can be summarized as follows: God will preserve the French people because they have returned to the true religion, to the worship of the only Master. By their behavior, the people induce God to intercede for them in the world. There is no indication in either Quillet or Chaumont that the revolutionaries assumed that Voltaire could be contrary to this principle. Quite the opposite, Chénier's hymn (quoted at the beginning of this chapter) clearly shows that at least some contemporaries firmly believed that Voltaire's philosophy was consistent with this principle.[99]

---

position. As charming and convincing as this hypothesis sounds, the here-mentioned sources tell another story: that the respective positions were considered equivalents.

98 AP 83, 720.

99 Another example that does not refer to Voltaire is the mayor of Paris, who claimed that the Supreme Being had instructed nature to give the French people a good harvest, in response to the decree of 18 Floréal. See Aulard, *Culte*, 288.

5   Voltaire and the Motley Crew of God Thinkers

In December 1793, a citizen named Darparens presented to the Committee of
Public Instruction his project of a textbook in the form of a catechism entitled
Principes élémentaires d'éducation républicaine (sic!).[100] Presumably to bring
his project to greater attention,[101] he had it printed thereafter on his own.[102] In
addition to the catechism, the print also contained a proposal for a frontispiece
that was to precede the later officially published work: On one side a "temple
of superstition" was to be destroyed by *sans-culottes*; on the other side, crowds
were to enter a building bearing the inscription "To the reason."[103] Both the
presentation of the project in December 1793 and the proposed pictorial elements of the frontispiece show that this project was a contribution to the Cult
of Reason. The second chapter of the catechism (the first one briefly, laconi-
cally and without any enthusiasm stated that the true republican only belongs
to his fatherland) taught readers that the Cult of Reason was the only adequate
cult to the Supreme Being. This cult consisted in "a pure morality, which will
turn the human race into a people of brothers."[104] This Cult of Reason was thus
anything but atheistic (as Robespierre claimed), and it was not the fatherland
that had to be adored here (as Aulard, Mathiez, and Ozouf would later claim).
It was rather just the only correct form of worshipping God. In this presentation, it resembled Robespierre's Cult of the Supreme Being in many ways. And
like Quillet in his account of the Festival of the Supreme Being, Darparens also
made use of the *philosophes* for his remarks on the proper worship of God. In
the 7th chapter, entitled *Historique révolutionaire* (sic!), Darparens enumerated
important revolutionary events and named the central revolutionary martyrs.
Then he also addressed the problem of the precursors of the revolution:

---

100   Actually, the presentation was to take place on 11 Frimaire Year 2 (12 December 1793)
       but was postponed until 27 Frimaire (17 December). See *Procès-verbaux du Comité
       d'Instruction Publique de la Convention Nationale*, ed. James Guillaume, vol. 3 (Paris: 1897),
       52 and 166.

101   He seems to have succeeded in this to a certain extent. The catechism was published
       again by the Parisian publisher C.-F. Galletti, under the title *Alphabet des Sans-culottes,
       ou Premiers élémens de l'éducation républicaine* (BnF, LB41-3844). This is possibly a pirated
       edition, which would explain the lack of author attribution.

102   See Darparens, *Principes élémentaires d'éducation républicaine; ouvrage dont le manuscrit
       a été lu et remis au comité d'instruction publique de la convention nationale, le 27 frimaire*
       (BnF, LB41-3590) (Paris: s.a.).

103   Darparens, *Principes*, 3–4.

104   Ibid., 8.

Q. Who are the men who prepared the Revolution with their writings?

A. Helvétius, Mably, J.J. Rousseau, Voltaire, Franklin.

Q. What do you call these great men?

A. Philosophers.

Q. What does this word mean?

A. A wiseman, friend of humanity.

Q. What do their works teach?

A. That one must adore the Supreme Being, be subject to the Laws, and love men.

Q. What else do they teach?

A. The practice of all the virtues, and that we must sacrifice what we hold dearest to the interests of the Fatherland.[105]

Darparens' textbook was by no means a religious catechism, such as priests and missionaries used for religious education. Darparens' goal was to provide a textbook for the education of citizens. Hence, some chapters dealt with problems of political theory, such as the right form of government or the question of the separation of powers.[106] However, Darparens saw the basis for the proper republican politics in the adoration of the Supreme Being and the morality resulting from it. According to Darparens, precisely this worship of God was also the first teaching of the *philosophes*. Questions of political theory, the questions of freedom and equality, the question of tolerance, all those problems on which scholars often concentrate were not attributed here at all or only peripherally and implicitly to the "friend of humanity." In any case, the separation of politics and religion still seems to be completely outside Darparens' horizon. The minutes of the Committee of Public Instruction did not mention any dismissive reaction at all to this project. Its members seemed to agree in the main with Darparens.[107]

With regard to our question about the reception of the *philosophes* during the revolution, something else is perplexing. Voltaire and Rousseau may somehow be lumped together when it comes to the question of God – Helvétius (as a materialist) certainly does not fit from today's majority perspective. But according to Darparens, Helvétius' first teaching was the same as that of Voltaire and Rousseau: That God exists and must be adored.

---

105   Ibid., 16.

106   See ibid., 11–12.

107   In fact, there was no reaction at all except to adjourn any discussion until a date when all "basic books" were to be discussed. See *Procès-verbaux*, 166.

6   Conclusion

In this chapter, I have presented a strand of a certain reception of Voltaire that clearly ran from 1791 to 1794 (and possibly beyond): Voltaire as a religious thinker. Even in the cases when Voltaire was not recalled by name, I have shown that everyone was quite aware who was quoted because the small number of the cited phrases from Voltaire's work were well-known and often attributed to Voltaire by name.[108] Furthermore, the examples of the *Notices sur la nouvelle Nomenclature des Rues à la Rochelle* from the end of 1794, and of the print showing Rousseau and Voltaire, who together refer to the Supreme Being, indicate that even in 1794 Voltaire was still considered a religious thinker and was united with Rousseau concerning this question. In the following points, I want to show to what extent the evidence provided here can enrich and differentiate the historiographies on the French Revolution and on deism: At least some revolutionaries appreciated Voltaire as a religious thinker beyond his commitment as a fighter for liberty and against the Church, and specifically used his authority to convince their contemporaries.

1)   The Cult of Reason was *not* atheistic to the extent that Robespierre and some scholars until today have claimed. Rather, Aulard is absolutely right in describing it as a variety of deism, and thus as a religious movement for most of the actors.

2)   Related to this, the sharp distinction between the Cult of Reason and the Cult of the Supreme Being is problematic. The opposition seems to have been more orchestrated by Robespierre than based on factual differences. The practice of referring to Voltaire and Rousseau was in both cults much the same and with similar frequency and, above all, with exactly the same quotations. In order to clarify this point once again, a schematic reading of Voltaire's two quotations will be given here in summary.

Seeking the difference between Voltaire and Rousseau in matters of religion, we have ascribed to Voltaire a rather rationalistic, and to Rousseau a rather affective-emotional understanding of religion. An intuitive division of these two understandings between the two cults would then rather see Voltaire as godfather for the Cult of Reason (focus on reason, but also anti-clericalism), while the Cult of the Supreme Being would

---

108   We have gone into two in some detail. But something similar could easily be shown for the *Mahomet* quotation about the equality of mortals, as it was read on a banner in the festival in honor of Voltaire. As indicated, this quotation also has religious implications and can be found in sources from both the Cult of Reason and the Cult of the Supreme Being.

rather have a guarantor in Rousseau (consoling function of the idea of immortality, but also officially decreed cult). In a similar way, the two sentences "If God …" and "Adore a God …" (although both penned by Voltaire) could be distributed between these two poles: The former, as a sort of logical-practical proof of God, would then stand more for a rationalist reading, the latter, as an instruction of a practical devotion to God, more for an affective-emotional one. This schematic (and admittedly very simplified) division regarding the two cults is now doubly challenged by the findings of this chapter. On the one hand, both *philosophes*, the rationalistic Voltaire as well as the affective-emotional Rousseau, were represented relatively equally in both cults. On the other hand, the "Voltairean Voltaire" ("If God …") was naturally quoted in the Cult of Reason, but also in the Cult of the Supreme Being, and conversely, the "Rousseauean Voltaire" ("Adore a God …") could also be found in both cults.[109] By showing here that both the Cult of Reason and the Cult of the Supreme Being referred to the same authorities (at least Voltaire and Rousseau), and even to the same phrases, it becomes clear that the difference between these two movements was more subtle than it has been previously considered. In any case, the divergence between these two cults is by no means what Robespierre himself claimed as an opposition (atheism vs. natural/civic religion). If there is one, it is a different accentuation in the concept of natural religion itself (see No. 6).

3) The apostrophizing of a "Voltairean" and a "Rousseauean Voltaire" showed that this chapter was not meant to be a reconstruction of Voltaire, or his philosophy of religion, or the question of how much of his "authentic" position was taken up by the revolutionaries. Rather, what was presented here can be read as a kind of reformulation of Chartier's hypothesis that the *philosophes* were "produced" first and foremost by the revolutionaries. By an extremely eclectic handling of the works of Rousseau and Voltaire (the quotations that were the focus here would have to be supplemented only by about ten further phrases), which was also characterized by an absolute decontextualization, the revolutionaries constructed a Voltaire and a Rousseau who ultimately agreed on the question of religion.

---

109 I apologize if the reader has become a little dizzy while reading this chapter. But to jump somewhat unconventionally back and forth between two quite easily chronologizable periods (fall/winter 1793/94 and early summer 1794) fits best to my intention to cross the more often separated phenomena of the Cult of Reason and the Cult of the Supreme Being.

4)   From the perspective of research on the history of religion in the French
     Revolution, the sources fanned out here show how profoundly the revo-
     lutionary cults were preoccupied with the question of God's existence
     and his role for society. The assertion of an emerging or even already
     completed "modern" separation between politics and religion, as schol-
     ars have partly represented the revolution, seems strangely inappropri-
     ate against this background. Would it not be more accurate to say that
     political means were used to enforce certain religious ideas? Or, maybe
     more adequately still, that politics and religion were (still) so intertwined
     that it was difficult to deal with one without the other? The French
     Revolution would then have to be described neither as a secularization
     movement nor as a phenomenon of political theology (or religion), but
     rather as a theopolitical event. In many ways, this would show the French
     Revolution to resemble more closely the Reformation of the 16th century
     than the laical France of the late 19th and 20th centuries. By referring
     to the Reformation, it also becomes clear that such a perspective by no
     means wants (or would be able) to negate the anti-clerical element that
     pervaded the revolution at least since 1791 (evidently at the celebration
     in Voltaire's honor). Rather, it helps to introduce a conceptual acuity that
     does not equate anti-clericalism and anti-Christianism with anti-religion
     or even atheism. And it also helps to avoid continuously dragging along
     the condemnatory judgements of contemporaries (Robespierre's accusa-
     tion of atheism against the Cult of Reason above all).

5)   From the perspective of research on deism, the revolutionary cults
     (including the Cult of Theophilanthropy established after 1794) open up
     a field to examine practiced deism beyond the history of ideas. The con-
     nection between Voltaire's and Rousseau's deisms and some protagonists
     of the French Revolution, shown here in principle, lead to further ques-
     tions, for instance: Which philosophical ideas of deism were adopted,
     and which were perhaps rejected by the practitioners? By which rituals,
     by which forms of worship, and by which symbols did the revolution-
     aries stage the deism of the *philosophes*? Who were the practitioners of
     these cults? How long-lived was such deism? What impact did it have on
     French Catholicism, which re-established itself from 1801? Moreover, it
     seems very important to nuance our understanding of deism. As I have
     shown, at least some revolutionaries contradicted our common under-
     standing of a deist God as a watchmaker, for they actively prayed to get
     his intervention. It seems that the core of revolutionary deism, with refer-
     ences to Voltaire and Rousseau, was not so much a passive image of God
     but rather the notion of a return to an original state of religion. A God

who intervenes in human affairs was fully compatible with this religious conception.

6) The commonly stated distinction between the two cults is now highly questionable. Is a differentiation then entirely impossible? A hypothesis based on the sources of this chapter can only be suggested here very cautiously: In both cults, the assumption of God's existence was commonly upheld. Also, as shown, the question of God-recognition and worship was virtually indistinguishable, at least in the sources presented here. A certain difference, however, is found with regard to the immortality of the soul.[110] The inscription "Death is an eternal sleep," which Joseph Fouché had written on a cemetery gate in Nièvre in fall 1793, was long considered one of the triggers for the dechristianization movement and thus, indirectly, for the Cult of Reason. But the position within the Cult of Reason toward this question was all but uniform: Darparens' catechism provides a very unpolemical rejection of the idea of life after death,[111] but De La Bastays pleaded in *Culte philosophique* for a future life,[112] and many other sources omitted this question completely. On the whole, it seems as if the question did not play a big role for the protagonists of the Cult of Reason, but it was clearly the other way round in the Cult of the Supreme Being. There, the commitment to an afterlife as part of Robespierre's double dogma belonged to the core inventory and is explicitly mentioned as such in almost all sources. It was not always treated in the polemical way that Robespierre did in his speech of 18 Floréal,[113] but there were references to it everywhere. The *Notices sur la nouvelle Nomenclature des Rues à la Rochelle* at the end of 1794 not only quoted the double dogma,[114] but made Voltaire himself into a decided advocate.[115]

---

110 On the long dispute about the immortality of the soul in France, see Martin Papenheim, "Die Dialektik der Unsterblichkeit im Frankreich des 18. Jahrhunderts," *Zeitschrift für Literaturwissenschaft und Linguistik* 18 (1988): 29–43; Martin Papenheim, *Erinnerung und Unsterblichkeit: Semantische Studien zum Totenkult in Frankreich (1715–1794)* (Stuttgart: 1992); Ann Thomson, *L'âme des lumières: le débat sur l'être humain entre religion et science; Angleterre-France (1690–1760)* (Seyssel: 2013); Ulrich Barth, "Seele," in *Handbuch Europäische Aufklärung. Begriffe – Konzepte – Wirkung*, ed. Heinz Thoma (Stuttgart: 2015), 465–474; Günther Mensching, "Die Sterblichkeit der Seele im französischen Materialismus," *Aufklärung* 29 (2017): 181–192.

111 See Darparens, *Principes*, 9.

112 De La Bastays, *Culte*, 1.

113 See *AP* 90, 135–6. Cf. *ŒRob* 10, 451–4.

114 *Notices*, 309.

115 Ibid., 201–2. According to Pomeau, *La Religion*, 405, Voltaire obviously struggled to decide clearly on this question.

However, this hypothesis – that the Cult of Reason is undecided but the Cult of the Supreme Being positions itself unequivocally regarding the question of an afterlife – hardly accomplishes what one would need to distinguish sharply between the two movements. Rather, it seems to highlight the rest of what has been said here: The Cult of the Supreme Being solidified certain tendencies in the Cult of Reason.

7) The concentration on Voltaire in this chapter also served, among other things, to question the common view that the revolution, since 1793 at the latest, was shaped primarily by Rousseau and his idea of a civil religion, which was then to be enforced in the Cult of the Supreme Being and was strongly linked to the Terror. My point here was not to drag Voltaire over from the rational-liberal camp into the irrational-ideologically deluded camp of the Terror period or, conversely, to absolve Rousseau of his anachronistic guilt, as it were, by approving Voltaire. Rather, I am concerned with seeking to understand the religious motivations of the revolutionaries and with interpreting the revolution as a religious reform movement. What the focus on continued references to Voltaire shows is that for many revolutionaries, neither the *philosophes* in general nor Voltaire in particular were concerned with eradicating religion – just as the revolutionaries themselves were not. This may be illustrated conclusively by an event of 17 Frimaire Year 2 (7 December 1793), which was presented in a letter to the National Convention ten days later. In this letter, the commune of Ferney-Voltaire apologizes: "we hope that you will not judge our zeal, our patriotism, and our civic spirit, by the modest amount of silverware that there was in the former church of this place."[116]

Indeed, in the fall of 1793, many communities in France sent their church silver to the National Convention as a patriotic gift. In doing so, they demonstrated their patriotism in two ways: On the one hand, they showed their anti-clerical attitude and, at the same time, their affection for the fatherland. The more church silver, so the simple logic, the greater the patriotism. The citizens of Ferney now explained their small yield thus: Voltaire, who had lived in their community for almost the last 20 years of his life, and could even be considered the "founder of this colony," had rebuilt the old church and dedicated it to God alone with the inscription "*Deo erexit / Voltaire MDCCLXI*,"[117] "and that he had not liked to enrich."[118] In short, Voltaire is to blame for the fact that the congregation cannot give more valuables from their church and so they tried to increase the

---

116   *AP* 81 (Paris: 1913), 593.
117   Sheu, *Voltaire*, 143.
118   *AP* 81, 593.

amount a bit more by private contributions. What is striking, but easily understandable against the background of what is presented here, is the following: Voltaire is not reprimanded for having rebuilt a church or rededicated it to God. Nor has Voltaire's authority suffered in any way – on the contrary, it is emphasized again at the end of the letter with one of his anti-clerical quotations.[119] A certain admiration even resonates in the apportionment of blame, because the citizens see that Voltaire had begun the process which the revolutionaries now instructed: he had cleansed but not enriched the church. The revolutionaries did not want to eliminate religion, but to purify it and return it to its origins, and they felt that Voltaire and Rousseau accompanied them in this endeavor in 1791, 1793, and 1794.

References

Primary Sources

Alphabet des Sans-culottes, ou Premiers élémens de l'éducation républicaine (BnF, LB41–3844).

Archives Nationales de France (Paris), AF/II/66, 489.

Archives parlementaires de 1787 à 1860. Recueil complet des débats législatifs & politiques des chambres françaises. Première série (1787 à 1799), 102 vols. (Paris: 1867–2012).

Arrivée de J.J. Rousseau aux champs elisées (BnF, IFN–6950589).

Chaussard, Pierre-Jean-Baptiste, *La France régénérée; pièce épisodique en vers et à spectacle, précédée d'un prologue* (BnF, YF–8582) (Paris: 1791).

Chronique de Paris 195 (14 July 1791).

Courrier de Paris dans les 83 départemens 26/12–13 (13 July 1791).

Darparens, *Principes élémentaires d'éducation républicaine; ouvrage dont le manuscrit a été lu et remis au comité d'instruction publique de la convention nationale, le 27 frimaire* (BnF, LB41–3590) (Paris: s.a.).

De Lamerville, Jean-Marie Heurtault, *Discours prononcé le jour de la fête de l'Être suprême dans la commune de Dun-sur-Auron, et dont le peuple a voté l'impression* (BnF, LB41–5417) (Bourges: s.a.).

De La Bastays, Lebeschu, *Culte philosophique* (BnF, LB41–846) (Paris: Year 2 [1793/94]).

Description de la fête de la Raison, célébrée pour la première fois à Strasbourg, le jour de la 3e décade de brumaire de l'an 2e de la République une, indivisible et démocratique (BnF, LB41–3528) (Strasbourg: s.a.).

---

119   "Our priests are not what vain people think; / our credulity makes their only science." See Voltaire, *Œdipe*, act 4, scene 1. Cf. *ŒCV* 2, 117.

Être suprême Peuple souverain République française (Paris, Musée Carnavalet, Inv.-No. G.26963) (Paris: 1794).

Féraud, Jean-François, *Dictionnaire critique de la langue française*, 3 vols. (Marseille: 1788).

Feuille villageoise 43 (21 July 1791).

Guillaume, James, *Procès-verbaux du Comité d'Instruction Publique de la Convention Nationale*, 8 vols. (Paris: 1891–1958).

Hymne. Sur la translation du corps de Voltaire au Panthéon. Par M. J. Chénier; Représentant du peuple. Musique de Gossec (BnF, VM7–16910) (s.l.: 1791).

Hymnes du Républicain à l'Éternel (BnF, YE–24340) (Paris: Year 2 [1793/94]).

Journal de Paris 194 (13 July 1791).

Le Maître de Claville, Charles-François-Nicolas, *Traité du vrai mérite de l'homme*, 2 vols. (Amsterdam: 1738).

Le Vieux Cordelier 2 (20 Frimaire Year 2 [12 December 1793]).

Massard, Jean Baptiste Félix, *Inscriptions du char pour la translation de Voltaire le XI juillet MDCCXCI* (BnF, G–162361) (Paris: 1791).

Notices sur la nouvelle Nomenclature des Rues de la Rochelle (BnF, LK7–3464) (La Rochelle: Year 3 [1794/95]).

Quillet, Cassius, *Rapport fait à la Societé révolutionnaire, de Rochefort, au nom de sa commission des fêtes décadaires* (London, British Library, 936.f.7.[14.]) (Rochefort: 1794).

Récit de la fête célébrée pour l'inauguration du temple de la Raison, dans la ci-devant cathédrale de Chartres, le 9 frimaire, l'an 2e. de la République, une & indivisible (BnF, LB41–3552) (Chartres: 1793).

Robespierre, Maximilien, *Œuvres de Maximilien Robespierre*, 11 vols. (Paris: 1912–2007).

Rousseau, Jean-Jacques, *Basic Political Writings*, trans. Donald A. Cress (Indianapolis: 1987).

Rousseau, Jean-Jacques, *Collection complète des œuvres de J.J. Rousseau*, 17 vols. (Geneva: 1780–1788).

Rousseau, Jean-Jacques, *Emile: or On Education*, trans. Allan Bloom (New York: 1979).

Socrate et Jean-Jacques, ou parallèle de Jean-Jacques Rousseau avec Socrate (BnF, MS–6099).

Voltaire, *Œuvres complètes de Voltaire. Nouvelle édition*, 52 vols. (Paris: 1877–1885).

Secondary Literature

Ages, Arnold, "Voltaire Rousseauiste?" *University of Windsor Review* 3 (1967): 62–8.

Aulard, François-Alphonse, *Le culte de la raison et le culte de l'être suprême: 1793–1794. Essai historique* (Paris: 1892).

Baker, Keith Michael, *Inventing the French Revolution: Essays on French Political Culture in the Eighteenth Century* (Cambridge, Eng.: 1999).

Baker, Keith Michael, *The French Revolution and the Creation of Modern Political Culture*, 4 vols. (Oxford: 1986–1992).

Barny, Roger, *Rousseau dans la Révolution: le personnage de Jean-Jacques et les débuts du culte révolutionnaire (1787–1791)* (Oxford: 1986).

Barth, Ulrich, "Seele," in *Handbuch Europäische Aufklärung. Begriffe – Konzepte – Wirkung*, ed. Heinz Thoma (Stuttgart: 2015), 465–474.

Beik, Paul H. (ed.), *The French Revolution. Selected Documents* (London: 1970).

Bell, David A., *The Cult of the Nation in France: Inventing Nationalism, 1680–1800* (Cambridge, Mass.: 2001).

Biver, Marie-Louise, *Fêtes révolutionnaires à Paris* (Paris: 1979).

Blum, Carol, *Rousseau and the Republic of Virtue: The Language of Politics in the French Revolution* (Ithaca: 1986).

Chartier, Roger, *Les origines culturelles de la Révolution française* (Paris: 1990).

Chartier, Roger, *The Cultural Origins of the French Revolution*, trans. Lydia G. Cochrane (Durham: 1991).

Constant, Pierre, *Les hymnes et chansons de la Révolution* (Paris: 1904).

Cotoni, Marie-Hélène, "La polémique contre les modernes matérialistes dans les professions de foi théistes de Rousseau," *La Lettre clandestine* 21 (2013): 191–211.

Cotoni, Marie-Hélène, "Mécréant ou chrétien? Les paradoxes dans la pensée religieuse de Jean-Jacques Rousseau," in *Jean-Jacques Rousseau (1712–2012): Matériaux pour un renouveau critique*, ed. Christophe Van Staen (Brussels: 2012), 143–157.

Culoma, Michaël, *La religion civile de Rousseau à Robespierre* (Paris: 2010).

Dagen, Jean, "Quel besoin Voltaire a-t-il de Dieu?" *La Lettre clandestine* 21 (2013): 213–227.

Delorme, Jean Jacques, *Histoire de la ville de Saint-Aignan (Loir-et-Cher)* (Saint-Aignan: 1846).

Di Rosa, Geneviève, *Rousseau et la Bible: pensée du religieux d'un philosophe des Lumières* (Leiden: 2016).

Furet, François, *Jean-Jacques Rousseau and the French Revolution: Jan-Patočka Memorial Lecture of the IWM 1994* (Vienna: 1994).

Furet, François, *Penser la Révolution française* (Paris: 1978).

Galliani, Renato, "Voltaire et les autres philosophes dans la Révolution: les brochures de 1791, 1792, 1793," *Studies on Voltaire and the Eighteenth Century* 174 (1978): 69–112.

Hidalgo, Oliver, "Voltaire und Rousseau: Zwei Antipoden im Kontext der Aufklärung und ihre Bedeutung für die Französische Revolution," in *Das Jahrhundert Voltaires: Vordenker der europäischen Aufklärung*, eds. Norbert Campagna and Rüdiger Voigt (Baden-Baden: 2020), 48–68.

Hulliung, Mark, *The Autocritique of Enlightenment: Rousseau and the Philosophes* (Cambridge, Mass.: 1994).

Israel, Jonathan I., *Democratic Enlightenment: Philosophy, Revolution, and Human Rights 1750–1790* (Oxford: 2012).

Israel, Jonathan I., *Revolutionary Ideas: An Intellectual History of the French Revolution from* The Rights of Man *to Robespierre* (Oxford: 2014).

Jacob, Margaret C., *The Radical Enlightenment: Pantheists, Freemasons and Republicans* (London: 1981).

Jacquet, Christian, *La pensée religieuse de Jean-Jacques Rousseau* (Louvain: 1975).

Kaiser, Thomas E., "This Strange Offspring of *Philosophie*: Recent Historiographical Problems in Relating the Enlightenment to the French Revolution," *French Historical Studies* 15 (1988): 549–562.

Labica, Georges, *Robespierre: Eine Politik der Philosophie* (Hamburg: 1994).

Lanson, Gustave, *Histoire de la littérature française* (Paris: 1898).

Lauritsen, Holger Ross, and Mikkel Thorup (eds.), *Rousseau and Revolution* (London: 2011).

Le Guicheux, Auguste, *Chroniques de Fresnay, Assé-le-Boisne, Douillet, Montreuil-le-Chétif, Saint-Aubin-de-Locquehay, Saint-Georges-le-Gaultier, Saint-Léonard-des-Bois, Saint-Ouen-de-Mimbré, Saint-Paul-le-Gaultier, Saint-Victeur* (Le Mans: 1877).

Leigh, Ralph A., "From the *Inégalité* to *Candide*: Notes in a Desultory Dialogue between Rousseau and Voltaire (1755–1759)," in *The Age of the Enlightenment: Studies Presented to Theodore Besterman*, ed. William Henry Barber (Edinburgh: 1967), 66–92.

Lepelletier, Almire René Jacques, *Histoire complète de la province du Maine depuis les temps les plus reculés jusqu'à nos jours*, 2 vols. (Paris: 1861).

Levine, Andrew, "Robespierre: Critic of Rousseau," *Canadian Journal of Philosophy* 8 (1978): 543–557.

MacDonald, Joan, *Rousseau and the French Revolution 1762–1791* (London: 1965; repr. 2013).

Manin, Bernard, "Rousseau," in *Dictionnaire critique de la Révolution française*, eds. François Furet and Mona Ozouf, vol. 4: *Idées* (Paris: 1992), 457–481.

Marti-Brander, Urs, *Rousseaus Schuld: Essays über die Entstehung philosophischer Feindbilder* (Basel: 2015).

Masson, Pierre-Maurice, *La religion de Jean-Jacques Rousseau*, 3 vols. (Paris: 1916).

Mathiez, Albert, "Robespierre et le culte de l'Être suprême," *Annales révolutionnaires* 3 (1910): 209–238.

Mathiez, Albert, *Les origines des cultes révolutionnaires: 1789–1792* (Paris: 1904).

McNeil, Gordon H., "The Anti-Revolutionary Rousseau," *The American Historical Review* 58 (1953): 808–823.

McNeil, Gordon H., "The Cult of Rousseau and the French Revolution," *Journal of the History of Ideas* 6 (1945): 197–212.

Mensching, Günther, "Die Sterblichkeit der Seele im französischen Materialismus," *Aufklärung* 29 (2017): 181–192.

Michelet, Jules, *Histoire de la Revolution française*, 7 vols. (*Œuvres complètes de J. Michelet*, 40 vols.) (Paris: 1893–1898).

Michelet, Jules, *History of the French Revolution*, trans. Charles Cocks (London: 1847).

Mornet, Daniel, *Les origines intellectuelles de la Révolution française: 1715–1787* (Paris: 1933).

Mostefai, Ourida, and John T. Scott (eds.), *Rousseau and L'infâme: Religion, Toleration, and Fanaticism in the Age of Enlightenment* (Amsterdam: 2009).

Ozouf, Mona, "Voltaire," in *Dictionnaire critique de la Révolution française*, eds. François Furet and Mona Ozouf, vol. 4: *Idées* (Paris: 1992), 523–539.

Ozouf, Mona, *La fête révolutionnaire: 1789–1799* (Paris: 1976).

Papenheim, Martin, "Die Dialektik der Unsterblickheit im Frankreich des 18. Jahrhunderts," *Zeitschrift für Literaturwissenschaft und Linguistik* 18 (1988): 29–43.

Papenheim, Martin, *Erinnerung und Unsterblichkeit: Semantische Studien zum Totenkult in Frankreich (1715–1794)* (Stuttgart: 1992).

Pappas, John, "Le Rousseauisme de Voltaire," *Studies on Voltaire and the Eighteenth Century* 57 (1967): 1169–1181.

Parker, Noel, "Religion and Politics: Voltaire's and Rousseau's Enlightenment Strategies," *Distinction: Scandinavian Journal of Social Theory* 7 (2006): 93–115.

Pečar, Andreas, and Damien Tricoire, *Falsche Freunde: War die Aufklärung wirklich die Geburtsstunde der Moderne?* (Frankfurt a.M.: 2015).

Perrochon, Henri, "Noé-Antoine-Abraham Bonjour (1731–1807): politique, stratégie et histoire des religions," *Revue historique vaudoise* 80 (1972): 33–47.

Pomeau, René, *La religion de Voltaire* (Paris: 1969).

Robisco, Nathalie-Barbara, *Jean-Jacques Rousseau et la Révolution française: une esthétique de la politique 1792–1799* (Paris: 1998).

Rockwood, Raymond, "The Legend of Voltaire and the Cult of the Revolution, 1791," in *Ideas in History. Essays Presented to Louis Gottschalk by His Former Students*, eds. Richard Herr and Harold T. Parker (Durham: 1965), 110–134.

Rockwood, Raymond, *The Apotheosis of Voltaire during the French Revolution*, unpublished Ph.D. dissertation (Chicago: 1931).

Schinz, Albert, *La pensée religieuse de Rousseau et ses récents interprètes* (Northampton, Mass.: 1928).

Schönpflug, Daniel, "La faute à Voltaire? Secularizations and the Origins of the French Revolution," in *Redefining the Sacred: Religion in the French and Russian Revolutions*, eds. Daniel Schönpflug and Martin Schulze Wessel (Frankfurt a.M.: 2012), 25–50.

Sheu, Ling-Ling, *Voltaire et Rousseau dans le théâtre de la Révolution française (1789–1799)* (Brussels: 2005).

Smyth, Jonathan, *Robespierre and the Festival of the Supreme Being: The Search for a Republican Morality* (Manchester: 2016).

Swenson, James, *On Jean-Jacques Rousseau: Considered as One of the First Authors of the Revolution* (Stanford: 2000).

Tate, Robert S., "Rousseau and Voltaire as Deists: A Comparison," *L'Esprit Créateur* 9 (1969): 175–186.

Thomson, Ann, *L'âme des lumières: le débat sur l'être humain entre religion et science; Angleterre-France (1690–1760)* (Seyssel: 2013).

Torrey, Norman, *The Spirit of Voltaire* (New York: 1938).

Trousson, Raymond, *Rousseau et sa fortune littéraire* (Paris: 1977).

Waldinger, Renée, *Voltaire and Reform in the Light of the French Revolution* (Geneva: 1959).

Waterlot, Ghislain (ed.), *La théologie politique de Rousseau* (Rennes: 2010).

CHAPTER 8

D'Holbach and Deism

Hasse Hämäläinen

1   Introduction

According to a received interpretation, baron d'Holbach rejects both the-ism (belief in a personal God) and deism (belief in a God not personal but manifested in empirical nature, the most influential representative of which in d'Holbach's intellectual milieu was Voltaire). This chapter evaluates the jus-tifications for this interpretation based on d'Holbach's main work, *Système de la Nature*.

After introducing the received interpretation in part two, the succeeding parts of this chapter show that d'Holbach knowingly fails to refute the intel-ligent design argument, which is the most famous argument that Voltaire used for deism. Part three concentrates on the "watchmaker" version of this argu-ment, and part four on its later, "biological" version. However, the fact that d'Holbach cannot refute the rationality of believing in a deist God based on what we know about nature does not yet imply that he must approve of deism, because *ethical reasons* for unbelief can warrant ignoring the possible *epis-temic reasons* for belief.

Although some of d'Holbach's arguments about achieving happiness can be interpreted as eliminating ethical grounds for approving deism, part five of this chapter claims that his other arguments do not support these readings. D'Holbach writes that he has nothing against believing in God provided that such belief does not entail socially harmful dogmas, as, in the end, spiritual beliefs are "not accessible to reason."[1] He even says that religion, just like gov-ernment, could be "reasonable" (*raisonnable*) if only it promoted people's hap-piness.[2] Using the concept of "happiness" (*bonheur*), d'Holbach refers to being in a state in which one wants to be.[3] Although d'Holbach argued that any existing theist religion undermines people's happiness, this does not mean that no reli-gion could be reasonable. A religion that does not have any dogmas, such as

---

1   Paul-Henri Thiry d'Holbach, *The System of Nature*, vol. 1, trans. Henry D. Robinson (Kitchener: 2010), 9.

2   Ibid., 169.

3   Ibid., 72.

Voltaire's deism, is reasonable. This part concludes that d'Holbach should thus not be read as an opponent of deism *tout court*.

Part six investigates why d'Holbach thought that the existing religions could not be reformed towards a reasonable religion but must be destroyed. It shows that d'Holbach's pessimism towards religious reform derives from his conception of the essence of traditional religions as forms of oppression. Part seven asks why d'Holbach, although he acknowledged reasonable deism, nevertheless chose atheism as his worldview. This part argues that even though reasonable deism would not undermine one's happiness and could even contribute to it, one can also be happy without such deism, according to d'Holbach. Thus, although we might have epistemic reasons to be deists, a happy atheist lacks an ethical reason to choose deism over atheism. For d'Holbach, only ethical reasons can motivate our choices because all our desires are desires for happiness.

2   D'Holbach: An Enemy of Deism?

Jean-Paul Thiry, baron d'Holbach, was not among the first atheists (people who do not believe in the existence of God) in Europe.[4] The first known atheist was the German pamphleteer Matthias Knutzen, who lived a century before him.[5] Even in France, d'Holbach was not among the first atheists. By the time of d'Holbach, atheistic arguments had circulated among the French reading public for over a century as *littérature clandestine*.[6] Among philosophical authors known outside this literature, already some three decades before d'Holbach, Julien Offray de La Mettrie had acquired notoriety as a promoter of a materialistic and deterministic conception of the human being. Among the regular guests at d'Holbach's *salon*, Claude-Adrien Helvétius and Denis Diderot had presented arguments that undermined religious belief some years earlier than the baron.[7]

Although d'Holbach scored no firsts among the pioneers of atheism, what makes him unique was the systemic and comprehensive character of his exposition of atheism and the work he put in promoting it. His great two-part work, *Système de la Nature*, true to its title, did not only focus on criticizing the nature of the human soul and showing the harmful implications of religion

---

4   *Pace* Michael J. Buckley, *At the Origins of Modern Atheism* (New Haven: 1989), 30.

5   Winfried Schröder (ed.), *Matthias Knutzen, Schriften und Materialien* (Stuttgart: 2010), 8.

6   For an overview of the history of the clandestine literature in France during the *ancien régime*, see e.g. Guido Canziani (ed.), *Filosofia e religione nella letteratura clandestina: secoli XVII e XVIII* (Milan: 1994).

7   See Claude-Adrien Helvétius, *L'Esprit* (Paris: 1758) and Denis Diderot, *Lettre sur les aveugles* (London: 1749).

on an individual's happiness. The *Système* also criticized the dogmatism of the existing religions, envisaging the world without a need for God. Shortly after its publication in London in 1770, under the name of d'Holbach's recently deceased friend Jean Baptiste de Mirabaud, this work became a bestseller and a point of reference for both atheists and apologists of religion alike.[8]

According to an assessment by Henry Vyverberg, La Mettrie, Helvétius and Diderot built the groundwork for the emergence of atheism as an acceptable philosophical worldview. However, "it was only d'Holbach who particularly stressed the universal roles of matter and motion, and who devised elaborate schemes of educational and legislative action as the foundations, together with experimental science, for a universal morality."[9] Unlike his predecessors, d'Holbach not only formulated arguments for atheism but arguably also presented a godless *alternative* to any form of religion, whether theistic or deistic. This alternative was based on a hope that one day, natural science will be able to trace our every belief – including our belief in the existence of God – back to our desires and desires to sensations, sensations to movements, and movements to the laws of nature.[10] And unlike the atheistic works of other *philosophes*, which were not widely perceived as threatening the position of deism as the most influential challenger to the established religion, the deists might have perceived d'Holbach differently. Even the arch-deist Voltaire was sufficiently interested in dedicating several letters and an essay to showing that "it is rather shameful to our nation that so many people have so quickly embraced such a ridiculous system" as d'Holbach's.[11]

According to Jonathan Israel, Voltaire's invectives against d'Holbach show that the deistic establishment had become finally afraid of the power of the atheistic arguments, as the *Système* had laid bare that they were more coherent

---

8   According to Mark Curran, "D'Holbach was the second most read *philosophe* after Voltaire. Out of 28219 prohibited books ordered by French booksellers from STN [Société typographique de Neuchâtel, a leading distributor of books prohibited by the royal censors – H.H.], 2903 were by Holbach." See *Atheism, Religion and Enlightenment in Pre-Revolutionary Europe* (Woolbridge: 2012), 5. Michael Buckley writes that d'Holbach's *Système* was "the most important demonstration of materialism and atheism until the middle of the twentieth century." See Buckley, *At the Origins of Modern Atheism*, 32, and Henri Lion, "Essai sur les oeuvres politiques et morales du Baron d'Holbach," *Annales revolutionnaires* 14 (1922): 89, which is the original source of this view.

9   Henry Vyverberg, *Human Nature, Cultural Diversity and the French Enlightenment* (New York: 1989), 13.

10   Buckley, *At the Origins of Modern Atheism*, 291.

11   See, e.g., Voltaire's letters D16666, D16602, 16673, 16693, 16736, 16678 in *Voltaire's Correspondence*, vol. 120, ed. Theodore Besterman (Oxford: 1974). The essay is titled "Dieu, Dieux," and is in Voltaire's *Questions sur l'encyclopedie*, vol. 15 (London: 1771).

than the deists' arguments. Israel claims that, on the one hand, there was the "moderate" deist Enlightenment spearheaded by Voltaire, and on the other, the "radical" atheistic current flowing from d'Holbach's *salon*.[12] As both sides targeted the Catholic Church, the deist camp usually tolerated the radicals to a certain extent. However, the appearance of the *Système* made the latter perceived as threatening Voltaire's pre-eminence.[13] Israel thinks, though, that "what chiefly antagonised Voltaire was not the irreligion but [the *Système*'s] anti-monarchical and anti-aristocratic orientation."[14]

Not many would agree with Israel regarding d'Holbach's opposition to monarchy or aristocracy, as this claim lacks sufficient textual basis.[15] D'Holbach nowhere claims that these institutions should not exist. In the only place of the *Système* where the baron, a wealthy aristocrat, discusses revolution, he writes:

> Princes sacrifice their true happiness, as well as that of their states, to these passions, to those caprices, which discourage the people, which plunge their provinces in misery, which make millions unhappy without any advantage to themselves.... The misery of a people produces revolutions: soured by misfortunes, their minds get into a state of fermentation, and the overthrow of an empire is the necessary effect.[16]

Instead of displaying opposition to monarchy or aristocracy, this passage *warns* monarchs and aristocrats against priests, who have always "breathed forth fanaticism and fury, and obliged [them] to disturb the public tranquility, every time there was a question of the interests of the invisible monarch of another life, or the real interests of his ministers in this."[17] That is, unless the rulers stop listening to the priests, a popular revolution shall happen. However, d'Holbach does not describe such a revolution as desirable.

A long interpretative tradition supports Israel's second point, though, that d'Holbach threatened deism more than his atheist colleagues and predecessors.

---

12   Jonathan I. Israel, *A Revolution of the Mind: Radical Enlightenment and the Intellectual Origins of Modern Democracy* (Princeton: 2011), 217.

13   See ibid., c. 6, esp. 208–217, and Jonathan I. Israel, *The Enlightenment that Failed: Ideas, Revolution, and Democratic Defeat, 1748–1830* (Oxford: 2019), 193–206.

14   Ibid., 164.

15   See Javier Peña Echeverría, "La teoría política de d'Holbach y sus presupuestos filosóficos," *Revista de Estudios Políticos* 179 (2018): 13–41. Cf. Anthony J. La Vopa, who notes that "quite a few" figures labelled as proponents of revolution by Israel did not oppose "aristocratic wealth and privilege." Anthony J. La Vopa, "A New Intellectual History? Jonathan Israel's Enlightenment," *The Historical Journal* 52 (2009): 729.

16   D'Holbach, *The System of Nature*, vol. 1, 174.

17   Ibid., 141.

According to this tradition, d'Holbach is the *philosophe* that most openly endorses atheism and considers it certain that *no* God exists.[18] Apart from Vyverberg, Buckley, and Israel, Alan Charles Kors writes that d'Holbach thus confirmed "the worst fears of the faithful about their age, dismaying deists."[19] Alain Sandrier labels d'Holbach as a "proselytiser of atheism" against deism in general and Voltaire in particular.[20] If publicly exposing the incoherence of deism was indeed d'Holbach's aim, it becomes understandable why Voltaire had to react to his work.

In order to evaluate whether d'Holbach's arguments against deism were so compelling that they could have made Voltaire afraid of him, we turn to Voltaire's design argument, of which he had two versions that can be dubbed as "watchmaker" and "biological." He considered these arguments the most robust demonstrations for the existence of God. Since Voltaire presented the former version two decades before the latter, we first assess d'Holbach's counterargument to it.

3   Voltaire's Watchmaker Argument and d'Holbach's Response

In his letter to canon lawyer Ludwig Martin Kahle (1744), Voltaire announced that reading Newton's theories has affirmed that he shall "always be convinced that a watch proves the existence of a watchmaker and that the universe proves the existence of a God."[21] At least since writing *Eléments de la philosophie de Newton* (1738), Voltaire had supported the view that "Newton's philosophy necessarily leads to the cognition of a Supreme Being, who created everything," as the system of the laws of nature that Newton has discovered is so coherent that

---

18   Alan Charles Kors, "Atheism of d'Holbach and Naigeon," in *Atheism from Reformation to the Enlightenment*, eds. Michael Hunter and David Wootton (Oxford: 1992), 273–300; Alain Sandrier, *Le style philosophique du baron d'Holbach. Conditions et contraintes du prosélytisme athée en France dans la seconde moitié du XVIIIᵉ siècle* (Paris: 2004); Michael LeBuffe and Emilie Gourdon, "Holbach," in *A Companion to Atheism and Philosophy*, ed. Graham Oppy (Oxford: 2019), 28–43.

19   Kors, "Atheism of d'Holbach and Naigeon," 274.

20   Sandrier, *Le style philosophique du baron d'Holbach*, 2.

21   Voltaire, "Lettre 1664," in *Œuvres complètes de Voltaire*, vol. 36 (Paris: 1880), 309. Notice that David Beeson and Nicholas Cronk attribute this famous passage to *Eléments de la philosophie de Newton*, and this misattribution has been present in scholarly discussion ever since. "Voltaire: philosopher or *philosophe*?" in *The Cambridge Companion to Voltaire*, ed. Nicholas Cronk (Cambridge: 2009), 63 n. 5.

it must be the work of an intelligent designer.[22] D'Holbach made a sustained attempt to address this argument in the second part of the *Système*, which contains an entire chapter dedicated to it. The counterargument that the baron presents in that chapter is as follows:

> [A]ll those who speak of the divine goodness, wisdom, and intelligence, which are shown in the works of nature; who offer these same works as incontestable proofs of the existence of a God, or of a perfect agent, are men prejudiced or blinded by their own imagination, who see only a corner of the picture of the universe, without the whole. Intoxicated with the phantom which their mind has formed to itself, they resemble those lovers who do not perceive any defect in the objects of their affection; they conceal, dissimulate, and justify their vices and deformities, and frequently mistake them for perfections.[23]

The problem of the deist conception of God for d'Holbach is that what it conceives as God's essential attributes are derived from the subjective perceptions of human beings. If one sees nature as a perfect system and thus a result of intelligent design, one's perception can be explained by one's "optimist" mental disposition.[24] However, "whenever one's machine becomes deranged":

> [T]he spectacle of nature, which, under certain circumstances, has appeared to them so delightful and so seducing, must then give place to disorder and confusion. A man of a melancholy temperament, soured by misfortunes or infirmities, cannot view nature and its author under the same perspective as the healthy man of sprightly humour and content with everything. Deprived of happiness, the peevish man can only find disorder, deformity, and subjects to afflict himself with; he only contemplates the universe as the theatre of malice or the vengeance of an angry tyrant.[25]

For d'Holbach, the above observation implies that "deists have no real ground to separate themselves from the superstitions."[26] According to him, the only relevant difference between a deist and a superstitious person is that, unlike the former, the latter has undergone hardships that have made him perceive

---

22 See Voltaire, "Éléments de la philosophie de Newton," in *Œuvres complètes de Voltaire*, vol. 22 (Paris: 1880), 403.

23 D'Holbach, *The System of Nature*, vol. 2, 76.

24 Ibid., 77.

25 Ibid.

26 Ibid., 80.

nature as "a valley of tears."[27] Consequently, the superstitious person is unable
to endorse the deists' idealistic view that nature is a perfectly rational system.
Hence d'Holbach concludes his criticism of the "watchmaker" argument in
this way:

> Let us conclude, then, that the man who is the most credulously supersti-
> tious reasons in a manner more consistent than those, who, after having
> admitted a God of whom they have no idea, stop all at once, and refuse to
> admit those systems of conduct which are the immediate and necessary
> result of this radical and primitive error.[28]

D'Holbach's conclusion suggests that insofar as a deist claims to believe in God
based on the perfection of nature but knowingly closes his eyes to any imperfections in nature, the deist is both irrational and inconsistent in his "optimism." An example of such a deist is Voltaire: as a philosopher, he believes
in an intelligent designer, but as a novelist, he had to admit in *Candide* that
based on our everyday experiences, "If this is the best of all possible worlds,
then what must the others be like?"[29] A superstitious person is also irrational,
but he is true to his experience and sees God as malicious. In this picture, an
atheist would be the only person who can both acknowledge reality and stay
rational by rejecting the existence of an evil God.

D'Holbach's counterargument to the watchmaker argument does not conclude that God does not exist but that the interpretation of nature does not
provide justifications for believing in the existence of God. The watchmaker
argument illegitimately assumes that one's subjective mental state and conception of God that results from it is shared by everyone else. Believing in God
based on such a false universalization undermines one's rationality regardless
of whether one naively assumes that the world is good or absurdly that God
is evil.

However, although d'Holbach's argument is internally consistent, it crucially
fails to expose Voltaire's *whole* argument for the intelligent designer. Voltaire
did not claim that the coherence of the laws of nature implies that nature is a

---

27   Ibid., 77.
28   Ibid., 81.
29   The whole passage reads: "If this is the best of all possible worlds, then what must the
      others be like? I wouldn't mind if I'd only been flogged. That happened with the Bulgars.
      But, o my dear Pangloss! You, the greatest of philosophers! Did I have to see you hanged
      without my knowing why?! O my dear Anabaptist! You, the best of men! Did you have
      to drown in the port?! O Miss Cunegonde! You pearl among daughters! Did you have to
      have your stomach slit open?!" Voltaire, *Candide and Other Stories*, trans. Roger Pearson
      (Oxford: 2006), 15.

perfect system in any moral or aesthetic sense. Furthermore, while d'Holbach presents the deist as thinking that the existence of the laws of nature *proves* the existence of a perfectly intelligent being, outside his letters to religious thinkers such as Kahle, Voltaire writes that they only show it is more *likely* that God exists than not:

> From [the watchmaker] argument, I cannot conclude anything more, except that an intelligent and superior being has likely prepared and shaped matter with some cleverness ... However profoundly I search my mind for the connection between the following ideas – it is likely that I am the work of a being more powerful than myself; therefore, this being has existed from all eternity; therefore, he has created everything; therefore, he is infinite, and so on – I cannot see the chain which leads directly to that conclusion. I can see only that there is something more powerful than myself, and nothing more.[30]

Based on the laws of nature, Voltaire thinks he can confidently say *no more* than that a powerful God likely exists. He thinks he cannot acknowledge that God must have any perfections the existing religions have traditionally attributed to the divine being, such as eternity, omnipotence and omnipresence. By skipping these essential qualifications that Voltaire adds to his watchmaker argument, d'Holbach makes it seem that Voltaire's philosophical deism is incompatible with the down-to-earth realism of *Candide*. However, suppose that these qualifications were not skipped. In that case, Voltaire could be read as consistently holding that although the world is organized according to the laws of nature and thereby presupposes an intelligent designer, there is no guarantee that this designer must be morally and aesthetically perfect or that it has designed the world in the best possible way.

Acknowledging the brutality of our daily reality is not inconsistent with thinking that the laws of nature presuppose an intelligent designer. It would be inconsistent if and only if the designer were to be concerned with the fortunes of humanity, but this is a claim that a deist does not need to make. Like d'Holbach, the deist can acknowledge the world's aesthetic and moral imperfections without rejecting God, but only rejecting, like Spinoza, the projection of any "human" mental states, such as benevolence (or malignancy) onto God. Thus, because Voltairean deism, *pace* d'Holbach, does not need to presuppose "optimism," d'Holbach's counterargument to the watchmaker argument fails to be conclusive.

---

30   Voltaire, *Traité de métaphysique* (Manchester: 1957), §2.

4   Voltaire's Biological Design Argument and Another
         Failed Response

In the aftermath of *Candide*, Voltaire might have come to think that apart from
the coherence of the laws of nature, there must be an argument for the existence of God that is less vulnerable to being overstretched by the "optimists" to
"prove" the perfection of everything. This argument is the "biological" design
argument. According to Voltaire, it is a biological fact that the existence of living beings presupposes a giver of life. In his *Dictionnaire philosophique portatif*
(1764) he makes it clear that:

> Atheism [the lack of belief in the existence of God] is very pernicious
> in those who govern, but also in the learned even where their lives are
> innocent because from their study they can exert influence on those in
> authority; that if atheism is not as harmful as fanaticism, it almost always
> proves deadly for virtue. There are now fewer atheists than ever, since
> the day when philosophers acknowledged that there is no growing thing
> without seed, no seed without design, and so on, and that wheat does not
> spring from putrefaction.[31]

Apart from winking at d'Holbach by suggesting that atheism is harmful to
morality, a point to which we shall return, Voltaire adds that the popularity of
atheism is waning. Atheism claims that life is spontaneously generated from
matter and it cannot acknowledge that every living being is born from a "seed"
that evidently contains a blueprint for that being. Only an intelligent designer
could have stuffed these seeds with blueprints for life; to think anything else
would beg the question. This observation inspired Voltaire to even conclude
that "it is perfectly evident to my mind that there exists a necessary, eternal,
supreme, and intelligent being. This is not a matter of faith, but of reason."[32]

If the confident tone of Voltaire's conclusions can be treated as an indica-
tor, he was more convinced with his biological design argument than with the
watchmaker version. However, d'Holbach's counterargument to this argument
is considerably shorter than his reply to the watchmaker argument. It does not
take even one entire paragraph in the first part of the *Système*:

---

31   Voltaire, "Athee, Atheism," in *Pocket Philosophical Dictionary*, trans. John Fletcher (Oxford:
       2011), 145–161.
32   Voltaire, "Faith," in *Philosophical Dictionary*, trans. William Dugdale (London 1843), 473
       (this chapter is not included in the *Dictionnaire philosophique portatif*, which was an ear-
       lier version of the same work).

If flour be wetted with water, and the mixture closed up, it will be found, after some little lapse of time, by the aid of a microscope, to have produced organised beings that enjoy life, of which the water and the flour were believed incapable: it is thus that inanimate matter can pass into life, or animate matter, which is in itself only an assemblage of motion. Reasoning from analogy, the production of a man, independent of the ordinary means, would not be more marvellous than that of an insect with flour and water. Fermentation and putrefaction evidently produce living animals.[33]

As his only argument against the biological design argument, d'Holbach appeals to the claimed empirical observation that combining "water and flour" can generate living organisms. He seems to think that this observation suffices to demonstrate that life – and by implication, human life – can arise without the influx of an immaterial cause such as a soul, spirit, or intelligent designer.

The observation that d'Holbach seems to regard as indisputable as Voltaire regards his conclusion was based exclusively on the experiments of John Needham published in French in 1750.[34] One of these experiments that he designed together with a *philosophe* Georges-Louis Leclerc de Buffon involved water and flour, and another used mutton broth as its source material. The test equipment was not sterilized in the former experiment, but in the latter, a broth sample was first boiled and then closed to a jar. In both cases, after a few days, Needham observed previously unseen "small worms" in the test sample, which, according to him, proved that living organisms could arise from non-living matter. However, by the time of d'Holbach, an Italian priest and natural scientist Lazzaro Spallanzani had famously and conclusively refuted the validity of these experiments by showing that if the jars were properly hermetically sealed and the boiling time extended from a few minutes to one hour, *no* "worms" appeared until the jar was opened to receive airborne lifeforms.[35] D'Holbach must have been aware of this refutation, but apparently, he chose to ignore it in his argumentation because without demonstrating that life can arise from non-living matter, he could not present a plausible alternative candidate for divinely designed "seeds" as the source of life.[36]

---

33   D'Holbach, *The System of Nature*, vol. 1, 21.

34   John Needham, *Nouvelles observations microscopiques* (Paris: 1751).

35   Lazzaro Spallanzani, *Saggio di osservazioni microscopiche concernenti il sistema della generazione* (Modena: 1765).

36   Needham thought that d'Holbach, a "false philosopher," was misusing the results of his experiments to demonstrate atheism, which they could not demonstrate. See

Voltaire understood that d'Holbach's argument failed. The fact that d'Holbach's atheism was "based on a false experiment made by an Irish Jesuit who has been mistaken for a philosopher" was why Voltaire judged his thought incoherent and "ridiculous."[37] Thus, we need to conclude that d'Holbach did not demonstrate why anyone should prefer his atheism to the kind of deism supported by Voltaire's arguments. On the one hand, d'Holbach could tolerate his failure to refute the watchmaker argument: the baron can claim that the concept of God who only designs the laws of nature but ignores what happens in the world makes the concept of God useless and apt to be removed from the language. Apart from calling Voltaire's God "useless," he also writes that "if God is to the human species what colours are to the man born blind, this God has no existence with relation to us ... let us not occupy ourselves with him."[38] On the other hand, d'Holbach's failure against the biological design argument is very problematic to his atheism. According to Winfried Schröder, the fact that atheists such as d'Holbach had no good counterarguments to deism, together with the fact that only theism and deism were able to explain the origin of life, prevented most people from taking d'Holbach's atheism or any other form of atheism seriously.[39]

Should we thus conclude that Israel is unjustified in claiming that Voltaire was directing verbal attacks against d'Holbach because he was afraid of the force of the baron's arguments, and concur with the assessment of Anthony La Vopa, according to whom Israel suffers a "failure to demonstrate the unity and coherence he claims for radical thought?"[40] In the case of d'Holbach, this conclusion would be too hasty. Contrary to his reputation as an atheist, d'Holbach does not argue for God's non-existence when attempting to refute the versions of the intelligent design argument. The lack of an argument for the non-existence of God in this context can suggest that we should seek his argument for atheism elsewhere. According to Kors, d'Holbach's view is that instead of discussing the possibility of the existence of God, we should "limit our language and thought to the superficial corporeal structure of actual experience" and argue that for the sake of maximizing our happiness, we should not believe in God even if the existence of God could not be demonstrated

Shirley A. Roe, "Voltaire Versus Needham: Atheism, Materialism, and the Generation of Life," *Journal of the History of Ideas* 46 (1985): 83.

37   Letter D16666 in *Voltaire's Correspondence*.

38   D'Holbach refers here to Diderot's *Lettre sur les aveugles* (London: 1749). See d'Holbach, *The System of Nature*, vol. 2, 36.

39   Schröder, *Ursprünge des Atheismus*, 315.

40   La Vopa, "A New Intellectual History?" 725.

impossible.[41] The next part will show that even this interpretation exaggerates the strength of d'Holbach's commitment to atheism, as he is not even confident that an atheist is necessarily happier than a non-optimistic, Voltairean deist.

5   D'Holbach's Ethical Argument for Atheism and Its Implications for Deism

The canon of the Cathedral of Notre-Dame, *abbé* Nicolas-Sylvestre Bergier concluded in his *Examen du matérialisme, ou Réfutation du Système de la nature* (1771) that when faced with the arguments of d'Holbach, there are only two options that a deist can choose from: "either to make common cause with the theologians or to accept a triumph of atheism."[42] In the light of the weaknesses of the baron's arguments against Voltaire's design arguments, Bergier's warning about the imminent threat of atheism to deism may appear ingenuine and purely rhetorical. Although Bergier might theoretically have failed to notice the weaknesses in d'Holbach's claims, such omission seems nevertheless highly unlikely for this most famous 18th-century apologist of the Catholic Church.

A more likely and charitable explanation for Bergier's stance and one supported by the text of the *Examen* would be that he thinks that d'Holbach's most threatening ideas are not those weak *epistemic* assertions that he throws against the design arguments. Instead, according to Bergier, the deist's motive for choosing to side with the theologians would be *ethical*: Bergier writes that according to the baron, "belief in God is the enemy of happiness," defined as "satisfying the desires of man."[43] If d'Holbach succeeded in convincing his readers that only atheism offers happiness, this offer would be a reason for many to choose unbelief over belief in God regardless of the baron's inability to refute the design arguments. Although according to Voltaire, there are "fewer atheists than ever" today due to this inability, Voltaire's opinion might not be sincere because why would he otherwise have dedicated so much effort to attacking d'Holbach and atheism? Both Bergier and Voltaire seem to think that the baron's practical considerations require counterarguments, unlike his theses against the design argument. Bergier claims, for example, that without

---

41   Kors, "Atheism of d'Holbach and Naigeon," 280.

42   Nicolas Sylvestre Bergier, *Examen du matérialisme, ou réfutation du Système de la nature*, vol. 1 (Paris: 1771), 489–491.

43   Ibid., 391.

assuming that God exists, we will not reach happiness but fall into depression, because no "earthly source of joy can satisfy the desires of man ... only religion offers man the hope for reaching happiness,"[44] and Voltaire stipulates that for us to be able to be happy in this unjust world, we need to postulate God as the guarantor of the punishment of evil and of the reward of virtue in the afterlife (even if there was no afterlife).[45]

D'Holbach's ethical argument against the existence of God in the *Système* is to be found in a series of statements scattered across his epistemic arguments. This can explain why it has received less scholarly attention than the latter. Alan Charles Kors, Michael LeBuffe and Emilie Gourdon are some of the few recent interpreters who treat it as the centrepiece of the *Système*. The argument emerges when we combine d'Holbach's following claims, each presented in a different location in the *Système*. First, he claims that "the source of man's unhappiness is his ignorance of Nature."[46] Then he says that "happy is [he] who knows how to enjoy the benefits of nature."[47] He adds to this that religious belief "precludes our research into the true cause of the effects which we see" and that religion offers "magical stories" as explanations for natural phenomena.[48] Treating these claims as premises, LeBuffe and Gourdon have arrived at the same conclusion as *abbé* Bergier. According to them, for d'Holbach, atheism "is an important part of the wise person's happiness and ... by contrast, the belief in God produces suffering."[49]

D'Holbach's above claims leave space for interpretative disagreement: manifesting the "notoriously imprecise" language of the *philosophes*,[50] the baron does not clarify what kind of epistemic attitude the rejection of religious belief that shall enable one to reach happiness is. For LeBuffe and Gourdon, this rejection means being sure that God does not exist. In contrast, according to Kors, it means merely not believing in the existence of God. D'Holbach's answer to his self-posed question "who is an atheist?" which LeBuffe and Gourdon fail to cite, clearly supports Kors. The baron writes: "no man can be certain of the existence of an inconceivable being, in whom inconsistent qualities are said to be united. In this sense, many theologians would be atheists."[51]

---

44   Ibid.
45   See Voltaire, "To Frederic, Prince Royal of Prussia: On God, Soul and Innate Morality," in *Voltaire in his Letters*, trans. Stephen G. Tallentyne (New York: 1919), 47–50.
46   D'Holbach, *The System of Nature*, vol. 1, 7.
47   Ibid., 12.
48   Ibid., 180.
49   LeBuffe and Gourdon, "Holbach," 33.
50   Vyverberg, *Human Nature*, 6.
51   D'Holbach, *The System of Nature*, vol. 2, 190.

This suggests that for d'Holbach, an atheist is not only one who knows that God does not exist but also whoever does not know if God exists – a position nowadays called "agnostic." Kors claims that d'Holbach's opposition to believing in the existence of God is motivated by "utilitarian" considerations.[52] That is, independently of the question of whether or not God exists, for the sake of maximizing our happiness, which d'Holbach defines as "any mode of existence of which man naturally wishes the duration, or in which he is willing to continue,"[53] we should abstain from believing in the existence of God.

Although Kors' claim about the agnostic character of d'Holbach's "atheism" has textual support – which renders his interpretation more justified than LeBuffe's and Gourdon's proposal – his other thesis, that d'Holbach prefers atheism to deism because only the former can maximize one's happiness, has less apparent textual foundations. So far, we have seen the baron claim that superstition results in unhappiness, but he does not claim anything similar about deism, which, even though sharing the same "real ground" with superstition, namely belief in God, is not identical to it.[54] Hence, Kors' thesis about d'Holbach's ethical argument for atheism rests only on the many passages in which the baron describes the negative contribution of *superstition* to one's happiness.[55]

However, in Kors' defence, there is one line in the *Système* that *could* be taken to imply that also deism harms one's happiness: "it is with the gods in heaven that the reform must commence; it is by removing these imaginary beings ... that we shall be able to promise ourselves to conduct man to a state of maturity."[56] By speaking about "gods" here, d'Holbach can refer to (also) non-Christian deities, including the deist God. The inconsistency between unjust reality and the mental images of the perfect God that d'Holbach attributes to deism can be interpreted as a sign of moral immaturity, and, presumably, an immature person cannot be happy. However, even if this line implied all these propositions, it could still refer only to the "optimist" deism, but not to the Voltairean deism according to which God is the author of the laws of nature without possessing any moral properties. Thus, although Kors is justified in interpreting d'Holbach's "atheism" as agnostic, he is not justified in claiming

---

52   Kors, "Atheism of d'Holbach and Naigeon," 275–280.

53   D'Holbach, *The System of Nature*, vol. 1, 72. Cf. the more Aristotelian formulation in vol. 2, 171: "The final end of man is self-preservation, and rendering his existence happy."

54   Ibid., 80.

55   Kors' citation is extremely general: "*Systeme* 1.1–12." Together, these chapters extend over 100 pages and in none of them does d'Holbach discuss deism. Kors, "Atheism of d'Holbach and Naigeon," 277 n. 8.

56   D'Holbach, *The System of Nature*, vol. 2, 150. However, Kors does not quote this passage.

that for d'Holbach, "above all else, the benefits that would accrue to humanity from adopting a materialist and atheistic world-view" make this worldview "preferable" to deism.[57]

As it is now clarified that d'Holbach's ethical argument for atheism does not undermine the non-optimistic deism of Voltaire, we can proceed to show that in the *Système*, he even expresses toleration for such deism. This attitude would be understandable if he regarded it (unlike the "optimist" deism and superstition) as a reasonable worldview. There are at least two passages in which such a view is expressed. The first of them is in the introduction to the *Système*:

> If [one] must have his chimeras, let him at least learn to permit others to form theirs after their own fashion; since nothing can be more immaterial than the manner of men's thinking on subjects not accessible to reason, provided those thoughts will not result in actions injurious to others: above all, let him be fully persuaded that it is of the utmost importance to the inhabitants of this world to be just, kind, and peaceable.[58]

The above passage states that belief in the existence of God, which for d'Holbach is a "chimera," can be tolerated provided that the believer does not want to force others to believe in her God and that her belief emphasizes justice, mutual kindness and peace above all religious dogmas. A religion like this would resemble Voltaire's non-optimist deism. On the other hand, d'Holbach's toleration of such deism is due to the inaccessibility of God to reason, which runs contrary to Voltaire's claims about the existence of God being "not a matter of faith, but of reason,"[59] and brings to the fore once more that the baron's stance towards the question of the existence of God is agnostic.

The second passage can be found towards the end of the first part of the *Système*. The tone of this passage lacks the derision of the first passage, in which religion was called a "chimera":

> Government and religion could be reasonable institutions only inasmuch as they equally contributed to the felicity of man: it would be folly in him to submit himself to a yoke from which these [sic! – H.H.] resulted nothing but evil: it would be rank injustice to oblige him to renounce his rights, without some corresponding advantage.[60]

---

57   Kors, "Atheism of d'Holbach and Naigeon," 275.
58   D'Holbach, *The System of Nature*, vol. 1, 9.
59   Voltaire, "Faith," in *Philosophical Dictionary*, 473.
60   D'Holbach, *The System of Nature*, vol. 1, 169.

Here d'Holbach admits the possibility of both government and religion becoming "reasonable" (*raisonnable*). Provided that they are reformed to start producing happiness instead of evil, this goal is achievable. The "evil" that religion produces must refer to the "ignorance of the true causes" that prevents the religious people from seeing the natural causes of events[61] and the "fear" and "trembling" they feel as a result of conceiving God, whom they consider the cause of natural events, as an "angry and cruel tyrant."[62] It can additionally refer to the gap between the "optimist" deists' benevolent God and brutal reality.[63] A reasonable religion would thus be religion without these implications, one that promotes natural science, a realistic conception of the world, and the lack of fear towards spiritual beings. Non-optimistic, Voltairean deism would tick all these boxes.

However, although it now seems that d'Holbach could consider Voltaire's deism as a tolerable and even approvable alternative for his agnostic unbelief, it is not yet clear why he does not acknowledge the possibility of reforming the existing "superstition" towards a reasonable religion. It is equally unclear why he is an atheist, even though none of his epistemological or ethical arguments can refute this deism. In the next part, these remaining issues will be investigated.

6   The Impossibility of Religious Reform

According to d'Holbach, the corrosive influence of the existing religions or "superstition" on society is not accidental but is due to the essence of superstition. We all pursue happiness or self-preservation, but we do not possess any "innate" conception of the ways of reaching this goal:

> It is never by any other means than by his senses, that beings become known to man, or furnish him with ideas; it is only in consequence of the impulse given to his body, that his brain is modified; or that his soul thinks, wills, and acts ... [W]hat is called moral sentiment, a moral instinct, that is, innate ideas of virtue, anterior to all experience of the good or bad effects resulting from its practice, are chimerical notions, which, like many others, have for their guarantee and base only theological speculation.[64]

---

61   E.g., ibid., vol. 2, 129.
62   Ibid., 76.
63   Ibid.
64   Ibid., 87.

Moral instinct is no more than speculation: we either learn all our ethical conceptions from our direct experience or by listening to others. The representatives of the existing religions also understand this and emphasize obediently attending to "priests or parents." However, according to d'Holbach, it is dangerous that priests and parents are regarded as authority figures, whom the less experienced are obliged to obey. "Without understanding and devoid of morals [they] impress on the ductile mind of their scholar those vices with which they are themselves tormented, and who transmit to them the false opinions which they have an interest in making them adopt."[65]

As a result of believing these ignorant epistemic authorities, one remains ignorant. Because one has never had an opportunity to learn what is conducive to his self-preservation from his parents and the priests, he is susceptible to paying attention to only those claims that *promise* him the most satisfaction with the least effort. Religion offers obedient people nothing less than eternal life in a blissful state with no toil. No pleasure can compare with this joy. The only price one has to pay to enjoy this heavenly happiness eventually is to ensure that one's children are taught "absolute obedience" to priests. The power of the priests, and the *raison d'etre* of any existing religion, is built on this pair of promises and obligations: the former draw ignorant people to the religion and the latter enable the religion to maintain its influence by keeping people ignorant.

The intergenerational circle of ignorance is "very useful to crafty theologians, but very injurious to society" because it makes people indifferent to improving their lives here on earth:[66]

> This irrational doctrine of a future life prevents [a man] from occupying himself with his true happiness; from thinking of ameliorating his institutions, of improving his laws, of advancing the progress of science, and of perfectioning his morals. Vain and gloomy ideas have absorbed his attention: he consents to groan under religious and political tyranny; to live in error, to languish in misfortune, in the hope, when he shall be no more, of being one day happier.... It is thus that the doctrine of a future life has been most fatal to the human species: it plunged whole nations into sloth, made them languid, filled them with indifference to their present welfare.[67]

---

65   Ibid., 112.
66   Ibid., 180.
67   Ibid., 138.

As all the existing religions depend on ignorance for their survival, there is no chance that any existing religion could be reformed to eschew promoting "the doctrine of another life which placed the government itself in a state of dependence upon the priest."[68] D'Holbach thinks that those who claim otherwise and suggest that "reforming" the existing religions is possible hail from "those countries where liberty of thought reigns; that is to say, where the civil power has known how to counterbalance superstition."[69] However, if one had to live in a country "where superstition, backed by the sovereign authority, makes the weight of its yoke felt, and imprudently abuses its unlimited power,"[70] one would see the true essence of religion: "oppression gives a spring to the soul, it obliges man to closely examine the cause of his sorrows; misfortune is a powerful incentive, that turns the mind to the side of truth ... it tears [the religion's] mask off."[71] Regardless of how "liberal" a country is and however rational and tolerant its religion pretends to be, if one day its priests had a chance to do what they truly wanted, the religion that they promote would turn out to be no different from the superstitious religion of any absolutist theocracy.

The existing religions have always resorted to oppressive measures to prevent the enlightened men from igniting doubt in people towards the authority of the priests. Even in the most "liberal" countries, where priests have not directly persecuted scientists and philosophers, they have made use of "the notion of spirits," which, according to d'Holbach, is "calculated to retard the progress of knowledge, since it precludes our research into the true cause of the effects which we see, by keeping the human mind in apathy and sloth."[72] By appealing to spiritual forces – that "no one has ever seen" but "which the priests claim to understand" – as the causes of things, the priests obfuscate empirical causes, and hence prevent people from perceiving the connections between cause and effect and that they are kept ignorant.[73] The extent of the attention that superstition has paid to undermine the pursuit of knowledge everywhere is in itself evidence, thinks d'Holbach, that if people's ignorance about their own best interest were remedied by natural science, all existing religions would collapse because people would finally grasp that the promises of the priests lack any tangible capacity to offer satisfaction to their desire for self-preservation.[74]

---

68   Ibid., 141.
69   Ibid., 140.
70   Ibid., 140–1.
71   Ibid., 140.
72   Ibid.
73   Ibid., vol. 1, 54.
74   Ibid., 55–6.

7   Deism for d'Holbach: Victorious in Theory, but Useless in Practice

Deism is not interested in promoting ignorance, unlike the existing religions, which, according to d'Holbach, could not survive without ignorance. True, a deist can be excessively optimistic like Dr Pangloss in Voltaire's *Candide*, and such excess might produce long-term harm to one's survival in the real world. However, a deist does not have to believe like Pangloss that this is the best possible world or even a decent world: Voltaire himself did not sympathize with his caricature of "the profoundest metaphysician in Germany."[75] Moreover, Voltairean deism that allows considering God an impersonal designer of the laws of nature and living beings bypasses d'Holbach's counterarguments to deism. Because d'Holbach could not show that atheism could explain the origin of the laws of nature and life, such deism can seem more rational than atheism. This is the "true scandal of atheism," as Winfried Schröder has concluded in his *Ursprünge des Atheismus*.[76]

If d'Holbach's arguments against Voltaire's deism were so weak, why then did Voltaire even bother to strike back at the baron? Instead of feeling threatened by d'Holbach's arguments, *pace* Israel, Voltaire could have been concerned for another reason. In his essay directed against d'Holbach, "Dieu, Dieux," he concludes, "When you venture to claim there is no God ... it must be demonstrated like a proposition in Euclid, or you build your system only on a 'maybe'."[77] This conclusion suggests that as a philosopher, Voltaire was committed to the pursuit of certainty. For him, reaching the certainty of the existence of God was no less than "the most interesting thing to humanity."[78] In d'Holbach's philosophy, in contrast, certainty is no longer treated as important.

D'Holbach shares the anti-rationalist orientation of his Scottish friend David Hume, a parallel that Kors has emphasized.[79] The baron wanted to exclude theoretical speculation, in particular the pursuit of certainty about the existence of God, from his philosophy because, as he writes:

> It is not given to man to know everything, it is not given him to know his origin, it is not given him to penetrate into the essence of things, nor to recur to first principles; but it is given him to have reason, to have good faith (*bonne foi*), to ingeniously allow he is ignorant of that which he

---

75   Voltaire, *Candide*, 80.
76   Schröder, *Ursprünge des Atheismus*, 315.
77   Voltaire, "Dieu, Dieux," 344.
78   Ibid.
79   Kors, "Atheism of d'Holbach and Naigeon," 297.

cannot know, and not to substitute unintelligible words and absurd suppositions for his uncertainty.[80]

In light of the above passage, d'Holbach might think that, like many philosophers, Voltaire is too confident in his reason, its ability to know things that cannot be empirically perceived. Instead of either acknowledging the existence of God or denying it, d'Holbach simply does not believe in God.

However, d'Holbach's agnostic atheism is not motivated by a belief that atheism must bring greater happiness than deism, *pace* Kors, but rather by a conviction that we do not *need* to believe in God in order to be happy. To become happy, one only needs to "regulate his pleasures" by accepting durable pleasures and refusing "all those of which the indulgence would be succeeded by regret or pain."[81] As Hume argued, an urge to know the cause of everything is of "secondary" importance to us compared to satisfying our desire to be happy. When our desire for happiness is satisfied, knowing the truth about the existence of God becomes superfluous to us: "during this state of mind, men have little leisure or inclination to think of the unknown, invisible regions."[82] Reflecting Hume's claim that "reason is the slave of passions,"[83] d'Holbach writes: "let us reply to those who unceasingly repeat, that the interest of the passions alone conducts us to atheism ... We shall, without hesitation, agree that only the interests and the passions of men excite them to make inquiries."[84]

If our desire for happiness can be satisfied without answering whether God exists, no passion shall motivate us to bother about this question, and thus we become "atheists" (or agnostics). Only superstitious and unhappy people can be ever genuinely interested in God.[85] The recalibration of the aim of philosophical inquiry from reaching certainty to producing happiness could explain why d'Holbach rejected even Voltairean, non-optimistic deism, although "all the good arguments"[86] supported it, and why Voltaire was so concerned about this rejection. If the radical project of d'Holbach's *salon* convinced enough people about the new aim of philosophy, Voltaire's deism would appear trivial to posterity. Indeed, d'Holbach suggests that trivializing even reasonable deism would show good faith (*bonne foi*). Opposed to any deist, d'Holbach refuses to

---

80   D'Holbach, *The System of Nature*, vol. 1, 51.
81   Ibid., 72.
82   David Hume, "Natural History of Religion," in *A Dissertation on the Passions and Natural History of Religion* (Oxford: 2007), 42.
83   David Hume, *Treatise on Human Nature* (Oxford: 2007), 266.
84   D'Holbach, *The System of Nature*, vol. 2, 143.
85   Ibid., 96.
86   Schröder, *Ursprünge des Atheismus*, 77.

value things only "pretended"[87] to be significant and admits that as a being that pursues happiness above all, "a man can only approve of that which procures for him his object or furnishes him the means by which it is to be obtained."[88] Thus, although d'Holbach does not succeed in refuting Voltairean deism, he does not see it as ethically warranted to believe in the existence of God, and this gives him a reason to ignore Voltaire's epistemic arguments for deism.

Acknowledgments

The work on this chapter has been supported by a grant from the National Science Centre in Poland, no. UMO-2018/31/B/HS1/02050, funding the research project *Between Secularization and Reform. Religious Rationalism in the Late 17th Century and in the Enlightenment*, at the Institute of Philosophy of the Jagiellonian University in Kraków. I would like to thank Anna Tomaszewska for her substantial editorial suggestions and Damien Tricoire for his comments that improved this chapter.

References

Beeson, David, and Nicholas Cronk, "Voltaire: Philosopher or *philosophe*?" in *The Cambridge Companion to Voltaire*, ed. Nicholas Cronk (Cambridge, Eng.: 2009), 47–64.

Buckley, Michael, *At the Origins of Modern Atheism* (New Haven: 1989).

Canziani, Guido (ed.), *Filosofia e religione nella letteratura clandestina: secoli XVII e XVIII* (Milan: 1994).

Curran, Mark, *Atheism, Religion and Enlightenment in pre-Revolutionary Europe* (Woolbridge: 2012).

Diderot, Denis, *Lettre sur les aveugles* (London: 1749).

Helvétius, Claude-Adrien, *L'Esprit* (Paris: 1758).

D'Holbach, Paul-Henri Thiry, *The System of Nature*, 2 vols., trans. Henry D. Robinson (Kitchener: 2010).

Hume, David, "Natural History of Religion," in *A Dissertation on the Passions and Natural History of Religion* (Oxford: 2007), 35–85.

---

87   See, e.g., d'Holbach, *The System of Nature*, vol. 1, 203, where natural philosophy is called "pretended science."

88   Ibid., 155. Cf. Ibid., 32: "all [our] passions, wills, actions have eternally [happiness] for their object and end."

Hume, David, *Treatise on Human Nature* (Oxford: 2007).

Israel, Jonathan I., *A Revolution of the Mind: Radical Enlightenment and the Intellectual Origins of Modern Democracy* (Princeton: 2011).

Israel, Jonathan I., *The Enlightenment that Failed: Ideas, Revolution, and Democratic Defeat, 1748–1830* (Oxford: 2019).

Kors, Alan Charles, "Atheism of d'Holbach and Naigeon," in *Atheism from Reformation to the Enlightenment*, eds. Michael Hunter and David Wootton (Oxford: 1992), 273–300.

La Vopa, Anthony J., "A New Intellectual History? Jonathan Israel's Enlightenment," *The Historical Journal* 52 (2009): 717–738.

LeBuffe, Michael, and Emilie Gourdon, "Holbach," in *A Companion to Atheism and Philosophy*, ed. Graham Oppy (Oxford: 2019), 28–42.

Lion, Henri, "Essai sur les oeuvres politiques et morales du Baron d'Holbach," *Annales révolutionnaires* 14 (1922): 89–98.

Needham, John, *Nouvelles observations microscopiques* (Paris: 1751).

Peña Echeverría, Javier, "La teoría política de d'Holbach y sus presupuestos filosóficos," *Revista de Estudios Políticos* 179 (2018): 13–41.

Roe, Shirley A., "Voltaire Versus Needham: Atheism, Materialism, and the Generation of Life," *Journal of the History of Ideas* 46 (1985): 65–87.

Sandrier, Alain, *Le style philosophique du baron d'Holbach. Conditions et contraintes du prosélytisme athée en France dans la seconde moitié du XVIIIᵉ siècle* (Paris: 2004).

Schröder, Winfried (ed.), *Matthias Knutzen. Schriften und Materialien* (Stuttgart: 2010).

Schröder, Winfried, *Ursprünge des Atheismus* (Stuttgart: 1998).

Spallanzani, Lazzaro, *Saggio di osservazioni microscopiche concernenti il sistema della generazione* (Modena: 1765).

Voltaire, *Candide and Other Stories*, trans. Roger Pearson (Oxford: 2006).

Voltaire, "Athee, Atheism," in *Pocket Philosophical Dictionary*, trans. John Fletcher (Oxford: 2011), 92–102.

Voltaire, "Éléments de la philosophie de Newton," in *Œuvres complètes de Voltaire*, vol. 22 (Paris: 1880).

Voltaire, "Faith," in *Philosophical Dictionary*, trans. William Dugdale (London 1843), 473–6.

Voltaire, "Lettre 1664," in *Œuvres complètes de Voltaire*, vol. 36 (Paris: 1880), 309–310.

Voltaire, "On the Existence of God," in *The Works of Voltaire*, vol. 21: *The Henriade: Letters and Miscellanies* (Paris: 1901), 238–250.

Voltaire, *Questions sur l'Encyclopédie*, vol. 15 (London: 1771).

Voltaire, "To Frederick, Prince Royal of Prussia: On God, Soul and Innate Morality," in *Voltaire in His Letters*, trans. Stephen G. Tallentyne (New York: 1919), 47–50.

Voltaire, *Traité de metaphysique* (Manchester: 1957).

Voltaire, *Voltaire's Correspondence*, 120 vols. (Oxford: 1974).

Vyverberg, Henry, *Human Nature, Cultural Diversity and the French Enlightenment* (New York: 1989).

CHAPTER 9

'A Matter of Dangerous Consequence': Molyneux and Locke on Toland

Ian Leask

William Molyneux's attitude to John Locke, as demonstrated by their correspondence, might appear to be that of a fawning acolyte: on the face of it, Molyneux's reverence at times leaves him almost prostrate. Certainly, Locke makes important changes to the *Essay Concerning Human Understanding* as a direct result of Molyneux's queries. Nonetheless, reading Molyneux's own account, there is no mistaking the seniority of Locke: in 1694, for example, Molyneux declares that "a man of greater candour and humanity [than Locke] there moves not on the face of the earth."[1] Three years later, Molyneux tells Locke (on 17th Sept. 1697) about the portrait of him (Locke) that hangs in his dining room in Dublin – and also that Robert Molesworth is wont to call by in order to "pay his Devotion"![2] (Even allowing for the exaggerated conventions of epistolary discourse, this depiction of philosophical worship remains strikingly strange.)

Despite the genuine reverence evidenced here, closer analysis of the Locke-Molyneux correspondence regarding the very particular case of John Toland, and the events and misadventures that characterized Toland's sojourn in Dublin in 1697, reveal a different aspect to Molyneux's attitude. As I want to show in this chapter, it seems that Molyneux refused to accept the "abandonment" of Toland that Locke more or less commands; moreover, he sought to defend Toland, in part, upon the basis of Locke's own philosophical-political principles – thereby showing himself to be (on this occasion, at least) more Lockean than Locke himself.

To make this case, I begin by providing some wider biographical and contextual information about both Molyneux and Toland. I then outline, first, the way in which Toland's most famous (or infamous) text, *Christianity Not Mysterious*,

---

1   See the autobiographical account that William Molyneux provides, in Capel Molyneux, *An Account of the Family and Descendents of Sir Thomas Molyneux* (Evesham: 1820), 78. (William) Molyneux also states, in the same paragraph, that "no age has seen a more admirable piece" than Locke's *Essay*.

2   John Locke, *The Correspondence of John Locke*, 8 vols. (Oxford: 1976–1989), v: 2312.

draws on important Lockean conceptions to construct its case against conventional religious views and, secondly, the kind of backlash that this "borrowing" produced, against Locke himself, as well as Toland. With this established, I offer a narrative account of the relevant sections of the Molyneux-Locke correspondence, showing Locke's increasing irritation with the trouble that Toland (and their perceived association) had generated. I conclude with more detailed focus upon the construction of a particular letter that "closes" the exchange between Locke and Molyneux regarding Toland; as already indicated, this may well show that Molyneux applies Lockean principles more consistently and evenly than their original author did.

1   Molyneux and Toland: Backgrounds

William Molyneux (1656–1698) was born in Dublin into a well-heeled Protestant, Anglo-Irish, family; his father was a lawyer and landowner, but also an accomplished mathematician. He attended Trinity College Dublin from 1671 to 1674, studying maths and science, and immersing himself in the work of Descartes, Gassendi and Bacon, and in the *Transactions* of the Royal Society of London. Although this was followed by three years of legal study at the Middle Temple in London, Molyneux's principal concerns remained philosophical and scientific. He translated Descartes' *Meditations* over the winter of 1679 and 1680; in 1684, he founded the Dublin Philosophical Society – an exceptionally important forum for stimulating and supporting philosophical and scientific discourse in Ireland; and, in 1692, he published his *Dioptrica Nova*, the result of ongoing research he carried out into various aspects of optics (from the refraction of light to the best techniques for lens-grinding).

Molyneux was elected Member of the Irish House of Commons, for Trinity, in 1692, and re-elected in 1695. This was a particularly turbulent period, in terms of the wider theological-political conjunction: the attempt to restore a Catholic monarchy in Britain and Ireland had been defeated; the Anglican Church was determined to cement its hegemony; Irish Protestants also wanted to ensure that their parliament in Dublin enjoyed "equal rights" alongside Westminster. It was within this context that Molyneux produced his *The Case of Ireland's Being Bound by Acts of Parliament in England, Stated*, in 1698.[3] The book, which made solid use of Molyneux's legal training (and, to some extent, his appreciation of Locke's political philosophy), set out the case for legislative independence for Dublin, and was duly condemned by the London parliament;

---

3   See Patrick Hyde Kelly's definitive edition of the text: *William Molyneux's* The Case of Ireland's Being Bound by Acts of Parliament in England, Stated (Dublin: 2018).

its subsequent status as a kind of *ur*-text of Irish nationalism may have been based on a slightly exaggerated assessment, however.[4]

Molyneux's correspondence, and friendship, with Locke started in 1692, when he sent the Englishman a copy of his *Dioptrica Nova*. So began a cordial and highly important epistolary association. Over the course of their correspondence, they discussed a diversity of issues, regarding money, politics, and education, for example; but the most important aspect of the discourse was regarding the substance of Locke's *Essay*. Locke sent Molyneux a copy of the first edition, and then he asked explicitly for suggestions and comments on how to improve a second edition. Most famously, this resulted in Locke adding the famous question of the blind man with restored sight, in Book 2 of Chapter 9.[5] But Molyneux's queries and injunctions also led Locke to add the chapter "Of Identity and Diversity" (Book 2, Chapter 27) to the second edition of the *Essay*, published in 1694. Locke also made substantial changes to his treatment of the agency entailed in suspending desires (Book 2, Chapter 21, of the second edition) as a result of Molyneux's comments – and, of course, of the respect in which Locke held the younger man.

The pair finally met in August 1698, when Molyneux was able to travel to England, as Locke's guest; he subsequently described the visit as "the Happiest Scene of my whole life."[6] Sadly, however, this was as far as their relationship would run: Molyneux died on the 11th of October 1698, aged 42, from kidney problems.[7]

John Toland was born in 1670, in the Inishowen peninsula, County Donegal, and raised an Irish-speaking Catholic (who may even have been the son of a priest); culturally and geographically, his origins could hardly have been more marginal. His intellectual prowess was immediately evident, however, and by converting to Protestantism at the age of 14 he was able to begin attending an Anglican school in Derry. He was awarded a scholarship to continue his studies at Glasgow University, after which various dissenting Presbyterians in London funded his further study in the Netherlands. Toland would spend his entire life in a state of privilege-less insecurity, continually struggling to find sponsorship, patronage or even just a few shillings from Grub Street.

---

4 See the General Introduction that Kelly provides to the 2018 edition of Molyneux's *Case of Ireland*, 1–52. See also, Ian McBride, "*The Case of Ireland* (1698) in Context: William Molyneux and His Critics," *Proceedings of the Royal Irish Academy: Archeology, Culture, History, Literature* 118c (2018): 201–230.

5 For the original question, see Locke, *Correspondence*, IV: 1609.

6 Ibid., VI: 2490.

7 For a fuller account of Molyneux's life and times, see John Gerald Simms, *William Molyneux of Dublin* (Dublin: 1982).

In Leiden and Utrecht, Toland absorbed new historical and critical methods of Scripture analysis which originated with Spinoza and were propounded by theologians like Philipp van Limborch and Jean Le Clerc; he also became acquainted with various early Enlightenment figures like Anthony van Dale and Benjamin Furly. Through these connections, Toland was able to make contact with John Locke, when he returned to England in 1693: van Limborch provided a formal introduction, writing from Amsterdam that

> The bearer of this is an Irishman, an excellent and not unlearned young man, who, being about to leave here for England, has solicited a letter to you, to be faithfully conveyed. If perchance you meet him you will find him frank, gentlemanly, and not at all of a servile character.[8]

Although we know that Toland certainly made the most of the introduction, and that the two met, we have little further, direct, information.[9] But what seems certain, nonetheless, is that Locke's work had a galvanizing effect on Toland, as he set to work on what would become a scandalous intervention in philosophical and theological discourse.

2   The Lockean Foundations of *Christianity Not Mysterious*

Toland's *Christianity Not Mysterious* was published, anonymously, in 1695, and again in 1696, with Toland's authorship acknowledged.[10] In large part, the text was heavily influenced by the critical-historical approach to Scripture that Toland had encountered, and absorbed, during his studies in the Netherlands, at the start of the decade. For example: the operative principle that governs the text, overall – namely, the refusal of any distinction between the categories "above" and "contrary" to reason – is probably derived from Spinoza's treatment of miracles, in chapter six of the *Theological-Political Treatise* (TTP); but Toland also draws from the TTP methodologically, in the very particular way

---

8   Locke, *Correspondence*, IV: 1640.

9   John Marshall, *John Locke: Resistance, Religion and Responsibility* (Cambridge, Mass.: 1994), 409, states: "It is quite likely that Toland had expressed deistic notions when they met [in 1693]."

10   The edition used here is Philip McGuinness, Alan Harrison and Richard Kearney (eds.), *John Toland's* Christianity Not Mysterious: *Text, Associated Works and Critical Essays* (Dublin: 1997). Hereafter CNM.

that Scripture is presented as its own interpreter (yet is simultaneously denied any transcendent or normative status).[11]

However, *Christianity Not Mysterious* was most notable, certainly in terms of its immediate anglophone reception, for its very particular use of important concepts that Locke had developed in his *Essay*. For example: Toland more or less plagiarizes Locke's definition of "Idea," as the "immediate object of the mind when it thinks";[12] he follows Locke directly in depicting simple ideas as resulting from the mind's receptivity to the effects of matter, and in differentiating the passive reception of simple ideas and the active reflection on the mind's operations;[13] and he provides his own versions of the Lockean distinction between sensation and reflection, and between intuition and reason.[14]

Probably most significant of all, though, was Toland's treatment of Locke's differentiation of real and nominal essences. For Locke, the fundamental properties that constitute a body – its "real essence" – are inaccessible to perception yet still the crucial supports for its observable, "nominal," essence: solidity and extension, for example, presuppose an unknowable yet ontologically necessary "substance." We can still have perfectly respectable, probabilistic reasoning about the empirical world; but we can only infer what its "ontological infrastructure" amounts to.[15]

Toland pounces on this Lockean distinction: it becomes a central tool – or even weapon – for his project. Following "an excellent modern Philosoper,"[16] he distinguishes the collection of knowable, corpuscular attributes and properties of a given entity from the "intrinsic constitution" that any such phenomenal manifestation requires. We know something to be extended, solid, divisible, smooth, hard, and so on; and we know that all of these qualities "depend" on there being some real essence which we infer rather than experience directly. Nonetheless, we do not conclude that, because objects have "deeper" aspects that we cannot know as such, we are dealing with anything "mysterious":

---

11 For fuller consideration of the influence of Spinoza on Toland's CNM, see Ian Leask, "Toland, Spinoza, and the Naturalisation of Scripture," in *Ireland and the Reception of the Bible: Social and Cultural Studies*, eds. Brad Anderson and Jonathan Kearney (London: 2018), 227–242.

12 CNM, 1.1.4; cf. John Locke, *An Essay Concerning Human Understanding* (Harmondsworth: 1997), 1.1.8 and 2.8.8.

13 See CNM, 1.1.4; cf. Locke, *Essay*, 2.2.2.

14 See CNM, 1.4.14; cf. Locke, *Essay*, 4.9.3.

15 See Locke, *Essay*, 2.23.3–5.

16 CNM, 3.2.16.

nothing can be said to be a Mystery, because we are ignorant of its real Essence, since it is not more knowable in one thing than in another, and is never conceiv'd or included in the Ideas we have of things, or the Names we give 'em.[17]

Accordingly, for Toland, the *theological* notion of mystery is rendered redundant: everything can be said to have an unknowable "core"; and so religious phenomena are unexceptional, in this regard. In Toland's own words:

no Christian doctrine, no more than any ordinary piece of nature, can be reputed a mystery because we have not an adequate or complete idea of whatever belongs to it ...[18]

Or again:

... nothing is a Mystery, because we know not its essence, since it appears that it is neither knowable in itself, nor ever thought of by us: so that the Divine Being himself cannot with more reason be accounted mysterious in this respect than the most contemptible of his creatures.[19]

What is more, Toland will employ this principle (or weapon) to bolster his Spinoza-inspired case against the category "*supra rationem,*" or "above reason." Locke may have provided Toland with the means for denying mystery, but, in Book Four of the *Essay*, he had also insisted that reason has nothing directly to do with matters of faith, that we can accept some propositions – such as the resurrection of the dead – as being "above reason," and that our certain knowledge is so limited that morality requires supra-rational, Biblical, guidance.[20] (In *The Reasonableness of Christianity*, Locke had also stressed that issues like salvation and atonement were necessarily above human comprehension.) Toland, pushing matters as far as he can, comes to regard "mystery" and "above reason" as synonymous terms: Lockean raw materials have been shaped into a blade for excising any trace of fideism.

---

17   CNM, 3.2.18.
18   CNM, 3.2.12.
19   CNM, 3.2.21.
20   See, for example, Locke, *Essay*, 4.13.23, and 4.18.7.

3   *Christianity Not Myterious*: A Lockean Scandal?

Locke's own *Reasonableness of Christianity* might have seemed Socinian enough, to his critics; but Toland's work had now exposed the full (and, for many, lamentable) implications of certain Lockean notions. In the eyes of conservative divines, an increasingly composite enemy emerged, with Toland merely confirming their worst fears about Locke.

It seems worth noting, in this respect, that so many of the multiple critical responses to *Christianity Not Mysterious* – for example, those by John Milner, Thomas Beverley, and Jean Gailhard[21] – lumped Locke with Toland and condemned both together. In turn, discourse about Locke himself rendered him Toland-tainted. In 1695, for example, the Calvinist minister John Edwards had offered a fairly disdainful critique of Locke's *Reasonableness of Christianity*, accusing it of aiding and abetting, not just Socinianism, but even atheism. Edwards followed up this text, *Some Thoughts concerning the Several Causes and Occasions of Atheism*, with further broadsides in each of the two succeeding years: *Socinianism Unmasked* and *The Socinian Creed*.[22] Throughout, Edwards asserted that Locke had reduced faith solely to belief in Jesus Christ as messiah, had denied original sin, had converted "trusting Christ's righteousness" into "assenting to truth," had allowed the mob to determine legitimate creed, and had consistently undermined Trinitarian doctrine (to the extent that Locke's version of Christianity was barely distinguishable from an Islamic equivalent!).

Locke penned an immediate reply to Edwards, claiming (probably falsely) that he had no knowledge of Socinian texts, and pointing out (reasonably) that his intention was to demarcate the minimum requirement of faith, not to proscribe all other credal formulae. Nonetheless, the assault was by no means a one-off: Thomas Burnet, John Norris, and John Sergeant, amongst other churchmen, would all publish similar, critical, tracts. Locke even began to suspect something of a conspiracy against him, as he confided to Molyneux in February 1697.[23]

By far the most serious attack, however, came from Edward Stillingfleet, the Anglican bishop of Worcester, in his 1696 *Discourse in Vindication of the Trinity*. The book's final chapter pounced on Toland, quite correctly perceiving Toland's

---

21   See Giancarlo Carabelli's magisterial *Tolandiana. Materiali bibliografici per lo studio dell'opera e della fortuna di John Toland (1670–1722)* (Florence: 1975), 27–30, 34–41, and 51–4, for fuller details of the contemporaneous responses to CNM.

22   See Victor Nuovo (ed.), *John Locke and Christianity. Contemporary Responses to* The Reasonableness of Christianity (Bristol: 1997), 209–235, for an edited compilation.

23   Locke, *Correspondence*, V: 2202.

radical intentions. But it also quite correctly perceived the source of so much of Toland's thinking: Locke's *Essay*. As far as Stillingfleet was concerned, Locke had provided Toland with the conceptual infrastructure for his assault on religion: if "substance" was unknowable but not mysterious, the same could apply to any Christian doctrine, like the Trinity. Stillingfleet recognized that Toland's "Notions are borrowed [from Locke] to serve other Purposes than [Locke] ... intended them";[24] nonetheless, he joined them together as "Gentlemen of this new way of reasoning."[25]

Stillingfleet was a far more substantial, and influential, opponent than so many of the other pamphleteers and preachers: his position and reputation in the Anglican Church were stellar; and Locke knew that his critique would act as a kind of theological vanguard. (Locke would later complain that "[s]ince a debate has arisen between the bishop of Worcester, who has attacked me on a far-fetched pretext, and myself, the cassocked tribe of theologians has been wonderfully excited against my book."[26]) Accordingly, Locke felt obliged to offer a thorough-going response, published early in 1697, in which he tried to stress that his *Essay* had nothing to do with Trinitarian debates, and that Stillingfleet was, in effect, blaming him for other authors' work.[27]

The argument rumbled on, often going round in circles. Stillingfleet published a response to Locke, in May 1697; Locke provided a second response, early in September of the same year; Stillingfleet gave a second "Answer," a few weeks later; and Locke published a *third* letter to Stillingfleet in May of the following year, 1698. Meanwhile, and in the midst of all of this, on May 17th, 1697, the Grand Jury of Middlesex had condemned Locke's *Reasonableness of Christianity*: very tellingly, it was "convicted" (as it were) alongside Toland's *Christianity Not Mysterious*; the jury's "presentment" deemed both books anti-Trinitarian and pro-Socinian, and likely to give rise to atheism.[28]

---

24   Edward Stillingfleet, *A Discourse in Vindication of the Doctrine of the Trinity* (London: 1696), 239.

25   Ibid., 234.

26   Locke, *Correspondence*, V: 2340.

27   Locke already had history, so to speak, with Stillingfleet. In 1680, Stillingfleet had published his *Mischief of Separation*, and then followed up with the *Unreasonableness of Separation*; his targets in both were dissenting Protestants who sought separation from the Church of England. Soon afterwards – very probably in early 1681 – Locke and his friend James Tyrell began compiling a 167-page reply, the "Critical Notes Upon Edward Stillingfleet's Mischief and Unreasonableness of Separation"; although unpublished, it seems that some of the themes treated would find more developed expression in the 1685 *Epistola*, the *Letter Concerning Toleration*. For discussion, see Marshall, *John Locke*, 95–117.

28   For discussion of the events, see Justin Champion, "Making Authority: Belief, Conviction and Reason in the Public Sphere in late Seventeenth-Century England," in *Libertenage*

So, in summary: throughout 1697, the pressure was mounting on Locke, especially because of his perceived association with Toland; and, as the tone of the exchanges with Stillingfleet makes plain, he had become increasingly defensive. Locke perceived himself to be under siege.[29]

4   Big Trouble: Toland in Dublin

With this wider background established, we can now turn to the Locke-Molyneux correspondence regarding Toland, and see how it provides specific evidence of Locke's aggressively wary attitude – but also of Molyneux's qualified sympathy.

The first reference to Toland comes on 16th March 1697, when Molyneux, writing from Dublin, tells Locke that he has been in discourse with "an ingenious man" about the nature of Stillingfleet's objections to Locke – the ingenious man's main point being that the bishop did not object directly to Locke's own ideas, but more to how they had been employed and "misused" by others, "particularly by the Author of *Christianity Not Mysterious*."[30] Molyneux points out that, however ingenious this point, it does not quite address the actuality: the bishop does directly oppose Locke's ideas, even if his objections are framed in terms of *Christianity Not Mysterious* (his direct objections come "on the occasion of the foresaid book," as Molyneux phrases it). In the same letter, Molyneux also tells Locke that he has learned that Toland is Irish, but that, at the time of writing, Toland is not resident in his homeland, and so he cannot report much more about him.

Very shortly afterwards, however, in late March 1697, Toland was back in Ireland: one of his patrons, the Whig politician John Methuen, had been appointed Lord Chancellor of Ireland, and Toland apparently had hopes of securing a job with him, as secretary. Accordingly, in a letter dated 6 April, Molyneux informs Locke that Toland is now resident in Dublin, and that they

---

et Philosophie au XVII siècle, eds. Antony McKenna and Pierre-François Moreau (Paris: 1999), 143–190. See also, Robert Todd Carroll, *The Common-Sense Philosophy of Religion of Bishop Edward Stillingfleet* (The Hague: 1975), 85.

29   See, for example, Roger Woolhouse, *Locke. A Biography* (Cambridge, Mass.: 2007), 372: "Locke was determined to rescue the *Essay* from any connection with ... Toland's rejection of things above reason"; or John Yolton, *John Locke and the Way of Ideas* (Oxford: 1956), 125–6: "Locke was loud in his protestations that he had been falsely coupled with Toland. He accordingly sought to dissociate his way of ideas from that used by such men as Toland."

30   Locke, *Correspondence*, V: 2221.

have met up. Toland, he reports, has been abroad (in the Netherlands) and has studied with Jean Le Clerc, the radical (and possibly Socinian) biblical scholar.[31] (Locke already knew about Toland's Dutch sojourn: as we have already seen, Philipp van Limborch, the liberal Remonstrant theologian, had provided the young Irishman with a written introduction to Locke in July 1693.) Above all, Molyneux notes that Toland says he knows Locke and that he holds him in the highest regard. Molyneux likes Toland, he says; but he also sounds a note of caution:

> I propose a great deal of satisfaction in his conversation; I take him to be a candid free thinker, and a good scholar. But there is a violent sort of spirit which reigns here [in Dublin], which begins already to shew it self against him; and I believe will increase daily, for I find the clergy alarmed to a mighty degree against him; and last Sunday he had his welcome to this city by hearing himself being harangued against out of the pulpit by a prelate of this country.[32]

Toland himself gives a fairly full account of his hostile reception in Dublin in his *Apology for Mr. Toland* and his *Defence of Mr. Toland*, both from 1697.[33] Two contextual points are worth noting, in terms of the severe hostility that Toland met: first, general clerical concerns about preventing heretical consequences of the Licensing Act lapsing, in 1695; and secondly, local opposition to Toland's sponsor, John Methuen (whom Jonathan Swift would describe as "a profligate rogue without religion or morals"!). *Christianity Not Mysterious* served as a kind of lightning-rod, it seems.

Locke's reply to Molyneux, of the 3rd of May 1697, seems notable for its barely concealed injunction to caution and distance (bound up with a very telling insult):

> I am glad to hear that [Toland] ... does me the favour to speak well of me on that side of the water, I have never deserved other of him, but that he should always have done so on this. If his exceeding great value of himself do not deprive the world of that usefulness, that his parts, if rightly conducted, might be of, I shall be very glad ... I always value men of parts and learning, and think I cannot do too much in procuring them

31   Ibid., v: 2240.

32   Ibid.

33   Both are contained in McGuinness, Harrison and Kearney (eds.), *John Toland's Christianity Not Mysterious*.

friends and assistance. But there may happen occasions when that may make one stop ones hand. And tis the hopes of what use young men give, that they will make of their parts, which is to me the encouragement of being concerned for them. But, if vanity increases with age, I always fear whither it will lead a man. I say this to you because you are my friend for whom I have no reserves, and think I ought to talk freely where you enquire, and possibly may be concerned; but I say it to you alone, and desire it may go no further. For the man [Toland] I wish very well, and could give you, if it needed, proofs that I do so. And therefore I desire you to be kind to him; but I must leave it to your prudence, in what way, and how far. If his carriage with you gives the promises of a steady useful man, I know you will be forward enough of your self, and I shall be very glad of it. For it will be his fault alone if he prove not a very valuable man, and have you not for his friend.[34]

Replying three weeks later, Molyneux thanks Locke for the "fresh marks of your kindness and confidence in me," and says that Locke's comments

perfectly agree with the apprehensions I had conceived of that gentle-man. Truly to be free, and without Reserve to you, I do not think His management since he came into this city has been so prudent; he has raised against him the clamours of all parties; and this not so much by his difference in opinion, but as by his unseasonable way of discours-ing, propagating, and maintaining it. Coffee-houses and public tables are not proper places for serious discourses relating to the most important truths. But when also a tincture of vanity appears in the whole course of a man's conversation, it disgusts many that have a due value for his parts and learning.[35]

As we can see, Molyneux is taking up Locke's case regarding Toland's supposed vanity. He goes on to speak about an unnamed Socinian of his acquaintance who, despite the nature of his beliefs, had such a quiet and modest nature that no-one had a word to say against him. The contrast that he sets up with Toland is striking: "I am very loath to tell you how far tis otherwise with Mr. T in this place; but I am persuaded it may be for his advantage that you know it, and that you friendly admonish him of it, for his conduct hereafter."[36] Molyneux

---

34   Locke, *Correspondence*, V: 2254.
35   Ibid., V: 2269.
36   Ibid.

hopes that Toland, or Mr. T, might be persuaded (by Locke) to be more prudent in terms of choosing his occasion and opportunity for holding forth, and
that he might avoid "running against the rocks" for no purpose, and inflaming
people against him.

Significantly, Molyneux also informs Locke about Toland's cavalier exploita-
tion of his contact and "relationship" with Locke:

> Mr. T also takes here a great liberty on all occasions to vouch your patron-
> age and friendship, which makes many [who] rail at him, rail also at you.
> I believe you will not approve of this, as far as I am able to judge by your
> shaking him off in your letter to [Stillingfleet] ... But after all this, I look
> upon Mr. T as a very ingenious man, and I should be very glad of any
> opportunity of doing him service, to which I think myself indispensably
> bound by your recommendation.[37]

However, Molyneux's plea is quickly given short shrift, and it becomes clear
that Toland is to be dropped like a dangerous contaminant: as Locke replies,
on 15 June 1697, a month after the Grand Jury's verdict,

> As to the gentleman, to whom you think my friendly admonishment may
> be of advantage for his conduct thereafter, I must tell you, that he is a
> man to whom I never writ in my life, and, I think, I shall not now begin.
> And, as to his conduct, tis what I never so much as spoke to him of.[38]

Locke continues by differentiating those people (like Molyneux, presumably)
to whom he feels genuinely close and friendly, and others (like Toland, presumably) whom he has let into his study, but not into his "heart and affection." He
says that Molyneux seems to feel "under some obligation of peculiar respect ...
on account of my recommendation to you" but adds that "this comes from
nothing but your own over-great tenderness to oblige me."[39] He continues:

> if I did recommend him, you will find it was only as a man of parts and
> learning for his age, but without any intention that that should be of any
> other consequence, or lead you any farther, than the other qualities you
> should find in him, should recommend him to you. And therefore, what-
> soever you shall or shall not do for him, I shall no way interest myself in.[40]

---

37   Ibid.
38   Ibid., v: 2277.
39   Ibid.
40   Ibid.

Locke says he knows that Molyneaux is a good friend to those who deserve his friendship, but he adds that "for those that do not [deserve it], I shall never blame your neglect of them."[41] And he finishes his consideration by saying he would not have taken up so much of his letter speaking about Toland if Molyneaux had not made plain that he wanted Locke "to give [him] light in these matters" – something which he has now done plainly and thoroughly.[42] The message is fairly unambiguous: drop Toland.

5   Molyneux's (Lockean) Defence of Toland

We might expect, given Locke's seniority, and Molyneux's deferential attitude, that this is where things would end. But, as I indicated in my introduction, we find a definite act of resistance in Molyneux's response to Locke's (apparent) order. To unpack this more thoroughly, I want to look in slightly more detail at the substance of this response, written on 20th July 1697.

Molyneux tells Locke that he is obliged for the confidence that Locke shows in him, "communicating your thoughts concerning Mr. T more freely than you would to every one."[43] Toland has "had his opposers here," Molyneux reports, and he then immediately begins to discourse on Peter Browne's 1697 response to Toland, *A Letter in Answer to a Book Entitled Christianity Not Mysterious, as also to all those who set up for Reason and Evidence in opposition to Revelation and Mysteries*. (Browne's reply, written while he was a Fellow at Trinity College Dublin, and apparently much admired by Narcissus Marsh, suggests that we cannot have clear and distinct ideas of certain religious phenomena, but that we can have *analogical* ideas – like those that a blind man might form of colours. It is worth mentioning, too, that Browne was responsible for drawing Dublin's legal authority's attention to *Christianity Not Mysterious*.)

Interestingly, though, the first (negative) point that Molyneux highlights is Browne's treatment of Locke himself (rather than Toland) – specifically, Locke's case that we cannot prove the immateriality of the soul. (Browne claims to "demonstrate" this, but does not, Molyneux says.) It is only after this brief discussion (of Browne on Locke) that Molyneux returns to his original point – the opposition and antagonism that Toland has engendered in Dublin. He then tells Locke that there are two reasons he can "never forgive" Browne for his treatment of Toland: first, the "foul language and opprobrius names he gives Mr. Toland," and, secondly, and more importantly, the way in which

---

41   Ibid.
42   Ibid.
43   Ibid. v: 2310.

Browne confuses and conflates the religious and the secular, by calling on the civil magistrate to punish Toland's irreligious contentions.[44]

With this point made, Molyneux immediately switches back to Locke: the kind of confusion demonstrated by Browne reminds him (or "minds him") of the treatment that Locke himself had faced, when his *Reasonableness of Christianity* was put before the Grand Jury of Middlesex. (Significantly, it was "charged," as it were, alongside Toland's *Christianity Not Mysterious*, as already mentioned, and also alongside a text called *A Lady's Religion* – for which Toland almost certainly wrote the preface.[45]) As Molyneux puts it, very succinctly: "[T]o make our civil courts judges of religious doctrines" is "a matter of dangerous consequence."[46] There is a hugely important principle at stake – one that transcends the particular case at hand.

It seems to me that this is exceptionally crafty, and philosophically astute, on Molyneux's part. In his narrative, he is conjoining the fate of Toland and Locke: both are being presented as the victims of unthinking religious prejudice. Locke is looking to drop Toland, completely; but Molyneaux's discourse binds them together as victims of the same prejudice. Locke wants to extricate himself from Toland; Molyneux is not letting this happen. More than this, though, Molyneux is invoking a Lockean principle to oppose the treatment that Locke and Toland have jointly suffered: religious issues, he insists, should not be decided by civil powers. As Locke had put it, in one of the founding statements of modernity, the first *Letter Concerning Toleration*, or *Epistola*, of 1685, church and state are "perfectly distinct and infinitely different"[47] – a church is a voluntary association concerned with saving souls (rather than with maintaining the social contract) – and, strictly speaking, civil rights and religious belief are wholly separate.

Molyneux's rhetorical and logical strategy is designed to show that, if it is wrong to put Locke's works on religion before a civil court, it is equally wrong to do the same to Toland. So where Locke is only too keen to abandon Toland, Molyneux is stressing that he should be defended, not just out of a general sense of this being somehow right, but, more specifically, on the basis of Locke's own, foundational, criteria. Of course, it seems deeply ironic that, within a few months of producing this subtle defence of Toland, Molyneaux would be prompted into writing his *Case of Ireland Being Bound*

---

44   Ibid.

45   The author uses the pseudonym "Adeisidaemon," or "without superstition"; Toland used the same name for the author of his 1700 poem *Clito*, and he employed the term as the title for his 1709 work, published alongside *Origines Judaicae*.

46   Locke, *Correspondence*, V: 2310.

47   John Locke, *A Letter Concerning Toleration and Other Writings* (Indianapolis: 2010), 24.

by Acts of Parliament in England, Stated in response to a pamphlet that was almost certainly the work of Toland: *A Letter from a Gentleman in the Country,* published in December 1697, and arguing against allowing Protestant Ireland more commercial independence (not least because of the "despotick tendencies" of the Protestant Irish).[48] Further consideration of the *Case of Ireland* is beyond our present scope, obviously enough. But what we can take from the Molyneux-Locke correspondence on Toland is that Molyneux was far more than some star-struck lackey and was in some respects a more consistent Lockean than the older Locke himself.

Moreover, and going beyond the particularities and personalities of the debate, I would suggest that the entire episode provides us with access to something like a tectonic shift that was occurring in European thought and culture. One could argue, like Jonathan Israel, that Locke's radicalism is hugely qualified (and even "grudging") in comparison to Toland's;[49] and there seems to be no question of Locke looking to "un-god" the world, as Toland would. Nonetheless, Locke, Molyneux and Toland – whatever their differences – were part of a vanguard that changed the conditions for the possibility of thinking and acting (not least by creating the space for a secular politics). Whether we think about this change in terms of the "historical *a priori*" of Foucault (who himself drew on the later Husserl), or Kuhn's "paradigm shift" (itself much indebted to Alexandre Koyré), or some entirely different frame, what we are confronted with here is striking "evidence" – a case study, in fact – of the crisis of theocracy and the very emergence of modernity, in all of the frictions and contradictions that this process entailed.

References

Browne, Peter, *A Letter in Answer to a Book Entitled Christianity Not Mysterious, as also to all those who set up for Reason and Evidence in opposition to Revelation and Mysteries* (Dublin: 1697).

Carabelli, Giancarlo, *Tolandiana. Materiali bibliografici per lo studio dell'opera e della fortuna di John Toland (1670–1722)* (Florence: 1975).

---

48   See Patrick Kelly, "A Pamphlet Attributed to John Toland and an Unpublished Reply by Archbishop William King," *Topoi* 4 (1985): 81–90, which also includes a reprint of the pamphlet: 84–5.

49   See, for example, Jonathan I. Israel, *Radical Enlightenment. Philosophy and the Making of Modernity 1650–1750* (Oxford: 2001), 265–6.

Carroll, Robert Todd, *The Common-Sense Philosophy of Religion of Bishop Edward Stillingfleet* (The Hague: 1975).

Champion, Justin, "Making Authority: Belief, Conviction and Reason in the Public Sphere in late Seventeenth-Century England," in *Libertinage et Philosophie au XVII siècle*, eds. Antony McKenna and Pierre-François Moreau (Paris: 1999), 143–190.

Israel, Jonathan I., *Radical Enlightenment. Philosophy and the Making of Modernity 1650–1750* (Oxford: 2001).

Kelly, Patrick, "A Pamphlet Attributed to John Toland and an Unpublished Reply by Archbishop William King," *Topoi* 4 (1985): 81–90.

Leask, Ian, "Toland, Spinoza, and the Naturalisation of Scripture," in *Ireland and the Reception of the Bible: Social and Cultural Studies*, eds. Brad Anderson and Jonathan Kearney (London: 2018), 227–242.

Locke, John, *The Correspondence of John Locke*, 8 vols. (Oxford: 1976–1989).

Locke, John, *An Essay Concerning Human Understanding* (Harmondsworth: 1997).

Locke, John, *The Reasonableness of Christianity. As Delivered in the Scriptures* (Oxford: 1999).

Locke, John, *A Letter Concerning Toleration and Other Writings* (Indianapolis: 2010).

Marshall, John, *John Locke: Resistance, Religion and Responsibility* (Cambridge, Mass.: 1994).

McBride, Ian, "*The Case of Ireland* (1698) in Context: William Molyneux and His Critics," *Proceedings of the Royal Irish Academy: Archaeology, Culture, History, Literature* 118c (2018): 201–230.

Molyneux, Capel, *An Account of the Family and Descendents of Sir Thomas Molyneux* (Evesham: 1820).

Molyneux, William, *William Molyneux's* The Case of Ireland's Being Bound by Acts of Parliament in England, Stated (Dublin: 2018).

Nuovo, Victor (ed.), *John Locke and Christianity. Contemporary Responses to* The Reasonableness of Christianity (Bristol: 1997).

Simms, John Gerald, *William Molyneux of Dublin* (Dublin: 1982).

Stillingfleet, Edward, *A Discourse in Vindication of the Doctrine of the Trinity* (London: 1696).

Toland, John, *John Toland's* Christianity Not Mysterious. *Text, Associated Works & Critical Essays* (Dublin: 1997).

Woolhouse, Roger, *Locke. A Biography* (Cambridge, Mass.: 2007).

Yolton, John, *John Locke and the Way of Ideas* (Oxford: 1956).

PART 3

Religious Enlighteners and Radical Reformers

∴

Locke's Reasonable Christianity: A Religious Enlightener's Theology in Context

Diego Lucci

1 Introduction

John Locke is well known as one of the major figures in the history of philosophy and political theory. He was also a biblical theologian, whose religious interests, concerns, and views permeate virtually all areas of his production and are expressed in his later theological writings, which represent the culmination of his studies.[1] Locke expounded his religious ideas unsystematically and at times ambiguously in his public as well as private writings on religion. Nevertheless, an accurate analysis of his reflections on scriptural revelation, salvation, divine judgment, and Christ's nature and mission demonstrates that his religion is an internally coherent, original, heterodox version of Protestant Christianity.

Locke was well acquainted with the theological debates and controversies of his time and had good knowledge of various theological traditions. His reliance on Scripture as the ultimate source in matters of religion and ethics, his moralist soteriology emphasizing good works and faith, his views on the soul's death and the resurrection of the dead for the Last Judgment, and his considerations on Trinitarian and Christological issues indeed denote various similarities with some heterodox currents of the early modern period. After the publication of his major book of theology, *The Reasonableness of Christianity* (1695), several critics, including, among others, the Calvinistic divine John Edwards, the latitudinarian Bishop Edward Stillingfleet, and the non-juror John Milner, called attention to several points in common between Locke's

---

1 Various monographs have highlighted the importance of Locke's religious views to his philosophical, moral, and political thought: see John Dunn, *The Political Thought of John Locke: An Historical Account of the Argument of the* Two Treatises of Government (Cambridge, Eng.: 1969); John Colman, *John Locke's Moral Philosophy* (Edinburgh: 1983); John Marshall, *John Locke: Resistance, Religion and Responsibility* (Cambridge, Eng.: 1994); Kim Ian Parker, *The Biblical Politics of John Locke* (Waterloo, ON: 2004); Victor Nuovo, *John Locke: The Philosopher as Christian Virtuoso* (Oxford: 2017). For a comprehensive treatment and reassessment of Locke's religion, see Diego Lucci, *John Locke's Christianity* (Cambridge, Eng.: 2021).

© KONINKLIJKE BRILL NV, LEIDEN, 2022 | DOI:10.1163/9789004523371_011

religious thought and anti-Trinitarian theories – particularly theories belonging to the Socinian theological tradition.[2] Socinianism was named after the Italian anti-Trinitarian and anti-Calvinist theologian Faustus Socinus, who, in the late 16th and early 17th century, played a major role in the development of the theology of the Minor Reformed Church of Poland, whose mostly German and Polish members were widely known as "Polish Brethren." Locke actually cited Socinian authors, texts, and concepts in his manuscripts quite frequently, for he was familiar with Socinian thought – not only with the ideas of Socinus and his immediate disciples, but also with the theories of 17th-century Polish Brethren who contributed significantly to the refinement of Socinian theology. Locke's public writings on religion also present several Socinian-like principles, as Edwards and Milner noted and as I explain below. Furthermore, some critics, including Stillingfleet, argued that Locke's agnosticism on substance and his rethinking of personal identity in non-substantialist terms promoted skepticism and supported anti-Trinitarianism. Locke had indeed departed from the traditional, scholastic, substantialist notions of substance and person, which, according to Stillingfleet, were crucial to the Trinitarian doctrine.

Socinianism was not the only heterodox theological current in which Locke was deeply interested. In fact, his views on justification and the atonement are largely in line with the Arminian tradition of thought, which was inaugurated by the Dutch anti-Calvinist theologian Jacob Arminius in the late 16th and early 17th century. According to Arminius and his followers, including, among others, the Dutch Remonstrants and the English latitudinarians, atonement is intended for all, and God's grace is *assisting* grace, which human beings are able to respond or resist. Locke knew Arminian theories thanks to the writings of Remonstrant authors such as Hugo Grotius and Philipp van Limborch (who was also a close friend of Locke's) and Arminian-influenced English books, such as William Chillingworth's *The Religion of Protestants* (1638) and the works of various latitudinarian divines. He found the Arminian stress on free will and moral works particularly appealing, and he shared with Arminian authors a view of the Law of Nature as rational and divine. Nevertheless, as I clarify in this chapter, Locke's theology, soteriology, and Christology present several differences from Socinianism and Arminianism and, thus, are neither Socinian nor Arminian proper.[3] In fact, Locke always made sure that his religious

---

2   On the debate on Locke's religion in the late 17th and 18th century, see Alan P.F. Sell, *John Locke and the Eighteenth-Century Divines* (Cardiff: 1997); John C. Higgins-Biddle, "Introduction," in John Locke, *The Reasonableness of Christianity, as Delivered in the Scriptures* (Oxford: 1999), xv–cxv.

3   On Locke's interest in Socinianism, see Higgins-Biddle, "Introduction," lviii–lx; John Marshall, "Locke, Socinianism, 'Socinianism,' and Unitarianism," in *English Philosophy in the Age of*

views were consistent with, and actually grounded in, the Scriptures, since he adhered to the Protestant principle of *sola Scriptura*, thereby regarding Scripture alone as the rule of faith. He even disassociated himself expressly from the Socinians and the Socinian-influenced English Unitarians of his time in his two vindications of the *Reasonableness*, which he wrote in response to Edwards' charges, and in his three replies to Stillingfleet. At any rate, he certainly benefited from his extensive knowledge of various theological currents, particularly when writing about the role of good works and faith in the pursuit of salvation, the resurrection of the dead, and the Trinitarian doctrine.

Briefly, Locke's version of Protestant Christianity was essentially rooted in his reading of Scripture, although being also influenced by various heterodox theological traditions. The main elements of Locke's Christianity, which I examine in this chapter, are his notion of scriptural revelation as a necessary complement to natural reason and an infallible and sufficient guide in moral and religious matters; his moralist soteriology, emphasizing both good works and faith; his views on the soul's death and the resurrection of the dead for the Last Judgment; and his unique Christology, which is Messianic but non-Trinitarian. When explaining, although unsystematically, his hermeneutical, soteriological, and Christological views, he described Christianity as "reasonable" – namely, as acceptable to natural reason (even though not completely in line with natural reason, because some revealed truths are above reason) and convenient to the pursuit of eternal salvation. To Locke as a theologian, it was indeed the moral, soteriological, and eschatological meaning of Scripture that mattered first and foremost, as I explain in this chapter.

2   Morality, Reason, and Revelation

In the year 1695, Locke decided to publish, albeit anonymously, his theological ideas in *The Reasonableness of Christianity*, a treatise devoted mainly to the subject of justification – namely, to what it is that "justifies" human beings who have sinned and, thus, enables their salvation. Before the publication of the *Reasonableness*, Locke was simply an inquirer who took notes on theological subjects in his private papers. However, his public writings on philosophy and politics also denote his religious concerns and interests, which permeate

---

Locke, ed. Michael A. Stewart (Oxford: 2000), 111–182; Stephen D. Snobelen, "Socinianism, Heresy and John Locke's *Reasonableness of Christianity*," *Enlightenment and Dissent* 20 (2001): 88–125. On the similarities and differences between Locke's religion and the Socinian and Arminian theological traditions, see Lucci, *John Locke's Christianity*.

virtually all his oeuvre. *An Essay Concerning Human Understanding* (1690) is actually not a secular book, since it tends toward theological investigation. In the *Essay*, Locke affirmed God's existence as the Creator and the Legislator of the eternal, universal, and rational moral law.[4] Moreover, he highlighted the important role of biblical revelation as "enlarging" natural reason, and he stressed the need to believe in things "above reason" revealed in Scripture, such as the existence of an afterlife, which natural reason cannot demonstrate.[5] Locke's emphasis on God's role as a lawgiver and on otherworldly rewards and sanctions as incentives to moral conduct denotes his preoccupation with the grounds of ethics – a preoccupation that eventually led him to turn to biblical revelation in search for solid foundations for morality.[6] In the *Essay*, he characterized morality as *"the proper Science, and Business of Mankind in general."*[7] He also placed morality *"amongst the Sciences capable of Demonstration."*[8] He regarded human beings as able to conceive of the existence of a divine moral law and the duty to comply with this law, given that we humans have "the *Idea* of a supreme Being, infinite in Power, Goodness, and Wisdom, whose Workmanship we are, and on whom we depend; and the *Idea* of our selves, as understanding, rational Beings."[9] He considered human beings capable of demonstrating the existence of a Divine Creator and Legislator through the argument from design and the anthropological argument. In this respect, he maintained that "the visible marks of extraordinary Wisdom and Power, appear so plainly in all the Works of the Creation, that a rational Creature, who will but seriously reflect on them, cannot miss the discovery of a *Deity*."[10] Moreover, considering that "bare *nothing can no more produce any real Being, than it can be equal to two right Angles*," he concluded that "from the Consideration of our selves, and what we infallibly find in our own Constitutions, our Reason leads us to the Knowledge of this certain and evident Truth, That *there is an eternal, most powerful, and most knowing Being*."[11] In the *Second Treatise of Civil Government* (1690), too, he referred to human beings' relation to God when affirming our moral duties:

---

4   John Locke, *An Essay Concerning Human Understanding* (Oxford: 1975), 89, 302–3, 619–621.
5   Ibid., 687–698.
6   Lucci, *John Locke's Christianity*, 25–48.
7   Locke, *Essay*, 646.
8   Ibid., 549.
9   Ibid.
10   Ibid., 89.
11   Ibid., 620–1.

> For Men being all the Workmanship of one Omnipotent, and infi-
> nitely wise Maker; All the Servants of one Sovereign Master, sent into
> the World by his order, and about his business; they are his Property,
> whose Workmanship they are, made to last during his, not one anoth-
> er's Pleasure…. Every one, as he is *bound to preserve himself,* and not to
> quit his Station wilfully, so by the like reason, when his own Preservation
> comes not in competition, ought he, as much as he can, *to preserve the
> rest of Mankind.*[12]

Locke considered the divine moral law, or in other words the Law of Nature, to
be rational and, thus, demonstrable through natural reason. He thought that
we humans, being God's rational creatures, are the bearers of the God-given
rational moral law, and he saw obedience to this law as a duty towards our
Creator and, hence, towards our fellow rational creatures who, being all naturally equal, have the same natural rights and duties. Therefore, he proposed a
sort of theistic and rationalist deontological ethics.[13] Nevertheless, Locke was
skeptical about the actual likelihood of demonstrating moral ideas through
natural reason and, thus, about the actual likelihood of providing morality with
scientific or theoretical foundations. He called attention to the difficulties that
natural reason faces when trying to demonstrate moral ideas – difficulties like
the complexity of moral ideas and their unfitness for sensible representation –
and he concluded that the imperfection and weakness of human nature prevent us from demonstrating moral ideas in the same way as we demonstrate
mathematical concepts.[14] Therefore, he turned to biblical revelation to establish morality on solid grounds in the *Reasonableness*, in which he wrote:

> 'Tis too hard a task for unassisted Reason, to establish Morality in all
> its parts upon its true foundation; with a clear and convincing light….
> Humane reason unassisted, failed Men in its great and Proper business
> of *Morality*. It never from unquestionable Principles, by clear deductions,
> made out an entire body of the *Law of Nature*.[15]

Locke thought that, besides being demonstrable by natural reason (at least in
principle), the Law of Nature was also revealed unambiguously in Scripture.
He even regarded Scripture as infallible and, hence, as trumping rational doubt

---

12   John Locke, *Two Treatises of Government* (Cambridge, Eng.: 1988), 271.
13   Lucci, *John Locke's Christianity*, 43–5.
14   Locke, *Essay*, 550–2.
15   Locke, *Reasonableness*, 148–150.

and sufficient to establish morality. This is why, in the year 1692, he did not accede to his friend William Molyneux's request to "think of Obleidging the World, with a *Treatise of Morals*, drawn up according to the Hints you frequently give in your Essay, of their being Demonstrable according to the Mathematical Method."[16] And when Molyneux reiterated this request in 1696, around one year after the publication of the *Reasonableness*, Locke answered that "the Gospel contains so perfect a body of ethics, that reason may be excused from that inquiry, since she may find man's duty clearer and easier in revelation, than in herself."[17]

Locke's turning to the Bible to find a convincing, Scripture-based theological ethics was also due to what he gave as the contingent reason for writing the *Reasonableness* – namely, his intention to disprove, on the one hand, antinomianism and, on the other, deism.[18] In *A Second Vindication of the Reasonableness of Christianity* (1697), he declared that a controversy that had "made so much noise and heat amongst some of the Dissenters" had drawn him "into a stricter and more thorough Enquiry into the Question about Justification," thereby prompting him to write the *Reasonableness*.[19] Whereas he never used the terms "antinomian" and "antinomianism" in the *Reasonableness* and its two vindications, in the above-quoted passage from the *Second Vindication* he was obviously referring to the antinomian controversy that involved several Nonconformist theologians in the first half of the 1690s. This controversy was triggered by the republication of the Civil-War Independent divine Tobias Crisp's *Christ Alone Exalted* (1643) by his son Samuel in the year 1690. This book argued that the elect were justified solely by God's eternal decree, the effects of which their good works and faith could not alter. Its republication provoked the reaction of the Presbyterians headed by Daniel Williams, who, in 1694, was removed from the Pinners' Hall lectureship and established the Salters' Hall lectureship. In the end, this controversy led to the dissolution of the "Happy Union" between Presbyterians and Independents in 1695, only four years after its start. Locke abhorred antinomian and, generally, predestinarian ideas. Although he avoided using the term "predestination" in the *Reasonableness* and its vindications, he denounced predestinarian views as unscriptural and unreasonable, because he saw belief in predestination as denying any role to good works in the pursuit of salvation.

---

16   Esmond S. de Beer (ed.), *The Correspondence of John Locke* (Oxford: 1976–1989), vol. 4: nos. 1530, 1538.
17   Ibid., vol. 5: nos. 2050, 2059.
18   Lucci, *John Locke's Christianity*, 16–25.
19   John Locke, *Vindications of the Reasonableness of Christianity* (Oxford: 2012), 34.

Locke also accused predestinarians of having provoked the reaction of others who maintained that "there was no Redemption necessary ... and so made Jesus Christ nothing but the Restorer and Preacher of pure Natural Religion; thereby doing violence to the whole tenor of the New Testament."[20] Here, Locke was referring to deists, and he indeed used the words "deist" or "deists" several times in the two vindications of the *Reasonableness*. In this regard, it is worth noting that, when Locke wrote the *Reasonableness* in 1695, the deist controversy in England was still in its germinal phase, although some prominent theologians of different stripes, such as Richard Baxter and Edward Stillingfleet, had already written against deism in the 1670s, and although the works of 17th-century thinkers commonly considered as deists, such as Edward Herbert of Cherbury and Charles Blount, were well known by the mid-1690s. Yet, Locke most probably had two other authors in mind when he wrote about deism in the *Reasonableness* and its vindications. One of these authors was the heterodox Jewish thinker Uriel Acosta, who committed suicide in 1640, after being expelled twice from the Jewish community of Amsterdam because he considered the doctrines and rituals of institutional religion incompatible with reason and Scripture and, at the same time, he saw the Law of Nature as universal and sufficient. Locke indeed labeled Acosta "the father and patriarch of the Deists" in a manuscript note of the mid-1690s.[21] The other "deist" whom Locke probably had in mind when writing the *Reasonableness* was the Irish-born freethinker John Toland, who sent several papers – probably drafts of his controversial book *Christianity Not Mysterious* (1696) – to Locke through their common friend John Freke in early 1695.[22] At any rate, Locke blamed deists for overestimating the capabilities of natural reason in religious and moral matters. According to Locke, deists believed that natural reason attains certain knowledge in all religious matters and actually grasps the Law of Nature, which they regarded as universal, eternal, and sufficient. Conversely, Locke conceived of morality as demonstrable in principle but actually unmonstrated by unassisted reason. Moreover, he considered most theological knowledge as falling within the scope of probability, not certainty (with the significant exception of our knowledge of God's existence, which, as I have explained above, is demonstrative and implies an understanding that we have duties towards our Creator). Locke indeed wrote in the *Essay* that "most of the

---

20   Locke, *Reasonableness*, 5.
21   Oxford, Bodleian Library, MS Locke d. 10, "Lemmata Ethica, Argumenta et Authores 1659," 33.
22   De Beer (ed.), *Correspondence*, vol. 5: nos. 1868, 1874. See Higgins-Biddle, "Introduction," xxvii–xxxvii; Lucci, *John Locke's Christianity*, 19–24.

Propositions we think, reason, discourse, nay act upon, are such, as we cannot have undoubted Knowledge of their Truth."[23] Therefore, in the numerous instances when we are unable to achieve *certainty*, we need to rely on *probability*.[24] This is also true in religious matters, since many things are "beyond the Discovery of our natural Faculties, and above *Reason*" and hence "are, when revealed, *the proper Matter of Faith*."[25] According to Locke, "it still belongs to *Reason*, to judge of the Truth of [a proposition's] being a revelation, and of the signification of the Words, wherein it is delivered."[26] Nevertheless, he explained:

> I do not mean, that we must consult Reason, and examine whether a Proposition revealed from God can be made out by natural Principles, and if it cannot, that then we may reject it; But consult it we must, and by it examine, whether it be a *Revelation* from God or no: And if *Reason* finds it to be revealed from God, *Reason* then declares for it, as much as for any other Truth, and makes it one of her Dictates.[27]

Briefly, as Nicholas Wolterstorff has aptly explained, in Locke "faith is not a mode of knowledge. It consists in believing things on the basis of one's belief that they have been revealed by God rather than on the basis of the premises of some demonstration."[28] In other words, faith is assent to merely *probable* matters of fact on the basis of the evidence of their being divine revelations. Locke clarified his notion of faith and his views on the relation between reason and revelation with the following words:

> For where the Principles of Reason have not evidenced a Proposition to be certainly true or false, there clear *Revelation*, as another Principle of Truth, and Ground of Assent, may determine; and so it may be Matter of *Faith*, and be also above *Reason*. Because *Reason*, in that particular Matter, being able to reach no higher than Probability, *Faith* gave the Determination, where *Reason* came short; and *Revelation* discovered on which side the Truth lay.[29]

---

23   Locke, *Essay*, 655.
24   Ibid., 661–2.
25   Ibid., 694.
26   Ibid.
27   Ibid., 704.
28   Nicholas Wolterstorff, "Locke's Philosophy of Religion," in *The Cambridge Companion to Locke*, ed. Vere Chappell (Cambridge, Eng.: 1994), 190.
29   Locke, *Essay*, 695.

This is a significant point of divergence between Locke and deist thinkers. John Toland in *Christianity Not Mysterious* and other writings and, in the 18th century, other deists and freethinkers such as Anthony Collins and Matthew Tindal judged probability to be an insufficient ground for faith and, thus, they regarded faith as a mode of knowledge. Accordingly, they subjected the content of Scripture to rational analysis and rejected the notion of truths above reason, as they argued that any truly divine revelation ought to be consistent with natural reason. On the other hand, Locke thought that both Scripture and natural reason are divinely given but scriptural revelation complements and sustains natural reason, in that scriptural revelation discloses more than unassisted reason can discover on its own. According to Locke, natural reason can ascertain the divine origin of a revelation, but divine revelation, particularly biblical revelation, comes in where unassisted reason cannot reach:

> *Reason* is natural *Revelation*, whereby the eternal Father of Light, and Fountain of all Knowledge communicates to Mankind that portion of Truth, which he has laid within the reach of their natural Faculties: *Revelation* is natural *Reason* enlarged by a new set of Discoveries communicated by God immediately, which *Reason* vouches the Truth of, by the Testimony and Proofs it gives, that they come from God.[30]

Concerning the divine origin of Scripture, Locke adopted the proof of scriptural authority that Socinus had formulated in *De Sacrae Scripturae auctoritate* (1588) and Grotius had repeated in *Pro veritate religionis Christianae* (1627).[31] According to this proof, the excellence of Christ's moral and salvific message, the agreement between Old Testament messianic prophecies and their fulfillment in the New Testament, and Christ's miracles show that the Bible is God's Revealed Word.[32] Therefore, given also the limitations of natural reason – limitations that, according to Locke, deists ignored – the Bible serves as a useful, and indeed necessary, guide for humanity in moral and soteriological matters.

---

30   Ibid., 698.

31   Faustus Socinus, *De Sacrae Scripturae auctoritate* (Raków: 1611), 5–36; Hugo Grotius, *Pro veritate religionis Christianae* (Paris: 1627), 83–4.

32   Locke, *Vindications*, 35. See Victor Nuovo, *Christianity, Antiquity, and Enlightenment: Interpretations of Locke* (Dordrecht: 2011), 53–73; Nuovo, *John Locke*, 220–5, 233–5; Lucci, *John Locke's Christianity*, 58–61.

3   The Pursuit of Salvation

Contra both antinomianism and deism, *The Reasonableness of Christianity* presents a Scripture-based moralist soteriology consistent with the Protestant irenic tradition of the "way of fundamentals."[33] Like Socinians, Arminians, latitudinarians, and other Protestant irenicists of the early modern period, Locke believed that the core of the Christian religion consists of a few fundamental principles, which are clearly revealed in Scripture, easily acceptable to all Christians, and necessary to salvation. Yet, Locke recognized that different churches had developed specific beliefs, dogmas, and practices based on their readings of the Scriptures. He indeed acknowledged the problem of the obscurity of many biblical texts. Thus, he admitted the possibility of mistakes in interpreting scriptural passages about non-fundamentals. Given that Scripture contains many passages liable to interpretation, he argued that searching for religious truth is more important than (often supposedly) finding and maintaining it. He even thought that error about non-fundamentals, if held after sincere search by a Christian perusing the Scriptures, could still lead to salvation.[34] Therefore, non-fundamental beliefs and practices, being unnecessary to salvation, ought not to cause hurtful tensions, pointless controversies, and divisive conflicts among Christians. However, whereas Locke's theory of the fundamentals presents important irenic implications, the main motivation behind this theory was his preoccupation with morality and salvation. In fact, he described adherence to the fundamental articles of Christianity, which he saw as unambiguously revealed in the Gospel, as necessary to salvation and as promoting moral conduct. He argued that "some of the Truths delivered in Holy Writ are very plain: 'Tis impossible, I think, to mistake their Meaning; And those certainly are all necessary to be explicitly believ'd."[35] These "very plain" truths are the three fundamentals of Christianity – faith in Jesus the Messiah, repentance for sin, and obedience to the divine moral law.

Locke saw Jesus' Messiahship as "the sole Doctrine pressed and required to be believed in the whole tenour of our Saviour's and his Apostles Preaching"[36] because faith in Jesus' Messiahship is essential to believe in his teaching. Christ affirmed the necessity of repentance for sin, which is "not only a sorrow for sins past, but (what is a Natural consequence of such sorrow, if it be real) a turning from them, into a new and contrary Life," entailing "a sincere Resolution

---

33   On Locke and the way of fundamentals, see Lucci, *John Locke's Christianity*, 67–76.
34   Locke, *Reasonableness*, 168–171; Locke, *Vindications*, 11–12, 44–5, 75–6, 174–7, 192–4, 230–3.
35   Locke, *Vindications*, 175.
36   Locke, *Reasonableness*, 109.

and Endeavour, to the utmost of our power, to conform all our Actions to the Law of God."[37] Without repentance for sin and the consequent effort to obey the divine moral law, it is impossible to pursue moral renovation and strive to live an exemplary life inspired by faith in Christ. Nevertheless, according to Locke, adherence to the fundamentals of Christianity is necessary but not sufficient to salvation. Although some of his critics, including, among others, John Edwards, accused him of creedal minimalism, Locke was far from reducing the Christian life to mere acceptance of the three fundamentals of Christianity or even only faith in Christ. According to Locke, faith in Jesus the Messiah, which entails repentance for sin and obedience to the divine moral law, is necessary to become a Christian, but is not enough to achieve salvation, as is explained in the *Reasonableness* and its two vindications. Even repentance and obedience, which result from faith in Jesus the Messiah, are not sufficient to salvation. According to Locke, the conscientious study of Scripture, too, is required to live a Christian life and obtain salvation, because acceptance of Jesus as the Messiah binds the faithful to Scripture as a whole, and not only to this simple article of faith and its consequences concerning the practice of morality. Therefore, Locke was far from being a creedal minimalist. In fact, according to Locke (who was not a deist), Jesus the Messiah taught much more than merely the need to repent for sin and obey the God-given Law of Nature.

Locke argued in the *Essay* and the *Reasonableness* that unassisted reason had never grasped the Law of Nature completely and perfectly because of human imperfection and weakness, the abuse of words by philosophers, and power politics and priestcraft. For this reason, God reaffirmed the Law of Nature through the covenant of works, establishing the Law of Moses. This law consisted of a ceremonial part, which had only temporary validity, and a moral part – "the Law of Works" – identical to the Law of Nature and, hence, universally binding and eternally valid. Being stated in clear terms in the Old Testament, the Law of Works was easily intelligible. Nevertheless, this law was excessively demanding in that it required perfect obedience. Moreover, this law did not offer any incentive to act morally.[38] Therefore, with the covenant of grace or covenant of faith, God established a new and final law – the Law of Faith – through Jesus the Messiah, who restored the Law of Nature in its entirety. However, the Law of Faith, although encompassing the Law of Nature, is not coextensive with the Law of Nature. Christ actually complemented the Law of Nature with important revelations, such as the promise of otherworldly rewards and sanctions, thereby providing a powerful incentive to act

37   Ibid., 111–112.
38   Ibid., 17–22.

morally (although, according to Locke, obedience to the divine moral law is still essentially a duty, as I have explained above).[39] This incentive to morality was also one of the main tenets of Socinian soteriology, since Socinus and his disciples argued that, before Christ's Coming, humankind had no assurance of an afterlife with rewards and punishments.[40] Locke described rewards and punishments in the afterlife as incentivizing the practice of morality not only in *The Reasonableness of Christianity*, but also in *A Paraphrase and Notes on the Epistles of St Paul*, which appeared posthumously in several volumes between 1705 and 1707. Yet, in the *Essay* and the *Reasonableness* he admitted that even those who believe in otherworldly sanctions are still liable to commit evil deeds, due to human weakness and imperfection. In fact, while stressing human rationality, Locke never ignored the limitations of human nature.[41] Therefore, he put emphasis on Christ's promise of God's forgiveness of the faithful, which makes salvation possible despite the limits of human nature. This is another point in common between Locke's religion and Socinianism. Rejecting the opinion that God necessarily has to punish sinners, Socinus and his followers maintained that God is merciful and omnipotent. Therefore, God can waive his right to punishment and forgive the sins of the repentant faithful who, during their life, sincerely attempt to abide by the divine law.[42] Likewise, Locke wrote in the *Reasonableness* that "by the Law of Faith, Faith is allowed to supply the defect of full Obedience; and so the Believers are admitted to Life and Immortality as if they were Righteous."[43] He argued that Christ "did not expect ... a Perfect Obedience void of all slips and falls: He knew our Make, and the weakness of our Constitution too well, and was sent with a Supply for that Defect."[44] This supply was faith:

> Christian Believers have the Privilege to be under the *Law of Faith* too; which is that Law whereby God Justifies a man for Believing, though by his Works he be not Just or Righteous, *i.e.* though he came short of Perfect

---

39   Ibid., 22–5, 110–112.

40   David Wootton, "John Locke: Socinian or Natural Law Theorist?" in *Religion, Secularization and Political Thought: Thomas Hobbes to J.S. Mill*, ed. James E. Crimmins (London: 1989), 39–67; Sarah Mortimer, "Human Liberty and Human Nature in the Works of Faustus Socinus and His Readers," *Journal of the History of Ideas* 70 (2009): 191–211.

41   Locke, *Essay*, 273–287, 356–7; Locke, *Reasonableness*, 19, 120, 130. See William M. Spellman, *John Locke and the Problem of Depravity* (Oxford: 1988), 57; Sell, *John Locke*, 230; Lucci, *John Locke's Christianity*, 92.

42   Sarah Mortimer, "Human and Divine Justice in the Works of Grotius and the Socinians," in *The Intellectual Consequences of Religious Heterodoxy, 1600–1750*, eds. Sarah Mortimer, John Robertson (Leiden: 2012), 75–94.

43   Locke, *Reasonableness*, 19.

44   Ibid., 120.

Obedience to the Law of Works. God alone does, or can, Justifie or make Just those who by their Works are not so: Which he doth by counting their Faith for Righteousness, *i.e.* for a compleat performance of the Law.[45]

The conviction that "God Justifies a man for Believing, though by his Works he be not Just or Righteous" led Locke to formulate, in the *Paraphrase*, a concept of saving faith as *fiducia* – namely, as trust in Jesus the Messiah, which entails reliance on Scripture.[46] However, in the *Paraphrase* Locke did not disavow the aforesaid notion of faith as assent, which he had explained in the *Essay*. Both notions of faith, as assent and *fiducia*, actually entail a commitment to biblical revelation and its salvific message, which emphasizes not only faith in Jesus the Messiah, but also repentance for sin and obedience to the divine moral law. Locke indeed disapproved of the principle of salvation by faith alone. As he explained in the *Reasonableness*, saving faith has practical consequences, in that it must be accompanied by repentance and obedience:

> [Jesus' followers] were required to believe him to be the *Messiah*; Which Faith is of Grace promised to be reckoned to them for the compleating of their Righteousness, wherein it was defective: But Righteousness, or Obedience to the Law of God, was their great business; Which if they could have attained by their own Performances, there would have been no need of this Gracious Allowance, in Reward of their Faith.... This Righteousness therefore, a compleat Obedience and freedom from Sin, are still sincerely to be endeavoured after. And 'tis no where promised, That those who persist in a wilful Disobedience to his Laws, shall be received into the eternal bliss of his Kingdom, how much soever they believe in him.[47]

In other words, faith will enable the faithful to receive "the Pardon and Forgiveness of Sins and Salvation,"[48] but only on condition that, during their life, they repent for their sins and endeavor to obey the God-given Law of Nature reaffirmed by Christ. This means that the justifying faith includes good works. Therefore, the concept of justification that is at the core of Locke's moralist soteriology, and that involves a stress on free will and individual responsibility,

---

45   Ibid., 20–1.
46   John Locke, *A Paraphrase and Notes on the Epistles of St Paul to the Galatians, 1 and 2 Corinthians, Romans, Ephesians* (Oxford: 1987), vol. 1: 136. See Arthur W. Wainwright, "Introduction," in Locke, *Paraphrase*, vol. 1: 41–3; Sell, *John Locke*, 87–8; Lucci, *John Locke's Christianity*, 93–4.
47   Locke, *Reasonableness*, 130.
48   Ibid., 133.

diverges from the Calvinist theory that Christ's righteousness, imputed by God to the faithful, justifies. Locke, like Socinians and Arminians, indeed believed that human beings are able to accept or resist God's assisting grace, although he deemed it reasonable and convenient to accept grace in order to pursue salvation.[49] However, Locke's position is closer to the Arminians' than the Socinians' understanding of justification. Locke's notion of the Law of Nature as divinely given, universally binding, and eternally valid actually differs from the Socinian view of the Law of Nature as partly contradicted and, hence, invalidated and replaced by the Revealed Law, which is the saving law. Locke's position on justification rather echoes the Arminian emphasis on the cooperation between human nature (with the recognition of the natural law as divine) and God's assisting grace in salvation.

4   Divine Judgment

Locke's moralist soteriology, accentuating the role of individual responsibility in the pursuit of salvation, entails the denial of original sin.[50] In *The Reasonableness of Christianity*, Locke blamed those who "would have all *Adam*'s Posterity doomed to Eternal Infinite Punishment for the Transgression of *Adam*, whom Millions had never heard of, and no one had authorized to transact for him, or be his Representative."[51] Moreover, in two manuscripts composed a few years before the *Reasonableness* – "Peccatum originale" (1692) and "Homo ante et post lapsum" (1693) – he rejected the view that Adam's sin was imputed to his posterity, he denied the fallen condition of humankind, and he described original sin as unscriptural, unreasonable, and incompatible with God's goodness and justice.[52]

Another place in Locke's oeuvre that denotes his stress on individual moral accountability and, hence, his refusal of original sin, is Chapter 27 of Book II of *An Essay Concerning Human Understanding* – a chapter composed for the second edition of the *Essay*, published in 1694. In this chapter, titled "Of Identity and Diversity," Locke formulated a non-substantialist account of personhood, explaining that personal identity is located in "consciousness [which] always

49   Dewey D. Wallace, "Socinianism, Justification by Faith, and the Sources of John Locke's *The Reasonableness of Christianity,*" *Journal of the History of Ideas* 45 (1984): 49–66; Lucci, *John Locke's Christianity*, 94–6.

50   Spellman, *John Locke*; Aderemi Artis, "Locke on Original Sin," *Locke Studies* 12 (2012): 201–219; Lucci, *John Locke's Christianity*, 96–105.

51   Locke, *Reasonableness*, 5.

52   John Locke, *Writings on Religion* (Oxford: 2002), 229–231.

accompanies thinking."[53] While the traditional Christian understanding of personal identity was based on Boethius' definition of "person" as an "individual substance of a rational nature,"[54] Locke did not provide a substantialist account of personhood because of his agnosticism on substance, including the thinking substance (or soul). According to Locke, substance is an unknown support or substratum of ideas that are "conveyed in by the Senses, as they are found in exteriour things, or by reflection on [the mind's] own operations," and that cannot "subsist by themselves."[55] Locke maintained that "we have no clear, or distinct *Idea* of that *thing* we suppose a Support."[56] Thus, whereas we are aware of our thoughts and have an idea of our thinking, which is an operation of the mind, we have no clear and distinct idea of the underlying entity in which our thinking takes place – namely, the thinking substance – and of its ontological constitution.[57]

While Locke's non-substantialist approach to personhood is the logical continuation of his agnosticism on substance, including the thinking substance, his consciousness-based theory of personal identity was also intended to complement and sustain his moral and theological commitments to a system of otherworldly rewards and sanctions.[58] This theory combines with his moralist soteriology in that it involves an understanding of moral accountability centered on the concept of consciousness. When focusing on the moral implications of his theory of personal identity, Locke called attention to one's awareness of one's deeds as crucial to recollect past events on Judgment Day, when everyone will need to have a clear idea of the reasons why they will be punished or forgiven and rewarded with eternal beatitude. Consciousness, extending "backwards to any past Action or Thought," actually enables the self, both in this life and upon resurrection for the Last Judgment, to recognize that "it is the same *self* now it was then; and 'tis by the same *self* with this present one that now reflects on it, that that Action was done."[59] Therefore, at the Last Judgment "the Sentence shall be justified by the consciousness all Persons shall have, that they *themselves* in what Bodies soever they appear, or what Substances soever that consciousness adheres to, are the *same*, that

---

53   Locke, *Essay*, 335.
54   Boethius, *Theological Tractates. The Consolation of Philosophy*, trans. Hugh F. Stewart, Edward K. Rand, and Stanley J. Tester (Cambridge, Mass.: 1978), 85.
55   Locke, *Essay*, 295.
56   Ibid., 297.
57   Ibid., 539–543.
58   Lucci, *John Locke's Christianity*, 106–133.
59   Locke, *Essay*, 335.

committed those Actions, and deserve that Punishment for them."[60] In this regard, drawing on a passage in 1 Cor. 14:25 ("And thus are the secrets of his heart made manifest"),[61] Locke maintained in *Essay* II.xxvii.22 that "in the great Day, wherein the Secrets of all Hearts shall be laid open, it may be reasonable to think, no one shall be made to answer for what he knows nothing of; but shall receive his Doom, his Conscience accusing or excusing him."[62] In *Essay* I.iii.8, Locke defined "conscience" as "our own Opinion or Judgment of the Moral Rectitude or Pravity of our own Actions."[63] If matched by a proper consideration of the divine moral law, one's moral judgment of one's actions is accompanied by a sound understanding of their righteousness or wrongness and, thus, by feelings of confidence and serenity in the case of good works, or by remorse in the case of misdeeds.[64] However, one's consciousness (which is *non-evaluative* awareness) of one's deeds is presupposed to one's moral evaluation of such deeds, both in this life and on Judgment Day.

Locke's comments on divine judgment in the *Essay* show his dislike of original sin. His persuasion that on Judgment Day "no one shall be made to answer for what he knows nothing of" and "every one shall receive according to his doings"[65] is indeed at odds with the view that human beings can be held accountable for another person's deeds, such as Adam's sin. Locke's stress on individual responsibility also clashes with the satisfaction theory of atonement, originating in medieval scholasticism and also adopted, and modified, by the Magisterial Reformers. According to the satisfaction doctrine, Christ suffered death on the cross as a substitute for human sin, thereby satisfying God due to his infinite merit. This doctrine is based on the idea of substitutionary atonement – namely, the idea that Jesus died for us, which is upheld by the Roman Catholic Church and the majority of Protestant churches. Locke was silent on satisfaction in the *Reasonableness*, but, in the *Second Vindication*, he described it as a "disputed" doctrine and observed that the word "satisfaction" is "a term not used by the Holy Ghost in the Scripture, and very variously explained by those that do use it."[66] Yet, he paid attention to this subject in some of his manuscripts, particularly in "Adversaria Theologica" – a notebook written, for the most part, shortly before the *Reasonableness* – and in "Redemtion, Death"

---

60   Ibid., 347.
61   In this chapter, all biblical quotes are from the King James Version (KJV).
62   Locke, *Essay*, 344.
63   Ibid., 70.
64   Ibid., 69–72.
65   Ibid., 344, 347.
66   Locke, *Vindications*, 227.

(*c*.1697). In these two manuscripts, Locke described Christ's death on the cross as necessary to confirm the truth of his doctrine. He wrote in "Adversaria":

> Christ by his death redeems us from sin in that his death is a demonstration of the truth of his doctrine & the great argument to bring them into an obedience to the Gospel whereby they leave sin & soe scape punishment. To restore the law of nature or natural religion almost blotted out by corruption god yields his son to death which is therefor cald a Ransome.... The first & principal end of Christs death is by being a proof of the Gospel to be a motive to holynesse, & for all such as it thus works on god accepts it as a Sacrifice & forgives their sins.[67]

This position on Christ's death is incompatible with the doctrine of satisfaction but is in line with the Arminian governmental theory of atonement, first formulated by Grotius and then refined by Limborch.[68] This theory also influenced 17th-century Socinians like Martin Ruar, Jonas Schlichting, and the editors of the final Latin edition of 1680 of the *Racovian Catechism*, Andrzej and Benedykt Wiszowaty, who deviated from Socinus' outright denial of the atonement.[69] According to the governmental theory of atonement, God offered Christ's death as a public display of how seriously he takes sin in order to uphold his moral government of Creation. In other words, Christ's physical death on the cross showed that God hated evil and loved justice. Moreover, Christ's death opened the way to reconciliation between God and humanity. Drawing on Paul's epistles, Locke described Jesus as the "second Adam," through whom God had offered immortality to humanity once again.[70] Locke, like Socinus and his followers, considered Jesus literally the Son of God,

---

67   Locke, *Writings on Religion*, 33. See also, the transcription of "Redemtion, Death," in Locke, *Reasonableness*, 205–8.

68   Hugo Grotius, *Defensio fidei Catholicae de satisfactione Christi adversus Faustum Socinum* (Leiden: 1617), 56–157; Philipp van Limborch, *Theologia Christiana* (Amsterdam: 1686), 224–241, 264–273.

69   The *Racovian Catechism* was first published, in Polish, in 1605 by some of Socinus' direct disciples based at Raków, the main site of the Minor Reformed Church of Poland until the expulsion of anti-Trinitarians from that country in 1658. It was translated into German in 1608 and into Latin for the first time in 1609, and it subsequently received several editions in various languages. For an English translation, see *The Racovian Catechism*, trans. Thomas Rees (London: 1818).

70   Locke, *Reasonableness*, 12. On Jesus as the "second Adam," see Rom. 5:12–21, 1 Cor. 15:20–23, and 1 Cor. 15:45–49. The definition of Jesus as the "second Adam" also appeared in the works of various English theologians of the mid-17th century, such as Jeremy Taylor, Robert Harris, and Thomas Bradley. See Lucci, *John Locke's Christianity*, 100.

miraculously born to a virgin. However, whereas the Socinians regarded Jesus as created mortal, commissioned as Messiah shortly before his ministry, and made immortal by divine miracle upon his death, Locke portrayed Christ as born immortal like God the Father and as being the Messiah since birth. According to Locke, Jesus chose to die in order to make his resurrection possible and, thus, to demonstrate his divine sonship and the existence of the Kingdom of God in the afterlife. In this regard, Locke, like the Socinians, described Christ's resurrection as what really matters in the economy of salvation, since Christ's resurrection is proof of eternal reward for the righteous.[71]

While rejecting original sin and diverging from the traditional satisfaction theory of atonement, Locke still admitted that Adam's Fall had impacted on human life because, following Adam's sin, humankind had become morally corrupt and had lost the immortality enjoyed in Paradise. In "Homo ante et post lapsum," Locke observed that, after the sin of Adam and Eve, their children were "infected." However, he explained that the moral "corruption" of humanity spread because of fashion and example in a world of covetousness, pride, and ambition. In other words, the "infection" or "corruption" of humankind was caused by merely environmental factors. Locke did not believe that humanity suffered from an *inherited* guilt or propensity to evil due to the Fall, given also his notion of the human mind at birth as "white paper, void of all Characters."[72] Yet, while denying that all human beings were "punished" for Adam's disobedience, Locke acknowledged that Adam and his posterity had become liable to suffer "a natural death" following Adam's sin, as is confirmed in Gen. 2:17 ("in the day that thou eatest thereof thou shalt surely die").[73] This means that Adam was immortal in Paradise. Locke's position, however, is ambiguous on whether Adam was created immortal or mortal. "Homo ante et post lapsum" and the introductory sections of the *Reasonableness* state that Adam was not created immortal, but, in Paradise, he was offered the means to attain immortality since God gave him a probationary law, which, regrettably, he transgressed. Nonetheless, the *Reasonableness* and the manuscript "Christianae Religionis Synopsis" (1702) also maintain that Adam was created immortal but became mortal and begot mortal children because of his disobedience. On this point, Locke wrote in the *Reasonableness*:

> *Adam* being the Son of God ... had this part also of the *Likeness* and *Image* of his Father, *viz*. That he was Immortal. But *Adam* transgressing

---

71   Locke, *Reasonableness*, 113–115. See Lucci, *John Locke's Christianity*, 100, 104–5, 158–9.

72   Locke, *Writings on Religion*, 231; Locke, *Essay*, 104.

73   Locke, *Writings on Religion*, 231; Locke, *Reasonableness*, 5.

the Command given him by his Heavenly Father, incurred the Penalty, forfeited that state of Immortality, and became Mortal. After this, *Adam* begot Children: But they were *in his own likeness, after his own image*; Mortal, like their Father.[74]

At any rate, despite Locke's ambiguity on Adam as created mortal or immortal, his views on human mortality are still consistent with his theory that humanity was not "punished" for Adam's sin. Locke indeed saw human mortality as simply inherent to the human condition "out of Paradise," and he argued that humanity "has no right to" immortality because "the state of Immortality in Paradise is not due to the Posterity of *Adam* more than to any other Creature."[75] Briefly, Locke, like Socinus and his disciples, did not see human mortality as punishment for Adam's sin, but merely as part of human nature. Adam's immortality, far from being natural, was only part of his condition in Paradise, which he lost when he had to leave it.

Locke believed that not only the human body, but also the soul is not naturally immortal. He maintained a sort of Scripture-based mortalism – more precisely, a version of thnetopsychism, as he argued that the soul dies with the body (because the soul cannot subsist without the body) and will be resurrected by divine miracle for the Last Judgment.[76] Mortalist views were quite common among early Christians but were subsequently rejected, in both Latin and Eastern Christianity, in favor of belief in the natural immortality of the soul. Mortalist ideas reemerged in the post-Reformation era, particularly among anti-Trinitarians and other radical Protestants.[77] Some Protestants actually saw mortalism as grounded in Scripture and compatible with Protestant principles, such as the rejection of Purgatory and the view that the soul's otherworldly fate depends exclusively on God – not on ecclesiastical authorities or other human agencies or intercessions. Even some of the Magisterial Reformers upheld mortalist ideas. For instance, whereas Calvin rejected all sorts of mortalism, and whereas mortalist views were foreign to the Arminian theological tradition, Luther advocated a "soft" version of mortalism known as psychopannychism, according to which the soul sleeps, and is unconscious although not literally "dead," until its awakening on Judgment Day.

---

74   Locke, *Reasonableness*, 113. See also Locke, *Writings on Religion*, 242–4.
75   Locke, *Reasonableness*, 9–11.
76   On Locke's mortalist ideas, see Lucci, *John Locke's Christianity*, 106–133.
77   On mortalism in early modern Europe, and particularly in Britain, see Norman T. Burns, *Christian Mortalism from Tyndale to Milton* (Cambridge, Mass.: 1972); Bryan W. Ball, *The Soul Sleepers: Christian Mortalism from Wycliffe to Priestley* (Cambridge, Eng.: 2008).

Locke's writings on religion – particularly the *Reasonableness*, the *Paraphrase*, the manuscript "Resurrectio et quae sequuntur" (*c.*1699), and various other private writings – present a version of thnetopsychism identical to that of Socinians such as Johann Crell, Jonas Schlichting, and the editors of the final Latin version of the *Racovian Catechism*. These authors' thnetopsychism affirmed conditional immortality while presenting annihilationist elements in that they argued that, after Christ's Second Coming and the general resurrection of the dead, the saved will be rewarded with eternal life while the unsaved will suffer a second, final death, thereby ceasing to exist permanently upon the Last Judgment.[78] Based mainly on 1 Cor. 15 and other Pauline texts, Locke maintained in the *Reasonableness* that the resurrection of the dead will take place only thanks to a divine miracle. He added that "Immortality and Bliss belong to the Righteous," who will be "re-instated in an Happy Immortality," while the wicked will experience a "second Death."[79] He expressed the same ideas in "Resurrectio et quae sequuntur," explaining that "all men by the benefit of Christ shall be restored to life," but the wicked "shall not live forever" because "the wages of sin is death," as is written in Rom. 6:23, while "the reward of the righteous is everlasting life."[80] Moreover, when commenting, in the *Reasonableness*, on the New Testament references to the punishment of the unsaved, he clarified that by "*Death*" it is meant "nothing but a ceasing to be, the losing of all actions of Life and Sense" – not "endless torment in Hell-fire" or "Eternal Life in Misery."[81] Drawing on 2 Thess. 1:9 ("Who shall be punished with everlasting destruction from the presence of the Lord, and from the glory of his power"), he added: "The state the unrighteous are at last destined to is a final cessation of life, *i.e.* of all sense perception and activity…. The punishment of those that know not God and obey not the gospel shall be *everlasting destruction*."[82] He made the same point in "Resurrectio et quae sequuntur," in which he maintained that, when mentioning the "corruption" of the unsaved in Gal. 6:8, Paul was referring to "the dissolution & final destruction of a thing whereby it ceases to be," and not "eternal life in torment."[83]

---

78   George H. Williams (ed.), *The Polish Brethren: Documentation of the History and Thought of Unitarianism in the Polish-Lithuanian Commonwealth and in the Diaspora 1601–1685* (Missoula: 1980), vol. 1: 106–7, 202–4, 237, 326; vol. 2: 407, 416, 616.
79   Locke, *Reasonableness*, 12, 104, 117.
80   Locke, *Writings on Religion*, 233.
81   Locke, *Reasonableness*, 7–8.
82   Ibid., 15.
83   Locke, *Writings on Religion*, 235–6.

Locke also denied that "the resurrection of the same body ... is an article of the Christian faith," as he explained in his third and last reply to Stillingfleet in 1699.[84] Based on 1 Cor. 15, he wrote in the *Reasonableness* that our "frail Mortal Bodies" will be changed into "Spiritual Immortal Bodies at the Resurrection."[85] He restated that "the saints shall then have spiritual & immortal bodys"[86] in "Resurrectio et quae sequuntur," in which, referring expressly to 1 Cor. 15, he explained:

> We shall all be changed in the twinkleing of an eye ... Because this corruptible thing must put on incorruption & this mortal thing put on immortality. how? by putting off flesh & bloud by an instantaneous change because ... Flesh & bloud cannot inherit the kingdom of god.... Men alive are flesh & bloud, the dead in the graves are but the remains of corrupted flesh & bloud. But flesh & bloud can not inherit the kingdom of god, neither can corruption inherit incorruption i e immortality.[87]

Since Locke regarded the soul and the body as interdependent although distinct, he thought that the resurrected souls of the saved will need incorruptible, "spiritual" bodies in order to "subsist perpetually" in a "state of immutable incorruptibility."[88] On the other hand, he abstained from speculating about the bodies of the wicked at the resurrection, given that "the Scripture ... is perfectly silent" on this subject.[89]

Briefly, Locke argued that the soul dies at physical death, when the mortal body does not sustain it anymore. He also maintained that the dead will be resurrected only by divine miracle for the Last Judgment. Moreover, he denied the resurrection of the same body. These elements of his mortalism imply that personal identity is neither in the soul, nor in the body, nor in a union of soul and body. As I have observed above, Locke stated that personal identity is in consciousness alone. In fact, consciousness alone, always accompanying thinking, can provide continuity to the self between physical death and the resurrection for the Last Judgment, regardless of the substance in which thinking takes place.

---

84   John Locke, *Works*, 12th ed. (London: 1824), vol. 3: 303.
85   Locke, *Reasonableness*, 115–116.
86   Locke, *Writings on Religion*, 232.
87   Ibid., 233.
88   Locke, *Paraphrase*, vol. 1: 254–5.
89   Locke, *Writings on Religion*, 237.

5   Christ and the Trinity

The originality and heterodoxy of Locke's religion are also manifest in what he wrote about Trinitarian and Christological issues.[90] He was silent on the Trinity in *The Reasonableness of Christianity*, although this book appeared in the midst of the Trinitarian controversy of the late 17th century – a controversy that involved Unitarian writers and Trinitarian apologists upholding different notions of the Trinity and that, therefore, caused significant turmoil in English religious, social, and political life. After publishing the *Reasonableness*, Locke obstinately abstained from clarifying publicly his position on the Trinity, even when Edwards and Stillingfleet pressured him to explain his views on this subject. Some of his critics saw the exclusion of Trinitarian belief from the fundamentals of Christianity as implicitly denying the Trinitarian dogma and, thus, as endorsing anti-Trinitarianism. In point of fact, Locke neither asserted nor rejected the Trinity in clear terms. However, the truth is that he was not a Trinitarian. Had he believed in the Trinity, he could have followed the example of his Arminian friend Limborch who, while considering the Trinitarian doctrine inessential to salvation, still affirmed belief in the Trinity, which he also defended against Socinian objections. But Locke's public as well as private writings on religion actually show that he held a non-incarnational, and hence non-Trinitarian, Messianic Christology, which presents both Socinian and Arian elements while being neither Socinian nor Arian proper. Thus, although he was not an "anti-Trinitarian" proper, in that he never denied the Trinity expressly and unambiguously in his public as well as private writings, he was certainly a "non-Trinitarian," since the Trinitarian doctrine plays no role in his version of Christianity.

The concept of an incarnational Christ is a crucial element of the doctrine of the Trinity and has important soteriological implications, which distinguish it from a merely Messianic Christology, as Victor Nuovo has noted:

> Although both make Christ the centre of salvation, a Messianic Christ achieves this goal through deeds, and, he being a king, the benefits of his saving activity are distributed to those who become his subjects after a judicial process; an incarnational Christ, although not inactive, accomplishes salvation through the communication of his divine being, which he makes available to his beneficiaries by becoming human.[91]

---

90   On Locke's Christology, see Marshall, "Locke, Socinianism"; Nuovo, *Christianity*, 75–101; Lucci, *John Locke's Christianity*, 134–173.

91   Nuovo, *Christianity*, 76.

In the *Reasonableness*, Locke emphasized faith in Jesus the Messiah, whom he portrayed as the center of salvation. When considering Christ's Messianic mission, he stressed Christ's office as a divinely appointed king who, upon his Second Coming, will deliver his kingdom to God the Father and reign with him forever.[92] Locke also took into account Christ's prophetic office in the *Reasonableness* and highlighted Christ's priestly office in the *Reasonableness* and in a manuscript note on the Epistle to the Hebrews.[93] Moreover, he described Christ as a mediator between God the Father and humanity and as a "second Adam," as I have explained above. On the other hand, he never wrote of Christ as "incarnated" or "divine" or a person of the Trinity, thereby eschewing an incarnational, Trinitarian Christology, although he consistently avoided denying the Trinity in explicit terms.

Despite his claim that his elucidation of Christianity was based on Scripture alone, and despite his attempts to disassociate himself from Socinians and Unitarians in his responses to his critics, Locke referred to anti-Trinitarian authors and theories in several letters to his friends and in various manuscript notes. In the late 1680s and early 1690s, he corresponded with Philipp van Limborch, Jean Le Clerc, and other intellectuals about various Unitarian works published in the late 1680s and early 1690s, such as Stephen Nye's *A Brief History of the Unitarians, Called Also Socinians* (1687) and Arthur Bury's *The Naked Gospel* (1690) – two books that contributed significantly to the aforesaid Trinitarian controversy of the late 17th century. Locke indeed owned a large number of anti-Trinitarian books, including, among others, the nine-volume *Bibliotheca Fratrum Polonorum* (1665–1692), which contained the works of Socinus and some of the leading Polish Brethren; three of the five volumes of Unitarian tracts published between 1691 and 1703; and the writings of all major Continental as well as English anti-Trinitarian authors of the early modern period. Moreover, he was friends with various anti-Trinitarians, such as the Unitarian leader Thomas Firmin, the merchant William Popple, who translated Locke's *Epistola de Tolerantia* (1689) into English, the theologian Samuel Crell, and Isaac Newton. He even interceded on Newton's behalf with Le Clerc when Newton intended to publish "An Historical Account of Two Notable Corruptions of Scripture." Newton privately held anti-Trinitarian ideas that can largely be ascribed to the Arian tradition, although he was also influenced by Socinian and Unitarian views, particularly concerning the denial of the scriptural grounds of Trinitarian belief. In "An Historical Account," Newton dismissed the authenticity of two biblical passages commonly alleged to

---

92   Locke, *Reasonableness*, 93–108.
93   Ibid., 120; Locke, *Writings on Religion*, 238–241.

substantiate the Trinitarian dogma – namely, 1 Tim. 3:16 and 1 John 5:7–8, the latter passage being the controversial Johannine Comma, already questioned by Erasmus and other scholars including various Socinians and other anti-Trinitarians. Newton sent "An Historical Account" to Locke in November 1690. He wanted this tract to be translated into French and published anonymously. Le Clerc accepted to translate and publish "An Historical Account" in a volume with other tracts. However, Newton later felt uncomfortable with the prospect of publishing his views on such a contentious issue and, in February 1692, he called off the publication of "An Historical Account," thereby upsetting Le Clerc. In the end, "An Historical Account" was published, posthumously and imperfectly, in 1754.[94]

Besides being receptive to research concerning scriptural passages of dubious authenticity, in his manuscripts Locke often called attention to the difficulty of inferring the Trinitarian doctrine from the Scriptures. In some notes taken in the notebook "Lemmata Ethica" in the mid-1690s, he made reference to anti-Trinitarian authors, such as the Socinians Johann Crell and Johann Ludwig von Wolzogen and the Unitarian Stephen Nye, when observing that in the Bible there is "scarce one text alledgd by the Trinitarians which is not otherwise expounded by their own writers."[95] Moreover, he stated that the Bible contains "a multitude of texts that deny those things of Christ which can not be denied of god; & that affirme such things of him that cannot agree to him if he were a person of god. In like manner of the holy ghost."[96] In this manuscript, he also denounced the "Platonic corruption" of Christianity, pointing out the "parallelism betwixt the Ancient or Genuine Platonick, and the Christian Trinity" and arguing that "the fathers before the Council of Nice speak rather like Arians than Orthodox."[97] Locke's dislike of the "Platonizing" of Christianity is also evidenced by his interest in the work of the heterodox Huguenot minister Jacques Souverain, author of *Le Platonisme dévoilé* (1700), whose anti-Trinitarian and anti-Platonic manuscript "Some General Reflections upon the Beginning of St. John's Gospel" Locke owned in a copy made by his amanuensis

---

94   For a modern edition, see Isaac Newton, "An Historical Account of Two Notable Corruptions of Scripture," in *The Correspondence of Isaac Newton*, ed. Herbert Westren Turnbull (Cambridge, Eng.: 1959–1977), vol. 3: 83–146. On Newton's anti-Trinitarianism and "An Historical Account," see Rob Iliffe, *Priest of Nature: The Religious Worlds of Isaac Newton* (Oxford: 2017), 354–389.

95   Oxford, Bodleian Library, MS Locke d. 10, 177.

96   Ibid.

97   Ibid., 167–8, 177.

Sylvester Brounower.[98] Locke also related anti-Trinitarian ideas in "Adversaria Theologica," in which, drawing mainly on the mid-17th-century English anti-Trinitarian John Biddle, he recorded only eight arguments supporting the Trinitarian doctrine and thirty-six arguments against it.[99]

Although Locke always refrained from clarifying his position on the Trinity, his public writings, too, denote his aversion to the Trinitarian doctrine. In the *Paraphrase*, he never mentioned the word "Trinity," but he interpreted in non-Trinitarian terms several Pauline verses often alleged in support of the Trinitarian dogma (e.g., Rom. 1:3–4, Rom. 9:5, 1 Cor. 1:2, and Eph. 3:9). Moreover, in both the *Reasonableness* and the *Paraphrase* he used the term "Son of God" as merely an equivalent for "Messiah." The *Paraphrase*, however, contains a passage indicating Arian-like belief in Christ's pre-existence to his human birth. In a note to Eph. 1:10, Locke indeed wrote that "'tis plain in Sacred Scripture, that Christ at first had the Rule and Supremacy over all, and was Head over all."[100] Satan's rebellion disrupted Christ's unitary rule and supremacy over all, but "Christ recovered this Kingdom, and was re-instated in the Supremacy and Headship, in the fullness of time ... at his death and resurrection."[101] Belief in Christ's pre-existence is foreign to Socinian Christology. Nevertheless, this note to Eph. 1:10 is far from affirming Trinitarianism, given also that Locke cited, as a gloss to Eph. 1:10, another Pauline passage – Col. 1:15–17, in which the Son is described as "the firstborn of every creature."[102] Therefore, the note to Eph. 1:10 in the *Paraphrase* denotes an Arian notion of Christ as pre-existent but created. Another, earlier passage in Locke's oeuvre, specifically in "Adversaria Theologica," apparently indicates belief in Christ's pre-existence. In the entries on Trinitarian issues in this manuscript, Locke endorsed only one argument, which stated that Christ's "spirit was in the ancient prophets."[103] This argument was based on 1 Peter 1:11 ("Searching what, or what manner of time the Spirit of Christ which was in them [i.e., the prophets] did signify, when it testified beforehand the sufferings of Christ, and the glory that should follow"). However, this argument can be interpreted as signifying that the Holy Spirit inspired first the ancient prophets and then Christ. This interpretation is supported by the manuscript "Note on John 3:34" that Locke wrote in the first half of the 1690s. In this note, he referred to "the fulnesse of the Godhead bodily"

98   Oxford, Bodleian Library, MS Locke e. 17, 175–223, "Some General Reflections upon the Beginning of St. John's Gospel."
99   Locke, *Writings on Religion*, 23–8.
100   Locke, *Paraphrase*, vol. 2: 616.
101   Ibid.
102   Ibid., 616–617.
103   Locke, *Writings on Religion*, 27.

dwelling in Christ as denoting the presence of the "Spirit of god" (that is, the Holy Spirit) in Christ.[104] Therefore, the note to Eph. 1:10 in the *Paraphrase* is the only place in the Lockean corpus that indicates incipient Arianism. Yet, Locke's Christological considerations, taken as a whole, do not warrant the conclusion that he was an Arian proper. Even the aforesaid note to Eph. 1:10 denotes a purpose typical of Socinianism, in that it presents a "focus on [Christ's] exaltation and on Christ's lordship following the resurrection…. Such focus was more distinctive of Socinian emphases than of Arian or Trinitarian emphases."[105]

In conclusion, Locke's Christology is neither Socinian nor Arian proper. It is an original, Scripture-based, non-incarnational and non-Trinitarian Messianic Christology, which is inherently coherent although Locke abstained from explaining it in systematic and unambiguous terms. In this regard, it is worth mentioning that Locke's obstinate public silence on the Trinity was due to irenic as well as prudential reasons. He indeed deemed it inappropriate and immoral to fuel pointless, divisive controversies about non-fundamentals, such as the then ongoing Trinitarian controversy. Moreover, he probably considered it unwise to cause himself unnecessary troubles with the ecclesiastical and political authorities, in a time when openly denying the Trinity could still lead to unpleasant consequences.

6   Conclusion

Locke's endeavor as a theologian was typical of a *biblical* theologian, who paid particular attention to the moral, soteriological, and eschatological meaning of Scripture. Whereas he wrote extensively about theological issues in his later years, his religious concerns, interests, and views also emerge from his philosophical and political works. Locke's oeuvre indeed shows what John Dunn has called "the intimate dependence of an extremely high proportion of Locke's arguments for their very intelligibility, let alone plausibility, on a series of theological commitments."[106] Thus, it is no accident that his intellectual struggle culminated in the public as well as private writings on religion that he composed in his later years and that present an original and internally coherent (albeit expressed unsystematically) version of Protestant Christianity. Locke's philosophical, political, and religious writings are actually an emblematic example of a heterodox way of thinking that is theological in nature. Given his emphasis on the interplay of natural reason and biblical revelation in

---

104   Oxford, Bodleian Library, MS Locke f. 30, fo. 43r, "Note on John 3:34."
105   Marshall, "Locke, Socinianism," 175.
106   Dunn, *Political Thought*, xi.

philosophical, political, moral, and theological matters, Locke was the archetype of a "religious Enlightener" endorsing reasonable belief as "the coordination of reason and revelation," which he regarded "as the two God-given 'lights'."[107] Accordingly, the religious dimension of Locke's thought calls into question the enduring stereotype of the Age of Enlightenment as a wholly secularized, or even irreligious, "Age of Reason."

Locke's religious ideas were mostly disregarded or even intentionally dismissed as unimportant by freethinkers and *philosophes* in the 18th century and were then largely ignored by historians until around half a century ago. However, Locke's religion attracted the attention of many 18th-century theologians, particularly in England, where it received not only criticism but also commendation, and where it had an impact on the growth of various Protestant movements, such as Unitarianism, Methodism, several Baptist churches, and various evangelical groups. On this point, as Stephen Snobelen has observed, "considering Locke's status as an icon and herald of the Enlightenment, this particular legacy of Locke is more than a little ironic."[108] In conclusion, Locke's theological production, while being still underestimated, is no less important than his philosophical and political theories, which his religious views conditioned significantly.

Acknowledgments

I am grateful to the MCAS – Maimonides Centre for Advanced Studies (DFG-FOR 2311) at the University of Hamburg for awarding me a Senior Research Fellowship held in 2021. This essay has significantly benefited from the resources and activities of the MCAS. I also wish to express my gratitude to my home institution, the American University in Bulgaria, for its continued support of my research. Furthermore, I thank the scholars who attended the lecture I gave on "Locke's Reasonable Christianity" on May 14, 2021, for the Institute of Philosophy at the Jagiellonian University. Special thanks go to Anna Tomaszewska and Hasse Hämäläinen for inviting me to give this lecture and to contribute a chapter to this collection of essays. The questions, comments, and suggestions I received after this lecture have been very helpful to the revision of this chapter.

---

107   David Sorkin, *The Religious Enlightenment: Protestants, Jews, and Catholics from London to Vienna* (Princeton: 2008), 12.

108   Snobelen, "Socinianism, Heresy," 97. On the reception of Locke's thought among 18th-century divines and churches, see Sell, *John Locke.*

References

Artis, Aderemi, "Locke on Original Sin," *Locke Studies* 12 (2012): 201–219.

Ball, Bryan W., *The Soul Sleepers: Christian Mortalism from Wycliffe to Priestley* (Cambridge, Eng.: 2008).

Bibliotheca Fratrum Polonorum quos Unitarios vocant, 9 vols. ("Irenopoli" [Amsterdam]: "post 1656" [1665–1692]).

Boethius, *Theological Tractates. The Consolation of Philosophy*, trans. Hugh F. Stewart, Edward K. Rand, and Stanley J. Tester (Cambridge, Mass.: 1978).

Burns, Norman T., *Christian Mortalism from Tyndale to Milton* (Cambridge, Mass.: 1972).

Bury, Arthur, *The Naked Gospel* (London: 1690).

Chillingworth, William, *The Religion of Protestants a Safe Way to Salvation* (Oxford: 1638).

Colman, John, *John Locke's Moral Philosophy* (Edinburgh: 1983).

Crisp, Tobias, *Christ Alone Exalted* (London: 1643).

De Beer, Esmond S. (ed.), *The Correspondence of John Locke*, 8 vols. (Oxford: 1976–1989).

Dunn, John, *The Political Thought of John Locke: An Historical Account of the Argument of the* Two Treatises of Government (Cambridge, Eng.: 1969).

Grotius, Hugo, *Defensio fidei Catholicae de satisfactione Christi adversus Faustum Socinum* (Leiden: 1617).

Grotius, Hugo, *Pro veritate religionis Christianae* (Paris: 1627).

Higgins-Biddle, John C., "Introduction," in John Locke, *The Reasonableness of Christianity, as Delivered in the Scriptures* (Oxford: 1999), xv–cxv.

Iliffe, Rob, *Priest of Nature: The Religious Worlds of Isaac Newton* (Oxford: 2017).

Limborch, Philipp van, *Theologia Christiana* (Amsterdam: 1686).

Locke, John, *Epistola de Tolerantia* (Gouda: 1689).

Locke, John, *An Essay Concerning Human Understanding* (Oxford: 1975).

Locke, John, *A Paraphrase and Notes on the Epistles of St Paul to the Galatians, 1 and 2 Corinthians, Romans, Ephesians*, 2 vols. (Oxford: 1987).

Locke, John, *The Reasonableness of Christianity, as Delivered in the Scriptures* (Oxford: 1999).

Locke, John, *Two Treatises of Government* (Cambridge, Eng.: 1988).

Locke, John, *Vindications of the Reasonableness of Christianity* (Oxford: 2012).

Locke, John, *Works*, 12th ed., 9 vols. (London: 1824).

Locke, John, *Writings on Religion* (Oxford: 2002).

Lucci, Diego, *John Locke's Christianity* (Cambridge, Eng.: 2021).

Marshall, John, *John Locke: Resistance, Religion and Responsibility* (Cambridge, Eng.: 1994).

Marshall, John, "Locke, Socinianism, 'Socinianism,' and Unitarianism," in *English Philosophy in the Age of Locke*, ed. Michael A. Stewart (Oxford: 2000), 111–182.

Mortimer, Sarah, "Human and Divine Justice in the Works of Grotius and the Socinians," in *The Intellectual Consequences of Religious Heterodoxy, 1600–1750*, eds. Sarah Mortimer, John Robertson (Leiden: 2012), 75–94.

Mortimer, Sarah, "Human Liberty and Human Nature in the Works of Faustus Socinus and His Readers," *Journal of the History of Ideas* 70 (2009): 191–211.

Newton, Isaac, "An Historical Account of Two Notable Corruptions of Scripture," in *The Correspondence of Isaac Newton*, ed. Herbert Westren Turnbull (Cambridge, Eng.: 1966), vol. 3: 83–146.

Nuovo, Victor, *Christianity, Antiquity, and Enlightenment: Interpretations of Locke* (Dordrecht: 2011).

Nuovo, Victor, *John Locke: The Philosopher as Christian Virtuoso* (Oxford: 2017).

Nye, Stephen, *A Brief History of the Unitarians, Called Also Socinians* (London: 1687).

Oxford, Bodleian Library, MS Locke d. 10, "Lemmata Ethica, Argumenta et Authores 1659."

Oxford, Bodleian Library, MS Locke e. 17, 175–223, "Some General Reflections upon the Beginning of St. John's Gospel."

Oxford, Bodleian Library, MS Locke f. 30, fo. 43r, "Note on John 3:34."

Parker, Kim Ian, *The Biblical Politics of John Locke* (Waterloo, ON: 2004).

The Racovian Catechism, trans. Thomas Rees (London: 1818).

Sell, Alan P.F., *John Locke and the Eighteenth-Century Divines* (Cardiff: 1997).

Snobelen, Stephen D., "Socinianism, Heresy and John Locke's *Reasonableness of Christianity*," *Enlightenment and Dissent* 20 (2001): 88–125.

Socinus, Faustus, *De Sacrae Scripturae auctoritate* (Raków: 1611).

Sorkin, David, *The Religious Enlightenment: Protestants, Jews, and Catholics from London to Vienna* (Princeton: 2008).

Souverain, Jacques, *Le Platonisme dévoilé* (Cologne [Amsterdam]: 1700).

Spellman, William M., *John Locke and the Problem of Depravity* (Oxford: 1988).

Toland, John, *Christianity Not Mysterious* (London: 1696).

Wainwright, Arthur W., "Introduction," in John Locke, *A Paraphrase and Notes on the Epistles of St Paul to the Galatians, 1 and 2 Corinthians, Romans, Ephesians* (Oxford: 1987), vol. 1: 1–88.

Wallace, Dewey D., "Socinianism, Justification by Faith, and the Sources of John Locke's *The Reasonableness of Christianity*," *Journal of the History of Ideas* 45 (1984): 49–66.

Williams, George H. (ed.), *The Polish Brethren: Documentation of the History and Thought of Unitarianism in the Polish-Lithuanian Commonwealth and in the Diaspora 1601–1685*, 2 vols. (Missoula: 1980).

Wolterstorff, Nicholas, "Locke's Philosophy of Religion," in *The Cambridge Companion to Locke*, ed. Vere Chappell (Cambridge, Eng.: 1994), 172–198.

Wootton, David, "John Locke: Socinian or Natural Law Theorist?" in *Religion, Secularization and Political Thought: Thomas Hobbes to J.S. Mill*, ed. James E. Crimmins (London: 1989), 39–67.

CHAPTER 11

Does Quakerism Qualify as Kantian Enlightened Religion?

Stephen R. Palmquist

1 What (and When) Is Enlightenment?

"Enlightenment is the human being's emergence from his self-incurred immaturity" (WA, 8:35; translation altered – S.R.P.). These oft-quoted words come at the beginning of Immanuel Kant's 1784 essay, *What Is Enlightenment?* The essay goes on to argue that, although the present Age – i.e. 18th-century Europe – prides itself on being enlightened, it has not actually reached that goal. The bulk of his short work sketches the path a society must tread if it is going to have any hope of growing up, casting aside the "hindrances" of cultural immaturity, and becoming enlightened. What is most striking about Kant's argument is that his ideal is not one that places Reason on a divine throne and requires the people to bow in subservience. Rather, Kant's 1781 *Critique of Pure Reason* had clipped reason's metaphysical wings, arguing that theoretical reason (i.e. *logic*) is powerless to give us *knowledge* of what matters most in life – i.e. of God, freedom, and immortality. Sophisticated metaphysical arguments must therefore give way to a simpler, *practical* (i.e. morally grounded) *faith*,[1] if we are to retain any sense of human life being ultimately meaningful. As a result, in *What Is Enlightenment?* Kant focuses most of his attention on encouraging increased efforts in education, especially within the church. In short, pastors need to be mature enough to recognize the limits of our ability to *know* ultimate truths if they are to help, rather than hinder, the task of bringing enlightenment to the public.

Kant's vision of a *humble* Enlightenment,[2] with reason's power circumscribed by an awareness of its own limits, did not reflect the *status quo* for his

---

1 For a detailed defense of the claim that Kant's famous confession in the Preface to the second edition of the first *Critique*, that he had to "deny *knowledge* in order to make room for *faith*" (KrV, B xxx, trans. S.R.P.), applies not just to practical reason but also to faith in the *theoretical* realm, see Stephen R. Palmquist, "Faith as Kant's Key to the Justification of Transcendental Reflection," *The Heythrop Journal* 25/4 (1984): 442–455.

2 On the importance of humility as one of the chief outcomes of the first *Critique*'s arguments, see KrV, A 830–1/B 858–9.

Age; rather, it attempts to *correct* what he saw as a serious error in a movement that was itself already well-established in his youth. For the Enlightenment ideals that Kant had learned during his education at the University of Königsberg (a university that was recently renamed "Immanuel Kant University") were not *essentially* different from the Scholasticism that dominated universities during the Middle Ages: it was Scholasticism with the new science, as instituted by Francis Bacon (1561–1626), René Descartes (1596–1650), and Isaac Newton (1643–1727), awkwardly grafted onto it.[3] The success of the new science in gaining reliable knowledge of the external world was challenging the role that religion had played for so long in European culture, as the guiding light for seekers after truth. How could religion survive in a world where science was gradually coming to be recognized as the most reliable pathway to truth?

Significantly, Kant wrote *What Is Enlightenment?* during the academic year *between* two years when he taught a course on Philosophical Theology.[4] In his lectures, he hints at the need for a more enlightened textbook that could be used for the purpose of training pastors to release the laity from their self-incurred immaturity. This makes it less surprising that his first book *after* completing the third *Critique* was *Religion within the Bounds of Bare Reason* (1793), which, as he says near the end of the first Preface (RGV, 6:10), is meant to fill this gap – i.e. he hopes his *Religion* will be adopted as a textbook for a course that pastors-in-training will be required to take near the end of their university studies. What were the *roots* of Kant's theory of enlightened religion?[5] As suggested by my title, this chapter will explore a much-neglected answer to this question: I will argue that the radical religious reformation effected by a group of British friends during the second half of the 17th century, which has come to be known as "Quakerism," is at the very least conceptually consistent with,

---

3   Kant frequently refers to the philosophy of "the schools"; in so doing, he is referring not to what we today call Scholastic philosophy, but to its successors in his own day: the metaphysical systems of Wolff and Baumgarten, which dominated the philosophy departments in Prussia throughout most of the 18th century.

4   For a detailed examination of the role of Kant's Lectures on Philosophical Theology in the development of his theory of religion, see Stephen R. Palmquist, "Kant's Lectures on Philosophical Theology – Training-Ground for the Moral Pedagogy of *Religion*?" in *Reading Kant's Lectures*, ed. Robert Clewis (New York: 2015), 365–390. I there point out that Kant probably taught the course four times: "once in the summer semester of 1774 and three times in the mid-1780s: the winter semesters of 1783/84 and 1785/86 and the summer semester of 1787" (ibid., 365). Kant completed *What Is Enlightenment?* in September 1784.

5   For an excellent account of the extent to which Kant's *Religion* contributed to various controversies related to the on-going Enlightenment project of constructing a rational religion, see Jonathan Head, "Kant's *Religion* as a Response to the Pantheism Controversy: Between Mendelssohn and Jacobi," *International Philosophical Quarterly* 61/1 (2021): 101–119.

and very well might have had some historical influence on, the development of Kant's mature theory of religion.

Kant was raised as a Pietist, and German Pietism was equivalent in many ways to the Quaker Movement in Great Britain. As Thomas Cattoi points out, "the Quaker emphasis on the inner light" is "much like the Pietist recovery of a more affective piety."[6] Allen Wood likewise affirms that the Pietism that arose "among German Lutherans ... resembles other 18th-century revivalist religious movements, such as Quakerism and Methodism in England,"[7] although Leslie Stevenson cautions that the particular *form* of Pietism that Kant experienced in his youth "had hardened into a somewhat fanatical insistence on stereotyped confessions of individual conversion" and that for this reason Kant reacted against his own religious upbringing during his early adulthood.[8] Before examining (in §2) the evidence for the controversial claim that Quakerism contributed to certain aspects of its early stages, we must identify *when* the Age of Enlightenment occurred.

While historians generally agree that the Enlightenment *ended* in 1800, the question of when it *began* has been answered in widely diverging ways. Without going into all of the various competing interpretations of historical facts, I suggest setting the movement's starting date at 1650, with its immediate pre-history coming in the preceding quarter century. In 1650, the Thirty Years War (1618–1648) has recently ended and Descartes, who had presented his famous *Cogito ergo sum* ("I think, therefore I am") argument in 1637, dies. Francis Bacon, whose *Novum Organum* introduced what we now call the inductive method as a new tool for scientific discovery, has already died (in 1626), while Newton's *Principia Mathematica* (1687) – undoubtedly a product of Enlightenment trust in a science that is thoroughly rational – will not be published for another 37 years.[9] With these dates (1650–1800) in mind, let us therefore examine the role played by Quakerism in the early stages of that movement. This will prepare us for an overview of Kant's theory of enlightened

---

6   Thomas Cattoi, "Conclusion," in *Quakers and Mysticism: Interdisciplinary Approaches to the Study of Mysticism*, ed. Jon R. Kershner (Cham: 2019), 245.

7   Allen W. Wood, *Kant and Religion* (Oxford: 2020), 9.

8   Leslie Stevenson, "Kant's Philosophy and Quakerism," *The Friends Quarterly* 33/2 (2002): 86; Leslie Stevenson, "Kant's Approach to Religion Compared with Quakerism," in *Kant and the New Philosophy of Religion*, eds. Chris L. Firestone and Stephen R. Palmquist (Bloomington: 2006), 211; Leslie Stevenson, *Open to New Light: Quaker Spirituality in Historical and Philosophical Context* (Exeter: 2012), 135.

9   *Encyclopedia Britannica*'s article on the Enlightenment (https://www.britannica.com/topic/history-of-Europe/The-Enlightenment#ref58391 [Accessed 21.04.2021]) says: "The perceptions and propaganda of the *philosophes* have led historians to locate the Age of Reason

religion (in §3), following which I shall conclude (in §4) by examining the extent to which Kant's enlightened religion resonates with Quakerism.

2   Early Quakerism: Is the "Inner Light" a Source of *Knowledge*?

Quakers traditionally date their religious movement from 1652, the year its founder, George Fox (1624–1691), experienced a vision on Pendle Hill in Lancashire, England – a vision of "a great people" gathered together to walk the new religious path that Fox had already been preaching around England for the previous five years.[10] After almost two decades of mostly itinerant ministry, during which its membership grew exponentially, in 1666 Fox established the current ordering of the Religious Society of Friends, with the aim of preventing it from becoming a typical hierarchical religious organization or from depending too much on any one person's strong personality. The early beginnings of Quakerism (1643–1666) therefore overlap with the decades that witnessed the rise of the Age of Enlightenment (1637–1688; see note 9). With this timeline in mind, let us look at some of the main features of Fox's new religious vision.

A founding principle of Quakerism is that an "inner light" is available to all human beings, although it may remain dormant in many, due to the restricting influence of society's traditions. Having been raised in Christian England, Fox interpreted this deeply personal experience as the immediate presence of Christ, but was convinced that every human being (including those who had never heard the Christian story) has what he sometimes called "that of God" within them. Unlike Catholics, who typically prioritize tradition and the authority of priests (and, ultimately, the Pope) as the most reliable guide for Christians to follow, and Protestants, who typically prioritize the Bible as the roadmap for proper belief and action, Fox and his friends were convinced that

---

within the 18th century or, more comprehensively, between the two revolutions – the English of 1688 and the French of 1789"; but the article goes on to argue that the *roots* of the Enlightenment go back to the late Renaissance, especially the scientific revolution inspired largely by Francis Bacon.

10   Fox relates the story of his vision in his *Journal*, first published in 1694 (George Fox, *The Journal of George Fox* (Cambridge: 1952), 103–5). His was one of many nonconformist religious movements that emerged during the English Civil War (1642–1651). For a description of the movement's early years, see "George Fox and the Quaker (Friends) Movement," https://www.georgefox.edu/about/history/quakers.html [Accessed 21.04.2021], which reports that Fox started his itinerant preaching in 1647, at age 23.

a divine Light presents all human beings (whether or not they are Christians) with the most reliable source of revealed Truth, because it is grounded in the individual's personal experience.

As Cattoi reports, this basic reliance on "inner illumination ... enabled [Fox] to cast aside creeds, liturgies, and university theology, and to know the divine 'experimentally'."[11] This language of "experiment" is closely related to Francis Bacon's emphasis on what we now call "induction," in his ground-breaking *Novum Organum* (first published in 1620, just four years before Fox's birth). Indeed, the early Quakers frequently emphasized the need to live "experimentally" by relying on whatever they experienced through the inward revelations of this divine Light. On this point, they saw themselves as following the same "experimental" philosophy that led Descartes and others to create the experiment of the Enlightenment, which takes *reason* to be the great light that shines on the human being's life-path, showing us the right way to live. This emphasis on first-hand, personal experience made the early Quakers, as one commentator explains, "unique [among other 'spiritualist' sects of the time] in maintaining the priority of the Light above the Bible and in keeping the Light distinct from reason."[12] In other words, George Fox and his friends did not buy into the doctrinal assumptions (which many today would call "fundamentalist") that most non-conformist religious groups in 17th-century Britain adopted,[13] but neither did they accept the competing assumption of early Enlightenment rationalism, that reason is all-powerful.

While most of the early Quakers were not scholars, and some used rhetoric that at times made them seem anti-academic,[14] there were some important exceptions. In a ground-breaking study of the relationships between early Quakers and the British empiricists who were responding to the rationalist underpinnings of the early Enlightenment, Laura Rediehs demonstrates that many of the early Quakers not only knew but in some cases actively engaged

---

11   Cattoi, "Conclusion," 246.

12   Laura Rediehs, "A Distinctive Quaker Theory of Knowledge: An Expanded Experiential Empiricism," *Quaker Studies* 21/1 (2016): 73.

13   Cattoi notes a contemporary "tension between 'universalist' and 'evangelical' Quakerism" (Cattoi, "Conclusion," 246). But in both traditions, "the Quaker vision resists this tendency [toward 'political fundamentalism'] and affirms the radical brotherhood of all men and women as children of the Christian God" (ibid., 246–7).

14   For instance, early Quakers tended to reject (or ignore) natural theology (Rediehs, "A Distinctive Quaker Theory of Knowledge," 74). Along these lines, Stevenson points out that Kant's stance on the "minimum of theology" (i.e. his claim that one does not need to possess certain knowledge that God exists in order to be authentically religious, but must merely accept the *possibility* that God exists) is a position often adopted by many Quakers (Stevenson, "Kant's Philosophy and Quakerism," 90).

with prominent British philosophers.[15] She details the case of Anne Conway (1631–1679), a British philosopher with connections to Henry More (1614–1687), the influential Cambridge Platonist, as well as to Robert Boyle and other top scientists of the day. Both Baruch Spinoza (1632–1677) and John Locke (1632–1704) likewise interacted with various Quakers from time to time. Even Gottfried von Leibniz (1646–1716) was familiar with the work of not only Conway but also other prominent Quaker intellectuals, such as Robert Barclay (1648–1690) and William Penn (1644–1718).

Rediehs argues that "Quaker thought" carries with it "[t]he seeds of a much more promising epistemology," which "provides better support [than competing western epistemologies] for both scientific and religious knowledge and furthermore harmonises the two."[16] In reconstructing this epistemology, which Rediehs calls "an expanded, experiential empiricism"[17] – expanded so that "empirical knowledge" includes personal experience of the "divine light," taken not literally but as a metaphor[18] for an otherwise mysterious correlate to other (natural) forms of inner sense – Rediehs collects significant evidence that various early Quakers may have actually influenced some of the aforementioned philosophers of the early Enlightenment, on both the empiricist and rationalist sides.[19] The most substantive area of possible influence – or, at the very least, overlapping theoretical frameworks – relates to the distinction between external and internal forms of sense-based knowledge, with inner sense further divided into two types: natural and supernatural. Locke's adoption of this framework for the senses is particularly noteworthy, given that he sometimes attended meetings sponsored by the "Lantern" discussion group in Rotterdam, which had developed out of a Quaker discussion group that was originally called "Inner Light."[20] Locke's essay puts forward precisely the same distinction that Barclay and other early Quakers had previously made, between natural forms of inner sense involving subjective experiences, ranging from emotion and conscience to mathematical reflection, and the divine Light that impresses itself on a person's inner sense during mystical experiences. (Locke's *Essay*, first published in 1689, refers in several passages to inward experience using the word "light."[21] At one point, for example, he describes revelation as

---

15   Rediehs, "A Distinctive Quaker Theory of Knowledge," 72ff.
16   Ibid., 71, 73.
17   Ibid., 67, 73, 87.
18   Ibid., 74.
19   Ibid. and Laura Rediehs, *Quaker Epistemology* (Leiden: 2019).
20   Rediehs, "A Distinctive Quaker Theory of Knowledge," 77n.
21   See John Locke, *Essay Concerning Human Understanding* (Oxford: 1975; first published 1698), book IV, c. XIX, §§11–14, 702–4. Rediehs says that Locke is likely thinking in such

an occurrence in which God "illuminates the Mind with supernatural Light" – an explicit reference to a Quaker-like description of divine revelation.[22]) After considering various parallels of this type, Rediehs concludes that it is at least "possible that Locke's contact with Quakers helped shape his views,"[23] not only on the nature of inner sense, but perhaps also on the relevance of the "light" metaphor itself to the budding En*light*enment philosophy.

Rediehs points out that not only Locke but later also David Hume (1711–1776) included internal as well as external sense in their understanding of what counts as experience; to this I would add that Kant, too, viewed inner sense (and its subjective mental correlate, inner *intuition*) as playing just as crucial a role in constituting empirical cognition as outer sense (and outer intuition). Rediehs admits that this notion of inner sense needs to be broadened to include what Quakers call the "inner light"; but in both cases, she argues, *experiential* knowledge is under consideration. To illustrate how early Quakers were using these terms *before* the British empiricists did, Rediehs quotes from several early Quakers. For example, three years before Locke's *Essay* appeared, Robert Barclay writes:

> The senses are either outward or inward; and the inward senses are either natural or supernatural: we have an example of the inward, natural sense in being angered or pacified, in love and hatred; or when we perceive and discern any natural truth ... or when we deduce any conclusion by the strength of natural reason, that perception also in a larger sense may be called an inward sense.[24]

---

passages of the light of *reason* as opposed to an explicitly *divine* light (Rediehs, "A Distinctive Quaker Theory of Knowledge," 76). However, these sections come in a chapter entitled "Of Enthusiasm," where Locke is explaining how to distinguish between rational and "enthusiastic" ways of experiencing this light. In §13, he clarifies that "Light, true Light in the Mind, is, or can be nothing else but, the Evidence of the Truth of any Proposition" (Locke, *Essay*, 703).

22   Locke, *Essay*, book IV, c. XIX, §14, 704. In the quoted sentence Locke is clarifying that experiencing the Divine Light need not result in enthusiasm, as long as we remember that in such revelatory experiences, God "does not extinguish that which is natural."

23   Ibid., 78.

24   Robert Barclay, "The Possibility and Necessity of the Inward & Immediate Revelation of the Spirit of God, Towards the Foundation and Ground of True Faith, Proved, in a Letter Writ in Latin to a Person of Quality in Holland; and Now Also Put Into English," *Truth Triumphant*, vol. 3 (Philadelphia: 1831; first published 1686), 569.

Barclay goes on to cite several examples of "an inward, supernatural sense": the "divine motions" which "the heart or soul of a pious man" experiences "as the voice or speech of God," "as a most pleasant and glorious" inwardly imagined object, "as a most sweet savour or taste," or "sometimes as an heavenly and divine warmness, or ... melting of the soul in the love of God."[25] That he took such experiences to be "the inward immediate revelation of God's Spirit in the heart"[26] may seem like a somewhat naïve claim by today's standards; but once we see that Locke and even Hume affirmed a similar view of inner sense, Barclay's statements can be understood as an early expression of an Enlightened mindset.

While most of the early Quaker writers were not *opposed* to reason, they were cautious about the extent to which some philosophers of their day were embracing it as the presumed solution to all human problems. Perhaps the best way to encapsulate the Quaker critique of the early Enlightenment would be to say that, while Fox and other early Quakers fully agreed that human beings are in need of a "light" to guide our path and that this light is to be found *within* the human being, they could not accept the Enlightenment assumption that *natural* human reason is adequate to serve as this light; rather, they believed that the light that we human beings find within ourselves has a transcendent source, in what is traditionally called "God." Still, as Rediehs points out, the early Quakers cared more about distinguishing themselves from other, more traditional forms of religious believers than from the philosophers of reason.[27] At some level they seem to have regarded Quakerism as an attempt to do for religion what they saw Enlightenment philosophy attempting to do for philosophy. Isaac Penington (1616–1679), for example, wrote a letter of concern to the Royal Society not long after it was established (in 1660), reminding them that knowledge obtained by reason tells us only "a literal relation or description" of things, whereas what really matters is to be able to "know things, not from an outward relation, but from their inward nature, virtue, and power."[28] For

---

25   These passages from Barclay, "The Possibility And Necessity Of The Inward & Immediate Revelation," 569, are quoted in Rediehs, "A Distinctive Quaker Theory of Knowledge," 77.

26   Robert Barclay, "An Apology for the True Christian Divinity, As the Same Is Held Forth and Preached by the People Called," in *Truth Triumphant*, vol. 2 (Glenside: 2002; first published 1676), 25; cf. Rediehs, "A Distinctive Quaker Theory of Knowledge," 79.

27   Ibid., 86.

28   Isaac Penington, "Some Things Relating to Religion Proposed to the Consideration of the Royal Society, so Termed," *The Works of Isaac Penington*, vol. iii (Glenside: 1996; first published 1668), 111; quoted in Rediehs, "A Distinctive Quaker Theory of Knowledge," 85. Here Penington comes close to prefiguring what Kant would later call the "primacy" of practical reason over theoretical reason.

Quakers, this inward light is just as reliable, just as *objective*, and just as subject to confirmation by experiment, as the new science was proving to be for the knowledge obtained from external sense. As Rediehs puts it, "Quaker epistemology emphasised a perceptual and experiential activity of knowledge: the relevant ideas are ... given by a source 'outside' the individual's natural mind.... The human activity of knowing, in both cases [internal as well as external sense], is to perceive what is 'objectively' given."[29]

An important point that Rediehs does not bring out is that, although the early Quakers did indeed emphasize the importance and the objectivity of the inner light, and although the views on internal sense defended by some empiricist philosophers may well have been shaped by their dialogues with early Quakers, the *focus* of Quaker faith and practice has never been on what we as human beings *know* but on what we do *not* know. This is why Quaker worship services consist mostly (if not entirely) of *silent* worship: the focus of Quaker theology is not on *any* objective knowledge that God allegedly imparts to the worshipper, but on the experience of *being known by God* (i.e. being held in the Light). This might *seem* passive, but it is passive only in an epistemological sense: what Quakers come to *know* in their silent worship is their own ignorance; and in so doing, they are impelled by the resulting humility to enter into active service to their society. As an expression of the priority of practice over dogma (see note 28), Quaker theology focuses on a set of "testimonies," the first and foremost of which is the *peace* testimony – the other key testimonies being simplicity, integrity, community, equality, and stewardship of the earth.

This admittedly tentative evidence that the first Quakers might have played some role in shaping the early Enlightenment, inasmuch as they developed a new approach to religion that was *oriented toward the inward light* in a way that empowers individuals to be genuinely free and mature, has some obvious resonances with Kant's own vision of enlightenment. Let us therefore now leap forward a century and examine the extent to which Kant's theory of what he calls "rational religion" may be consistent with Quakerism.

---

29   Ibid., 81. For Kant, too, givenness in intuition (either sensible or pure) is a key requirement for objectivity. On Kant's theory of intuition, especially as it relates to mathematics, see Stephen R. Palmquist, "A Priori Knowledge in Perspective: (I) Mathematics, Method and Pure Intuition," *The Review of Metaphysics* 41/1 (1987): 3–22.

3   Kant's (Quakerly?) Critique of the Enlightenment: Religion as
        Reason's Savior

That historians widely regard the Enlightenment as ending in 1800 is highly appropriate, inasmuch as this happens to be the very same year when Kant's last self-written publication appeared.[30] This coincidence is significant because those who promoted the Age of Enlightenment prior to Kant often tended to promote an unfettered trust in the reliability of human reason to solve human problems; although Kant obviously saw himself as a pro-Enlightenment thinker, his thoroughgoing critique of reason's power to fulfil this mission contributed significantly to the movement's demise – a rather ironic historical twist that the elderly Kant himself saw coming, with considerable dismay. For the fundamental message of Kant's Critical System is that, although theoretical reason empowers us to do empirical science with a high degree of reliability, provided we have sense-based evidence for our systematically organized theories, logical systems of thought will fall like houses of cards if they are *not* grounded in sensibility. If, as Kant argued in all three *Critiques*, reason must be *practical* (i.e. moral) in order to justify belief in God, freedom, and immortality (and thus, on Kant's view, in order to make life ultimately meaningful), then a divide opens up between science (theoretical reason) and religion (practical/moral reason) that is difficult (if not impossible) to bridge.

Hinting at the need for something like Rediehs' reconstructed Quaker epistemology, Cattoi suggests the possibility that "a close look at the Quaker tradition will reveal that its understanding of our experience of the divine can offer a way forward beyond the Kantian epistemic impasse that relegates the divine beyond the reach of our cognitive faculties."[31] Evaluating this claim requires answers to two preliminary questions. First, do Quakers make epistemic claims

---

30   As I shall explain below, Kant's final publication, significantly for our purposes, deals with mysticism. Of course, the German idealists were already becoming active during the 1790s. Their diverse efforts were united by their mutual attempt to get beyond Kant, and they all agreed that they could not do so by returning to the naïveté of the Enlightenment. When Heinrich Heine famously called Kant the "arch-destroyer in the realm of thought" (*Religion and Philosophy in Germany* [Boston: 1959; based on the 1882 edition], 109), he was not accurately reflecting *Kant's own* view of metaphysics, for Kant himself firmly believed he was putting metaphysics on a new and more secure foundation – but he *was* accurately reporting the effect Kant's Copernican revolution in philosophy had on the metaphysics that had come before him, which had served as the philosophical foundation for the Enlightenment. In other words, Kant *was* the arch-destroyer of the Enlightenment's devotion to all-powerful reason.

31   Cattoi, "Conclusion," 242.

that challenge Kant's Critique of the Enlightenment's trust in reason? And second, does Kant's epistemology lack a satisfactory way of accounting for what Quakers claim to experience? We are in need of a distinctively Quaker epistemology only if we answer *both* questions positively. That is, if *either* (1) Quakers do not claim to overstep Kant's account of the limits of reason's powers *or* (2) Kant's epistemology already makes room for a Quaker-type experience of the divine[32] – or, of course, if both (1) and (2) are true – then Rediehs and Cattoi may be attempting to reinvent the wheel. Or even worse, if they are seeking a rehabilitation of pre-Kantian metaphysics, they may be transforming Quaker experience into something its founders never meant it to be and/or into something for which Kantian epistemology *would* stand as an impasse. In this section, I will argue for a negative answer to *both* questions. In so doing, I shall intentionally extend the meaning of the question given in this chapter's title, so that it refers to more than just traceable historical *influence*; for the remainder of this chapter my focus on the Quakerly "roots" of Kant's theory of religion will entail a search for *conceptual affinity* – whether or not any historical influence actually took place.

In both Prefaces to his *Religion* Kant refers to the book's task as an "experiment [*Versuch*]," whose goal was to "hold the [biblical] revelation as a historical system up to moral concepts in a merely fragmentary way, and to see whether this system does not lead back to the same pure rational system of religion as a system independent and sufficient for actual religion" (RGV, 6:12). Kant is here explicitly following an experimental method that, as Brandon Love has argued, had been given its first systematic formulation in Francis Bacon's *Novum Organum* and its definitive statement in the *Port Royal Logic* (1662).[33] While we have no evidence that Kant had actually read any Quaker writings, his dependence on the same (Baconian) experimental method suggests that they, at the very least, shared a common (empiricist) influence. They

---

32   Rediehs ("A Distinctive Quaker Theory of Knowledge," 70–1) may not agree with Cattoi ("Conclusion," 242) when it comes to the alleged "Kantian epistemic impasse," for she laments at one point that Kantian epistemology "lost" to Hume in the 20th century, inasmuch as the logical positivists backed Hume. Her lament may be unwarranted, however, given that logical positivism had a relatively short life-span, and is now generally recognized as being self-defeating. Moreover, as I argue in my forthcoming book, *Kant's Critical Science: Precursor to Scientific Revolutions*, Kant had a profound influence on the various post-Kantian scientific revolutions of the 19th and 20th centuries. It may well be that Rediehs would accept a reconstructed Kantian epistemology – i.e., one that is open to what I call Critical mysticism (see below) – as essentially equivalent to her own proposed Quaker epistemology.

33   Brandon Love, *Kant's Baconian Method as a Transformation of Aristotelian Transcendental Philosophy – A Propaedeutic* (Hong Kong: 2018).

also shared a suspicion against any claim that bare reason (i.e. reason without input from some first-hand experience) can establish knowledge, as illustrated by their mutual tendency to downplay the importance of natural theology (see note 14, above) – this being, of course, one of the three areas of traditional metaphysics that Kant's epistemic restrictions challenge.

In numerous past publications I have set forth what I call an "affirmative interpretation" of Kant's theory of religion.[34] As the details of my reading of Kant's theory are readily available elsewhere (see, e.g., note 34), I shall not repeat them here. Suffice it to say that on my reading of *Religion within the Bounds of Bare Reason*, Kant is not attempting to reduce religion to nothing but morality, but is attempting to *raise* morality to the status of religion, and in so doing, to show how historical religious traditions can *save* Enlightenment reason from the fate of being irrelevant to human destiny. In the course of constructing his argument regarding the nature of authentic (i.e. enlightened[35])

---

34   Stephen R. Palmquist, *Kant's Critical Religion: Volume Two of Kant's System of Perspectives* (New York: 2019; first published 2000), included revised and updated versions of nine previously published journal articles covering various aspects of Kant's theory of religion (see, e.g., note 37 below). Stephen R. Palmquist, *Comprehensive Commentary on Kant's Religion within the Bounds of Bare Reason* (Chichester: 2016), presents a thoroughly revised version of Pluhar's 2009 translation of Kant's *Religion*, divided into snippets of (roughly) one or a few sentences each, and comments on the various grammatical/translation, interpretive, and scholarly issues that arise out of each passage. In order to keep the length of the *Commentary*'s main text to just 500 pages, I had to write numerous other journal articles concurrently, wherein I defend in detail the interpretive positions stated more succinctly in the *Commentary*.

35   That Kant identified true religion with enlightened religion is evident from a quick look at his eight uses of forms of the word "enlighten" in *Religion*. First, he bemoans the fact that "lately the word enlightenment" (like "virtue") "has often been boastfully misused and ... ridiculed" (RGV, 6:57), but reassures his reader that ultimately such misuse "can do it no harm." He then testifies to the universality of true religion (indicating that, contrary to the accusation some interpreters level against Kant, he did *not* view enlightenment as a purely European phenomenon) when he says, while discussing the moral interpretation of Scripture, that "the *Indians* do the same with the interpretation of their *Veda*, at least for the more enlightened part of their people" (RGV, 6:111). (Later in the same passage, however, he does refer to European culture as "the most enlightened part of the world" and praises it for regarding Scripture "as the worthiest, and now ... the only, instrument for the unification of all human beings into one church" (RGV, 6:112); he finds this acceptable "because to the people no teaching that is based on bare reason seems suitable as an unchangeable standard.") He goes on to clarify that teachers of the various historical faiths can participate in this one true (enlightened) religion as long as they are willing to view their own traditions as temporary means to the end of rational faith, "until, with time, by dint of the true enlightenment (a lawfulness emerging from moral freedom) [which] has [then] gained the upper hand, one can with everyone's concordance exchange the form of an abasing means of coercion for a church form that is appropriate

religion, Kant introduces numerous terms that can hardly be understood apart from the assumption that they refer to *immediate experiences* that a religious person has: having *experienced* evil within ourselves, we can *empower* ourselves to recover our originally good "predisposition" to moral goodness only by *encountering* a divine Word that impresses itself upon our reason as an "archetype"[36] of perfection.

My most recent book, *Kant and Mysticism: Critique as the Experience of Baring All in Reason's Light* (2019), refines and updates one of the main features of the interpretation of Kant's theory of religion that I have been defending since the 1980s:[37] just as Kant saw his Critical philosophy as having a two-sided

---

to the dignity of a moral religion, namely the form of a free faith" (RGV, 6:123n). Even in non-Christian faiths such as Judaism, he adds, "[t]his wisdom presumably also helped to enlighten this people through concepts of virtue" (RGV, 6:128). In discussing the delusions that tend to corrupt church practice, he writes: "It is a psychological phenomenon that the adherents of a confession [of faith] in which there is somewhat less statutory [material] to believe feel ennobled thereby, as it were, and more enlightened, even though they still have retained enough of it in order not indeed to be entitled to look down with contempt (as, after all, they really do) from their supposed height of purity upon their brethren in church delusion" (RGV, 6:173n). (If Rediehs' Quaker epistemology entails that an experience of the inner light imparts *empirical cognition* of objective truths, then Kant's criticism here might apply to Quakers, who were openly critical of the delusions being promoted by their Christian "brethren." Kant could use them to illustrate his point that less deluded religious believers tend to look down on more deluded ones, even though they themselves remain in the grip of *some* religious delusion.) After defining delusion as dependent "on the order in which one binds" moral faith with statutory/ revealed faith, which Kant calls "two good things," he adds: "It is in this distinction ... that true *enlightenment* consists; the service of God thereby becomes first of all a free [and] hence moral service" (RGV, 6:179). Finally, near the end of the book Kant quotes from 1 Cor. 1:26–7 to emphasize the necessarily universal nature of enlightened religion: "It is equitable, it is reasonable, to accept that not merely 'wise men after the flesh,' scholars and rationalizers, will be called to this enlightenment in regard to their true wholeness – for the entire human race is supposed to be capable of this faith – but [also] 'the foolish things of the world'" (RGV, 6:181).

36   Cattoi notes that for the Greek Fathers of the Church, "the purpose of the Christian life ... is ... to reconfigure our inner life according to the model of Christ's" (Cattoi, "Conclusion," 244). This seems fully compatible with what Kant describes as the reconfiguring of our moral lifestyle in response to an encounter with the archetype.

37   My efforts to demonstrate the affinity between Kant's philosophy and a *refined* form of mysticism date back to the late 1980s, when I composed a pair of articles on the topic shortly after completing my doctoral dissertation: "Kant's Critique of Mysticism: (1) The Critical *Dreams*," *Philosophy & Theology* 3/4 (1989): 355–383 and "Kant's Critique of Mysticism: (2) The Critical Mysticism," *Philosophy & Theology* 4/1 (1989): 67–94. Unfortunately, both articles were published with literally hundreds of errors that the editors introduced into the manuscripts, rendering large portions of the first paper, in particular, virtually unintelligible. Chapters II and X of my *Kant's Critical Religion* presented

implication for metaphysics (i.e. it not only destroys the old, "speculative" metaphysics, but also paves the way for a new, *moral* metaphysics), so also his philosophy has a two-sided implication for mysticism. Kant frequently hinted at this two-sided implication, but perhaps due to the Enlightenment's general antipathy toward anything mystical, he only explicitly worked out its negative side. As a result, Kant is well-known for reproaching any form of mysticism that he called "delirious"[38] – i.e. any appeal to mystical experience that causes a person to be *deluded* about what human experience can and cannot establish as scientifically valid "empirical cognition" – yet his many moving ways of acknowledging the value and potential profundity of *non*-cognitive mystical experiences typically go unnoticed. In hopes of calling attention to Kant's morally grounded mystical side, I have coined the term "Critical mysticism," to refer to any way of experiencing the divine that does not overstep the epistemological and moral restrictions of Kant's Critical philosophy.

If my arguments about Kant's Critical mysticism are correct, then we are left with two possibilities: either Quaker epistemology is actually *consistent* with Kant's Critical principles, in which case the search for further conceptual resonances between Kant's theory of religion and Quakerism will make perfect sense, or else Quakers make knowledge-claims that overstep Critical restrictions, in which case Kant and Kantians would have to classify any epistemology that defends such an approach as "delirious." On my reading of Quaker literature, its writers rarely, if ever, make *epistemic* claims of the sort that would need to *overcome* the so-called "impasse" that Kant's epistemic restrictions allegedly impose on religious believers. Rather, Quakerism offers an example of precisely the sort of religious experience that, as Carl A. Wilmans put it in a 1797 letter to Kant,[39] a "true Kantian" can not only tolerate but openly welcome.

---

revised and updated versions of the same arguments and supplemented them (in Chapter XII) with a new argument interpreting Kant's *Opus postumum* as the culmination of his Critical mysticism. *Kant and Mysticism: Critique as the Experience of Baring All in Reason's Light* (Lanham: 2019) thoroughly repackages and further updates these three chapters, adding a new Introduction and Conclusion that clarify various aspects of my claims. The March 2021 issue of *Kantian Review* includes a symposium in which five scholars assess the plausibility of my arguments, to which I respond in the article: "Responses to Critics: What Makes Mysticism Critical? (Or: What Makes Critique Mystical?)," *Kantian Review* 26/1 (2021): 137–162.

38   I translate Kant's term, *Schwärmerei*, as "delirium." I defend the superiority of this translation over the usual alternatives, "fanaticism" and "enthusiasm," in *Comprehensive Commentary*, 520–1.

39   For Kant's correspondence with Wilmans, see Br, 12:202, 207, 230, 259, 277 and 279–280. Allen W. Wood ("Translator's Introduction" to Kant's *Preface to Reinhold Bernhard Jachmann's Examination of the Kantian Philosophy of Religion*, in *Religion and Rational*

Wilmans had just finished a doctoral dissertation (in Latin), entitled *On the Similarity between Pure Mysticism and the Kantian Religious Doctrine* (Halle, 1797), a copy of which he sent to Kant in hopes of piquing Kant's interest. He succeeded: Kant was so impressed by this comparison that he published Wilmans' lengthy letter as an Appendix to his 1797 book, *The Conflict of the Faculties* (see 7:69–75), adding only a brief comment of his own, explicitly praising "this young man" as a scholar "from whom much can be expected" (7:69n.), while cautioning that, by reproducing his letter, "I do not mean to guarantee that my views coincide entirely with his."[40] Kant was also sufficiently impressed by the comparison that he asked his friend and former research assistant, Reinhold Bernhard Jachmann (1767–1843), who had since become a Lutheran pastor, to write a book-length response to Wilmans' intriguing claims. Jachmann responded by writing a book entitled *Examination of the Kantian Philosophy of Religion in Respect of the Similarity to Pure Mysticism which Has Been Attributed to It*, and he asked Kant to write a Preface. In January of 1800, Kant complied by writing up a short Preface – his last solely authored publication. Whereas Jachmann had argued that Wilmans was radically mistaken to think that Kant's Critical philosophy is consistent with some forms of mysticism, Kant's Preface remains conspicuously neutral on the question of whether Wilmans himself

Theology [Cambridge, Eng.: 1996], 331) says that Wilmans "pestered Kant with a series of letters"; but of Kant's two known replies to Wilmans' four letters, the only extant one (Br, 12:279–280) shows no sign of annoyance. Quite to the contrary, after apologizing for his delay in replying, due to his busy schedule and the ailments of age, and offering some mild criticism of a point Wilmans had made about the distinction between reason and understanding, Kant concludes his short reply by conceding that Wilmans' "daring assertions could, under certain modifications, produce something which, with further elaboration and more precise definition of your ideas, might lead to a third, more tenable principle – for which I wish [you] luck with sincere friendship." For a more balanced assessment of Kant's last self-written publication, see Stephen R. Palmquist, "Preface to Reinhold Bernhard Jachmann's *Examination of the Kantian Philosophy of Religion in Respect of the Similarity to Pure Mysticism which Has Been Attributed to It*," in *The Cambridge Kant Lexicon*, ed. Julian Wuerth (Cambridge, Eng.: 2021), 712–713.

40   Some commentators read Kant's proviso as his way of implying that he does not endorse the idea of comparing his theory of religion with mysticism. But that comparison is the main point of Wilmans' entire letter! If Kant did not endorse *that*, why would he have bothered to devote such a substantial chunk of his book to promoting Wilmans' work? Before making the comparison between Kant and certain mystics, the bulk of Wilmans' letter offers summaries of Kant's various theories and brief comments on their implications. It therefore seems far more plausible to assume that Kant added his proviso to warn readers that he did not always agree with the accuracy of Wilmans' rather sketchy *background summaries* of his Critical theories. This seems especially likely, given the fact that, in his only extant letter to the young scholar, Kant's only criticism of Wilmans' position relates to his interpretation of the term "understanding," *not* to his proposal regarding the consistency of Kant's position with mysticism (see note 39 above).

was guilty of promoting the specific type of (impure) mysticism that Kant now calls "counterfeit philosophy" (PKR, 8:441); instead, he strikes a middle path that carefully avoids explicitly endorsing Jachmann's extreme rejection of Wilmans' claims. Calling Jachmann "a most treasured friend," Kant concludes his last published work with the nuanced words: "Not that [Jachmann's book] in any way needs a recommendation on my part; rather, I would [in writing this Preface] merely add to this book the seal of my friendship toward the author as an everlasting memento" (PKR, 8:441).

Notwithstanding Jachmann's rejection of the notion of a "Kantian mysticism," Kant is not opposed to talking *as if* we know that God speaks to us or leads us in a particular way; rather, he carefully and explicitly targets his epistemic restrictions against those who claim to possess *empirical cognition* of various facts about God and, on this basis, to be able to *control* God (e.g. through certain rituals) or to *determine* God's judgement in some way. Wilmans' aforementioned letter to Kant does an excellent job of bringing out this implication of Kant's theory of religion. Significantly, however, it ends by *contrasting* the "separatists," whose mysticism he believed was fully Kantian, "from Quakers": although "their religious *principles*" overlap with those of the Quakers, Wilmans' mystics differ in "the way they apply them to their everyday life; for example, they adopt no distinctive dress and pay both their state and church taxes." Kant famously argues that human beings have a duty to obey the law of the land,[41] so Wilmans' point here is that, whereas Kant might disapprove of those Quakers who intentionally broke the law by withholding taxes that were destined to be used to support war and violence,[42] the group of mystics he has in mind are *more* Kantian in the sense that they do not go to such extremes by intentionally breaking the law.

In *Kant and Mysticism* I argue that Kant's epistemology readily acknowledges a role for "immediate experience" (which I also refer to as *encounter*) as a component of ordinary, reliable "empirical cognition": Kant argues that the latter is always a form of *mediate* experience, because our immediate encounter with the world through inner and/or outer sense must be placed under the ordering conditions of the twelve categories in order to rise to the status of

---

41   See, e.g., Stephen R. Palmquist, "Kantian Conditions for the Possibility of Justified Resistance to Authority," in *The Right to Resist: Philosophies of Dissent*, eds. Mario Wenning and Thomas Byrne (London: 2022; forthcoming).

42   While Wilmans' (implied) point is a good one, I have argued in "Kantian Conditions for the Possibility of Justified Resistance to Authority" that Kant does support acts of civil disobedience in some limited circumstances. That is, the willingness of some Quakers to break the law when it conflicts with morality is not necessarily something that Kant would censure.

being *cognized*. What many Kant scholars ignored until fairly recently[43] is that Kant openly recognizes that sometimes immediate experiences (i.e. encounters with ourselves or with something beyond ourselves) might occur *without* being subjectable to the categories. Once we recognize that Kant acknowledges a legitimate place for such encounters, it seems evident that the Quaker epistemology that Rediehs seeks to reconstruct on behalf of Barclay and other early Quakers would have more affinity to Kant's epistemology than to Locke's. Because the British empiricists do not distinguish between uses of inner sense that can and cannot be adequately conceptualized – i.e. because they do not clearly distinguish between (what I would call) an *encounter* with the divine through the revelation of an inward Light and the empirical *cognition* of (say) a triangle as one pictures it in inner sense – their epistemology does not resonate well with the way Quakers typically describe their experience. An experience of the inner light in Quaker silence is *wordless* and as such does not allow itself to be cognized as empirical knowledge. Rediehs underestimates the significance of this feature of the Quaker mystical experience, while nevertheless acknowledging that her reconstructed Quaker epistemology interprets the term "experience" as "broad enough to include ethical, aesthetic, relational, and religious experience."[44] Such a wide range of experience is obviously far too broad to qualify as Kantian "empirical cognition"; it is not for that reason *unKantian*, though it might for that reason be inappropriate to call it an "epistemology," *per se*.

As Rediehs puts it: "The Quakers were seldom as negative towards human reason as some of their critics tended to think, but they did emphasise the limits of natural reason."[45] In this sense, they were surely closer to Kant than to Locke or any of the other early Enlightenment philosophers.[46] Barclay, for example, says that the immediate experience of God to which Quakers testify occurs "as we wait in that *pure and undefiled Light of God* (that proper and fit *organ*), in which they are received."[47] This somewhat ambiguous reference to an "organ" appears to be metaphorical, as it does not obviously refer literally to any part of the human body. As such, Barclay seems to have in mind something close to what Kant means by his special term, *Gesinnung* (which I translate as

---

43   The recent debate over whether or not Kant's theory of cognition allows intuition to have a constitutive role as nonconceptual content has largely remedied such past neglect. See Stephen R. Palmquist (ed.), *Kant on Intuition: Western and Asian Perspectives on Transcendental Idealism* (New York: 2019).

44   Rediehs, "A Distinctive Quaker Theory of Knowledge," 93.

45   Ibid., 82.

46   As Melvin Keiser puts it: "The spiritual light ... works through, not separate from, reason." "Touched and Knit in the Life: Barclay's Relational Theology and Cartesian Dualism," *Quaker Studies* 5/2 (2001): 153; quoted in Rediehs, "A Distinctive Quaker Theory of Knowledge," 83.

47   Barclay, "An Apology for the True Christian Divinity," 54.

"conviction"[48] but is more commonly rendered "disposition"). For as Rediehs puts it: "Barclay (along with other Quaker writers of this time) argued that the spiritual sense can initially be clouded or blocked, and a personal transformation brought about by 'forsaking iniquity' is required before the spiritual sense is activated."[49] On the basis of claims such as this, Rediehs calls Quaker epistemology "a distinctive view of the Inward Light, cast as an experiential faculty."[50] Just as Barclay claims that the human capacity for experiencing the immediate Presence of God (i.e. the ability to see all things "in the Light," as Quakers say) may require a person to experience a conversion from their old way of life to a new way of life, so also Kant acknowledges that the evil conviction that human beings all start off with will cause human beings to deceive themselves until we experience a conversion of heart that empowers us to view ourselves as holy, or at least as being virtuous (which now takes on the religious meaning of being on the *path* to holiness).

Another term Kant associates closely with the reformed religious conviction is "conscience" (*Gewissen*). Kant controversially claims that conscience *cannot err* (RGV, 6:185–7), but this initially shocking claim seems more plausible once we recognize that the German word in question means "certain" (as in "definitely not mistaken") when written as an adjective (i.e. as *gewissen*). Like many Quakers, Kant writes at times as if conscience and/or our conviction function as an "organ" (or mental faculty, as Kant would put it). Admittedly, he shies away from associating either of these with inner sense, as this would seem perilously close to an affirmation of intellectual intuition, which Kant repeatedly rejects (see e.g. RGV, 6:175). But when Quaker writers associate their experience of the inner light with inner sense, they are surely not affirming what *Kant* means by intellectual intuition: they are not claiming to create *empirical* objects merely by thinking them. Consider, for example, these words of Penington: "There is a witness of and from God in every conscience; which, in his light, power, and authority, witnesseth for him, and against that which is contrary to him ... From this witness proceeds the true and well-grounded religion in the mind towards God ..."[51]

Given that Kant himself uses the metaphor of light no less than five times in *Religion*, twice in an explicitly Quakerly way, it seems plausible to suggest that the overall spirit of his approach to "true religion" as *enlightened* religion is at least *conceptually* rooted in Quaker-like terminology. In the Second Piece he

---

48   See Stephen R. Palmquist, "What is Kantian *Gesinnung*? On the Priority of Volition over Metaphysics and Psychology in Kant's *Religion*," *Kantian Review* 20/2 (2015): 235–264; Palmquist, *Comprehensive Commentary*, 520.

49   Rediehs, "A Distinctive Quaker Theory of Knowledge," 80.

50   Ibid., 90.

51   Quoted in Rediehs, "A Distinctive Quaker Theory of Knowledge," 84, from Penington, "Some Things Relating to Religion," 108.

associates "good and evil" with "the kingdom of light and the kingdom of darkness" (RGV, 6:60n.; cf. John 8:12), respectively, later adding (RGV, 6:87) that "the
evil spirit often disguises himself as an angel of light." Moreover, employing the
clothing metaphor that is implicit in his book's title, Kant clarifies in the Third
Piece that enlightened religion requires mature human beings to see beyond
the immaturity of childhood religion: "The cloaks under which the embryo first
formed itself into the human being must be cast off if he is now to step into
the light of day" (RGV, 6:121). That is, although children take the myths, rituals,
and symbols of their historical religious tradition at face value, the enlightened
adult sees the deeper meanings that lie at the core of such traditions – in a nut-
shell, conscience-inspired goodness by conviction. Kant is not at all suggesting
that we must cast off *experience* of God; far from it.[52] Rather, he is encouraging
his readers to shed the "cloaks" of historical faith that, if taken as the core of
true religion, tend to *block* people from having the kind of immediate, life-
giving experience that can alone suffice to effect a revolution of the heart.

On two occasions in the Fourth Piece Kant expresses his view of enlightened religion by employing the Quaker concept of an "inward light." First, after
referring to church councils and other optional supplements to pure rational
faith, he adds: "Concerning this scholarship, or its antipode, the inward light to
which any layperson can also lay claim, it is still impossible to see how many
changes yet lie in store for faith on their account; and this cannot be avoided
as long as we seek religion not within us but outside us" (RGV, 6:167). Here
Kant is explicitly contrasting the religion of scholarship, which is bound to
hinder the cause of enlightenment if taken as a necessary guide to people's
faith, with those who "seek religion ... within us": while being guided by "the
inward light" is the more enlightened approach, it too runs the risk of leading
people astray, if we regard the Light as an *external* influence rather than as an
internally manifested (and thus moral) light. Accordingly, *Religion*'s concluding paragraph exhorts us:

---

52   Stevenson, after asking whether perhaps Kant "had a blindspot" when it came to the issue
      of the possibility of religious experience of God, answers by rightly pointing out that
      "Kant does not deny that we can have deeply significant experiences – in *some* sense of
      the term – which involve awareness of some aspect of things that transcends our ordinary
      perception or scientific knowledge." Stevenson, *Open to New Light*, 150. He suggests that
      what Kant meant "is that there can be an *indirect* experience of God through" various
      ways of experiencing sensible (e.g. beautiful) things (ibid., 152). He then proceeds to offer
      quotes from several prominent Quaker writers, each illustrating that the *way* Quakers
      tend to talk about their inward experiences of God is, for the most part, entirely con-
      sistent with Kant's cautious insistence that we not claim to have established empirical
      cognition on this basis.

It is no wonder, then, if [people] publicly complain that religion still contributes so little to the reformation of human beings, and that the inward light ("under a bushel") of those pardoned ones is not willing to shine also outwardly through good works, and indeed (as according to this pretense of theirs one could indeed require) to shine *preferentially* in front of other naturally honorable human beings, who, [to put it] short and sweet, take up religion not as a substitution for, but as furtherance of, the virtuous conviction that actively appears in a good lifestyle.

RGV, 6:201

As I shall argue in the concluding section of this chapter, on this point Quakerism is as Kantian as it is in its insistence on inward experience being the core of true religion; for Quakers have from the very outset been outspoken defenders of freedom, justice, and various types of morally motivated social action.[53]

4   Further Resonances: Simplicity in Quakerism and Kantian Rational Faith

Among the relatively few scholars who have addressed the issue of how Quakerism relates to philosophy in general and to Kant's philosophy in particular, none has surpassed the excellent work of the British Quaker philosopher, Leslie Stevenson.[54] Stevenson acknowledges many features of the wide-ranging

---

53   Countless examples could be cited here, but perhaps one will suffice: the 1947 Nobel Peace Prize was awarded to two Quaker groups for their work during and in the immediate aftermath of World War Two.

54   Although there have been several prominent Quaker philosophers, none (other than Stevenson) has devoted much attention to Kant. Stevenson points out that John Macmurray (1891–1976) was a Quaker, though it seems he joined the Society only in his old age (*Open to New Light*, 153). Perhaps the most well-known academic philosopher who was openly Quaker and who devoted much of his writing to Quaker-related topics was Rufus Jones (1863–1948). (Some would regard William Penn as the first Quaker philosopher, but he was never trained as such, nor did he have an academic career, and his writings were more theological than philosophical. Much the same could be said of Sophia Hume [1702–1774].) Co-founder of general systems theory, Kenneth E. Boulding (1910–1993), was a life-long Quaker and is sometimes regarded as a philosopher, but his academic affiliation was as an economist. One reason Quakerism has produced so few influential philosophers, no doubt, is that it emphasizes social activism far more than intellectual or academic understanding. Thus, for example, many would regard Jim Corbett (1933–2001) as an exemplary Quaker philosopher, yet he published little (if anything) that would be of interest to most academic philosophers. Similarly, the great

overlap between the concerns of Kantian and Quaker religion, some of which I have pointed out in the foregoing overview.[55] Nevertheless, he highlights one (alleged) bone of contention between the two: "Kant saw no validity in religious experience."[56] However, as I have argued elsewhere and summarized in the previous section, Kant's well known *criticisms* of mysticism tell only part of the story as to how his philosophical system relates to mystical experience. Stevenson himself concedes that the objections Kant raises against mystical experience might arise mainly from the difficulty of *explaining* what is happening when a person testifies to experiencing (for example) "the promptings of love and truth in [one's] heart."[57] Stevenson connects Kant's categorical imperative (especially in its second formulation, the formula of respect for humanity) with one of the key principles of Quaker faith, "that everyone has 'that of God' within them."[58] Another key principle of Kantian ethics, which Kant hammers home in the first few pages of the first edition Preface to his *Religion*, is that morality precedes (in the sense of not being dependent on) religion, yet it *leads to* religion because we human beings are unable to live up to the high standards set by the categorical imperative without some kind

---

Korean Quaker, Ham Seok-heon (1901–1989), might be regarded as a philosopher, but he was primarily an historian, poet, and political activist.

55 Stevenson's "Kant's Approach to Religion" and *Open to New Light* are successively revised and extended versions of the same basic argument he initially defended in "Kant's Philosophy and Quakerism." In *Open to New Light*, Stevenson summarizes his argument as follows: "The constitution and practice of the Religious Society of Friends seem pretty close to Kant's requirements. There is no appeal to authoritative revelation or miracles, no rituals except the practice of meeting for an hour of silent worship, and no sacraments ... There are no professional priests or pastors" (ibid., 138). Moreover, Quakers tend to be ecumenical (ibid., 141), downplaying the role of theology, such that "there is no mention of the doctrine of the divinity of Christ" (ibid., 140). Stevenson later explains that the tendency Quakers have to shy away from "such highly intellectual inquiry" is a direct result of the fact that they tend to place "a corresponding emphasis on the practical character of true religion" (ibid., 142). Quakers therefore have no creeds or required statements of faith (ibid., 143–4); instead, they have *testimonies* that relate directly to how one acts in the world. Stevenson adds: "Like Kant, Quakers have not insisted on the doctrine of incarnation, i.e. the metaphysical identification of Jesus with God" (ibid., 146), though I would add that Quakers (*also* like Kant – see Stephen R. Palmquist, "Could Kant's Jesus Be God?" *International Philosophical Quarterly* 52/4 (2012): 421–437) allow for the possibility that Jesus *could* be divine and welcome Friends to adopt such a belief if they see fit, without it being a litmus test for true faith.

56 Stevenson, "Kant's Philosophy and Quakerism," 91.

57 Ibid., 92, quoting from the Quaker pamphlet, *Advices and Queries*, number 1. For his further elaboration on and assessment of Kant's apparent rejection of religious experience, see Stevenson, "Kant's Approach to Religion."

58 Stevenson, "Kant's Philosophy and Quakerism," 86.

of *extra-rational* support. This two-sided claim is entirely consistent with the Quaker conviction that, even though human beings have within themselves a source of truth that is independent of any traditional religious doctrine, we still need the support of a community of faith in order to live authentically.

Kant's claim that what is *essential* for enlightened religion is what he calls "rational faith," such that the particular doctrines of any given *historical* faith (i.e. any religious tradition) are optional extras, is also consistent with the fundamental Quaker principle (or "testimony") of simplicity. Admittedly, simplicity is not a word that is often associated with Kant's philosophy, yet at its heart this was surely his goal. As he states near the end of the first *Critique*, readers should not be surprised if it seems that, after over 800 pages of complex philosophical argument, what the *Critique* ends up supporting boils down to what common human beings already believe (KrV, A 830–1/B 858–9). This illustrates Kant's conviction that enlightened philosophy must be *humble* rather than sophisticated. This, indeed, is why the Critical System focuses on reason's *limits*. Even Kant's *Religion*, filled as it is with complicated attempts to grapple rationally with the paradoxical tensions we find in human nature, offers ample evidence that what Kant means by "*rational* religion" is *simple* religion. As Kant puts it, introducing authentic religion to "human beings whose heads – crammed with statutory dogmas – have become almost unreceptive to the rational religion, must always be much more difficult than if one had intended to bring this religion to the reason of untutored but also uncorrupted human beings" (RGV, 6:162–3). In other words, historical traditions introduce innumerable *complexities* into their account of what it means to be religious, whereas rational religion keeps it simple and requires nothing but an inwardly attested conviction to be good, as evidenced by one's lifestyle, thereby demonstrating that one's good-heartedness is genuine.

Two obvious examples of Kant's attempt to make religion simple are his insistence that the "*one* (true) *religion*" be simple enough to serve as the rational grounding for "many kinds of *faith*" (RGV, 6:107) and his call to Christians, in particular, to rid the church of the complexities of hierarchy, because clerical power-structures only hinder the progress of true religion. Similarly, as Cattoi rightly notes, Quakerism is well-suited to "become a meeting point of many traditions";[59] this is precisely due to its refusal to require its members to believe any specific set of doctrines, which, in Kant's terms, belong to the complexities of "historical faith." That is, Quakerism models Kant's ideal historical faith by allowing each member to embrace whatever doctrinal beliefs he or she finds conducive to promoting goodness. Cattoi specifically asks "whether

---

59   Cattoi, "Conclusion," 241.

the tensions within Quakerism merely reflect or actually challenge the modern epistemological shift ... toward the Kantian turn to the subject."[60] Instead of opting for the former, as I have argued above, he claims that the Quaker "understanding of our experience of the divine can offer a way forward beyond the Kantian epistemic impasse that relegates the divine beyond the reach of our cognitive faculties." He later adds: "The last two centuries have labored under the Kantian distinction between pure and practical reason, effectively relegating the divine into a sphere that transcends the reach of sensory perception." The result has been a choice, either "to accept secularism" or "to embrace a rather sterile fideism, stripped of all experiential content."[61] While Cattoi is correct that much of the post-Kantian history of philosophical theology has indeed faced enlightened religious people with just such an undesirable choice, he fails to acknowledge the recent scholarship that has demonstrated that this dichotomy was not of *Kant's own* making, any more than George Fox's.

Fortunately, Cattoi comes close to recognizing the Quakerly roots of Kant's position when he continues:

> Perhaps the tendency of early Quakers to view the inner light as something utterly immaterial, and therefore as something that is not perceived by the senses, somehow anticipated this Kantian divide. If this is the case, Quakerism may also contain some antidotes to the post-Kantian tendency to reject the insights of mystical experience or to regard mystical experience of the divine as simply impossible.[62]

As so often happens in such discussions, Cattoi bases his entire account of Kant on the first and second *Critiques*; had he attended to the third *Critique* and Kant's *Religion*, especially in its recent "affirmative" interpretations,[63] he may well have described essentially the same position as Kantian Quakerism, rather than as the Quaker "antidote" to the secularism-or-fideism choice, allegedly required by Kant's epistemology. For Cattoi's Quaker antidote focuses on

---

60   Ibid., 242.
61   Ibid., 247.
62   Ibid.
63   See notes 34 and 37, above, for references to my key works promoting an affirmative interpretation. For other prominent works in this new school of Kant interpretation, see John E. Hare, *The Moral Gap: Kantian Ethics, Human Limits, and God's Assistance* (Oxford: 1996); Firestone and Palmquist, *Kant and the New Philosophy of Religion*, especially the Editors' Introduction; Chris L. Firestone and Nathan Jacobs, *In Defense of Kant's Religion* (Bloomington: 2008); Lawrence Pasternack, *Routledge Philosophy Guidebook to Immanuel Kant's* Religion within the Boundaries of Mere Reason: *An Interpretation and Defense* (London: 2014); Wood, *Kant and Religion*.

a pair of ideas that Kant himself defends in *Religion*: first, that "the distinction between pure and practical reason" must be bridged in such a way that "the natural order is again invested with cues of God's providential presence in the cosmos." And second, "that the mystical experience of the individual always takes place in the context of a community of believers."[64] I have elaborated on these very aspects of Kant's theory of religion in great detail in several of my previous publications (see note 34, above), so I will not repeat those details here. Cattoi even uses the very same metaphor as Kant uses to describe the church: in a Quaker Meeting, he says, Friends are to be "fellow members of the human family."[65] Kant himself, immediately after setting forth the four requirements of the true church (i.e. universality, integrity, freedom, and holding only these requirements as unchangeable), adds that its political constitution is best "compared with the structure of a household (family)" (RGV, 6:102).[66]

Kant's focus on morality as the essence of religion is surely one of the key roadblocks that prevents his approach to being religious from becoming as widely accepted as he hoped it would become. This hindrance to the feasibility of taking Kant's theory of religion seriously is partially overcome once we recognize that, as I first argued in a 1992 article, he does not reduce religion to morality, but raises morality to the level of religion.[67] Another step toward rendering Kant's theory as a view that actual religious people can embrace is to recognize that when Kant talks about morality, he is referring primarily not to some external code of behavior, but to what nowadays typically goes by the name "spirituality." Along these lines, Cattoi observes that Quakerism tends to attract those who are "spiritual, but not religious."[68] Just as Rediehs insists

---

64   Cattoi, "Conclusion," 247.

65   Ibid.

66   Commenting on this passage, Wood suggests, in good Quakerly fashion, that an even better model for Kant's ideal church structure would be *friendship* (Allen W. Wood, *Kant's Ethical Thought* [Cambridge: 1999], 316). The first requirement is virtually identical to the Quaker emphasis on authentic religion as universal. The emphasis of the Religious Society of Friends on simplicity likewise resonates with Kant's second requirement, while their peace testimony is based on an understanding of church-state relation that is virtually identical with Kant's third requirement. Moreover, although I have not had space to develop this point here: a key subordinate theme in Kant's *Religion* is the importance of moral pedagogy in the church, which resonates well with the Quaker emphasis on education.

67   See Stephen R. Palmquist, "Does Kant Reduce Religion to Morality?" *Kant-Studien* 83/2 (1992): 129–148.

68   Cattoi, "Conclusion," 248. Cattoi illustrates this point by noting the existence of what he calls "Quagans – neo-pagan Quakers." That the Religious Society of Friends welcomes people of all faiths to become members, without requiring them to give up whatever beliefs or rituals they may still treasure from their past affiliations, is a practical application of

that the Quaker experience of the inward light is an objective confirmation of an experiential faith,[69] so also Stevenson observes that moral cognition is "for Kant just as objective as [the cognition] of mathematics and science, but they have a different *kind* of truth."[70]

In conclusion, then, we have seen that in several important respects Kant's enlightened religion *does* have Quaker roots. Historically, Quakerism arose at the very outset of the Enlightenment, and its emphasis on the "inward light" may well have influenced some of the earliest Enlightenment philosophers: and when the Enlightenment ended in 1800, the year of Kant's last publication (a Preface that carefully avoids endorsing a book's categorical denial of the possibility of mystical experience), this was largely *because* Kant had placed firm (but Quakerly) limits on that movement's pretentious agenda. He did not do so, however, without also providing a way forward that entails the promotion of a radically new vision of what it means to be religious – a vision that has remarkable resonances with Quakerism. In short, the Enlightenment had transferred the *divine* Light of Quakerism into a *human* power that many believed could do without any immediately experienced God; so, by putting that movement to death, Kant can be seen as restoring the need for inward experience that had been at its Quakerly core at the movement's beginning. As I have argued, Kant's vision of an inwardly experienced, revolutionary "moral religion" deeply resonates with, and gives philosophical expression to, the spiritually oriented vision of revolutionary religion that the early Quakers had preached at the Enlightenment's very outset.

Acknowledgments

An earlier version of this chapter was presented as an online lecture for a seminar on "Enlightenment and Religion," sponsored by the research project, "Between Secularization and Reform: Religious Rationalism in the Late 17th Century and in the Enlightenment," based at the Institute of Philosophy of Jagiellonian University in Kraków, Poland. I would like to thank the participants of that seminar for their helpful feedback on that earlier version. Thanks also for the feedback provided by those who attended a talk I gave on Kant and

---

  Kant's view that the church will include "all well-meaning human beings" (RGV, 6:152), regardless of which historical faith they may embrace.

69 Rediehs, "A Distinctive Quaker Theory of Knowledge," 80–1. Such an objectivity claim is most plausible in the context of a *gathered* Meeting for Worship, where each participant can test his or her experience by relating it to that of the group.

70 Stevenson, *Open to New Light*, 137.

Quakerism at a gathering sponsored by the Hong Kong Monthly Meeting of the Religious Society of Friends.

References

Barclay, Robert, "The Possibility and Necessity of the Inward & Immediate Revelation of the Spirit Of God, Towards the Foundation and Ground of True Faith, Proved, in a Letter Writ in Latin to a Person of Quality in Holland; and Now Also Put Into English," *Truth Triumphant*, vol. 3 (Philadelphia: 1686/1831).

Barclay, Robert, "An Apology for the True Christian Divinity, As the Same Is Held Forth and Preached by the People Called," in *Truth Triumphant*, vol. 2 (Glenside: 1676/2002).

Cattoi, Thomas, "Conclusion," in *Quakers and Mysticism: Interdisciplinary Approaches to the Study of Mysticism*, ed. Jon R. Kershner (Cham: 2019), 241–8.

Firestone, Chris L., and Nathan Jacobs, *In Defense of Kant's Religion* (Bloomington: 2008).

Firestone, Chris L., and Stephen R. Palmquist (eds.), *Kant and the New Philosophy of Religion* (Bloomington: 2006).

Fox, George, *The Journal of George Fox* (Cambridge: 1694/1952).

Hare, John E., *The Moral Gap: Kantian Ethics, Human Limits, and God's Assistance* (Oxford: 1996).

Head, Jonathan, "Kant's *Religion* as a Response to the Pantheism Controversy: Between Mendelssohn and Jacobi," *International Philosophical Quarterly* 61/1 (2021): 101–119.

Heine, Heinrich, *Religion and Philosophy in Germany* (Boston: 1882/1959).

Kant, Immanuel, "Preface to Reinhold Bernhard Jachmann's *Examination of the Kantian Philosophy of Religion*," in *Religion and Rational Theology* (Cambridge, Eng.: 1996), 333–4 (PKR, 8).

Kant, Immanuel, "The Conflict of the Faculties," in *Religion and Rational Theology* (Cambridge, Eng.: 1996), 239–327 (SF, 7).

Kant, Immanuel, *Religion within the Bounds of Bare Reason* (RGV, 6), in *Comprehensive Commentary on Kant's Religion within the Bounds of Bare Reason*, trans. (revising Wernar Pluhar's 2009 translation) Stephen R. Palmquist (Chichester: 2016).

Kant, Immanuel, "An Answer to the Question: What Is Enlightenment?," in *Practical Philosophy* (Cambridge, Eng.: 1996), 15–22 (WA, 8).

Keiser, R. Melvin, "Touched and Knit in the Life: Barclay's Relational Theology and Cartesian Dualism," *Quaker Studies* 5/2 (2001): 141–164.

Locke, John, *Essay Concerning Human Understanding* (Oxford: 1975).

Love, Brandon, *Kant's Baconian Method as a Transformation of Aristotelian Transcendental Philosophy – A Propaedeutic* (Hong Kong: 2018).

Palmquist, Stephen R., "Kantian Conditions for the Possibility of Justified Resistance to Authority," in *The Right to Resist: A Philosophy of Dissent*, eds. Mario Wenning and Thomas Byrne (London: 2022; forthcoming).

Palmquist, Stephen R., "Preface to Reinhold Bernhard Jachmann's *Examination of the Kantian Philosophy of Religion in Respect of the Similarity to Pure Mysticism which Has Been Attributed to It*," in *The Cambridge Kant Lexicon*, ed. Julian Wuerth (Cambridge: 2021), 712–713.

Palmquist, Stephen R., "Responses to Critics: What Makes Mysticism Critical? (Or: What Makes Critique Mystical?)," *Kantian Review* 26/1 (2021): 137–162.

Palmquist, Stephen R., *Kant and Mysticism: Critique as the Experience of Baring All in Reason's Light* (Lanham: 2019).

Palmquist, Stephen R., *Comprehensive Commentary on Kant's Religion within the Bounds of Bare Reason* (Chichester: 2016).

Palmquist, Stephen R., "What is Kantian *Gesinnung*? On the Priority of Volition over Metaphysics and Psychology in Kant's *Religion*," *Kantian Review* 20/2 (2015): 235–264.

Palmquist, Stephen R., "Kant's Lectures on Philosophical Theology – Training-Ground for the Moral Pedagogy of *Religion*?" in *Reading Kant's Lectures*, ed. Robert Clewis (New York: 2015), 365–390.

Palmquist, Stephen R., "Could Kant's Jesus Be God?" *International Philosophical Quarterly* 52/4 (2012): 421–437.

Palmquist, Stephen R., *Kant's Critical Religion: Volume Two of Kant's System of Perspectives* (Aldershot: 2000; reprinted New York: 2019).

Palmquist, Stephen R., "Does Kant Reduce Religion to Morality?" *Kant-Studien* 83/2 (1992): 129–148.

Palmquist, Stephen R., "Kant's Critique of Mysticism: (2) The Critical Mysticism," *Philosophy & Theology* 4/1 (1989): 67–94.

Palmquist, Stephen R., "Kant's Critique of Mysticism: (1) The Critical *Dreams*," *Philosophy & Theology* 3/4 (1989): 355–383.

Palmquist, Stephen R., "A Priori Knowledge in Perspective: (I) Mathematics, Method and Pure Intuition," *The Review of Metaphysics* 41/1 (1987): 3–22.

Palmquist, Stephen R., "Faith as Kant's Key to the Justification of Transcendental Reflection," *The Heythrop Journal* 25/4 (1984): 442–455.

Pasternack, Lawrence, *Routledge Philosophy Guidebook to Immanuel Kant's Religion within the Boundaries of Mere Reason: An Interpretation and Defense* (London: 2014).

Penington, Isaac, "Some Things Relating to Religion Proposed to the Consideration of the Royal Society, so Termed," in *The Works of Isaac Penington*, vol. 3 (Glenside: 1996), 106–124.

Rediehs, Laura, *Quaker Epistemology* (Leiden: 2019).

Rediehs, Laura, "A Distinctive Quaker Theory of Knowledge: An Expanded Experiential Empiricism," *Quaker Studies* 21/1 (2016): 67–94.

Stevenson, Leslie, *Open to New Light: Quaker Spirituality in Historical and Philosophical Context* (Exeter: 2012).

Stevenson, Leslie, "Kant's Approach to Religion Compared with Quakerism," in *Kant and the New Philosophy of Religion*, eds. Chris L. Firestone and Stephen R. Palmquist (Bloomington: 2006), 210–229.

Stevenson, Leslie, "Kant's Philosophy and Quakerism," *The Friends Quarterly* 33/2 (2002): 85–92.

Wilmans, Carl Arnold, *De similitudine inter Mysticismum purum et Kantianam religionis doctrinam* (University of Halle doctoral dissertation: 1797).

Wood, Allen W., *Kant and Religion* (Oxford: 2020).

Wood, Allen W., *Kant's Ethical Thought* (Cambridge: 1999).

Wood, Allen W., "Translator's Introduction" to Kant's *Preface to Reinhold Bernhard Jachmann's* Examination of the Kantian Philosophy of Religion, in Immanuel Kant, *Religion and Rational Theology* (Cambridge, Eng.: 1996), 331.

CHAPTER 12

Radical Critics and Religious Enlighteners: The Cases of Edelmann and Kant

Anna Tomaszewska

1   Enlightenment and Religion

A well-entrenched *cliché* labels the Enlightenment an age of reason. An equally established narrative, especially strong on a part of the Protestant spectrum of religious traditions, questions the rational nature of religion and even regards religion as the opposite of reason. Against this background, the all too obvious question would be raised of how "enlightened values" can be reconciled with religious faith, if only such a reconciliation could be effected. Hence, some scholars, following Max Weber's diagnosis of modernity,[1] have featured the epoch as secular, that is, witnessing the unleash of processes leading to the diminishing of the influence of religion on individual lives (ethics) and to the separation between church and state (politics).[2] In a recent account, Margaret Jacob claims that "the Enlightenment was an eighteenth-century movement of ideas and practices that made the secular world its point of departure."[3] Yet this approach has repeatedly been challenged in favour of a picture showing the Enlightenment and religion as deeply intertwined.[4] The term "religious Enlightenment" has been coined, which captures the preoccupation

---

1   For the influence of Weber's theory of secularization on modern debates, in which the increase in "modernity and rationality" would be seen as conducive to the demise of religiosity, see Charles Taylor, *A Secular Age* (Cambridge, Mass.: 2007), 307.

2   An example of a narrative connecting secularization and rationalization, enriching the debate with the claim about the pivotal role of Spinoza in sparking the process, can be found in Jonathan I. Israel, *Radical Enlightenment: Philosophy and the Making of Modernity, 1650–1750* (Oxford: 2001).

3   Margaret C. Jacob, *The Secular Enlightenment* (Princeton: 2019), 1.

4   This intertwinement of the Enlightenment and religion is the subject of Jeffrey D. Burson's *The Culture of Enlightening. Abbé Claude Yvon and the Entangled Emergence of the Enlightenment* (Notre Dame: 2019). According to Burson, "theological debates over the nature of faith were the ironic origins of the Enlightenment, just as texts and debates produced by the Radical Enlightenment … were themselves deeply anchored in early modern theological disputation" (ibid., 25). See also Anton M. Matytsin and Dan Edelstein (eds.), *Let There Be Enlightenment. The Religious and Mystical Sources of Rationality* (Baltimore: 2018).

© KONINKLIJKE BRILL NV, LEIDEN, 2022 | DOI:10.1163/9789004523371_013

of the enlightened thinkers with topics from which the relation between the human being and transcendence would not be expunged.[5] According to David Sorkin, for example, "contrary to the secular master narrative ... modern culture also has religious roots,"[6] one of the reasons for this state of affairs being that the Enlightenment "made possible new iterations of faith."[7]

The categories of the secular and the religious Enlightenment essentially overlap with another distinction, which scholars have embraced following Jonathan Israel's seminal work, namely, the distinction between the radical and the moderate Enlightenment. Neither Jacob nor Israel in his more recent works presents the radical Enlightenment as inimical to *all* forms of religiosity, as they claim that it would make an exception for pantheism and some anti-Trinitarian Christian, or Socinian, doctrines,[8] yet like so many other authors in the field, they emphasize the radicals' criticism of those kinds of religion that would be considered politically pernicious, perpetuating alliance between church and state. In particular, the radical Enlightenment would target *revealed* religion, which it often associated with superstition, making space for a "true religion" originating in reason or reducible to rational activity – in contradistinction to the religious enlighteners acknowledging reason and revelation as equally legitimate sources of "true religion," and even willing to accept truths that transcend human comprehension and are thus called *supra rationem*.[9]

In this chapter, I intend to show that the boundaries between the radical enlighteners' approach to religion and the religious impulse in the Enlightenment – hence between the secularizing tendency, on the one hand, and the reformatory zeal, on the other – could occasionally be remarkably

---

5   See David Sorkin, *The Religious Enlightenment. Protestants, Jews, and Catholics from London to Vienna* (Princeton: 2008).

6   Ibid., 21.

7   Ibid., 3.

8   According to Jacob, pantheism, "although so profoundly secular in its orientation," relied on the imagery and idiom of mysticism. Margaret C. Jacob, *The Radical Enlightenment: Pantheists, Freemasons and Republicans* (London: 1981), 223. On the "alliance" between Spinozism and Socinianism, see Jonathan I. Israel, *A Revolution of the Mind. Radical Enlightenment and the Intellectual Origins of Modern Democracy* (Princeton: 2010), c. 1. On the connection between Spinoza and heterodox Christians (the so-called Collegiants), see Jonathan I. Israel, "Spinoza and Early Modern Theology," in *The Oxford Handbook of Early Modern Theology, 1600–1800*, eds. Ulrich L. Lehner, Richard A. Muller, and Anthony G. Roeber (New York: 2016), 577–593. For a critical appraisal of Leo Strauss's association of the radical Enlightenment with atheism, see Jonathan I. Israel, "Leo Strauss and the Radical Enlightenment," in *Reading between the Lines – Leo Strauss and the History of Early Modern Philosophy*, ed. Winfried Schröder (Berlin: 2015), 9–28.

9   John Locke provides an example of the "religious" *and* "enlightened" stance along these lines. See Diego Lucci, *John Locke's Christianity* (Cambridge: 2021).

thin or as much as blurred. This pertains to thinkers one could subsume under the broad category of religious rationalists.[10] Here I will study two such cases, representative of the German Enlightenment in its budding and declining stages, respectively: Johann Christian Edelmann (1698–1767) and Immanuel Kant (1724–1804). Though Edelmann enjoyed a reputation of the most radical Spinozist in Germany before Lessing[11] and Kant established a new method of philosophical criticism that was to ensure resistance to "materialism, fatalism, atheism" and "freethinking unbelief" (KrV, B xxxiv), widely associated with Spinoza at the time,[12] they share noteworthy commonalities when it comes to their reading of the Christian revelation, which suggests the influence of the Platonic, or Neoplatonic, tradition. In two subsequent sections, I will zoom in on their reinterpretation of one crucial element of the Christian doctrine, that is, the dogma of Incarnation, in order to bring these commonalities to the fore; before that, though, let us look at some more general features shared by the two thinkers.

Edelmann and Kant originated from a shared religious background, that is, pietism. This fact is telling insofar as the 18th century witnessed peculiar susceptibility of some religious reformers, dissatisfied with the turn taken by the Protestant Reformation, especially in the Lutheran Church, to the ideas of Spinoza. Frederick C. Beiser avers that "almost all the early Spinozists in Germany were the unhappy children of the Protestant Counter-Reformation ... bitterly disillusioned with the cause of the Reformation" which "had gone astray and betrayed its own principles."[13] One of the causes of their dissatisfaction was the growing institutionalization of faith and the tightening of the

---

10   For a brief description of the tendency and its adherents, see Ian Hunter, "Kant's *Religion* and Prussian Religious Policy," *Modern Intellectual History* 2/1 (2005): 11 and 14; Leszek Kołakowski, *Świadomość religijna i więź kościelna: studia nad chrześcijaństwem bezwyznaniowym XVII wieku* (Warsaw: 2009), 150.

11   Leo Bäck, *Spinozas erste Einwirkungen auf Deutschland* (Berlin: 1895), 35.

12   References to Spinoza's "atheism" are present throughout the early modern compendia such as Pierre Bayle's *Dictionnaire historique et critique* (Rotterdam: 1697) and Johann Anton Trinius' *Freydenker Lexicon* (Leipzig: 1759), where Spinoza is depicted as one who systematized and popularized the views of other "atheistic" authors, among them: Epicurus, Giordano Bruno, Lucretius, Petronius, Vanini, Hobbes, John Toland and the Socinians. Yet attributing atheism to an author would often have polemical purport, "atheism" being used as a smear word against one's ideological adversaries. This point is well illustrated by Jakob Friedrich Reimann's *Historia universalis atheismi et atheorum* (Hildesiae: 1725), which, apart from reputed freethinkers like "Casimir Lyszincki," "Adrianus Curbachius," "Matthias Knutzen" and "J.C. Wachterus," lists Christian authors such as Martin Luther and Nicolas Malebranche as suspected of advocating atheism.

13   Frederick C. Beiser, *The Fate of Reason. German Philosophy from Kant to Fichte* (Cambridge, Mass.: 1987), 50–1. See also Israel, "Spinoza and Early Modern Theology."

bonds between state and clerical authorities, the very same processes against which the early Lutherans rebelled as corrupting the Catholic Church. Both Edelmann and Kant were anti-clerical thinkers, though their critiques of the church would differ in scope and degree: while the former denied any positive role to the church, which he accused of perpetuating a false notion of God,[14] the latter construed the church as a form of the ethical community, yet without identifying the church thus conceived with any existing ecclesiastical institution. (For such an identification to be possible, a church would have to satisfy four criteria, as listed in *Religion within the Boundaries of Mere Reason*, namely, universality, purity, freedom, and unchangeableness (RGV, 6:101–2)). Undermining the role of the church as mediator between man and God implied the need to reconceive the divine as immediately accessible to the human being, somehow "present" in her heart, mind, reason, or conscience. Edelmann and Kant alike would locate the source of divinity in human reason. Yet, while the former identified reason with God "in us," the latter would ascribe divine-like characteristics to reason as legislator for morality, a move which comes most patently to the fore in his late unfinished project published as the *Opus postumum*.[15]

However, a concern arises with regard to an apparent disparity between Kant and Edelmann at a fundamental level, which may undermine the plausibility of comparing their ideas on religious matters. For, on the one side, there is an author of a comprehensive philosophical system underpinned by the critical method which aims to serve the investigation of the limits of human rational capacities. On the other side, we shall encounter a less prominent figure of a Protestant theologian, restless in his "constant search for the religious and spiritual foundations" and prone to succumb to paranoid mental states along the way.[16] Why should we consider these two figures jointly and in relation to each other? What would be the expected benefits of such a comparison?

---

14   Thus, for example, according to Edelmann, priests, whom he dubs "blind guides" (*blinde Leiter*), misleadingly instruct the faithful that God lives in "houses of stone or wood" and do not know the real God but "only serve a phantasy" (*dem Gedanken-Bilde*). Johann Christian Edelmann, *Die Göttlichkeit der Vernunft, in einer kurtzen Anweisung zu weiterer Untersuchung der ältesten und vornehmsten Bedeutung des Wortes ΛΟΓΟΣ* (Berleburg: 1742), 6 (all quotations from this work are in my translation – A.T.).

15   For more details on this move, see Anna Tomaszewska, "Kant's 'Deification' of Reason in the *Opus postumum*: An Attempt at Reconciling God and Autonomy," in *Perspectives on Kant's Opus postumum*, eds. Giovanni Pietro Basile and Ansgar Lyssy (New York: forthcoming).

16   Annegret Schaper, *Ein langer Abschied vom Christentum. Johann Christian Edelmann (1698–1767) und die deutsche Frühaufklärung* (Marburg: 1996), 151 (trans. A.T.).

The comparative strategy adopted in this chapter can be justified as follows. First, a reason related to the method of developing intellectual history can be adduced: studying "minor" or "background" figures, such as Edelmann, can be deemed to form part of the programme which Martin Mulsow has labelled "philosophical micro-history." This is a method of studying the history of ideas which seeks to derive the "big picture" from details of individuals' biographies against particular social and historical contexts.[17] We can thus learn more about the radical and the religious Enlightenment by investigating the intellectual activity of people like Edelmann. Second, there is an important historical-philosophical reason to make an attempt at comparing the two thinkers: Edelmann was among the first who set in motion the process of rationalizing religion that would find its apex in German Idealism a century later. He is therefore one of the founding fathers of the idea of secularization conceptualized by Georg Wilhelm Friedrich Hegel. According to Annegret Schaper, Edelmann's *Göttlichkeit der Vernunft* should be recognized as

> the first German work of the religiously motivated Enlightenment in the 18th century which occupied itself with collecting the etymological evidence of the notion of "*logos*" in various ecclesiastical as well as philosophical doctrines, and thereby in fact set in motion this new reception of Neoplatonism in the age of enlightenment, whose historical-philosophical development would culminate in the 19th century with Hegel's conception of the "world-spirit."[18]

Finally, there is the exegetical rationale behind the comparison at issue: reading Kant in light of Edelmann's ideas shall enable us to bring out the radical potential of Kantian thought, ignored by those who read it as offering conceptual means to defend Christianity against the secularizing tendencies of the Enlightenment.[19]

---

17   Martin Mulsow, *Moderne aus dem Untergrund. Radikale Frühaufklärung in Deutschland 1680–1720* (Hamburg: 2002), 29–30.

18   Schaper, *Ein langer Abschied*, 156 (trans. A.T.).

19   For an overview of "secular" and "religious" readings of Kant's account of religion, see Chris L. Firestone and Nathan Jacobs, *In Defense of Kant's Religion* (Bloomington: 2008), part 1.

2   The Divinity of Reason: Edelmann's Turn to Rational Religion

Behind Edelmann's critique of institutional religion, there might have been a personal motive: a failed attempt to earn a position in the Lutheran Church.[20] It could also be inspired by his acquaintance with some works of the Christian heterodoxy. Thus, the reading of Gottfried Arnold's *Kirchen- und Ketzerhistorie* shaped Edelmann's criticism of the church in *Unschuldige Wahrheiten* (1735– 1743),[21] while reading Spinoza's *Theological-Political Treatise* brought him to question the divine origin of Scripture in a three-volume dialogue between "Lichtlieb" and "Blindling" – the light-lover and the blind – published as *Moses mit aufgedeckten Angesichte* (1740). Edelmann's critique of religion, like Spinoza's, starts from biblical exegesis, and heavily relies on the text of the Bible, as is the case with *Die Göttlichkeit der Vernunft* (1742). The drafting of the latter would be prompted by the following course of events: In the late 1730s Edelmann joined the activities of a radical Pietist "Community of the Inspired," led by a self-proclaimed prophet, Johann Friedrich Rock. The Community, whose members claimed to have direct encounter with God, resided in Berleburg, where Edelmann moved to work on a translation of the Bible. He came into conflict with the Community, which triggered a spiritual crisis, to be overcome only by the discovery that "God is reason."

Die Göttlichkeit der Vernunft builds on the exegetical point that "Λογος" in the Prologue to John's Gospel should be rendered as "reason" (*Vernunft*), rather than "word" (*Wort*). The frontispiece of the 1742 edition of the work shows the following inscription:

> In the beginning was reason, and reason was with God
> and God was the reason. It was in the beginning with God:
> All things came into being through it
> and without it nothing would have come into being
> which has come into being.[22]

---

20   See Rüdiger Otto, "Johann Christian Edelmann's Criticism of the Bible and its Relation to Spinoza," in *Disguised and Overt Spinozism around 1700*, eds. Wiep van Bunge and Wim Klever (Leiden: 1996), 174.

21   Schaper, *Ein langer Abschied*, 154. For a comprehensive account of Edelmann's intellectual biography, see Walter Grossmann, *Johann Christian Edelmann. From Orthodoxy to Enlightenment* (The Hague: 1976); Walter Grossmann, "Johann Christian Edelmann's Idea of Jesus," *Harvard Theological Review* 60 (1967): 375–389; Otto, "Johann Christian Edelmann's Criticism of the Bible."

22   Edelmann, *Die Göttlichkeit der Vernunft*, frontispiece.

The mistranslation of "*Λογος*" around 180 AD by a group of theologians Edelmann labels "*Αλογη*" resulted in distorting the original message of Christianity[23] and facilitated, as he contends, the emergence of a power-thirsty caste of priests, perpetuating errors to their own benefit. Edelmann's story of the priestly fraud reflects a theme commonly addressed by the early modern critics of revealed religion, to be found for instance in John Toland's *Christianity Not Mysterious*,[24] and also echoes that lineage of religious criticism which advanced the "religion-as-imposture" thesis. To legitimate his critique of the clergy, Edelmann invokes early Christian authors who apparently shared his view on the biblical *Λογος*. The long list of these authors includes: Amelius, Justin Martyr, Athenagoras, Clement of Alexandria, Gregory of Nyssa, Origen, John Damascene, Dionysius the Areopagite, and Ignatius of Antioch; their translators and compilers such as Ambrosius Ferrarius and Isaac Casaubon; and the Renaissance humanist Marsilio Ficino. Anchoring his ideas to a respectable tradition, Edelmann launches an attack not just on the post-Nicene Christianity, but primarily on Lutheran theologians and ministers, whom he accuses of propagating spurious faith which relies on the senses and imagination – hence is immersed in the "darkness of the flesh"[25] – because they urge that reason should be subjugated, or "taken captive" (*gefangen nehmen*).[26] According to Edelmann, by equating God with "word," contingent upon the one who utters or otherwise employs it, the ecclesiastics created for themselves the possibility not only to use religion as an instrument of manipulating the ignorant many, but also to subordinate God to the institution of the church, its arbitrary rules and statutes; they thus invented a religion based on, and appealing to, their own imagination.[27]

---

23   Ibid., 22–3.

24   Drawing on the anti-clerical motive of religious criticism, Toland wrote: "Now their own Advantage being the Motive that put the Primitive Clergy upon reviving Mystery, they quickly erected themselves by its Assistance into a separate and politick Body." John Toland, *Christianity Not Mysterious: Or, a Treatise Shewing, That There Is Nothing in the Gospel Contrary to Reason, nor above It: and That No Christian Doctrine Can Be Properly Called a Mystery* (London: 1696), 166. On the source of the charge of imposture against religion, levelled by freethinkers, see Winfried Schröder, "The Charge of Religious Imposture in Late Antique Anti-Christian Authors and their Early Modern Readers," *Intellectual History Review* 28/1 (2018): 23–34.

25   Edelmann, *Die Göttlichkeit der Vernunft*, 21.

26   Ibid., 14. Cf. ibid., 157.

27   Cf. ibid., 37.

Edelmann contrasts the distant God living in "houses of stone or wood,"[28] a picture created by the ecclesiastics, with the "living God" in us – a phrase he uses throughout *Die Göttlichkeit der Vernunft* – who manifests, or reveals, himself in our own reason.[29] The claim about God "indwelling" our reason defines the position which Walter Grossmann has called rational spiritualism,[30] and which can be characterized thus: insofar as it manifests God "in us," reason testifies to the unity of our – human – essence with God. What makes us human beings is thus of divine nature and God "lives," that is, exists "in us" in the mode of reason. Due to our ontological unity with God, we also have direct epistemic access to the divine, that is, such access that does not require discursive cognition. Remarkably, though, Edelmann's metaphors of light and the sun, in which he refers to reason as the "sunbeam of justice" (*Strahl der Sonne der Gerechtigkeit*),[31] indicate that he does not construe God, or reason, as an object of cognition, but rather as the "medium," or the condition, of cognition and moral judgment. Clearly, Edelmann's metaphors strike a Platonic note, alluding to the analogy of the sun in Book 6 of *The Republic* (506e–509b),[32] but they also connect with various breeds of early modern mysticism instantiated by the doctrines of "inner light" and propagated by the Dutch Collegiants like Pieter Balling or by the English Quakers.[33] Since it is through our reason that we are united with God, Edelmann does not conceive of the *unio mystica* as an experience undergone by some and unavailable to others, or private. Rather, the unity with God must be universal, shared by all human beings with one another and even with Christ, who is therefore "our brother."[34] In other words, insofar as we are rational, we participate in universal revelation. Based on universal revelation, faith consists in obedience to reason, as do virtue and duty. "Obedience to reason," avers Edelmann, "was thus the faith of the first Christians."[35]

---

28   Ibid., 6.

29   On the "living God" (*der lebendige Gott*), see, e.g., ibid., 5, 15, 35, 82, 99.

30   Grossmann, "Johann Christian Edelmann's Idea of Jesus," 382.

31   Edelmann, *Die Göttlichkeit der Vernunft*, 68.

32   Plato, *Republic*, trans. C.D.C. Reeve (Indianapolis: 2004), 201–5.

33   On Balling and "inner light" mysticism, see Kołakowski, *Świadomość religijna i więź kościelna*, c. 3, sec. 9. On Quaker religiosity, see Leslie Stevenson, "Kant's Approach to Religion Compared with Quakerism," in *Kant and the New Philosophy of Religion*, eds. Chris L. Firestone and Stephen R. Palmquist (Bloomington: 2006), 210–229.

34   Edelmann, *Die Göttlichkeit der Vernunft*, 170.

35   Ibid., 146–7. The author attributes to Clement of Alexandria the idea that virtue demands that one subject one's "whole life" to reason.

Edelmann's conception of the universality of divine revelation implies the equality of all human beings with regard to faith, and so the eradication of not only interconfessional, but also interreligious differences. It also implies that the contents of the "true religion" cannot be determined by particular occurrences in time and space, that is, by historical revelation. Yet these consequences are not supposed to have anti-religious purport; on the contrary, they are aimed to reinforce the claim about the universality of the Christian faith. "Christians," says Edelmann, "did not begin to emerge in the world from today or yesterday onwards, but from the very beginning they have been everywhere and in all times."[36] Since there had been Christians before the appearance of Jesus, Christianity must have adopted guises delivered by different philosophical and religious traditions – and in fact, urges Edelmann, it did appear already under the guise of the philosophy of Plato:

> John and Plato would think identically about God, as we will learn below from Justin Martyr and in particular from Clement of Alexandria. For they knew well that God is not the God of the Jews and Christians alone, but also of the heathens, and that the external ceremonies of Christianity do not make up the main work of religion.[37]

If the content of the Christian faith is not provided by historical revelation, the question arises about Edelmann's interpretation of the doctrine of Incarnation constituting the core of (the orthodox) Christianity. Does his rational spiritualism allow any space for this doctrine? Moreover, what is the status of Jesus of Nazareth in Edelmann's view; in particular, can he consider Jesus to be God? Interestingly, a positive answer to the first question, albeit qualifiedly so, does not entail a similar answer to the second one: for while Edelmann offers a reinterpreted version of the dogma of Incarnation, he denies divinity to Jesus as a particular historical figure in the traditional (that is, post-Nicene) Christian sense in which he would be identified as a "God-man" and the "Son of God." We shall now investigate these two issues – the Incarnation and the status of Jesus – more closely.

Recall Edelmann's claim that God manifests himself in our own reason. Thus, if Jesus was a human being, he must have manifested the divine reason in his life – and indeed he did so in an admirable degree: "the living God revealed himself under no other name than that of reason in our brother

---

36   Ibid., 96.
37   Ibid., 26.

Jesus."[38] The Nazarene provides therefore the paradigm of a rational human being "in whose person the eternal reason, in all its fullness, has established an abode [for itself]."[39] What we share with Jesus is not only humanity, though, but both the human and the divine nature in which we equally participate. The Incarnation of God in the human being, if one may so put it, is thus universal. Precisely for this reason Jesus cannot be regarded as essentially distinct from other human beings and thus as the "Son of God." For there is no other "son" of the "living God," according to Edelmann, "than the divine reason, lasting in God and proceeding from God, which ... has revealed itself, full of grace and truth, not only in Christ, the firstborn of all creatures, but also in all his brothers."[40] Thus, the "Son of the Father" is identical with "his mind/ his reason/ his wisdom,"[41] and this is the proper meaning of "$\Lambda o\gamma o\varsigma$" in John's Gospel. Remarkably, some statements of Edelmann suggest that he thinks that the $\Lambda o\gamma o\varsigma$ constitutes not only the essence of human beings, but also the principle of all reality as such. For instance, he says: "the Son of God is nothing but the reason of the Father insofar as it discloses itself as visible and active in the shaping and generation of things ... For the Son of God is nothing but the mind and reason of the Father."[42]

In light of the foregoing, not only can we establish the existence of affinities between Pietist Edelmann and some Christian dissenters belonging to the "*cercle Spinoziste*," such as Jarig Jelles, the author of the preface to Spinoza's *Opera posthuma* (1677), in which he attempted to assimilate Spinoza's thought with Christianity,[43] but we can also explain Edelmann's vehement objection to trinitarian Christianity. Comparing the Trinity to a "three-headed beast" of ancient Pomeranians, Edelmann points out that Scripture stays silent about "three persons in a unique and undivided divine entity," which must then amount to no more than "a meaningless monstrosity of the priests."[44] His *Glaubens-Bekentniß* (1746), in which Edelmann puts together over a dozen theses about Jesus, only confirms this antitrinitarian agenda. Little wonder, then,

---

38   Ibid., 170.

39   Ibid., 99.

40   Ibid., 16–17.

41   Ibid., 135–6.

42   Ibid., 130.

43   Jelles equates Christ (that is, the "Son of God") with the divine $\Lambda o\gamma o\varsigma$ or wisdom. See his preface to: Benedict de Spinoza, *Opera posthuma* (Amsterdam: 1677), ***3. For an account of the views of "Spinoza's circle," see Henri Krop, "The Secularism of Spinoza and his Circle," in *The Sources of Secularism. Enlightenment and Beyond*, eds. Anna Tomaszewska and Hasse Hämäläinen (Cham: 2017), 71–99.

44   Edelmann, *Die Göttlichkeit der Vernunft*, 108–9.

that the edition[45] would be printed together with Johann Jacob Rambach's polemical essay against the Socinians, titled *Vindiciae satisfactionis Christi a frivolis accusationibus Catechismi Racoviensis* (1734).

Accordingly, in his 1746 book, Edelmann confesses belief in Jesus a "true man" who in all respects was endowed with human nature and properties.[46] Jesus, says Edelmann, differed from "others, his equals," only in this that he had received exceptional gifts and virtues from God, which is why he earned the name of Christ.[47] His disciples used this name to emphasize Jesus' excellence, in accordance with a Jewish custom. Jesus never referred to himself as the son of God, but rather as the son of man.[48] Moreover, when he called God his father, he did so in the same sense as we do when we turn to God as "our father," that is, metaphorically. For to think of God as having sons is to think of him in a pagan manner.[49] The main aim of Jesus was to bring unity among human beings, divided by dissenting opinions, and so to put an end to religious strife.[50] Jesus did not strive to establish a new institutional religion but wanted to ensure peace among people; for human beings are capable of inflicting harm upon each other but they cannot act against God.[51] This means that there is no need to restore the relation between human beings and God after the "fall of Adam," since the relation has never been truly broken. Yet Jesus deserved the name of saviour since he attempted to liberate people from the yoke of their desires.[52] He suffered ignominious death on the cross, because the clergy were concerned that he would turn the people against them and undermine the authority of ecclesiastical institutions.[53] Thus, the meaning of the crucifixion was principally political.

Edelmann confesses to believe that Jesus resurrected spiritually (*nach dem Geiste*) and would come again in the same spirit to "thousands of his witnesses" in his times as well as nowadays,[54] yet he declines to believe in the resurrection of Jesus in body (*nach dem Fleische*). To back his claims, he resorts – as usual – to biblical exegesis: Peter, he observes, who witnessed the events before and after Jesus' death, does not mention his bodily resurrection; on the

---

45   As available in the National Library of Sweden (Kungliga biblioteket) in Stockholm.
46   Johann Christian Edelmann, *Abgenöthigtes jedoch Andern nicht wieder aufgenöthigtes Glaubens-Bekentniß* (s.l.: 1746), 93.
47   Ibid., 101.
48   Ibid., 122–3.
49   Ibid., 136.
50   Ibid., 143.
51   Ibid., 147.
52   Ibid., 164.
53   Ibid., 182–3.
54   Ibid., 190.

contrary, he speaks about the teacher having risen in spirit. Apart from John, who reports the events in the third person, all three evangelists were no eyewitnesses of the death of Jesus. Besides, Edelmann goes on, stories about people rising from the dead, in the literal sense, can be found in earlier authors, such as Plato (in whom, according to Clement of Alexandria, we can find a report on the rising of Zoroaster), Herodotus (reporting on a "pious fraud" of a certain "Zamolride"[55]), and Theophilus (who adduces a story about Asclepius rising after being struck by a thunderbolt). All these supposedly miraculous events would be fabricated to deceive credulous masses into believing in supernatural powers of the protagonists of the events; and Christians could not be any worse in their methods of acquiring supporters.[56]

Edelmann rejects therefore the literal meaning of Resurrection but allows a kind of metaphorical interpretation of this Christian dogma. Thus, insofar as his claims are based on a certain reading of Scripture, he can be said to adhere to revealed religion, although his reading consists ultimately in adjusting revelation to reason. Accordingly, he abandons the suprarational sense of revelation, that is, the sense which the Christian orthodoxy would consider essential for their creed. The notion of religion advocated by Edelmann is then close to Spinozist in that he offers a thorough reinterpretation of the Bible along the lines of rationalist tenets and reduces religion to "living by the guidance of reason."[57] Yet is not Edelmann's account deflationary, rendering his idea of Christianity a mere cover-up for a patently atheistic position?

What this question suggests may seem plausible only if we abstract from the context in which the account was developed. But Edelmann's thought, as Grossmann points out, is embedded in the tradition of radical Protestantism.[58] Rüdiger Otto also emphasizes the theological bent of this thought.[59] It is after all noteworthy that Edelmann justifies most of his startlingly heterodox conceptions by invoking passages from the Bible. Reading a heterodox position as promoting an atheist agenda would require, as Winfried Schröder has noted, that an interpreter deny to take an author's claims at face value; yet such an

---

55   As the index and the register of printing errors evidence, though, Edelmann means to
        refer to Zamolxis, a Geto-Dacian divinity.
56   Edelmann, *Glaubens-Bekentniß*, 191–6.
57   Spinoza's definition of religion runs thus: "Whatever we desire and do, whereof we are the
        cause insofar as we know God, I refer to Religion [*religio*]. The desire to do good which
        derives from our living by the guidance of reason, I call Piety [*pietas*]." Baruch Spinoza,
        "Ethics," in *Complete Works* (Indianapolis: 2002), 339.
58   Grossmann, "Johann Christian Edelmann's Idea of Jesus," 378–9.
59   Otto, "Johann Christian Edelmann's Criticism of the Bible," 188.

approach makes room for possible misinterpretations.[60] Arguably, conflating heterodoxy with atheism, one may fail to recognize what actually makes for the special character of a heterodox position; one also risks employing the term "atheism" in a polemical rather than descriptive fashion, characteristic of religious apologists committed to a strictly confessional point of view.

3   The Prototype and Jesus: Kant's Rationalization of the
       Christian Dogma

Unlike Edelmann, Kant did not attempt to speak as a theologian but, as he makes clear in his reply to Frederick William II, later added to the preface to *The Conflict of the Faculties*, as a philosopher – a theorist of natural reason – who only "cite[s] some biblical texts to corroborate certain purely rational teachings in religion" (SF, 7:8). Kant would not aim to prove that Christianity is a rational and universal religion; rather, less boldly, he sought to show that many, if not most, of the Christian tenets can be made compatible with the "religion of reason" (RGV, 6:12–13). Yet, this subtle difference notwithstanding, Kant's philosophical (re)interpretation of Christianity takes him close to the picture advocated by the radical Pietist from Berleburg. As we shall see, also Kant provides arguments against equating the historical Jesus with the "Son of God," and thereby thwarts the possibility of accommodating Incarnation within his rational religion. Moreover, Kant's rendering of the "Son of God" as a symbol of moral regeneration available to the human being insofar as she participates in the idea of moral perfection – the "prototype of a humanity well-pleasing to God" (RGV, 6:119) – reveals distinct Platonic (or Neoplatonic) overtones.

In the second preface to the *Religion*, Kant explains his method of the philosophical investigation of religion, illustrated by a metaphor of two concentric circles. This method involves two steps. First, a revealed religion becomes divested of its historical, empirical, and therefore contingent elements, to see whether at the "core" of the religion, represented by the "inner circle," something can be found to which one may attribute a purely rational origin. Second, it is checked whether the "outer circle," representing the historical parts of religion, does not "lead back to the same pure rational system of religion" when considered in light of "moral concepts" (RGV, 6:12). Thus, the method of Kant's critical philosophy of religion consists essentially in an attempt to unearth the

---

60   See Winfried Schröder, *Ursprünge des Atheismus: Untersuchungen zur Metaphysik- und Religionskritik des 17. und 18. Jahrhunderts* (Stuttgart: 2012), 21–44.

rational *foundations* of religion and to translate the elements of historical revelation into the concepts of "pure moral faith" (RGV, 6:112).

The results of the application of the method emerge in Part Four of Kant's *Religionsschrift*. In a section titled "The Christian Religion as Natural Religion," invoking an association with Jesus, Kant writes of a teacher that "was the first to advocate a pure and compelling religion" and "made this universal religion of reason the supreme and indispensable condition of each and every religious faith" (RGV, 6:158). Then, he adduces passages from the Gospel of Matthew which supposedly corroborate the unity between revelation and rational faith. Concluding the section, he translates the Great Commandment into the idiom of the "universal religion of reason," formulating the following injunctions: "Do your duty from no other incentive except the unmediated appreciation of duty itself" and "Love every one as yourself, i.e. promote his welfare from an unmediated good will, one not derived from selfish incentives" (RGV, 6:160–1). Echoing Hermann Samuel Reimarus' critique of the figure of Jesus as the purported Christian messiah,[61] Kant denies the need for miracles to certify the truth of religion (RGV, 6:162) which the "divinely disposed teacher" (RGV, 6:65) is supposed to have introduced in the world, since the religion has purely rational credentials. In the teacher, he avers, we can recognize the "founder of the first true church," but not "the *founder* of the *religion* which, free from every dogma, is inscribed in the heart of all human beings" (RGV, 6:159). Historical revelation, as embodied in the story of Jesus of Nazareth, can thus serve as an instrument of introducing rational religion – an *ancilla* of reason – provided that it has been purified from its suprarational residue, such as miracles.

However, the core of Christianity as revealed religion contains a doctrine "above reason" (*supra rationem*). This is the doctrine of Jesus the "Son of God" as "messiah" sent by his "Father" to restore the relation between God and humanity, damaged after the "fall of Adam" which symbolizes the original choice of evil by the human being, consisting in disobedience to the divine lawgiver. What is suprarational in this doctrine is the idea that God adopted human nature and, in the person of Jesus Christ, sacrificed himself for the sins

---

61   Charles Voysey (ed.), *Fragments from Reimarus Consisting of Brief Critical Remarks on the Object of Jesus and his Disciples as Seen in the New Testament* (London: 1879). For a comparison of Kant's and Reimarus' ideas on revealed religion, see Manfred Kuehn, "Kant's Jesus," in: *Kant's Religion within the Boundaries of Mere Reason. A Critical Guide*, ed. Gordon E. Michalson (Cambridge: 2014), 156–174. Kuehn claims that Kant approximates the "Neologists," a group of German enlightened theologians who sought to "empty" revealed religion "of all historical content and to fill it with purely rational content instead." Ibid., 157.

of humanity. In line with Kant's method, to show the compatibility of Christian revelation with the religion of reason would require a "translation" of this core doctrine into the language of pure moral faith. Indeed, much of the idiom Kant uses in Part Two of the *Religion* suggests that he attempts to carry out the translation, and a number of commentators who have subscribed to the "*Religion* – as – Translation" thesis have also recognized a rationalized version of Christ's vicarious atonement in Kant's doctrine of the "prototype" of morally perfect humanity.[62] For, without mentioning Jesus by name, Kant employs descriptions which would originally refer to Jesus and which could be found in John's Gospel and the Nicene Creed, such as "God's only-begotten Son" (RGV, 6:60), "'the *Word*' (the *Fiat!*) through which all other things are, and without whom nothing that is made would exist" (ibid.), one who "has *come down* to us from heaven" and "taken up humanity" (RGV, 6:61), and in whom "'God loved the world'" (RGV, 6:60). Yet, while Kant associates these expressions with "the prototype of moral disposition in its entire purity" (RGV, 6:61) and "the good and pure disposition" (RGV, 6:70–1), he does not attribute divinity to the figure he calls the "teacher of the Gospel" (e.g. RGV, 6:128, 134, 162, 195, 201) or the "teacher of the one and only religion" (RGV, 6:85), in which we can identify the *historical* Jesus. This is to say that he does not equate Jesus with the prototype, which means that eventually he fails to "rationalize" the Incarnation.

Kant's rationale for not attributing divine nature to the teacher of morality is twofold: epistemic and moral. The former draws on the phenomenon of "moral opacity," that is, the fact that we are capable of determining with certainty neither the moral character of another person nor even our own character (cf. RGV, 6:63). Since "outer experience yields no example adequate to the idea" of a morally perfect human being, which "always resides only in reason," none of the witnesses of the actions of Jesus could legitimately claim that the Nazarene instantiated the *ideal* of moral perfection in his life, even if they were entitled to an inference to the moral disposition of Jesus, "though not with strict certainty" (RGV, 6:63). Additionally, for some contemporary readers of the Christian Scriptures, this certainty could be undermined by popular kinds of religious criticism: the story of Jesus as one of the three "impostors" (the other two being Moses and Muhammad) or Reimarus' "Wolfenbüttel Fragments" depicting Jesus as a teacher of morality whose agenda, overall innocuous, was

---

62   See, for example, Otfried Höffe, "Holy Scriptures within the Boundaries of Mere Reason: Kant's Reflections," in *Kant's* Religion within the Boundaries of Mere Reason. *A Critical Guide*, 15; Firestone and Jacobs, *In Defense of Kant's* Religion, 48; Lawrence R. Pasternack, *Kant on* Religion within the Boundaries of Mere Reason (London: 2014), 6.

exploited by the apostles with a view to political gain.[63] Furthermore, attributing divinity to the historical Jesus would only result in mounting "mysteries": for apart from being unable to explain the presence of the "prototype" in our reason, we would also be unable to explain the existence of such a "God-man" (SF, 7:39; cf. RGV, 6:63).

Kant's moral argument challenging the doctrine of Incarnation highlights the practical irrelevance of the doctrine. Accordingly, regarding the nature of a figure like Jesus, Kant avers:

> Not that we would ... absolutely deny that he might also be a supernaturally begotten human being. But, from a practical point of view any such presupposition is of no benefit to us, since the prototype which we see embedded in this apparition must be sought in us as well (though natural human beings).
>
> RGV, 6:63–4

The existence of a "supernaturally begotten human being" cannot have practical purport because we are not to be motivated by an *empirical* instantiation of moral perfection – should such an instantiation be anyhow cognitively available to us – but by the very idea of moral perfection which we can discover in our reason. To demand that such an instantiation be provided, according to Kant, testifies to "moral unbelief" (RGV, 6:63), an attitude in which one denies necessarily binding force to the moral law and requires additional incentives to be able to follow it. Thus, should we approximate the moral ideal only if it were exemplified by an existing agent, the moral disposition embodied by the ideal as such would turn out to have no compelling motivational force for us and following the ideal – as well as morality in general – would be conditional upon contingent facts.

By declining to identify the prototype with the historical Jesus, Kant may seem to endorse a position analogous to Edelmann's, which has been dubbed rational spiritualism. The key tenet of this position, as we have seen, is that due to our rationality we have direct access to, or a relation with, God. Edelmann rejects external mediators in the relation. In one of the opening passages of *Die Göttlichkeit der Vernunft*, he addresses the reader thus: "Do you not know that you are the temple of God and that you can find this Lord, invisible to the external animal eyes, as close as in yourself?"[64] The kind of universal Christianity that Edelmann promotes can – and indeed should – do without any external

---

63   Cf. footnote 61. See also Winfried Schröder, "The Charge of Religious Imposture."
64   Edelmann, *Die Göttlichkeit der Vernunft*, 6.

signs or symbols of the divine as belonging to the repository of the spurious faith based on the senses and imagination. Kant, however, does not recommend abandoning external signs and symbols in religion altogether: due to "a peculiar weakness of human nature" (RGV, 6:103), recourse to sensibility, also in the religion of reason, remains indispensable. According to Allen Wood, for example, on Kant's account of religion, symbols are requisite to make the contents of ideas cognitively accessible to us: a symbol is what "gives us experiential access to what it symbolizes."[65] Thus, Kant's point in the argument for the practical irrelevance of Incarnation is not that the historical Jesus of Christian revelation can be dispensed with as of no value to rational religion, but rather that it is not the empirical representation of the moral ideal that provides the right kind of motivation for our actions. In other words, Jesus cannot motivate us to strive for moral perfection, but he can provide, as it were, an occasional cause for us to be motivated by the ideal itself.

As much as Edelmann, though, Kant suggests that we share our human nature with the moral teacher; the historical Jesus was "one of us," even if his conduct manifested a better disposition than the disposition which could be attributed to the vast majority of human beings. If he were divine, says Kant, he "could *not* be presented to us as an example to be emulated" (RGV, 6:64). Mired in radical evil, we could not hope to be able to strive for the moral ideal, should it be necessary to be God in order to follow it. Therefore, the doctrine of Incarnation, if construed as a constituent element of faith, rules out the possibility of moral progress. This must then be the case with the orthodox Christianity, too.

Kant's distinction between the prototype of morally perfect humanity and the historical Jesus mirrors the Platonic distinction between the ideal and the empirical, and the absence of the accommodation of Incarnation within his rational religion seems to have Platonic (or Neoplatonic) underpinnings, analogous to those which can be uncovered in Edelmann's account. According to Christopher Firestone and Nathan Jacobs, with his conception of the prototype that "resides in our morally-legislative reason" (RGV, 6:62), Kant represents a position which can be called "transcendental Platonism."[66] For the way in which he describes the prototype approximates his construal of the Platonic idea. In Pölitz lecture notes, for instance, he states:

---

65   Allen W. Wood, *Kant and Religion* (New York: 2020), 151. Cf. Kant's remarks on "a *schematism of analogy*" in RGV, 6:65.

66   Firestone and Jacobs, *In Defense of Kant's* Religion, 157–164.

> The term *idea* ... signifies a concept of reason insofar as no possible expe-
> rience can ever be adequate to it. Plato thought of the divine ideas as
> the archetypes of things, according to which these things are established,
> although, to be sure, they are never posited as adequate to the divine
> idea. For example, God's idea of the human being, as archetype, would be
> the most perfect idea of the most perfect human being. Particular indi-
> viduals, as particular human beings, would be formed in accord with this
> idea, but never in such a way that they completely correspond to it.
>
> v-Phil-Th/Pölitz, 28:1058–9

As we have seen, Kant features the prototype as an idea which no outer experience can yield an adequate example to (cf. RGV, 6:63). The reason why experience cannot be identical with an idea, in Kant's view, can be found in his
Orientation essay (1786), where he claims that "the *concept* of God" which "can
be met with only in reason ... must serve to *gauge*" whether what presents itself
to us as divine revelation satisfies "the characteristics required for a Deity"
(WDO, 8:142; italics A.T.). A rational concept, such as the prototype, provides
a standard by means of which empirical instantiations of the concept can be
assessed (cf. v-Phil-Th/Pölitz, 28:993–4 and KrV, A 315/B 372); it must therefore
be constitutively prior to a particular instantiation. The historical Jesus cannot
be identical with the prototype of morally perfect humanity because recognizing Jesus' moral disposition presupposes the "presence" of the prototype in our
reason. In other words, the standard by means of which an experience can be
assessed cannot derive from experience.

Yet it can be objected that the argument from criterion, while establishing
that an idea must be independent from, and prior to, its empirical instantiation, does not suffice to establish that an empirical object cannot adequately
correspond to the idea. Jesus as the "Son of God" might have been the only
existing morally perfect human being. Why would Kant not endorse this
option? The answer, it seems to me, lies in an underlying Platonic assumption,
namely, the conviction that only ideas, and not empirical objects, can embody
(the maximum degree of) perfection. This assumption does not invalidate
Kant's injunction that we accomplish the morally flawless disposition on our
own: for he emphasizes that "it is our universal human duty to *elevate* ourselves
to this ideal of moral perfection" (RGV, 6:61) and that "we *ought* to conform to
it" (RGV, 6:62). This idiom suggests, quite explicitly, that empirical objects – or
finite human beings – may, according to Kant, assimilate themselves to, or imi-
tate, the rational idea, rather than become identical with it.

However, an objection to the above "Platonic" reading of the prototype might
also be raised, and that along the following lines: Whereas Kant construes the

prototype as an idea in our moral-practical reason – the contents of which we are aware of as long as we are moral agents – he conceives of Plato's ideas as archetypes in *God's* mind, emphasizing that they "flowed from the highest reason, through which human reason partakes in them" (KrV, A 313/B 370). Accordingly, whereas for Plato ideas are independent of the human mind, for Kant the existence of the moral ideal hinges on the existence of the human mind. Yet there are exegetical reasons to think that Kant considers the prototype, too, independent of the human mind: for he contends that "we are not its authors" and that "the idea has ... established itself in the human being without our comprehending how human nature could have ever been receptive of it" (RGV, 6:61). Hence, we "discover" the prototype in us, as given together with our moral awareness, instead of creating this idea.

Still, though, one may notice that whereas for Kant the prototype is immediately given to us in our morally legislative reason, he denies any cognitive access to divine archetypes. In a note on "philosophical enthusiasm" he clearly rejects the vision of ideas in God, whereby such archetypes would be made available to us (cf. HN, 18:437–8). Does he then, in Part Two of the *Religion*, fall into the trap of dogmatic thinking, which he would earlier criticize? To address this worry, it suffices to point out that Kant's critique of Plato ranges over the area of theoretical philosophy, whereas the conception of the prototype belongs into moral-practical considerations. This is consistent with the critical project which allows investigating the ideas of reason without positing the existence of their objects. The ideas are real but in the practical sense, that is, as furnishing the constituents of our rationality and enabling us to exercise our moral agency. The prototype, in particular, is to motivate us to struggle against our innate, though self-incurred, propensity to evil.

Finally, from this practical-philosophical perspective, there is a sense in which Kant himself can be attributed the view that we "intuit ourselves in God," which he ascribes to Plato and later, in the *Opus postumum*, to Spinoza (OP, 22:56). The phrase "to intuit oneself in God" suggests the awareness of the presence of the archetype of a human being in the divine mind. Given Kant's conception of God in which God is defined as "the moral law itself, as it were, but thought as personified" (v-Phil-Th/Pölitz, 28:1075–6), the archetype of a human being in the divine mind can be envisaged as humanity "desired" by God – a being embodying the moral law – that is, as "a humanity well-pleasing to God" (RGV, 6:119). Put otherwise, when we "intuit ourselves in God," we reflect on human nature from the divine perspective (recall Spinoza's *sub specie aeternitatis*),[67] that is, as "morally good, and ... we find in God the uncreated

---

67   Cf. Spinoza, "Ethics," 376–8.

exemplar of perfect humanity."[68] Conceiving of ourselves from the viewpoint of an entity embodying the moral law – or, less metaphorically, seeing ourselves in light of the moral law – we become aware of the human *telos*. Thus, vision in God in the practical-philosophical sense amounts to a metaphor of our awareness of the requirements that human nature imposes on us insofar as it is considered a moral nature.

4   Concluding Remarks

The above-outlined ways of reinterpreting Incarnation, which would require debarring suprarational elements from this pivotal Christian doctrine, may evince some influence of ideas that can be traced back to Spinoza who defined religious faith in terms of "living by the guidance of reason." Yet, while Spinoza has been predominantly associated with the origins of the radical Enlightenment,[69] bringing about religious criticism and a "package" of secular ideas,[70] none of the thinkers discussed above would explicitly promote an anti-religious agenda. Rather, in the spirit of the "religious Enlightenment," they ventured a "reform" of religion along rationalist lines. Do the examples of these thinkers show the inadequacy of the opposition between the secular and the religious in relation to the Enlightenment; or that the categories of the radical and the moderate Enlightenment are in the end semantically empty? Regardless of how these questions are answered, they point to the complex nature of the relation between the Enlightenment and religion. I shall conclude by illustrating this complexity in three remarks concerning the relation at issue.

1)   Spinoza's influence on religion in the "age of lights" reaches further than merely inspiring radical critics of religion, like Theodor Ludwig Lau,[71] Friedrich Wilhelm Stosch[72] and John Toland.[73] His ideas would also spark changes in Christian orthodoxy itself. According to Walter Sparn,

---

68   Firestone and Jacobs, *In Defense of Kant's* Religion, 163. Cf. Wood, *Kant and Religion*, 126–7.

69   Sorkin, *The Religious Enlightenment*, 4.

70   Jonathan I. Israel, *Enlightenment Contested. Philosophy, Modernity, and the Emancipation of Man, 1670–1752* (New York: 2006), 866. See also: Jacob, *The Secular Enlightenment*, Prologue.

71   Bäck, *Spinozas erste Einwirkungen*, 67.

72   Ibid., 56.

73   Ian Leask, "Toland, Spinoza and the Naturalisation of Scripture," in *Ireland and the Reception of the Bible: Social and Cultural Studies*, eds. Brad Anderson and Jonathan Kearney (London: 2018), 227–241.

"it is exactly in confrontation with Spinoza that the Protestant orthodoxy arrived at the limits of its capacities. This confrontation with Spinoza belongs to the most important processes that brought this orthodoxy to its historical end ..."[74] Spinoza helped to bring back into focus such pillars of Protestantism as reliance on Scripture as the source of religious instruction, perused by an individual mind endowed with "natural light," and the immediacy of the relation between human beings and God. We have found both aspects of the Protestant doctrine in Edelmann and Kant. The former would read the Bible as a theologian and a "searching" believer, the latter – as a philosopher who embarked on the project of a critique of reason. Also, whereas Edelmann believes that God reveals himself to us directly through our own reason, Kant endorses the conception of rational revelation – "a revelation (though not an empirical one) permanently taking place within all human beings" (RGV, 6:122), which "must *precede all other* revelation and serve for the estimation of outer revelation ..." (V-Phil-Th/Pölitz, 28:1117). Briefly, like Spinoza, both thinkers claim that it is our rationality that takes us closer to God.

2) There might be a sense, though, in which the work of Kant and Edelmann alike can be read as promoting an anti-religious agenda. This sense emerges from Leo Strauss' description of the radical Enlightenment as "the critique of Revelation" originating in Greek antiquity, in particular, among the Epicureans.[75] Although I have been arguing for Platonic, and not Epicurean, overtones manifesting themselves in the thought of these two protagonists of the German Enlightenment, both Kant and Edelmann engage in a critique of *revealed* religion. As we have seen, they venture to purify Christianity from the kind of *supra rationem* dogmas that are best represented by the doctrine of Incarnation. However, on Strauss' construal, which establishes a stark opposition between reason and faith – between Athens and Jerusalem, to draw on the title of one of Strauss' works – rational religion might have constituted a covert attempt at smuggling atheism. The problem with this construal – apart from its buying into the polemical strategy of the orthodox against religious heterodoxy and demanding that we do not take claims made by early modern authors at face value – is that it seems to contentiously narrow

---

74 Walter Sparn, "Formalis Atheus? Die Krise der protestantischen Orthodoxie, gespiegelt in ihrer Auseinandersetzung mit Spinoza," in *Spinoza in der Frühzeit seiner religiösen Wirkung*, eds. Karlfried Gründer and Wilhelm Schmidt-Biggemann (Heidelberg: 1984), 29 (trans. A.T.).

75 Leo Strauss, *Spinoza's Critique of Religion* (New York: 1982), 35–52.

religion to those of its expressions that come close to various forms of fideism or even religious fundamentalism. If religion as such stands in opposition to reason, then any attempt to rationalize a religion will be regarded as an advocacy of unbelief, even if disguised in religious idiom.

3) From yet another angle, the source of the secularizing impulse may lie elsewhere than the anti-religious agenda defining the critique of revelation according to Strauss. Namely, it may accompany the reformatory intent emerging within or alongside the Christian tradition itself.[76] Dislodging the dogmatic foundations of Christianity, as well as detaching Christianity from the institutional framework in which it had thus far been entrenched, was the price Edelmann was ready to pay for rendering Christianity a universal religion. Kant would also pay this price for showing that the unity between reason and faith is possible – and that without turning reason into an *ancilla theologiae*. Secularization would thus be an inevitable by-product of a religious reform that both thinkers seem to have had in view and which would eventually consist in devising a new enlightened religion.

Acknowledgments

The work on this chapter has been subsidized by a grant from the National Science Centre in Poland, no. UMO-2018/31/B/HS1/02050, funding the research project *Between Secularization and Reform. Religious Rationalism in the Late 17th Century and in the Enlightenment*, at the Institute of Philosophy of the Jagiellonian University in Kraków. I would like to thank Hasse Hämäläinen for his helpful comments on an earlier draft of this chapter.

References

Bäck, Leo, *Spinozas erste Einwirkungen auf Deutschland* (Berlin: 1895).

Bayle, Pierre, *Dictionnaire historique et critique* (Rotterdam: 1697).

Beiser, Frederick C., *The Fate of Reason. German Philosophy from Kant to Fichte* (Cambridge Mass.: 1987).

---

76 For a sociological argument supporting the claim about the Christian roots of secularization, see Graeme Smith, "Talking to Ourselves: An Investigation into the Christian Ethics Inherent in Secularism," in *The Sources of Secularism*, 229–244.

Burson, Jeffrey D., *The Culture of Enlightening. Abbé Claude Yvon and the Entangled Emergence of the Enlightenment* (Notre Dame: 2019).

Edelmann, Johann Christian, *Abgenöthigtes jedoch Andern nicht wieder aufgenöthigtes Glaubens-Bekentniß* (s.l.: 1746).

Edelmann, Johann Christian, *Die Göttlichkeit der Vernunft, in einer kurtzen Anweisung zu weiterer Untersuchung der ältesten und vornehmsten Bedeutung des Wortes ΛΟΓΟΣ* (Berleburg: 1742).

Firestone, Chris L., and Nathan Jacobs, *In Defense of Kant's Religion* (Bloomington: 2008).

Grossmann, Walter, *Johann Christian Edelmann. From Orthodoxy to Enlightenment* (The Hague: 1976).

Grossmann, Walter, "Johann Christian Edelmann's Idea of Jesus," *Harvard Theological Review* 60 (1967): 375–389.

Höffe, Otfried, "Holy Scriptures within the Boundaries of Mere Reason: Kant's Reflections," in *Kant's Religion within the Boundaries of Mere Reason. A Critical Guide*, ed. Gordon E. Michalson (Cambridge, Eng.: 2014), 10–30.

Hunter, Ian, "Kant's *Religion* and Prussian Religious Policy," *Modern Intellectual History* 2/1 (2005): 1–27.

Israel, Jonathan I., "Spinoza and Early Modern Theology," in *The Oxford Handbook of Early Modern Theology, 1600–1800*, eds. Ulrich L. Lehner, Richard A. Muller and Anthony G. Roeber (New York: 2016), 577–593.

Israel, Jonathan I., "Leo Strauss and the Radical Enlightenment," in *Reading between the Lines – Leo Strauss and the History of Early Modern Philosophy*, ed. Winfried Schröder (Berlin: 2015), 9–28.

Israel, Jonathan I., *A Revolution of the Mind. Radical Enlightenment and the Intellectual Origins of Modern Democracy* (Princeton: 2010).

Israel, Jonathan I., *Enlightenment Contested. Philosophy, Modernity, and the Emancipation of Man 1670–1752* (New York: 2006).

Israel, Jonathan I., *Radical Enlightenment: Philosophy and the Making of Modernity, 1650–1750* (Oxford: 2001).

Jacob, Margaret C., *The Secular Enlightenment* (Princeton: 2019).

Jacob, Margaret C., *The Radical Enlightenment: Pantheists, Freemasons and Republicans* (London: 1981).

Kant, Immanuel, *Notes and Fragments* (Cambridge, Eng.: 2005) (HN, 14–23; Refl, 14–19).

Kant, Immanuel, *Critique of Pure Reason* (Cambridge, Eng.: 1998) (KrV, A/B).

Kant, Immanuel, "Groundwork of the Metaphysics of Morals," in *Practical Philosophy* (Cambridge, Eng.: 1996), 37–108 (GMS, 4).

Kant, Immanuel, "What Does It Mean to Orient Oneself in Thinking?" in *Religion and Rational Theology* (Cambridge, Eng.: 1996), 1–18 (WDO, 8).

Kant, Immanuel, "Religion within the Boundaries of Mere Reason," in *Religion and Rational Theology* (Cambridge, Eng.: 1996), 39–215 (RGV, 6).

Kant, Immanuel, "The Conflict of the Faculties," in *Religion and Rational Theology* (Cambridge, Eng.: 1996), 233–327 (SF, 7).

Kant, Immanuel, "Lectures on the Philosophical Doctrine of Religion," in *Religion and Rational Theology* (Cambridge, Eng.: 1996), 335–451 (V-Phil-Th/Pölitz, 28).

Kant, Immanuel, *Opus postumum* (Cambridge, Eng.: 1993) (OP, 21–22).

Kołakowski, Leszek, *Świadomość religijna i więź kościelna: studia nad chrześcijaństwem bezwyznaniowym XVII wieku* (Warsaw: 2009).

Krop, Henri, "The Secularism of Spinoza and his Circle," in *The Sources of Secularism. Enlightenment and Beyond*, eds. Anna Tomaszewska and Hasse Hämäläinen (Cham: 2017), 71–99.

Kuehn, Manfred, "Kant's Jesus," in *Kant's* Religion within the Boundaries of Mere Reason. *A Critical Guide*, ed. Gordon E. Michalson (Cambridge: 2014), 156–174.

Leask, Ian, "Toland, Spinoza and the Naturalisation of Scripture," in *Ireland and the Reception of the Bible: Social and Cultural Studies*, eds. Brad Anderson and Jonathan Kearney (London: 2018), 227–241.

Lucci, Diego, *John Locke's Christianity* (Cambridge, Eng.: 2021).

Matytsin, Anton M., and Dan Edelstein (eds.), *Let There Be Enlightenment. The Religious and Mystical Sources of Rationality* (Baltimore: 2018).

Mulsow, Martin, *Moderne aus dem Untergrund. Radikale Frühaufklärung in Deutschland 1680–1720* (Hamburg: 2002).

Otto, Rüdiger, "Johann Christian Edelmann's Criticism of the Bible and its Relation to Spinoza," in *Disguised and Overt Spinozism around 1700*, eds. Wiep van Bunge and Wim Klever (Leiden: 1996), 171–188.

Pasternack, Lawrence R., *Kant on* Religion within the Boundaries of Mere Reason (London: 2014).

Plato, *Republic*, trans. C.D.C. Reeve (Indianapolis: 2004).

Reimann, Jakob Friedrich, *Historia universalis atheismi et atheorum* (Hildesiae: 1725).

Schaper, Annegret, *Ein langer Abschied vom Christentum. Johann Christian Edelmann (1698–1767) und die deutsche Frühaufklärung* (Marburg: 1996).

Schröder, Winfried, *Ursprünge des Atheismus: Untersuchungen zur Metaphysik- und Religionskritik des 17. und 18. Jahrhunderts* (Stuttgart: 2012).

Schröder, Winfried, "The Charge of Religious Imposture in Late Antique Anti-Christian Authors and their Early Modern Readers," *Intellectual History Review* 28/1 (2018): 23–34.

Smith, Graeme, "Talking to Ourselves: An Investigation into the Christian Ethics Inherent in Secularism," in *The Sources of Secularism: Enlightenment and Beyond*, eds. Anna Tomaszewska and Hasse Hämäläinen (Cham: 2017), 229–244.

Sorkin, David, *The Religious Enlightenment. Protestants, Jews, and Catholics from London to Vienna* (Princeton: 2008).

Sparn, Walter, "Formalis Atheus? Die Krise der protestantischen Orthodoxie, gespiegelt in ihrer Auseinandersetzung mit Spinoza," in *Spinoza in der Frühzeit seiner religiösen Wirkung*, eds. Karlfried Gründer and Wilhelm Schmidt-Biggemann (Heidelberg: 1984).

Spinoza, Benedict de, "Ethics," in *Complete Works*, trans. Samuel Shirley (Indianapolis: 2002), 213–382.

Spinoza, Benedict de, *Opera posthuma* (Amsterdam: 1677).

Stevenson, Leslie, "Kant's Approach to Religion Compared with Quakerism," in *Kant and the New Philosophy of Religion*, eds. Chris L. Firestone and Stephen R. Palmquist (Bloomington: 2006), 210–229.

Strauss, Leo, *Spinoza's Critique of Religion*, trans. Elsa M. Sinclair (New York: 1982).

Taylor, Charles, *A Secular Age* (Cambridge, Mass.: 2007).

Toland, John, *Christianity Not Mysterious: Or, a Treatise Shewing, That There Is Nothing in the Gospel Contrary to Reason, nor above It: and That No Christian Doctrine Can Be Properly Called a Mystery* (London: 1696).

Tomaszewska, Anna, "Kant's 'Deification' of Reason in the *Opus postumum*: An Attempt at Reconciling God and Autonomy," in *Perspectives on Kant's Opus postumum*, eds. Giovanni Pietro Basile and Ansgar Lyssy (New York: forthcoming).

Trinius, Johann Anton, *Freydenker Lexicon* (Leipzig: 1759).

Voysey, Charles (ed.), *Fragments from Reimarus Consisting of Brief Critical Remarks on the Object of Jesus and his Disciples as Seen in the New Testament* (London: 1879).

Wood, Allen W., *Kant and Religion* (New York: 2020).

CHAPTER 13

The Gospel of the New Principle: The Marcionian Leitmotif in Kant's Religious Thought in the Context of Thomas Morgan and the German Enlightenment

Wojciech Kozyra

> Wir wissen nicht, in wessen Hände sich Marcions Gabe widerfinden wird.
>
> MARTIN BUBER

∴

This chapter aims to present Kant's understanding of Christianity and Judaism in the context of Marcion's theology, which proclaims the urgent need to radically purify Christianity from Judaism and the Jewish God.[1] I posit that Kant is the only representative of the philosophy of the German Enlightenment who argues – along Marcionian lines – for the thesis that to realize its essence, Christianity must *entirely* discard its Jewish heritage. Regarding the Enlightenment predecessors of Kant's Marcionism, I will discuss the telling affinity – so far only ambivalently hinted at in modern scholarship – between his and Thomas Morgan's ideas concerning Judaism and Christianity. Additionally, I will establish a polemical point against the claim that Kant possesses some abstract – i.e. creed-neutral – theory of rational religion. I will argue that what he does have is a theory of Christianity *as* a religion and a theory of Judaism *as* an anti-religion. I will start with outlining Marcion's original idea and its problematic history.

---

1 Cf. Paul Fletcher, "Towards Perpetual Revolution: Kant on Freedom and Authority," in *The Politics to Come: Power, Modernity and the Messianic*, eds. Arthur Bradley and Paul Fletcher (London: 2010), 70; cf. also J. Kameron Carter, *Race. A Theological Account* (New York: 2008), 107. Both authors draw on the connection between Kant and Marcionism, although only *en passant*.

1   Marcionism: The Doctrine and Its History

Isidor of Pelusium wrote:

> Just as there is only one single creator of both the beautiful moon and
> the even more beautiful sun, there is also only one single legislator of
> both the Old and the New Testaments, who gave the laws wisely and with
> respect to temporal circumstances.[2]

This fifth-century motto epitomizes what Marcion – a second-century
Christian monk born in Sinope – fought against. He formulated the idea of
a radical incommensurability between the New Testament and the Hebrew
Bible. Surely, he thought, the God who helps Joshua to eradicate the people of
Jericho cannot be identical to the God of Jesus, who teaches to turn the other
cheek.[3] Accordingly, Marcion postulated the necessity of founding autonomous Christianity without its Jewish component. Marcion's idea was not, of
course, incorporated into Christianity as we know it, which did preserve in its
sacred canon the Hebrew Bible as the Old Testament. Marcionism first met
with the critique of Justin Martyr to be later vehemently refuted by Tertullian
in *Adversus Marcionem*. In this work, Tertullian concedes "that one order did
run its course in the old dispensation under the Creator and that another is on
its way in the new under Christ." He does "not deny that there is a difference
in the language of their documents, in their precepts of virtue, and in their
teachings of the law." However, he insists that "all this diversity is consistent
with one and the same God."[4] Tertullian opposes Marcion's dualism of the evil
God of the Hebrew Bible and the "good and excellent"[5] deity of Jesus, who is
to lead his people to absolute spiritual renewal free of the yoke of Judaism. He
does so scripturally by emphasizing the moral content of the Old Testament
(e.g., the Decalogue) as well as philosophically – by invoking the logic of God's
necessary uniqueness.

In this way, *via* Tertullian and other Church Fathers, Marcion became
the emblem of the radical theologico-ethical rupture between Judaism and
Christianity, which Gershom Scholem once described as "metaphysical

---

2   Jan Assmann, *Moses the Egyptian. The Memory of Egypt in Western Monotheism* (Cambridge,
    Mass.: 1998), 71.
3   See Bart D. Ehrman, *Lost Christianities: The Battles for Scripture and the Faiths We Never Knew*
    (New York: 2003), 106.
4   Tertullian, *The Five Books Against Marcion*, trans. Peter Holmes (Edinburgh: 1878), 176.
5   Ibid., 4–10.

antisemitism in its profoundest and most effective form."[6] Marcionism was largely marginalized after the canonization of the Hebrew Bible and it was not until the Reformation that it made a gradual return to the forefront of Christian consciousness.[7] It fitted well with the Lutheran promise of renewed Christianity free from excessive ritualism and arbitrary authority. However, this argument was formulated in its final form as late as the first half of the 20th century, when a luminary of Lutheran theology, Adolf von Harnack, published *Marcion: The Gospel of the Alien God*. In this work, Harnack argues that the traditional Christian canon was erected in defiance of Marcion. For Harnack, not only early Christians but also their God were alien to the world – "alien" (*fremd*) meaning new and hitherto unknown. This God of "morality and goodness," who had nothing in common with the cruel and arbitrary God of the Jews, was to lead its people toward authentic dejudaized Christianity.[8] It is evident that Harnack's book is not only a work of scholarship – it also clearly pursues a strictly theologico-ideological aim. Marcion was the father of "the great undertaking on behalf of Christianity,"[9] which consisted in the religion of Jesus relinquishing everything that stems from the Jews. In turn, Harnack sees himself as the fulfilment of the Reformation's promise of restoring pure (Marcionian) Christianity and his book attempts to bring this process to its completion.

This Marcionian-Lutheran theme was abused by the Nazi ideology.[10] In the third edition of *Der Mythus des 20. Jahrhunderts* (1934), Alfred Rosenberg first explains to his critics that he does not dream about the reintroduction of the "cult of Wotan" and strives only to free Christianity from its Jewish features,[11] and later recalls with dismay his discussion with the "learned theologians" who held fast to the "dubious spiritual dregs of the Old Testament."[12] And so, over a dozen years after Harnack's *Marcion*, Rosenberg still had to persuade the theologians of his day that the "desert demon"[13] of the Hebrew

6   See Adam Sutcliffe, *Judaism and Enlightenment* (Cambridge, Mass.: 2003), 157.

7   Cf. Antonius H.J. Gunneweg, *Vom Verstehen des Alten Testaments. Eine Hermeneutik* (Göttingen: 1988), 42–85.

8   Adolf von Harnack, *Marcion. The Gospel of the Alien God*, trans. John E. Steely and Lyle D. Bierma (Durham: 1990), 22.

9   Cf. ibid., 24.

10   Cf. Micha Brumlik, *Die Gnostiker. Der Traum von der Selbsterlösung des Menschen* (Frankfurt: 1992), 89–90; cf. also Richard Steigmann-Gall, *The Holy Reich. Nazi Conceptions of Christianity, 1919–1945* (New York: 2003), 13–51.

11   Alfred Rosenberg, *Der Mythus des 20. Jahrhunderts* (Munich: 1934), 6–13.

12   Ibid., 31.

13   Ibid., 294.

Bible stands in irreconcilable opposition to Jesus' gospel of love.[14] Rosenberg also explicitly mentioned Marcion as a praiseworthy early denier of the "so-called Old Testament."[15] He did not have to wait long until a group of academic theologians committed to the cause of the comprehensive dejudaization of Christianity appeared – the Institute for the Study and Elimination of Jewish Influence on German Church Life was created in 1939. Moreover, in the same year the Reich's Minister of Ecclesiastical Affairs Hanns Kerrl tried to unify the evangelical community in Germany. The "ecumenical ground" he envisaged was described in the *Godesberger Erklärung* – point "b" of the document insisted that Christianity is neither a continuation nor a completion of the Jewish religion. On the contrary, it forms "an unbridgeable religious opposition to Judaism."[16] Its Nazification, however, did not prevent the Marcionian leitmotif from reappearing in the post-Shoah thought.[17]

In the foregoing outline of the fate of Marcion's idea, I have deliberately omitted the Enlightenment, to which I will now turn and which I will discuss with Kant as its focal point.

2   Marcionism in Kant's Thought

In the *Religion within the Boundaries of Mere Reason* (1793/1794), Kant states:

> *Jewish* faith stands in absolutely no essential connection, i.e. in no unity of concepts, with the ecclesiastical faith whose history we want to consider, even though it immediately preceded it and provided the physical occasion for the founding of this church (the Christian). The *Jewish faith*, as originally established, was only a collection of merely statutory laws supporting a political state; for whatever moral additions were *appended* to it … do not in any way belong to Judaism as such. Strictly speaking Judaism is not a religion at all but simply the union of a number of individuals who, since they belonged to a particular stock, established themselves into a community under purely political laws, hence not into a church.
>
> RGV, 6:125

---

14   Ibid., 607.
15   Ibid., 75–6.
16   Susannah Heschel, *The Aryan Jesus. Christian Theologians and the Bible in Nazi Germany* (Princeton: 2008), 81.
17   Richard Faber, *Political Demonology. On Modern Marcionism* (Eugene: 2018).

Kant dogmatically claims that Judaism is by essence deprived of morality and whatever moral elements can be detected in it must be of foreign, that is, Greek origin (RGV, 6:127–8). For this reason he denies that Judaism amounts to a "Church," which is a polemical point against Moses Mendelssohn, who argued in *Jerusalem* – well-known to Kant – for an inclusive understanding of church-hood.[18] Not being a (moral) church, Judaism is a mere politico-ethnical entity and as such cannot be considered a part of the "universal history of the Church," which is how Kant restructures the notion of *historia sacra* (RGV, 6:124–7). For Kant, this history "cannot ... begin ... anywhere but from Christianity," which means "a total abandonment of ... Judaism," and is "grounded on an entirely new ['alien' in Harnack's parlance – W.K.] principle" (RGV, 6:127–8). Kant contrasts this (moral) principle with an "evil principle" (RGV, 6:93). At the beginning of the *Religion* both principles receive an abstract-moral interpretation, but later the Christian Church emerges as the embodiment of the former and the Jewish Synagogue – of the latter. Kant says that to "the people of God in accordance with the laws of virtue [i.e. Christians – W.K.] ... we can oppose the idea of a band [*Rotte*; cf. *Rotte Korach* from Luther's translation of the Bible – W. K.] under the evil principle – a union of those who side with that principle for the propagation of evil [i.e. the Jews – W.K.]. It is in the interest of evil to prevent the realization of the other [i.e. moral-Christian – W.K.] union" (RGV, 6:99–100). For Kant, the Synagogue not only lies outside the realm of the morally inspired *Ecclesia,* but it also – as essentially lacking morality[19] – stands in a radically antagonistic relation to the intrinsically moral church *and yet as a matter of fact it is considered a part of Christianity* (we will see shortly how much Kant bemoans this state of affairs; RGV, 6:106).[20] Kant contrasts particularistic, political, and "heteronomous" Judaism attuned only to the attainment of earthly goods (RGV 6:79) with universalistic Christianity, which through Christ for the first time "placed the chief work in [morality – W.K.]" (RGV, 6:127). He further explains that "Christianity has the great advantage over Judaism of ... coming *from the mouth of the first teacher* not as a statutory but as a moral religion" (RGV, 6:167). Kant's emphasis on Jesus being "the first teacher" can be read as a radicalization of Gotthold Ephraim Lessing's claim, who in *The*

---

18   See Moses Mendelssohn, *Jerusalem: Or, on the Religious Power and Judaism*, trans. Allan Arkush (Hanover: 1983), 41.

19   In a recent paper, James Haring aptly notes that Kant's image of Judaism cannot be described as merely "amoral" instead of "immoral." James Haring, "Judaism and the Contingency of Religious Law in Kant's Religion within the Boundaries of Mere Reason," *Journal of Religious Ethics* 48/1 (2020): 82.

20   Elsewhere Kant also describes Judaism as a "devasted state which stands in the way of the Kingdom of Heaven" (RGV, 6:138).

Education of the Human Race considered Jesus to be a "better instructor"[21] who came to continue the divine mission of Moses when humanity was already ripe for "the *second* great step in its education [italics W.K.]."[22] Moreover, according to Lessing, the second stage of human development – Christianity – will also give way to a subsequent (final) stage of mankind's ascendance in the future, as Judaism gave way to Christianity.[23] This Joachimian[24] theme in Lessing is countered by Kant's moralized Marcionism: authentic moral revelation is perpetual and as such became articulated by Jesus in the form of religion, that is, as moral duties commanded by God (RGV, 6:153–4). In this way, Kant subsumes Lessing's third stage of human progress – in which humanity is to "love virtue for its own sake"[25] – under Christianity and given that he rejects Judaism as the first stage, he consequently announces Christianity to be not only the beginning but also the end of humanity's "true enlightenment" (RGV, 6:179, 122; see also EAD, 8:339). It is crucial to explain this duality of Kant's notion of Christianity in more detail. To this end, let us consult two fragments from the *Religion* and *The Conflict of the Faculties*, respectively.

The *Religion*:

[E]ven though ... a historical faith attaches itself to pure religion as its vehicle, yet, if there is consciousness that this faith is merely such and if, as the faith of a church, it carries a principle for continually coming closer to pure religious faith until finally we can dispense of that vehicle, the church in question can always be taken as the true one.

RGV, 6:115

The Conflict:

I hear biblical theologians cry out in unison against the very idea of a philosophical interpretation of Scripture. Philosophical exegesis, they say, aims primarily at a natural religion, not Christianity. I reply *that Christianity is the Idea of religion, which must as such be based on reason and to this extent be natural.*

Italics W.K.; SF, 7:44

---

21   Gotthold Ephraim Lessing, "The Education of the Human Race," in *Philosophical and Theological Writings*, trans. H.B. Nisbet (New York: 2005), 231.

22   Ibid.

23   Ibid., 234–6.

24   See Ernst Bloch, "On the Original History of the Third Reich," trans. Neville Plaice, Stephen Plaice, in *The Frankfurt School on Religion*, ed. Eduardo Mendieta (New York: 2005), 29.

25   Lessing, "The Education," 237.

In the first fragment Kant depicts Christianity as the first religious institution with correct self-knowledge. Christianity is credited here with a self-conception according to which it understands itself – in its positive features – only as a means for a dialectical induction of the religion of reason. "Dialectical" is used here in the Hegelian sense: Christianity must realize itself as a moral religion of reason through abolishing itself as a statutory entity. It must, therefore, achieve self-fulfillment through self-abolishment, which Hegel will later assume to be the core idea of dialectics.[26] As the second fragment indicates, when Kant attempts to provide a definition of Christianity, he defines it as a rational (i.e. moral) religion. While "biblical theologians" strive for rescuing Christianity from dissolution in natural religion, Kant insists that Christianity in essence is *nothing but* natural religion. Therefore, the moral religion of reason to which the church must lead is not something different from Christianity – on the contrary, it is Christianity's self-fulfillment *as* Christianity.

This is Kant's dual conception of Christianity which tends to be overlooked by scholars who prefer to read Kant as developing a creed-neutral notion of rational religion. Such interpretations are, however, frustrated with Kant's notorious rendition of Christianity as a carrier of this religion and his categorical exclusion of Judaism from such a possibility. The frustration is usually eliminated by putting Kant's discriminatory theoretical behaviour down to some extra-rational factors like, most commonly, Christian nurture.[27] In this way, Kant's theory of religion "as such" comes out as not anti-Jewish, and its denigration of Judaism is explained "externally." Motivated by this reading, Bettina Stangneth points to an inconsistency at the point when the philosopher states that the "euthanasia of Judaism is pure moral religion" (SF, 7:53). Were Kant loyal to his theory, Stangneth argues, he would have to say that "also euthanasia of Christianity occurs in favour of rational religion."[28] My thesis, however, is that Kant remains consistent here. He only gives an expression to his view of Judaism as an immoral anti-religion and to his respective notion of the authentic moment of Christianity as identical with religion in the strict sense of the term, according to which there is only one "purely moral" religion "valid for all worlds" (RGV, 6:85). Judaism is not only not a religion in this sense, but also it

---

26   In line with this, Haring shows that Kant plays out the Thomistic scheme of the relation between Mosaic and ecclesiastical law within Christianity alone (Haring, "Judaism and the Contingency of Religious Law," 85–8). This is exactly why Kant needs to endow Christianity with a dynamic double-identity.

27   See e.g. Bettina Stangneth, "Antisemitische und Antijudaistische Motive bei Immanuel Kant? Tatsachen, Meinungen, Ursachen," in Horst Gronke, Thomas Meyer, Barbara Neisser (eds.), *Antisemitismus bei Kant und anderen Denkern der Aufklärung* (Würzburg: 2001), 69–74.

28   Ibid., 43.

is not – and cannot be – a church, that is, the means of religion, due to its irrevocably heteronomous character. As it will shortly become clear, by claiming that pure moral religion comes about in the wake of Judaism's "euthanasia," Kant says that the elimination of Judaism from Christianity allows for the latter's self-realization which is now hindered by the former's stubborn presence within Christianity. When Christianity shakes off its Jewish elements – so the argument goes – it will be free to release its moral essence as a natural religion.

Perhaps the most sustained effort to level out Kant's notions of historical Christianity and Judaism has come from Stephen R. Palmquist, most recently, in his article "How Political is the Kantian Church?"[29] Palmquist states that Kant "takes authentic Christianity as an illustration of the true church and contrasts it with both Judaism and various forms of historical Christianity, as examples of false churches."[30] Palmquist, however, misses the dialectical nature of Kant's Christianity and hence he severs Christianity from what Kant considers its fulfillment *as* Christianity: the moral religion of reason. This is also why he equates historical Christianity with Judaism while not being sensitive to the difference between these institutions that Bruce Rosenstock expressed thus: "[for Kant] both Judaism and historical Christianity fall on the side of hell [i.e. positivity – W.K.], but ... *only Judaism makes hell its preferred dwelling place* [italics W.K.]."[31]

Let us now analyze the following exemplarily Marcionian sequence from the *Religion*. Kant explains that the pathological state of Protestant orthodoxy consists in the excess of "domination" (*imperium*) over "service" (*ministerium*). He first quotes a statement from an unknown source, which is nevertheless perfectly intelligible given Kant's Marcionian agenda: "blind with respect to nature, it [the Protestant church – W.K.] scrambles to gather the whole antiquity above its head and buries itself under it." He later gives a diagnostic hint about Protestantism's predicament:

> First, the procedure prudently followed by the first propagators of Christ's doctrine to procure for it introduction among their people is taken to be a part of religion itself, valid for all times and all peoples, so that we ought to believe that *every Christian must be a Jew, whose Messiah has come*; it

---

29   Stephen R. Palmquist, "How Political is the Kantian Church?" *Diametros* 17/65 (2020): 95–113.

30   Ibid., 101.

31   Bruce Rosenstock, *Philosophy and the Jewish Question. Mendelssohn, Rosenzweig, and Beyond* (New York: 2010), 80. Cf. Wojciech Kozyra, "Kant on the Jews and their Religion," *Diametros* 17/65 (2020): 43.

is not however altogether coherent to say that a Christian is not really bound by any law of Judaism ... yet must accept the entire holy book of this people on faith as divine revelation given to all human beings.

RGV, 6:165–6

The first part asserts that the apostles used the Hebrew Bible in order to facilitate spreading Jesus' teachings among the Jews. However, this "prudent" strategy – i.e. deriving Christianity from Judaism – was later mistakenly considered "to be a part of a religion itself" (Jewish scriptures were sealed as Christianity's sacred books), which in Kant's view is the cause of a lingering confusion within the Christian religion. This confusion, which Protestantism erratically perpetuates, constantly inclines Christian churches toward replacing moral *ministerium* with political *imperium*. Obviously, this situation will continue until Christianity consistently bans Judaism from within its midst and therefore returns to what Harnack presented as original Marcionian Christianity. If it does not do so, Christians have no option but to conceive of themselves "as Jews whose Messiah has come." The second part of the excerpt clearly testifies to Kant's desire to see Christianity to be free from Judaism. Kant points to an inconsistency between, on the one hand, claiming that the Mosaic law is not binding to Christians (as Luther emphatically emphasized in the wake of calling *Halakha* the "Jewish Saxon mirror"[32]) and, on the other, insisting on the divine authority of the Hebrew Bible. It follows that consistency would demand the decanonization of the Old Testament. The above fragment is annotated by an important footnote:

Mendelssohn very ingeniously makes use of this weak point of the customary picture of Christianity to pre-empt any suggestion of religious conversion made to a son of Israel. For, as he said, since the faith of the Jews is, according to the admission of the Christians, the lower floor upon which Christianity rests as the floor above, any such suggestion would be tantamount to asking someone to demolish the ground floor in order to feel at home on the second. His true opinion, however, shines through quite clearly. He means to say: first remove Judaism from your *religion* ... and we shall be able to take your proposal under advisement. (In fact nothing would then be left over, except pure moral religion unencumbered by

---

32   See Christoph Schulte, *Die jüdische Aufklärung. Philosophie, Religion, Geschichte* (Munich: 2002), 55.

statutes[33]) ... In any case, the sacred books of this people will no doubt always be preserved and attended to, though not for the sake of religion, yet for scholarship.[34]

> RGV, 6:166–7n.

At the beginning of this statement Kant refers to Mendelssohn's use of the traditionally Christian supersessionist theology as a polemical weapon against Christians. In *Jerusalem* Mendelssohn argued against August Cranz' proselytist zeal by stating that he – as a Christian – is committed to a charitable interpretation of the Old Testament for it is *his* holy book and the "lower floor" of *his* religious edifice.[35] The idea that Christianity fulfills Judaism in the name of Judaism is precisely what Kant calls a "weakness" of mainstream Christianity. Firstly, it does not give the Jews any animus to convert, for why should they exchange one statute for another? Christianity as a "messianic faith" (SF, 7:52) will thus not deliver on the Jewish conversion.[36] Secondly, this "customary picture of Christianity" keeps the religion in the state of "self-inflicted immaturity" (to refer to Kant's famous definition of enlightenment). For Kant, Christianity must mature and gain autonomy in the wake of leaving the "upper floor" of the Judeo-Christian edifice and build its religious structure anew from purely moral elements in defiance of heteronomous Judaism. Accordingly, at the end of the excerpt Kant prophesizes an optimal future situation in which Jewish scriptures will be studied only as secular history.

In line with his main argument, Kant drops the identity of God across the Testaments and announces the Hebrew Bible as the offspring of an undertaking that is deliberately heteronomous and therefore anathematic to Christianity's moral notion of God. He writes:

---

33 The bracketed sentence further supports my previous claim that the "euthanasia" of Judaism amounts for Kant to pure moral religion, that is, the authentic Christianity.

34 Kant is mistaken as to Mendelssohn's "true opinion." It is indeed quite preposterous to suggest that Mendelssohn – a committed *Halakha*-observer – would consider conversion if Christianity purified itself from Judaism. Essentially, the same mistake was committed by Kant in his letter to Mendelssohn, where Kant, after studying *Jerusalem*, praises its author for advocating the curtailment of Judaism of its non-moral elements which, in fact, this book does not feature (Kant finally acknowledged Mendelssohn's orthodoxy with distaste in SF, 7:53). In the case of Lazarus Bendavid, the same happened. See Ian Hunter, "The Early Jewish Reception of Kantian Philosophy," *Modern Intellectual History* (2020): 13.

35 Mendelssohn, *Jerusalem*, 87.

36 Kant's rejection of the "dream of a conversion of all Jews [*allgemeine Judenbekehrung*]" (SF, 7:52) is more an expression of his negative attitude towards messianic-Jewish Christianity than of his liberal ideology.

> It can hardly be doubted that ... the Jews ... must have had a faith in a future life, hence had their heaven and hell, for this faith automatically imposes itself upon everyone by virtue of the universal moral predisposition in human nature. Hence it must have come about *intentionally* that the lawgiver of this people, though portrayed as God himself, did not *wish* to show the least consideration for the future life – an indication that his intention was to found only a political and not an ethical community.
>
> RGV, 6:126

Kant is referring here to a popular Enlightenment idea of William Warburton, expressed in *The Divine Legation of Moses*, in which – to use Jan Assmann's words – Warburton "pursued a rather strange plan."[37] Indeed, he claimed that because the afterlife is not mentioned in the Old Testament, and because this idea is so attractive to the human mind, Moses must have been sent by God, for if this were not the case, he would have had to mention the afterlife in order to render his message acceptable. In the absence of such references, his success can only be explained under the assumption of his divine legation. However, like most of Warburton's interlocutors, Kant remained unconvinced. For him, the fact that the idea of the soul's immortality imposes itself on every human being due to their "moral predisposition" proves only that the lack of the respective moral content in Judaism has been programmatic and not accidental. Therefore, Judaism in its pretense to religiosity suppresses the human moral need and as such could not have come from a true moral deity – in fact, its legislator, Moses, used the concept of God merely as a "juridical fiction," as it were, which was to give proper sanction to his legal code.

There remain two considerations in support of Kant's Marcionian theological profile. Let us start with his neglect of the prophets, which is significant because they form the most crucial theological bridge between the Testaments. Kant never mentions the moral message of the prophets and refers to them only either in a purely political context (SF, 7:80),[38] or implicitly – as transitory means for facilitating the acceptance of Jesus' doctrine among the Jews. Interestingly, even the "radical" Spinoza writes about Jeremiah, who prophesies the coming of Jesus, as the moral teacher who will "inscribe the law ... in hearts."[39] Spinoza's "radical Protestantism" – to refer to the title of Graeme

---

37 Assmann, *Moses*, 96.

38 For references to the political notion of the messiah, see RGV, 6:125, 138.

39 Benedict Spinoza, *Theological-Political Treatise*, trans. Jonathan I. Israel, Michael Silverthorne (New York: 2007), 163. See a relevant discussion in Graeme Hunter, *Radical Protestantism in Spinoza's Thought* (New York: 2017), 51–69.

Hunter's significant book[40] – seems then less radical than Kant's in that it is not Marcionian. This is not to say that Kant does not grapple with the seemingly moral content of the Old Testament. He notices, for example, that morality can be inferred from the Decalogue, but explains (here agreeing with Spinoza) that the Ten Commandments are given by Moses not as a moral law, which appeals to the inner moral disposition of a human being, but as a mere statute, which demands actions that take place only in conformity with the law (unlike moral actions *effected* by the law) that Kant's ethics deems "merely legal" (RGV, 6:125–7). In the case of the prophets, however, Kant does not reiterate this ploy and simply ignores the moral import of the prophetic writings. This is especially vivid in that while ethically condemning the notion of the cross-generational culpability present in the Mosaic law (RGV, 6:126), he does not draw upon the book of Ezekiel where the prophet introduces the individual-based model of moral responsibility.

The last remaining issue to be discussed in this section is Kant's devaluation of monotheism. On various occasions Kant claims that the Jews should not be given such credit for their monotheism because their unique God is deprived of moral qualities, discriminates against non-Jewish nations, demands blind obedience, and even commands immoral deeds.[41] Kant warns that "we should not place too much weight on the fact that [the Jews] set up, as universal ruler of the universe, a one and only God who could not be represented by any visible image" (RGV, 6:127).[42] This God – Jehovah – is not a moral God who is "necessary for religion." Kant continues by stating that the creedal focus on morality is

> more likely to occur with a faith in many … mighty invisible beings, if a people were somehow to think of them as uniting, in spite of their "departmental" differences, in deeming worthy of their pleasure only those human beings who adhere to virtue with all their heart, than when faith is dedicated to but one being, who, however, makes of a mechanical cult the main work.
>
> RGV, 6:127

---

40   Ibid.

41   See, e.g., Kant's discussion of the binding of Isaac in SF, 7:63–4.

42   Here Kant revokes his praise of the rejection of idolatry in Judaism, which he expressed in the *Critique of Judgment* published three years before the *Religion* (KU, 5:274; see also HN, 23:104.).

Kant expresses his preference for morally tainted polytheism over supposedly morality-free Jewish monotheism. The Marcionian motif is apparent here, because Marcion – like Kant – compromises monotheism (which he was criticized for by Tertullian) by postulating two deities: the moral deity of Jesus and the immoral deity of the Hebrew Bible. In Kant's "naturalized Marcionism," analogously, we deal with two principles: the immoral principle fostered by Judaism and the moral principle pursued by Christianity. Notably, Sebastian Moll writes in the introduction to his monograph devoted to Marcion that "Marcion's second God, the God of the New Testament, formed a clear antithesis to the Old Testament God, but *he did not in any way replace him.*"[43] It is important to bear in mind that in Kant the moral principle proclaimed by Jesus also does not replace the immorality of Judaism. On the contrary, it stands against it in a state of immediate and irreconcilable tension.

3   The German Enlightenment and the Continuity between Judaism and Christianity

There exist three positions concerning Judaism in the philosophy of the German Enlightenment. The first position is represented by German Jews like Moses Mendelssohn and Saul Ascher, who defend Judaism's eligibility for modernization. The second one considers Judaism to be an "anachronism"[44] that gave way to Christianity. The third position claims that Judaism is not even an anachronism, if being an anachronism presupposes a state of bygone validity, a view which – as discussed in the previous section – is defended by Kant. Moreover, Kant is largely isolated in this view, because philosophically important figures among his Christian contemporaries who discussed this issue subscribed to the second position (in various ways and with various caveats). I will now show that the important German Enlighteners affirmed the existence of a moral or theologico-historical continuity between Judaism and Christianity. My aim is to undermine the practice of grouping Kant's ideas of Judaism with the views of his Christian German contemporaries under the general category of "Christian anti-Judaism."[45] Kant's Marcionism vividly stands out against the background of his theologically "orthodox" peers (at least with respect

---

43   Sebastian Moll, *The Arch-Heretic. Marcion* (Tübingen: 2010), 3.

44   Johann G. Hamann, "Golgotha and Sheblimini!" in *Writings on Philosophy and Language*, trans. Kenneth Hayes (New York: 2007), 201.

45   Cf. Josef Bohatec, *Die Religionsphilosophie Kants in der* Religion innerhalb der Grenzen der bloßen Vernunft. *Mit besonderer Berücksichtigung ihrer theologisch-dogmatischen Quellen* (Hamburg: 1938), 467.

to the commensurability between Judaism and Christianity), which will become evident from its juxtaposition with the relevant ideas presented in what follows.

I have already touched upon Kant's disagreement with Lessing's view defended in *The Education of the Human Race* about the divine legation of Moses and Judaism being an integral – although invalidated by the advent of Christianity – part of humanity's moral and religious progression. I shall therefore turn first to Reimarus's case, because it is particularly interesting in Kant's context.

Kant repeatedly praises Reimarus for his outstanding formulation of the cosmological proof for God's existence from *Abhandlungen von den vornehmsten Wahrheiten der natürlichen Religion* (BDG, 2:161; KU, 5:476–7). Hence it seems that for Kant at a certain period Reimarus was no less than a classic of natural theology. At the same time, Reimarus harboured unequivocally subversive beliefs at the margin of his conservative intellectual activity. After his death in 1768, his clandestine writings were published anonymously in the years 1774–1778 by Lessing as *Fragmente des Wolfenbüttelschen Ungenannten*.[46] In the *Fragmente*, Reimarus did to the New Testament what Spinoza did to the Old Testament – he historicized it and consequently debunked its claim to transcendence. He depicted Jesus as an instigator, who can secure support for his cause only among the lower classes of the Jewish community, while its priestly and pharisaic elite rejects his advocacy. Its members were right, says Reimarus, in thinking that Jesus' activity can bring Roman repression upon the Jewish nation, and they simply did not want it to happen.[47] Their hostility toward Jesus is therefore fully understandable. Still, the main object of Reimarus' critique are the apostles. After the crucifixion of the alleged messiah, they do not want to return to their pre-revolutionary routine and so they make up Jesus-God around whom they found their movement.[48] Nevertheless, Reimarus still holds Jesus in high esteem as a teacher of morality. However, unlike Kant, he does not take the moral message of the New Testament to separate itself categorically from the Old Testament. He writes:

> The goal of Jesus's sermons and teachings was a proper active character, a changing of the mind, a sincere love of God and of one's neighbor ... These are not great mysteries or tenets of the faith that he explains, proves, and preaches; they are nothing other than moral teachings and

---

46   Kant knew this book. See RGV, 6:82; see also Bohatec, *Die Religionsphilosophie Kants*, 497.
47   Hermann S. Reimarus, *Fragments from Reimarus*, trans. Charles Voysey (London: 1879), 25–6.
48   Ibid., 66–7.

duties intended to improve man inwardly and with all his heart ... But he does not explain these things anew ... To the same extent that he wished to see the law fulfilled and not done away with in respect to his own person, he shows others how the whole law and the prophets hang on these two commandments: that one love God with all his heart, and his neighbour as himself, and that consequently *the repentance and improvement of man is contained in the essence of the Old Testament.*[49] (Italics W.K.)

Reimarus sees the gospel of natural religion in the Old Testament as well; Jesus' message or his "principle" (*vide* Kant) is neither new nor "alien" (*vide* Harnack). It is that same moral message of the Old Covenant (expressed for example in the Noachide Laws) that Jesus just articulated "better than had ever been done."[50] The gospel of the New Testament is therefore not directed against the Old Covenant, but only develops its core moral features. Moreover, Reimarus openly attacks Marcionian sentiment:

> I cannot avoid revealing a common error of Christians who imagine that ... [Jesus'] purpose in his role of teacher was to reveal certain articles of faith that were in part new and unknown, thus establishing a new system [*Lehrgebäude*] of religion while on the other hand doing away with Jewish religion.[51]

We can see that Reimarus does not support Christianity's "moving out" from the "upper floor" of the Judeo-Christian edifice. He calls such attempts the mistake of Christians – a mistake which Kant will later commit. In conclusion, for Reimarus there surely exists a "unity of concepts" between Judaism and Christianity: the latter only elaborates on what was already present in the former and does not introduce an "entirely new principle."

Karl Leonhard Reinhold was the most prominent popularizer and supporter of Kant's first *Critique*, which he cherished as a "gospel of pure reason."[52] At the same time, he developed his own thinking independently from his master. An example of this is provided by Reinhold's views concerning religion presented in *Die Hebräischen Mysterien: Oder die älteste religiöse Freymaurerey* (1788), which the author probably sent to Kant.[53] In this work, Reinhold – himself a

---

49   Hermann S. Reimarus, *Reimarus: Fragments*, trans. Ralph S. Fraser (London: 1970), 69–70.

50   Ibid., 68.

51   Ibid., 71.

52   Karl L. Reinhold, *Letters on the Kantian Philosophy*, trans. James Hebbeler (New York: 2005), 49.

53   Assmann, *Moses*, 129.

mason – situates the development of religious spirit at the advent of masonic lodges. His main point is that the masonry is in possession of the means to satisfactorily realize the idea of a rational religion. The core of the "mysteries" of rational religion, however, is known to Christianity as well as to Judaism. In Reinhold's narrative, Moses steals the mysteries from Egyptian priests and announces them to his people, whose mission from then on would be to spread them worldwide.[54] Although Reinhold does not spare the Jews – mostly rabbis – various invectives, he still admits that masons (and obviously Christians too) must be grateful to "Hebraism"[55] for their enlightenment (*Erleuchtung*). Reinhold does not theorize any radical antagonism within the history of mankind's spiritual improvement. He sees the notion of natural religion as a perennial idea, which has been historically accessed by various social groups – most recently, and most promisingly for Reinhold, by the masonry.

Schiller's famous piece *Die Sendung Moses* (1790), which in its basic features (like the Egyptian narrative) is a summary of *Hebräischen Mysterien*, delivers one of the most politically optimistic treatments of the Jews and Judaism available among the established philosophers of the *Spätaufklärung* (the usual denigration of the exodus and the rabbinic Jews notwithstanding). With respect to its religious content, Schiller follows Reinhold in acknowledging in his essay the positive influence of Hebrew monotheism on humanity in general and on Christians – whose religion is "grounded" in "the religion of the Hebrews" – in particular.[56] He stresses very strongly that the Jews can be rightly credited for that[57] – a point that Kant will later repudiate, quite plausibly, in response to Schiller. Even though the very title of Schiller's *Die Sendung Moses* is an obvious polemic against Warburton's *The Divine Legations of Moses* (the German translation of this book appeared in 1751 and was entitled *Göttliche Sendung Mosis*), Schiller takes pains to assure that the *Halakha* – although it was Moses' initiative – was instituted in the name of the true religion and is by no means "based on a lie." Jehovah is the "true God," whose image was presented at Sinai in a form fit for the "deplorable" spiritual level of his Jewish addressee.[58] Accordingly, for Schiller, Mosaic legislation was "grounded in truth"[59] so that "the future reformer" (i.e. Jesus) will not have to annul the whole "basic

54   Karl L. Reinhold, *Die Hebräischen Mysterien: Oder die älteste religiöse Freymaurerey* (Leipzig: 1788), 37–40.

55   Ibid., 84.

56   Friedrich Schiller, "Die Sendung Moses," *Thalia* 3/10 (1790): 3.

57   Ibid.

58   Ibid., 28.

59   Ibid.

constitution" (*Grundverfassung*) when he attempts to improve religious con-cepts.[60] Schiller also does not envisage a Kantian-Marcionian radical rebuild-ing of Christianity by means of eradicating Judaism from it.

Two other proto-romantics subscribed to the idea of a substantial com-mensurability between Judaism and Christianity – Johann Georg Hamann and Johann Gottfried Herder. In his immediate reaction to Mendelssohn's *Jerusalem*, Hamann writes in *Golgotha and Sheblimini!* addressing a Christian reader: "I would wish, for the sake of our mutual safety in the upper floor, no such lose ground and sandy bottom for the new and tough theory of Judaism."[61] Hamann refers to the passages from *Jerusalem* about Christianity being Judaism's "upper floor," which also caught Kant's attention, as we have seen before. And yet while Kant polemizes with Mendelssohn by claiming that Christianity should constitute itself anew as a moral entity in opposition to Judaism, Hamann is happy to adopt the two-floors theory, which he wants, however, to see improved. This improvement proceeds along the lines already indicated by Reinhold and Schiller. It consists in elevating the elements of ancient "Hebraism," like God's promise to Abraham (the focal point of Hamann's discussion[62]) at the cost of the supposedly legalistic and confused Mosaic "Judaism," which failed dramat-ically in the attempt to gain self-knowledge. Hebraism understood this way, or "genuine Judaism,"[63] as Hamann prefers to call it, is the spiritual and historical ancestor of the universal message of Christianity; it is a "vehicle of the mystery," "the shadow of good things to come,"[64] while Christianity itself "recognizes no other shackles of faith than the sure word of prophecy within the most ancient documents of the human race."[65]

In this last fragment, Hamann refers to Herder's work *Älteste Urkunde des Menschengeschlechts*. Indeed, Herder's notion of the relation between Judaism and Christianity is essentially in accord with Hamann's. In his most mature work devoted to this issue, *Vom Geist der ebräischen Poesie* (1782) Herder insists that the Hebrew scriptures mark "the beginning of the enlight-enment of the human race."[66] In another passage, Herder almost *verbatim* negates point "b" of the *Godesberger Erklärung* when he states that "the New

---

60   Ibid., 36.
61   Hamann, *Golgotha and Sheblimini!* 180.
62   Ibid., 166.
63   Ibid., 185.
64   Ibid., 181.
65   Ibid., 185.
66   Johann G. Herder, *Vom Geist der ebräischen Poesie. Eine Anleitung für die Liebhaber der-selben, und der ältesten Geschichte des menschlichen Geistes. Erster Theil* (Stuttgart: 1827), 40.

Testament is grounded in the Old, for Christianity springs from Judaism."[67] He asserts further the existence of the prophecy of Christ within the Old Testament and defends its morality against the blunt and ahistorical ethical standard of some Enlightenment critiques (Morgan's included[68]). Like Hamann, he also emphasizes the crucial role of Abraham (yet, unlike Hamann, he extends his interpretative charity to Moses) as the forerunner of Jesus' universal gospel and writes that the post-Mosaic Jews mistook their "separation from other nations"[69] for a political privilege and a promise of political reign over all peoples.[70] Herder concludes by saying that the Jews, once God's beloved children, are now openly his enemies.[71] However, he does forcefully argue to the conclusion that the Jews and their religion form a substantial (although bygone) part of humanity's development.

The philosophers discussed above *instrumentalized* Judaism for the sake of the "education of the human race," to use Lessing's phrase. It can be argued that at the time it was a peculiar way of expressing sympathy toward Judaism, at least in contrast with Kant's Marcionian theology, which claimed that Judaism cannot be treated even as an obsolete means of benefiting mankind. But what is the source of Kant's nonconformist Marcionian idea concerning the relation between Judaism and Christianity, given that the philosophy of the German Enlightenment supported the competing view? I will answer this question in the last section of this chapter.

4   The Antecedents of Kant's Marcionism: Thomas Morgan

There exists evidence in light of which Kant's Marcionism becomes historically intelligible, even if we never catch Kant studying *Adversus Marcionem*. The most important Enlightenment precedent for Kant's Marcionism can be found in *The Moral Philosopher* (1737) written by an English deist and the "Marcion of his times,"[72] Thomas Morgan. In a classical *Geschichte*

---

67   Ibid., 13.
68   Johann G. Herder, *Vom Geist der ebräischen Poesie. Eine Anleitung für die Liebhaber derselben, und der ältesten Geschichte des menschlichen Geistes. Zweiter Theil* (Stuttgart: 1827), 7.
69   Ibid., 67.
70   Ibid., 12–13.
71   Ibid., 81.
72   Jan van den Berg, "English Deism and Germany: The Thomas Morgan Controversy," *Journal of Ecclesiastical History* 59/1 (2008): 48.

des englischen Deismus G.V. Lechler characterized Morgan's theology as Marcionian.[73] Harnack also deems Morgan a restorer of Marcionism in the era of Enlightenment.[74] However, telling and numerous similarities – with respect to their Marcionian content – between Morgan's and Kant's views on Judaism and Christianity have so far escaped the attention of scholars. The only firm statement of the affinity known to me comes from a theologian Karl Friedrich Stäudlin, Kant's contemporary to whom the philosopher dedicated *The Conflict of the Faculties*. In the *Geschichte der Sittenlehre Jesu* from 1799, Stäudlin precedes his critique of Kant and Morgan with a note that "Morgan had argued [for the 'immoral' and 'irreligious' nature of Judaism – W.K.] on more or less the same grounds as Kant in our times."[75] Contemporarily, Jan van den Berg admits that "the value of the Old Testament for the great philosopher [i.e. Kant – W.K.] is likewise [like for Morgan – W.K.] less than the New Testament."[76] But to say no more than that is to miss the peculiarity of Kant's view on the Old Covenant. Every Christian then and now – in a more or less mindful way – has elevated the New Testament over the Old. The specificity of Kant's view, however, consists in the fact that his attitude toward the Old Testament is not "typically Christian" (i.e. supersessionist) but Marcionian in nature and as such entirely devalues the Hebrew Bible as a carrier of religion for the sake of Christianity's moral renewal. Morgan was the only philosopher of the Enlightenment who expressed this idea with comparable force (or even greater force due to better theological training). This merits closer attention, especially because Morgan's Marcionian views, as Berg shows, were popular in the German *Aufklärung* and attracted wide audience. However, these views were still suppressed, as evidenced by the fact that Morgan's *opus magnum* has never been translated into German, in contrast to a number of *Gegenschriften* produced by various English Enlighteners.[77] Morgan's religious thought met with resistance from the mainstream German theology of the early Enlightenment.[78] Here, the most important figure is Siegmund Jacob Baumgarten of Halle, a chief theologian of the period. In the years 1746–1766

---

73   Gotthard Victor Lechler, *Geschichte des englischen Deismus* (Stuttgart: 1841), 387.

74   Harnack, *Marcion. The Gospel of the Alien God*, 220–1.

75   Karl F. Stäudlin, *Geschichte der Sittenlehre Jesu* (Göttingen: 1799), 128.

76   Van den Berg, "English Deism and Germany," 58.

77   Ibid., 56.

78   The so-called "radical Enlightenment" in Germany, on the other hand, did happen to harbour originally Marcionian ideas about a "genuine contradiction between Christian and Jewish religion." See e.g. Johann G. Wachter, *Der Spinozismus im Jüdenthumb* (Amsterdam: 1699), 253–6.

Baumgarten published a number of works in which he criticized Morgan.[79] Closer to Kant's environment, in 1740 Martin Knutzen, who had the most influence on young Kant in Albertina,[80] published the acclaimed *Philosophischer Beweis von der Wahrheit der christlichen Religion* directed at refuting English deism, Morgan's in particular.[81] Another acquaintance of Kant's (his neighbour since 1769),[82] a controversial theologian named Johann August Starck, could also have provided Kant with some knowledge about Marcionism and Morgan, as well as influencing his general view of Christianity.[83] Last but not least, from among the circle of Kant's friends, in the already mentioned *Älteste Urkunde des Menschengeschlechts* (read by Kant),[84] Herder mentions Marcion disapprovingly among other "Gnostics" who distinguish themselves through a peculiar hostility toward Moses and the Old Testament.[85] In turn, between the years 1760–1782 in Kant's home city of Königsberg, there successively appeared a monumental theological study of Knutzen's associate, Theodore Christoph Lilienthal, who often polemically referred to Morgan's theology.[86] Apart from that, moderately Marcionian (or, for that matter, Morganian) themes can be observed in the *Abhandlung von Freier Untersuchung des Canon* (1771–1776) written by a famous representative of neology, Johann Salomo Semler,[87] not unfamiliar to Kant.[88] In this work, Semler argues that only a part of the Old

---

79   Jan van den Berg, "English Deism and Germany," 53–4. Unsurprisingly, the mainstream early German Enlightenment in general stood firmly for the substantial connection between Judaism and Christianity. See Haim Mahlev, "Kabbalah as Philosophia Perennis? The Image of Judaism in the German Early Enlightenment: Three Studies," *The Jewish Quarterly Review*, 104/2 (2014): 234–257.

80   See Manfred Kuehn, *Kant. A Biography* (New York: 2001), 78.

81   Martin Knutzen, *Philosophischer Beweis von der Wahrheit der christlichen Religion* (Nordhausen: 2005), 11.

82   Kuehn, *Kant*, 225.

83   See Johann A. Starck, *Betrachtungen über das Christenthum* (Berlin: 1780), 138, 281; see also ibid., 69.

84   Kuehn, *Kant*, 223–4.

85   Johann G. Herder, *Älteste Urkunde des Menschengeschlechts: eine nach Jahrhunderten enthüllte heilige Schrift. Erster Band* (Tübingen: 1806), 397–403.

86   Van den Berg, "English Deism and Germany," 54.

87   Indeed, Semler reacted critically to what he considered Reimarus' overemphasis of the affinities between Christianity and Judaism. See Johann Salomo Semler, *Beantwortung der Fragmente eines Ungenanten insbesondere vom Zweck Jesu und seiner Jünger* (Halle: 1780), 37–43. Yet he still did not give up entirely on the commensurability between the Covenants. Cf. Andreas Lüder, *Historie und Dogmatik. Ein Beitrag zur Genese und Entfaltung von Johann Salomo Semlers Verständnis des Alten Testaments* (Berlin: 1995), 226–240.

88   See Ludwig E. Borowski, *Darstellung des Lebens und Charakters Immanuel Kant's* (Königsberg: 1804), 171. The importance of Semler's theological views for Kant is emphasized by Bohatec. See Josef Bohatec, *Die Religionsphilosophie Kants* (Hamburg: 1938), 27.

Testament is divinely inspired, while the rest is directly (morally) opposed to Christianity.[89] The "freedom" of the inquiry of Christianity's holy scriptures means for Semler precisely the freedom to revise the status of the Hebrew Bible as divine revelation. Although the book does not mention Morgan, it does occasionally refer to Marcion.[90]

A short note on Kant's attitude toward neology is in place here. Kant writes in *The Conflict* that the "name of [neologians] is justly hated" (SF, 7:34). Most probably, he refers to Semler, who supported the so-called Wöllner's edict of 1788, which curtailed the freedom of speech in Prussia and because of which Kant was forbidden to publish works on religious matters – this is suggested by the political context of Kant's statement. Besides politics, however, there was yet another thing that separated Kant from the neologians' attempt at "rationalizing" Christian tradition – consistency. Kant *consistently*, i.e. *radically*, eliminated Judaism from Christianity, while neologians, in accordance with their "popular" inclination toward syncretism,[91] would stop halfway like Semler, who was still willing to consider Judaism a "mixture of politics and moral religion."[92] For Kant, a thinker for whom "to be consistent is the greatest obligation of a philosopher" (KpV, 5:24), such half-measures must have been distasteful (as we have seen, he takes Judaism to be "no religion at all"). The syncretism of the neologians is further confirmed by neology's founding father, Johann Friedrich Wilhelm Jerusalem, who remains one of the two figures also worth mentioning here, whose books Kant kept in his private library.[93] It is not an accident that Semler dedicated his plea for restricting the boundaries of the Christian canon to Jerusalem. In his most important book, *Betrachtungen über die vornehmsten Wahrheiten der Religion*, Jerusalem argues that the "Christian religion possesses power which is entirely its own and independent from the mosaic religion."[94] However, he does not drive this argument to its Kantian

89   See a discussion in Marianne Schröter, "Johann Salomo Semler und das Alte Testament," in *Christentum und Judentum. Akten des Internationalen Kongresses der Schleiermacher-Gesellschaft in Halle, März 2009*, eds. Roderich Barth, Ulrich Barth and Claus-Dieter Osthövener (Berlin: 2012), 125–141.

90   Johann S. Semler, *Abhandlung von Freier Untersuchung des Canon: nebst Antwort auf die Tübingische Vertheidigung der Apocalypsis* (Halle: 1771), 170, 208. Furthermore, Semler's is the first defence of the accuracy of Marcion's version of the Gospel of Luke present in the *Vorrede über Markions Evangelium* that preceded one of his translations. See Dieter T. Roth, *The Text of Marcion's Gospel* (Leiden: 2015), 8.

91   Kant condemns the syncretism of the so-called *Popularphilosophie* (neologians included), e.g., in KpV, 5:25.

92   Semler, *Abhandlung*, 57–8.

93   See Arthur Warda, *Immanuel Kants Bücher* (Berlin: 1922), 43.

94   Johann F.W. Jerusalem, *Betrachtungen über die vornehmsten Wahrheiten der Religion. Zweiter Teil* (Frankfurt: 1775), viii.

end. In *Briefe über die mosaischen Schriften und Philosophie*, he openly criticizes Morgan's denigration of Moses[95] and defends the authenticity of the prophetic writings.[96] He also asserts the divine provenance of Judaism and its "partial" belonging to Christianity.[97] The second figure is Johann David Michaelis, a very prominent orientalist and Biblical scholar from Göttingen. Kant kept in his library Michaelis' *Einleitung in die göttlichen Schriften des Neuen Bundes* in which Marcion is repeatedly presented as a heretic who mistreats the apostolic writings.[98] Michaelis also sheds some light on Marcion's theology – he notes that Marcion rejected the Old Testament together with the prophets who proclaimed God to the Jews as "powerful" rather than "good."[99] All things considered, Kant must have had several occasions to come in contact with Marcion's or Morgan's ideas. Especially that in his later years he is reported to have developed a serious interest in Church history.[100] In this light, Kant's Marcionism ceases to be an enigma, but still retains its dissentient quality.

In the remainder, I will analyze the relationship between Kant's and Morgan's views on Judaism and Christianity and make a case for a deep affinity between their ideas.

Morgan's book is presented in the form of a dialog between the philosopher Philalethes and a "Jewish Christian," Theophanes. Theophanes is one of the mainstream Christians whom Kant considers the "Jews whose Messiah has come." These "Judaizing Christians," according to Morgan, work in favour of "founding Christianity on Judaism"[101] and therefore want to "preserve certain ceremonies and rituals "as necessary Parts of Religion."[102] Religion, however, as Morgan (and Kant) understand it, does not allow any positivity as its indispensable component, because its concept is exclusively moral.[103] In regard to the Old Testament, at the crucial point in the dialog, Philalethes asks his interlocutor: "I would ... ask, whether the Christian Revelation is contained in the Books of the *Old Testament*, or whether *Moses* and the Prophets understood and taught the revealed Doctrines of Christianity?"[104] Theophanes answers:

---

95   Johann F.W. Jerusalem, *Briefe über die mosaischen Schriften und Philosophie* (Braunschweig: 1762), 4.

96   Ibid., 6.

97   Ibid., 7.

98   Johann D. Michaelis, *Einleitung in die göttlichen Schriften des Neuen Bundes. Erster Theil* (Göttingen: 1788), 38.

99   Ibid., 7.

100   Borowski, *Darstellung*, 172.

101   Thomas Morgan, *The Moral Philosopher in a Dialog between Philalethes a Christian Deist, and Theophanes a Christian Jew* (London: 1737), 185.

102   Ibid., v.

103   Ibid., viii, 18, 85, 94, 99, 206.

104   Ibid., 19.

"Not, indeed, clearly, explicitly and literally but darkly, obscurely and under Types and Shadows."[105] To this Philalethes sarcastically retorts:

> Literal *Judaism* then, it seems, was figurative Christianity, and literal Christianity is mystical *Judaism*; the Letter of the Law was the Type of the Gospel, and the Letter of the Gospel is the Spirit of the Law ... *Moses* was the Shadow of Christ, and Christ is the Substance of *Moses*.[106]

As I showed in the previous section, the view that "Christ is the substance of Moses" and that the Old Testament is pregnant with the New Testament resonates with Kant's major philosophical peers. For Kant and Morgan, on the other hand, this position is deeply mistaken. For them, Moses (i.e. the Old Covenant), far from anticipating Christ, adopts the role of Christ's moral antagonist and, therefore, of the enemy of religion. Philalethes presents his program accordingly:

> The Question ... to be debated ... shall be this, whether the positive and ceremonial Law of *Moses* ... was originally a divine Institution or Revelation from God, to be afterwards nullified, abolished and set aside by another Revelation; or, whether it was originally a mere Piece of carnal, worldly Policy?[107]

Here Morgan presents an alternative between traditionally supersessionist understanding of Judaism and his own conception of it as a religiously and morally valueless entity, thus attempting – like Kant – to shape the Christian of the future who is no longer a Kantian "Jew whose Messiah has come." When Theophanes attempts to employ the accommodationist strategy and argues that the political character of the Mosaic law does not exclude its divine origin,[108] Theophanes asks rhetorically, as he often does,

> whether God can establish Iniquity by Law or whether a Law which ... introduced and confirmed a State of civil and religious Blindness and Bigotry, Tyranny and Slavery, could, in the same Judgment, have been originally a divine Institution, and an immediate Revelation from God?[109]

---

105   Ibid.
106   Ibid.
107   Ibid., 23.
108   Ibid., 31.
109   Ibid., 32.

Clearly, the moral notion of God, which for Morgan and Kant is "necessary for religion," cannot be reconciled with the discriminatory[110] Jehovah from the Hebrew Bible. Consequently, in view of the moral corruption of Judaism theorized by him, Morgan claims the right to be a pure Christian, a Christian who is not a Jew and who grounds his faith only in the moral gospel of the New Testament.[111] Therefore, instead of continuity between the Covenants, we have a Marcionian rupture between the Hebrew Bible and the New Testament in both Morgan and Kant.

Kant's way of explaining the apostolic reference to the Hebrew Bible is also Morganian. Morgan says that by making these references the apostles wanted to fight the pharisees with their own weapon,[112] and so the link to the Jewish antiquities was a temporary means of pursuing the cause of the new religion. As we have seen, for Kant the apostles also referred to the books of the Old Testament – which were later mistakenly assumed to be a part of Christianity – only to win supporters among the Jews. Accordingly, both thinkers admit that as long as Christianity confers an autotelic meaning upon its positive elements (i.e. those of the Jewish origin), it will be unable to present the Jews with a convincing case for conversion. As Morgan says, "it will be impossible for the Christians ever to convince the *Jews* upon *Jewish* Principles."[113]

After hearing a lot about Christianity being identical with morality, confused Theophile finally asks Philalethes what, according to him, remains out of Christianity as it is commonly experienced.[114] In his reply Philalethes provides an utterly Kantian description of Christianity: "I take Christianity – he says – to be that most complete and perfect Scheme of moral Truth and Righteousness, which was first preached to the World by Christ."[115] After two hundred and fifty pages, Theophile enquires further: "I would still be glad to know ... how you would distinguish [Christianity] from the Religion of Nature?"[116] Philalethes gives his final answer:

---

110   Ibid., 51.
111   Ibid., 359. It should be kept in mind, however, that this does not mean that Kant's contemporaries had to give up the moral notion of God to preserve the commensurability of the Testaments. What they did give up instead is the uncompromising and absolute notion of morality (as announced by Jesus) that Kant and Morgan share. For these two thinkers, Jesus' moral message understood in this way makes it impossible to historize and therefore appropriate the Sinaitic revelation to the progressive scheme of humanity's development.
112   Ibid., 51.
113   Ibid., 359.
114   See ibid., 96.
115   Ibid.
116   Ibid., 346.

And I, in Return, would be glad to know, when you have thrown out the Religion of Nature, what Christianity you would have left, or what Christianity or the Gospel Revelation is as distinguished from natural Religion, or the Obligations of moral Truth and Righteousness?[117]

On the one hand, Morgan characterizes Christianity as the "most perfect scheme" of morality, that is, a doctrinal vehicle[118] of the moral world to come, which understands itself as such; on the other hand, he identifies the "moral truth" of natural religion with Christianity itself, as he polemically reverses Theophanes' question and asks what remains of *Christianity* after one removes its moral essence. For Morgan, like for Kant, Christianity is not different from natural religion. On the contrary, the latter *is* the former at the point of its fulfillment. Interestingly, Kant uses the term "schema" in a similar context. He says that a "particular community" with a correct self-understanding, that is, a visible (and to that extent positive) church "that strives after the consensus of all human beings in order to establish an absolute ethical whole," can be called a "schema" – i.e. a "visible representation" – of an "ethical community," meaning the invisible (purely moral) church (RGV, 6:96), in which "Christianity's true first purpose" that "was none other than the introduction of a pure religious faith" finds realization and radically differentiates itself from Judaism (RGV, 6:131–2).

In light of the foregoing, it becomes clear that Morgan and Kant both share (in general and in detail) the Marcionian commitment to morally revolutionize Christianity at the cost of placing Judaism – an "eternal scandal,"[119] not merely an "anachronism" – as its total opposite.

5   Conclusion

Kant gave the clearest expression to Marcion's main idea in the entire German Enlightenment, second only to Morgan when it comes to the Enlightenment as such. By supporting this thesis, this chapter moves the framework linking Marcion and German philosophy from the period of German Idealism to Kant. As I have already noted, Harnack points out that Morgan revived Marcionism in the Enlightenment. However, later on Harnack omits the German Enlightenment and moves on to Schleiermacher and Hegel, claiming

---

117   Ibid., 346–7.
118   Cf. ibid., 408.
119   Ibid., 255.

that only those thinkers philosophically adapted Marcionism.[120] There is a similar tendency in Micha Brumlik's *Deutscher Geist und Judenhaß* – Marcion appears in Brumlik's discussion of Schleiermacher and Schelling, but is absent from the fragments on Kant.[121] Jan van den Berg, in turn, does not mention Kant at all in his just-published monograph on Morgan, even though the book discusses Morgan "as a Harbinger of the Disparagement of the Old Testament" in Germany.[122] If philosophically rendered Marcionism is a popular theme in German Idealism, it is worth pointing out that it has its origin in the most important impulse of this intellectual current, that is, Kant's philosophy. The Marcionian trope was preserved in Kant's religious thought against the spirit of its times and survived various antagonisms between Kant and his idealistic followers.

Acknowledgments

This chapter is a result of the research project no. 2020/37/N/HS1/02922, financed by the National Science Centre in Poland.

References

Assmann, Jan, *Moses the Egyptian. The Memory of Egypt in Western Monotheism* (Cambridge, Mass.: 1998).

Beck, Lewis W., *Early German Philosophy. Kant and his Predecessors* (Cambridge, Mass.: 1969).

Bendavid, Lazarus, *Etwas zur Charakteristik der Juden* (Leipzig: 1793).

Bloch, Ernst, "On the Original History of the Third Reich," trans. Neville Plaice, Stephen Plaice, in *The Frankfurt School on Religion*, ed. Eduardo Mendieta (New York: 2005), 21–41.

Bohatec, Josef, *Die Religionsphilosophie Kants in der* Religion innerhalb der Grenzen der bloßen Vernunft. *Mit besonderer Berücksichtigung ihrer theologisch-dogmatischen Quellen* (Hamburg: 1938).

Borowski, Ludwig E., *Darstellung des Lebens und Charakters Immanuel Kant's* (Königsberg: 1804).

---

120   Harnack, *Marcion, The Gospel of the Alien God*, 220.

121   Micha Brumlik, *Deutscher Geist und Judenhaß. Das Verhältnis des philosophischen Idealismus zum Judentum* (Munich: 2002).

122   Jan van den Berg, *A Forgotten Christian Deist. Thomas Morgan* (New York: 2021), 162–8.

Brumlik, Micha, *Deutscher Geist und Judenhaß. Das Verhältnis des philosophischen Idealismus zum Judentum* (Munich: 2002).

Brumlik, Micha, *Die Gnostiker. Der Traum von der Selbsterlösung des Menschen* (Frankfurt a.M.: 1992).

Carter, Kameron J., *Race. A Theological Account* (New York: 2008).

Ehrman, Bart D., *Lost Christianities: The Battles for Scripture and the Faiths We Never Knew* (New York: 2003).

Faber, Richard, *Political Demonology. On Modern Marcionism*, trans. Therese Feiler, Michael Mayo (Eugene: 2018).

Fletcher, Paul, "Towards Perpetual Revolution: Kant on Freedom and Authority," in *The Politics to Come: Power, Modernity and the Messianic*, eds. Arthur Bradley and Paul Fletcher (London: 2010), 57–78.

Gunneweg, Antonius H.J., *Vom Verstehen des Alten Testaments. Eine Hermeneutik* (Göttingen: 1988).

Hamann, Johann G., "Golgotha and Sheblimini!" in *Writings on Philosophy and Language*, trans. Kenneth Hayes (New York: 2007), 164–205.

Haring, James, "Judaism and the Contingency of Religious Law in Kant's *Religion within the Boundaries of Mere Reason*," *Journal of Religious Ethics* 48/1 (2020): 74–100.

Harnack, Adolf, *Marcion. The Gospel of the Alien God*, trans. John E. Steely and Lyle D. Bierma (Durham: 1990).

Herder, Johann G., *Älteste Urkunde des Menschengeschlechts: eine nach Jahrhunderten enthüllte heilige Schrift. Erster Band* (Tübingen: 1806).

Herder, Johann G., *Vom Geist der ebräischen Poesie. Eine Anleitung für die Liebhaber derselben, und der ältesten Geschichte des menschlichen Geistes* (Stuttgart: 1827).

Heschel, Susannah, *The Aryan Jesus. Christian Theologians and the Bible in Nazi Germany* (Princeton: 2008).

Hunter, Graeme, *Radical Protestantism in Spinoza's Thought* (New York: 2017).

Hunter, Ian, "The Early Jewish Reception of Kantian Philosophy," *Modern Intellectual History* (2020): 1–28.

Jerusalem, Johann F.W., *Betrachtungen über die vornehmsten Wahrheiten der Religion. Zweiter Teil* (Frankfurt: 1775).

Jerusalem, Johann F.W., *Briefe über die mosaischen Schriften und Philosophie* (Braunschweig: 1762).

Kant, Immanuel, "Religion within the Boundaries of Mere Reason," in *Religion and Rational Theology* (Cambridge, Eng.: 1996), 39–217 (RGV, 6).

Kant, Immanuel, "The End of All Things," in *Religion and Rational Theology* (Cambridge, Eng.: 1996), 217–233 (EAD, 8).

Kant, Immanuel, "The Conflict of the Faculties," in *Religion and Rational Theology* (Cambridge, Eng.: 1996), 233–329 (SF, 7).

Kant, Immanuel, *Critique of Judgment*, trans. Werner S. Pluhar (Indianapolis: 1987) (KU, 5).

Kant, Immanuel, "The Only Possible Argument in Support of a Demonstration of the Existence of God," in *Theoretical Philosophy, 1755–1770* (Cambridge, Eng.: 1992), 107–195 (BDG, 2).

Knutzen, Martin, *Philosophischer Beweis von der Wahrheit der christlichen Religion* (Nordhausen: 2005).

Kozyra, Wojciech, "Kant on the Jews and their Religion," *Diametros* 17/65 (2020): 32–55.

Kuehn, Manfred, *Kant. A Biography* (New York: 2001).

Lechler, Gotthard V., *Geschichte des englischen Deismus* (Stuttgart: 1841).

Lessing, Gotthold E., "The Education of the Human Race," in *Philosophical and Theological Writings*, trans. H.B. Nisbet (New York: 2005), 217–241.

Lüder, Andreas, *Historie und Dogmatik. Ein Beitrag zur Genese und Entfaltung von Johann Salomo Semlers Verständnis des Alten Testaments* (Berlin: 1995).

Mahlev, Haim, "Kabbalah as Philosophia Perennis? The Image of Judaism in the German Early Enlightenment: Three Studies," *The Jewish Quarterly Review* 104/2 (2014): 234–257.

Mendelssohn, Moses, *Jerusalem: Or, on the Religious Power and Judaism*, trans. Allan Arkush (Hanover: 1983).

Michaelis, Johann D., *Einleitung in die göttlichen Schriften des Neuen Bundes. Erster Theil* (Göttingen: 1788).

Moll, Sebastian, *The Arch-Heretic. Marcion* (Tübingen: 2010).

Morgan, Thomas, *The Moral Philosopher in a Dialog between Philalethes a Christian Deist, and Theophanes a Christian Jew* (London: 1737).

Palmquist, Stephen R., "How Political is Kantian Church?" Diametros 17/65 (2020): 95–113.

Reimarus, Hermann S., *Abhandlungen von den vornehmsten Wahrheiten der natürlichen Religion* (Hamburg: 1772).

Reimarus, Hermann S., *Fragments from Reimarus*, trans. Charles Voysey (London: 1879).

Reimarus, Hermann S., *Reimarus: Fragments*, trans. Ralph S. Fraser (London: 1970).

Reinhold, Karl L., *Letters on the Kantian Philosophy*, trans. James Hebbeler (New York: 2005).

Reinhold, Karl L., *Die Hebräischen Mysterien: Oder die älteste religiöse Freymaurerey* (Leipzig: 1788).

Rosenberg, Alfred, *Der Mythus des 20. Jahrhunderts* (Munich: 1934).

Rosenstock, Bruce, *Philosophy and the Jewish Question. Mendelssohn, Rosenzweig, and Beyond* (New York: 2010).

Roth, Dieter T., *The Text of Marcion's Gospel* (Leiden: 2015).

Schiller, Friedrich, "Die Sendung Moses," in *Thalia* 3/10 (Leipzig: 1790): 3–38.

Schröter, Marianne, "Johann Salomo Semler und das Alte Testament," in *Christentum und Judentum. Akten des Internationalen Kongresses der Schleiermacher-Gesellschaft in Halle, März 2009*, eds. Roderich Barth, Ulrich Barth and Claus-Dieter Osthövener (Berlin: 2012), 125–141.

Schulte, Christoph, *Die jüdische Aufklärung. Philosophie, Religion, Geschichte* (Munich: 2002).

Semler, Johann S., *Abhandlung von freier Untersuchung des Canon* (Halle: 1771).

Semler, Johann S., *Beantwortung der Fragmente eines Ungenannten insbesondere vom Zweck Jesu und seiner Jünger* (Halle: 1780).

Spinoza, Benedict, *Theological-Political Treatise*, trans. Jonathan I. Israel, Michael Silverthorne (New York: 2007).

Stangneth, Bettina, "Antisemitische und Antijudaistische Motive bei Immanuel Kant? Tatsachen, Meinungen, Ursachen," in *Antisemitismus bei Kant und anderen Denkern der Aufklärung*, eds. Horst Gronke, Thomas Meyer, Barbara Neisser (Würzburg: 2001), 11–125.

Starck, Johann A., *Betrachtungen über das Christenthum* (Berlin: 1780).

Stäudlin, Karl Friedrich, *Geschichte der Sittenlehre Jesu* (Göttingen: 1799).

Steigmann-Gall, Richard, *The Holy Reich. Nazi Conceptions of Christianity, 1919–1945* (New York: 2003).

Sutcliffe, Adam, *Judaism and Enlightenment* (Cambridge, Mass.: 2003).

Tertullian, *The Five Books Against Marcion*, trans. Peter Holmes (Edinburgh: 1878).

Van den Berg, Jan, *A Forgotten Christian Deist. Thomas Morgan* (New York: 2021).

Van den Berg, Jan, "English Deism and Germany: The Thomas Morgan Controversy," *Journal of Ecclesiastical History* 59/1 (2008): 48–61.

Wachter, Johann G., *Der Spinozismus im Jüdenthumb* (Amsterdam: 1699).

Warda, Arthur, *Immanuel Kants Bücher* (Berlin: 1922).

Index

Abraham   136, 335–336
Acosta, Uriel   243
Adam (first man)   136, 254–255
    fall of   104, 254, 304, 307
    sin of   143, 250, 252, 254–255
Adams, Abigail   61
Adams, John   64–65
afterlife   87, 150, 174, 189–190, 209, 240, 248, 254, 329
agnostic   82, 85, 94, 210–212, 216
agnosticism
    on substance   238, 251
Al-Farabi, Abu Nasr Muhammad ibn Muhammad   29
d'Alembert, Jean le Rond   16, 35
Ambrosius Ferrarius   300
Amelius   300
Ancien Régime. See also Old Regime   106, 131, 134, 152, 156, 198 n. 6
anti-Christianism   188
anti-clericalism   19, 145, 161, 166, 186, 188
anti-religion   188, 319, 325
anti-Trinitarianism   238, 258, 260 n. 94
anti-Trinitarians   253 n. 69, 255, 259–260
antinomianism   242, 246
Aquinas, Thomas   8, 73
archetype   86, 278 n. 36
    divine   312
    of human being   86, 312
    of perfection   278
Arianism   262
Aristotelianism   106, 113
Arminianism   10, 238
Arminians   112, 246, 250
Arminius, Jacob   238
Arnold, Gottfried   5, 299
Artigas-Menant, Geneviève   145
Ascher, Saul   331
Assmann, Jan   329
atheism   5–6, 18, 55, 102, 120, 134–135, 140, 153, 162, 169, 173, 175, 179, 187–188, 198–199, 201, 205, 206 n. 36, 207–210, 215–216, 226, 295 n. 8, 296 n. 12, 306, 314
    accusation of   50, 173, 188, 225
    agnostic   210, 216
    arguments for   199, 207, 210–211

Athenagoras   300
atomism   30
atonement   224, 238, 252–254, 308
Augustine (Saint)   8, 54, 73, 104
Aulard, François-Alphonse   168, 177–178, 184, 186

Bacon, Francis   23, 220, 267–268, 269 n. 9, 270, 276
Bailyn, Bernard   59
Baker, Keith Michael   88, 90
Balling, Pieter   301
Banks, Bryan   37
Barclay, Robert   271–273, 282–283
Baumgarten, Alexander Gottlieb   267 n. 3
Baumgarten, Siegmund Jacob   337–338
Baxter, Richard   243
Bayle, Pierre   29, 50, 52–54, 105–106, 108, 113–114, 135, 138, 149, 155–156
Beccaria, Cesare   62
Becker, Carl   18, 69
Beiser, Frederick C.   296
Bendavid, Lazarus   328 n. 34
Benedictines   24–25
Benítez, Miguel   30 n. 44
Bergier, Nicolas-Sylvestre   208–209
Berkeley, George   53
Bernard, Jean-Frederick   4
Beverland, Adriaan   104–105
Beverley, Thomas   225
Bible   4, 17, 27, 48–49, 103–104, 145, 242, 245, 260, 269–270, 299, 305, 314, 323
    Hebrew   320–322, 327–328, 331, 337, 339, 342
Biddle, John   261
Blount, Charles   243
Bodin, Jean   133–134, 136, 153
Boethius   251
Boileau, Nicolas   75–77
Bonjour, Noé Antoine Abraham   180 n. 90
Bossuet, Jacques-Bénigne   75–76, 85
Bossuet's circle   75–78, 80, 89
Boswell, James   53, 107
Boulding, Kenneth E.   285 n. 54
Boyle, Robert   271
Bradley, Thomas   253 n. 70

Brissot de Warville, Jacques-Pierre   91–93, 95

Brounower, Sylvester   261

Browne, Peter   231–232

Brumlik, Micha   344

Brunet, Pierre   69

Bruno, Giordano   296 n. 12

Brutus   176, 179

Buckley, Michael   199 n. 8, 201

Buffier, Claude G.   25

Buffon, Georges-Louis Leclerc de   32, 167 n. 35, 206

Bulman, William J.   21

Burgersdijk, Franco   113

Burke, Edmund   46

Burman, Franciscus   105

Burnet, Thomas   225

Burson, Jeffrey   3, 8, 70 n. 7, 294 n. 4

Bury, Arthur   259

Butterwick, Richard   19

Calas, Jean   178

Calvin, John   104, 255

Calvinists   28, 103
   Dutch   113

Cartesianism   109, 135–136, 138, 152, 154
   and Enlightenment   152
   radical   154
   reception of   106

Cartesians   31, 135
   radical   113

Casaubon, Isaac   300

Cassirer, Ernst   18

Catholicism   17, 22, 24, 72, 113, 175
   Enlightenment   23, 25
   French   188
   Reform   23–25
   revolutionary   70

Cattoi, Thomas   268, 270, 275–276, 278 n. 36, 287–289

cercle Spinoziste (also Spinoza's circle)   7, 303

Chalier, Marie Joseph   176, 179

Challe, Robert   9, 134, 136–157

Charles II   104

Chartier, Roger   167, 187

Chaussard, Pierre-Jean-Baptiste   173

Chénier, André   183

Chénier, Marie-Joseph   161

Chillingworth, William   238

China   72, 79, 89

Christianity   6–8, 10, 35, 48, 72, 93–94, 101, 103, 111, 120, 145–146, 154, 168 n. 37, 225, 239, 258–260, 298, 300, 302–303, 305–306, 314–315, 319–322, 324–328, 331, 333–335, 337–339, 342–343
   critique of   3, 137
   dejudaization of   321–322
   Eastern   255
   fundamentals of   246–247, 258
   historical   326
   and Judaism   10, 319–320, 325–328, 331–333, 335–337, 338 n. 79, 87, 340
   Latin   255
   Marcionian   321, 327
   as morality   342–343
   as natural religion   325, 343
   orthodox   302, 310
   Protestant   10, 237, 239, 262
   reasonable   239
   as revealed religion   307
   sectarian. See heterodoxy   47
   trinitarian   303
   universal   309, 323, 335

Church (church(es))   4, 74, 101, 103, 145, 166, 169, 178, 186, 190–191, 232, 266, 287, 289 n. 66, 290 n. 68, 297, 323, 325–326, 343
   Anglican (of England, English)   48, 220, 226
   Baptist   263
   Catholic (Roman)   23, 72, 139, 200, 208, 252, 297
   Christian   323, 327
   councils   284
   critics (critique) of   3, 174, 297, 299
   Fathers   73, 103–104, 139, 278 n. 36, 320
   Gallican   32
   history   47, 340
   institutional   156, 300
   invisible and visible   343
   Lutheran   5, 74, 296, 299
   practice   278 n. 35
   Protestant   252, 326
   Reformed
      Dutch   103, 111, 118
      Minor, of Poland   238, 253 n. 69

silver   190
and state   74, 101, 103, 232, 289 n. 66,
   294–295
true   289
Cicero   136
clandestine   30–31, 131, 132 n. 4, 7, 135–136,
   153, 156, 332
   literature   3, 132, 198 n. 6
   manuscripts   5, 9, 30, 32, 34, 132–135
clandestinity
   philosophical   134
Clement of Alexandria   300, 301 n. 35, 305
Cocceians   27–28, 112
Cocceius, Johannes   27
Colardeau, Charles-Pierre   179 n. 87
Coleman, Charly   3, 17, 37
Collegiants   49, 111, 295 n. 8, 301
Collins, Anthony   31, 107, 245
colonialism   81
Community of the Inspired   299
Condorcet, Marie Jean Antoine Nicolas de
   Caritat, Marquis of   82–85, 165 n. 25,
   172 n. 56
confessionalization   101
Conrad, Sebastian   35
conscience   49–50, 54–56, 61, 74, 77, 85–86,
   89, 146, 181, 183, 252, 271, 283, 297
   national   61
   natural light of   52
   rights of   139
Conway, Anne   271
Corbett, Jim   285 n. 54
cosmopolitanism   115–116, 118
Cranz, August   328
Crébillon, Claude-Prosper Jolyot de   179
   n. 87
creedal minimalism   247
Crell, Johann   256, 260
Crell, Samuel   111, 259
Crisp, Samuel   242
Crisp, Tobias   242
Crousaz, Jean-Pierre de   180 n. 90
Cult of Reason   9, 169, 174–175, 179–180, 184,
   186–190
Cult of Theophilanthropy   188
Cult of the Supreme Being   9, 79, 169–170,
   172–173, 175–178, 180–181, 184, 186–187,
   189–190

Curbachius, Adrianus. *See* Koerbagh,
   Adriaan   296 n. 12

Danton, Georges Jacques   172 n. 56
Darparens   184–185, 189
Davies, Simon   19
De La Bastays, Lebeschu   173–174, 189
de Neufville, Christina   111
de Pinto, Isaac   108
de Sales, François   3
de Vallone, Yves   134, 151
Decalogue   94, 320, 330
dechristianization   166, 169, 189
Declaration of Independence   46
Declaration of the Rights of Man and of the
   Citizen   93–94
deism   5–6, 9, 93, 102, 134–135, 139, 151–152,
   153, 155–156, 164, 168, 178, 183, 186, 188,
   197–201, 207–208, 210–212, 215–217,
   242–243, 246
   arguments against   201, 207, 215
   Cartesian   152
   clandestine   135–136, 143, 153
   English   338
   non-optimistic   211–212, 216
   optimist   210–211
   philosophical   204
   radical   136, 152
   reasonable   198, 216
   revolutionary   188
Descartes, René   23, 31 n. 46, 53, 113, 135,
   148–149, 152, 154–156, 220, 267–268, 270
Desgabets, Robert   154 n. 86
Desmoulin, Camille   174
Diderot, Denis   6–7, 16, 26, 32–35, 77, 81–82,
   107, 134, 198–199
Dionysius the Areopagite   300
disenchantment   5, 101
divine law(s)   70–71, 73, 78–79, 81, 87, 90–91,
   93–94, 248
divine light   270–271, 272 n. 21, 22, 290
Dominicans   75
du Marsais, César Chesneau   35, 134, 136
Dunn, John   262
Durkheim, Emile   37

Edelmann, Johann Christian   4–5, 10,
   296–306, 309–310, 314–315

Edelstein, Dan   3, 20–21, 70
Edwards, John   225, 237–239, 247, 258
empiricism   9, 53, 135, 138, 151
Encyclopédie   32, 34–35, 84, 110
Engelberts, Matthias (Engelbertus)   117
Engelhard, Nicolaus   111
Enlightenment   1–10, 15–23, 24 n. 25, 25–27,
      29, 33–37, 46–47, 49, 52–53, 58, 65,
      68–72, 76, 90, 101, 116, 134–135, 152, 154,
      156, 165, 167, 263, 268–270, 275–276, 279,
      290, 294–295, 298, 313, 322, 337, 343
   American   19
   Catholic   3, 22–24, 70
   Counter-   7
   Dutch   102, 107–109, 112–113
   early   9, 17, 50, 105, 222, 270–271, 274, 282,
      337
      critique of   273
      Dutch   105
      German   338 n. 79
   European   53, 106
   French (*also* Francophone)   19, 32–33,
      35, 37, 68, 74–75, 85
   German   10, 296, 314, 319, 331, 336, 343
   humble   266
   moderate   7, 153, 200, 295, 313
   radical   4, 6–7, 9, 16, 21, 26, 28, 33, 105,
      107, 112–113, 131, 134–135, 152–153, 295,
      298, 313–314, 337 n. 78
   and religion   1, 9, 294, 313
   religious   2, 10, 22–23, 25, 70, 152–153,
      294–295, 298, 313
   secular   4, 16, 37, 46, 50–51, 153, 295, 313
   and secularization   5, 8–9, 15–17, 21, 28,
      30, 34, 71, 94
enlightenment (process)   2 n. 4, 15, 175, 266,
      274, 277 n. 35, 278 n. 35, 284, 328, 334
   entangled   26, 33
enlightenments   19–20, 26
   national   20
   religious   22, 25, 36
enthusiasm   272 n. 22, 279 n. 38
   philosophical   312
Epicureanism   7 n. 38, 30, 32 n. 46
Epicureans   3, 314
Epicurus   296 n. 12
Erasmus of Rotterdam   103, 119, 260
Erdozain, Dominic   8

Espinoza, Gabriel   19
essences
   free creation of   154 n. 86
   nominal and real   223
Eugene of Savoy, Prince   134
experience(s)   53, 213, 271–277, 278 n. 35,
      279, 282–284, 290, 301, 311
   immediate   278, 281–282
   inward   271, 284 n. 52, 285, 290
   mediate   281
   mystical   271, 279, 282, 286, 290
   personal   48, 269–271
   religious   29, 38, 279, 284 n. 52, 286 n. 57
experimental method   276
experiment(s)   110, 206, 270, 274, 276

faith(s)   3, 8, 26, 33, 48–52, 92, 140, 151,
      154, 224–225, 239, 245–247, 249, 259,
      266 n. 1, 278 n. 35, 284, 287, 289 n. 68,
      296, 302, 310, 314–315, 342
   as assent   244, 249
   Christian   145, 302
   experiential   290
   good (*bonne foi*)   216
   and good works   237, 239, 242, 249
   historical   277 n. 35, 284, 287, 290 n. 68
   in Jesus. *See also* Christianity,
      fundamentals of   246–247, 249, 259
   justifying   249
   as knowledge   245
   Law of   247
   moral   278 n. 35, 308
   as obedience to reason   301
   practical   266
   Quaker   274, 286
   rational   277 n. 35, 284, 287, 307
   religious   1, 46–47, 294, 313
   revealed   278 n. 35
   salvation by   48, 249
   saving   249
   spurious   300, 310
   true   286 n. 55
fanaticism   162, 174–175, 279 n. 38
Fell, Margaret   48
Fénelon, François   3, 75–77, 80
Ferrone, Vincenzo   21, 36
Ficino, Marsilio   300
fideism   224, 288, 315

Firestone, Christopher   310
Firmin, Thomas   259
Fix, Andrew   49
Fleury, Claude   75
Fontenelle, Bernard le Bovier de   134
Foucault, Michel   233
Fouché, Joseph   189
Fox, George   10, 48, 269–270, 273, 288
Franklin, Benjamin   179
Frederick William II   306
freedom   58, 80, 117, 266, 275, 285
    divine   148
    and equality   185
    as a feature of true church   289, 297
    human   80, 90, 147, 149
    of inquiry   339
    of the press   85
    sense of   144
    of speech   339
Freemasonry   157
Freke, John   243
Fréret, Nicolas   134
freethinkers   106, 120, 245, 263, 296 n. 12,
    300 n. 24
fundamentalism (religious)   315
Furly, Benjamin   222

Gailhard, Jean   225
Galland, Antoine   75
Gassendi, Pierre   3, 220
Gay, Peter   6–7, 18–19, 53, 69
general will   47, 61, 86, 87 n. 70
German Idealism   115, 298, 343–344
God   9–10, 17, 25, 28, 30, 34, 49, 51–53, 68,
    70, 72–73, 77, 86, 88–89, 92–94, 106,
    112, 117–118, 139, 141, 144, 146, 149–151,
    162–164, 174–175, 177, 180, 182–183, 185,
    187–188, 190–191, 197, 199, 203–204,
    209–211, 215, 238, 240–242, 244,
    247–248, 250, 252–255, 272–274, 281,
    297, 299–303, 304, 307, 309–310, 312,
    314, 320–321, 328–330, 335–336, 340,
    342
    attributes of   140, 147, 202
    belief in   50, 82, 140, 172 n. 54, 197, 203,
        207–208, 210–211, 216, 275
    City of   95
    commandments of   29, 324

concept (conception) of   148, 154–155,
    167, 173–174, 177, 182–183, 202–203, 207,
    212, 312, 329
creation of eternal truths   147, 155
deist   197, 202, 207, 210, 212, 215
design argument   197, 201–208, 215, 240
do ut des   183
doctrine of univocity   141, 144, 148
evil   203, 320
existence of   5, 82, 92, 140, 148, 169, 171,
    173, 175, 177–178, 185, 188–189, 198–199,
    201, 203–205, 207, 209–211, 215–217,
    240, 270 n. 14
experience of   48, 282, 284, 290
the Father   254, 259, 304
forgiveness of   248
and French nation   94, 162, 183
goodness of   82, 147, 149, 250
government by   70, 78
idea of   155, 175, 180
in us   297, 301
intervening in the world   153, 183, 188
Jehovah   330, 334
Jewish   319, 321
as judge   147, 155
Kingdom of   50, 254
knowledge of   177, 182, 243, 266
as lawgiver   240, 247, 249
love of   48
mind of   312
non-existence of   150, 201, 207, 209–210
personal   147, 197
of philosophers   53
presence of   283, 289
proof(s) of   175, 182, 187, 332
rational   155
reference to   68, 71, 77, 95, 163
thinkers of   167, 169
transcendent   9, 149
unity with   301
vision in   138, 141–142, 154, 312–313
voice of   50
as watchmaker   183, 188
will of   87 n. 70, 148, 155
word of   48–49, 245
worship of   181–182, 184–185, 189
Goethe, Johann Wolfgang   114
Gomarists   112

Gordon, Thomas   57, 59–60
Gossec, François-Joseph   161, 162 n. 14
Gourdon, Emilie   209–210
grace   247, 250
    assisting   238, 250
    distribution of   151, 154
    fall from   74, 104
    salvific   17
Great Awakening   72
Gregory of Nyssa   300
Grossmann, Walter   301, 305
Grotius, Hugo   73, 104, 238, 245, 253
Gut, Przemysław   28
Guyon, Jeanne-Marie   3

Halakha   327, 328 n. 34, 334
Hamann, Johann Georg   335–336
Hamilton, Alexander   63–64
Hampton, Alexander J.B.   37
Hardenberg, Friedrich von   37
Haring, James   323 n. 19, 325 n. 26
Harnack, Adolf von   321, 323, 327, 333, 337,
    343
Harris, Robert   253 n. 70
Hämäläinen, Hasse   9, 25
Hébert, Jacques-René   172 n. 56
Hegel, Georg Wilhelm Friedrich   298, 325,
    343
Heine, Heinrich   275 n. 30
Heinsius, Daniel   104
Helvétius, Claude-Adrien   7, 167 n. 35, 179
    n. 87, 185, 198–199
Hemsterhuis, Frans   108, 114, 118–119
Hemsterhuis, Tiberius   119
Henry IV   54
Herbert of Cherbury, Edward   243
Herder, Johann Gottfried   335–336, 338
Hermeticism   30–31
Herodotus   305
heterodoxy   4–5, 258, 306
    Christian   299
    religious   5–6, 314
Hill, Christopher   47–49
Hirsi Ali, Ayaan   1
histoire croisée   26
Hobbes, Thomas   50, 60, 113, 135, 296 n. 12
Holbach, Paul-Henri Thiry, baron d'   3, 6–7,
    9, 112, 134, 138, 140, 197–217

Holy Spirit   48–50, 261–262
Hooft, Pieter C.   104
Houdon, Jean-Antoine   160
Hölderlin, Friedrich   37
Hudson, Wayne   153
Huguenots   139
human nature   18, 47, 56, 58–59, 61, 64, 73,
    77, 241, 248, 250, 255, 287, 304, 307, 310,
    312–313
humanity   17, 21, 23, 34, 54, 204, 245, 254–255,
    303, 308, 324, 332, 334, 336, 342 n. 111
    and God   253, 259, 307, 312
    happiness of   34
    morally perfect   308, 310–311
    respect for   286
    theology (religion) of   29, 35
Hume, David   6–7, 52–53, 63–64, 134, 215–216,
    272–273, 276 n. 32
Hume, Sophia   285 n. 54
Hunt, Lynn   34, 37
Hunter, Graeme   330
Husserl, Edmund   233
Hussites   70, 80

Ignatius of Antioch   300
immanent frame   4, 5 n. 25
immortality   187, 253–256, 266, 275
    of the soul   171, 173, 178, 189, 255, 329
Incarnation   8, 151, 286 n. 55, 296, 302–303,
    306, 308–310, 313–314
Independents   242
induction   270
intellectual intuition   283
inward (inner) light   48, 56, 269, 272, 274, 278
    n. 35, 282–284, 290, 301
irenic (Protestant tradition)   246, 262
irreligion. See atheism   5
Isidor of Pelusium   320
Israel, Jonathan   6–8, 28, 30 n. 44, 50–51,
    105–106, 112, 131, 134–135, 152, 199–201,
    207, 215, 233, 295

Jachmann, Reinhold Bernhard   280–281
Jacob, Margaret   4, 30 n. 44, 68–69, 71, 74, 131,
    294–295
Jacobi, Friedrich Heinrich   114
Jacobins   171–172
Jacobites   87

Jacobs, Nathan   310
James II   87
Jansenism   72
Jansenists   24–25, 33, 76–77
Jefferson, Thomas   46, 56, 61–62, 64–65
Jelles, Jarig   5, 303
Jeremiah (prophet)   329
Jerusalem, Johann Friedrich Wilhelm
    339
Jesuits   3, 23–24, 31–33, 71–72, 74–76
Jesus Christ   8, 10, 28, 48–50, 86, 145–146,
    237, 245–250, 252–254, 259, 261–262,
    269, 301–311, 320–322, 324, 327, 329,
    331–334, 336, 341, 342 n. 11
  divinity (deity) of   286 n. 55, 302, 320, 331
  incarnational   258
  as messiah   225, 246–247, 249, 259
  pre-existence of   261
  as second Adam   253, 259
  Second Coming   256
  as Son of God   253, 303 n. 43, 307, 311
  as teacher of morality   308, 323, 329
Johannine Comma   260
John Damascene   300
John Paul II (Pope)   1
Johnson, Erica   37
Johnson, Samuel   53
John the Apostle   305
Judaism   10, 136, 278 n. 35, 319–320, 323–329,
    330 n. 42, 331–337, 338 n. 79, 87, 339–343
  elimination from Christianity   326–327,
    328 n. 33, 34, 335, 339
  as immoral   323 n. 19, 325, 331
  as political organization   323
  three positions on   331
Judgment Day. See Last Judgment   251–252,
    255
Jullien, Marc-Antoine   172 n. 54
justification   238–239, 249–250
Justin Martyr   300, 320

Kahle, Ludwig Martin   201, 204
Kant, Immanuel   6, 8, 10, 15, 25, 114–116,
    118, 266–269, 270 n. 14, 272, 273 n. 28,
    274–290, 296–298, 306–312, 314–315,
    319, 322–344
Kantianism   114, 116
Karel, Gijsbert   114

Keiser, Melvin   282 n. 46
Kerrl, Hanns   322
Kinker, Johannes   115
Kloek, Joost   107
Knutzen, Martin   338
Knutzen, Matthias   198, 296 n. 12
Koenig, Samuel   111
Koerbagh, Adriaan   102
Kors, Alan Charles   3, 201, 207, 209–210,
    215–216
Koyré, Alexandre   69, 233
Kozyra, Wojciech   10
Kuehn, Manfred   307 n. 61
Kuhn, Thomas   233

La Bruyère, Jean de   75–77
La Mettrie, Julien Offray de   32, 198–199
La Mothe Le Vayer, François de   131
Lamourette, Adrien   2
Last Judgment   146, 237, 239, 251, 255–257
latitudinarians   238, 246
Lau, Theodor Ludwig   313
La Visclède, Antoine-Louis de
    Chalamont   180 n. 90
La Vopa, Anthony   200 n. 15, 207
law(s) of nature   30, 57, 199, 201, 203–205,
    207, 210, 215, 238, 241, 243, 247, 249–250
Leask, Ian   9
Le Barbier, Jean-Jacques François   94
LeBuffe, Michael   209–210
Lechler, Gotthard Victor   337
Le Clerc, Jean   222, 228, 259–260
Lehner, Ulrich   3, 22
Leibniz, Gottfried Wilhelm   29, 271
Le Mercier de la Rivière, Pierre-Paul   80, 82
Lepeletier, Loius Michel   176, 179
Lepelletier, Almire René Jacques   177 n. 76
Lessing, Gotthold Ephraim   296, 323–324,
    332, 336
Levellers   56
libertinism   76, 131
liberty   52, 58, 63, 149, 162, 165, 186
  of fatherland   177
Lilburne, John   56
Lilienthal, Theodore Christoph   338
Limborch, Philipp van   222, 228, 238, 253,
    258–259
Lipsius, Justus   103

littérature clandestine. See clandestine,
    literature 198
Locke, John   8–10, 23, 47, 51–53, 56–58, 65,
    106, 114, 135, 151, 219–233, 237–263,
    271–273, 282, 295 n. 9
Logos (Λογος)   49–50, 299–300, 303
Louis XIV   137, 152
Love, Brandon   276
Lucci, Diego   10
Lucretius   120, 296 n. 12
lumières naturelles. See natural light   140
Luther, Martin   255, 296 n. 12, 323, 327
Luzac, Elie   108
Łyszczyński, Kazimierz (*also* Casimir
    Lyszincki)   5, 296 n. 12

Mabillon, Jean   75
Mably, Gabriel Bonnot de   88–91, 93
Macmurray, John   285 n. 54
Madison, James   63
Maimonides (Moses ben Maimon)   29, 33
Malebranche, Nicolas   23, 29, 53, 135–140,
    142–144, 146–148, 151, 154–155, 296 n. 12
Marat, Jean-Paul   176, 179
Marcion   319–322, 331, 338–340, 343–344
Marcionism   319–321, 324, 331, 336–338, 340,
    343–344
Marsh, Narcissus   231
materialism   18, 28, 30, 55, 135
    Epicurean   33
    modern   26
    one-substance   28
    vitalistic   30–31
Mathiez, Albert   168, 184
Matytsin, Anton   3
McKenna, Antony   132
McMahon, Darrin   21
Mendelssohn, Moses   2, 10, 323, 328, 331, 335
Mércier, Sébastien   165 n. 25
Meslier, Jean   134
Methodism   263
Methuen, John   227–228
Michaelis, Johann David   340
Middle Ages   72, 87, 133, 156, 267
Mijnhardt, Wijnand W.   107–109
Milner, John   225, 237–238
Mirabaud, Jean Baptiste de   31, 199
Mirabeau-Tonneau (André Boniface Louis
    Riquetti de Mirabeau)   94

Molesworth, Robert   219
Moll, Sebastian   331
Molyneux, William   9, 219–221, 225, 227–233,
    242
monotheism   330–331, 334
Montaigne, Michel de   135
Montesquieu, Charles Louis de Secondat
    32, 106, 135
moral law   153, 240, 309, 312–313, 330
    divine   240–241, 246–249, 252
morality   61, 71–72, 77, 147–148, 151, 153–155,
    178, 185, 205, 224, 240–242, 246–248,
    281 n. 42, 286, 189, 297, 309, 323, 330,
    336, 342–343
    of Christ   145
    demonstrability of   243
    as the essence of religion   289
    foundations for   155, 240–241
    political   177
    of reciprocity   54
    as religion   277, 289
    teacher of   308, 332
Moravian Brethren   111
More, Henry   271
Morgan, Thomas   10, 319, 336–344
mortalism   255, 257
    psychopannychism   255
    thnetopsychism   255–256
Mortier, Roland   31
Mosaic law. *See also* Moses: Law of   327,
    330, 341
Moses   308, 324, 329–330, 332, 334, 336, 338,
    340–341
    Law of   247
Muhammad (prophet)   308
Mulsow, Martin   131, 298
mystery (theological)   224
mysticism   275 n. 30, 278 n. 37, 279–281, 286,
    295 n. 8, 301 n. 33
    Critical (*also* Kantian)   276 n. 32, 279, 281
    early modern   301

National Convention   169–171, 172 n. 54,
    175–176, 190
nationalism   116
    Dutch   118
    Irish   221
    modern   20

natural law 2, 50, 54–55, 57–58, 70, 72–77, 79–80, 83–84, 90–95, 111
    divine 75, 78–79, 250
natural light 29, 52, 82, 154, 314
natural philosophy 18, 23, 25 n. 26, 38, 109–110, 115, 217 n. 87
Naudé, Gabriel 131
Needham, John 206
neologians (also neologists) 307 n. 61, 339
neology 338–339
New Testament 28, 55, 103, 139, 145, 245, 256, 320, 332–333, 337, 341–342
Newtonianism 109–110, 113, 115
Newton, Isaac 23, 29, 106, 110–111, 201, 259–260, 267–268
Nieuwentijt, Bernard 110
Norris, John 225
Nuovo, Victor 258
Nye, Stephen 259–260

occasionalism 144, 151, 154
Ockerse, Willem Anthony 117
Old Regime. See also Ancien Régime 81, 90
Old Testament 245, 247, 320, 327–333, 336–338, 340–342
Origen 300
orthodoxy 49, 328 n. 34
    Calvinist 27
    Christian 305, 313
    Protestant 326
    Reformed 28
    religious 18
Otto, Rüdiger 305
Overton, Richard 56
Ovid 104
Ozouf, Mona 168, 184

Paganini, Gianni 5, 9
Paine, Thomas 62–63, 112
Palmquist, Stephen 10, 326
pantheism 135, 153, 295
Pantheismusstreit 114
Pascal, Blaise 140–141, 149
passions 61–63, 77, 86, 89
    tyranny of 47
patriotism 190
Paul the Apostle 48, 93, 253, 256
Penington, Isaac 273, 283

Penn, William 55, 271, 285 n. 54
Perrault, Charles 75
personal identity 238, 250–251, 257
Pestel, Friedrich Wilhelm 111
Peter the Apostle 304
Petronius 105, 296 n. 12
Petsch, Johannes 111
Philhellenism 114, 119
philosophes 3, 6–7, 9, 19, 21, 24 n. 25, 34–36, 75, 77, 81, 114, 120, 164–165, 167, 172 n. 57, 182, 184–185, 187–188, 190, 199, 209, 263
    false 171–172
    radical 27
physico-theology 110
physiocracy 78, 81–83, 84 n. 54, 85, 95
physiocrats 78, 81, 83–85, 89–90
Picart, Bernard 4
Pietism 268, 296
Pietist(s) 74–75, 268, 299, 303, 306
    radical 4, 299, 306
Plato 119, 302, 305, 312
Pluche, Abbé Noël Antoine 25
Pocock, John Greville Agard 19, 22
Polignac, Melchior de 107
Polish Brethren 238, 259
political liberalism 3, 18 n. 9
Popple, William 259
predestination 146–147, 242
pre-enlightenment 131
Presbyterians 221, 242
Price, Richard 112
Priestley, Joseph 112
prisca theologia 16, 36
probabilism 71
property rights 89, 92
Protestantism 17, 101, 221, 314, 326–327
    modern 118
    radical 305, 329
Providence 88–89, 155
Pufendorf, Samuel 74

Quakerism 10, 267–269, 273–274, 279, 285, 287–291
Quakers 10, 48, 269–276, 278 n. 35, 279, 281–283, 284 n. 52, 285, 286 n. 55, 290, 301
    (Religious) Society of Friends 48, 269, 289 n. 66, 68, 291

Quesnay, François 78–80, 85, 89
Quillet, Cassius 181–184

Racine, Jean 75, 77
radicalism 6, 28, 132, 152, 233
Rambach, Johann Jacob 304
rational spiritualism 301–302, 309
rationalism 52, 111, 135, 140, 154, 157
    anti-Christian 136
    Cartesian 53, 137–138
    Christian 136
    dogmatic 142
    early Enlightenment 270
rationalists
    Christian 50
    religious 296
Raynal, Guillaume-Thomas 78, 81
reason 2, 9–10, 23, 34, 47, 49–56, 61–62, 77,
        85, 92, 135–136, 138, 140–142, 146–149,
        152, 154–155, 186, 211, 216, 243, 266, 270,
        272 n. 21, 273, 275–276, 278, 287, 295,
        297, 299–302, 307–311, 314, 325, 326
    age of 7, 46, 263, 294
    authority of 141
    bare 277
    catechism of 156
    and Christian belief 146
    contrary to 222
    critical 8
    critique of 275, 314
    cult of. See also Cult of Reason 46
    dictates of 153
    divine 142, 155, 302
    empirical 18
    Enlightenment 277
    and faith 3, 8, 49, 151, 224, 314–315
    festival (feast) of 174, 179
    as God 10, 53, 297, 299, 301
    and history 155
    human 56, 142, 155–156, 273, 275, 297
    ideas of 312
    and intuition 223
    as legislator 297, 312
    limits of 65, 276, 287
    natural 10, 16, 28–29, 153, 239–241, 243,
        245, 262, 273, 306
    natural light of 29
    notions of 136
    practical 266 n. 1, 273 n. 28, 275, 288, 312

    primacy of 138, 141
    pure 140, 150, 288
    and religion 8, 35, 52, 294, 315
    and revelation 135–136, 244, 262, 295,
        305
    of state 72
    theoretical 266, 273 n. 28, 275
    truths above 222, 224, 239–240, 245, 307
    truths of 139
    unassisted 54, 243, 245, 247
    universality of 132, 141, 152, 154
    univocity of 148
Rediehs, Laura 270–276, 278 n. 35, 282–283,
        289
Reformation (reformation) 7 n. 38, 188, 321
    political 152
    Protestant 6, 296
    radical 10, 267
    legal 61
reform 2, 65, 76, 81
    of beliefs 150
    movements 5, 70, 72, 190
    physiocratic 81, 83
    political 90
    religious (of religion) 8–10, 190, 198, 313,
        315
    of society 77, 80
Régis, Pierre-Sylvain 154 n. 86
Reimarus, Hermann Samuel 8, 307–308,
        332–333, 338 n. 87
Reinhold, Karl Leonhard 333–335
religion 1–4, 7–10, 17, 23 n. 24, 27–29, 34–35,
        48, 51–52, 56, 69, 101, 116, 118, 145, 150,
        152, 155, 161, 164, 166–168, 182–183,
        186–188, 190–191, 197–199, 209, 211–214,
        226, 232, 236–238, 248, 256, 258, 262–
        263, 267, 273–275, 277, 284, 286–287,
        289–290, 294–295, 298, 300, 305–307,
        310, 313, 315, 319, 321–322, 324–326, 333,
        336–337, 340–342
    artificial 139, 142
    Christian 137, 140, 146, 246, 327–328
    civil (civic) 87, 156, 170, 187, 190
    critique of 6, 106, 133, 168 n. 37, 295, 299,
        313
    definition of 305 n. 57, 324
    enlightened (Enlightenment) 2, 10,
        267–269, 277–278, 283–284, 287, 290,
        315

historical 137, 139
history of 31, 34, 134, 188
of humanity 29
as imposture 300
moral 156, 290, 325–326, 328 n. 33
and morality 277, 286, 289
national 136
natural 9, 17, 29, 34, 70, 134, 136, 139,
    147, 150, 153–154, 164, 174, 187, 325–326,
    333–334, 343
of nature 136
notion (concept) of 2, 8, 35, 169, 305
organized (institutional) 3, 50, 243, 299,
    304
philosophy of 166, 187, 306
political 69, 168–169
and politics 69, 152, 166, 168, 185, 188
positive 154–155, 164, 181
rational 9, 136, 138, 140, 153, 154 n. 86,
    155–156, 214, 267 n. 5, 274, 287,
    306–307, 310, 314, 319, 325, 334
of reason 136, 157, 308, 310, 325–326
reasonable 9, 197–198, 212
revealed 6, 8–9, 55, 102, 106, 116, 136, 139,
    141, 146, 179, 295, 300, 305–307, 314
state 2
theory of 267 n. 4, 268, 276–279, 280
    n. 40, 281, 289, 325
true 30, 35, 162, 183, 277 n. 35, 283–285,
    287, 295, 302, 334
universal 8, 30, 289 n. 66, 306, 315
Remonstrants 111, 238
Renaissance 6, 30–31, 73, 133, 135, 156, 269
    n. 9, 300
republicanism 70, 85, 95, 176
    American 58
    classical 88
republicans 84, 90
Resurrection (resurrection) 305
    of Jesus 8, 146, 254, 304
    of the dead 224, 237, 239, 251, 256–257
revelation 23, 73, 116, 135–136, 153, 155, 179,
    244, 271, 282, 286 n. 55, 295, 305, 307
    biblical (scriptural) 10, 237, 239–241,
        245, 249, 262
    Christian 296, 308, 310
    critique of 315
    divine 244–245, 272, 302, 311, 339
    historical 10, 302, 307

moral 324
rational 314
Sinaitic 342 n. 111
suprarational 305
universal 301
revolution 9, 83, 160, 162 n. 15, 163, 165–167,
    171 n. 50, 172–173, 176, 178, 182 n. 97,
    184–185, 188, 190, 200
    American 59, 112
    Atlantic 37
    Batavian 112–113
    Copernican 115, 275 n. 30
    cultural 8, 15–16, 36, 38
    English 87, 95
    French 37, 68–70, 82, 90–91, 95, 102, 112,
        120, 164–165, 167–169, 177, 186, 188
    of heart 284
    religious 37
    scientific 8, 33, 69, 269 n. 9
    theological 17, 30, 34, 36
revolutionary 21 n. 15, 37, 68, 70, 91, 95,
    111–112, 161, 165, 167–169, 184, 188, 290
    cult(s) 167–168, 188
    elites 168
    festive culture 161, 169
    government 172 n. 57
    martyrs 176, 184
    politics 69
    societies 163
    theater 160
Robespierre, Maximilien 94–95, 163 n. 19,
    169–175, 177 n. 76, 178, 184, 186–189
Rock, Johann Friedrich 299
Rockwood, Raymond 160 n. 6, 161
Roman law 72, 75, 93
Rosenberg, Alfred 321–322
Rosenstock, Bruce 326
Rousseau, Jean-Jacques 6–7, 46–47, 52,
    54–56, 61, 65, 77–78, 82, 85–94, 112,
    114, 164–167, 169–179, 181–182, 185–188,
    190–191
Ruar, Martin 253
Rufus, Jones 285 n. 54
Rush, Benjamin 65

salvation 25, 48, 146, 153, 224, 237, 239, 242,
    246–250, 254, 258–259
Sandrier, Alain 201
Satan 146, 261

Scaliger, Joseph   103–104
Schaper, Annegret   298
Schelling, Friedrich Wilhelm Joseph   344
Schiller, Friedrich   334–335
Schlegel, Friedrich   37
Schleiermacher, Friedrich   343–344
Schlichting, Jonas   253, 256
Schmaltz, Tad   154 n. 86
Schmidt, James   21
Schneider, Eulogius   179
Scholasticism   252, 267
Scholem, Gershom   320
Schröder, Winfried   5, 132, 207, 215, 305
Schulz, Johann Heinrich   4–5
Scripture(s)   2, 4, 10, 48, 70, 73–74, 80,
       222, 237, 239–243, 245–247, 249, 255,
       259–260, 262, 303, 314
    Christian   308, 339
    divine origin of   245, 299
    interpretation of   239, 277 n. 35, 305
       critical-historical   222
       as its own interpreter   223
    Jewish (Hebrew)   327–328, 335
    sect of philosophy. See philosophes   16, 33
secularism   18, 25, 27, 119, 288
secularization   1–2, 8–9, 15–17, 21, 26, 28–30,
       34, 37, 50, 65, 68–69, 71, 82, 85, 94,
       101–102, 114, 119, 188, 294 n. 1, 2, 298, 315
Seignelay, Jean-Baptiste Colbert   137
Semler, Johann Salomo   338–339
Seok-heon, Ham   286 n. 54
Sergeant, John   225
's Gravesande, Willem Jacob   109–110, 114
Sheehan, Jonathan   4, 17, 34 n. 50
silence (as a way of worship)   180–182
    Quaker   282
simplicity (Quakerism)   274, 287, 289 n. 66
sin   46–48, 53–54, 56, 63, 65, 143–144,
       246–249, 252–253
    original   54, 73, 77, 138, 143, 151, 154, 225,
       250, 252, 254–255
Sirven, Jean-Paul   178
skepticism   53–54, 82, 135, 151, 238
Skinner, Quentin   50
slavery   73, 81, 83, 112, 177
    critique of   81 n. 43
Smith, Blake   37
Snobelen, Stephen   263

social contract   46–47, 55, 59, 63, 232
société populaire   171 n. 50, 175–176, 179, 181
Socinianism   10, 111, 225, 238, 248, 262,
       295 n. 8
Socinians   239, 246, 250, 253–254, 256,
       259–260, 296 n. 12, 304
Socinus, Faustus   238, 245, 248, 253, 255, 259
Socrates   170 n. 48
Sonnleithner, Mathias   9
Sorkin, David   2, 8, 22, 25, 295
soteriology   238
    moralist   10, 237, 239, 246, 249–251
    Socinian   248
Souverain, Jacques   260
Spallanzani, Lazzaro   206
Sparn, Walter   313
Spinoza, Baruch (Benedict)   3, 5, 7, 9, 26–31,
       33, 47, 49–50, 53, 101–102, 105–106,
       111–113, 134–135, 151, 156, 204, 222, 223
       n. 11, 224, 271, 294 n. 2, 295 n. 8, 296,
       299, 303, 305 n. 57, 312–314, 329–330,
       332
Spinozism   7 n. 38, 9, 26, 27 n. 33, 33, 106,
       109–110, 135, 138, 149, 295 n. 8
Stangneth, Bettina   325
Starck, Johann August   338
state of nature   56–57, 73, 85, 91
Stäudlin, Karl Friedrich   337
Stevenson, Leslie   268, 270 n. 14, 284 n. 52,
       285–286, 290
Stillingfleet, Edward   225–227, 237–239, 243,
       257–258
Stoicism   136
Stosch, Friedrich Wilhelm   313
Strauss, Leo   6, 135, 295 n. 8, 314–315
Stroumsa, Guy   29
Suárez, Francisco   74–75, 80, 85, 94
substance   238, 251
    as nature (in Spinoza)   28–29
    as substratum (in Locke)   223, 226, 251
    thinking   251, 257
superstition   35, 51–52, 54, 78, 184, 210–212,
       214, 295
supra rationem. See reason, truths above
       224, 295, 307, 314
Supreme Being   85–87, 89, 92–94, 170, 177,
       178 n. 76, 180, 183, 185–186
    Festival of   169–170, 175, 181, 184

Swift, Jonathan 228
syncretism 339

Taylor, Barbara 51
Taylor, Charles 1 n. 3, 4–5, 17, 37, 68
Taylor, Jeremy 253 n. 70
Temple, William 107
Temple of Reason 174, 179–180, 183
Terrasson, Jean 134, 136
Terror 163 n. 19, 166, 170 n. 44, 173, 190
Tertullian 320, 331
testimonies (in Quakerism) 274, 286 n. 55
theism 9, 197, 207
theocracy 70, 78, 80–82
    absolutist 214
    crisis of 9, 233
    enlightened 70
theology 16–17, 23, 34–35, 47, 53–54, 104,
        116, 237–238, 286 n. 55
    anti-modernist 52
    Catholic 71
    Christian 3, 27, 34 n. 50, 52, 119, 141–143,
        146, 151, 154–155
    deconfessionalization of 17
    dogmatic 54
    Greco-Roman 33
    historicization of 17
    Jewish 33
    Lutheran 321
    Marcionian 319, 336–338, 340
    modernist 118
    natural 17, 32, 270 n. 14, 277, 332
    philosophical 138, 147, 267, 288
    and philosophy 33, 35, 138, 154
    political 46, 188
    Quaker 274
    radical 48
    revealed 151
    Socinian 238
    supersessionist 328, 341
Theophilus 305
Thomasius, Christian 74
Thomism 73, 75, 95
Thomson, Ann 31
Tindal, Matthew 245
Tocqueville, Alexis de 37
Toland, John 9, 30–31, 157, 219–233, 243, 245,
        296 n. 12, 300, 313
Tomaszewska, Anna 10, 25

Touber, Jetze 27
Trapman, Hans 102
Trenchard, John 60
Tricoire, Damien 9
Trinitarianism 261
Trinity 8, 49, 146, 226, 258–259, 261–262,
        303
Turgot, Anne-Robert-Jacques 81–85
Tyrell, James 226 n. 27

ultramontanists 24
Unitarianism 263
Unitarians 239, 259

van Bunge, Wiep 9
van Dale, Anthony 222
van den Berg, Jan 337, 344
van der Capellen tot den Poll, Joan Derk 111,
        118
van der Marck, Frederick Adolf 111
van der Wyck, Johan 103
van de Wijnpersse, Dionysius 116
van Effen, Justus 108, 117
van Hamelsveld, IJsbrand 117
van Hemert, Paulus 115
van Heusde, Philip Willem 102, 116–117, 119
van Hogendorp, Dirk 114, 118
Vanini, Lucilio 296 n. 12
Van Kley, Dale 16, 23
van Leenhof, Frederik 27
van Musschenbroek, Pieter 109
van Rooden, Peter 101, 103
van Sas, Nicolaas C.F. 107, 109
van Woensel, Pieter 102, 120
van Zuylen, Belle 108
Vartanian, Aram 152
Velema, Wyger 119
Vermij, Rink 27
Vernet, Jacob 2
Virieu, François-Henri de 94
virtu(es) 58–59, 61, 80, 89, 105, 177, 209,
        301, 304
    burgerlijke 108–109
    civic (also social) 76, 156 n. 88
    national 65
    as obedience to reason 301
    religious 156 n. 88
    revolutionary 37
Voetians 27, 112

Voetius, Gijsbert   27
Voltaire (François-Marie Arouet)   6–9,
        16, 36, 46–47, 52–55, 65, 77–78, 81,
        106–107, 110, 134–135, 153, 155, 157,
        160–167, 169, 172–183, 185–191, 197–201,
        203–209, 211–212, 215–217
voluntarism   154 n. 86, 155
Vossius, Isaac   104
Vyverberg, Henry   199, 201

Wachterus, J.C. (Wachter, Johann Georg)
        296 n. 12
Wade, Ira   30 n. 44
Warburton, William   2, 329, 334
Weber, Max   101, 294
Werner, Michael   26
Wielema, Michiel   105, 111
Williams, Daniel   242
William v   112
Wilmans, Carl A.   279–281
Winckelmann, Johann Joachim   114, 119
Winstanley, Gerard   47, 49
Winterer, Caroline   19

Wiszowaty, Andrzej   253
Wiszowaty, Benedykt   253
Wolff, Betje   111
Wolff, Christian   111, 267 n. 3
Wolffianism   111–112
    Dutch   113
Wöllner's edict   339
Wollstonecraft, Mary   51
Wolterstorff, Nicholas   244
Wolzogen, Johann Ludwig von   260
Wood, Allen   268, 289 n. 66, 310
Wood, Gordon   58, 65
worship   150, 179, 181, 183–185, 188– 189
    interior (inward)   156, 182
    public   156
    silent   10, 274
Wyttenbach, Daniel   116

Yvon, Abbé Claude   4, 70 n. 7

Zimmermann, Bénédicte   26
Zoroaster   305